Land and Ancestors

AMSTERDAM ARCHAEOLOGICAL STUDIES 4

Other titles in the series:

N. Roymans (ed.)
From the Sword to the Plough
Three Studies on the Earliest Romanisation of Northern Gaul
ISBN 90 5356 237 0

T. Derks
Gods, Temples and Ritual Practices
The Transformation of Religious Ideas and Values in Roman Gaul
ISBN 90 5356 254 0

A. Verhoeven
Middeleeuws gebruiksaardewerk in Nederland (8e-13e eeuw)
ISBN 90 5356 267 2
(in Dutch)

Forthcoming (1999):

J. Bazelmans
By Weapons Made Worthy
Lords, Retainers and Their Relationship in Beowulf
ISBN 90 5356 325 3

Land and Ancestors

CULTURAL DYNAMICS IN THE URNFIELD PERIOD AND THE MIDDLE AGES IN THE SOUTHERN Netherlands

EDITORS

F. THEUWS & N. ROYMANS

AMSTERDAM UNIVERSITY PRESS

Lay-out: Damiaan Renkens, Amsterdam and Wouter Kool, Leiden
Cover design: Kok Korpershoek, Amsterdam
Cover illustration: Large-scale settlement research in an *es*-complex with a *plaggen* soil

ISBN 90 5356 278 8

CONTENTS

V

PREFACE

Since the beginning of the 1980s, the IPP, together with the AIVU has been carrying out archaeological research in the sandy areas of the Southern Netherlands. This volume offers a series of reports of investigations done as part of the South Netherlands project. These include the final reports of archaeological fieldwork as well as some contributions by historians associated with the project. The book focuses on the presentation of primary data on the one hand. On the other hand we have attempted to link the analyses of these data with broader, more abstract discussions. With this objective in mind, it was decided to present the book in the English language.

We wish to thank all persons and institutions who have contributed to the South Netherlands project over the past years. We would like to mention here the many students and local volunteers who bore the brunt of the fieldwork every year. We are also grateful to various municipalities and the province of North Brabant for subsidizing the excavations. Furthermore, we thank everyone who helped to realise this volume, and in particular, Christine Jefferis, who translated the articles into English or corrected them, and Paul van der Kroft, who did most of the drawings.

The publication of this volume also takes place within the framework of the project 'Settlement and landscape in the Maas-Demer-Scheldt region'. This project is supported (in part) by the Foundation for History, Archaeology and Art History, which is subsidized by the Netherlands Organization for Scientific Research (NWO).

ABBREVIATIONS

AAG	Afdeling Agrarische Geschiedenis, Wageningen
AIVU	Archeologisch Instituut der Vrije Universiteit, Amsterdam
AB	Archaeologia Belgica
AK	*Archäologisches Korrespondenzblatt*
APL	*Analecta Praehistorica Leidensia*
BAR	British Archaeological Reports
BROB	*Berichten van de Rijksdienst voor het Oudheidkundig Bodemonderzoek,* Amersfoort
IPP	Instituut voor Pre- en Protohistorische Archeologie, Amsterdam
IPL	Instituut voor Prehistorie, Leiden
NAR	Nederlandse Archeologische Rapporten
OMROL	*Oudheidkundige Mededelingen van het Rijksmuseum van Oudheden,* Leiden
PPS	*Proceedings of the Prehistoric Society*
PSHAL	*Publications de la Société Historique et Archéologique dans le Limbourg*
ROB	Rijksdienst voor het Oudheidkundig Bodemonderzoek, Amersfoort
STIBOKA	Stichting voor Bodemkartering, Wageningen

Long-term perspectives on land and people in the Meuse-Demer-Scheldt region (1100 BC-1500 AD). An introduction

Nico Roymans / Frans Theuws

I   INTRODUCTION

Since 1980 the IPP has been conducting a regional archaeological research project in the sandy landscape of the South Netherlands.[1] The central goal is the study of the long-term relationship between people and their land from the Late Bronze Age into the Late Middle Ages (c 1100 BC-1500 AD). Attention is focused on:

a. the study of changing settlement patterns in relation to agrarian systems, demographic developments and changes in the physical landscape;
b. the way in which social relations in societies are reflected in the development of the landscape, and how the organization of the landscape contributes to the formation and consolidation of social (power) positions;
c. the study of the cognitive-ideational dimensions of the association of man with the landscape.

The study area was originally limited to the region southwest of Eindhoven (de Kempen), to be expanded later to the entire sandy plateau of the South Netherlands and North Belgium, or the area between the rivers Meuse, Demer and Scheldt. From the very beginning there has been close collaboration with the Archeologisch Instituut of the Vrije Universiteit of Amsterdam. Since 1996, research is also done in association with the 'Maaskant project' of the Instituut voor Prehistorie in Leiden[2] as part of a multiple project, financed by the Netherlands Organization for Scientific Research.

---

[1] On the development of the South Netherlands project in the last two decades, see Roymans 1996, where further references are given.

[2] Cf. Fokkens 1996.

From the start, large-scale excavations of settlements have played a central role in the project as the most important method of acquiring data. Optimum use was made of the possibilities offered by the sandy regions for excavating large areas (see below). In contrast, field surveys and remote-sensing techniques have played a limited role until recently, mainly because many archaeological sites in this region are covered by man-made *plaggen*-soils of late-medieval origin.[3]

2   SOME LONGUE-DURÉE STRUCTURES IN THE RELATIONSHIP BETWEEN MAN AND ENVIRONMENT IN PLEISTOCENE SAND AREAS

The region between the rivers Meuse, Demer and Scheldt is, from the point of view of landscape and geography, a well-defined area (fig. 1). It includes the gently undulating sand plateau of North Belgium and the South Netherlands which was formed in the course of the Pleistocene. Under the relatively dry conditions of the Late Glacial period, a polar sandy desert with an extremely sparse vegetation developed here. A layer of fine sands was then deposited by the wind, which covered the older fluvial deposits: the coversands. The thickness of the coversand layer can vary considerably, but is generally between 0.5 and 1.5 m.

The landscape of the Meuse-Demer-Scheldt area forms part of a chain of large coversand plateaus or *Geestlandschaften* situated along the southern part of the North Sea and separated from it by a belt of Holocene peat and clay areas (fig. 1). The *Geestlandschaften* themselves are separated by wide river valleys. From south to north these are the Flemish sand plateau, the Meuse-Demer-Scheldt area, the Veluws-Utrechts Plateau, the Drents Plateau, the Lower Saxonian *Geest* region, and the *Geest* area of the Elbe-Weser triangle.[4]

Seen from an agrarian perspective, the Pleistocene sand landscapes of the Northwest European Plain have two structural constraints for habitation and subsistence resulting from the physical conditions of soil and climate. In the first place, the *Geestlandschaften* are characterized by oligotrophic soils; they are mineralogically poor. Fields cannot be permanently cultivated here without heavy additional manuring. A structural shortage of manure was the main limiting factor for plough agriculture until the introduction of artificial fertilizer in the 19th century. A second feature of coversands is their vulnerability to soil degradation as a result of human intervention. The natural vegetation in the later prehistoric period originally consisted of deciduous forest, which was connected to a brown podzolic soil or *moderpodzol* soil.[5] As a result of cutting down parts of the forest for arable land and using the the woodland as a *Waldweide* and source of leaf fodder for cattle, a more open landscape gradually developed. The forest floor, which was originally relatively fertile, quickly lost its fertility after reclamation due to the washing out of humus. This process led to a gradual expansion of the heath vegetation and − with it − the acidification and podzolization of the soil.[6] This process of degradation − sometimes even of desertification − particularly affected the coarse sand zones in the landscape with a low loam content. Since the Bronze Age, a heath vegetation can be seen here in the pollen diagrams, al-

[3] Systematic field surveys were carried out by the AIVU in the 1970s, but with disappointing results for many periods. However, they will play an important role in the near future, especially in the micro-regional projects within our study area, where we have a better grip on the specific formation processes and biases of the archaeological record in different parts of the landscape. See the discussion in chapter 3.

[4] Cf. Waterbolk 1979; Slofstra e.a. 1982, 10.

[5] Cf. Theuws/Verhoeven/Van Regteren Altena 1988, 247.

[6] Cf. the discussion in Spek 1993; Hüppe 1996, 17.

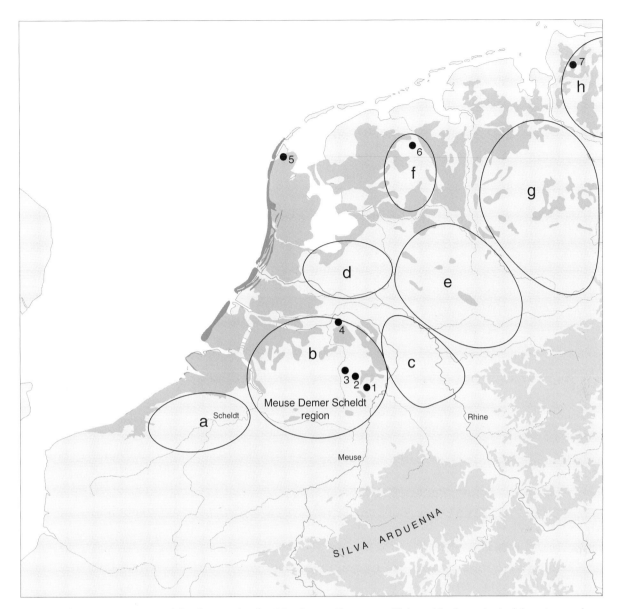

Fig. 1. Pleistocene coversand landscapes in the Northwest European Plain with the principal locations where large-scale settlement research has been carried out (total uncovered area >5 ha).
a Flemish sand plateau; b Meuse-Demer-Scheldt region; c Meuse-Rhine region; d Veluws-Utrechts Plateau; e East Netherlands/Westphalian sand plateau; f Drents Plateau; g Lower Saxonian sand region; h Elbe-Weser triangle
1 Weert (13 ha); 2 Someren (20 ha); 3 Geldrop (8.5 ha); 4 Oss (40 ha); 5 Texel (11.5 ha); 6 Peelo (7 ha); 7 Flögeln (11 ha)

though the relative importance of this through time is difficult to establish.[7] The expansion of the heathland reached its culmination in the Late Middle Ages, and until well into the 19th century virtually treeless heaths were characteristic of the landscape of the sandy areas (fig. 2).

The features outlined above of the coversands and the environmental dynamics associated with them had a major impact on the structure of the societies developing here and their agricultural sys-

[7] For the earliest expansion of heath on the sandy soils   Groenman-van Waateringe 1980 and Hüppe 1996.
     in the Northwest-European Plain, see Casparie/

Fig. 2. Nineteenth-century heath landscape at Overpelt (North Belgium) with urnfield barrows. Painting by J. du Fief, c 1870. Collection Koninklijke Musea voor Kunst en Geschiedenis, Brussels (copyright Instituut voor het Archeologisch Patrimonium).

tems. The image is dominated in all phases by mixed agrarian strategies, often with an emphasis on extensive animal husbandry.[8] We always find that large sections of the landscape, particularly the waste lands, were in use as pastureland. The prospects for intensifying cereal cultivation were very limited. The sandy areas therefore never belonged to the classic arable production landscapes such as the adjoining loess regions in the south. The relative importance of stockbreeding in the sandy regions is especially evident in times of integration in supraregional economic systems, when part of the agrarian production was intended for external markets. Both in the Roman period and in the Late Middle Ages this production for external markets was achieved by intensifying the stockbreeding sector. Although arable production was also intensified, it retained the nature of subsistence farming, intended primarily to meet internal demographic growth.[9]

[8] Following Bieleman (1992, 12) we speak of an extensive agrarian practice when a large area of land is used in proportion to the volume of labour and capital imput. We refer to intensive agriculture whenever a large amount of labour and capital is used in proportion to the area of land. Bieleman emphasises the relative meaning of the terms *intensive* and *extensive*; they can only be defined in relation to each other.

[9] For the Roman period, cf. the discussion in Roymans 1996, especially ch. 3.3.3, on the transformation of agrarian regimes in the Lower Rhine area, including the sandy regions. Here, cattle and horse breeding seem to have been the motor of the market-oriented sector of native agriculture in the Roman period. This is indicated by the increasing length of the native farmhouses in the course of the 1st and 2nd centuries. Archaeobotanical investigation of cultivated crops shows that the Roman influence on native arable farming in the sandy areas was limited. There is hardly any evidence of adaptations to the specific demands of urban and military centres, where wheat (in particular spelt and bread-wheat) was the main food crop. Native agriculture continued to cultivate the traditional pre-Roman spectrum of crops, dominated by emmer, millet and especially barley. In the Late Middle Ages, an intensification of cereal (rye) cultivation takes place in the sandy areas, but this was mainly in order to meet local demand and especially to cater for the internal population growth. Production for external markets was largely realized by intensifying pas-

The constant emphasis on stockbreeding did not only apply to the economic sphere, but also had an effect on the social organization and the system of ideas and values of the societies concerned. In many periods we can speak of a pastoral ideology which transcends the economic significance of stockbreeding. Take, for example, the deeply-rooted tradition (from the Bronze Age until subrecent times) of sheltering man and cattle in one and the same house (*Wohnstallhaus*), the prominent place of cattle in all kinds of ritual repertoires, and the popularity of the native-Roman cult of Hercules in the Lower Rhine area. For the Late Middle Ages, one can refer to the etymology of *heerdgang* – the local term for the small settlements or hamlets in which most of the population lived – which refers to the herdsman appointed by each hamlet to lead the cattle every day to the common pasture lands.[10] This term illustrates that the social-economic organization of these settlements was largely geared to the communal management of a large herd of cattle.

The always limited population density of the sandy areas, the emphasis on a pastoral ideology and the restricted opportunities for feeding a substantial non-agrarian population, meant that urban centres here did not develop until the Late Middle Ages and then only to a limited extent (fig. 9), and that before then, in the Roman period, they were completely absent.[11] Mentally too, the population of the sandy areas generally belonged to the periphery of urban culture and its associated life-style.

French *Annales* historians have demonstrated that environment has a considerable impact on the ordering of a culture, also indirectly, via social and ideational structures.[12] Despite the existence of important environmental factors, which are responsible for a series of *longue-durée* structures in habitation and land use, the social and cultural development of the sandy regions is anything but static. On the contrary, throughout time we find a pattern of constantly changing socio-cultural constellations against the background of these long-term structures. There is also a creative association of people with the structural constraints of landscape and climate within the scope of much broader cultural dynamics (fig. 8). The latter is especially evident in the variety of ritual repertoires with continually changing emphases which we find in each period. These may be associated with settlements, cemeteries, rivers or marshes, and later also with monumental sanctuaries and churches. The ritual repertoires are the contexts *par exellence* within which the central ideas and values of a society or group are expressed and in which the social and cosmological order is given shape.

3   PLEISTOCENE SAND LANDSCAPES AND THEIR ARCHAEOLOGICAL POTENTIAL

The main reason why this project is concentrated on the Meuse-Demer-Scheldt region is the potential of this landscape for regional research from the perspective described above. However, we would first

---

toral farming, especially sheep breeding for the Flemish and Brabant textile industry (Theuws 1989, 188-206).

[10] On the tradition of *Wohnstallhäuser* and the significance of cattle in ritual repertoires in the Lower Rhine region, see Roymans 1996, 51 ff, 72 ff, with further references. On the pastoral connotations of the Lower Rhine cult of Hercules Magusanus in the Roman period, see Roymans 1996, 88 ff; Derks 1998, 102 ff.,

113. About the etymology of *heerdgang*, cf. Behets 1969, 24-26; Molemans 1986, 88-89; Leenders 1996, 43-44.

[11] Cf. Roymans 1995, 55-58, for the Roman period. For the Middle Ages, see Bonenfant 1962; Theuws 1989, 195-197. For the archaeology of a late-medieval town in the interior of the Meuse-Demer-Scheldt region, see Arts 1994.

[12] Braudel 1978 (1949), 23 ff; Bintliff 1991, 11.

Fig. 3. Large-scale settlement research in an *es*-complex with a *plaggen*-soil.

like to consider two important limitations on archaeological research in the sandy areas. Compared with the archaeology of the Holocene wetlands, these are the poor conservation of organic material and the fact that the old habitation levels at archaeological sites always have been ploughed in younger phases. For this reason, the excavation level is several decimetres below the original surface, where only the dug in features can be recorded. These limiting factors mean that part of the original patterns in the archaeological record, in particular those from pits and ditches, can no longer be traced.

Against these adverse aspects for archaeological research in the sandy areas, there are important advantages. There are few cultural landscapes in Northwest Europe which provide such favourable prospects for diachronic large-scale investigation as the sandy areas. By using mechanical diggers and because of the absence of complex stratigraphies (generally just one excavation level is sufficient) large areas can be excavated in a relatively short time and with limited funds (fig. 3). Traces from the Bronze Age up to and including the Late Middle Ages are usually clearly visible. The possibility of investigating large areas in a short space of time makes sand excavations attractive for the study of long-term patterns in the association of man with the landscape. This diachronic perspective is best realized in micro-regional projects in which the entire cultural landscape is the object of research: not only settlements and cemeteries, but – via off-site archaeology – also stream valleys, moors, local depressions, field complexes etc.[13]

[13] Examples of such microregional projects are the excavations at Oss (Fokkens 1996), Someren (Kortlang, this volume) and Weert (Roymans/Tol 1996).

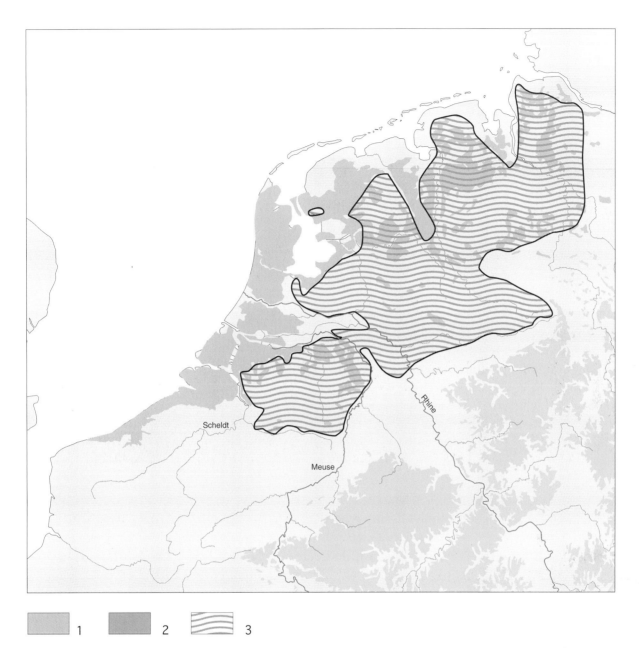

Fig. 4. Distribution of *plaggen* soils (*essen*) in the Northwest European Plain. After Pape 1970.
1 land above 300 m; 2 coastal peat areas; 3 area with plaggen soils

For an efficient use of the archaeological potential of the sandy areas, it is essential to take the pre-modern cultural landscape, such as that formed in the Late Middle Ages, as a starting point. The Meuse-Demer-Scheldt region has, of old, consisted of a finely divided landscape of stream valleys and marshy depressions with coversand plateaus in between. The pre-modern landscape has three main elements.[14] The first is the villages and hamlets with arable lands nearby on the coversand plateau. The field complexes on the sandy soils of the Northwest-European plain are characterized by man-

---

[14] Kakebeeke 1968; Behets 1969, 51-62; Molemans 1986; Roymans/Tol 1996, 7-16; Theuws, this volume; De Bont 1993.

made *plaggen* soils, called *essen* (fig. 4). These are the product of centuries-old fertilization with a mixture of heath and grass sods and animal manure. A second landscape element consists of the pasture- and haylands in the stream valleys, which were usually reclaimed for the first time in the Late Middle Ages. The third and in surface area by far the most important element of the pre-modern landscape is the extensive wastelands or heaths.[15]

For the study of the long-term settlement history of the sandy areas, it is important to differentiate between the habitation trajectory of the (pre-modern) heaths and that of the arable complexes.[16] Recent research has shown that habitation from the Late Iron Age until into the High Middle Ages is almost entirely concentrated in the zone of the present-day *essen*. By contrast, habitation from the Bronze Age until into the Middle Iron Age is more regularly distributed across the zones of the *essen* and the heaths. The concentration of settlement from the Late Iron Age in the zone of the medieval fields is mainly the result of the process of soil degradation described above. This process reached a peak during the transition from the Early to the Middle Iron Age, and affected the coarse-sand zones in the landscape in particular. Most of the settlements here were abandoned, after which the zones in question continued to exist until modern times as wastelands with an open forest or heath vegetation. The more loamy sand plateaus were less sensitive to this type of soil degradation and it was here that settlement was concentrated from the Late Iron Age on.

The large-scale archaeological research of the past decennia in the South Netherlands has focused on the *essen*. Almost all excavations of more than 5 hectares are located on sand plateaus which had been in use as arable land since the Late Middle Ages. The largest excavations are those at Oss (c. 40 ha.), Someren (20 ha.), Weert (13 ha.) and Geldrop (8.5 ha.).[17] Together with the excavations at Peelo (7 ha.), Texel (11 ha.) and Flögeln (11.5 ha.) they are among the largest investigations in the *Geestlandschaften* of the Northwest European Plain (fig. 1). The recent boom in the development of large-scale settlement research in the sandy areas however is not only determined by considerations of a scientific nature. It must also be understood in the context of the large-scale destruction of old cultural landscapes, and in particular, the arable fields, by the massive development of housing estates and industrial zones. With the exception of the research at Flögeln in North Germany which has been financed by the *Deutsche Forschungsgemeinschaft*,[18] all the great sand excavations have been rescue excavations.

4 DIFFERENT PERSPECTIVES ON THE STUDY OF THE CULTURAL LANDSCAPE

Recent research on past cultural landscapes has brought with it a proliferation of perspectives that are in sharp contrast to the unidimensional approach of 20 years ago.[19] This unidimensional approach was mainly rational-economic in character, as exemplified by the site catchment analysis formulated by Vita-Finzi and Higgs.[20] Contemporary critique on this approach remained well within the limits of

[15] See for example Theuws, this volume, figs 5 and 6.

[16] Roymans, in prep.; Gerritsen, in prep.

[17] Although the excavations at Oss and Weert are located in medieval arable complexes, the loam content of the local sandy soil is so high that the system of sod-manuring was not practised here. There is no question of a *plaggen* soil here.

[18] Zimmermann 1992.

[19] See for instance the many contributions in the Durch journal *Archaeological Dialogues*. Among them: Kolen 1995; Roymans 1995a; Lemaire 1997; Bradley 1997; Derks 1997.

[20] Vita-Finzi/Higgs 1970.

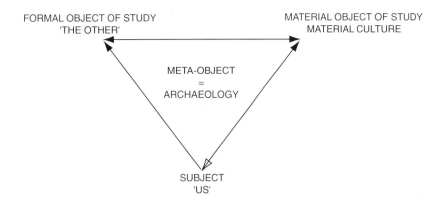

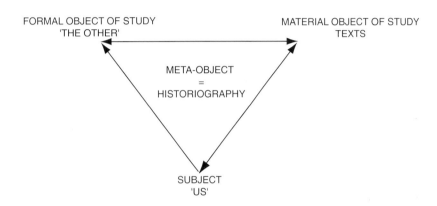

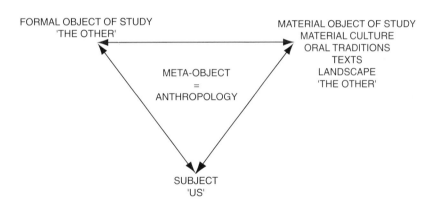

Fig. 5. The relations between formal object, material object and subject in archaeology, history and anthropology.

the 'processual paradigm'.[21] However, it has been realized that the environment is not just a stage for socio-economic practices, but is part of the cosmological order: environment became landscape. It was even realized that next to 'practical' landscapes there were 'thought of' landscapes and that part of the practices were responses to landscapes of the mind. Now archaeologists often work with the idea that several landscapes existed in the same physical environment at the same time. We also started to realise the problematic character of the use of modern concepts in analysing old landscapes, that land-

21   Flannery 1976, 91-95.

scapes have a cultural biography because of the long-term existence of elements from the past. Now we talk of mythical landscapes, religious landscapes, mindscapes, seascapes and townscapes.

In order to organize their thoughts modern scholars tend to isolate different dimensions of ancient landscapes and define different perspectives on them. So, the economic, social, ideational and religious dimensions can be studied from a rational-economic, marxist, structuralist or post-modern perspective. In this volume too, economic, social and religious dimensions are identified. However we have to realize that these are dimensions defined on the basis of modern classifications. We have to ask ourselves to what extent they correlate to ancient classifications involving the landscape. Serious trouble can be expected. But on the other hand, if we still see it as one of our objectives to (re)construct ancient thoughts on the landscape and ancient representations of man-landscape relations, how can we identify these on the basis of a geographical ordering or on the basis of morphological characteristics alone? And what is our own role in this (re)construction? The essential triangular relationship of any archaeological research is even more important in the analysis of the cultural landscape, for we still live in these landscapes and have developed a set of relations with them, although many of them are only a palimpsest of the past ones. The triangle consists of the relations between our formal object (the 'others' in the past), our material object (material culture and landscapes) and the subject ('us') (fig. 5).[22] Our problem is that the other cannot inform us anymore about his/her views on or the uses of the landscape in the way an anthropologist is informed by the other during fieldwork.[23] Neither are we informed in the way an historian is informed through texts on uses of and views on the landscape.[24] In fig. 5 the triangular relations for archaeology, history and anthropology are given. The direction of the arrows indicate the dominant informative/interpretative relations. Often the distinction between history, archaeology and anthropology is presented nowadays as the arbitrary result of a historical process since the 18th century without having much meaning for modern interdisciplinary scholars. The formal object is the same, the material objects are different but stand on an equal footing and we (historians and archaeologists) are the same, that is we are scholars operating in modern western ideology (although differences are easy to see).[25] However, statements like these ignore the different relationships in the triangle presented above. Any (re)construction of past ideas on the landscape using (re)constructed landscapes from the past and elements therein as a sole source (as many of us are condemned to do so) is always the result of the interaction of the modern subject and the remains of past landscapes. They are invented landscapes presented as 'conceptions of the past' or 'dwellers' perspectives'[26] etc. The last perspective, also termed the 'bottom up perspective'[27] is gaining some importance in archaeology.[28] It is suggested that in understanding ancient landscapes 'the key (...) is the way in which men dwell or inhabit an environment, thus adopting a 'dwelling perspective'. So we may be capable of understanding a societies landscape by presuming that it is structured from

[22]   Harmsen 1968, 10-14.

[23]   For that reason the (American, processualist) adage 'archaeology is anthropology or is nothing' (Binford 1972, 20) was a mistake. Archaeology is archaeology is archaeology said Clarke (see Austin/Thomas 1997 (1990), 47-51) and he may have been right for other reasons than he put forward, namely because of the different relations in the triangle for archaeology and anthropology.

[24]   I assume that textual information (that is information we receive through language) is of a different nature (but not less complex) than information we extract from material culture only. For instance we react differently towards textual and material constructions of identities in the past.

[25]   Austin/Thomas 1997 (1990), 76.

[26]   Lemaire 1997.

[27]   Hoppenbrouwers 1992.

[28]   For instance: Austin/Thomas 1997 (1990).

the perspective and the way of life of the people that dwell in it'.[29] It is a problematic perspective. It may be a perspective appropriate for the analysis of the landscape of small-scale prehistoric societies, but what about those of the Roman empire or the Middle Ages? How literally do we have to take the dwelling perspective? Lemaire's lines seem to indicate a rather literal approach. We know from written texts that specific medieval landscapes are not just the product of those who lived in them. Far-away 'owners' (either lay or ecclesiastical) were also involved in the creation of the physical as well as the social and ideational dimensions of the landscape, for instance by accumulating landed property and creating large estates. New taxation systems imposed from outside may have important consequences for cultural landscapes (see section 1.5). Non-dwellers even were involved in the oral structuring of the local landscape by intervening in the naming of settlements and other elements. Or are the owners of estates that lived hundreds of kilometres away to be considered members of the dwelling community? On the other hand should we understand the 'dwelling perspective' as a means 'to recover the experience of dwelling as our primary mode of being in the world' in contrast to a rational scientific attitude?[30] Such a perspective is an interesting project for developing present and future attitudes towards a historical cultural landscape, but can it help us in understanding and interpreting past landscapes and past ideas on them?

Different perspectives on the cultural landscape emerge from different sets of relations in the triangles presented above and different theoretical stands in interpreting the relations. Is materially organized behaviour to be considered more important than a system of ideas in interpreting the relation between the other and his physical world? In our system of ideas, materialism seems to have taken a dominant position. What importance is given to routine daily action in the interpretations? What possibilities for personal reflection and related possibilities for personal action do we think subjects in different social horizons in the past had?

This volume is a first attempt in the South Netherlands project to deal with these problems on the basis of ordinary archaeological material which most of the members of the archaeological community have to deal with (incomplete settlements and cemeteries, poor ecological information, a small fraction of the past material culture, etc.). We have not solved many problems yet. What we did is gather an immense body of data (archaeological, historico-geographical, toponymical, textual, oral, pedological) that is only partially published and hardly interpreted in relation to ideas formulated here.[31] The combined use of texts and material culture force us to consider these problems and see what happens when literate and non-literate societies that are chronologically apart, but are present in the same region, are dealt with in a combined effort. In order that readers understand some of the basic problems we have, we choose to combine data publications with those in which it is attempted to interpret this material at a higher level of abstraction. The case studies do have a common element, that is they relate to an aspect of the ideological dimension of past cultural landscapes, more precisely how parts of the environment were claimed, how landed property was structured on the local level, and how these claims were represented by different groups, thereby creating 'landscape'. In our conviction that claims on the environment are to be studied in relation to its use a number of contributions also deal with that aspect.

In experimenting in this way in a region that we choose to call our laboratory, we hope to be able to create an 'ideal' project for the study of past cultural landscapes. It is not strictly archaeological, nor is it historical or geographical. It is ... (we have no name) in the sense that in the analysis the three tri-

[29] Ingold 1993.
[30] Lemaire 1997, 11-12.
[31] Roymans 1996b.

angles presented above are put on top of each other (the scheme will then have a three-dimensional character in a graphical sense and a multidimensial character in analytical sense) and that all types of relations between the components of the triangles are analysed on the basis of material culture, texts and oral information told and sung by old inhabitants.

5   ANCESTORS AND THE CULTURAL CONSTRUCTION OF CLAIMS ON LAND. A LONG-TERM PERSPECTIVE

Within the scope of this study, we shall take a closer look at one theme. It is a first attempt on the basis of present insights and available data to show how, in the course of time (from the Bronze Age until into the Late Middle Ages) claims on land were made and represented by groups and individuals, and the extent to which land formed part of exchange relations. In the research into the changing cultural association with land in the Meuse-Demer-Scheldt area, however, we quickly encounter several fundamental problems which must be dealt with first.

The first problem is of a theoretical nature. Concepts such as economy, culture, landscape and also ownership or property have their own specific framework in modern (capitalist) society. This means that these concepts cannot be used just like that in the analysis of pre-modern societies.[32] In the modern Western world, all the emphasis lies on economic aspects in the representations of the value of land. Land is an alienable commodity which can be rented or sold via a real estate market, where price-making takes place via the mechanisms of supply and demand. From historical research into pre-modern societies and from anthropological research into non-western societies, it appears that, in these cases, we should take into account the different ideas and values concerning property and the alienability of land. The notion of property was less absolute, less exclusive and less related to the economic value of the land.[33] In studying early-medieval society, Rosenwein analyses property and property relations in terms of a series of overlapping claims.[34] The use of the term 'claims' offers better opportunities to study diffuse and less static appropriations of land in pre-modern societies, as well as the social and cosmological embedding of these claims.

A second problem is a methodical one. How can archaeologists make statements on an abstract subject such as property relations and ideas on them in late pre- and protohistoric societies within a certain area? Archaeological information on the association of man with the landscape is, after all, essentially spatial in character and often concerns use rather than the representations of claims connected with it. The step from the interpretation of spatial patterns in abstract social and ideational aspects as claims on land and property relations is not an easy one. In the Middle Ages, socio-political forms of organization such as the parish, the demesne and the aldermen's court do not necessarily have identical spatial structures. Conversely, identical spatial stuctures need not imply identical social structures. An example is the pattern of single-phase 'wandering farmsteads' discussed below, known from late prehistory as well as from the Early Middle Ages, but which are organized within very different societal contexts. Another example is that in the Early Middle Ages, an archaeologically defined settlement type[35] may correspond in one case to a manorial centre (Bladel) and in another case to a secondary settlement within a demesne (Dommelen, Geldrop).

---

[32] Cf. the more general discussion in Lemaire 1997. See also Van den Brink 1996, 53-56.

[33] Theuws 1991, 304 ff.; Rosenwein 1989; Hoppen-brouwers 1992, 287-294.

[34] Rosenwein 1989, IX and 152.

[35] Theuws 1989, 180-187.

We are aware of the methodical problems involved in outlining a long-term perspective of the way in which claims on land were made and expressed in the past. Nevertheless we wish to make an attempt on the basis of an interdisciplinary approach. We are able to arrive at meaningful statements along three lines:

a. by means of archaeological investigation of the spatial organization of the landscape, the lay-out of settlements and cemeteries as well as of individual farmyards. It is assumed that the constantly changing spatial patterns enable conclusions to be drawn on changing property relations or claims on land by groups or individuals in the past.
b. by making use of historical studies on use, ownership and exchange of land in the study area in the Early and Late Middle Ages, firstly as a specific source of knowledge for these periods but also (in combination with the archaeological information) as a source of inspiration when studying older periods.
c. by the use of anthropological studies on the social and cosmological embedding of land use and claims on land in non-western societies based on agriculture, in which a real estate market is lacking. We use the anthropological studies as a source of inspiration, and not as a means of identifying cross-cultural commonplaces.

The long-term outline of the cultural association with land in the study area which follows is based on a combined use of various categories of information. Basically, all statements remain hypothetical, and their strength is determined by the extent to which they are based on various types of evidence. Particularly with anthropological insights, there is always the question of to what extent they are relevant to pre-modern societies in our study area. These insights only become significant when they can be related to patterns in the archaeological and historical record. In this way we hope to demonstrate that archaeologists can contribute to discussions on cultural constructions of claims on land in the past. Moreover, archaeologists are able to add a depth of time to their analyses which exceeds by far the potential of anthropological and historical research. This may be the surplus value of a regional archaeological project with interdisciplinary themes of research.

For the sandy areas of the Meuse-Demer-Scheldt region, the Urnfield period, covering the Late Bronze Age and the first half of the Iron Age, is a phase of demographic expansion and agrarian intensification, connected with the introduction of the *celtic field* system. Settlement in the sandy areas is characterized by a dispersed pattern of small, open settlements with a diffuse structure (fig. 6; Roymans/Kortlang, this volume, fig. 3).[36] The average settlement consisted of 3 to 6 more or less isolated farmsteads which were generally used for only one generation. After about 20 years the houses were rebuilt elsewhere in the direct neighbourhood. Referring to some excavations in the sandy areas of the Northern Netherlands, we may assume that this 'shifting' of farmsteads took place within large *celtic field* complexes.[37] This model of a regular shifting of farmsteads throughout the arable complex of a local community provides leads for the study of native conceptions about claims on land. The bond of individual families with specific plots of land seems to have been very loose, and was probably not inheritable. The emphasis lay entirely on collective ownership and forms of land use; the land, even the arable fields, seem to have been held in common and the strong pastoral component in the agrarian system further strengthened the collective basis of landownership (common pasture lands).

[36] Cf. the discussion in Schinkel 1995, I, 260 ff.; Roymans 1996a, 53-54, with further references; Gerritsen, in prep.
[37] Cf. Schinkel 1995, I, 260 ff.; Kortlang, this volume.

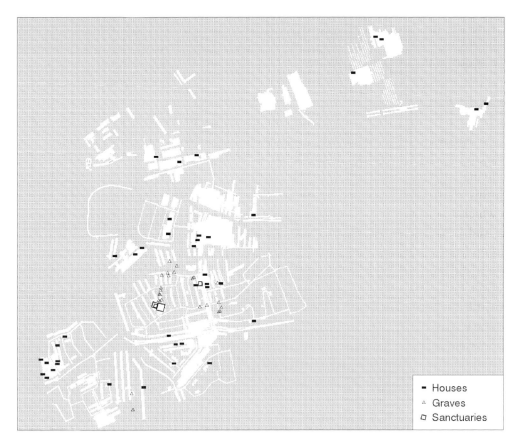

Fig. 6. The distribution of farmsteads and other features dating to the Middle Iron Age (500-250 BC) at Oss. The diffuse pattern is probably the result of only three to four wandering farmsteads which together formed a local community. The area presented measures c 2 × 2 km. After Fokkens 1996, fig. 3.

Anthropological studies show that in non-Western cultures the environment is part of a cosmological ordering, that is represented in a certain way. A key role in the social and cosmological order of many tribal societies is attributed to the ancestors. They are often considered to be the real owners of the land,[38] an idea that is continually made topical in rituals of exchange, or are represented as the source of the land held by a family.[39] Claims on land are often rooted in myths and presented as part of a sacred order created by the ancestors. As collective ancestral property, the land is so closely connected with the identity and constitution of the local community that it may be regarded as one of the most fundamental 'inalienable possessions'.[40] These land claims of local communities were, in turn, generally embedded in the claims of larger tribal groups with their own name and identity on a certain territory, given to them by their ancestors.[41]

This cosmological embeddedness of the bond between people and their land in tribal societies with a limited social differentiation is difficult to demonstrate archaeologically in our study area. However, the study of spatial aspects of the mortuary ritual of Urnfield groups offers leads.[42] The burial system is, after all, the ideal ritual context for linking the social world with the cosmological and ancestral

[38] De Coppet 1988; Friedman 1984 (1975), 170 ff.; Bloch 1984 (1975), 208 ff; Tilley 1996, 220.

[39] Geary 1994 (1986), 78 ff.; Gurevich 1992 (1987), 201-202, 205.

[40] For this term, cf. Weiner 1992.

[41] Cf. the discussion in Roymans 1990, 18 ff.

[42] Cf. Roymans/Kortlang, this volume.

world. From the Late Bronze Age until into the Middle Iron Age we find local communities each with their own collective cemetery. These monumental urnfields, consisting of a compact cluster of barrows of varying shape and size, were situated in the centre of the territory belonging to the local community, often in the middle or on the edge of the *celtic field* complex in which the farmsteads lay scattered. Recent excavations have focused attention on the presence of a long barrow of extreme size in the oldest centre of several urnfields. Such monumental long barrows can be interpreted as 'founder burials', which were the foci of the local ancestor cult. In their paper, Roymans and Kortlang argue that, in view of their spatial disposition, the urnfields played a crucial part in the relation between the living community and the land. The cemeteries symbolized the ancestral claims on the land and with this the existence and identity of the living community. They formed a powerful medium through which a local community defined itself with regard to outsiders.

For the Bronze and Iron Age societies in the study area, we should probably imagine a series of overlapping claims on land. Individual households would have had claims (though not inheritable) on specific plots of land which they cultivated and on which their farmstead stood. In addition, the local community as a whole had a claim on land which, on a supralocal level, was embedded in the territorial claims of (sub-)tribal groups. The ultimate claim on land, however, lay – we assume – with the ancestors. The material basis of social power in Urnfield society depended on the control of human labour and mobile wealth (cattle, prestigious bronzes), while private landed property may not have played any role. Land did not enter the circulation sphere and could not be accumulated like moveable goods. The notion of land as an alienable possession that could be the object of exchange transactions probably did not fit into the conceptual framework of Urnfield society.

In the course of the Late Iron Age and the Roman period, fundamental changes take place in the study area in the organization and use of land, and perhaps also in views on the ownership of land.[43] After a period of demographic decline from the end of the Urnfield period, the Late Iron Age and Roman period again are a phase of population growth. At the same time, however, one is confronted with a drastic reduction in the potential arable area as a result of soil degradation in the preceding phase. Habitation starts to concentrate in smaller parts of the landscape: the plateaus with sandy soils whose loam content is relatively high. Agrarian intensification probably occurs in these areas. The extensive system of *celtic field* agriculture seems to make way for a system of *Dauerackerland* with a periodical fallow period.[44]

Important changes in the internal spatial structure of the rural settlements are connected with these developments. In the course of the Late Iron Age and the beginning of the Roman period, the previously outlined pattern of open settlements with shifting farmsteads gradually makes way for structured and nucleated settlements with fixed locations, often surrounded by a ditched enclosure (fig. 7).[45] Within these settlements, individual farmsteads are increasingly rebuilt on the same spot. All this implies a close and inheritable bond between individual households and specific yards, probably also plots of arable land, and suggests a more stable spatial organization. The occurrence of linear ditch systems between sites also points to a greater and more stable spatial organization of the landscape.[46]

[43] The following theme is discussed more extensively in Roymans, in prep.; Gerritsen, in prep.

[44] The greater density of native-Roman settlements in the inhabtied parts of the landscape makes it clear that the traditional *Celtic field* form of agriculture with

arable complexes of over 50 hectares could no longer be practised here. For other indications for arable intensification, see Roymans 1996, 76 ff.

[45] Slofstra 1991.

[46] Cf. Fokkens 1996, 209 and fig. 4.

Fig. 7. General plan of the native-Roman settlement at Hoogeloon (1st-3rd century AD), with a Roman-style villa built in the 2nd century. After Slofstra 1991, fig. 22.

In the Late Iron Age more hierarchical tribal formations are seen in the study area, due to the expansion of clientship relations and the intensification of local warfare or raiding. In this respect, reference can also be made to the first appearance in the Late Iron Age of cult places with an evident regional significance (Empel, Kessel). The rituals performed here played a central role in the reproduction of ideas and values underlying the more hierarchical social organization. It is assumed that, under these conditions, the control of land also began to play a part in the power positions of elite families. Via the mechanisms of inheritance, marriage and the use of force, successful warrior elites were able to accumulate land and use it (as well as other valuable objects) to bind people to them according to the principles of gift exchange.

Although the developments described above are not fully visible until the Roman period, they started in the Late Iron Age. One cannot regard them simply as a product of Romanization. Nevertheless, it is beyond question that integration in the Roman empire entailed fundamental changes. A new aspect is that the Roman authorities claimed the Lower Rhine area as part of the Roman empire. From this, they would have derived the right to intervene in local property relations, in certain situations. Take, for example, land alienation in connection with the construction of the military infrastructure in the Lower Rhine frontier zone. The settlement of the Batavians in the Dutch river area and the adjacent part of the Meuse-Demer-Scheldt region, which is assumed to have taken place after the conclusion of an official treaty with Rome, must have included the reordering of claims on land. Generally speaking, the Roman authorities respected local indigenous claims on land. There are no indications in the Meuse-Demer-Scheldt region for a large-scale intervention in the property relations, for example in the form of a mass alienation and redistribution of land. Habitation consisted almost exclusively of native settlements, which had often developed as early as the Late Iron Age.[47]

Recently, reference has been made to the specific character of the process of Romanization of native societies in the Lower Rhine frontier zone, which also included the sandy areas. These were societies with a specific regime of ideas and values very different from that of Gallic groups in southern Gaul, which was based on an articulation of pastoral and martial cultural traditions and practices.[48] Among these groups one finds specific interpretations of (Gallo-)Roman cultural forms. In contrast to the southern loess areas, there was no transformation here into a villa-dominated rural landscape. More than 95% of the rural settlements can be qualified as non-villa sites of the native type. Production for external groups outside the region (urban and especially military populations) was mainly achieved by intensifying the pastoral component of the agrarian system. In addition, we should consider the role of Roman taxation; certain taxation systems encouraged private forms of landownership and contributed to the formalization of property relations. The question, however, is to what extent was taxation in the Lower Rhine area linked with landownership. There is evidence that taxation here consisted primarily of supplying manpower for the Roman army.[49]

Our temporary conclusion is that for the Meuse-Demer-Scheldt area, despite its position within the boundaries of the Roman empire, we must reckon with a strong continuity of tribal conceptions concerning landownership. We should not overestimate the degree of 'commoditization' of landed property in the Roman period, certainly not in these northern non-villa landscapes. There would have been little room for a commercial exchange of land via a 'real estate market'. The principle that landed property could be rented or sold for money and was therefore alienable, was poorly developed here. Most transactions of landed property probably remained embedded in social relations connected with succession, marriage relations, gifts to clients, etc.[50]

The question remains of how far existing collective claims on land by local groups were broken down, and how the path was cleared for an expansion of private landownership. The moral acceptance of the principle of private landed property that could be accumulated and could be the object of exchange transactions presupposes changes in the cosmological embedding of landownership. The notion that land basically belonged to the ancestors of a local community and was therefore inalienable would certainly have been weakened. Possibly the ancestor cult was less linked with the local community as a collective, and more with separate families (as in the Middle Ages; see below). Families which were able to accumulate landed property may have distinguished between what they regarded as the inalienable core of their ancestral heritage and the land that was less closely bound up

---

[47] Important in this context is the occurrence of fragments of glass Late La Tène armrings in many native-Roman settlements.

[48] Roymans 1996a.

[49] Cf. the discussion in Roymans 1996, ch. 3.3.4.

[50] Roymans 1996, 83.

with the identity of the family. At any rate, the greater role of landed property in the hands of certain families will certainly have articulated with other groups' claims on land. Referring to the situation in the Early Middle Ages (see below), we must take into account the rights of use of dependent peasant families and collective claims by local communities on the extensive complexes of waste pasturelands for their cattle. Collective forms of landownership and management no doubt continued to be of great importance.

The medieval habitation[51] of the Meuse-Demer-Scheldt sand plateau starts around the middle of the 6th century.[52] Up to now no indications for settlement have been found from the late 5th and first half of the 6th centuries. It is often thought that the Frankish settlers, arriving from the Meuse valley or regions to the south, colonized an empty forested landscape. Considering such a landscape as "empty" is a modern perspective, accustomed as we are to the idea of an objectified landscape, devoid of mythical dimensions. The 6th-century landscape will not have been empty: it was probably considered to be inhabited by ancestors of previous dwellers, by spirits and other dwellers of a metaphysical nature; before colonisation it will have been structured by stories told and names given from outside the region (especially rivers and streams and the region as a whole). Some evidence indicates that the colonists dealt with the metaphysical dwellers in the landscape.

The colonists settled on small, high-lying sand plateau's and lived in dispersed settlements of only one or two farmsteads. However, on the local level they formed burial communities that in the middle of the 7th century were no larger than 4 to 6 families, and used a single cemetery. In fact this looks like the Early Iron Age settlement pattern (dispersed settlement, single cemetery). The structure of the cemeteries may vary: in some of them individual families are clearly represented, in others not. The importance attached to representing single families in relation to the burial community as a whole may therefore differ from burial group to burial group. How these groups were organized internally and to what extent the families were related cannot be established yet. Neither can we establish whether they are part of communities organixed at a higher level involving several local groups. What we can see, on the basis of a few indications, is that ancestors of previous inhabitants of the region were dealt with. The early-medieval cemetery at Hoogeloon is located on the site of a prehistoric (probably Bronze Age) burial mound. The excavation of a Bronze Age barrow near Hapert revealed younger graves too, which in view of their structure, are most probably early-medieval. At Someren, the three large barrows (and possibly others too) of the Iron Age cemetery were left untouched in the Early Middle Ages, although the area surrounding it was probably in use as arable by the inhabitants of the Merovingian and Carolingian settlements nearby. In the Carolingian age a smithy was set up right between the barrows.[53] One may wonder whether this is a coincidence in view of the supernatural connotations that iron-working has in the Early Middle Ages. Locating Merovingian cemeteries on sites with remains from the past (a common feature in northern Gaul) or respecting old barrows, may be seen as a strategy of relating old and new ancestors in a specific territory devoid of living people but full of metaphysical dwellers.

[51] This section, sketchy as it is, relates to the sand areas in the Meuse Demer Scheldt area, not to the valleys of the Meuse or the peat and clay areas in the north-west.

[52] For the Early Middle Ages see: Theuws 1988; Theuws 1991; Theuws 1993 and Theuws 1994, Leenders 1996, 101-199. The period and the problems addressed here will be dealt with extensively in Theuws, in prep.

[53] Roymans/Kortlang 1993, 35 (in this publication it was dated to the Roman period, a C14 date points to a later date in the Carolingian period, communication N. Roymans).

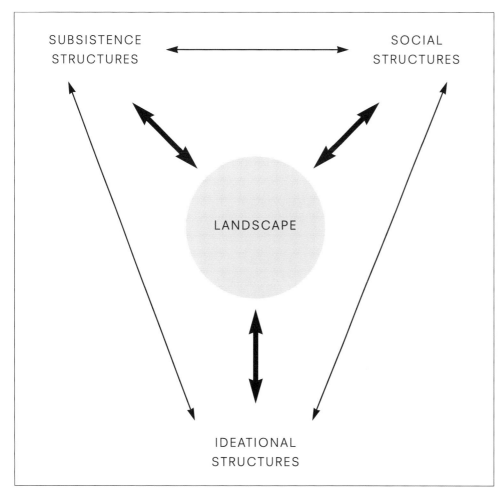

Fig. 8. The role of the landscape as a reference point in the social, the economic and the ideational ordering of a society. After Roymans 1996, fig. 34.

The settlement pattern drastically changes in the second half of the 7th century. New nucleated settlements appear, involving dwellers already present as well as newcomers. The old settlements seem to disappear. The emergence of the new settlements can be linked with a process of accumulation of landed property in the hands of a few families, the development of large property complexes and the organization of these as *villae*. Some of the elite families might be of local origin; other owners might be outsiders from northern Gaul. An interesting feature is that in the new nucleated settlements some people are buried in the farmyard. This is always at least an important man, probably the founding father of the farmstead. In some cases other members of the family of his or the following generation are buried next to or on top of him. A possible explanation for this practice is that individual families in a symbolic way substantiate their new claims on the farm and the land (in new settlements) by creating an ancestral order through the burial ritual and the creation of a family burial ground. However, the old cemeteries were still in use and at the time of the second generation of burials in the farmyard there were churches in the region too. The inhabitants must have had a choice as to where to bury their deceased relatives (in the farmyard, in the old cemetery, in a churchyard or even outside the region). Several burial grounds were therefore in use at the same time. It is certain that members of a single family were buried in at least two, possibly three different places. Each location stood for a different group. It can be hypothesized that each burial ground was related to a specific type of (overlapping) claims on the landscape. It can also be expected that the use of several burial grounds and the creation of different 'layers' of ancestors is part of a complex symbolic strategy to define the different contemporary communities (social as well as spiritual): the family, the ancient local group or burial community, the new estate and the community gathered around the local saint (that is, one in which social distinctions in "real life" are obliterated to some extent). The strategy will have been different for various social groups like the owners of estates and the local dwellers, and different interpretations will have existed for specific ritual practices.[54] The claims on (parts of) the landscape must have been different for both groups and must have overlapped, but it seems clear that, for both groups, the family is considered the prime 'owner' of important parts of the land. Individuals always needed the consent of other family members (that is heirs) even when donating the land to a religious institution. How the idea of family property related to communal forms of use and ownership of parts of the landscape is difficult to establish for the Early Middle Ages on the basis of archaeological evidence alone.

The first half of the 8th century saw a gradual change as well: building traditions changed, farmyard and settlement layout changed, the settlement pattern changed and large property complexes were donated to religious institutions.[55] In the Carolingian period a settlement pattern emerged in which the local nucleated settlements continued to exist, although in some cases on a small scale so that the element of nucleation is hardly visible anymore, and new dispersed farmsteads appeared in the landscape in the eastern part of the Meuse-Demer-Scheldt area. Most of the settlements formed part of large estates and were in the hands of faraway monasteries (Corbie in Picardy (Northern France), Lorsch (not far from Mainz), Echternach (in Luxembourg), Crespin (Northern France), Chévremont (near Liège in the Meuse Valley in Belgium), Sint Truiden (not far to the south of the region in Belgium) and possibly Sint Servatius in Maastricht) or they were in the hands of the Pippinid (later Carolingian) family. The organization of the estates did not only involve the agricultural production, it was the framework for the social organization, the religious practices and the ideological ordering of the landscape. In the view of high-ranking ecclesiastics like Hincmar of Reims, the villa was the ideal ordering of the countryside, a God-given order which should not be subject to human interventions.[56]

The lack of archaeological data on burial grounds or cult places in the Meuse-Demer-Scheldt region for this period and the very simple layout of the farmsteads (one building and one well) makes it difficult to analyse Carolingian communities in the region in the same way as it is possible for the previous or the following periods. It is expected that there was a shift in emphasis from subsistence arable farming and pig-keeping to a pastoral economy, in which raising cattle and sheep and probably horses for the large abbeys is important. For the time being it is the only plausible explanation for the changes in the cultural landscape and the intensive interest of abbeys in this remote region unsuited for large-scale arable farming. If this is the case, it is not just the group of dwellers that created the new landscape, it is the group of distant landowners as well. In the Carolingian period the landscape must have been valued differently, when its 'openness' (in relation to keeping cattle, sheep and horses) was important in comparison to its 'closeness' (pigs) in the previous period. Whether the environment was actually a closed, forested landscape in the Merovingian period is another matter; the place-names, almost entirely related to forest, indicate that this element was indeed highly valued then.

[54] For instance the burial near a church in the centre of an estate may have been interpreted in a different way by the members of the elite, the local dwellers and the clergy.

[55] For this last aspect see: Bijsterveld 1989a; Bijsterveld 1989b; Theuws 1991; Theuws/Bijsterveld 1991.

[56] Devroey 1985; Devroey 1986, Theuws 1991.

Settlement names related to open parts of the landscape are hardly encountered. The possible shift in emphasis towards a more pastoral way of life may have been connected with the development of different forms in the claims on land and different representations of them. However we lack sufficient data to expand on this theme here.

After a period of decline in the late 9th and 10th century, a period of rapid expansion starts, especially in the first half of the 12th century, a period of transformations in the region.[57] The old local centres still exist but the bulk of the population lives on new farmsteads scattered over the high-lying, relatively fertile soils or in small loosely structured hamlets. Churches had already existed in estate centres since the Carolingian age or the 10th century, but now many chapels or small churches are built in this period in the secondary centres of the estates. The importance of these newly re-vitalized local communities is stressed by the creation of new cemeteries there. The living and the majority of the dead are no longer geographically separated. Some of these cemeteries are older than the chapels that were built on them in the 12th and 13th centuries. The proliferation of the dead over the landscape out of the centre of the estate is not just a result of the growth of the population. In this period too, it may stand in relation to the development of local communities and the gradual dissolution of the estate, and again the ancestors play an important role in the symbolic construction of these new local communities. Although it is not entirely correct to create such a dichotomy, one could state that the 'profane' structure of the estate as an organizing principle in the landscape was replaced by a 'religious' one centring on the parish. This idea is supported by the evidence in the charters in which, since the middle of the 13th century, individual settlements are often located in a parish. It is also supported by the fact that in the 14th century the territorial marker par excellence is the church tower. These are rare in the 12th and 13th centuries. Built by now in an open landscape they are a new element. Although the landscape is flat in some places, cases are known from the 19th century where one could see twelve of them from the same spot.[58] One could state that the landscape is represented as a Christian landscape.

In the same period, land will have been an important medium in defining the family, its identity and its social status. It is an important element in the exchange cycle between the living and the dead (the ancestors) as described by Geary.[59] It is the ancestors who are the providers of life, of wealth through their gift of land to the next generation and an identity through the gift of names. In the Meuse-Demer-Scheldt region this is the case too, as is clear from the analysis by Bijsterveld of the meaning attached to land by local and regional elites who donate parts of their land to the monastery of Postel. Land and identity are merged in the names of elite families that refer to specific places in the landscape. Land is eternal and is therefore (next to gold) the ideal gift to God and provision for the ancestors that are re-membered in prayer by the religious community. So a mythical and Christian landscape is created in which parcels of land, each with their symbolic connotations, in the hands of religious institutions (or rather saints[60]), elite families and local dwellers are intermingled.[61] It is this landscape that is confronted with a new perspective on it, related to the development of a non-rural segment in society.

---

[57] In the last ten years there has been an enormous increase in studies of the Meuse Demer Scheldt region in this period. See among others: Theuws/ Verhoeven/Van Regteren Altena 1988; Verhoeven/ Theuws 1989; Theuws/Bijsterveld 1991; Steurs 1993; Bijsterveld 1997; Bijsterveld this volume. The bibliographies of these studies provide further examples of recent work. A comprehensive bibliography of publications on archaeological settlement research has now been prepared.

[58] For the church towers see Strijbos 1995.

[59] Geary 1994 (1986).

[60] See the title of Bijsterveld 1989b, which refers to a statement that the lands of Echternach are actually owned by Willibrord.

[61] Rosenwein 1989.

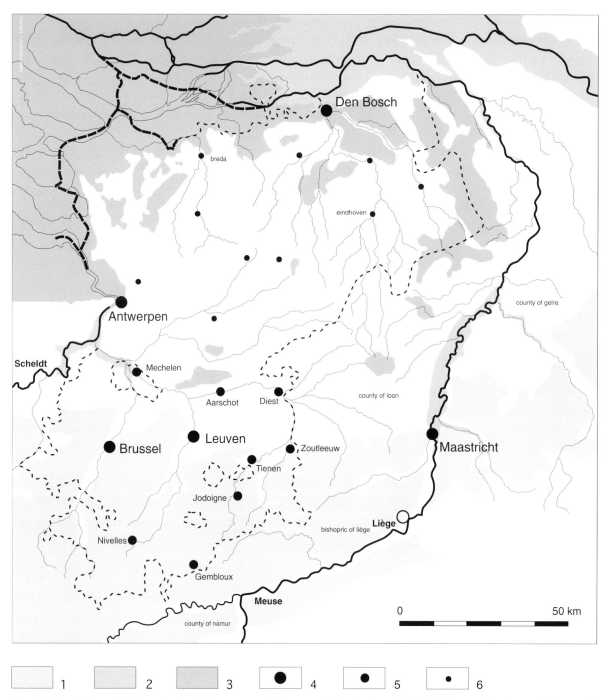

Fig. 9. The duchy of Brabant in the 13th century. In the south the fertile, urbanised löss area, in the north the sand area dominated by heath lands.

1 löss; 2 river clay areas; 3 peat areas; 4 major city; 5 minor city; 6 small town ('*ville neuve*')

Although the Meuse-Demer-Scheldt region was never a completely forested area in the Middle Ages and had always had stretches of open heathland, the landscape now became entirely open, main-ly as a result of a drastic increase if sheep-raising in order to produce wool. The incorporation of the region in the duchy of Brabant with its urbanized southern part (fig. 9), where arable farming on loess soils dominated the agricultural practice, and textile industry grew in the cities, may have triggered off this process of intensification. It led to sweeping changes in the cultural landscape in the 13th century. The landscape of scattered farmsteads disappeared, new hamlets came into being, situated on the edges of the low-lying parts in the landscape. The arable fields were manured in a new way (with *plaggen* manure) allowing for permanent use of the entire area for growing rye and for a higher productivity per hectare, although less fertile lands were still kept in use as arable, though not permanently. Brook valleys were reclaimed. Although the local economy was based on a system of mixed farming, the important factor was the pastoral element. This is indicated by the fact that the contemporary noun for the hamlet was *heerdgang* which contains the element *heerde,* which referred to the shepherd of the common flock grazing on the common grounds.[62] The sheep brought wealth, they created the need for a new territorial awareness in remote parts of the landscape in a way that had not existed before. The church towers substantiated these changes and the outer circle of the landscape as defined by Roymans was structured with stories and legends as well as names.[63] The village as a socio-cosmological structure came into being, and the landscape became fixed. However, the morphological structure of the village is not that of a nucleated settlement as in many other parts of Europe. It consists of a conglomerate of hamlets distributed over the parish.

Arable farming remained a subsistence activity on fields that were parcelled out. This parcelling out (which can be observed archaeologically) gives the impression that 'private', absolute or individual property emerged and that the idea of familial property gradually disappeared.[64] If this was the case, it could be related to the gradual development of a modern, rational economic attitude towards the landscape. It is an old matter of debate.[65] As far as the Meuse-Demer-Scheldt region is concerned, a few remarks have to be made to qualify this hypothesis regarding property. First of all, next to individual property there was communal property of large parts of the landscape (heaths, roads, squares with tree on them, etc.). Second, archaeological evidence seems to indicate that the arable fields were parcelled out, which suggests the existence of individual private property, though the presence of arable layers covering many fields crossing their borders, indicates a common use. So the *idea* of individuality may have been coupled with the *practice* of communality for the arable fields. Third, in addition to these aspects of socio-economic practice there are the representations of the origins of property and products of the land. The products are represented as having a supernatural origin (that is God, for which he is thanked in specific religious rituals) and not so much the product of peasant labour. Fourth, it was expected that the rational economic perspective on the landscape led to the development of selling and buying of land and a real estate market, and that land had acquired a 'price'. However, Vangheluwe's research clearly demonstrates that this is not really the case in the core of the Meuse Demer Scheldt region.[66] Almost all land changed hands within the family sphere and through inheritance. The idea of individuality in property does not seem to be developed well in the Late Middle Ages in the Meuse-Demer-Scheldt region. Fifth, it is to be expected that new taxation systems in the Late Middle Ages and Early Modern Period that are based on a 'modern' concept of private property instead of being based on productivity (like the tithes) brought with them important changes in land use. For instance, many farmers had landed property that partly consisted of unfertile

[62] Behets 1969, 24-26.

[63] Roymans 1995a.

[64] Not all property of persons will have fallen in the category family property, but a core of it, related to the history and identity of the family. This core of landed property will have had a changing composition over the generations. For instance the land reclaimed by a person may not be family property in his generation, but may have become so after his children inherited it.

[65] See also Hoppenbrouwers 1992.

[66] See Vangheluwe this volume. However the Kempen region is a remote area, far from major towns. In rural areas nearer to towns, a real estate market may have developed (Hoppenbrouwers 1992, 380-392).

lands that they used once a while. When taxation is based on property, these lands are very expensive while they are taxed as property but their productivity is low or non-existent. Thus the development of a new taxation system based on property and use[67] intervenes in the conception of claims on the landscape and may have had serious consequences for the use and layout of the landscape. Sixth, the creation of a new mythical landscape in which witches, dwarfs, gnomes and sometimes the devil participated, indicates that changes were present in the way the landscape was perceived, but still one can doubt whether the process of objectification and demythification of the landscape had really started by then. Among the group of metaphysical dwellers in the landscape, those who lived under the surface had a special importance: it was with them that one had to keep up good relations andthey had to be dealt with in the proper way. The earth dwellers might be linked with the ancestors, and the special relation that people had with them might indicate that they still valued good relations with past ancestors. In fact the stories were still told in the late 18th and 19th century when they were recorded. It is assumed that they originate from the Late Middle Ages (possibly 13th century or earlier?). The stories still had meaning then. We suspect that drastic changes in the perception of the landscape occurred no sooner than the 19th century in the Meuse-Demer-Scheldt region. This does not mean that that century saw the end of local mythical landscapes. Even after the Second World War, when the Dutch part of the Meuse-Demer-Scheldt region was subject to intense changes in the landscape as a result of integration in the European common market, with its implications for the organization of agricultural production, new mythical landscapes were created in order to define an modern identity located in a changing landscape based on the values of the Catholic church and those of simple agricultural communities. In this process ancient dwellers played an important role again, each of them related to a part of the set of values: the Romans as bringers of Christianity and the heathen Franks as the simple, but honest, though not entirely civilized people.[68] It is not just modernization, but also modern rational scientific archaeology that partly destroyed this mythical landscape, though elements from it still lead a persistent life to prove that, even in our day, different (historical) landscapes exist at the same time, and that rational scientific archaeology has not and cannot make up for the loss it brought with it.

The result of the above analysis is not a simple evolutionist development, but a surprisingly complex pattern. From late prehistory until into the pre-modern period we observe an articulation of different forms of claims on land. In no phase can one speak of the exclusive ownership of land by a certain group or institution. There always appears to be a system of multiple overlapping claims, increasingly so for the younger periods. It may also be concluded that in all the periods of the time span studied, the concept of ancestors plays a crucial part in the way in which claims on land are represented. Moreover, there is always a cosmological embedding of the bond between people and the land.

[67] Behets 1969, 43-47.

[68] This theme will be dealt with more extensively in a volume on the excavations of the medieval settlements at Geldrop by F. Theuws.

Fig. 10. Location of the excavated sites or historical places discussed in this volume.
1 Beegden; 2 Mierlo-Hout; 3 Someren; 4 Kessel; 5 Hulsel; 6 Postel; 7 Eersel

6   COMMENTS ON THE PAPERS

In the above more general discussion, reference has repeatedly been made to contributions in this volume. We would now like to discuss the content of the various contributions and their connection in more detail. Central to the project is the study of long-term developments from the Late Bronze Age until into the Late Middle Ages. This long time span is also covered by the archaeological field-work. In this book, the emphasis has, for practical reasons, been placed on two periods: the Late Bronze Age/Iron Age and the Middle Ages.

The first five articles focus on the analyses of the mortuary ritual in the Urnfield period. Urnfields were traditionally one of the most characteristic archaeological features in the sand landscape of the Lower Rhine. Several hundred cemeteries have been localized, and these have played an important part in creating an image of the Late Bronze Age and Early Iron Age societies. It was observed that the study of these cemeteries had come to a standstill and that is was characterized by conceptual poverty. One of the aims of the South Netherlands project is to give a new incentive to urnfield research.

In the first, synthesizing contribution by Roymans and Kortlang, a new theoretical framework is presented which may open up new lines of research into the urnfields. Their line of argument may be summarized as follows:

a. the Urnfield period is a period of demographic expansion and agrarian intensification;

b. this results in increasing pressure on the land;

c. this leads to new cultural mechanisms for regulating the changing association with the land; for example, changes in kinship ideology, new marriage rules and a greater emphasis on the collective identity of local communities in relation to outside groups;

d. the mortuary ritual associated with the urnfields forms the main ritual context within which these social and ideological changes are expressed.

Subsequently, in the contributions of Roymans, Tol and Kortlang, concrete case studies are given in the form of reports of urnfield excavations at Beegden, Mierlo-Hout and Someren (the latter two in combination with settlement research). These excavations belonged to the new series of urnfields recently excavated as part of the South Netherlands project.[69] The cemeteries of Someren and Beegden, in particular, are of great importance as models. Someren is the first location in the Northwest-European plain where a complete urnfield has been excavated together with a substantial part (ca 20 hectares) of the settlement territory associated with it. This provides unique possibilities for analysing the relation between cemetery and settlement. The small, but completely excavated urnfield of Beegden offers exceptional opportunities for spatial analyses which shed new light on the social and ideological aspects of the mortuary ritual. Thanks to these new excavations we get an idea of the active role played by the burial ritual in the creation and reproduction of the social and cosmological order of local communities.

Ter Schegget's study draws our attention to the existence in late pre- and protohistory of other ritual repertoires which are perhaps also connected with the burial system. It is clear that, in the Iron Age, not all the members of local communities were buried in regular cemeteries. In the northeast Netherlands, we have the phenomenon of bog bodies. Furthermore, throughout the Netherlands stray human bones are regularly found among Iron Age settlement material. In recent years there has been increasing evidence that human remains were also deposited in large and small rivers in later prehistoric times. However, there has not yet been any systematic attention for this category of material from rivers. One first convincing dataset which might trigger off the discussion is the bone material from a large ritual find complex from the Meuse at Kessel. The greater part appears to date from the later Iron Age, but other periods are also represented.

The systematic archaeological study of the Middle Ages in the Meuse Demer Scheldt area only started after 1980 with the excavation of a number of settlements like those at Dommelen, Bladel and Hulsel. Later, the excavations at Geldrop and Someren and numerous smaller ones in the 1990s added substantially to the knowledge and brought about revisions of the models created in the first 10 years. This research started in a Dutch archaeological context that stressed environmental conditions as a dominant factor in human existence. This was an understandable point of departure for an archaeology rooted in the wetlands of the western Netherlands, where environmental conditions changed dramatically from time to time in pre- and protohistory. However, conditions were very different in the sandy areas of the south, and from the onset of the programme in 1980 we stressed that social and economic conditions and religious practices should be in the foreground of research. We cooperated closely with historians and the first 10 years (1980-1990) were in fact spent entirely on creating a body of basic knowledge on medieval material culture and the landscape in the Meuse Demer Scheldt region. In order to correlate

---

[69] Three other urnfields have been excavated in 1997 and 1998: Weert-'Raak', Roermond-'Musschenberg' and Sittard-'Hoge Veld'. First reports of the results are in preparation

26

archaeological research to historical research we focused on the analysis of changing property and power relations and the landed property structure on the local level and changes in settlement patterns. The first results were very promising. We could easily prove that the medieval peasant society in the Meuse Demer Scheldt area, although far removed from medieval centres, was not a immobile society, but that it was transforming all the time. It also became clear that there were correlations in the transformations of settlement patterns and local power and property relations. The archaeological research triggered off new historical research into the Early and High Middle Ages of the region as well. This had virtually come to a standstill because of the idea that in this backward region nothing interesting happened and that there were insufficient sources to do proper historical research. However, perspectives changed and the region now proved to have excellent possibilities to analyse cultural processes. The juridical–institutional perspective lost its primary position in research and after 15 years of excavations and study we are grasping the opportunities of an enlarged body of evidence (material as well as textual), a combination of intensive archaeological and historical research and the development of new perspectives on medieval society.[70] However, the Middle Ages is a vast area of study, and basic research had only been carried out for some periods in it, and much excavated material is still unpublished. A first attempt to analyse the archaeological evidence in terms of cultural processes, moving away from a processual perspective, is made for the Merovingian period in relation to the analysis of the *villa* as an organizing structure for society as a whole, instead of seeing it as a means of organizing agricultural production alone.[71] Other studies were aimed at (re)constructing basic historical developments[72] (for instance establishing who were the main power holders in the region and their strategies of gaining or holding power in relation to settlement) or at the study of property relations and settlement patterns at the local level.[73] Our present activities are twofold: we try to publish the basic material from excavations and try to develop new perspectives on the analysis of the cultural landscape in the region. For the study of the Middle Ages, a close encounter with historians and with texts is again envisaged.[74]

The medieval contributions in this volume do not differ in character so much because some of them are written by historians and one by an archaeologist as because of the perspectives used.

[70] Between 1990 and 1996 excavations took place but activities aimed at interpreting the medieval material virtually came to a standstill because those originally involved had to turn to other projects. The new project 'Settlement and landscape in the Meuse Demer Scheldt region' takes up this research again.

[71] Theuws 1991.

[72] Theuws/Bijsterveld 1991.

[73] See for instance the contributions in Verhoeven/Theuws 1989.

[74] In a recent contribution to the debate on the nature of medieval archaeology, Austin complained about the historical agenda of medieval archaeology. What he probably means is a specific historical agenda, because there are many historical agendas. He pleads for a medieval archaeological agenda of its own and wants to shake off the historical yoke: 'If medieval historians, however, continue to assert the dominance of the word over the material and if they continue to use history as a prop to the present institutional arrangements of power, then we should not bother with the dialogue and we can leave them bricked up by their own hand in their own ivory towers'(Austin 1997 (1990). Maybe his stand is determined by his fixation on power relations and not for instance on mentalities and systems of ideas on the socio-cosmological order. We have never felt the relation between medieval history and medieval archaeology to be so negative. We often worked within an historical agenda by choice, because (anthropologically informed) medieval historians since 'Annales times' perhaps asked more interesting questions than some of our fellow archaeologists. That processual archaeology (as an alternative to the historical agenda) has not been 'accepted' by medieval archaeologists is not so much because of their working within a historical agenda as because of their working within an intellectual environment where they could easily 'feel' the shortcomings of processual archaeology

Theuws' contribution, written eight years ago, aims at publishing archaeological data and reflects the perspectives of the regional research project at the end of the 1980s. The contribution focuses on the analysis of the relation between the cultural landscape and property relations throughout the Middle Ages on the local level in one village. It stresses the importance of the prolonged presence of a single landowner (the abbey of Sint Truiden in Belgium), the disappearance of its direct involvement in the village and the transformation in the layout of the settlement and landscape in the 13th century. The study is intended to be one of several in order to grasp local developments on the basis of which studies departing from new perspectives can be carried out.[75]

Bijsterveld analyses the meaning of the gift of landed property by local and regional aristocrats to the monastery of Postel for the process of defining their position vis à vis the community in the region as well as in relation to the supernatural world. He analyses the spiritual and socio-political intentions of the donors. Eternal life is sought after by donating 'eternal' land, originating from the ancestors, to the monastery. Bijsterveld's analysis provides new insights into the conceptualization and valuation of land and landed property in the region.

Vangheluwe's contribution contrasts with Bijsterveld's study in that it analyses the structure of non-aristocratic landed property in the 'post-feudal' Late Middle Ages, when aristocratic property has almost disappeared. Religious institutions still retain a number of large, leased out farmsteads but their local influence has disappeared almost completely. A detailed analysis of the rent registers of the Duke of Brabant shows the effects of the major transformations in society and the cultural landscape in the 13th century. What remains is a small-scale society, with small hamlets and small farmsteads that have no more than 2.4 ha. cultivated land (arable and hayland) on average, but one which finds itself in economic prosperous circumstances. Intensification of production led to a total fragmentation of the cultivated lands. The study also shows that there is no such thing as a commodification of the land in the late-medieval or early-modern period. Most land is still family-held and passed on through heritage, not through a real estate market and buying and selling.

The three studies provide a first insight into the structure of property relations, conceptualizations of landed property and the valuation of land. It is a start. In the near future we will have to publish basic evidence on the one hand and analyse the practical use and symbolic ordering of the landscape and the underlying concepts and values on different levels on the other hand. Other themes present themselves, such as the symbolic use of money in relations where claims on the land are involved as well as in relations with the supernatural world.

It has been said before and we will repeat it here again: after many years of collecting data and doing basic research on the local level it is time to try out new developments in thinking in archaeology and history on the cultural landscape in a concrete case. The Meuse Demer Scheldt region seems to be a perfect laboratory for this and we are confident of living up to expectations.

without really being able to describe them. Discussions on the pluriformity of culture already raged in French medieval history when processual archaeology with its emphasis on adaptation to the environment as an important condition for human life, was presented as a novelty in Europe (Le Goff 1970). Austin pleads for a more archaeological agenda for medieval archaeologists in which ideas formulated by prehistorians are included. My guess is that when medieval archaeologists turn to the same intellectual sources outside archaeology used by these prehistorians and to historians as well, they will come up with something even more interesting, for there is a lot of guessing for the prehistorian where there is reading for the medieval archaeologist.

[75] Theuws, in prep; Huybers, in prep.

REFERENCES

Arts, N., (ed.) 1994: *Sporen onder de Kempische stad. Archeologie, ecologie en vroegste geschiedenis van Eindhoven 1225-1500*, Eindhoven.

Austin, D., 1997 (1990): The 'proper study' of medieval archaeology, in D. Austin/L. Alcock (eds), *From the Baltic to the Black Sea. Studies in Medieval archaeology*, London/New York, 9-42.

Austin, D./J. Thomas, 1997 (1990): The 'proper study' of medieval archaeology: a case study, in D. Austin/L. Alcock (eds), *From the Baltic to the Black Sea. Studies in Medieval archaeology*, London/New York, 43-78.

Behets, J., 1969: *De plattelandsgemeente in het graafschap Loon en het omliggende van de vroege middeleeuwen tot aan de Franse revolutie*, Bokrijk (Bokrijkse Berichten 10).

Bieleman, J., 1992: *Geschiedenis van de landbouw in Nederland 1500-1950*, Meppel.

Binford, L. 1972: Archaeology as Anthropology, in L. Binford, *An archaeological perspective*, New York, 20-32.

Bintliff, J., 1991: The contribution of an Annaliste/structural history approach to archaeology, in J. Bintliff (ed.), *The Annales school and archaeology*, Leicester, 1-33.

Bijsterveld, A.-J.A., 1989a: Een zorgelijk bezit. De benedictijnenabdijen van Echternach en St. Truiden en het beheer van hun goederen en rechten in Oost-Brabant, 1100-1300, *Noordbrabants Historisch Jaarboek* 6, 7-44.

Bijsterveld, A.-J.A., 1989b: «Sinte Willebrordus eygen». Het bezit van de abdij van Echternach in Texandrië (Nederland en België), circa 700-1300, in G. Kiesel/J. Schroeder, (eds), *Willibrord. Apostel der Niederlände. Gründer der Abtei Echternach. Gedenkgabe zum 1250. Todestag des angelsächsischen Missionars*, Luxembourg, 271-290.

Bijsterveld, A.J.A., 1997: Een nieuwe orde? De politieke en religieuze ontwikkelingen in het Maas-Demer-Scheldegebied in de elfde en twaalfde eeuw en de stichting van norbertijnenabdijen in het tweede kwart van de twaalfde eeuw, in S. van de Perre (ed.), *Norbertijnen in de politiek. Verslagen van de zevende contactdag. Abdij van 't Park zaterdag 26 april 1997*, Brussel, 9-38.

Bonenfant, P., 1962: La fondation de «villes neuves» en Brabant au Moyen Age, *Vierteljahrschrift für Sozial and Wirtschaftsgeschichte* 49, 145-170.

Bont, Chr. de, 1993: '...Al het merkwaardige in bonte afwisseling...'. Een historische geografie van Midden- en Oost-Brabant, Waalre, 67-106.

Bradley, R., 1997: Working the land: imagining the landscape, *Archaeological Dialogues* 4, 39-52.

Braudel, F., 1978 (1949): *The Mediterranean and the Mediterranean World in the Age of Philip II*, 1-2, Glasgow.

Brink, G. van den, 1996: *De grote overgang. Een lokaal onderzoek naar de modernisering van het bestaan. Woensel 1670-1920*, Nijmegen.

Casparie, W.A./W. Groenman-van Waateringe, 1980: Palynological analysis of Dutch barrows, *Palaeohistoria* 22, 7-65.

Coppet, D. de, 1985: ...Land owns people, in R.H. Barnes/D. de Coppet/R.J. Parkin (eds), *Context and levels. Anthropological essays on hierarchy*, Oxford (Jaso Occasional Papers 4), 78-90.

Derks, T., 1998: *Gods, Temples and ritual practices. The transformation of religious ideas and values in Roman Gaul*, Amsterdam (AAS 2).

Derks, T., 1997: The transformation of landscape and religious representations in Roman Gaul, *Archaeological Dialogues* 4, 126-163 (including discussion).

Devroey, J.-P., 1985: Les premiers polyptyques rémois VIIe-IXe siècles, in A. Verhulst, (ed.), *Le grand domaine aux époques mérovingienne et carolingienne/Die Grundherrschaft im frühen Mittelalter*, Gent, 78-97.

Devroey, J.-P., 1986: Réflections sur l'économie des premiers temps carolingiens (768-877): grands domains et action politique entre Seine et Rhin, *Francia* 13, 475-488.

Flannery, K., (ed.), 1976: *The early mesoamerican village*, New York.

Fokkens, H., 1996: The Maaskant project. Continuity and change of a regional research project, *Archaeological Dialogues* 3, 196-215.

Friedman, J., 1984 (1975): Tribes, states and transformations, in M. Bloch (ed.), *Marxist analyses and social anthropology*, London (ASA Studies), 161-202.

Geary, P., 1994 (1986): Exchange and Interaction between the Living and the Dead in Early Medieval Society, in P.J. Geary, *Living with the Dead in the Middle Ages*, Ithaca/London, 77-92 (earlier as: Échanges et relations entre les vivants et les morts dans la société du Haut Moyen Age, *Droit et Cultures* 12, 1986, 3-17).

Gerritsen, F., in prep.: *Late Bronze Age and Iron Age societies in the Meuse-Demer-Scheldt region* (Ph.D. thesis, Vrije Universiteit, Amsterdam).

Goff, J., Le, 1977: *Pour une autre Moyen Age. Temps, travail, et culture en occident: 18 essais*, Paris.

Gurevich, A., 1992 (1987): Semantics of the medieval community: 'farmstead', 'land', 'world', in A. Gurevich, *Historical anthropology of the Middle Ages*, Cambridge, 200-209.

Huybers, T., in prep: *The ethnography of the 'peasant' household in the High Middle Ages in the Meuse Demer Scheldt region* (Ph.D. thesis, University of Amsterdam).

Harmsen, G., 1968: *Inleiding tot de geschiedenis*, Bilthoven.

Hoppenbrouwers, P.C.M., 1992: *Een middeleeuwse samenleving. Het land van Heusden (ca. 1360 - ca. 1515)*, Wageningen (AAG Bijdragen 32).

Hüppe, J., 1996: Zur Entstehung der Heiden in der Bronzezeit, *Die Kunde* 47, 13-20.

Ingold, T., 1993: The temporality of the landscape, *World archaeology* 25, 152-174.

Kakebeeke, A., 1968: Some observations about habitation and parcelling in the hamlet Schadewijk, municipality of Eersel (North-Brabant), *Geografisch Tijdschrift* 12, 190-204.

Kolen, J., 1995: Recreating (in) nature, visiting history. Second thoughts on landscape reserves and their role in the preservation and experience of the historic environment, *Archaeological Dialogues* 2, 127-159.

Leenders, K.A.H.W., 1996: *Van Turnhoutervoorde tot Strienemonde. Ontginnings- en nederzettings-geschiedenis van het noordwesten van het Maas-Schelde-Demergebied (400-1350)*, Zutphen.

Lemaire, T., 1997: Arcaheology between the invention and the destruction of the landscape, *Archaeological Dialogues* 4, 5-38.

Molemans, J., 1986: De Kempische gemeente, *Brabants Heem* 38, 77-94.

Pape, J.C., 1970: Plaggen soils in the Netherlands, *Geoderma* 4, 229-255.

Rosenwein, B., 1989: *To be the neighbour of Saint Peter. The social meaning of Cluny's property, 909-1049*, Ithaka/London.

Roymans, N., 1995a: The cultural biography of urnfields and the long-term history of a mythical landscape, *Archaeological Dialogues* 2, 2-38.

Roymans, N., 1995b: Romanization, cultural identity and the ethnic discussion. The integration of Lower Rhine populations in the Roman empire, in J. Metzler/M. Millett/N. Roymans/J. Slofstra, *Integration in the Early Roman West. The role of culture and ideology*, Luxemburg, 47-64.

Roymans, N., 1996a: The sword or the plough. Regional dynamics in the romanisation of Belgic Gaul and the Rhineland area, in N. Roymans (ed.), *From the sword to the plough. Three studies on the earliest Romanisation of Northern Gaul*, Amsterdam (Amsterdam Archaeological Studies, 1), 9-126.

Roymans, N., 1996b: The South Netherlands project. Changing perspectives on landscape and culture, *Archaeological Dialogues* 3, 231-245.

Roymans, N., in prep.: *Changing settlement patterns and environmental dynamics in the Meuse-Demer-Scheldt area from the Bronze Age to the Middle Ages.*

Roymans, N./F. Kortlang, 1993: Bewoningsgeschiedenis van een dekzandlandschap langs de Aa te Someren, in N. Roymans/F. Theuws (eds), *Een en al Zand. Twee jaar graven naar het Brabantse verleden*, 's-Hertogenbosch, 22-41.

Roymans, N./A. Tol 1996 (eds): *Opgravingen in Kampershoek en de Molenakker te Weert. Campagne 1995*, Amsterdam (Zuidnederlandse Archeologische Rapporten 4).

Schinkel, K., 1994: *Zwervende erven. Bewoningssporen in Oss-Ussen uit Bronstijd, IJzertijd en Romeinse tijd* 1, Leiden (Ph.D. thesis, University of Leiden).

Slofstra, J./H.H. van Regteren Altena/N. Roymans/F. Theuws 1982: *Het Kempenprojekt. Een regionaal-archeologisch onderzoeksprogramma*, Waalre.

Slofstra, J., 1991: Changing settlement systems in the Meuse-Demer-Scheldt area during the Early Roman period, in N. Roymans/F. Theuws (eds), *Images of the past. Studies on ancient societies in Northwestern Europe*, Amsterdam (Studies in Prae- en Protohistorie, 7), 132-199.

Spek, Th., 1993: Milieudynamiek en locatiekeuze op het Drents Plateau (3400 v.Chr. - 1850 na Chr.), in J.N.H. Elerie/S.W. Jager/Th. Spek (eds), *Landschapsgeschiedenis van de Strubben/Kniphorstbos. Archeologische en historisch-ecologische studies van een natuurgebied op de Hondsrug*, Groningen, 169-236.

Steurs, W., 1993: *Naissance d'une région. Aux origines de la Mairie de Bois-le-Duc. Recherches sur le Brabant septentrional aux 12e et 13e siècles*, Bruxelles (Académie royale de Belgique. Mémoire de la Classe des lettres. Collection in-8°, 3e série tome 3).

Strijbos, H., 1995: *Kerken van Heren en Boeren. Bouwhistorische verkenningen naar de middeleeuwse kerken in het kwartier van Kempenland* (Bijdragen tot de studie van het Brabantse Heem 37), 's-Hertogenbosch.

Theuws, F., 1988: *De archeologie van de periferie. Studies naar de ontwikkeling van bewoning en samenleving in het Maas-Demer-Schelde gebied in de vroege middeleeuwen*, Amsterdam.

Theuws, F.C., 1989: Middeleeuwse parochiecentra in de Kempen 1000-1350, in A. Verhoeven/F. Theuws (eds), *Het Kempenprojekt 3. De Middeleeuwen centraal*, Waalre (Bijdragen tot de studie van het Brabantse heem 33), 97-216.

Theuws, F., 1991: Landed property and manorial organisation in Northern Austrasia: some considerations and a case study, in N.Roymans/F. Theuws (eds), *Images of the past. Studies on ancient societies in Northwestern Europe*, Amsterdam (Studies in Prae- en Protohistorie, 7), 299-407.

Theuws, F., 1993: Heren en boeren in vroeg-middeleeuws Geldrop, in N. Roymans/F. Theuws (ed.), *Een en al Zand. Twee jaar graven naar het Brabantse verleden*, 's-Hertogenbosch, 88-104.

Theuws, F., 1994: Elites and the transition from Merovingian to Carolingian, in P.O. Nielsen/K. Randsborg/H. Thrane, (eds), *The archaeology of Gudme and Lundeborg, Papers presented at a conference at Svendborg, october 1991*, 195-201.

Theuws, F., in prep.: *Frankish transformations. Actions and thoughts of aristocrats and peasants in the pagus Texandrië (6th-8th centuries).*

Theuws, F./A.-J. Bijsterveld, 1991: Der Maas-Demer-Schelde-Raum in ottonischer und salischer Kaiserzeit, in H.W. Böhme (ed.), *Siedlungen und Landesausbau zur Salierzeit*, Sigmaringen, (Römisch-Germanisches Zentralmuseum, Monographien Band 27) I 109-146.

Theuws, F./A. Verhoeven/H.H. van Regteren-Altena 1988: Medieval settlement at Dommelen I-II, *BROB* 38, 229-430.

Thomas, R., 1997: Land, kinship relations and the rise of enclosed settlement in first millennium B.C. Britain, *Oxford Journal of Archaeology* 16, 211-218.

Tilley, Chr., 1996: *An ethnography of the Neolithic. Early prehistoric societies in southern Scandinavia*, Cambridge (New studies in archaeology).

Verhoeven, A./F. Theuws, (eds), 1989: *Het Kempenprojekt 3. De Middeleeuwen centraal*, Waalre (Bijdragen tot de studie van het Brabantse Heem 33).

Vita-Finzi, C./E.S. Higgs, 1970: Prehistoric economy in the Mt. Carmel area of Palestine: site catchment analysis, *Proceedings of the Prehistoric Society* 36, 1-37.

Waterbolk, H.T., 1979: Siedlungskontinuität im Küstengebiet der Nordsee zwischen Rhein und Elbe, *Probleme der Küstenforschung im südlichen Nordseegebiet* 13, 1-21.

Weiner, A., 1992: *Inalienable possessions. The paradox of keeping-while-giving*, Berkeley,/Los Angeles/Oxford.

Westering, W. van de, 1988: Man-made soils in the Netherlands, especially in the sandy area's ('plaggen soils'), in W. Groenman van Waateringe/M. Robinson. (eds), *Man-made soils* (BAR, Int.Ser. 410), 5-19.

Zimmermann, W.H., 1992: Die Siedlungen des 1. bis 6. Jahrhunderts nach Christus von Flögeln-Eekhöltjen, Niedersachsen. Die Bauformen und ihre Funktionen, *Probleme der Küstenforschung im südliche Nordseegebiet* 19.

Urnfield symbolism, ancestors and the land in the Lower Rhine region

Nico Roymans/Fokko Kortlang[1]

I   INTRODUCTION: URNFIELD RESEARCH IN THE LOWER RHINE REGION

The monumental barrow cemeteries or urnfields from the Late Bronze Age and Early Iron Age traditionally belong to the most characteristic archaeological phenomena of the sandy landscapes in the Lower Rhine region. Up to the '70s our knowledge of the inhabitants of that time of the sandy areas was almost entirely determined by the study of these cemeteries. Concepts like *'Niederrheinische Grabhügelkultur'*, 'Urnfield culture' and 'Urnfield period' bear witness to this.[2] Though our knowledge

[1] This research was carried out within the framework of the project 'Settlement and landscape in the Maas-Demer-Scheldt region'. The project is supported (in part) by the Foundation for History, Archaeology and Art History, which is subsidized by the Netherlands Organisation for Scientific Research (NWO). We would like to thank the other members of the project for having discussed with us the ideas put forward in this study. We also thank Jos Bazelmans for reading the manuscript and making comments on it.

[2] The two last-mentioned terms suggest close cultural links with the Central European Urnfield Cultures. Desittere (1968), basing himself on the study of the grave pottery, considered the Lower Rhine Urnfield group to be a subgroup of the Central European Urnfield Culture. However, the Lower Rhine urnfield groups have many specific characteristics that are rooted in local Middle Bronze Age B traditions. Therefore, they cannot simply be regarded as a subgroup of the Central European Urnfield complex. The term *Niederrheinische Grabhügelkultur* is used to emphasize the particular cultural identity of this region. See the discussion in Kersten 1948; Verwers 1969; Roymans 1991, 14; Ruppel 1995. Furthermore, it should be noted that the term 'Urnfield period' in the Lower Rhine area refers to the Late Bronze Age as well as the Early Iron Age (Ha C/D).

has substantially broadened in the past three decades with information on settlements, the agrarian economy and the circulation of bronze objects, the cemeteries keep playing a dominant role in the images we create of Late Bronze Age and Early Iron Age society. Nevertheless it should be stated that the archaeological potential of these urnfields has still hardly been used.[3] A short overview of the history of urnfield research in the area between the rivers Meuse, Demer and Scheldt may elucidate this.

The 'hey-day' of urnfield archaeology is the period between 1850 and 1960. It is the sad story of hundreds of barrow cemeteries which were clearly visible in the heathlands at that time and which were destroyed by reclamation activities and 'urn-digging'. Only a few cemeteries were systematically investigated by archaeologists. These early excavations are, however, of limited importance: not a single cemetery was excavated completely, and many burials had already been plundered by urn-diggers. Physical-anthropological research of cremated bones did not exist, and the zones between individual barrows were (also because of the limited technical and financial means) rarely excavated. These older excavations are clearly unsuitable for answering a series of basic questions that archaeology now poses, like that of the demographical composition of the population, and the size, spatial structure and development of the cemetery. The answer to these basic questions is a prerequisite for raising more complex questions concerning the symbolism of grave-fields and grave monuments in the framework of the social and cosmological order of Lower Rhine Urnfield populations. In the Lower Rhine area, but also elsewhere in the Northwest European Plain, these topics have hardly received any attention to date. In this regard, urnfield research is still in its infancy.

If we want to enhance urnfield research, it is necessary to excavate several new cemeteries more or less completely. The problem is, however, that well-preserved monumental urnfields are no longer available in the zones of the former heathlands. The cemeteries that are left there have all been plundered or seriously disturbed in the past, and because of their actual legal protection they are not available for research. The investigation of cemeteries in another zone of the pre-industrial cultural landscape offers better perspectives: the zone of the traditional arable complexes or 'essen' of the hamlets and villages. The 'essen archaeology', which started in the '60s but has only got into its stride since the late '80s,[4] has produced several examples of urnfields that are hidden underneath thick *plaggen* layers; every year there are some newly-discovered cemeteries that are destroyed by building activities. The urnfields situated underneath these *plaggen* soils are often fairly well preserved; most burials are still intact, while the presence of ditched peripheral structures makes it rather easy to reconstruct the form and size of the original grave monuments. Moreover, the investigation of urnfields underneath the *essen* often makes it possible to excavate parts of the corresponding settlements, as at Someren, Mierlo-Hout and St.-Oedenrode.[5] For our future modelling of the social and ideational organisation of Lower Rhine Urnfield groups we are primarily dependent on the possibilities offered to us by the *essen* archaeology, and therefore these should be used optimally.

In analysing the urnfields from the Lower Rhine region we are confronted with a rich variety of mortuary practices and symbols that refer to a complex of ideas and values concerning the social organisation and the relationship with the supernatural order. Up to now no attempts have been made

---

[3] Until recently, the emphasis was laid on typochronology of pottery and grave structures and research into the origins of the Lower Rhine Urnfield culture from a cultural historical perspective. Cf. for example Kersten 1948; Desittere 1968; Verwers 1969; idem 1972; Kooi 1979; Verlinde 1985; Wilhelmi 1974; idem 1983.

[4] Cf. Roymans 1996, 236 ff.

[5] Kortlang, this volume; Tol, this volume; Van Bodegraven 1991, respectively.

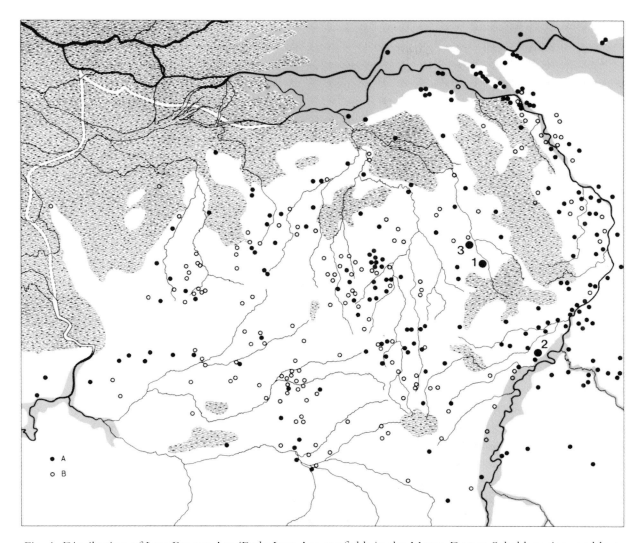

Fig. 1. Distribution of Late Bronze Age/Early Iron Age urnfields in the Meuse–Demer–Scheldt region, and location of the urnfields of Someren (1), Beegden (2) and Mierlo-Hout (3). After Roymans 1991, fig. 21.
A cemetery known from an excavation and/or preserved urns; B cemetery only known from old find reports

to understand these practices and symbolism. Anyway, this would hardly have been possible, as the quality of the information concerning the Lower Rhine urnfields is rather poor, and has only shown a substantial improvement during the last years. A major precondition is the availability of several completely excavated cemeteries, where we have sufficient grip on chronology, and where we can relate the variation of grave structures to the results of physical-anthropological analyses of the cremation remains. Within the Meuse–Demer–Scheldt area, Beegden and Someren (fig. 1) belong to the first cemeteries to meet these conditions. They allow us, in combination with the evidence from some other cemeteries, to formulate hypotheses that can direct further research and stimulate discussion.

   Starting point of this study is the idea that the mortuary ritual is embedded in the wider system of ideas and values of a society. It is part of an all-embracing ritual cycle of life an death, in which groups give their view on the social order and the wider cosmos. The mortuary ritual and the material culture associated with it, are media via which a perception of social reality is presented, and which actively contribute to the creation of this reality.[6] This makes the mortuary ritual an important element in the creation and reproduction of the socio-cosmic order.

Discussions concerning the symbolism of urnfields and of specific categories of grave monuments only make sense when they are placed in the broader context of the Lower Rhine Urnfield culture, and particularly its formative stage in the Late Bronze Age. Therefore we first have to pay attention to this broader cultural context.

2 DEMOGRAPHICAL EXPANSION, TERRITORIALITY AND THE FORMATION OF THE LOWER RHINE URNFIELD CULTURE

In the sandy landscapes of the Lower Rhine area, the Late Bronze Age (Ha A2/B1) is the formative period of what is called the *Niederrheinische Grabhügelkultur*. This term refers to a complex of cultural changes, of which the most important archaeological manifestations are:

a. the introduction of a new mortuary ritual that is materialised in 'urnfields', i.e. cremation cemeteries with stable locations, in which most members of a local community of 3 to 6 households are interred under individual barrows of varying shape and size. The cremation rite, the use of urns, the construction of barrows and (though less frequent) the placing of secondary interments in tumuli, are continuations of local Middle Bronze Age traditions. Major differences with the mortuary ritual of Middle Bronze Age groups are the introduction of a new type of grave (the long barrow or 'long-bed'; fig. 5), and the use of collective cemeteries by households forming a burial community. This is in contrast to the Middle Bronze Age when tumuli are widely spaced over the territory of a local group and are probably burial places of individual family units. They are indicated as 'family barrows', also because they have been intensively used for secondary burials of adults as well as children.[7]

b. the introduction of a new repertoire of ceramics, in which smooth-walled, decorated pottery takes a prominent place (particularly in grave contexts).[8] This is in contrast to the non-complex Middle Bronze Age pottery. However, we can also observe a certain continuity between Middle Bronze Age ceramics and the Late Bronze Age coarse ware (*Grobkeramik*).

c. an important intensification of the bronze circulation via the participation in Atlantic and Central-European exchange networks. Via these networks, Lower Rhine groups gain access to a wide range of bronze objects, including prestigious weaponry (swords in particular).

d. the gradual introduction of a more advanced system of arable farming, commonly indicated as *celtic-field* agriculture. In the sandy landscapes, *celtic fields* can be characterized as large arable complexes with a systematic layout, reflecting a considerable degree of collective organisation by the local community.

[6]   Cf. Hodder 1994, 74; Tilley 1996, 215 ff.; Diepeveen, in press, ch. 2.

[7]   Cf. the discussion in Roymans/Fokkens 1991, 12 ff. Theunissen (1993) warns us that we should not forget that only a small number of the deceased (c. 15%) is represented in the Middle Bronze Age barrows. The mortuary ritual of the majority of the population remains archaeologically intangible (flat graves around the tumuli?). This is in contrast to the Urnfield period when the great majority of the population is buried in the cemeteries.

[8]   Desittere 1968; Ruppel 1995; Van den Broeke 1991.

A New (Late Bronze Age) practices

– long-term clustering of graves of members of a local group of
  several families at one location in the landscape
– most members of the local group are buried in the urnfield
  and receive individual grave monuments
– great differentiation in the size of grave monuments
– introduction of a new type of monument: the long grave
– introduction of new pottery types

B Continuity of Middle Bronze Age B traditions:

– continuity of barrow ritual
– continuity of the cremation rite and the use of urns
– limited re-use of barrows for secondary burials
– limited continuity in grave pottery (coarse ware)

Table 1. The mortuary ritual of Lower Rhine Urnfield groups.

In the Lower Rhine region, the cultural changes described above take place in the course of the Late Bronze Age and should be seen in relation to each other. Archaeologists have repeatedly tried to interpret these changes. At first, great emphasis was laid on the immigration of Central-European Urnfield groups.[9] This migration hypothesis, however, was pushed into the background as new research produced more indications for a gradual development of the mortuary ritual, pottery, house-building, and settlement system from the Middle to the Late Bronze Age. It is now accepted that the formation of the Lower Rhine Urnfield Culture should be understood in terms of a transformation of local Middle Bronze Age society. The Lower Rhine populations demonstrate in their material culture a high degree of autonomy with regard to the Central European Urnfield Culture. This idea of a separate cultural identity is expressed in the term *Niederrheinische Grabhügelkultur*, introduced by Kersten in 1948.

What is the driving force behind these societal and cultural dynamics in the Late Bronze Age? In models used for explaining the social changes in Northwestern Europe a central role is often ascribed to the exchange and consumptive use of bronze objects in generating more hierarchical and competitive social formations. In this contribution we argue that the changes in the mortuary ritual are an expression of the way society copes with social problems emerging from a continuous demographical expansion and increased pressure on land. To elaborate on this thesis, we use results of urnfield investigations as well as large-scale research of settlements.

We start with the assumption that there is a territorial structure in Urnfield societies in the Northwest European Plain. Each local community of c. 3 to 6 families has its own territory, which includes an urnfield, a *celtic-field* complex (in which the dispersed farmsteads are situated), and a peripheral zone of uncultivated land, used for grazing cattle, collecting wood, etc. In the sandy landscapes the urnfields can be used for quantifying and mapping these territories.[10] For the Meuse-Demer-Scheldt region, 85 territories from the Late Bronze Age and 168 from the Early Iron Age can be reconstructed on the basis of an inventorisation of urnfields.[11] If we want to compare this evidence

---

[9]   E.g. De Laet 1974, 376 ff.

[10] Cf. Waterbolk 1987, 191 ff.

[11] Roymans 1991, 66-72. The great majority of the Late

Bronze Age urnfields continued to be used in the
Early Iron Age.

with the distribution of the population in the preceding Middle Bronze Age, we only have the barrows at our disposal. Middle Bronze Age communities, however, do not have a tradition of common cemeteries with a stable location. Barrows – isolated or in small groups – are distributed over a considerable part of the territory of a local community; the burial places frequently changed their location, probably in combination with a regular shifting of individual farmsteads. In order to get an impression of the number of cemeteries and indirectly of the number of territories, we consider those barrows with a distance of less than 1,5 km to each other and which are not separated by valleys of local streams or moors, as parts of one single cemetery.[12] Thus we arrive at a total of 55 Middle Bronze Age 'cemeteries' or territories for the Meuse-Demer-Scheldt region (fig. 2). The number of tumuli per case varies from 1 to 30.[13]

On the basis of the evidence summarised in figure 2, we can give a characterisation of the changing pattern of land-use in the Meuse-Demer-Scheldt region in the Bronze Age and Early Iron Age. In the Middle Bronze Age, population density – compared to that in the Urnfield period – was relatively low. Availability of land does not yet seem to have been a critical factor in the reproduction of society. In this pre-*celtic field* phase, we should probably imagine small dispersed field systems, which were used rather extensively and which were connected with individual farmsteads. These primary domestic units had a considerable degree of autonomy in the management of the land. This is suggested by the isolated position of the farmsteads and the connected 'family barrows', that lay dispersed over the territory of a local group.

Compared to the Middle Bronze Age, the Urnfield period is a phase of powerful demographical expansion, which reaches a maximum in the Early Iron Age (figs. 1 and 2). Relying on the number of urnfields in relation to the number of Middle Bronze Age cemeteries, one might speak of a three-fold increase in the number of settlement territories in the course of the Urnfield period.[14] The increase in the number of urnfields reflects a process of continuous foundation of new settlements by fission of small groups of people from the already existing communities. Relying on the urnfield evidence, it can be argued that more than half of the local communities were founded in the course of the Early Iron Age; the urnfields of Beegden, Someren and Mierlo-Hout are concrete examples for this. In the course of the Urnfield period the sandy landscapes of the Lower Rhine region reach a level of population density that is rarely surpassed in later periods of agrarian expansion, like the Roman period and the Early Middle Ages. There is a process of 'filling up' the landscape with small groups of 3 to 6 families each.

---

[12]   Cf. Waterbolk 1987, 211.

[13]   Beex 1989; Theunissen, in prep. It is important to realise that the great majority of the urnfields as well as the Middle Bronze Age tumuli in the Meuse-Demer-Scheldt region have been discovered in the (former) heathlands, where they manifested themselves as monumental structures. This means that both the distribution maps of urnfields and Middle Bronze Age barrows are subject to the same set of biases related to 'heath-land-archaeology'. No doubt many new cemeteries and groups of barrows can be expected under the thick *plaggen* soil of the medieval arable lands. The chance that an urnfield remained undiscovered in the heath-lands will have been considerably smaller than the chance that a single Middle Bronze Age tumulus remained unnoticed. This difference is to some degree compensated by the fact that Middle Bronze Age barrows were scattered over the settlement territory of a local group; the chance that one of these tumuli is documented is considerably higher.

[14]   It is surprising to see that Waterbolk (1987, 195, 211) observes a similar three-fold increase in the number of settlement territories in Drenthe (northeastern Netherlands). He counts 68 cemeteries/territories from the Middle Bronze Age and 185 from the Urnfield period.

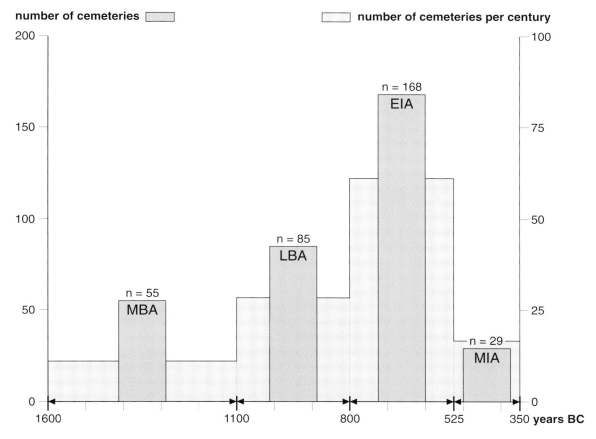

number of cemeteries ☐   ☐ number of cemeteries per century

Fig. 2. Diagram showing the number of territories per sub-period in the Meuse-Demer-Scheldt region, based on a sample of 210 urnfields and 55 Middle Bronze Age 'cemeteries'.
MBA = Middle Bronze Age, LBA = Late Bronze Age, EIA = Early Iron Age, MIA = first half of the Middle Iron Age

The increasing pressure on the land as a consequence of demographical expansion must have had its impact on the territorial organisation. The survey evidence suggests that the foundation of new settlements often did not take place in an 'empty' no man's land, but was realised at the cost of the territories of already existing settlements.[15] These continuous territorial reorganisations will have resulted in a reduction of the average size of the territories of local communities in the course of the Urnfield period. However, these territories were used more intensively now than in the Middle

---

[15] It is probably no coincidence that both the sites of the urnfields of Beegden and Mierlo-Hout, which start in the beginning of the Early Iron Age, have produced evidence for habitation in the Middle Bronze Age (respectively Roymans, this volume; Tol, this volume). Another example is the site of the urnfield of Haps (Verwers 1972). Furthermore, there is no evidence for a 'colonisation' of certain zones of the landscape during the Urnfield period that had been systematically avoided in the Middle Bronze Age. Recent large-scale excavations in the zones of the medieval arable lands or *essen* (generally corresponding with loamy sand plateaus) show that these sections of the landscape, too, were already occupied and claimed in the Middle Bronze Age. Cf. the excavations at Dommelen, Haps, Geldrop, St.-Oedenrode and Hoogeloon, which all have produced some Middle Bronze Age habitation remains.

Bronze Age. It is within this framework that we should understand the introduction of *celtic-field* agriculture. The development outlined above predicts that territoriality becomes a more important principle. There will have been an increased commitment to land, and more emphasis is laid on defining claims on land. We suggest that in the Late Bronze Age control over land instead of over labour became the most important factor for the reproduction of local domestic groups.

This increased pressure on land will have had its effects on the social organisation of local groups; it stimulated the development of social mechanisms to regulate the changing relationship with land.[16] In tribal societies, kinship-ideology is the most obvious mechanism for this. In the Urnfield period, claims on land will have been more strictly controlled and restricted by kinship-ideology than was the case in the preceding Middle Bronze Age. Using ethnographic evidence, we may think of changes in marriage rules, in patterns of inheritance, and in relations between maternal and paternal claims on offspring and resources.[17] Via such strategies, which often led to the development of a more 'closed' kinship structure, the transmission of rights on land could be restricted.

It is against the background of these social and demographical developments that we would like to discuss the significance and role of urnfield ritual and symbolism. In our model, urnfield ritual is connected with the competition between local kin groups over the control of labour and, above all, land.

3   URNFIELDS, ANCESTORS AND TERRITORIALITY

Large-scale settlement research carried out at Someren, Weert, St.-Oedenrode and Mierlo-Hout[18] has demonstrated that the dispersed farmsteads were situated directly around the cemetery, probably in the *celtic fields* (fig. 3). Urnfields (being the location where the remains of the ancestors had their resting-place), were in a spatial, but also in an ideational sense in the centre of the land cultivated and inhabitated by the living community. The cemetery, with its compact and monumental shape and stable location, symbolised the collective identity of each local group. In the small communities living in dispersed farmsteads, the urnfields provided a long-term community focus. They were a fixed reference point providing continuity and stability to the local group, and as such forming a counterbalance to the discontinuities that frequently occurred in the domestic sphere because of the practice of abandonment and small-scale displacement of farmhouses.

Moreover, the monumental urnfields functioned as territorial markers. Because of their physical appearance in the rather open landscape at that time, as well as the oral traditions attached to them, the urnfields symbolised the transcendental claim of a local community and its ancestors on a certain territory. This in a period in which the population density increased and in which territoriality became an important principle. As such, the cemeteries played an active role in the territorial ordering of the landscape.

---

[16]   The claim of newly-found communities on their territory will not always have been recognised by surrounding groups, and will frequently have given rise to conflict. Possibly, such conflicts were at the base of the short-lived use of some urnfields. The Beegden cemetery, for example, was already given up after two generations.

[17]   Cf. the studies of Friedman (1984) on the Kachin in Upper Birma, and Bloch (1984) on the Merina and Zafimaniry in Madagascar. See also the discussions in Hodder 1992, 67 ff.; Tilley 1996, 336; Thomas 1997.

[18]   Weert: Roymans/Tol 1996. Mierlo-Hout: Tol, this volume. St. Oedenrode: Van Bodegraven 1991. Someren: Kortlang, this volume.

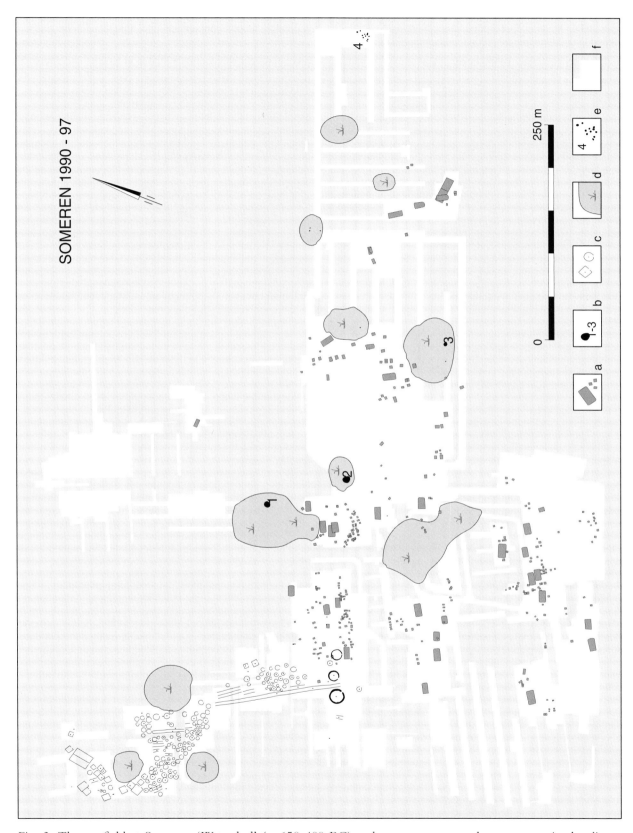

Fig. 3. The urnfield at Someren-'Waterdael' (c. 650–400 BC) and contemporary settlement traces in the direct surroundings.
a farmhouse with outbuildings; b well; c urnfield; d marshy depression; e storage pits; f excavated area

The Lower Rhine urnfields reflect an ideology in which the emphasis lies on the collectivity of the local group instead of the separate families as the constituent elements. This suggests that the inheritance and access to land will have been strongly regulated at the level of the local group. Central in the cosmology of the Lower Rhine burial communities is the notion of ancestors. Ancestral authority is intensively fused with the existence of the living group, including its claim on a certain territory. The living community, and particularly the local family heads, were responsible for the correct management of the ancestral land and the observance of all duties regarding the ancestors and their funeral sites.[19]

4 SYMBOLISM OF LONG BARROWS AND OTHER GRAVE TYPES

The discussion above concerned the place of the urnfield *as a whole* in the cosmology of the local group. A second point of attention concerns the meaning of the *internal* structure of the urnfields, and particularly the variation in shape and size of the grave monuments. This refers to ideas and values about the internal organisation of local groups.

It is obvious that the great majority of the members of a local community were buried in the urnfield, and that most persons received individual graves. Furthermore it is important to notice that each urnfield shows the same basic variety of grave structures. Characteristic is a small group of long graves and a great majority of round barrows, and in addition to these, some flat graves and secondary interments in tumuli.[20] This variety refers to social distinctions and associated ideas that are basic for each local group, and which are part of the collective ideological framework. It is of crucial importance that for some Lower Rhine urnfields we can dispose of physical-anthropological analyses of the cremations.[21] These offer us the possibility to relate the variation of grave monuments to the age and sex of the deceased.

A first general remark concerns the mortuary ritual of young children and in particular newborns. Although they are always underrepresented, it is signicant that this age-group is present in the urnfields, and in different contexts: in combination with adults in multiple interments, in single interments in flat graves, or in primary and secondary burials in barrows. It can be concluded that young children and even newborns were already considered members of the community, as some of them received a place in the collective cemetery.

Flat graves (burials without a barrow) are encountered in most urnfields, although their number is

---

[19] Cf. the study of De Coppet on the relationship between the land tenure system and the socio-cosmic order in Melanesian society. In Melanesian cosmology, "land is clearly not simply soil, but rather an entity always fused with the ancestors, under whose joint authority the living are placed" (De Coppet 1988, 81). See also the discussion in Tilley 1996, 220, 236, and Friedman 1984 (1974), 170 ff.

[20] In the final stage of the Lower Rhine Urnfield period (5th century BC) rectangular or square ditched grave enclosures appear. These are not further discussed here.

[21] Respectively for the urnfields of Beegden (contribution M. Hoogland in this volume), Someren-Waterdael (Kortlang, this volume; determination L. Smits), Berkel-Enschot (Kleij 1993; determination L. Smits), St.-Oedenrode-Haagakkers (Van der Sanden 1981; determination Van der Sanden), Wijk bij Duurstede (Hessing 1989; determination M. Hoogland). Less reliable are the physical-anthropological determinations of P. Jansens for the urnfields of Neerpelt-De Roosen and Donk (Van Impe e.a. 1973; Van Impe 1980).

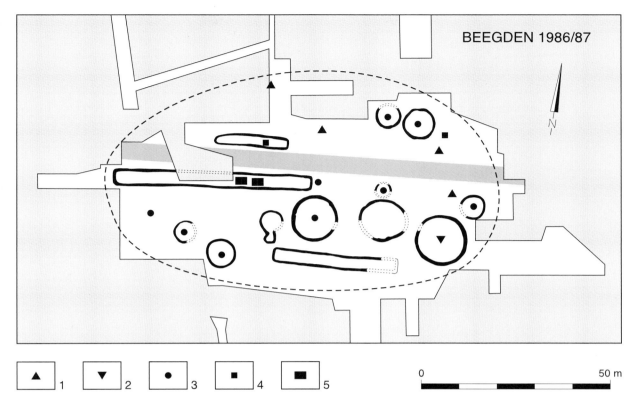

BEEGDEN 1986/87

▲ 1 ▼ 2 ● 3 ▪ 4 ■ 5   0 ___ 50 m

Fig. 4. The Beegden cemetery: results of the physical–anthropological analyses.
1 child; 2 juvenile; 3 adult; 4 double interment (adult + child); 5 multiple interment >4 persons

relatively low. Both adult males and females were interred in the flat graves, but most striking is the overrepresentation of children. In Beegden, 5 of the 7 flat graves contained the remains of a child (fig. 4) (once in combination with an adult), and at St.-Oedenrode, children were interred in 6 of the 7 identified cremations from flat graves.[22] In the Middle Bronze Age, child burials predominantly occur as secondary interments in tumuli. Though this tradition is still practised in the urnfield period (cf. below), we see a tendency now to bury children in flat graves.

By far the major part of the grave monuments are round barrows of varying size. Most of them are smaller (<10 m diameter) than the tumuli of the Middle Bronze Age, however almost every urnfield also produces specimens that are larger. Urnfield barrows normally contain one central interment. Not infrequently, however, one or two secondary interments are found in the peripheral zone or in the circular ditch. Analyses of the cremation remains demonstrate that both adult males and females were interred in these barrows. Children, too, are sometimes encountered as primary interments, particularly in tumuli of small size.[23] More often they occur here in combination with an adult, or – as has been observed above – as a secondary interment.

[22] St.-Oedenrode: Van der Sanden 1981, graves 33, 34, 35, 57, 62, 63. Children are also prominently present among the flat graves in the cemetery of Wijk bij Duurstede: Hessing 1989, graves 21, 24, 43, 44, 66, 93. Furthermore, many child burials have been en-

countered among the 'flat graves' of the cemetery at Donk, but some of these graves may have been eroded tumulus burials (Van Impe 1980).

[23] Cf. Neerpelt, graves 132 and 140 (Van Impe/Beex/ Roossens 1973, 30-31). Donk, graves 80 and 81 (Van

43

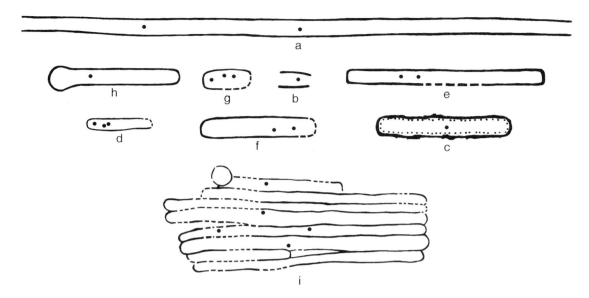

Fig. 5. Some long-beds with cremation burials from Lower Rhine urnfields. Scale 1:1000.
a Someren, grave 5; b idem grave 3; c Neerpelt-'De Roosen', grave 104; d Hilvarenbeek, graves 45/48/51;
e Beegden, graves 9/22; f Weert-'Boshover Heide', grave C7; g idem, grave C16; h Valkenswaard, grave 46;
i cluster of long-beds from Goirle

A central point in our discussion concerns the symbolism of long barrows (fig. 5). These are elongated earthen banks, enclosed by a ditch and usually containing one or more burials on the longitudinal axis.[24] In the Lower Rhine region, long-beds represent a regular element in almost every urnfield; in the few cemeteries where they are lacking, this seems due to an incomplete excavation. Long-beds are characteristic for both the early (Late Bronze Age) and the later phase (Early Iron Age) of the Lower Rhine Urnfield culture. However, it is possible to distinguish early from younger variants; those from the Late Bronze Age have rounded ends, while those with open or rectangular ends date to the Early Iron Age.

The long-beds have not always been interpreted as grave monuments. Clusters of long-beds (see fig. 5-i) were initially considered as ritual fields, and before that they were sometimes interpreted as cult places.[25] As cremation burials have been frequently found on the longitudinal axis of these structures, there is no doubt any longer about their function as a burial monument.

Impe 1980). Berkel-Enschot, grave 38 (Kleij 1993). St.-Oedenrode, graves 4 and 17 (Van der Sanden 1981).

[24] Cf. the references in Roymans, this volume, note 6. Long barrows are a typical phenomenon of the Urnfield cultures in the Northwest-European Plain (*Niederrheinische Grabhügelkultur* and the related Ems culture to the North). Outside this area more or less similar phenomena are known from barrow cemeteries in the Trier region (Haffner 1976, 115-116, n. 448; Nortmann 1992, 23 ff.) and from the Champagne/Ardennes district in Northeastern France (Lambot 1996, 23 ff.). As a rule, only one or two long-beds per cemetery are present here. These are not interpreted as normal grave structures, but as cult monuments for the local community (cf. Lambot 1996). The only exception are the long-beds from the urnfield of Mülheim near Koblenz, which functioned as grave monuments (Röder 1943).

[25] Cf. Verwers 1966b, 55-56; idem 1975, 32-33 (ritual fields). Willems 1936, 71 ff (cult places).

On the basis of a series of observations we will argue that long graves had a prominent position within the mortuary ritual of the Lower Rhine Urnfield culture:

a. long graves are always a small proportion of the total number of graves in a cemetery. In Beegden there is a ratio of ca. 1:9 (taking into account some lost burials); in the almost completely excavated urnfield of Someren the ratio is ca. 1:12; in Mierlo-Hout 1:13, in Knegsel ca. 1:10, and in the excavated parts of the urnfield of Weert-'Boshoverheide' ca. 1:9.

b. some recent excavations of urnfields have yielded a long-bed of extreme length (> 50 m), which seems to belong to the earliest structuring elements of the cemetery. In Beegden, a long-bed of 52,5 m occupies a dominant position directly to the south of the reconstructed road (fig. 4). In Someren long-bed no 5 with a length of 145 m belongs to the oldest elements of the urnfield (fig. 3). A cluster of ca. 40 grave monuments is clearly associated with the central interment on the longitudinal axis of this long-bed; this grave has determined the further development of the cemetery in an eastward direction. An urnfield with a long-bed of 180 m in the oldest zone has been excavated recently at Weert-'Raak'. Such long graves of extreme size from the oldest phase of the cemetery can be interpreted as 'founder burials'.[26]

c. ditches of long-beds, in contrast to those of round barrows, sometimes contain rich ceramic material in the form of sherds of beakers and dishes (fig. 6).[27] These point to special ritual activities, probably ceremonial feasting.

d. though most urnfield barrows are individual grave monuments, long-beds contain more often than round barrows 2 or 3 graves; these are commonly situated on the longitudinal axis of the monuments (fig. 5).[28] Moreover it has been demonstrated that graves from long-barrows sometimes contain the remains of several individuals. It mostly concerns an interment of an adult and a child. Such double graves, however, frequently occur in urnfields without having a special connection with long-beds.[29] Highly exceptional are the graves with the cremated remains of four and seven persons respectively,

[26] It should be noticed that the examples mentioned above come from cemeteries that start in the Early Iron Age. Future excavations will have to show whether these long-beds of extreme length already occur in the Late Bronze Age. A long grave of at least 63 m and according to an interment on its axis dating to the Late Bronze Age, is known from the centre of the urnfield of Donk (Van Impe 1980, grave 29). This long-bed has, probably together with some eroded long-beds, determined the later development of the urnfield. In the Northern Netherlands, the earliest long-beds (Ha A2) attract attention because of their monumental timber structures rather than their length.

[27] This observation particularly concerns long barrows from the Late Bronze Age. We refer to the crushed pottery from some recently excavated long-beds at Weert-Boshoverheide. Sherds of at least 14 pots were found at the bottom of the ditches of long-bed C7. Cf. also Verwers 1975, 26 ff., 31 (Hilvarenbeek); Verlinde 1985, 245, 253.

[28] Examples of long barrows containing several burials in the Southern Netherlands: Weert-Boshoverheide, graves C-7 and C-16 (fig. 5-f,g), Hilvarenbeek, graves 45/48/51 (fig. 5-d; Verwers 1975), Someren, grave 5.1-2 (fig. 5-a), Valkenswaard, graves 2/8 (Brunsting/ Verwers 1975), Beegden, graves 9/22 (fig. 5-e). See also Verlinde 1985, 244, 255, 259.

[29] Graves with the remains of two persons are known from the urnfield of Someren, graf 142 (within circular ditch; Kortlang, this volume), Neerpelt, grave 56 (within circular ditch; Roosens/Beex 1961, 56), Wijk bij Duurstede, grave 23 (flat grave) and 34 (secondary burial within circular ditch; Hessing 1989), Weert-Boshoven, grave C7a (long-bed; fig. 11-f), Beegden, grave 15 (flat grave) and 10 (long-bed), Donk, graves 38 and 67 (flat graves?; Van Impe 1980). See also Cuijpers 1994 and Wilhelmi 1988 on the occurrence of double graves in urnfields in Overijssel and Westphalia.

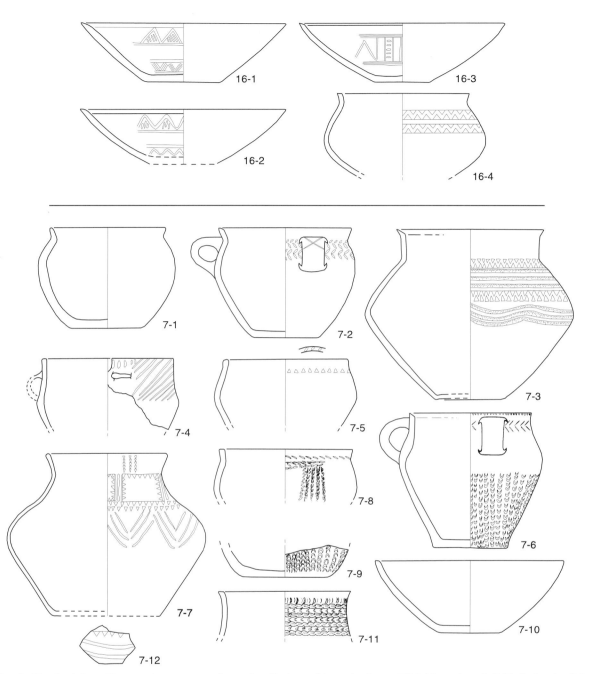

Fig. 6. Crushed Late Bronze Age pottery from the ditches of long-bed no. C16 (above) and C17 (below) of the urnfield of Weert-Boshoverheide. See also fig. 5. Scale 1:4. The pottery probably refers to a practice of ceremonial feasting.

both from the largest long-bed at Beegden (fig. 4). Assuming that both burials are more or less contemporary,[30] we are dealing here with the remains of 11 individuals. It is difficult to accept (also taking into account the small size of the Beegden community) that all these persons died and were cremated

---

30   This long-bed is the only grave monument with more
     than one burial in the cemetery of Beegden.

46

			date	child	juvenile	adult indet	adult female	adult male
1	Weert-Boshoven	grave C-16a	LB	-	-	1	-	-
		grave C-16b	LB	-	-	-	-	1
		grave C-16c	LB	-	-	-	-	1
2	Weert-Boshoven	grave C-7a	LB	-	-	1	-	1
3	Weert-Raak	grave 43	EIA	-	-	-	1?	-
4	Weert-Raak	grave 40	EIA	-	-	-	-	1?
5	Berkel-Enschot	grave 66	EIA	-	-	-	-	1?
6	Beegden	grave 10	EIA	1	-	-	-	1
7	Beegden	grave 9	EIA	2	-	-	2	-
		grave 22	EIA	3	-	-	2+1?	1
8	Someren-Waterdael	grave 3	EIA	-	-	-	-	1
9	Someren-Waterdael	grave 5.1	EIA	-	-	-	-	1?
		grave 5.2	EIA	-	-	1	-	-
10	Someren-Waterdael	grave 10	EIA	-	-	-	-	1?
11	Someren-Waterdael	grave 119	EIA	-	-	1	-	-
12	Someren-Waterdael	grave 121	EIA	-	-	-	-	1
13	Someren-Waterdael	grave 175	EIA	-	-	-	-	1
14	Wijk bij Duurstede	grave 6a	EIA	-	-	1	-	-
		grave 6b	EIA	-	1	-	-	-
		grave 6c	EIA	1	-	-	-	-

Table 2. Physical–anthropological determinations of crematory remains from 14 long barrows in the Lower Rhine region.

at the same moment.[31] Here, we should consider the possibility of (partially) secondary burials. It is interesting that the long-bed in question, being one of the oldest and most monumental grave structures of the urnfield, can be interpreted as a founder burial. Members of the family group that first settled at this location may have interred here the remains of close relatives who at first had been buried in the cemetery of the community from which they had split off. Another option is that we are dealing with the remains of some members of the Beegden community whose interment was postponed until interment in a founder burial became possible. The above practices indicate that long graves, more than the other graves, symbolised the family collective and are therefore not strictly individual.

e. long-beds are sometimes widely spread over the urnfield, in other cases they are joined together constituting small groups. Within the same cemetery there may be several clusters of long-beds, which sometimes are more or less contemporary. This suggests that there were several persons within a local community who after their death were qualified for being buried in a long-bed.

f. on the basis of the physical-anthropological investigation of the cremation remains of 14 long-beds from the Lower Rhine region (table 2), some first conclusions can be drawn concerning the age and sex of the persons buried in them. The long-beds seem to be meant primarily for adults; if children are present it is always in combination with adults. Furthermore it appears that mainly adult men are connected with the long barrows. Only at Weert-'Raak' an adult woman may have been interred. At Beegden, too, some adult women have been encountered, but the same long-bed also contained the remains of an adult man.

[31] This would have meant a catastrophic reduction of the Beegden community, which is estimated at c. 19 persons (see above).

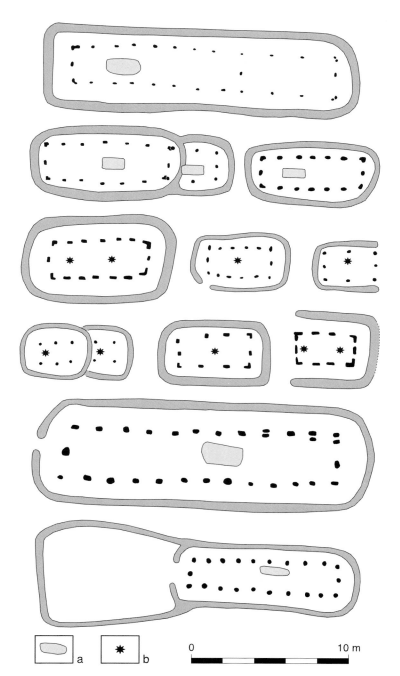

Fig. 7. Long barrows with timber structures from the Northern Netherlands and Warendorf, Westphalia. After Kooi 1982, fig. 2; Wilhelmi 1983, fig. 9.
a inhumation burial; b cremation burial

a ▭
b ✳
0   10 m

On the basis of the above observations we suggest that the long barrows are grave monuments for to adult persons (predominantly males) who may have been the heads of small families; as such the long barrows have a more 'collective' significance than the other graves.[32] Within a local community, there will have been several family heads at the same time. The small, compact clusters of long-beds within

[32]   It is this collective significance as a focus in the ancestor cult of a family group which makes it easy to explain that in the Trier and the Champagne/Ardennes regions the long-beds did not function as graves, but as a cult place for the local community. Cf. the discussion and references in note 24.

urnfields (fig. 5-i) can be interpreted as the graves of a series of successive heads of a particular family. It is an indication that within an urnfield specific families used a certain zone for a longer time.

This interpretation of the long graves can be taken further if we see them as the symbol for a house, which in its turn is a metaphor for the basic family-unit.[33] In the world of the living, the house formed the domicile of each family and was the symbol of the social position of a family head. After the death of a family head, he was buried in his 'house', thus providing for continuity between the world of the living and the dead. The hypothesis that the long-beds were associated with houses is based on the elongated form of the earthen grave monuments, which reminds us of the Bronze Age long houses of the Northwest European plain. A second argument is the occurrence of rectangular timber buildings in the oldest long barrows (Ha A2/B1) in urnfields of the adjacent Ems-culture in the Northern Netherlands and Westphalia (figs. 7 and 8).[34] As a rule these mortuary houses contain one or two graves. In the course of Ha B1 the timber structures disappear, and it is exactly in this phase that the long-bed tradition begins in the Lower Rhine urnfields.[35]

In the mortuary ritual the construction of a long grave refers to the position of a person as head of a 'house' or family-unit. Long-beds that can be interpreted as founder burials are notable for their excessive length, their multiple interments, and their situation in the earliest core of the urnfield, often determining there the later spatial development of the cemetery or part of it. The great length of these founder burial monuments can symbolise the position of the deceased not only as head of his own family, but also – at a higher level – of the other families of the local community in their relationship towards the ancestors. In the case of the Beegden urnfield (fig. 9) this would mean that the adult male buried in the long-bed 9/22 of family *A* also represented the families *B* and *C* in the ritual communication with the ancestors.

These local family leaders, who were buried in long graves after their death, were together responsible for the management (including the regulation of the inheritance) of the ancestral land, and the carrying out of the rituals associated with this, in which the relations with the ancestors were reproduced. We are not only thinking here of funeral rites, but also of fertility rites.[36] So, the family heads played a central role in the reproduction of the relations between the ancestors, the land, and the living group.

---

[33] Here we are inspired by Hodder's studies (1992; 1994) on the relationship between long barrows and long houses in Neolithic megalith cultures in Atlantic Europe.

[34] Kooi 1979; Verlinde 1985, 243-248; Wilhelmi 1983, 11-14. Little is known about the internal structure of the mortuary houses. In a few cases, the presence of a 'forecourt' or an interruption in the enclosing ditch suggests that the entrance was at the short end of the building. Within the Maas-Demer-Scheldt region a long-bed with an internal post-structure is known from Knegsel (Braat 1936) and Neerpelt (fig. 5-c). However, the disposition of the postholes makes a reconstruction into a roofed building highly improbable. We are dealing here with a configuration of isolated posts.

[35] This relatively late appearance of long graves in the Lower Rhine region, makes it possible to consider this grave type an innovation taken over from Urnfield groups ('Ems culture') in the Northern Netherlands and Westphalia. There, Wilhelmi (1987, 75, Abb. 1) suggests a relationship between the long-beds from the Urnfield period and the causeways lined with posts leading to monumental Middle Bronze Age barrows. The concrete evidence, however, is far from conclusive.

[36] In many tribal cosmologies, products of the land are perceived as a gift from the ancestors, an idea that is continually made topical in rituals of exchange. Cf. e.g. De Coppet 1988; Friedman 1984 (1974), 170; Tilley 1996, 220.

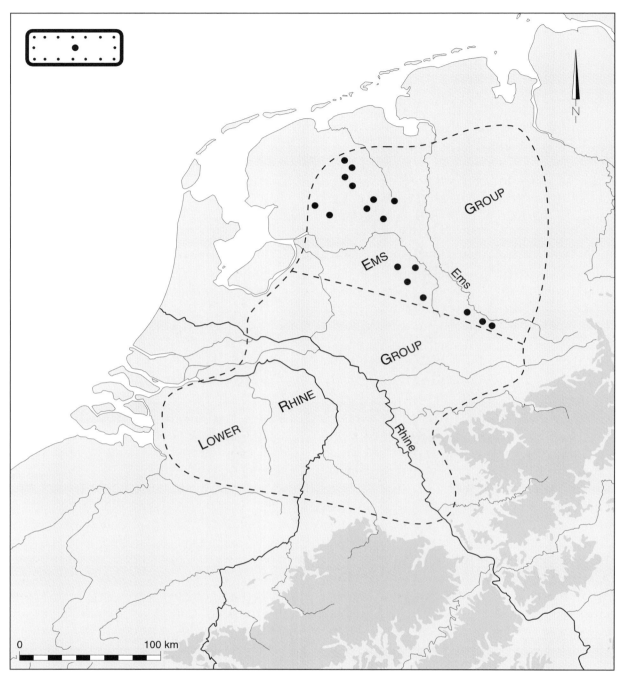

Fig. 8. Urnfield groups in the Northwest European Plain and the distribution of Late Bronze Age long barrows with timber structures (the latter after Wilhelmi 1983, fig. 11).

If we accept that long-beds in urnfields can be associated with heads of families, a comparison can be made with the mortuary ritual of the preceding Middle Bronze Age. At that time local groups of several families did not have a common burial place; each household had its own 'family barrow', situated near the farmhouse. It is assumed that the central graves in these tumuli were reserved for fami-

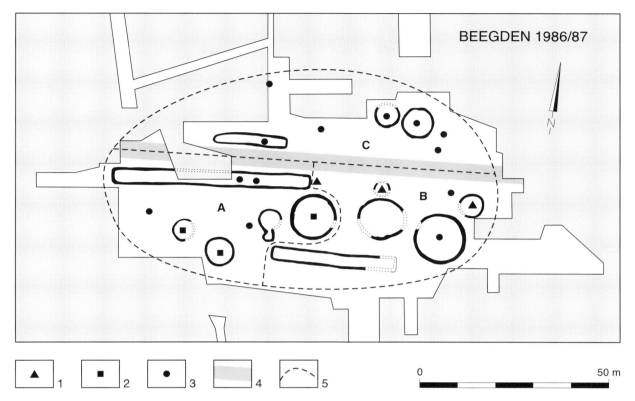

Fig. 9. The Beegden urnfield: some spatial patterns.
1 *Schräghals* pots with a decoration of dellen and grooved lines; 2 *Schräghals* pots with a decoration of one or two zigzag lines; 3 other graves; 4 probable prehistoric road; 5 general boundary of the urnfield, and internal boundaries of three clusters of graves probably corresponding to different families

ly heads, while part of their relatives were interred in secondary burials.[37] In the Late Bronze Age, family heads receive more individual grave monuments, in this case the long-beds. The greatest point of difference, however, is that from the Late Bronze Age onwards the individual families within a territory start to use a collective cemetery. In our opinion, these burial communities – although they manifest themselves for the first time now – do not represent newly formed social units, but are continuations of more loosely structured local groups of the Middle Bronze Age. In the Middle Bronze Age, too, we can speak of territories, inhabited by several families living in more or less isolated farmsteads. However, the territorial organisation was less sharply defined, and the relationship between the separate families less close. Individual households had a greater autonomy in the management of the land. This is indicated by the spatial organisation of the settlements (dispersed farmsteads), the mortuary ritual (family barrows situated near the farmsteads), and probably also the field system (small, dispersed plots of arable land connected with individual farmsteads instead of large *celtic-field* complexes with a considerable level of collective regulation).

In our model (fig. 10) the formation of new burial communities and the gradual introduction of a new mortuary ritual in the Late Bronze Age are an expression of the way the society dealt with the social problems that emerged from the increased demographical expansion and the growing pressure

37   Theunissen 1993; idem, in prep. See also Lohof 1994,
      107, 116 for the Northern Netherlands.

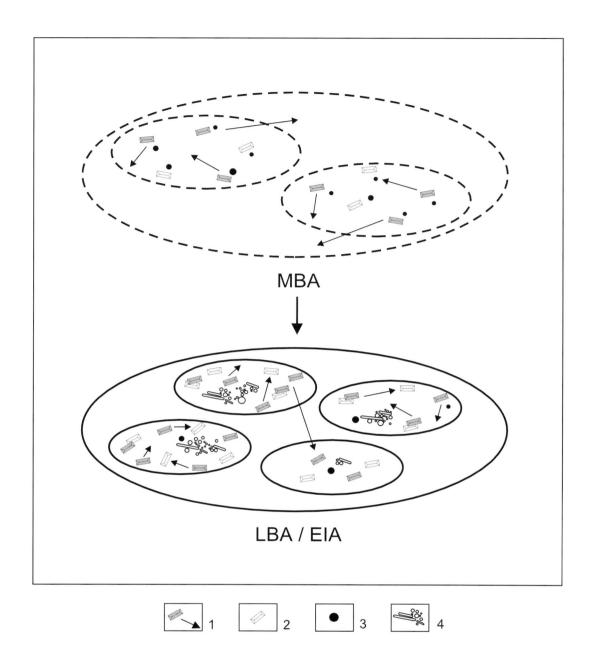

Fig. 10. Model of the territorial organisation of some local groups in the Middle Bronze Age (above) compared to that in the Urnfield period (below). In the Middle Bronze Age the territories of local groups are relatively large, and boundaries are only weakly defined, allowing much space to autonomous decision-making by individual households. In the course of the Urnfield period territorial boundaries become more fixed and territories tend to be smaller; collective cemeteries at one single location replace the old system of dispersed 'family-barrows'.
1 farmstead (household), shifting to a new location after some time; 2 farmstead from earlier habitation phase; 3 Middle Bronze Age 'family barrow'; 4 urnfield

on the land. Everything indicates that territoriality becomes an important notion. It is within this framework that the introduction of long-beds can be understood. It is no coincidence that their appearance concurs with the transition from a family-oriented mortuary ritual towards a more community-oriented one. The long-beds, with their metaphorical reference to the long house and the social unit residing in it, arose from the desire to express the identity of individual families within the new collective cemeteries.

We may conclude that in the urnfield ritual the emphasis is on the collective. Indeed, urnfields largely consist of individual grave monuments, but these figure within a strongly collective setting. Urnfields reproduce the ideal of the stable, kinship-based social order, given by the ancestors, in which each individual had its specific place. It is within this framework that we should understand the great variation in form and size of the grave structures. Because of its references to the sacred descent ideology, the mortuary ritual plays an active role in strategies to restructure or reduce claims on land. The latter had become necessary as a result of demographical developments and the growing pressure on territorial organisation. The continuous foundation of new settlements in the course of the Urnfield period (see above) points to the presence of a descent ideology on the level of local domestic groups that excluded a considerable part of the offspring from rights to the existing land; for them fission was the only alternative. This kinship or descent ideology had a great impact on social organisation, as it formed a social charter providing a blueprint for marriage rules, relations between maternal and paternal claims on resources, and also on patterns of inheritance.

Concrete archaeological evidence for a substantial change in the descent ideology in the Urnfield period is, of course, hard to give. Interesting, however, is the strong emphasis on adult males as family heads in the Urnfield period (see table 2), while in the Middle Bronze Age this position was equally accessible for adult women and men. This is suggested by the sex determinations of primary interments in Middle Bronze Age barrows; the first data demonstrate that adult males and females are equally represented here.[38] In the Urnfield period, the strong association of long-beds with adult males may indicate a development towards a more 'closed' kinship system.

5 RITUAL DEPOSITIONS OF WEAPONS IN THE LOWER RHINE URNFIELD SOCIETY

In this paragraph we will make some remarks about changing depositional practices concerning weapons during the Urnfield period, and their relationship with the mortuary ritual. In the Lower Rhine region there is a strong tradition of ritual depositions in rivers. We are confronted with the existence of a sword-bearing warrior elite, that remains invisible in the Late Bronze Age urnfields. Then we see that in the beginning of the Early Iron Age (Ha C) this warrior elite does manifest itself in the mortuary ritual. This raises the question how ideological structures connected to the weapon depositions articulate with the ideas and values that are central in the mortuary ritual outlined above.

In the Late Bronze Age there is an important tradition to depose bronzes in rivers. We are badly informed about the archaeological contexts of the often prestigeous bronzes, and it is only in general terms that we can make some remarks. We are mostly dealing with axes, spearheads and swords, which have often been deposited in the water in an undamaged state. A recent inventory of swords

---

[38] Theunissen 1993, table 4. There are also some child
burials among the primary interments.

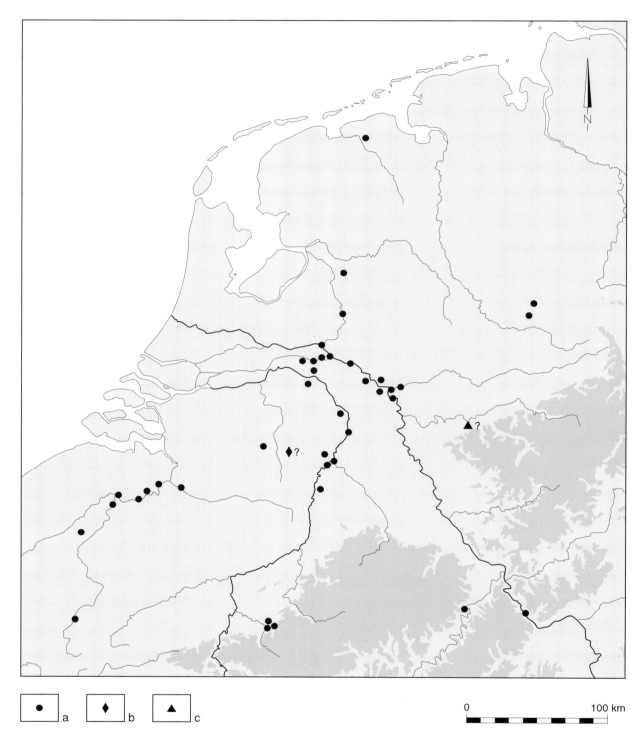

Fig. 11. Distribution of Ha B2/3 swords in the Lower Rhine region. After Roymans 1991, fig. 6, with some additions.

a river or moor find; b grave find; c hoard find

from the Ha B2/3 phase in the Lower Rhine area produced more than 30 examples, almost all from rivers.[39] Although depositions also occur in smaller rivers, there is a clear concentration in the valleys of the Meuse, Scheldt and Waal/Rhine (fig. 11). Sometimes there is a clustering at specific locations, e.g. near the confluence of the Roer and the Meuse at Roermond.[40] This depositional practice of weaponry in rivers has been explained mainly in sociopolitical terms until now. It is related to local chieftains who had access to interregional networks of bronze exchange and therefore could exercise some control over the bronze supply of Lower Rhine groups.[41]

Less central in the discussions held to date was the question towards the symbolism of rivers and river depositions in the cosmology of Urnfield groups. Two interpretations can be distinguished. Firstly, this is the votive offering hypothesis. It starts from the assumption that rivers were associated with deities (as documented in the later Gallic and Gallo-Roman religion), to whom offerings were brought in the context of a votive ritual.[42] The second hypothesis supposes that the river depositions have a funerary connotation.[43] The cemetery was only the place where the mortal remains of the ancestors rested; the soul or spirit of the deceased made a journey to an 'Other World', where the ancestors resided. In this context the river may have been perceived as an entrance to this 'Other World'. Continuing this line of argument, there may have existed a tradition to deposit the personal weapons of a deceased not with his mortal remains in the grave, but in a river via which the spirit of the dead person was thought to depart for the Other World. Though Late Bronze Age weapons are almost completely lacking in the Lower Rhine urnfields, there may have been a connection with a funerary ideology in this case.[44]

The interpretation of these dredge finds from rivers remains problematical, as long as we have no better information about context and find associations. Our attention is immediately focused upon the metal objects, but these may have been associated originally with human and animal bones, pottery, etc.[45] Weapons from rivers may have been part of larger ceremonial find complexes of supralocal significance, although there is still little concrete evidence for this in the Lower Rhine area.

Even though we can only guess at the ideas behind the river depositions, archaeologists using prestige goods models have pointed to the social-political dimension of this ritual display of wealth. Point

[39] Roymans 1991, 20-26, and appendix 1. Swords are almost unknown from graves or hoards from dry land, an indication that the river finds constitute a meaningful analytical category.

[40] Although the distribution pattern is certainly also determined by the varying intensity of the dredging activities, it does seem representative. Cf. the discussion in Roymans 1991, 24-25.

[41] Cf. Roymans 1991, 28 ff.

[42] Cf. e.g. Roymans 1990, 84 ff.; Derks 1995, 112 ff.

[43] Cf. the discussion in Bradley 1990, 99-109. Torbrügge (1970-71, 87, 91 ff.) already argued in 1971 that river depositions were funerary hoards, as the deposition of weapons in particular alternates from grave contexts in one period to river contexts in the other period, and vice versa. Warmenbol (1996) considers the rich find complex with many bronzes and pottery in the bed of the Lesse in the Han cave (B) as the result of a funerary rite and a chthonic cult. The cave would have been conceptualised as an entrance to the Other World.

[44] Following Bradley (1990, 107) we might even go a step further and hypothesize the existence (alongside the normal cremation rite practised in the urnfields) of an alternative way of disposal of dead bodies or parts of bodies in rivers. In this regard we can point to evidence for an excarnation-rite in the Iron Age in the Lower Rhine region (unburnt human bones from settlement contexts; cf. Roymans 1990, 242 ff.) and recent finds of large numbers of unburnt human bones of Iron Age date associated with weapons in the river Maas at Kessel (Ter Schegget, this volume).

[45] This seems to have been the case in the Thames valley in Southeast England (Bradley 1990, 108 ff.) and the river Lesse at the Han cave (Warmenbol 1996).

of departure is the competitive element present in it. Assuming that the river depositions occurred in the presence of a larger audience, this kind of (semi-funerary?) gatherings formed a public arena for the competition among local groups and their chieftains. This depositional practice was subjected to a considerable degree of collective control.[46] Local elites could win prestige by destroying part of their wealth, without being a threat to the strongly collective basis of the societal system.

The crucial question, however, remains why the deposition of weapons was kept out of the context of the urnfields in the Late Bronze Age. Perhaps the explanation should be sought in the association of the weapons with the martial domain of male competition and small-scale warfare, carried out outside one's homeland. This martial association was at odds with the ideas and values which were central in the domestic domain of urnfield ritual. Here, the emphasis was on the themes of death, life and fertility, and on the ideal of the stable kinship order, given by the ancestors, which gave each individual its fixed place. Within this domestic arena focused on the cemetery, there was a denial of the domain of warfare and elite competition. The mortuary ritual therefore expresses an egalitarian ideology to some extent. Indications for the presence of an elite above the level of the local burial community are lacking in the Late Bronze Age urnfields in the Lower Rhine area, which is not, of course, a representative reflection of the social organisation.

As said above, martial ideology is almost completely kept outside the Late Bronze Age urnfield ritual; it was probably a taboo to place weapons in graves. This changes in the Gündlingen phase and particularly in Ha C, when imported swords, sometimes in combination with bronze vessels, wagon parts and horse-gear, are encountered in a small group of elite burials in the Lower Rhine region. As far as we know, these warrior graves are connected with monumental tumuli, which are usually part of larger urnfields.[47] It is remarkable that up to now no associations are known with long graves. Weapon burials and long barrows seem to have had different social and ideological connotations.

How this switch in the ritual deposition of weapons from rivers to graves should be understood, remains a point of discussion. Bradley states that in a period of increased social instability the grave ritual and the water ritual may have functioned as alternative arenas for the competitive deposition of fine metalwork.[48] For emerging elites, whose power position is still unstable, the mortuary ritual can be an attractive medium for developing more individual-directed social strategies.[49] Thus, the excessive display of status in some Ha C elite burials may indicate problems concerning the transmission of social positions and claims from the deceased to their next of kin. This transmission apparently was not self-evident, and the mortuary ritual was used to strengthen the instable social positions of certain elite families at crucial moments.

Especially for the beginning of the Early Iron Age, we can point to some factors that have put pressure on the social order in the Lower Rhine region, and which may offer an explanation for the changing depositional practices. First, the demographical expansion and the foundation of new settlements in the Lower Rhine sandy regions reach a peak in the first half of the Early Iron Age (fig. 2), and thus also the social stress connected with it. Secondly, there is the introduction in the Lower Rhine region of a powerful set of symbols of a new, martial elite ideology, inspired on the Central-European Hallstatt culture. The combination of factors mentioned above may have been at the base

---

[46] Roymans 1991, 30.

[47] There are several arguments for assuming that the elites buried in a number of rich Ha C graves in the Lower Rhine region do not represent an immigrant group, but are the descendants of the local Late

Bronze Age elites. Cf. the discussion in Roymans 1991, 49 ff.

[48] Bradley 1990, 102.

[49] Kristiansen 1996, 262

of the shift in the ritual deposition and the break with the old taboo on placing weapons in graves. This new trend marks the increased importance of the martial domain, but it was only of short duration; in Ha D almost nothing is left of the tradition of rich warrior burials in the Lower Rhine urnfields.

When prestigious weapons and other symbols of elite status disappear from the graves, this may mean that the power position of elites has stabilised and is no longer a subject of discussion. In contrast to the core area of the Hallstatt culture, such a development does not seem to have taken place in the Lower Rhine region in Ha D. In other archaeological contexts, too, indications for a rich elite are absent in Ha D. The old urnfield symbolism with the associated ideas and values and typical kinship ideology remains in use during the entire Early Iron Age. It is not before the transition to the Middle Iron Age (5th century BC) that major changes occur, but these are beyond the scope of this discussion.

6 SUMMARY

In this study we have tried to present a model of urnfield symbolism in relation to the social developments in the area of the *Niederrheinische Grabhügelkultur*. The rise of urnfield ritual and (connected with it) the formation of new burial communities with collective cemeteries in the Late Bronze Age are seen as an expression of the way society copes with social problems emerging from a continuous demographical expansion and increased pressure on land. Increasing claims on land and the higher commitment to territory led to a redefinition of the social organisation of local communities. Characteristic for the Late Bronze Age is a greater emphasis on the collective regulation and control of the use of land by local groups than was the case in the Middle Bronze Age. The transmission of rights on land was probably restricted via the descent-ideology. The introduction of a more 'closed' kinship structure stimulating fission, may have been the driving force behind the explosive growth of the number of newly founded settlements in the course of the Urnfield period. The mortuary ritual (because of its direct link with the world of the ancestors) provided an ideal context for the propagation and reproduction of a new kinship order, in which the position and rights of each individual were specified much more than before.

Evidence for an elite above the level of local family leaders is almost completely lacking in the Late Bronze Age mortuary ritual. According to the river finds, however, a higher social level did exist in the Lower Rhine Urnfield culture; that of a sword-bearing warrior elite, whose position was partly based upon control of the exchange networks with external groups. The domain of elite competition was connected with non-domestic ritual, materialised in the weapon depositions in rivers. It is in Ha C that the old taboo on the deposition of weapons in graves was broken by a warrior elite that was integrated in the exchange networks with Central European Hallstatt groups. This elite – introducing a new set of symbols for a martial ideology – used the mortuary ritual as the medium for propagating its ambitions.

In the model presented here, the cultural changes connected with the formation of the *Niederrheinische Grabhügelkultur* are for an important part triggered by demographical growth. This growth was made possible by the gradual introduction of a more intensive system of plough agriculture, i.e. the *celtic-field* system. In a general sense, many archaeologists have stressed the importance of demographical expansion in explaining cultural change, particularly the formation of more complex societal systems. In most cases, however, the potential of each society to creatively respond to demographical expansion is seriously underestimated. Moreover, it often remains unclear how increased pressure on land may lead to changing social and ideational structures, or vice versa. In this case-study we have investigated how a society from its specific historical context deals with the social problems resulting from an increased pressure on land. We have described how this factor may lead to a series of transformations of social and ideological structures. The cultural patterns outlined are probably highly cultural-specific, and in that sense this model may help us to better understand the great regional differentiations within the continental Urnfield cultures.

REFERENCES

Beex, W.F.M., 1989: *Archeologische vondsten en vindplaatsen uit de Vroege en Midden Bronstijd in het Maas-Demer-Schelde-gebied*, Amsterdam (unpublished MA thesis University of Amsterdam).

Bodegraven, N. van, 1991: Nederzettingssporen uit de late bronstijd en de vroege ijzertijd op de Everse Akkers in St.-Oedenrode, in H. Fokkens/N. Roymans (eds), *Nederzettingen uit de bronstijd en de vroege ijzertijd in de Lage Landen*, Amersfoort (NAR 13), 129-139.

Bloch, M., 1984 (1974): Property and the end of affinity, in M. Bloch (ed.), *Marxist analyses and social anthropology*, London (ASA Studies), 203-228.

Braat, W.C., 1936: Een urnenveld te Knegsel (Gem. Vessem), *OMROL* 17, 38-47.

Bradley, R., 1990: *The passage of arms. An archaeological analysis of prehistoric hoards and votive deposits*, Cambridge.

Broeke, P.W. van den, 1991: Nederzettingsaardewerk uit de late bronstijd in Zuid-Nederland, in H. Fokkens/N. Roymans (eds), *Nederzettingen uit de Bronstijd en de Vroege IJzertijd in de Lage Landen*, Amersfoort (NAR 13), 193-211.

Brunsting, H./G.J. Verwers 1975: Het urnenveld bij Valkenswaard, prov. Noord-Brabant, *APL* 8, 53-77.

Butler, J.J., 1969: *Nederland in de Bronstijd*, Bussum (Fibulareeks, 31).

Coppet, D. de, 1985: ...Land owns people, in R.H. Barnes/D. de Coppet/R.J. Parkin (eds), *Contexts and levels. Anthropological essays on hierarchy*, Oxford (JASO Occasional Papers 4), 78-90.

Cuijpers, A.G.F.M., 1994: *Crematieresten uit de Late Bronstijd en Vroege IJzertijd in Overijssel*, Amersfoort (ROB Interne Rapporten 10).

Derks, T., 1995: *Goden, tempels en rituele praktijken. De transformatie van religieuze ideeën en waarden in Romeins Gallië*, Amsterdam (phil. doc. thesis University of Amsterdam).

Desittere, M., 1968: *De urnenveldencultuur in het gebied tussen Neder-Rijn en Noordzee; periodes HA A en B*, Gent (Dissertationes Archaeologicae Gandenses 11).

Diepeveen, M., in press: *Mensen, ideeën en goederen. Een symbolische en sociale analyse van het grafbestel van de elite in de Vroeg-La Tène-periode in de Marne-Moezelregio*, Amsterdam (phil.doc. thesis University of Amsterdam).

Engels, A./L. van Impe 1985: Het urnenveld op de Dorperheide te Kaulille, *AB* 1, nr 2, 33-35.

Fontijn, D., 1996: Socializing landscape. Second thoughts about the cultural biography of urnfields, *Archaeological Dialogues* 3, 77-87.

Friedman, J., 1984 (1974): Tribes, states and transformations, in M. Bloch (ed.), *Marxist analyses and social anthropology*, London (ASA Studies), 161-202.

Haffner, A., 1976: *Die westliche Hunsrück-Eifel-Kultur*, Berlin (Römisch-Germanische Forschungen 36).

Hessing, W.A.M., 1989: Wijk bij Duurstede 'De Horden': Besiedlung und Bestattungen aus der frühen Eisenzeit, *BROB* 39, 297-344.

Hodder, I., 1992: *Theory and practice in archaeology*, London.

Hodder, I., 1994: Architecture and meaning. The example of Neolithic houses and tombs, in M. Parker Pearson/C. Richards (eds), *Architecture and Order*, London/New York, 73-86.

Holwerda, J.H., 1913: *Das Gräberfeld von 'de Hamert' bei Venlo*, Leiden.

Impe, L. van, 1980: *Urnenveld uit de Late Bronstijd en de Vroege IJzertijd te Donk*, Brussel (AB 224).

Impe, L. van/G. Beex/H. Roosens 1973: *Het urnenveld op 'De Roosen' te Neerpelt*, Brussel (AB 145).

Kersten, W., 1948: Die Niederrheinische Grabhügelkultur, *Bonner Jahrbücher* 148, 5-81.

Kleij, P., 1993: *Voorlopig verslag opgraving Berkel-Enschot*, Tilburg (ITHO Archeologische Reeks 4).

Kooi, P.B., 1979: *Pre-Roman urnfields in the north of the Netherlands*, Groningen.

Kristiansen, K., 1996: Die Hortfunde der jüngeren Bronzezeit Dänemarks. Fundumstände, Funktion und historische Entwicklung, in *Archäologische Forschungen zum Kultgeschehen in der jüngeren Bronzezeit und frühen Eisenzeit Alteuropas*, Regensburg/Bonn, 255-270.

Laet, S.J. de, 1974: *Prehistorische kulturen in het zuiden der Lage Landen*, Wetteren.

Lambot, B., 1996: *Cartes postales aériennes de Champagne-Ardenne. 3000 ans d'histoire vus du ciel*, Reims (Société Archéologique Champenoise, memoire no. 11).

Lohof, E., 1994: Tradition and change. Burial practices in the Late Neolithic and Bronze Age in the north-eastern Netherlands, *Archaeological Dialogues* 1, 98-118.

Marschall, A./K.J. Narr/R. von Uslar 1954: *Die vor- und frühgeschichtliche Besiedlung des Bergischen Landes, Neustadt an der Aisch (Beihefte der Bonner Jahrbücher,* 3).

Modderman, P.J.R., 1964: The chieftain's grave of Oss reconsidered, *Bulletin van de Vereeniging tot bevordering der kennis van de antieke beschaving* 39, 57-62.

Nortmann, H., 1992: Eine Bestattung der ausgehenden Urnenfelderzeit bei Idenheim, Kreis Bitburg-Prüm, *Trierer Zeitschrift* 55, 15-24.

Röder, J., 1943: Der Kreisgrabenfriedhof von Mülheim, Ldkr. Koblenz, *Germania* 27, 1-20.

Roosens, H./G. Beex 1961: *De opgravingen in het urnenveld "De Roosen" te Neerpelt in 1960*, Brussel (AB 58).

Roosens, H./G. Beex 1962: *Het onderzoek van het urnenveld "De Roosen" te Neerpelt in 1961*, Brussel (AB 65).

Roymans, N., 1990: *Tribal societies in Northern Gaul. An anthropological perspective*, Amsterdam (Cingula 12).

Roymans, N., 1991: Late Urnfield societies in the Northwest European Plain and the expanding networks of Central European Hallstatt Groups, in N. Roymans/F. Theuws (eds), *Images of the Past. Studies on ancient societies in Northwestern Europe*, Amsterdam (Studies in Prae- en Protohistorie 7), 9-89.

Roymans, N., 1996: The South Netherlands project. Changing perspectives on landscape and culture, *Archaeological Dialogues* 3, 231-245.

Roymans, N./H. Fokkens 1991: Een overzicht van veertig jaar nederzettingsonderzoek in de Lage Landen, in H. Fokkens/N. Roymans (eds), *Nederzettingen uit de bronstijd en de vroege ijzertijd in de Lage Landen*, Amersfoort (NAR 13), 1-19.

Roymans, N./A. Tol 1996: Veranderende bewoningspatronen in het Land van Weert, in N. Roymans/A. Tol (eds), *Opgravingen in Kampershoek en de Molenakker te Weert*, Amsterdam (Zuidnederlandse Archeologische Rapporten 4), 7-16.

Ruppel, Th., 1995: Stand und Aufgaben der Spätbronzezeitforschung im Niederrheinischen Raum, in *Beiträge zur Urnenfelderzeit nördlich und südlich der Alpen*, Bonn (Monographien Römisch-Germanisches Zentralmuseum Mainz 35), 109-120.

Sanden, W.A.B. van der, 1981: The urnfield and the Late Bronze Age settlement traces on the Haagakkers at St.-Oedenrode (province of North Brabant), *BROB* 32, 307-328.

Theunissen, E.M., 1993: Once again Toterfout-Halve Mijl, *APL* 26, 29-43.

Theunissen, E.M., in prep.: *Midden Bronstijd-samenlevingen in het zuiden der Lage Landen. Een her-evaluatie van het begrip 'Hilversum-cultuur'*, (phil. doc. thesis University of Leiden).

Thomas, R., 1997: Land, kinship relations and the rise of enclosed settlement in first millennium B.C. Britain, *Oxford Journal of Archaeology* 16, 211-218.

Tilley, Chr., 1996: *An ethnography of the Neolithic. Early prehistoric societies in southern Scandinavia*, Cambridge (New studies in archaeology).

Torbrügge, W., 1970-1971: Vor- und frühgeschichtliche Flussfunde. Zur Ordnung und Bestimmung einer Denkmälergruppe, *Berichte der Römisch-Germanischen Kommission* 51-52, 1-46.

Verlinde, A.D., 1985: Die Gräber und Grabfunde der späten Bronzezeit und frühen Eisenzeit in Overijssel IV, *BROB* 35, 231-411.

Verwers, G.J., 1966a: A Late Bronze Age/Early Iron Age urnfield at Goirle, prov. Noord-Brabant, *APL* 2, 33-48.

Verwers, G.J., 1966b: Non-circular monuments in the southern Dutch urnfields, *APL* 2, 49-57.

Verwers, G.J., 1966c: Tumuli at the Zevenbergen near Oss gem. Berghem, prov. Noord-Brabant, *APL* 2, 27-32.

Verwers, G.J., 1969: The beginning of the Late Bronze Age in the Lower Rhine Area, *BROB* 19, 17-25

Verwers, G.J., 1972: Das Kamps Veld in Haps in Neolithikum, Bronzezeit und Eisenzeit, *APL* 5.

Verwers, G.J., 1975: Urnenveld en nederzetting te Laag Spul, gem. Hilvarenbeek, prov. Noord-Brabant, *APL* 8, 23-43.

Warmenbol, E., 1996: L'or, la mort et les Hyperboréens. La bouche des Enfers ou le Trou de Han à Han-sur-Lesse, in *Archäologische Forschungen zum Kultgeschehen in der jüngeren Bronzezeit und frühen Eisenzeit Alteuropas*, Regensburg/Bonn, 203-234.

Waterbolk, H.T., 1987: Terug naar Elp, in F.C.J. Ketelaar (ed.), *De historie herzien. Vijfde bundel 'Historische Avonden'*, Hilversum, 183-215.

Wilhelmi, K., 1974: Zur Verbreitung und Ausrichtung schlüssellochförmiger Grabanlagen der jüngeren Bronzezeit Nordwestdeutschlands, *Archäologisches Korrespondenzblatt* 4, 339-347.

Wilhelmi, K., 1983: *Die Jüngere Bronzezeit zwischen Niederrhein und Mittelweser*, Marburg (Kleine Schriften aus dem Vorgeschichtlichen Seminar Marburg 15).

Wilhelmi, K., 1987: Zur Besiedlungsgenese Englands und des nordwestlichen Kontinents von 1500 vor bis Christi Geburt, *Acta Praehistorica et Archaeologica* 19, 71-84.

Wilhelmi, K., 1988: Anthropologisches zur Bronze- und Eisenzeit in Nordwestdeutschland, *Archäologische Mitteilungen aus Nordwestdeutschland* 11, 3-24.

Willems, W., 1936: *De vóór-Romeinse urnenvelden in Nederland*, Maastricht.

Workshop of European Anthropologists 1980, *Journal of Human Evolution* 9, 517-549.

The Early Iron Age urnfield of Beegden

Nico Roymans (with a contribution by Menno Hoogland)

1   INTRODUCTION

The monumental barrow cemeteries or urnfields from the Late Bronze Age and Early Iron Age traditionally belong to the most characteristic archaeological phenomena of the sandy landscapes in the Lower Rhine region. Our knowledge of these urnfields is mainly based on the investigation of a series of cemeteries that were situated in the (former) heathlands. As stated in the previous article,[1] the scientific importance of these excavations is limited: not a single cemetery was excavated completely, while many burials had already been plundered by urn-diggers. Physical-anthropological research of cremated bones did not exist, and the zones between individual barrows were (also because of the limited technical and financial means) rarely excavated. These older excavations are unsuitable for answering a series of questions that archaeology now poses, like that on the demographical composition of the population, the size, spatial structure and chronological development of the cemetery, and the symbolism of the grave-field as a whole and of individual grave monuments.

---

[1]   Roymans/Kortlang, this volume.

Fig. 1. Geographical situation of Beegden in the Netherlands.

If we want to develop urnfield research, it is necessary to excavate several new cemeteries according to modern standards. The investigation of cemeteries in that part of the landscape where the traditional arable fields or 'essen' of the pre-modern hamlets and villages are situated offers the best conditions for this. The urnfields situated underneath the *plaggen* layer are often fairly well preserved; most burials are still intact, while the presence of ditched peripheral structures makes it rather easy to reconstruct the form and size of the original grave monuments. Moreover, the investigation of urnfields underneath the *essen* often makes it possible to excavate parts of the corresponding settlements too. For our future modelling of the social organisation and mental order of Lower Rhine Urnfield groups we are primarily dependent on the possibilities offered to us by the *essen* archaeology.

It is against the background of the above remarks that I would like to present the investigation of an urnfield at Beegden. It was discovered underneath the *plaggen* layer of an *es* complex in the Meuse valley in the Dutch province of Limburg and it has been excavated almost completely. Because of its short period of use, the rich variety of grave structures and the predominantly intact graves, this urnfield is important in the debate concerning the mortuary ritual and grave symbolism of Urnfield communities in the Lower Rhine region.[2]

[2]   The rescue excavations at Beegden would not have been a success without the enthousiast support of the Venlo amateur archaeologists R. Machiels and W. Alberts, and of a number of former students of the Instituut voor Pre- en Protohistorische Archeologie of the University of Amsterdam, in particular J. Schotten, J. Deeben, W. Beex and E. Vreenegoor. Furthermore I would like to thank mr. H. Stoepker, at that time provincial archaeologist of Limburg, for the support he gave us.

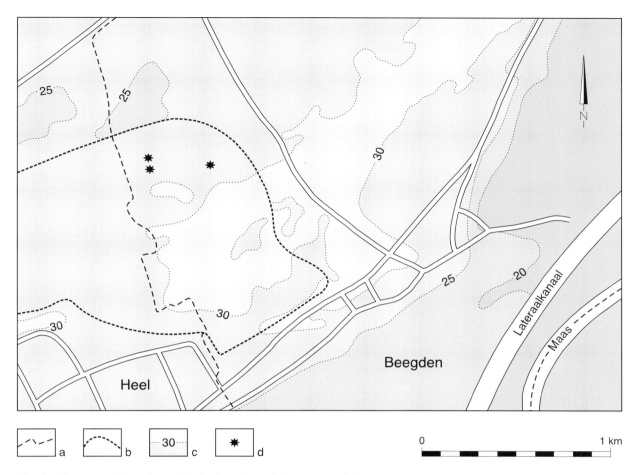

Fig. 2. The area of Beegden with the location of the excavated sites.
a municipal border; b edge of gravel pit; c land above 30 m +NAP; d excavated sites

2   THE EXCAVATION

In November 1986 Wolf Alberts and Jacob Schotten (Venlo) discovered an Early Iron Age urn with cremation remains on a site near the edge of a large gravel pit at Beegden (fig. 1). More fragments of urns and cremated bones were found in the surrounding area, which made it clear that they were deal-ing with an urnfield. This discovery and in particular the acute threat of destruction to the cemetery were the immediate cause for a series of short rescue excavations, carried out by the author in 1986 and 1987 under the auspices of the State Archaeological Service (Rijksdienst voor het Oudheidkundig Bodemonderzoek).[3] The site is situated at the western side of a broad, pleistocene sand ridge on the left bank of the river Meuse, c. 6 km southwest of the town of Roermond (fig. 2). In the '80s, large-scale gravel extraction had created an artificial lake in the area between the villages of Panheel and Beegden. In 1987 this gravel extraction was concentrated in the municipality of Beegden, in the zone where the urnfield was discovered (fig. 3). Until then, that area was part of the vast arable fields of the villages of Beegden and Heel. Judging from the pottery sherds found in the lowest levels of the *plaggen* layer at the excavation site, this zone was reclaimed in the Late Middle Ages. At different locations a

---

[3]   For a provisional report, see Roymans 1988.

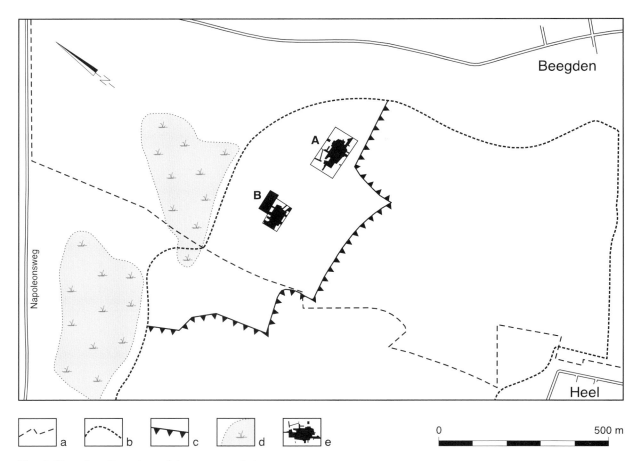

Fig. 3. Beegden. Location of the excavated sites.
a municipal border; b actual border of gravel pit; c edge of gravel pit in march 1987; d swamp; e excavated area
A urnfield; B rural settlement Late Iron Age/Roman period

more or less similar soil profile was documented. Underneath a dark *plaggen* layer of ca. 50 cm there is a brownish cultivation layer of 10-40 cm thick, which could not be dated. We are probably dealing with the remains of an older arable soil. Underneath this brown cultivation layer there was the clean yellow sandy subsoil, in which the brown-coloured archaeological features could be easily identified.

The acute threat to the site and the minimal financial means caused us to follow an adapted research strategy. It was decided to excavate in short campaigns of 3 to 4 days. After finishing the excavation of the urnfield, attempts were made to find traces of the corresponding settlement in the surrounding area. This led to the discovery of a small rural settlement from the Late Iron Age and Roman period, which was partly excavated (fig. 3, B).[4]

In addition, a concentration of some 15 pits was found in the northeastern zone of the urnfield (fig. 4). These contained pottery sherds, burnt pieces of stone, and some flint artefacts belonging to a later phase of the Middle Bronze Age and indicating the presence of habitation there. We are probably dealing with the remains of a farmhouse, of which most of the post-holes were eroded by later ploughing to such an extent that it is impossible to reconstruct the house. These Middle Bronze Age settlement remains are not further discussed here.

---

[4]   See Roymans 1988.

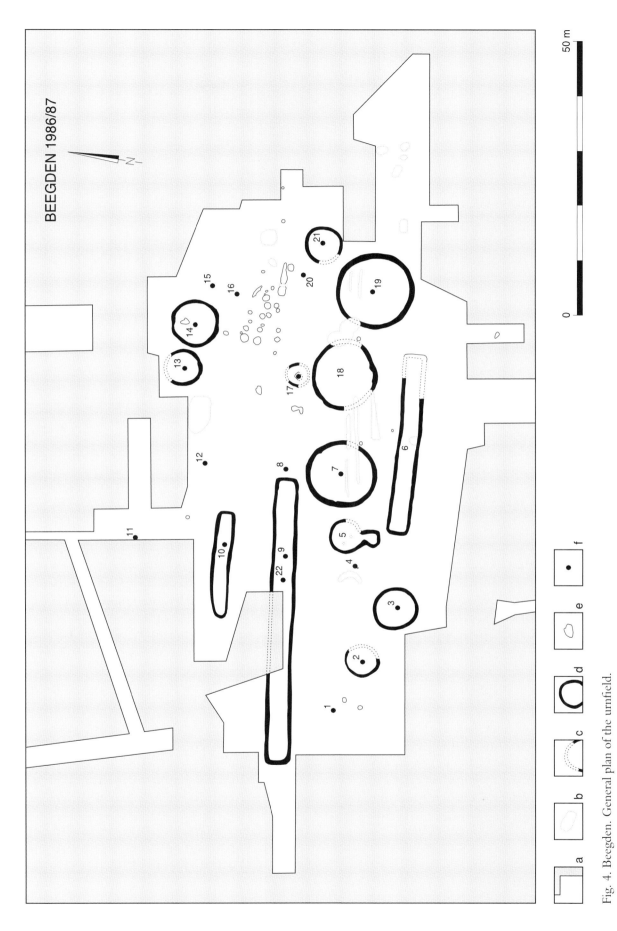

BEEGDEN 1986/87

50 m

Fig. 4. Beegden. General plan of the urnfield.
a excavated area; b recent disturbance; c reconstructed features; d ditch of grave monument; e post-hole or pit; f cremation burial

67

3 DESCRIPTION OF THE CEMETERY

The urnfield was almost completely excavated in three short campaigns at the end of 1986 and the beginning of 1987, during which an area of 0,75 ha was uncovered (figs. 3 and 4). Until shortly before our investigation, the cemetery must have been more or less intact, as it was covered by a protective arable layer. The upper parts of some urns were lost as a consequence of medieval ploughing, but there are no indications that graves were destroyed completely. It is significant that in almost all grave monuments the central interment was still present. Shortly before the start of the excavation, however, the site was disturbed by a bulldozer, which removed part of the arable topsoil. In retrospect the damage was less severe than expected; only in the centre of the urnfield were a few interments destroyed and some structures damaged. Before the start of the excavation amateur archaeologists collected sherds with cremation remains of two urns in the soil that was removed by the bulldozer. Later, one of these urns could be ascribed to the circular monument no. 7, while the other (appendix, grave 0) probably belonged to the structure no. 6 or 18.

3.1 MODE OF INTERMENT

Nineteen 19 graves have been found, including the two last-mentioned interments (fig. 4). In all cases we are dealing with a cremation ritual, in which the human bones were collected at the place of the pyre after cremation, and subsequently interred at the cemetery in a shallow pit. The cremation remains were almost completely free of charcoal, and therefore must have been carefully picked out at the pyre. In two cases (graves 9 and 10) it was observed that some pyre remains and cremated bones were scattered over the urn. Concerning the mode of interment, a first distinction can be made between urn graves and graves without a ceramic container. It is remarkable that this cemetery, with one possible exception, contained urn burials (95%) exclusively. In three cases a second pot was placed over the urn as a cover (graves 2, 9 and 19). The exception is the heavily disturbed grave 4, which only contained a minimal amount of cremated bone; this may have been an urnless interment. Secondly, a distinction can be made between burials situated within a grave monument (a ditched structure), and those which did not have a peripheral structure. Of the 22 graves (including three ditched structures – nos. 5, 6 and 18 – where the central interment was destroyed by a bulldozer) there are 8 (36%) flat graves and 14 (64%) which are associated with a grave monument. Furthermore it can be observed that no interments or grave goods were encountered in the ditches that surrounded the grave monuments.[5]

3.2 GRAVE MONUMENTS

The grave monuments (all marked by ditched structures) can be subdivided into three groups:

a. 9 circular ditches, with an outer diameter varying between 4,5 and 13,5 m. Originally these enclosed low barrows, which were levelled during the later medieval reclamation of the site.

---

[5] This is in agreement with Verwers' (1972, 50-51) observations on the Early Iron Age urnfield of Haps.

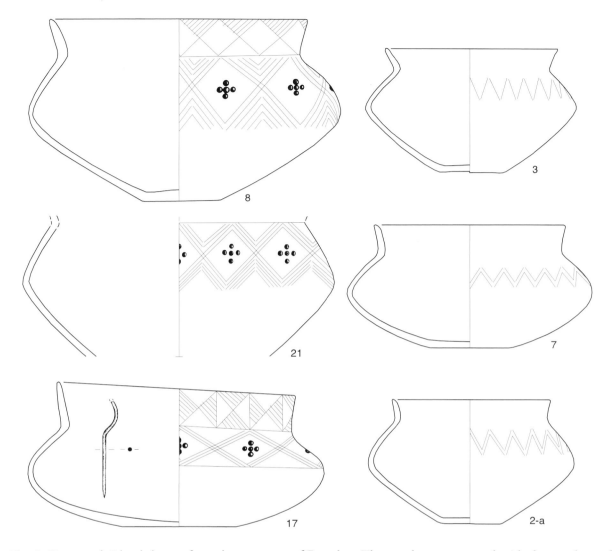

Fig. 5. Decorated *Schräghals* pots from the cemetery of Beegden. The numbers correspond with the numbers of the graves. Scale 1:4. Iron pin scale 1:3.

Important for their dating (see below) is that the ditches do not have any interruptions, except as a consequence of recent disturbances. A central interment was encountered within 8 circular ditches.

b. 3 elongated ditched structures or 'long-beds' (Dutch: *langbedden*), with outer lengths of 19, 32,5 en 52,5 m respectively, and an average outer width of 4 m. They are east-west oriented and mostly have rectangular ends. Within two of the structures, 1 respectively 2 graves were discovered on the longitudinal axis. These elongated ditches originally surrounded earthen banks or long barrows, as appears from the investigation of urnfields situated in heathlands where the monuments were still intact.[6]

[6]   See examples from De Hamert (Holwerda 1913), Valkenswaard (Brunsting/Verwers 1975, 63), Goirle (Verwers 1966a, 40), Zevenbergen (Verwers 1966c, 29, tumulus 2), Weert-Boshoven (unpublished) and Kallmuth (Marschall e.a. 1954). Cf. also Verwers 1966b, 55-56.

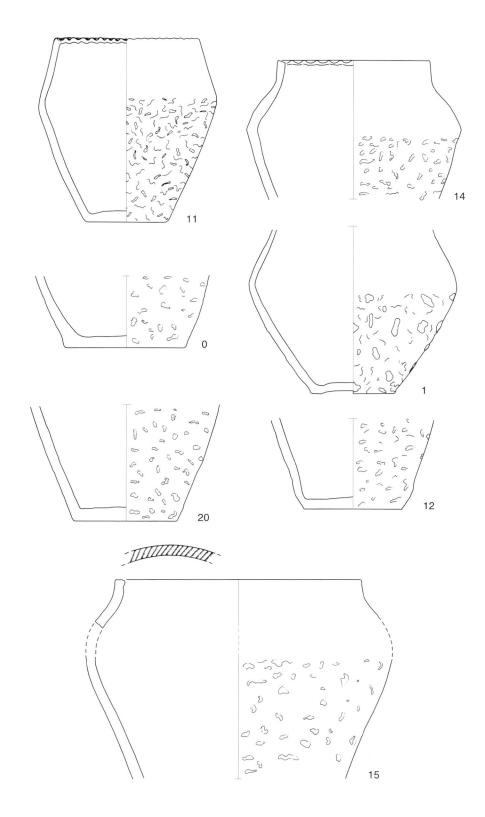

Fig. 6. Harpstedt pottery from the cemetery of Beegden. The numbers correspond with the numbers of the graves. Scale 1:4.

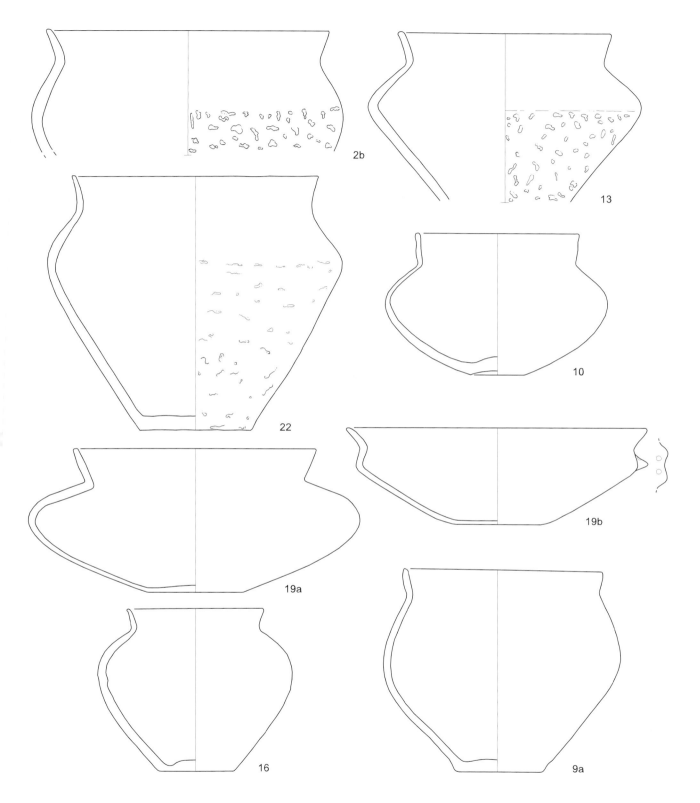

Fig. 7. *Schräghals* pots (nos. 2b, 10, 13, 19a, 22), a carinated dish (no. 19b), and other smooth-walled pots (no. 9a, 16) from the cemetery of Beegden. The numbers correspond with the numbers of the graves. Scale 1:4.

c. 1 keyhole-shaped ditch with an outer diameter of 6,25 m, or 8,75 m if the annex is included. The central interment was lost.

The interpretation of the 8 graves without ditched structures is problematic. Theoretically, they might originally have been covered with low barrows, but it is more probable that they were flat graves. We will see below that children are strongly represented in this category of burials.

3.3   POTTERY

The cemetery has produced 22 pots: 19 urns and 3 pots that were used as a cover. In all cases they are hand-made products which are in a bad, fragmentary condition; sometimes the upper part has disappeared because of medieval ploughing. Thanks to the professional work of W. Alberts some pots have been restored. The pottery from this cemetery fits well into the ceramic repertoire of the Lower Rhine urnfield culture (*Niederrheinische Grabhügelkultur*). Present are:
- 12 *Schräghals* pots (figs. 5 and 7).[7] They are carefully smoothened, with the exception of 3 examples which have a roughened (*besmeten*) belly.
- 1 sharply carinated dish, smooth-walled, with a perforated knobbed ear (fig. 7, no. 19b).
- 7 Harpstedt-like pots (fig. 6); high biconical pots with a roughened belly, a smoothened shoulder, and sometimes with finger-tip imprints on the rim.
- 2 high smooth-walled pots with rounded belly and outstanding neck (fig. 7, nos. 9a and 16).

Apart from the rim decoration with finger-tip imprints of some Harpstedt-like pots, decoration only occurs on *Schräghals* pottery. Three examples have an identical geometric decoration on the shoulder and neck, consisting of a combination of parallel or intersecting lines in the form of triangles and lozenges and groups of 5 impressed dots (*dellen*) (fig. 5, nos. 8, 17, 21). This decoration motif is unknown from other urnfields in the Southern Netherlands and Northern Belgium,[8] indicating that we are dealing with local ceramic products. The pots may even have been made by one and the same person. The same observation can be made for a group of three other *Schräghals* pots with an identical decoration of 1 or 2 zigzag lines on the shoulder (fig. 5, nos. 2a, 3, 7).

4   THE DATING OF THE CEMETERY

A date for this cemeterey can be obtained in different ways. A first lead is offered by the typochronology of the pottery. The dominance of *Schräghals* pots and roughened pots in *Harpstedter Stil* (together

[7] Harpstedt- and *Schräghals* pots are conventional terms for two characteristic types of pottery from the Early Iron Age in the Lower Rhine region. Although these terms are avoided by some archaeologists (Van den Broeke 1987, 29; Verlinde 1985) we still use them here in the conventional sense.

[8] An Early Iron Age sherd with a somewhat similar decoration of *dellen* and grooved lines is known from Geleen (Van den Broeke 1980, 110. fig. 5.2). Related Iron Age pottery decorated with groups of *dellen* in combination with zigzag lines has also been found on the eastern bank of the Rhine in the German Lower Rhine area (Marschall e.a. 1954,198, Abb. 25). For *Schräghals* pots with parallel zigzag lines on the shoulder, see Marschall et al. 1954, 221, Abb. 55.

86% of the ceramic material), clearly points to a date in the Early Iron Age; the types mentioned are characteristic for this period. The carinated dish with a perforated knobbed ear also dates to the Early Iron Age.[9] Equally important is the absence of typical Late Bronze Age pottery (pots with a cylindrical neck, with *Kerbschnitt* decoration, etc.) as well as ceramics characteristic for the Middle Iron Age (e.g. 'Marne' ceramics and barrel-shaped roughened pots). The *Schräghals* urn of grave 17 also contained an iron *Kropfnadel*, the head of which was lost (fig. 5, no. 17). Such pins are well-known from Early Iron Age contexts in the Lower Rhine region.[10]

A second lead for the dating is offered by the typochronology of the grave monuments in the Lower Rhine region. The circular ditches from the Late Bronze Age differ from those from the Early Iron Age in that the latter often have an interruption at the southeastern side, while the former are always 'closed'. Interrupted circular ditches are absent in the Beegden cemetery, which argues in favour of a date in or close to the Late Bronze Age. Until recently, long barrows were almost exclusively known from the Late Bronze Age, but new evidence shows that they also occur frequently in the Early Iron Age, as at Posterholt, Neerpelt, Someren, Mierlo-Hout and Wijk bij Duurstede.[11] They often distinguish themselves by their rectangular or open ends from the long-beds of the Late Bronze Age, which have rounded ends. Keyhole-shaped ditches are rare in the Lower Rhine region. They are characteristic for urnfields in the Northeastern Netherlands and Westphalia, where they are generally dated in the Late Bronze Age.[12]

A third lead for the dating is offered by the study of the mode of interment. Typical for the Early Iron Age in the Lower Rhine region is the predominance of interments in urns, while in the Late Bronze Age and Middle Iron Age urnless graves prevail.[13] The Beegden cemetery, with its extremely high percentage of urn graves (95%), clearly belongs to the Early Iron Age. The recently excavated urnfield at Someren, which was used in the period between c. 650-400 BC, almost exclusively produced urnless interments.[14] This indicates that the use of urns is particularly characteristic for the first phase of the Early Iron Age.

On the basis of the study of the pottery and the mode of interment the Beegden urnfield can be dated in the Early Iron Age. The presence of certain types of grave monuments, however, clearly points to Late Bronze Age traditions. A combination of the various dating elements argues for a positioning in an early phase of the Early Iron Age, roughly corresponding to the period 775-650 BC.[15] A

[9] Van den Broeke 1980, 109; Van den Broeke 1987, 106 (fig. 6-5).

[10] Cf. Verwers 1972, 158 and Abb. 32 (Ha D-grave with dagger and arrow heads from Haps); Hessing 1989, 318 (Early Iron Age grave from Wijk bij Duurstede); Modderman 1964, 59, fig. 3-10a/b (2 iron *Kropfnadel* with *Bombenkopf* from the Ha C elite burial at Oss); Engels/Van Impe 1985, 35 (Early Iron Age grave from Kaulille).

[11] Willems 1983, 221-225 (Posterholt); Van Impe/Beex/ Roosens 1973 (Neerpelt); Hessing 1989 (Wijk bij Duurstede); Tol, this volume (Mierlo-Hout); Kortlang, this volume (Someren). See also Verlinde 1985, 259-62.

[12] Butler 1969, 82, fig. 37; Wilhelmi 1974, Abb. 1; idem 1983, fig. 13; Verlinde 1985, 263-67. In the Southern Netherlands, a 'keyhole-shaped' long-bed is known from the urnfield of Valkenswaard (Brunsting/Verwers 1975, 57, 63) and Haps (Verwers 1972, grave O3), and a (prehistoric?) 'keyhole-shaped' ditch from the cemetery from the Roman period at Oss-'Ussen' (Van der Sanden, in: Van der Sanden/Van den Broeke 1987, 74 (fig. 4), 76).

[13] Verwers 1969, 59-61; idem 1972, 44; Van Impe 1983, 76.

[14] Kortlang, this volume.

[15] The start of the Early Iron Age in the Lower Rhine region is dated around 775 BC (Gündlingen phase in Central Europe): cf. the discussion in Roymans 1991, 36-37.

more exact dating is impossible because of the limited chronological resolution of the archaeological material. However, the great uniformity of the ceramic material, and particularly the presence of some series of pots with an identical decoration (fig. 5), which seem to have been made by the same person, suggest that the cemetery was used some 25 to 50 years, corresponding to one or two generations.

5   PHYSICAL–ANTHROPOLOGICAL STUDY OF THE CREMATION REMAINS

(MENNO HOOGLAND)

Eighteen cremations from the Beegden urnfield have been subjected to physical-anthropological analyses in order to study the age and sex composition of the group buried in the cemetery. Attention has also been paid to the possible occurrence of multiple interments and of animal bones among the cremation remains.

5.1   METHOD OF RESEARCH

A first point of interest is the fragmentation of the material, which can be indicated in two ways. The first method records the lower limit of the fragmentation, while the second shows the average size of the fragments. The cremations were sieved using a 3 and 10 mm sieve in order to make a distinction between a large fraction (>10 mm), a small fraction (3 to 10 mm) and a residue (<3 mm). The weight of the large fraction, represented in a percentage, indicates the degree of fragmentation of a cremation (see table 1, column 3).

For the age and sex determination, the fragments larger than 10 mm are sorted out according to the different regions of the skeleton. These are: neurocranium (part of the skull that contains the brains), viscerocranium (facial part of the skull), axial skeleton (vertebral column, sacrum, pelvis, clavicle and scapula), diaphysis of the long bones, epiphysis (joint) of the long bones, and an indeterminable residual group. The weight percentages of the different categories give us an indication of the degree to which these are represented. The multiple occurrence of fragments within one category is also noted. In most cases it concerns the epiphyses and fragments of the skull, among them pars petrosa. The occurrence of pretrosal bones (part of the os temporale in which the internal auditory organ is situated) appears to be the best evidence for determining multiple interments. Next the colour, the fracture pattern, and the size are recorded for each category. The first two variables can be used to reconstruct the temperature of the pyre. The last variable provides an impression of the average size of the fragments.

The variables used for the age-determinations are: the stage of eruption of the teeth, the stage of wear of the teeth, and the stage of fusion of the epiphyses and the cranial sutures. For individuals up to the age of 16 years, the development of the teeth provides the best indications, and for persons between 14 and 21 the stage of fusion of the epiphyses is conclusive. The age-determination of adults mainly depends on the obliteration of the sutures and the wear of the teeth, which give a rather unprecise outcome. For subadult individuals the results are reliable, but age-determinations based on the obliteration of the sutures have a wide margin and often only provide a lower limit of the age.

The sex determinations are based on a number of morphological characteristics of the skull and the pelvis. The latter are difficult to determine in case of cremations, as large fragments are required for this. Here the guidelines that were established by the *Workshop of European Anthropologists* have been

grave	grams	%>10mm	fragm.	number of ind.	age	sex morphol.	sex pars pet.	conclusion
1	452	50%	2-3	1	>18	2xM	1xN	M
2	719	45%	2-3	1	>18	–	–	–
3	1453	43%	1-3	1	18-30	2xF	–	F
7	205	(89%)	2	1	>18	–	–	–
8	758	43%	1–3	1	>18	–	–	–
9	2127	68%	2-4	4	0-1	–	–	–
					7-11	1xM	1xF	?
					>18	1xF	1xF	F
					30-40	–	2xF	F
10	1554	69%	3-4	2	4-7	–	1xF	?
					25-35	2xN,2xM	1xN,1xM	M
11	212	49%	2-3	1	8-10	–	–	–
12	183	51%	2-3	1	4-8	–	–	–
13	638	57%	2-3	1	25-35	3xF,1xN	–	F
14	523	34%	2-3	1	>18	-	–	–
15	896	27%	2	2	2-4	–	1xF	?
					>18	–	–	–
16	53	19%	1-2	1	3-5	–	–	–
17	1330	33%	2	1	18-30	–	–	–
19	1117	34%	2	1	14-18	1xF	–	F?
20	35	11%	1-2	1	0-3	–	–	–
21	1002	24%	1-2	1	>18	–	–	–
22	3407	75%	3-4	7	2-4	–	–	–
					8-12	1xF	2xF	?
					8-12	–	1xM?	?
					>18 } >18 } >18 } 30-40 }	8xF,3xM	4xF,1xM, 1xF?	2xF,1xM, 1xF?

Table 1. Beegden. Summary of the physical–antropological data per cremation burial.

followed. This method is supplemented by the analysis of the petrosal bone, according to the method of Wahl.[16] The reliability of the results depends on the number of variables that are available and their mutual consistency. If the outcome seems reliable, this is indicated by a F or M, otherwise with F? or M? In case of contradictory or non–discriminative outcomes the result of the sex determination is N.

5.2   RESULTS

The cemetery has produced 18 urns with cremation remains.[17] Their weight varies from 35 to 3407 g, with an average of 926 g.[18] The number of individuals, however, is higher than 18 because of the

[16]   Wahl 1982.
[17]   The disturbed grave no. 14 was not included in the analysis because of the minimal quantity of cremated bone (6 gr).

[18]   The average weight of the interments must have been higher originally, as a number of cremations were incomplete due to medieval ploughing.

presence of four multiple interments: two with two persons each, one with four, and one with the remains of seven individuals (see below). Therefore, the total number of persons represented is 29.

The degree of fragmentation is expressed by the percentage of the fraction larger than 10 mm. This varies from 11 to 89% with an average of 46%.[19] This high percentage is due to the fact that most graves were relatively well-preserved. The two lowest scores are determined by the young age of the persons involved, respectively 0-3 and 3-5 years.

The degree of incineration of the 18 interments is almost the same, between the beginning of phase III and the end of phase IV. This corresponds to temperatures between 550° and 700°C. Within each cremation the burning of the different parts of the skeleton is equal, and the same is true for the remains of different individuals in the multiple interments. Only in grave 22 a number of fragments, possibly of the same person, were cremated at a lower temperature.

Of the 29 persons in this urnfield (table 2), 17 reached the adult age (18 years or older). There are 11 children: one newborn, one aged between 0 and 3 years, three between 3 and 5 years, two between 4 and 8, and four between 8 and 12 years. One individual belongs to the juvenile age group (14-18 years). The age of the adults could not be determined precisely because of the lack of unambiguous indications. For 11 of the 17 adults it could only be said that they were older than 18-21 years. The age of the other adults could be further specified as between 18 and 30 years (two cases), between 25 and 35 (two cases), and between 30 and 40 years (two cases). These determinations, however, mostly indicate the lower age limits and do not exclude a higher age.

	number	
children (0-14)	11	(38%)
juveniles (14-18)	1	(3%)
adult males	3	(10%)
adult females	6	(21%)
adults indet.	8	(28%)
total	**29**	**(100%)**

Table 2. Beegden. Composition of the cemetery population according to age and sex.

For 9 adults fairly reliable sex determinations can be given: six females and three males. In two other cases, both females, the outcome is less trustworthy. For five other individuals no reliable sex determinations can be presented on the basis of the pars petrosa, as the persons involved were of subadult age. In most of these cases, however, the low metrical values of the (not fully grown) petrosal bones suggest a female status. These results are not included in the conclusion.

Finally it can be observed that no animal bones were encountered among the cremation remains.

---

[19] The extremely high percentage (89) for grave no. 7 is not representative, as in this case the cremation remains were collected by hand.

It is necessary to comment on the graves with multiple interments. In two cases (burials nos. 10 and 15) the urn contained remains of an adult and a child. In burial 10 there were 4 petrosal bones; one pair belonged to an adult and another immature pair to a child. The occurrence of dental elements of a child confirmed this conclusion and provided an age of 4-7 years. This cremation is a double interment of an adult man and a child. Burial 15 contained one petrosal bone of a young individual, and other remains of a subadult person as well as of an adult. The dental elements provide an age of 2-4 years for the child. The exact age and sex of the adult person could not be determined.

More interesting was the identification of the cremated bones from graves 9 and 22, both belonging to the largest long-bed of the Beegden cemetery. Burial 9 contained 4 petrosal bones; two form a full-grown pair, one is a full-grown specimen, and another one is immature. They point to the presence of at least 3 persons including one child. Among the dental remains there are elements of at least three different developmental stages; that of a newborn, that of a child aged 7-11 years, and the adult stage. The obliteration of the sutures provided an age of 30-40 years for one of the adults. We may conclude that the urn of burial 9 comprised the remains of two children aging 0-1 and 7-11 years, and two adults, both females, one of which aged 30-40 years.

The cremation remains of burial 22, which were excellently preserved in an urn, contained the remains of even more persons. There were 9 petrosal bones. Three of them are immature and belong to at least two children. The remaining 6 form two pairs and two single specimens, representing at least four adult persons. The dental remains contain elements of at least three developmental stages: that of a child aged 2-4 years, of a child aged 8-12 years, and the full-grown stage. From the study of the epiphyses we may conclude that the cremation – besides a child aged 2-4 years and several adults – contained two children aged 8-12 years. Furthermore, the suture obliteration points to at least one individual aged 30-40 years. The analyses of the petrosal bones resulted in the determination of the sex of four adults: two females, one probable female, and one male. The morphological analysis confirms the presence of several females and at least one male. The combination of these data gives a total number of at least 7 individuals who were interred in this grave.

6   A DEMOGRAPHICAL RECONSTRUCTION

If we consider the composition of the cemetery population (table 2), two observations can be made. First, there appears to be an underrepresentation of newborn children (only one certain case). Children make up 38%, while in pre-modern societies their proportion mostly fluctuates between 45 and 65%.[20] Second, there is an overrepresentation of women among the adults (six females to three males). The number of adults whose sex could not be determined is, however, so large that no final conclusions can be drawn from this.

The results of the physical-anthropological research provide some evidence for a demographical reconstruction of the living community. We assume that the cemetery is excavated almost completely; on all sides the boundaries seem to have been reached (fig. 8).[21] The minimal number of graves is 22,

---

[20]   Cf. Caselitz 1986, 169 ff; Hessing 1989, 327.

[21]   This is confirmed by some trial trenches and the fact that no new burials have been found during the removal of the top-soil by a bulldozer on the adjacent grounds.

including the three lost burials within the ditched enclosures nos. 5, 6 and 18. Assuming that some graves in the northern zone have been missed or were destroyed during earlier digging activities, a correction factor of 15% is introduced. This brings the estimated maximum number of graves to 25.

The formula of Acsadi and Némeskeri is a much used means for demographical reconstructions of a living community on the basis of burial evidence. The formula is:

$$P = k \times (D \times e)/t.$$

P represents the average number of persons of the living community. k is a correction factor, which, for the Beegden cemetery, is estimated at 1.1. This is based on the fact that newborn children are underrepresented in the Beegden cemetery.[22] D indicates the number of interments, and e the average age expectancy of a person at the moment of birth. This is usually fixed at 25 years in pre-modern societies. T is the number of years the cemetery was in use.

Table 3 shows a calculation of the size of the Beegden population, using the above formula. Two different values have been employed for t and three for D. The period the cemetery was used (t) is estimated at 25 and 50 years, thereby covering the margins that are given by the archaeological evidence (see above). The number of interred persons (D) is estimated at 30, 35 and 40. In each case we are proceeding from a (reconstructed) total number of 25 graves. For 18 burials the cremation remains have been analysed; together they produced the remains of 29 individuals. Taking into account the remaining 7 burials, one arrives at a total of 35 to 40 individuals, depending on the presence or absence of other graves with multiple interments. The case of a total of 30 is based on the assumption that most of the persons encountered in graves 9 and 22 represent secondarily interred persons who may have come from elsewhere, and in that case they cannot be included here (see the discussion below).

e = 25	D = 30	D = 35	D = 40
t = 25	33	39	44
t = 50	17	19	22

Table 3. Beegden. Calculation of the average size of the living population, using different figures for the total number of interments (D) and the duration of the cemetery (t). The average life expectancy (e) is 25 years.

According to the calculations in table 3, we should imagine an average population of minimally 17 to maximally 44 persons in Beegden. The most probable is (proceeding from a duration of the urnfield of 50 years, and a reconstructed number of 35 interments) an average living population of 19 individuals. This figure may correspond to three families of c. 6 persons each. The image created in this way is that of a small urnfield, used for only a few generations by a local group of probably three families. If we try to translate this demographical reconstruction into settlement terms, then this may correspond to the occupants of three farmhouses. By analogy with the situation elsewhere in the Meuse-Demer-Scheldt region (Someren, St.-Oedenrode, Mierlo-Hout, Oss), we may assume that these farmhouses were lying more or less dispersed in the direct surroundings of the cemetery, and that they periodically shifted their location.[23]

---

[22] This is conform the situation relating to many other Iron Age cemeteries in the Northwest European Plain. Cf. Hessing 1989, 327; Caselitz 1986, 169 ff.

[23] Cf. Schinkel 1994, I, 254 ff. (Oss); Kortlang, this volume (Someren); Tol, this volume (Mierlo-Hout); Van Bodegraven 1991 (St.-Oedenrode).

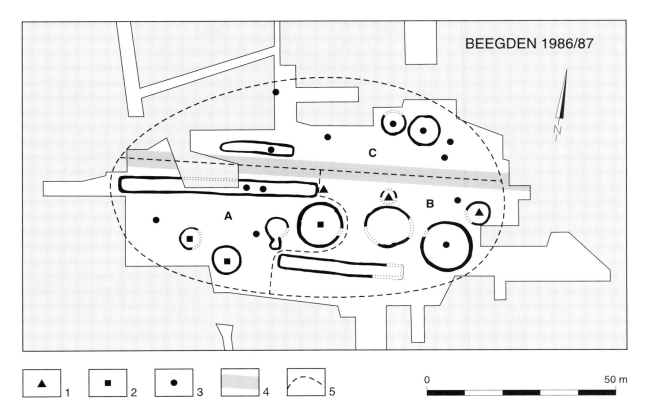

BEEGDEN 1986/87

Fig. 8. The Beegden urnfield: spatial patterns.
1 *Schräghals* pots with a decoration of dellen and grooved lines (fig. 5, left); 2 *Schräghals* pots with a decoration of one or two zigzag lines (fig. 5, right); 3 other graves; 4 probable prehistoric road; 5 general boundary of the urn-field, and internal boundaries of three clusters of graves which probably correspond to different families

7   SOME OBSERVATIONS ON SPATIAL ORGANISATION

The above demographical interpretation is indirectly confirmed by the layout of the cemetery, with its large open spaces between the individual burials. This pattern differs from that of most other urnfields in the Lower Rhine region, which show a dense packing of grave monuments, being the result of a long period of use covering several centuries. In Beegden we get a picture of a cemetery in its initial phase. The process of condensation of the graves, i.e. of filling in the open spaces between the oldest burials, has hardly started here. As the cemetery was given up after only two generations, it occupies an excep-tional place within the series of urnfields that have been excavated in the Lower Rhine region.

A second point of interest is the probable presence of a prehistoric road within the cemetery. In their analyses of urnfield plans, Dutch archaeologists have frequently noticed the occurrence of nar-row 'empty' or feature-less zones, which can be interpreted as roads.[24] In Beegden an east-west ori-

---

[24]   Kooi 1979, 152-166; Verlinde 1985, 388-89. Cf. also   urnfield of Well-'De Hamert'.
       Holwerda (1913), describing prehistoric roads in the

no.	monument	mode of interment	weight crem.	age	sex	grave goods
1	flat grave	urn	452	>18	M	–
2	circular ditch	urn + cover	719	>18	–	–
3	circular ditch	urn	1453	18-30	F	–
4	flat grave	heap of bone	6	–	–	–
5	keyhole-shaped ditch	–	–	–	–	–
6	long-bed	–	–	–	–	
7	circular ditch	urn	205	>18	–	–
8	flat grave	urn	758	>18	–	–
9	long-bed	urn + cover	2127	0-1	–	–
				7-11	–	
				>18	F	
				30-40	F	
10	long-bed	urn	1554	4-7	–	–
				25-35	M	–
11	flat grave	urn	212	8-10	–	–
12	flat grave	urn	183	4-8	–	–
13	circular ditch	urn	638	25-35	F	–
14	circular ditch	urn	523	18-80	–	–
15	flat grave	urn	896	2-4	–	–
				18-80	–	–
16	flat grave	urn	53	3-5	–	–
17	circular ditch	urn	1330	18-30-	iron pin	
18	circular ditch	–	–	–	–	–
19	circular ditch	urn + cover	1117	14-18	F?	–
20	flat grave	urn	35	0-3	–	–
21	circular ditch	urn	1002	18-80	–	–
22	long-bed	urn	3407	2-4	–	bronze,
				8-12	–	indet.
				8-12	–	
				18-80		
				18-80	F,F	
				18-80	F?,M	
				30-40		

Table 4. Beegden. Overview of the principal archaeological data per grave.

ented, ca. 10 m wide 'empty' strip can be observed that divides the cemetery into two halves (fig. 8). This strip probably marks the trajectory of a prehistoric road, on both sides of which the cemetery developed.

A third remark concerns the patterns in the distribution of some pottery types within the cemetery. Roughened pots of the Harpstedt type are found both in the northern and in the southern part of the urnfield. In contrast, the decorated, smooth-walled *Schräghals* pots all come from the southern part. Two groups of pots with an identical decoration can be distinguished (fig. 5), which are clustering in separate zones (fig. 8). Such patterns may have been the result of families who produced their own pots and buried their dead in a specific part of the cemetery.

A final observation, concerns the location of the long barrows. These structures appear to have a rather heterogeneous orientation in the urnfields which is determined by the local topography, in particular the situation on a sand-ridge or along a prehistoric road.[25] The latter seems to be the case at Beegden, where the orientation of the three long-beds is determined by the road trajectory. Moreover, it can be noticed that the relation between long-bed and other graves is almost equal on both sides of the road: 7 graves including 1 long-bed north of the road, and 15 graves including 2 long-beds at the southern side.[26] It is even possible to identify the three families, deduced from the demographical evidence, in the layout of the cemetery (fig. 8). The cluster of graves north of the road, including one long-bed, may correspond with family *A*. South of the road family *B* and *C* may correspond with the southeastern and the southwestern cluster respectively, each with one long-bed and a group of pots probably made by the same hand.

8   SUMMARY AND DISCUSSION

This study offers an analysis of an almost completely excavated urnfield on the west bank of the Meuse at Beegden. The burial place, dating to the beginning of the Early Iron Age, shows the typical characteristics of the cremation cemeteries of the *Niederrheinische Grabhügelkultur*: a great variety of grave structures (long graves, round barrows, flat graves) and an extreme scarcity of grave goods. The cemetery occupies a special position in modern research, because it was only used for a short period of time (c. two generations) by a small group of probably three families. The short period of use, the considerable variation of grave structures and the predominantly intact graves make that the Beegden cemetery will play an important role in discussions about the social and ideological meanings of the Lower Rhine urnfield ritual.[27]

The Beegden urnfield, for example, offers important evidence for the social and symbolic interpretation of the long graves. Though most urnfield barrows are individual grave monuments, long-beds contain more often than round barrows 2 or 3 graves; these are commonly situated on the longitudinal axis of the monuments.[28] Moreover it has been demonstrated that graves from long-barrows sometimes contain the remains of several individuals. Most often it concerns an interment of an adult and a child. Such double graves, however, frequently occur in urnfields without having a special connection with long-beds.[29] Highly exceptional are the graves with the cremated remains of four and seven persons respectively, both from the largest long-bed at Beegden (fig. 8). Assuming that both burials are more or less contemporary,[30] we are dealing here with the remains of 11 individuals. It is

[25] Verlinde 1985, 245 ff., 259, 261.

[26] The proportion of long-beds will have been somewhat smaller if we take into account that some flat graves or round barrows are lost. A ratio of ca. 1:9 seems more realistic.

[27] Cf. the more general discussion in Roymans/ Kortlang, this volume.

[28] Examples of long barrows containing several burials in the MDS-area: Weert-Boshoverheide, graves C-7 and C-16 (Roymans/Kortlang, this volume, fig. 11-f,g), Hilvarenbeek, graves 45/48/51 (Verwers 1975), Someren, grave 5.1-2 (Kortlang, this volume), Valkenswaard, graves 2/8 (Brunsting/Verwers 1975), Beegden, graves 9/22. See also Verlinde 1985, 244, 255, 259.

[29] Graves with the remains of two persons are known from the urnfield of Someren, graf 142 (within circular ditch; Kortlang, this volume), Neerpelt, grave 56 (within circular ditch; Roosens/Beex 1961, 56), Wijk bij Duurstede, grave 23 (flat grave) and 34 (secondary burial within circular ditch; Hessing 1989), Weert-Boshoven, grave C7a (long-bed; Roymans/Kortlang, this volume, fig. 11-f), Beegden, grave 15 (flat grave) and 10 (long-bed), Donk, graves 38 and 67 (flat graves?; Van Impe 1980). See also Cuijpers 1994 and Wilhelmi 1988 on the occurrence of double graves in urnfields in Overijssel and Westphalia.

[30] This long-bed is the only grave monument with more than one burial in the cemetery of Beegden.

difficult to accept (also taking into account the small size of the Beegden community) that all these persons died and were cremated at the same moment. This would have meant a catastrophic reduction of the Beegden community, which can be estimated at c. 19 persons (see above). We should consider the possibility of (partially) secondary burials. It is interesting that the long-bed in question, being one of the oldest and most monumental grave structures of the urnfield, can be interpreted as a founder burial. Members of the family group that first settled at this location may have interred here the remains of close relatives who at first had been buried in the cemetery of the community from which they had split off. Another option is that we are dealing with the remains of some members of the Beegden community whose interment was postponed until interment in a founder burial became possible. The above practices indicate that long graves, more than the other graves, symbolised the collective of the family and are therefore not strictly individual.

Appendix

Descriptive catalogue of the graves and grave monuments

Grave 0   Fragments of an urn with cremation remains, found in disturbed soil before the start of the excavation. Probably originating from the 'empty' ditched structure of no. 6 or 18. Pottery: bottom and wall fragments of a Harpstedt(?) pot with roughened belly (fig. 6-0).

Grave 1   (f. 106). Without peripheral structure. Cremation remains (452 g) in an urn. Pottery: bottom and wall fragments of a Harpstedt pot with roughened belly and smoothened shoulder and neck (fig. 6-1).

Grave 2   (f. 112). Situated in the centre of a circular ditch (outer diameter 8 m) with a recent disturbance at the eastern side. Cremation remains (719 g) in an urn. Pottery: a) bottom, wall and rim fragments of a *Schräghals* pot with a decoration of two grooved zigzag lines on the shoulder. Polished surface (fig. 5-2a); b) wall and rim fragments of a *Schräghals* pot, placed upside down over the urn. Roughened belly; smoothened shoulder and neck (fig. 7-2b).

Grave 3   (f. 63). Situated in the centre of a closed circular ditch (outer diameter 12 m). Cremation remains (1453 g) in an urn. Pottery: bottom, wall and rim fragments of a *Schräghals* pot with a decoration of a grooved zigzag line on the shoulder. Polished surface (fig. 5-3).

Grave 4   (f. 17). Without peripheral structure. Cremation remains (6 g) in a shallow pit; sherds of an urn have not been found.

Grave 5   Keyhole-shaped ditch with an outer diameter of 6.25 m, with annex 8.75 m. Central interment lost because of recent digging activities.

Grave 6   Long-bed (outer width 4 m, outer length 32.5 m). The eastern end has largely disappeared because of recent digging activities. The interment is also lost. Some stray fragments of an urn with cremation remains (see grave 0) may originate from this structure.

Grave 7   (f. 3). Situated in the centre of a circular ditch (outer diameter 12.5 m) with a recent disturbance at the eastern side. Cremation remains (205 g) in an urn. Pottery: bottom, wall and rim fragments of a *Schräghals* pot with a decoration of two grooved zigzag lines on the shoulder. Polished surface (fig. 5-7).

Grave 8   (f. 1). Without peripheral structure. Cremation remains (758 g) in an urn. Pottery: *Schräghals* pot with a geometric decoration on the shoulder and neck, consisting of a combination of parallel or intersecting lines in the form of triangles and lozenges and groups of 5 '*dellen*'. Polished surface (fig. 5-8).

Grave 9   (f. 18). Situated on the longitudinal axis of a long-bed (outer width 4 m, outer length 52.5 m). Cremation remains (2127 g) in an urn. Pottery: a) bottom, wall and rim fragments of a high pot with rounded belly and outstanding neck. Polished surface (fig. 7-9a); b) wall and rim fragments of a *Schräghals* pot, placed upside down over the urn. Smoothened surface (not drawn).

Grave 10   (f. 23). Long-bed (outer width 3.5 m, outer length 32.5 m). Excentric interment on the longitudinal axis. Cremation remains (1554 g) in an urn. Pottery: *Schräghals* pot with smoothened surface (fig. 7-10).

Grave 11   (f. 24). Without peripheral structure. Cremation remains (212 g) in an urn. Pottery: bottom, wall and rim fragments of a Harpstedt pot. Roughened belly; smoothened shoulder and neck; finger-tip imprints on the rim (fig. 6-11).

Grave 12   (f. 114). Without peripheral structure. Cremation remains (183 g) in an urn. Pottery: bottom and wall fragments of a Harpstedt(?) pot with roughened belly (fig. 6-12).

Grave 13   (f. 62). Situated in the centre of a circular ditch (outer diameter 6.5 m) with a recent disturbance at the northern side. Cremation remains (638 g) in an urn. Pottery: wall and rim fragments of a *Schräghals* pot with roughened belly and smoothened shoulder and neck (fig. 7-13).

Grave 14   (f. 52). Situated in the centre of a closed circular ditch (outer diameter 8.5 m). Cremation remains (523 g) in an urn. Pottery: wall and rim fragments of a Harpstedt pot with roughened belly, smoothened shoulder and neck and fingertip imprints on the rim (fig. 6-14).

Grave 15   (f. 69). Without peripheral structure. Cremation remains (896 g) in an urn. Pottery: wall and rim fragments of a Harpstedt pot with roughened belly, smoothened shoulder and neck, and slant imprints on the rim (fig. 6-15).

Grave 16 (f. 55). Without peripheral structure. Cremation remains (53 g) in an urn. Pottery: bottom, wall and rim fragments of a pot with rounded belly and outstanding neck. Smoothened surface (fig. 7-16).

Grave 17 (f. 0-1). Situated in the centre of a circular ditch (outer diameter 4.5 m) which is partially destroyed by recent digging activities. Cremation remains (1330 g) in an urn. Pottery: bottom, wall and rim fragments of a *Schräghals* pot with a geometric decoration on the shoulder and neck, consisting of a combination of parallel or intersecting lines in the form of triangles and lozenges and groups of 5 '*dellen*'. Polished surface (fig. 5-17). Metal: iron *Kropfnadel*, the head of which is missing. Found between the cremation remains (fig. 5-17).

Grave 18 Circular ditch (outer diameter 12.5 m) with a recent disturbance at the eastern and western side. The central interment is lost. Stray fragments of an urn with cremation remains (see grave 0) may originate from this structure.

Grave 19 (f. 67). Situated in the centre of a closed circular ditch (outer diameter 13.5 m) with a recent disturbance at the western side. Cremation remains (1117 g) in an urn. Pottery: a) bottom, wall and rim fragments of a *Schräghals* pot. Smoothened surface (fig. 7-19a); b) bottom, wall and rim fragments of a sharply carinated dish, with a knobbed ear with two perforations on the shoulder. Placed upside down over the urn. Polished surface (fig. 7-19b).

Grave 20 (f. 30). Without peripheral structure. Cremation remains (35 g) in an urn. Pottery: a) bottom and wall fragments of a Harpstedt(?) pot with roughened belly (fig. 6-20).

Grave 21 (f. 13). Situated in the centre of a circular ditch (outer diameter 6.5 m) with a recent disturbance at the western side. Cremation remains (1002 g) in an urn. Pottery: wall fragments of a *Schräghals* pot with a geometric decoration on the shoulder, consisting of a combination of parallel or intersecting lines in the form of triangles and lozenges and groups of 5 '*dellen*'. Polished surface (fig. 5-21).

Grave 22 Found on the longitudinal axis of the same long-bed as in which grave 9 was found. Cremation remains (3407 g) in an urn. Pottery: *Schräghals* pot. Slightly roughened belly; smooth-walled shoulder and neck (fig. 7-22). Metal: a cremated bone fragment with a green corrosion spot points to the presence of a bronze object during the cremation.

REFERENCES

Bodegraven, N. van, 1991: Nederzettingssporen uit de late bronstijd en de vroege ijzertijd op de Everse Akkers in St.-Oedenrode, in H. Fokkens/N. Roymans (eds), *Nederzettingen uit de bronstijd en de vroege ijzertijd in de Lage Landen*, Amersfoort (NAR 13), 129-139.

Broeke, P.W. van den, 1980: Een rijk gevulde kuil met nederzettingsmateriaal uit de IJzertijd, gevonden te Geleen, prov. Limburg, *APL* 13, 100-113.

Broeke, P.W. van den, 1987: Oss Ussen. Het handgemaakt aardewerk, in Van der Sanden/Van den Broeke 1987 (eds), 101-119.

Brunsting, H./G.J. Verwers 1975: Het urnenveld bij Valkenswaard, prov. Noord-Brabant, *APL* 8, 53-77.

Butler, J.J., 1969: *Nederland in de Bronstijd*, Bussum (Fibulareeks, 31).

Caselitz, P., 1986: Die menschlichen Leichenbrände des jüngerbronze- und ältereisenzeitlichen Gräberfeldes im 'Wangelister Feld', Stadt Hameln, Kr. Hameln-Pyrmont, *Neue Ausgrabungen und Forschungen in Niedersachsen* 17, 157-180.

Cuijpers, A.G.F.M., 1994: *Crematieresten uit de Late Bronstijd en Vroege IJzertijd in Overijssel*, Amersfoort (ROB Interne Rapporten 10).

Engels, A./L. van Impe 1985: Het urnenveld op de Dorperheide te Kaulille, *AB* 1, nr 2, 33-35.

Hessing, W.A.M., 1989: Wijk bij Duurstede 'De Horden': Besiedlung und Bestattungen aus der frühen Eisenzeit, *BROB* 39, 297-344.

Holwerda, J.H., 1913: *Das Gräberfeld von 'de Hamert' bei Venlo*, Leiden.

Impe, L. van, 1980: *Urnenveld uit de Late Bronstijd en de Vroege IJzertijd te Donk*, Brussel (AB 224).

Impe, L. van, 1983: Het oudheidkundig bodemonderzoek in Donk (gem. Herk-de-Stad) 1977-1982, in *Miscellanea Archaeologica in honorem H. Roosens*, Brussel (AB 255), 65-94.

Impe, L. van/G. Beex/H. Roosens 1973: *Het urnenveld op 'De Roosen' te Neerpelt*, Brussel (AB 145).

Kooi, P.B., 1979: *Pre-Roman urnfields in the north of the Netherlands*, Groningen.

Marschall, A./K.J. Narr/R. von Uslar 1954: *Die vor- und frühgeschichtliche Besiedlung des Bergischen Landes*, Neustadt an der Aisch (Beihefte der Bonner Jahrbücher, 3).

Modderman, P.J.R., 1964: The chieftain's grave of Oss reconsidered, *Bulletin van de Vereeniging tot bevordering der kennis van de antieke beschaving* 39, 57-62.

Roymans, N., 1988: Beegden, in H. Stoepker (ed.), Archeologische kroniek van Limburg over 1987, *PSHAL* 124, 346-363.

Roymans, N., 1991: Late Urnfield societies in the Northwest European Plain and the expanding networks of Central European Hallstatt Groups, in N. Roymans/F. Theuws (eds), *Images of the Past. Studies on ancient societies in Northwestern Europe*, Amsterdam (Studies in Prae- en Protohistorie 7), 9-89.

Sanden, W.A.B. van der/P.W. van den Broeke (eds) 1987: *Getekend zand. Tien jaar archeologisch onderzoek in Oss-Ussen*, Waalre (Bijdragen tot de studie van het Brabantse heem 31).

Schinkel, C., 1994: *Zwervende erven. Bewoningssporen in Oss-Ussen uit Bronstijd, IJzertijd en Romeinse tijd. Opgravingen 1976-1986*, Leiden (unpubl. dissertation University of Leiden).

Verlinde, A.D., 1985: Die Gräber und Grabfunde der späten Bronzezeit und frühen Eisenzeit in Overijssel IV, *BROB* 35, 231-411.

Verwers, G.J., 1966a: A Late Bronze Age/Early Iron Age urnfield at Goirle, prov. Noord-Brabant, *APL* 2, 33-48.

Verwers, G.J., 1966b: Non-circular monuments in the southern Dutch urnfields, *APL* 2, 49-57.

Verwers, G.J., 1966c: Tumuli at the Zevenbergen near Oss gem. Berghem, prov. Noord-Brabant, *APL* 2, 27-32.

Verwers, G.J., 1969: The beginning of the Late Bronze Age in the Lower Rhine Area, *BROB* 19, 17-25.

Verwers, G.J., 1972: Das Kamps Veld in Haps in Neolithikum, Bronzezeit und Eisenzeit, *APL* 5.

Verwers, G.J., 1975: Urnenveld en nederzetting te Laag Spul, gem. Hilvarenbeek, prov. Noord-brabant, *APL* 8, 23-43.

Wahl, J., 1982: Leichenbranduntersuchungen: Ein Überblick über die Bearbeitungs- und Aussagemöglichkeiten von Brandgräbern, *Prähistorische Zeitschrift* 57, 1-125.

Wilhelmi, K., 1974: Zur Verbreitung und Ausrichtung schlüssellochförmiger Grabanlagen der jüngeren Bronzezeit Nordwestdeutschlands, *AK* 4, 339-347.

Wilhelmi, K., 1988: Anthropologisches zur Bronze- und Eisenzeit in Nordwestdeutschland, *Archäologische Mitteilungen aus Nordwestdeutschland* 11, 3-24.

Willems, W.J.H., 1983: Archeologische kroniek van Limburg over de jaren 1980-1982, *PSHAL* 119, 197-291.

Workshop of European Anthropologists 1980, *Journal of Human Evolution* 9, 517-549.

Urnfield and settlement traces from the Iron Age at Mierlo-Hout

Adrie Tol

I   INTRODUCTION

The village of Mierlo-Hout (fig. 1) is situated in the eastern part of a cover-sand plateau which is bordered by the stream valleys of the Schotense Loop and the Goorloop (fig. 2).[1] Up to the middle of the 20th century, large sections of the plateau were exploited as arable lands or *essen* (fig. 3). In re-

---

[1] Figs. 2 and 3 are based on the soil map of the Netherlands, map 51 Eindhoven Oost (STIBOKA 1981); the geomorphological map of the Netherlands, map 51 Eindhoven Oost (STIBOKA 1981); the *Chromotopografische Kaart des Rijks*, sheet 671, surveyed in 1898 and published in 1912 and again published as: *Historische atlas van Noord-Brabant*, Den Ilp, 1989; and a hand-drawn map of Mierlo and 't Hout from 1800 (by courtesy of L. Leijsen, Heemkundekring Myrle).

Fig. 1. The location of Mierlo-Hout (mun. of Helmond).

cent years the arable area has gradually been redeveloped as a residential area and an industrial site. The *es* complex of *Snippenscheut*, southwest of the village church of Mierlo-Hout, was also turned into a residential area (fig. 4). While the site was being prepared for building in April 1992, members of the archaeological society *Vereniging Helmont* discovered some circular ditches indicating the presence of a prehistoric cemetery. Due to the rapid intervention of Helmond's town archaeologist N. Arts and thanks to subsidies from the Helmond council, a rescue excavation was started in time. It was carried out in 1992 and 1993 by the Institute for Pre- and Protohistoric Archaeology (IPP) of the University of Amsterdam, under the scientific direction of N. Roymans. The author was in charge of the day-to-day field management, assisted by R. Van Genabeek.[2] The fieldwork lasted for a total of 6 months, during which an area of c. 3 ha. was excavated. The higher sections of the site were excavated entirely, whereas the adjoining lower areas were investigated by means of several trial trenches (fig. 4).

First of all a cemetery was dug up which had been in use in two different periods, namely the Early and the beginning of the Middle Iron Age (c. 750 - 450 BC) and again in the Late Iron Age and Roman period (c. 150 BC - 225 AD; fig. 5). Inside this cemetery, traces were also found of a tumulus, probably dating to the Middle Bronze Age. In addition, five locations with settlement traces from the Iron Age and the Roman period were discovered immediately outside the cemetery. Three other locations with settlement traces from the Iron Age, at 400, 600 and over 1000 m from the cemetery respectively, had previously been excavated. So far, only a preliminary survey of the excavation results has been published.[3] This article aims to give a definitive analysis of the cemetery from the Early

[2]   We are grateful to Nico Arts (mun. of Helmond) for his support in organizing the excavations. Thanks are due to Piet Derks, Fokko Kortlang, archaeology students of various institutes and members of the *Vereniging Helmond* for their help in the field. We would particularly like to mention amateur archaeologists Henk Goossens and René Willems, without whom the excavations would never have reached a successful end.

[3]   Roymans/Tol 1993. See also Tol 1993.

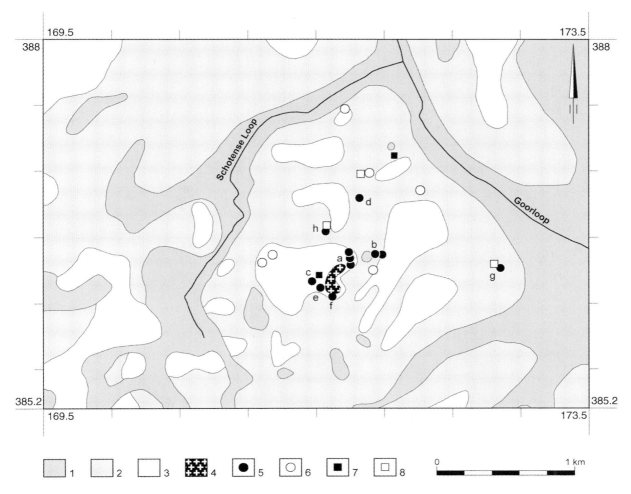

Fig. 2. Mierlo-Hout. Geomorphological reconstruction of the landscape with the location of the urnfield and findspots from the Iron Age and the Roman period.

1 stream valleys and marshes; 2 cover-sand plateau; 3 idem, higher parts; 4 urnfield; 5 site with traces of an Iron Age farmyard; 6 site with a concentration of Iron Age pottery (probable farmyard); 7 site with settlement traces from the Roman period; 8 site with surface finds from the Roman period (probable settlement); a to h sites mentioned in the text

and beginning of the Middle Iron Age, and of the related settlement traces.[4] The cemetery and the settlement traces from the Late Iron Age and Roman period will be discussed later in another article.

The Mierlo-Hout urnfield is incomplete and heavily eroded, making it of limited use for social analysis. The Mierlo-Hout excavations however, are relevant to Lower Rhine urnfield research in three respects. First we have an urnfield which, though incomplete, is reconstructible as far as size and period of use are concerned, making it suitable for a demographic reconstruction. Second, the cemetery provides important evidence for the study of the 'cultural biography' of urnfields. It contains a

[4]   I wish to thank Nico Roymans for his critical comments on the earlier drafts of the manuscript.

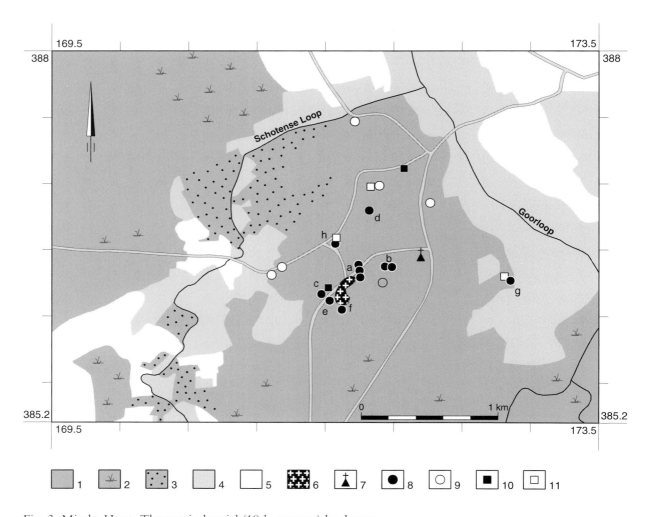

Fig. 3. Mierlo-Hout. The pre-industrial (19th-century) landscape.
1 heathland; 2 peat moor; 3 forest; 4 hayfields; 5 arable land with *plaggen* soils; 6 urnfield; 7 village centre with church; 8 site with traces of an Iron Age farmyard; 9 site with a concentration of Iron Age pottery (probable farmyard); 10 site with settlement traces from the Roman period; 11 site with surface finds from the Roman period (probable settlement); a to h sites mentioned in the text

Middle Bronze Age barrow and it is a good example of the re-use of an urnfield in the Late Iron Age and Roman period, after a discontinuity of c. 300 years. Finally, there is the possibility to analyse the relation between the cemetery and the corresponding settlement within the limits of a reconstructible *Siedlungskammer*. It are these three topics which will be central in the description and analysis of the urnfield, given below.

The *Snippenscheut* site holds a central position on the cover-sand plateau, on the southeast edge of a local sandy ridge bordering a zone of damp soils (fig. 2 and 5). Having been abandoned in the course of the Roman period, the site was probably again reclaimed in the High Middle Ages.[5] During reclamation the soil was deeply dug, and the burial mounds which had been visible until then were levelled. At the same time the highest part of the sandy elevation in the south was cut off down to the clean sandy subsoil. The sand may have been conveyed to depressions elsewhere on the site. During or shortly after the reclamation, a ditch was dug along the southeast flank of the sandy ridge. This could be traced for a distance of 25 m and served to demarcate the arable complex and as drainage. In the Late Middle Ages or later, the ditch was replaced by another slightly more northerly one, which was excavated over a distance of 75 m.[6]

Because the arable complex consists of relatively poor soil, the fertility of the area was sustained by means of heath sods mixed with manure. This method of fertilization was continued until into the last century, resulting in a 50 to 60 cm thick *plaggen* soil. Other agrarian activities also left their mark. In the 18th or 19th century, two broad zones were laid out with elongated pits for the purpose of horticulture ('*beddencultuur*'). Other activities in the (pre-)modern period are evidenced by the sand extraction pits which are found all over the area. The disturbances due to asparagus cultivation in the southwest section of the site are of recent date. All these medieval and post-medieval interventions have resulted in the relatively serious erosion of pre-medieval traces underneath the *plaggen* soil. The arable land at the *Snippenscheut* site shows that preservation conditions under *essen* are not always ideal.[7]

3   DESCRIPTION OF THE CEMETERY

At the beginning of the Early Iron Age a cemetery was laid out on a sandy ridge, and remained in use for about three centuries (fig. 6). Its outer limits were established in almost every direction. In the south and east, the cemetery borders low, wet ground; in the west and northeast settlement traces from the Iron Age were found at several locations immediately outside the urnfield.[8] Only the northwest boundary was difficult to determine, though several postholes indicating settlement traces near grave 26 suggest that the cemetery did not continue much further here.[9] We may state that the size of the urnfield is reconstructible. It extends for a length of 285 m by a maximum width of 110 m, and is oriented more or less southwest-northeast. Of the c. 1.75 ha. large cemetery, 40% has been lost due to post-medieval human activities. Particularly the central part and the southeast and southwest bor-

[5]   The oldest medieval finds from the arable topsoil and from a ditch (see below) on the *Snippenscheut* are sherds of Paffrath and Brunssum-Schinveld pottery and Proto-stoneware, dating from the end of the 12th and beginning of the 13th century.

[6]   The ditch fill produced material from the first half of the 17th century.

[7]   Cf. the introductory remarks in Roymans/Kortlang, this volume.

[8]   The bounds of the depression southwest of the cemetery were established by means of borings. The other wet soils lie within the limits of the excavation and were recognizable by the brown B-horizon of a humus podzol.

[9]   The numbering of the graves refers to the numbering in the catalogue (appendix) and the general plan (annex 1).

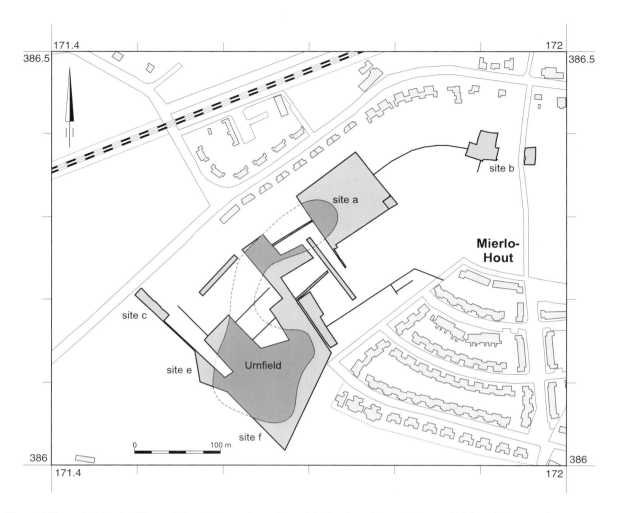

Fig. 4 (Above). Mierlo-Hout. The *Snippenscheut* site with the location of the urnfield and sites with Iron Age settlement traces (a–c, e–f).

Fig. 5 (Right). Mierlo-Hout. General plan of the urnfield and the cemetery from the Late Iron Age and Roman period. Scale 1:2000.

der zones have been badly eroded (fig. 6). That there were originally graves in these zones is evident from the small lumps of cremation remains found scattered here. In the relatively intact part of the cemetery (60%), 165 graves and burial monuments were excavated, which fit in the tradition of the Lower Rhine urnfields.

3.1   MODE OF INTERMENT

From the 165 grave structures 49 cremation graves were recovered (table 1). The cremation remains from graves 36 and 87 were interred in an urn (fig. 7). In 30 graves, the burnt bones were buried in a more or less compact lump in a pit (Dutch: *beenderblok*), possibly originally in a covering of organic material. Among the cremation remains there is generally little charcoal. This means that the burnt

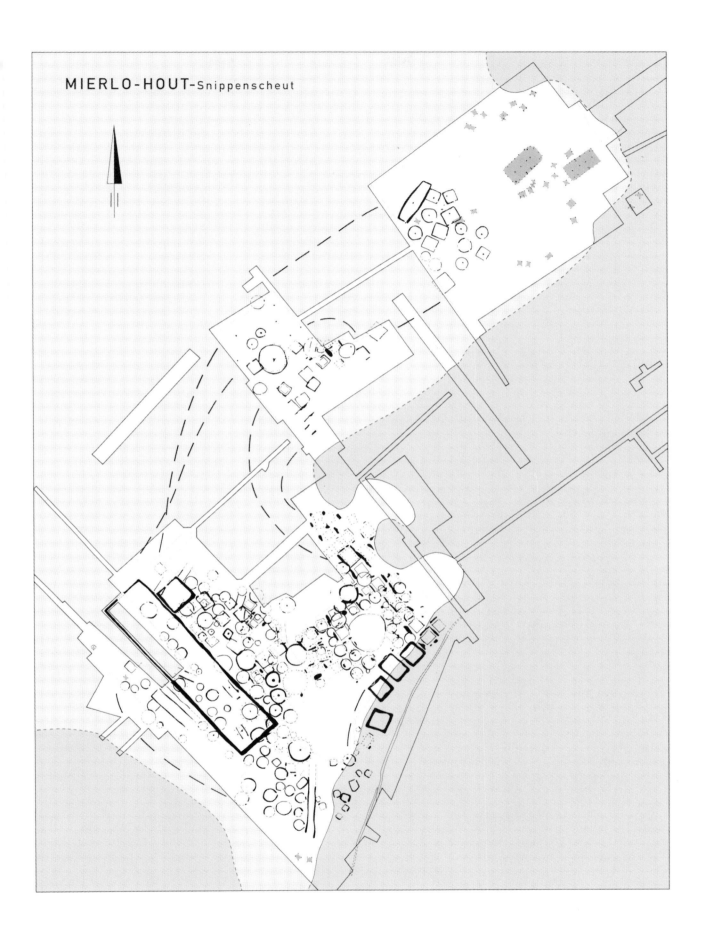

MIERLO-HOUT-Snippenscheut

MIERLO-HOUT-Snippenscheut

Fig. 7. Urn with cremation remains from grave 36. Photograph T. Welten.

bones were carefully picked out of the pyre remains. The only exception is grave 53, where the burial pit was filled with charcoal and scattered pyre remains.[10] In sixteen cases the quantity of pyre remains was too small to provide information about the mode of interment.

In most cases the cremation remains were interred in a shallow, round or oval pit with a diameter of approximately 0.35 m. Two burial pits (6 and 76) were more rectangular in form and considerably larger, 1 × 0.6 m and c. 1.8 × 0.6 m respectively.

3.2   GRAVE MONUMENTS

The 165 grave structures found were recognizable by the peripheral ditches which surrounded the original barrows and by the interment of cremations. Many of the ditches stood out from later soil formation on the site as strips of light-grey or brown sand. The original ditch fill was often completely eroded and its course could only be seen as a strip of iron concretions and fibres developed in the subsoil below the original ditch.

Fig. 6. Mierlo-Hout. General plan of the graves and grave monuments belonging to the urnfield. Scale 1:2000.
1 ditch structure with cremation grave; 2 ditch structure, partly reconstructed; 3 Iron Age building; 4 reconstructed boundary of the cemetery; 5 boundary of recent disturbance; 6 unexcavated area; 7 depression (wet soil)

---

[10]   Dutch: *brandafvalgraf*. Cf. Verlinde 1987, 211.

	number	with cremation burial
circular ditches	127 (77%)	26
post-circle	1 (1%)	–
long-beds	13 (8%)	4
rectangular ditches	9 (5%)	4
cremations in peripheral ditches	2 (1%)	2
flat(?) graves	13 (8%)	13
total	**165 (100%)**	**49**

Table 1. Mierlo-Hout. Overview of the types of grave structures and graves from the urnfield.

Fig. 8. (Right) Selection of grave monuments from the urnfield of Mierlo-Hout. The numbering corresponds with the numbering of the graves. Scale 1:200.

The following types of grave monuments were established (table 1):

a. 127 circular ditches. This form is by far the best represented. Most have an outer diameter varying from 2.5 to 8.5 m (outer measurements). The smallest monument is only 1.75 m, while the largest ditches have a diameter of 10 and 17 m respectively. A total of 71 circular ditches originally had an interruption (fig. 8, no. 141). The orientation of these interruptions varies from 80 to 190 degrees from the north (fig. 9). The majority (80%) is between 95 and 145 degrees, i.e. between east and south-southeast. Four ditches (67, 75, 84 and 164) are closed, five others (36, 37, 91, 128 and 133) are probably also closed (fig. 8, no. 75). For 47 circular ditches the possible presence of an interruption could no longer be established, due to subrecent disturbances. Remains of an interment were only found inside 26 circular ditches, and these interments were more or less centrally situated. Graves 33 and 47 were clearly dug excentrically. These were possibly secondary burials at the edge of the barrow. Five monuments with circular ditches are conspicuous for their unusual construction. In one case (grave 58) traces were found in the peripheral ditch of a row of small closely-set posts (fig. 8, no. 58); in four other cases (45, 77, 123 and 165) the ditches on the outer side had been surrounded by a circle of widely-spaced posts (fig. 8, no. 77).

b. 1 post-circle. The peripheral structure of barrow 132 consisted of a circle of widely-spaced posts with a diameter of 11 m (fig. 8, no. 132).

c. 13 elongated ditched structures or 'long-beds', which originally also enclosed mounds in the form of earth banks. They are scattered over the urnfield. Their orientation shows considerable variation (fig. 9), apparently connected with the relief of the sandy ridge and the direction in which the cemetery expanded. In ten cases these are long-beds of the 'Someren type', consisting of two parallel ditches with open ends (fig. 8, no. 50).[11] Their width fluctuates between 3 and 5 m; their length between 4.5 and c. 30 m. One long-bed has two four-post structures at its north end (fig. 8, no. 88), which may have been the remains of funerary structures. In three

---

11   Cf. Kortlang, this volume.

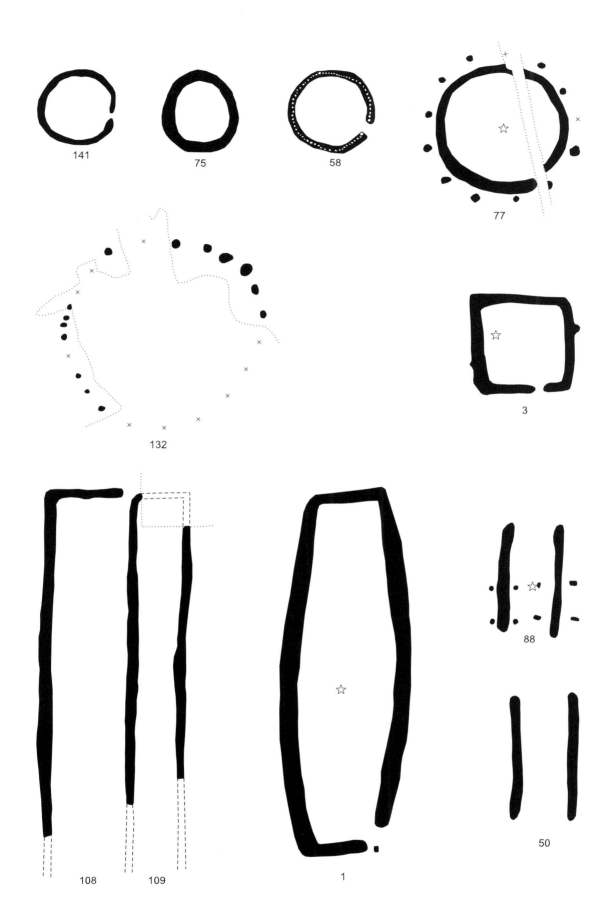

141

75

58

77

132

3

108   109

1

88

50

97

monuments of the Someren type, a cremation grave was found in the middle of the longitudinal axis or slightly excentric. In the southwest section of the urnfield there are two connected long-beds, c. 22 m in length, with rectangular ends in the north (fig. 8, no. 108/109). An a-typical 'boat-shaped' long-bed is situated at the northeast edge of the cemetery (fig. 8, no. 1). This ditched structure, 19 m in length and 7 m in width, has an interruption in the southeast corner. A post-hole at this spot suggests that the opening was closed off with an isolated post. In the middle of the ditched structure was a cremation grave. On the basis of its elongated form this monument has been included among the long-beds. However, the curved long sides and the opening in the southeast corner are unknown from other long-beds in the Lower Rhine region. There is a link with the rectangular ditched structures discussed below.

d. 9 rectangular or square ditches, with sides varying from 3.75 to 6.75 m (fig. 8, no. 3). They often have an opening in the southeast corner or side. A cluster of eight monuments is found at the northeast end of the cemetery (fig. 13). In the southwest border zone there is one rectangular ditched structure.

e. 2 graves in peripheral ditches. Graves 17 and 64 are secondary interments in the ditch of a rectangular and a circular grave monument respectively.

f. 13 flat graves or possible flat graves, i.e. without peripheral ditches.[12] In three cases (nos. 6, 7 and 166) these were certainly flat graves. Due to the erosion of the cemetery this cannot be stated with any certainty in the case of the remaining graves. They may originally have had a peripheral ditch which was destroyed later.[13] There is also the possibility that there was no peripheral structure around the barrow. This may apply to the six 'isolated' graves in the northern border zone of the urnfield. They have a wide and regular distribution, at 6 to 10 m intervals.

In and at the edge of the cemetery there are several clusters of postholes which cannot be interpreted.[14] In the northeast, west and southwest border zones there are several four-post structures. In view of the proximity of settlement traces in the north and west, these are probably the outbuildings of neighbouring farmhouses. These buildings probably date from the Iron Age.

3.3 POTTERY AND OTHER GRAVE GOODS

The graves contain very few finds. Apart from two urns, they did not yield much more than some cremated animal bones, two complete cups, some sherds of burnt pottery and some secondarily burnt iron and bronze fragments (table 2). The two unburnt cups may be regarded as containers for grave gifts. The burnt finds are probably remains of pots (containing food or drink?), pieces of meat and metal objects (personal adornments attached to the clothing of the deceased?) from the funeral pyre.

---

[12] The dating of 11 of these graves poses a problem. They did not yield any finds and were not cut by younger graves from the Roman period. These findless graves are included in the urnfield because most of the native-Roman graves did contain grave goods, and many of them lie outside the zone of the native-Roman cemetery.

[13] For example in the case of graves 76, 82, 126 and 127.

[14] In the southern section of the urnfield there are two (findless) concentrations of 40 and 6 post-holes respectively (c. 30 cm in diameter, and c. 35 cm deep), in which no recognisable structure could be seen, but some of which are cut by grave monuments from the urnfield (annex 1). In view of the imprecise dating and problematic interpretation of these features they are not discussed here.

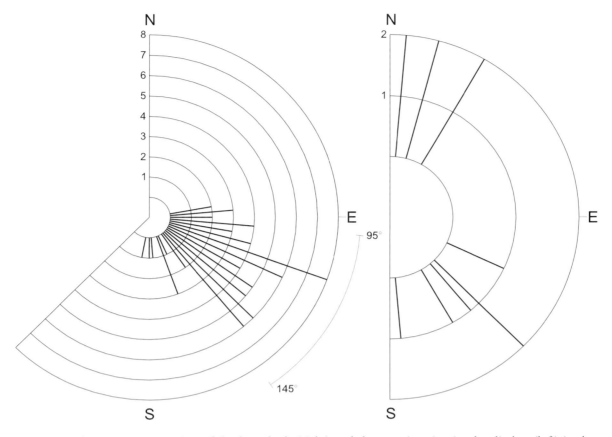

Fig. 9. Mierlo-Hout. Orientation of the long-beds (right) and the openings in circular ditches (left) in degrees from the north. The orientations are expressed to the nearest 5 degrees.

Together with the collecting of the cremated human bones, they were picked out of the remains of the pyre and buried. The extreme dearth of grave goods is a general characteristic of Lower Rhine urnfields.

The ditch fill (if present) of all grave structures was scraped out and examined for finds. This produced c. 80 'stray' sherds – most of them secondarily burnt –, of at least 23 pots and one iron fragment, and unburnt sherds from eight (partly) complete pots. The burnt finds were possibly also the remains of objects from the funeral pyre. They were not collected and ended up by chance in the ditches. The unburnt, sometimes complete pots on the other hand would have been intentionally deposited in the peripheral ditches (table 2). Bowl 24a, for instance, had first been broken and then the sherds were scattered in the circular ditch around grave 24.[15] In all cases, only one or two pots were involved. Larger depositions of pottery, as known from the ditches of several long-beds at Weert-Boshoverheide, were not found.[16]

[15]   Per grave every individual object is identified by a small letter.

[16]   Cf. Roymans/Kortlang, this volume, fig. 6.

grave	monument	from grave	from ditch
1	long-bed	sherds (secondarily burnt), fragments of two iron objects, burnt bones (rib) of pig or sheep	–
5	circular ditch	–	cup
6	flat grave	cup	–
8	circular ditch	sherds (secondarily burnt)	–
24	circular ditch	–	bowl
28	flat? grave	burnt bones (left foreleg) of pig	–
33	circular ditch	sherds (secondarily burnt)	–
48	circular ditch	cup	–
53	long-bed	sherds of cup (secondarily burnt)	–
60	circular ditch	–	dish
79	circular ditch	sherd (secondarily burnt)	–
87	circular ditch	molten bronze fragments	–
108	long-bed	–	dish + pot
119	circular ditch	–	bowl + pot
130	circular ditch	–	pot

Table 2. Mierlo-Hout. Overview of grave goods (urns excluded) and depositions of pottery in peripheral ditches.

In total, fragments of at least 40 pots were discovered in the graves and ditches of the urnfield. Thirteen pots were complete or almost complete, i.e. two urns, one burnt and two unburnt cups from graves, and eight pots from ditches. Only the (partly) complete pots are discusses below, as are two isolated sherds from ditches which are useful for dating purposes (fig. 10):[17]

– 1 polished *Schräghals* pot (36a).
– 1 smooth-walled, biconical pot with slightly outstanding neck (130b).
– 3 Harpstedt-like pots, with a roughened belly, a smoothened shoulder and neck, and finger-tip impressions on the rim (87a, 119b and 108b).[18]
– 1 barrel-shaped cup, with a roughened belly and a smoothened neck (6a).
– 2 smooth-walled cups, one with an outstanding neck (48a) and one with a vertical neck and comb decoration on the belly (53a).
– 1 conical cup, with a polished surface and a groove-line under the rim (5a).
– 1 biconical bowl, with a roughened belly and polished neck (24a).
– 1 smooth-walled bowl with vertical comb decoration (119a).
– 1 sharply-carinated dish with outstanding neck and on the belly a decoration of horizontally grooved lines (60a).
– 1 smooth-walled dish with an inverted rim (Dutch: 'haakrand'); the belly is decorated with vertical grooved lines (108a).[19]
– 1 rimsherd from a barrel-shaped pot with a smoothened neck and an inward-facing rim (1e).
– 1 rimsherd from a barrel-shaped pot with a smoothened neck and finger-tip impressions on the rim and belly (42a).

[17] We are grateful to Peter van den Broeke (IPL) for his help in identifying the pottery.
[18] Pot 108b was very fragmented and could not be re-constructed. Only a rimsherd is depicted.
[19] Van den Broeke 1984, note 10.

The urnfield produced four metal objects:
- 3 small unidentifiable iron and bronze fragments, two are grave goods (1b, 87b) and one is an isolated find from a ditch (fig. 10, 4a)
- 1 fragment of the end of an iron bar with rounded rectangular profile (length 1.6 cm) and a perforation, probably for the attachment of a metal (?) ring (fig. 10, 1c).

3.4 DATING OF THE URNFIELD

In order to date the urnfield more precisely, various types of information can be used. A first indication is the variation in grave monuments, which, to some extent, has chronological significance in the Lower Rhine area. Significant is the difference between closed circular ditches and those with an interruption. The latter variant is characteristic of the Early and Middle Iron Age, while closed circular ditches mainly occur in the Late Bronze Age and, less frequently, in the Early Iron Age.[20] In the Mierlo-Hout cemetery 90% of the circular ditches has an ancient interruption, indicating a dating in the second half of the Urnfield period. The round grave monuments surrounded by a post-circle also provide dating information. In the Lower Rhine area, they are only found in the Early Iron Age, particularly the 8th and 7th centuries BC.[21] Finally, the rectangular ditched structures in the Lower Rhine area are dated to the beginning of the Middle Iron Age (c. 525-400 BC), thus belonging to the youngest phase of the cemetery.[22]

A second lead is provided by the typochronology of the pottery. The range of forms points to a post-Bronze Age date, since characteristic forms from this period are lacking. The Harpstedt-like pots,[23] the *Schräghals* pot,[24] the carinated dish and the dish with a '*haakrand*'[25] certainly belong to the Early Iron Age. The conical cup fits the tradition of Marne ceramics and dates from the beginning of the Middle Iron Age.[26] The barrel-shaped pottery probably dates from the Middle or Late Iron Age.[27] The remaining pottery cannot be dated more precisely than Iron Age.

A third indication for dating is provided by the variation in mode of interment. At Mierlo-Hout, the large majority of interments has no ceramic container; only two urn graves were found. Verwers states that in the Late Bronze Age and Middle Iron Age urnless burials predominate in the Lower Rhine urnfields, whereas in the Early Iron Age burials in urns are dominant.[28] However, it seems increasingly apparent that – at any rate in the eastern part of the Meuse-Demer-Scheldt region – urn graves are mainly dominant around the transition Late Bronze Age/Early Iron Age, and that already in the Early Iron Age there is a shift towards urnless burials. It is, for example, striking that the urnfields of Beegden (775-650 BC) and the excavated section of Someren-'Philips Kampeerterrein'

[20] Verwers 1972, 36; Verlinde 1987, 199.

[21] Cf. the urnfields of Kaulille (Engels/Van Impe 1985), Nederweert (Appelboom 1952), Neerpelt (Van Impe *et al.* 1973), Ravels (Annaert 1984), Someren-'Philips Kampeerterrein' (Modderman 1955 and 1963) and Someren-Waterdael (Kortlang, this volume), which all date from the Early Iron Age. See also Van der Sanden 1994, 204, and table 15.

[22] Hulst 1966, 81-82; Verwers 1972, 36-37; Verlinde 1987, 204-206; Roymans 1991, 65; Kortlang, this volume.

[23] Verlinde 1987, 347-349; Roymans, this volume.

[24] Verlinde 1987, 342; Roymans, this volume.

[25] Van den Broeke 1984, 86.

[26] A similar specimen from Oss-Ussen dates from the 5th century BC. Personal communication P. van den Broeke.

[27] Barrel-shaped pots are mainly found in Oss-Ussen after the transition Early/Middle Iron Age (Van den Broeke 1987, fig. 5c).

[28] Verwers 1972, 44.

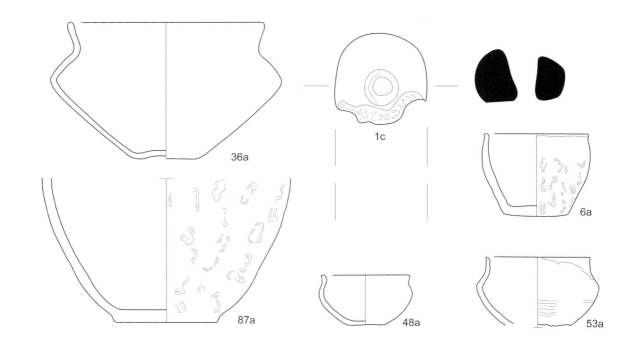

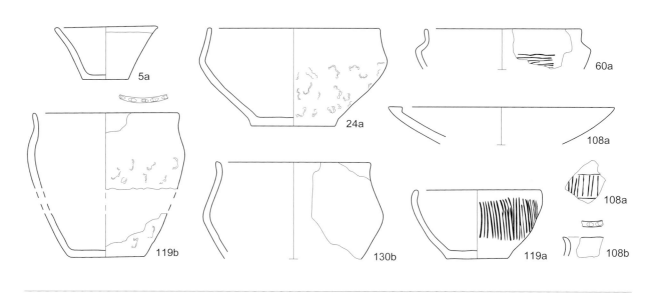

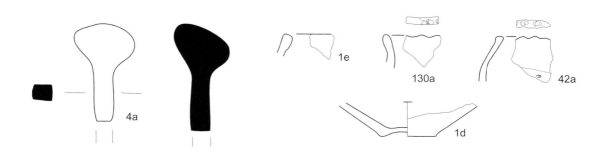

Fig. 10. Pottery and metal objects (1c and 4a) from the urnfield of Mierlo-Hout. Top: urns and grave-goods; centre: (in part) complete pots from ditches; below: isolated sherds and metal objects from ditches. The numbering corresponds with the numbering of the graves. Pottery scale 1:4, metal objects scale 1:1.

	grave context	C14 date	years BC (2 sigma)
1	burial within long-bed	2570 ± 80 BP (GrN-19885)	834 - 468/462 - 412
17	burial in fill of square ditch	2500 ± 30 BP (GrN-19886)	784 - 516/434 - 424
112	fill of circular ditch	2510 ± 35 BP (GrN-20594)	793 - 489/440 - 425
140	burial within circular ditch	2495 ± 35 BP (GrN-20595)	789 - 414
150	fill of circular ditch	2520 ± 40 BP (Grn-20596)	797 - 440

Table 3. Overview of the C14 dates from the urnfield of Mierlo-Hout. The dates have been converted into calendar years with a probability of 95.4% (2 sigma).

(8th/7th century BC) have almost exclusively urn graves, while that of Someren-Waterdael (650-400 BC) produced hardly any urn graves.[29]

A final clue is provided by five C14 dates of charcoal from three cremation graves and from the fill of two circular ditches (table 3). Converted into calendar years, they correspond with a probability of 95.4% (2 sigma) to the period 834-412 cal BC.[30] The dates of graves 1 and 17 are particularly important, since they confirm that the youngest cluster of graves with rectangular ditches in the northeast still belongs to the Urnfield period (see below).

The typochronology of the burial monuments, the (scarce) find material, the mode of interment and the C14 dates indicate that the date of the urnfield of Mierlo-Hout corresponds to the Early and beginning of the Middle Iron Age. The predominance of open circular ditches and the absence of characteristic Late Bronze Age forms among the pottery argue against an origin in the Late Bronze Age. The occurrence of grave monuments with post-circles and closed circular ditches points to an origin at the beginning of the Early Iron Age. The virtual absence of urn burials, though, would support an origin at an advanced stage of the Early Iron Age. However, burials in urns are underrepresented. In the most seriously disturbed southeast section of the cemetery, which is probably the oldest part (see below), there would originally have been more urn burials.[31]

It is likely that the cemetery was in use at the beginning of the Early Iron Age, i.e. the 8th century BC. From the presence of square grave monuments and pottery from the Middle Iron Age it may be concluded that the cemetery was certainly used until into the 5th century. The C14 dates also allow a continuation in the use of the cemetery until into the 5th century. In particular the dating of the charcoal from grave 17 is important in this respect, because it concerns a secondary interment in a square ditch, thus representing one of the youngest graves. All these indications point to the abandonment of the cemetery in the 5th century BC. The earliest graves from the Late Iron Age/native-

[29] Beegden: Roymans, this volume; Someren-'Philips Kampeerterrein': Modderman 1955, idem 1963; Someren-Waterdael: Kortlang, this volume.

[30] The C14 dates were calibrated with the help of the CALIB calibration programme of the Centre for Isotope Research of the Rijksuniversiteit Groningen.

[31] In the oldest zone of the urnfield (the southeast part), the central interment of only 17% of the grave monuments has been preserved, compared with 38% in the remaining area.

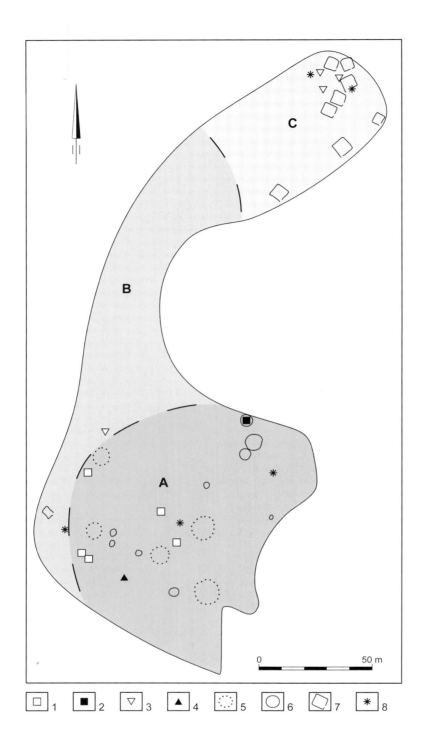

Fig. 11. Dating elements and chronological zoning of the urnfield.
1 Early Iron Age pottery; 2 urn grave from the Early Iron Age; 3 Middle Iron Age pottery; 4 urn grave, no pre-cise dating; 5 post-circle; 6 closed circular ditch; 7 rectangular ditch; 8 location C14 date; A zone with predom-inantly 8th/7th-century graves; B zone with predominantly 6th-century graves; C zone with predominantly late 6th/5th-century graves

Roman cemetery date from the 2nd century BC.[32] These are situated in the southern and oldest zone of the urnfield, about 200 m from the youngest urnfield graves in the northeast. There would appear to be a discontinuity of some 300 years in the use of the cemetery (see below). It may be concluded that the Mierlo-Hout urnfield was used for roughly three centuries, from c. 750 to 450 BC.

3.5 STRUCTURE AND DEVELOPMENT OF THE URNFIELD

If we translate the above dating elements into a spatial picture, there appears to be a horizontal stratigraphy in the cemetery (fig. 11). Three chronological zones can be distinguished. In the southeast section of zone A there are the oldest grave monuments (with post-circles and 'closed' circular ditches) and the urn graves, but no elements from the Middle Iron Age. This zone represents the oldest phase of the cemetery, dating from c. 750 to 600 BC. Zone C in the northeast corner of the cemetery contains most of the youngest features: the rectangular and square ditched monuments and the pottery from the Middle Iron Age are clustered here. This zone dates from the late 6th/5th century. The intermediate zone B is largely disturbed, but it is likely that most of the graves from the 6th century were situated here.

Within zone A a subdivision is possible. It is striking that most of the largest monuments are situated in the east part: a long-bed c. 30 m in length and burial mounds 10, 11 and 17 m in diameter, two of which with a post-circle. If we take into account the fact that there were originally graves in the disturbed sections as well, a picture emerges for this part of the cemetery of closely-packed, small circular ditches grouped around several larger barrows.

The development of the urnfield can now be more or less reconstructed (fig. 11). In the initial phase (c. 750 BC), several large burial monuments were erected in zone A. Subsequently, the intermediate empty spaces were filled up with smaller circular ditches. After this concentration around the oldest monuments, the cemetery expanded in a northeasterly direction in the 6th century BC. In the late 6th/5th century, the graves were mainly dug in zone C, but still also in zone B. It is certain that in the 5th century no burials took place in the oldest zone. Finally, in c. 450 BC, the cemetery fell into disuse. The urnfield of Someren-Waterdael shows an almost parallel development, starting in the Early Iron Age and continuing until into the beginning of the Middle Iron Age.[33]

3.6 PHYSICAL-ANTHOPOLOGICAL STUDY OF THE CREMATION REMAINS

The cremation remains of 40 of the 49 interments recovered, were examined for age and sexual characteristics.[34] At the same time the degree of burning and extent of fragmentation was investigated.

The cremations vary in weight from 1 to 1036 gr., with an average of 120 gr. (table 4). This low weight can be explained by the fact that the upper part of most graves was destroyed by ploughing in

[32] To the earliest phase of the cemetery belongs a large rectangular ditched enclosure 85 x 21 m in size, which may possibly be interpreted as a 'Viereckschanze' (fig. 5). Among the scanty find material of the earliest graves are fragments of several glass La Tène bracelets and an iron *fibula* from the Middle La Tène period.

[33] Kortlang, this volume.

[34] The remains of 9 burials were too insufficient for physical-anthropological research. We are grateful to Liesbeth Smits (IPP, Amsterdam) for the physical-anthropological analyses of the cremation remains. For the research method used, see Menno Hoogland's

grave	weight (gr.)	%> 10 mm	fragmentation	age	sex morphol.
1	955	37%	2-5	43-52	F? (3)
2	21	52%	2-4	>18?	–
3	1	–	–	–	–
5	4	–	–	–	–
7	20	45%	3-3	–	–
10	97	74%	1-4	–	–
13	43	42%	2-3	>18?	–
17	155	52%	2-5	–	–
18	35	–	2-4	>18?	–
22	23	57%	1-1	–	–
24	8	–	–	>18?	–
25	2	–	–	–	–
26	5	–	–	–	–
27	270	63%	1-6	–	–
28	347	42%	4-4	40-60	M (2)
29	6	–	–	–	–
33	19	74%	2-4	>18?	–
36	852	65%	5-8	24-29	M (5)
38	6	–	–	>12	–
47	1	–	–	–	–
48	855	49%	1-6	30-50	M (3)
53	10	–	–	–	–
54	9	–	–	–	–
64	3	–	–	–	–
70	13	–	–	>12	–
73	2	–	–	–	–
76	77	42%	1-5	>18	–
77	27	74%	2-3	–	–
79	28	64%	2-3	–	M (1)
87	689	42%	2-5	20-40	F? (3)
88	47	35%	1-4	>18	–
120	1036	52%	3-6	>35	M (3)
123	24	58%	1-3	–	–
125	6	–	–	–	–
126	18	–	–	–	–
127	20	50%	1-2	–	–
139	52	52%	1-4	>18	–
140	322	94%	1-4	>18	–
149	29	53%	1-3	–	–
160	4	–	–	–	–

Table 4. Mierlo-Hout. Summary of the physical-anthropological data per cremation burial.

grave	monument	mode of interment	weight crem.	age	sex
1	long-bed	heap of bone	955	43-52	F?
2	rectangular ditch	heap of bone	21	>18?	–
13	circular ditch	heap of bone	43	>18?	–
18	circular ditch	heap of bone	35	>18?	–
24	circular ditch	heap of bone	8	>18?	–
28	flat grave?	heap of bone	347	40-60	M
33	circular ditch	heap of bone	19	>18?	–
36	circular ditch	urn	852	24–29	M
38	circular ditch	heap of bone	6	>12	–
48	circular ditch	heap of bone	855	30-50	M
70	circular ditch	heap of bone	13	>12	–
76	flat grave?	heap of bone	77	>18	–
79	circular ditch	heap of bone	28	>18	F?
87	circular ditch	urn	689	20-40	F
88	long-bed	heap of bone	47	>18	–
120	circular ditch	heap of bone	1036	>35	M
139	circular ditch	heap of bone	52	>18	–
140	circular ditch	heap of bone	322	>18	–

Table 5. Mierlo-Hout. Overview of the cremation remains identified according to age and sex.

the Middle Ages. Only four interments (1, 36, 48 and 120) were reasonably intact. Their average weight is around 900 gr. This is still considerably less than the 2 to 3 kg of bone remains which are generally left after cremating an adult corpse. Presumably it was not considered necessary for the cremation remains to be completely collected and buried. In the case of grave 36, a selection may have been made: fragments of both legs are lacking in the urn.

The degree of fragmentation (expressed in the percentage of fragments larger than 10 mm) was on average 55%, with 35 and 94% as extreme values.[35] These percentages correspond well with what is known from other Lower Rhine urnfields.[36] The great variation is the result of differences in the care taken when collecting the cremated bones from the remains of pyres on the one hand, and the condition of preservation of the graves on the other.

The degree of burning of the cremations is generally in phases IV and V. This means that the bone remains were exposed to a temperature of between 650 and 800°C.

The 40 graves excavated contain the remains of the same number of individuals; no multiple interments were found. The age of 18 individuals was established (table 5). These were exclusively adults, with the possible exception of graves 38 and 70 (juveniles?). It was only possible to determine the sex of seven adults with any certainty: three women and four men.

contribution in Roymans, this volume.

[35] The (minimal) cremation remains collected by hand in the case of some burials are not included.

[36] Cf. Beegden (Roymans, this volume) and Wijk bij Duurstede (Hessing 1989, 323).

	number	
children (0-14)	–	(0%)
juveniles (14-18)	2?	(11%)
adult males	4	(22%)
adult females	3	(17%)
adult unidentified	9	(50%)
total	**18**	**(100%)**

Table 6. Mierlo-Hout. Composition of the determined graves according to age and sex.

3.7   THE DEMOGRAPHY OF THE LOCAL COMMUNITY

On the basis of the archaeological and physical-anthropological data it is possible to reconstruct the composition and size of the living community. A basic assumption is that the greater majority of the local population was buried in this urnfield. For an analysis of the composition of the population there are only 18 interments identified according to age and/or sex at our disposal (table 6). Apparently both men and women were buried in the cemetery, but not children. No value need be attached to the latter conclusion. Though children (particularly newborns) are underrepresented in Lower Rhine urnfield populations, they are present.[37] In Mierlo-Hout the children were possibly buried in small burial mounds or in shallow flat graves which were lost during the rigorous (post-)medieval digging activities.[38]

In order to estimate the size of the living community linked with the urnfield of Mierlo-Hout, Acsádi and Nemeskéri's formula can be applied.[39] It is of crucial importance that the limits of the cemetery are known, so that the original number of graves can be reconstructed. The formula is: $P = k \times (D \times e)/t$. P stands for the average size of the living community. k is a correction factor, necessary if part of the community was not buried in the communal cemetery. From research into other urnfields in the Lower Rhine region it appears that newborns, in particular, are less frequently found than might be expected on demographic grounds. This underrepresentation of newborns is generally in the region of 10%.[40] We assume that this number is also applicable to the Mierlo-Hout urnfield ($k = 1.1$). D stands for the total number of individuals buried. Since large sections of the urnfield are disturbed and only few cremation graves were found, it is only possible to give an estimate of the total number of persons buried. In the section investigated (60%), 150 burial monuments and 15 graves without peripheral structures (flat graves, graves under low mounds, as well as secondary interments in barrows or peripheral ditches) were discovered. The number of graves without peripheral structures will have been higher here originally. If, as in 116 (77%) of the 150 burial monuments, the cen-

---

[37]   Child graves are found for example in the urnfields of St. Oedenrode (Van der Sanden 1981, 325), Berkel-Enschot (Kleij 1993); Neerpelt-De Roosen (Van Impe et al. 1973, 24) and Beegden (Roymans, this volume).

[38]   Of the 31 circular ditches with a diameter less than 4.5 m, not one yielded identifiable cremation remains. In other urnfields, child graves appear to be well represented among the flat graves (cf. Roymans/Kortlang, this volume).

[39]   Acsádi/Nemeskéri 1970.

[40]   Hessing 1989, 327; Roymans, this volume. We expect the infant mortality to be c. 40-50%.

1		2	
e=25	275	290	305
200	38	40	42
300	25	27	28
400	19	20	21

Table 7. Mierlo-Hout. Calculation of the average size of the living population using varying figures for the totalnumber of interments (2) and the number of years the cemetery was used (1). The average life expectancy (*e*) is 25 years.

tral grave had disappeared, a number of flat graves and secondary burials will undoubtedly also have been lost. One must also take into account the occurrence of burials in which more than one individual was interred.[41] An additional loss of 30 graves is therefore reasonable. This would bring the number of persons buried in the area investigated to c. 195. The interments from the completely destroyed section must be added to this number. This section accounts for about 40% of the urnfield. Assuming a slightly lower density (75%) of graves, this means that another 95 graves were situated here. The total size of the urnfield may then be estimated at 290 graves. *e* is the average life expectancy at birth. For prehistoric societies, this is generally estimated to be c. 25 years, an age mainly determined by the high degree of infant mortality. *t* stands for the period of use of the cemetery. It has been stated above that the urnfield was in use from c. 750 to 450 BC.

The estimation of the size of the community belonging to the urnfield of Mierlo-Hout is shown in table 7. Three values were taken for both *t* and *D*. The Mierlo-Hout community appears to have consisted of 19 to 42 persons on average, or 3 to 7 families of an average of 6 persons. An average size of 27 persons or 5 families is the most likely, assuming a period of use of 300 years and a total number of 290 persons interred.

3.8 CULTURAL BIOGRAPHY OF THE NECROPOLIS

This section deals with the 'cultural biography' or long-term history of the Mierlo-Hout urnfield. The point of departure was Roymans' study,[42] in which he shows that urnfields often have a long history as 'sacred' places which play an important part in the cosmology of local communities. The attitude of inhabitants towards urnfields has changed considerably throughout time, and the Mierlo-Hout cemetery provides interesting prospects for analysing such a biography.

The oldest burial monument at the Snippenscheut site consists of traces of a barrow, probably from the Middle Bronze Age, built on one of the highest parts of the sandy ridge (annex 1: A). The mound itself was levelled in the Middle Ages and, more recently, a section of the remaining ground plan was disturbed by small-scale sand extraction. What remains are parts of the peripheral structure consisting of a ditch and traces of a post-circle. The monument has two phases (fig. 12). The oldest phase was a mound surrounded by a circular ditch c. 12.5 m in diameter. Part of the ditch was only visible as a

---

[41] Cf. the cemetery of Beegden (Roymans, this volume).   [42] Roymans 1995; see also Fontijn 1996.

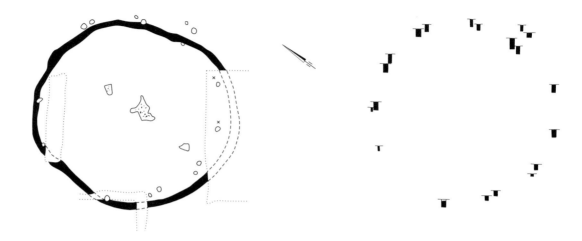

Fig. 12. Plan of the Middle Bronze Age barrow. In the centre several spots with charcoal. Scale 1:200, depths 1:100.

path of iron concretions in the subsoil beneath the original ditch. Later, partly over the ditch, a circle of widely-spaced paired posts (12 m in diameter) was set out around the mound.[43] No interments were found. It is possible that several vague features with tiny lumps of charcoal are the remains of these.

A more precise dating of the burial monument is only possible on typochronological grounds, since there are no finds and the charcoal found was insufficient for a C14 analysis. Circles of paired posts only occur in the Kempen area, where 17 mounds of this type have been excavated. A barrow at Someren-'Philips Kampeerterrein' belongs to the Early Iron Age,[44] but all other specimens are dated to the beginning of the Middle Bronze Age (c. 1700 BC).[45] The Mierlo-Hout specimen there-fore probably dates from the Middle Bronze Age. The tumulus is situated in a zone of the cemetery which exclusively contains graves from the transition from the Early to the Middle Iron Age. In this period, burial monuments with post-circles are no longer constructed. The presence of a Middle Bronze Age tumulus indicates contemporaneous settlement in the immediate surroundings, but no traces of this have been found.

More than 9 centuries after the construction of the above tumulus (c. 750 BC), the site was again brought into use as a cemetery. It is striking that other Lower Rhine cemeteries from the Urnfield period were also laid out near older tumuli. Examples are the urnfields of Goirle, De Hamert, Haps, Meerlo, Nijmegen-Kops Plateau, Knegsel, Oss-Zevenbergen, Toterfout-Halve Mijl and Veldhoven-De Heibloem.[46] During the construction of these cemeteries the older burial mounds were practically

[43] The post-circles probably originally consisted of 10 paired posts and two single ones; of these, 20 post-holes still remain. Two paired posts lie behind each other.

[44] Modderman 1963.

[45] Glasbergen 1954, 43-44; Beex 1989, 21-23, 30.

[46] Goirle: Verwers 1966a, 35-36, tumulus 39; Haps: Verwers 1972, 13-31; Meerlo: Verwers 1964, 17-24 and Verwers 1966b, 6-8, tumulus I; Nijmegen-Kops Plateau: Fontijn 1996, 79-80; Knegsel-Huismeer: Beex 1952, 17; Oss-Zevenbergen: Verwers 1966c, 27-32; Toterfout-Halve Mijl: Glasbergen 1954; Veldhoven-De Heibloem: Modderman/Louwe Kooijmans 1966, 21-23 and fig. 5.

never destroyed. Some older barrows were even re-used in the Early Iron Age for new burials.[47]

The urnfield was in use until 400 BC at the latest. In the Late Iron Age (c. 150 BC) the urnfield was again brought into use as a burial place by a local community. The absence of finds from the period 400-150 BC, and the situation of the first Late Iron Age graves in the oldest part of the urnfield, point to a hiatus in the use of the necropolis of at least 250 years. This means that the Mierlo-Hout cemetery belongs to the group of native-Roman cemeteries in the Lower Rhine area which were built at the site of an older urnfield.[48] The burial monuments from the Urnfield period appear to have been respected as far as possible in the Roman period. However, the northwest and northeast border zone containing less monumental grave structures was used as arable land in the Late Iron Age and Roman period.

The native-Roman cemetery was abandoned in about 225 AD. The nucleus of the abandoned cemetery continued to be respected until the reclamation in the High Middle Ages.[49] Finally, around 1200, the cemetery was levelled and the site converted into arable land.

With its above long-term history, the Mierlo-Hout cemetery fits into the large group of Lower Rhine urnfields with a long tradition as a sacred place. The general pattern for the pre-medieval period is that of a positive appraisal and 'mental' appropriation of ancient necropoles by the Late Iron Age and native-Roman population.[50] Only during the 12th- and 13th-century reclamations did the attitude towards these old relics in the landscape change; many of them were destroyed and came under the plough. Roymans suggests that this large-scale destruction of ancient sacred monuments is connected with the more intensive Christianization of the local population in this period.[51]

4   SETTLEMENT TRACES FROM THE IRON AGE

From parallels elsewhere in the Lower Rhine area it appears that urnfields were situated in the centre of the territory of the local community.[52] This is also the case at Mierlo-Hout. Here, the territory probably extended over the entire sandy plateau between the Schotense Loop and the Goorloop. This plateau can be regarded as a *Siedlungskammer,* with the valleys of both brooks forming natural boundaries. It occupies an area of c. 5 km², which corresponds well with the size of territories of other urnfield communities, such as those estimated for parts of Overijssel, Drenthe and the Kempen (Southeast Brabant).[53]

The five families which on average constituted the Mierlo-Hout community, would each have occupied a farmhouse. These farmhouses had an average life span of c. 25 years, after which they were rebuilt at another location in the immediate surroundings.[54] During the settlement in the Early and beginning of the Middle Iron Age, which lasted for three centuries, a total of c. 60 farmhouses must have been built on the cover-sand plateau. Around the urnfield 8 sites have so far been localized with

[47] Examples are Haps (barrows H-4 and H-1), Veldhoven-de Heibloem (barrow 101) and Oss-Zevenbergen (tumulus I).

[48] Cf. Roymans 1995, appendix 1.

[49] The highly podzolized features of the Iron Age and native-Roman grave monuments suggest that the site consisted of waste land with a poor heath(?) vegetation until the medieval reclamation.

[50] Cf. the discussion in Roymans 1995 and Fontijn 1996.

[51] Roymans 1995, 9-21.

[52] Roymans/Fokkens 1991, 11-13; Van Bodegraven 1991; Kortlang, this volume; Roymans/Kortlang, this volume.

[53] Verlinde 1987, 324; Kooi 1979, 170; Slofstra 1991, 149.

[54] Roymans/Fokkens 1991, 11.

site	farmyards	farmhouses	outbuildings	date
a	2 or 3	2	30	Middle/Late Iron Age
b	2	1?	6	Iron Age
c	1	-	5	Early Iron Age
d	1	1	1	Early Iron Age
e	1	-	2	Iron Age
f	1	-	2	Iron Age
g	1	-	1	Iron Age
h	1	-	1?	Iron Age

Table 8. Overview of the excavated sites with settlement traces from the Iron Age at Mierlo-Hout.

settlement remains possibly contemporaneous with the urnfield (table 8): five locations with settlement traces from the Iron Age, two from the Early Iron Age and one location with traces from the Middle or Late Iron Age (fig. 2). The excavated settlement traces are discussed below.

4.1 SITE A

Directly outside the northeast end of the cemetery, at the edge of the sandy plateau the remains of two farmhouses and 30 outbuildings were recorded (fig. 13). The two farmhouses measure 17 × 8.5 m and 14.5 × 7.5 m respectively (fig. 14). Both have a row of four roof-supporting posts on the longitudinal axis. The walls originally consisted of a double row of posts. The outer row supported the overhanging roof, the inner row was dug in less deeply so that only a few post-holes have been preserved. The entrances were opposite each other in the middle of the long sides. Based on their characteristic construction, the two house-plans may be identified as belonging to the Haps type. Farmhouses of this type appear in the South Netherlands in the course of the 5th century BC and are found until the Late Iron Age.[55] This rough dating cannot be made more precise because there is a total absence of finds.[56]

Around the farmhouses the plans of 30 outbuildings used for storage were excavated. They can be divided into 26 four-post structures and 4 six-post structures. The size of the first group varies from 1.4 × 1.8 m to 2.3 × 2.3 m. The size of the second group varies from 2.5 × 1.8 m to 3 × 2.5 m. Outbuildings or *spiekers* of four or six posts are characteristic of the Iron Age. Their distribution suggests that they in part belonged to the two farmhouses, and date from the Middle or Late Iron Age. One indication for this is a rimsherd from a dish from the Middle or Late Iron Age (fig. 15), found in the posthole of an outbuilding.[57]

[55] Verwers 1972, 79-93; Schinkel 1994, part I, 96-97, and part II, 3-15.

[56] A C14 analysis of charcoal from a posthole of the northern farmhouse produced a dating of 3550 ± 70 BP (GrN-19884). We assume that this is due to contamination with older charcoal.

[57] Identification P. van den Broeke.

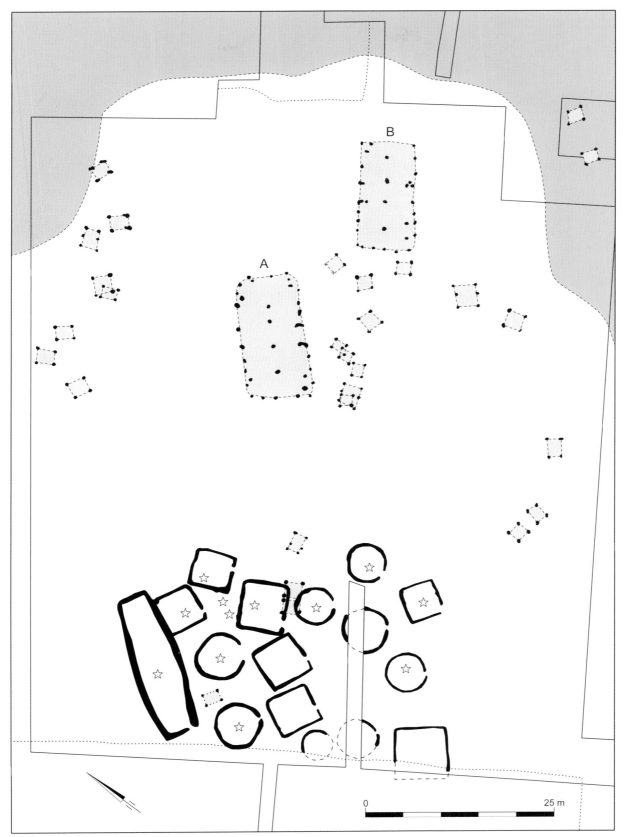

Fig. 13. Site a. Survey of the settlement traces and adjacent urnfield graves. Scale 1:500.

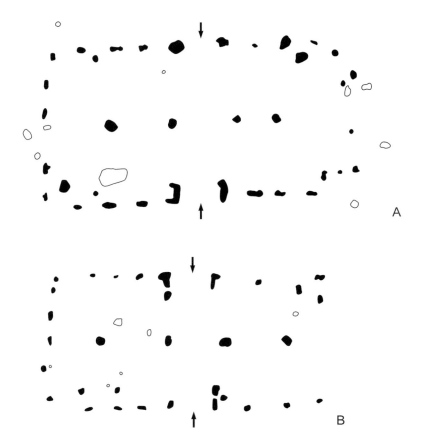

Fig. 14. House-plans of site a. The entrances are indicated by arrows. Scale 1:200.

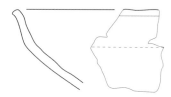

Fig. 15. Site a. Potsherd from a posthole of a granary. Scale 1:2.

Cluster a represents the remains of certainly two almost completely excavated farmyards, each consisting of a farmhouse and several outbuildings. The northern group of outbuildings probably belongs to a third yard whose main building lies outside the excavated area. It is uncertain whether the farmyards were contemporaneous, and also which outbuildings belonged to which farmhouse. Since there are no artificial boundaries, we have here open farmyards with a diffuse structure.

Fig. 16. (Right) Site b. Survey of the settlement traces. Scale 1:400.

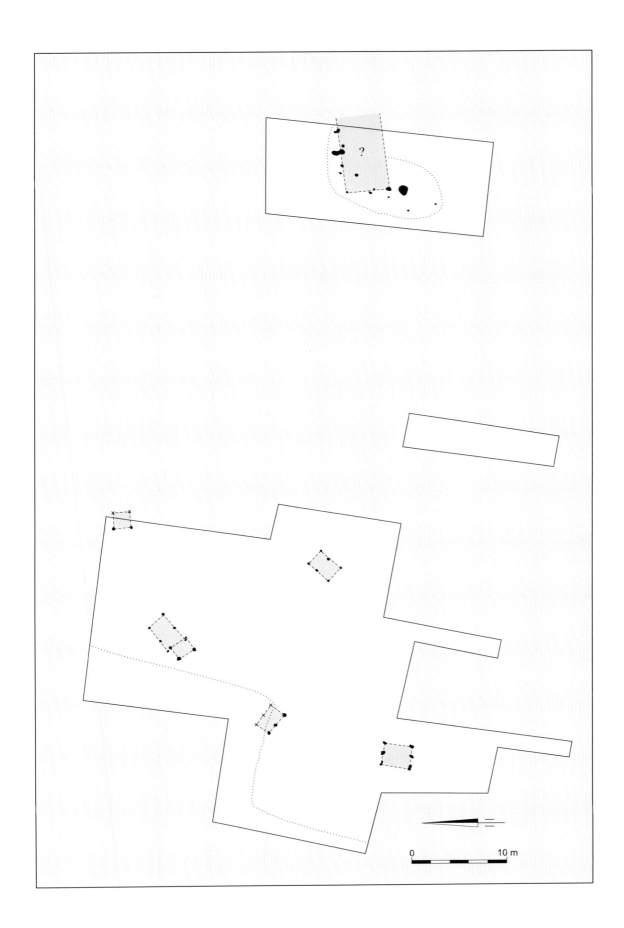

?

0   10 m

The settlement traces of site b are situated 300 m east of site a, and are separated from it by a deep depression. The site has only been excavated fragmentarily (fig. 16). The traces found consist of the remains of six outbuildings and possibly the west section of a house-plan (with traces of an entrance?).[58] Among the outbuildings there are 4 six-post and 1 four-post granary. The few sherds from the postholes cannot be more precisely dated than 'Iron Age'. The traces probably belong to at least two farmyards.

C. 80 m northwest of the cemetery, settlement traces from the Early Iron Age and the Roman period were discovered. These belong to the border zone of a settlement site which appears to extend further in a westerly direction. Many pottery sherds from the Iron Age and Roman period were collected during field surveys here, as was a fragment from a glass La Tène armring. At this site a strip of 50 × 12 m was excavated (fig. 17) with traces from the Iron Age and Roman period.[59] Only the Iron Age features are discussed here: the remains of five outbuildings and a well. Traces of the main buildings belonging to them were not found, but may be expected directly outside the excavated zone.

Among the five outbuildings there are one four-post and two six-post structures. The plan of the north six-post building contained eight sherds of (mainly roughened) handmade pottery which indicates a date in the Iron Age. Though the other outbuildings were without finds, they probably also date from the Iron Age, since granaries are rare in the Roman period.

The southwest well (fig. 17, no. 1) also belongs to the Iron Age, but can be more precisely dated. It was dug in a small natural depression and has a funnel-shaped mouth (fig. 18). The bottom of the well is oval in shape (1.5 × 0.65 m) and had a revetment of closely set, sharpened stakes (fig. 18). At a higher level, the remains of a wattle wall could be seen between the stakes. The well contained c. 375 potsherds, over 300 stone fragments, several quernstone fragments of tephrite and large lumps of daub. Almost all the material had been secondarily burnt. The majority of the finds came from the bottommost part of the secondary infill; only 10% originated from the fill of the well and a few from the packing-soil. In figure 19, the majority of rim fragments and some unusual sherds are shown. Only the sherds that are usefull for dating purposes will be discussed. A sherd from the packing-soil, with small carved lines on the rim, can be dated to the Late Bronze Age or Early Iron Age (fig. 19, no. 13).[60] The sherds from the well-fill cannot be more precisely dated than 'Iron Age' (fig. 19, nos. 14 and 15). The pottery from the secondary infill has a greater dating value (fig. 19, nos. 1 to 12). Sherds of a *Schräghals* pot decorated with a group of impressed dots ('*dellen*') and a knobbed ear date from the Early Iron Age (fig. 19, nos. 8 and 11).[61] The sherd with the hooked rim ('*haakrand*') (fig. 19, no. 10) and a fragment of a semi-cylindrical salt container (fig. 19, no. 5) are characteristic for the second half of the Early Iron Age.[62] Further, because barrel-shaped pots are lacking and tripartite shapes predominate, the material from this layer can be dated to the period 650-575 BC (phase c of

---

[58] These traces were recorded during building activities in 1989 by the Vereniging Helmont. The information was made available by H. Goossens.

[59] A main building and a well date from the Roman period.

[60] Personal communication P. van den Broeke.

[61] Verlinde 1987, 342; Van den Broeke 1987, 106 and fig. 6:5 respectively.

[62] Van den Broeke 1987, 36; and idem, 37, respectively.

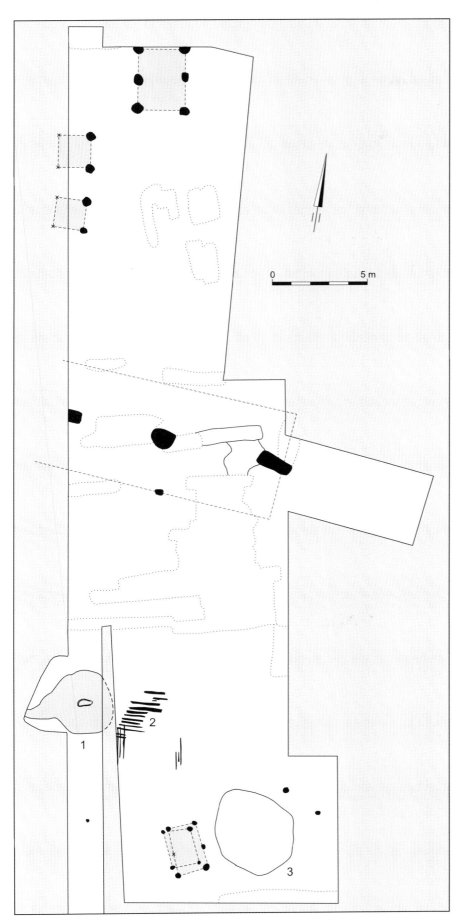

Fig. 17. Site c. Survey of the settlement traces. 1 to 3 structures mentioned in the text. Scale 1:200.

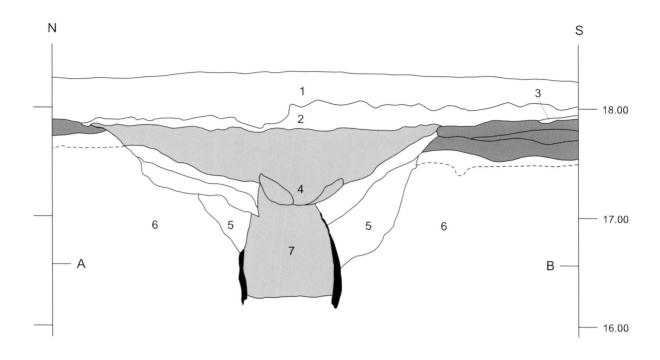

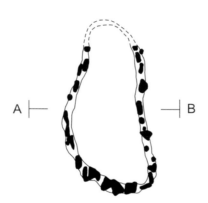

Fig. 18. Site c. Section of the Early Iron Age well. Below: plan of the wooden structure at 16.56 m + NAP (Normal Amsterdam Level). Scale 1:30.

1 arable *plaggen* soil; 2 arable layer from the Iron Age; 3 wind-blown sand with ard marks; 4 secondary infill; 5 packing-soil; 6 cover-sand with podzol soil; 7 well-fill with lumps of burnt daub

Oss-Ussen). On grounds of the typochronology of the pottery from the well-fill and the secondary infill, the well can be dated to the period 700-575 BC.

After the well had become abandoned and filled up, the depression was covered with a thin layer of wind-blown sand (fig. 18, no. 3). The site was subsequently brought into use as arable land. In the lower parts of the depression the arable layer was well-preserved. In the wind-blown sand layer immediately under the arable soil, ard marks were observed, showing two predominant directions at right angles to each other (fig. 17, no. 2). The arable layer contained a great deal of secondarily burnt stone fragments and sherds of Iron Age pottery, and was intersected by a 3rd-century AD well (fig. 17, no. 3).

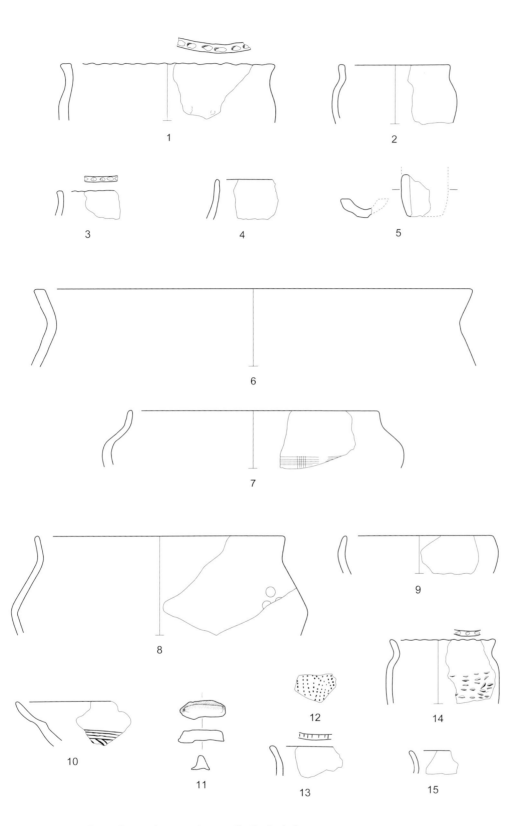

Fig. 19. Site c. Pottery from the Early Iron Age well. Scale 1:4.

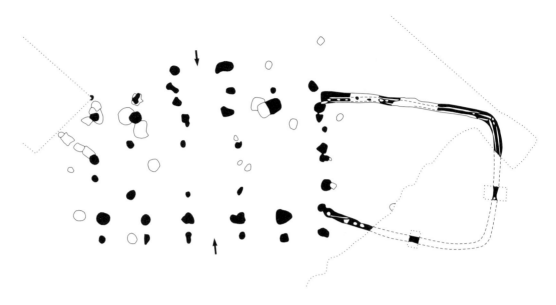

Fig. 20. Site d. Early Iron Age house-plan with annex. The entrances are indicated by arrows. Scale 1:200.

4.4   SITE D

C. 600 m north of the cemetery the remains of an isolated farmyard was found, consisting of the plan of an aisled farmhouse and a six-post granary.[63] The farmhouse, which was built on a small sand dune, is 12 m long and 8 m wide (fig. 20). In the interior there are three pairs of opposing post-holes, probably the remains of three trusses. The walls are marked by a double row of posts. In the middle of the long sides there is an entrance, the north part of which has an extension. The west half probably had a dwelling function and the east half was used as a byre. On the east side traces of an annex were found, marked by a U-shaped trench structure containing traces of horizontally laid planks supported by stakes vertically hammered in. This (unroofed) annex probably also served to pen cattle. The farm-house plan yielded ten sherds of handmade pottery, including a rim fragment of a *'lappenschaal'*, a rim fragment with finger-tip impressions, three wall fragments with finger-tip impressions and a earthen-ware spindle whorl (fig. 21). Based on this pottery, the farmhouse can be dated in the Early Iron Age.[64]

4.5   SITES E, F, G AND H

In the west (site e) and south (site f) border zone of the cemetery, 2 four-post structures were exca-vated (fig. 6). Approximately 1 km east of the urnfield (site g) a granary was discovered during a trial excavation in 1987 at a location where previously a concentration of Iron Age pottery had been col-

[63] The excavation results were previously published in Verwers 1991, 116-119.

[64] Identification P. van den Broeke, in Verwers 1991. Three-aisled farmhouses from the Early Iron Age are well-known in the Lower Rhine area (Roymans/ Fokkens 1991, 6-10). No parallels for the annex have so far been found.

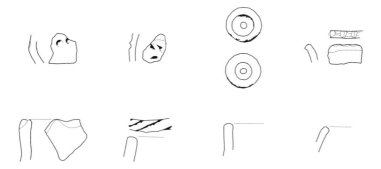

Fig. 21. Site d. Iron Age pottery from postholes belonging to the farmhouse.

lected during field surveys. About 300 m north of the cemetery, postholes of a granary were found at a building site in 1993, which contained some fragments of Iron Age pottery (site h). These four locations with settlement traces probably represent an equal number of farmyards from the Iron Age.

4.6   WANDERING FARMSTEADS

In figure 3 the locations of the eleven farmyards from the above-mentioned sites are shown; two of these are certainly contemporaneous with the urnfield and nine possibly so. In addition, six sites are represented with smaller and larger concentrations of Iron Age pottery, collected as surface finds by local amateur archaeologists.[65] They also point to the presence of settlement traces. At sites g and h, which at first only produced surface finds, this could be demonstrated by a trial excavation. The real number of sites with settlement traces in the vicinity of the urnfield will have been much greater. They are difficult to trace, because they are generally covered by a thick *plaggen* layer.

The traces of habitation from the Iron Age are found scattered over almost the entire cover-sand plateau. As far as we can tell, they always seem to represent single-phased farmsteads with an open structure, consisting of a main building and several outbuildings ('granaries'). We are confronted here with the pattern of 'wandering house-sites' characteristic of late-prehistoric settlement on the sandy areas of the Northwest-European plain.[66] On average, there would have been c. 5 contemporaneous farms on the plateau in Mierlo-Hout. One might expect that, in accordance with the pattern of other Early Iron Age settlements in the Lower Rhine area, they moved with some regularity (about every 25 years). This 'wandering' of the farms probably took place within the limits of the celtic field complex which would have been situated at that time around the fixed position of the urnfield.[67]

The diffuse and highly dynamic character of the Iron Age habitation around the Mierlo-Hout urn-field gives rise to the question of the definition and workability of the concept 'settlement' with this system of wandering house-sites. Some authors refer to every location with traces of one or more house-sites as a settlement.[68] The extreme consequence of this interpretation of the term 'settlement'

---

[65]   Information provided by Henk Goossens.

[66]   Roymans/Fokkens 1991.

[67]   Cf. the discussion in Schinkel 1994; Kortlang, this volume.

[68]   E.g. Slofstra 1991.

would be that at Mierlo-Hout 60 settlements could be expected around the urnfield! We prefer to reserve the term settlement for the entire territory of a local community within which the farms shift their location. In this way the diffuse and dynamic character of Early/Middle Iron Age habitation which distinguishes it from patterns of habitation from younger periods, is best expressed.

5   SUMMARY

In 1992 and 1993, a large-scale rescue excavation was carried out by the IPP on the *es*-complex *Snippenscheut* at Mierlo-Hout (municipality of Helmond). Attention was focused on a cemetery which was used in the Early and beginning of the Middle Iron Age (c. 750 - 450 BC) and then again in the Late Iron Age and Roman period (c. 150 BC - 225 AD; not discussed here), and some locations with settlement remains from the Iron Age and the Roman period.

The oldest element in the cemetery is the plan of a Middle Bronze Age tumulus. At the beginning of the Early Iron Age, a new cemetery was set up on the site. The cemetery was almost completely excavated, with the exception of several sections which had previously been destroyed. The urnfield was used in the period between c. 750 and 450 BC. The burial ritual is characterized by a considerable variation in the size and shape of burial structures (long-beds, round barrows, post-circles, rectangular ditched enclosures, flat graves), and the virtual absence of grave goods. Because of this, the cemetery fits into the traditions of the urnfields of the *Niederrheinische Grabhügelkultur*. Despite the destruction of large sections of the urnfield in later periods, it was still possible to estimate the total number of graves. On the basis of this estimate, the average size of the living community associated with the urnfield was determined as five families of an average of six persons. The habitation, although only fragmentarily investigated, has a diffuse nature. It is the familiar pattern of largely isolated, single-phased farmsteads which regularly changed their location on the sandy plateau around the urnfield. The locations of about eleven farmsteads were discovered, but calculations show that about 50 more may be expected, scattered over the surrounding area.

Appendix

Descriptive catalogue of the graves and grave monuments

Explanatory notes

The numbers of the graves or grave monuments correspond to the numbers on the general plan (annex 1). Per grave every individual object is identified by a small letter. If finds were indeterminable they were not counted as individual objects, except if they represented the only finds recovered. All lengths and diameters of grave monuments are outside measurements. Unless otherwise stated, the graves of the urnfield all consist of a pit with a 'heap of cremated bone' (Dutch: *beenderblok*). The interruptions in the ditches are all ancient openings. f. = feature number.

Grave 1   Round pit (f. 10-32) with cremation remains (955gr) and some burnt fragments of a rib of a sheep or pig (3 gr). Situated in the centre of a 'boat-shaped' long-bed (length 20 m, width 7 m) (fig. 8). The peripheral ditch has an interruption with a post-hole at the southeast corner. The southeast side is connected to the square ditch of grave 2. Among the cremation remains: a) 4 secondarily burnt pottery fragments; b) fragment of an indet. iron object (length 25 mm, rectangular cross-section 3 x 2 mm); c) the end of an iron bar with a rounded-rectangular cross-section (16 x 9 mm) and a perforation, probably for the fixing of a metal ring (fig. 10, no. 1c). From the ditch-fill: d) 1 secondarily burnt bottom fragment of a pot with a smoothened belly and a concave bottom (fig. 10, no. 1d); e) 1 smooth-walled rim fragment of a barrel-shaped pot (fig. 10, no. 1e); – 10 secondarily burnt pottery fragments (indet.). C14 date of charcoal from the interment: 2570 ± 80 BP (GrN-19885), 834-412 cal BC (2 sigma).

Grave 2   Shallow pit (f. 10-40) with few cremation remains (21 gr). Situated excentrically within a square ditch (5.5 x 5.5 m) with an interruption on the southeast side. Connected to the 'boat-shaped' ditch of grave 1. A small, shallow pit with some charcoal was found next to the interment.

Grave 3   Shallow pit (f. 6-109) with few cremation remains (1 gr). Mode of interment uncertain. Situated excentrically within a square ditch (5.5 x 5.5 m) with an interruption on the southeast side (fig. 8). From the ditch-fill: a) 1 secondarily burnt wall fragment of a sharply carinated pot (fig. 10, no. 3a).

Grave 4   Round pit (f. 6-110) with few cremation remains (not collected). Mode of interment uncertain. Situated somewhat excentrically within a rectangular ditch (6.5 x 7 m) with an interruption on the southeast side. From the ditch-fill: a) fragment of an iron pin (length 25 mm, square cross section) with a head (fig. 10, no. 4a).

Grave 5   Disturbed shallow pit (f. 6-79) with few cremation remains (4 gr). Mode of interment uncertain. Situated in the centre of a circular ditch (diameter 6.75 m) with an interruption on the southeast side. Pottery from the ditch-fill: a) a small conical cup with a smoothened surface and a grooved line below the rim, placed upside down (fig. 11, no. 5a); b) 1 smoothened wall fragment; 1 wall fragment (indet.).

Grave 6   Rectangular pit (f. 6-77; 1 x 0.6 m) with cremation remains (lost). Without peripheral structure; probably a flat grave. Pottery among the cremation remains: a) a barrel-shaped cup with a roughened belly and a smoothened shoulder and neck (fig. 10, no. 6a).

Grave 7   Shallow pit (f. 6-78) with few cremation remains (20 gr). Without peripheral structure; probably a flat grave.

Grave 8   Large (sub)recent pit (f. 6-125) with few cremation remains (not collected). Mode of interment uncertain. Situated within a circular ditch (diameter 5.25 m) with an interruption on the southeast side. Pottery from the (sub)recent pit: a) 2 secondarily burnt, roughened wall fragments; 2 wall fragments (indet.).

Grave 9   Square ditch (6.25 x 6.25 m) with an interruption on the southeast side. Central interment lost.

Grave 10   Disturbed shallow pit (f. 6-123) with cremation remains (97 gr). Situated in the centre of a circular ditch (diameter 6.5 m) with an interruption on the southeast side.

Grave 11   Rectangular ditch (6 x 5.5 m) with an interruption on the southeast side. Central interment lost.

Grave 12   Northern part of a circular ditch (diameter 4 m), probably with an interruption on the southeast side.

Grave 13   Shallow pit (f. 12-7) with cremation remains (43 gr). Situated somewhat excentrically within a circular ditch (diameter 5.5 m) with an interruption on the south.

Grave 14   Circular ditch (diameter 6.25 m) with an interruption on the southeast side. Central interment lost.

Grave 15   Part of a circular ditch (diameter c. 5.5 m) with an interruption on the southeast side. Central interment lost.

Grave 16   Shallow pit (f. 12-8) with few cremation remains (not collected). Mode of interment uncertain. Situated in the centre of a square ditch (5 x 5 m) with an interruption at the southern corner.

Grave 17   Shallow pit (f. 12-5-1) with cremation remains (155 gr). Interment in the south side of the peripheral structure of grave 16. C14 date of charcoal from the grave pit: 2500 ± 30 BP (GrN-19886), 784-516 en 434-424 cal BC (2 sigma).

Grave 18   Shallow pit (f. 12-150) with cremation remains (35 gr). Situated somewhat excentrically within a circular ditch (diameter 5.5 m) with an interruption on the southeast side.

Grave 19   Rectangular or square ditch (7.5 x ?m) with a recent disturbance at the west side and an interruption in the south corner. Traces of a post-hole were found on the bottom of the ditch, near the interruption. Central interment lost.

Grave 20   Rectangular or square ditch (6.75 m x ?m) with a recent disturbance at the northern side and an interruption in the southern corner. A large feature (depth c. 5 cm) with charcoal was found within the ditched structure. Central interment lost.

Grave 21   Circular ditch (diameter 6.25 m) with a recent disturbance at the northwest side and an interruption on the east side. Central interment lost.

Grave 22   Shallow pit (f. 11-8) with few cremation remains (23 gr). Without peripheral structure.

Grave 23   Shallow pit (f. 11-9) with few cremation remains (not collected). Mode of interment uncertain. Without peripheral structure.

Grave 24   Shallow pit (f. 11-36) with few cremation remains (8 gr). Situated in the centre of a circular ditch (diameter 4.5 m) with an interruption on the east side. Pottery from the ditch-fill: a) 5 bottom fragments, 34 wall fragments and 4 rim fragments of a conical bowl with a roughened belly and a smoothened neck (fig. 10, no. 24a). The fragments were distributed over the entire ditch.

Grave 25   Shallow pit (f. 11-40) with few cremation remains (2 gr). Mode of interment uncertain. Situated in the centre of a circular ditch (diameter 5 m) with an interruption on the south side. Pottery from the ditch-fill: a) 1 roughened wall fragment, secondarily burnt; b) 1 smoothened wall fragment.

Grave 26   Shallow pit (f. 11-18) with cremation remains (5 gr). Without a peripheral structure.

Grave 27   Disturbed pit (f. 6-131) with cremation remains (270 gr). Without a peripheral structure.

Grave 28   Round pit (f. 6-153) with cremation remains (347 gr) and burnt fragments of the left foreleg (humerus, radius, ulna, carpale and scapula) of a pig (22 gr). Without a peripheral structure.

Grave 29   Shallow pit (f. 6-138) with cremation remains (6 gr). Mode of interment uncertain. Without a peripheral structure.

Grave 30   Long-bed (width 3 m, length > 4.5 m) with open ends. The northern part shows a recent disturbance. Central interment lost.

Grave 31   Circular ditch (diameter?) with a recent disturbance at the northwest side. Presence of an interruption is uncertain. Central interment lost.

Grave 32   Southern part of a recently disturbed circular ditch (diameter ?) with an interruption (orientation?). Central interment lost.

Grave 33   Shallow pit (f. 16-3) with cremation remains (19 gr). Situated excentrically within an oval-shaped circular ditch (diameter 6.5-7.75 m) with an interruption on the southeast side. Pottery among the cremation remains: a) 4 secondarily burnt wall fragments.

Grave 34   Oval-shaped circular ditch (diameter 5-6.25 m) with an interruption on the south side. Central interment lost.

Grave 35   Circular ditch (diameter 6.5 m) with an interruption on the east side. Central interment lost.

Grave 36   Round pit (f. 8-47) with cremation remains (852 gr) in an urn. Situated in the centre of a probably closed circular ditch with a recent disturbance on the southwest side. Pottery: a) *Schräghals* pot with smoothened surface and concave base (fig. 10, no. 36a).

Grave 37	Probably closed circular ditch (diameter 9 m) with recent disturbances on the northwest and southeast sides. Central interment lost. Pottery from the ditch-fill: a) 1 secondarily burnt wall fragment.
Grave 38	Shallow pit (f. 8-2) with cremation remains (6 gr). Mode of interment uncertain. Situated in the centre of a circular ditch (diameter 7 m) with an interruption on the southeast side. Large parts of the ditch have been recently disturbed.
Grave 39	Parts of a disturbed circular ditch (diameter 7.75 m). Presence of an interruption is uncertain. Central interment lost.
Grave 40	Parts of the ditches of a disturbed long-bed (width 3.5 m, length 7 m) with open ends. Central interment lost.
Grave 41	Parts of a disturbed long-bed (width 3.75 m, length 7 m) with open ends. Central interment lost.
Grave 42	Circular ditch (diameter 5.5 m) with an interruption on the southeast side. Central interment lost. Pottery from the ditch-fill: a) 1 rim fragment of a barrel-shaped pot with smoothened neck and finger-tip impressions on rim and belly (fig. 10, no. 42a); 1 secondarily burnt wall fragment (indet.).
Grave 43	Circular ditch (diameter 5.5 m) with an interruption on the southeast side. The northeastern part has been recently disturbed. Central interment lost.
Grave 44	Parts of a recently disturbed circular ditch (diameter 5 m). Presence of an interruption is uncertain. Central interment lost.
Grave 45	Circular ditch (diameter 6.5 m) with an interruption on the southeast side and surrounded by a circle of originally 11 post-holes (5 are lost). Central interment lost.
Grave 46	Circular ditch (diameter 3.5 m) with an interruption on the southeast side. Central interment lost.
Grave 47	Shallow pit (f. 1-114) with few cremation remains (1 gr). Mode of interment uncertain. Situated excentrically within a circular ditch (diameter 5 m) with an interruption on the southeast side.
Grave 48	Round pit (f. 1-121/1-97) with cremation remains (855 gr). Situated in the centre of a circular ditch (diameter 7.5 m) with an interruption on the east side. Pottery among the cremation remains: a) small cup with outstanding rim (fig. 10, no. 48a).
Grave 49	Circular ditch (diameter 5.5 m) with an interruption on the east side. Central interment lost.
Grave 50	Long-bed (width 3.5 m, length 6.75 m) with open ends (fig. 8). Central interment lost. Pottery from the ditch-fill: a) 1 secondarily burnt wall fragment.
Grave 51	Circular ditch (diameter 4 m) with an interruption on the east side. The northern part has been recently disturbed. Central interment lost.
Grave 52	Circular ditch (diameter 6.5 m) with a recent disturbance at the northeast side. Presence of an interruption is uncertain. Central interment lost.
Grave 53	Round pit (f. 1-84) with cremation remains (10 gr). Situated somewhat excentrically within a long-bed (width 3.5 m, length 4.5 m) with open ends. Pottery among the cremation remains: a) rim and wall fragments of a secondarily burnt cup with comb decoration on the belly (fig. 10, no. 53a).
Grave 54	Shallow pit (f. 1-81) with cremation remains (9 gr). Situated within a circular ditch (diameter 6.5 m) with an interruption on the southeast side.
Grave 55	Circular ditch (diameter 3 m) with an interruption on the east side. Central interment lost.
Grave 56	Circular ditch (diameter 5 m) with recent disturbances at the north and east sides. Presence of an interruption is uncertain. Central interment lost.
Grave 57	Circular ditch (diameter 3.75 m) with an interruption (orientation?). The northeast side shows a recent disturbance. Central interment lost.
Grave 58	Circular ditch (diameter 4.75 m) with an interruption on the east side. The traces of 66 sharpened stakes were found on the bottom of the circular ditch (fig. 8). Central interment lost.
Grave 59	Long-bed (length >8 m, width?) with open ends, largely disturbed in recent times. Central interment lost.
Grave 60	The western part of a largely disturbed circular ditch (diameter 5 m). The presence of an interruption is uncertain. Central interment lost. Pottery from the ditch-fill: a) rim and wall fragments of a sharply carinated dish with outstanding neck and on the belly a decoration of horizontally grooved lines (fig. 10, no. 60a).

Grave 61   Circular ditch (diameter 4 m.) with a recent disturbance at the southwest side. The presence of an interruption is uncertain. Central interment lost.

Grave 62   Circular ditch (diameter 5 m) with a recent disturbance at the southwest side. The presence of an interruption is uncertain. Central interment lost.

Grave 63   Circular ditch (diameter 5.25 m) with a recent disturbance at the southwest side. The presence of an interruption is uncertain. Central interment lost.

Grave 64   Shallow pit (f. 1-25) with few cremation remains (3 gr), in the circular ditch of grave 63. Mode of interment uncertain.

Grave 65   Circular ditch (diameter 3 m) with a recent disturbance at the west and south side. The presence of an interruption is uncertain. Central interment lost.

Grave 66   Shallow pit (f. 1-2) with few cremation remains (not collected). Mode of interment uncertain. Situated in the centre of a circular ditch (diameter 2.75 m) with a disturbance at the south side. The presence of an interruption is uncertain.

Grave 67   Closed circular ditch (diameter 3.4 m). Central interment lost.

Grave 68   Circular ditch (diameter 8.25 m), the southwest part of which is disturbed in Roman times (ditch R-49). The presence of an interruption is uncertain. Central interment lost.

Grave 69   Circular ditch (diameter 8.8 m) with an interruption on the east side. Central interment lost. Pottery from the ditch-fill: a) 1 roughened wall fragment; 2 secondarily burnt wall fragments (indet.).

Grave 70   Shallow pit (f. 1-50) with cremation remains (13 gr). Situated in the centre of a circular ditch (diameter 4.75 m) with an interruption on the east side.

Grave 71   Parts of a circular ditch (diameter 2.75 m) with an interruption on the southeast side. Central interment lost. Pottery from the ditch-fill: a) 1 roughened wall fragment.

Grave 72   Circular ditch (diameter 5.5 m) with an interruption to the east. Central interment lost.

Grave 73   Shallow pit (f. 9-1) with few cremation remains (2 gr). Mode of interment uncertain. Situated excentrically on the longitudinal axis of a long-bed (length 7 m, width 3.75 m) with open ends.

Grave 74   Circular ditch (diameter 5.75 m) with an interruption on the southeast side. Central interment lost.

Grave 75   Closed circular ditch (diameter 3 m) (fig. 8). Central interment lost.

Grave 76.   Cremation remains (77 gr) in a disturbed rectangular pit (f. 9-3), length c. 1.75 m and width 0.6 m. Probably a flat grave.

Grave 77   Disturbed pit (f. 9-11) with cremation remains (27 gr). Situated in the centre of a circular ditch (diameter 7.2 m) with an interruption on the southeast side. The peripheral ditch is surrounded by a circle of originally 13 postholes (3 are disturbed by the Roman-period ditch R-49) (fig. 8).

Grave 78   Circular ditch (diameter 6.5 m) with an interruption on the southeast side. Central interment lost. Pottery from the ditch-fill: a) 1 smoothened rim fragment.

Grave 79   Shallow pit (f. 9-5) with cremation remains (28 gr). Situated excentrically within a circular ditch (diameter 5 m) with a Roman-period disturbance at the east and south side (ditch R-49). The presence of an interruption is uncertain. Pottery among the cremation remains: a) 1 secondarily burnt wall fragment.

Grave 80   Few cremation remains (2 gr) in disturbed soil. Situated in the centre of a circular ditch (diameter 5.7 m) with an interruption on the southeast side. Mode of interment uncertain. Pottery from the ditch-fill: a) 2 secondarily burnt wall fragments.

Grave 81   Southwest parts of a largely disturbed circular ditch (diameter 4.75 m). The presence of an interruption is uncertain. Central interment lost.

Grave 82   Shallow pit (f. 8-5) with few cremation remains (not collected). Without a peripheral structure.

Grave 83   Parts of a disturbed long-bed (width 3 m, length >7.25 m). Central interment lost.

Grave 84   Closed circular ditch (diameter 3.25 m). Central interment lost.

Grave 85   Circular ditch (diameter 4.1 m) with an interruption on the southeast side. Central interment lost. Pottery from the ditch: a) 1 wall fragment.

Grave 86   Circular ditch (diameter 5.5 m) with an interruption on the southeast side. Central interment lost. Pottery from the ditch-fill: a) 1 secondarily burnt, roughened wall fragment; 1 wall fragment (indet.).

Grave 87   Round pit (f. 27-10) with cremation remains (689 gr) in an urn. Situated within a circular ditch (diameter 4.75 m), parts of which have been recently disturbed. The presence of an interruption is uncertain. Pottery: a) bottom and wall fragment of a roughened, probably Harpstedt-like pot (fig. 10, no. 87a), used as an urn. Metal among the cremation remains: b) some fragments of molten bronze (indet.).

Grave 88   Shallow pit (f. 25-1) with cremation remains (47 gr). Central interment on the longitudinal axis of a long-bed (length 6.2 m, width 3 m) with open ends (fig. 8). Two four-post structures were found at the north end of the long-bed. Pottery from the ditch-fill: a) 2 secondarily burnt wall fragments; 1 indet. pottery fragment.

Grave 89   The northeastern part of a largely disturbed circular ditch (diameter ?). The presence of an interruption is uncertain. Central interment lost.

Grave 90   Circular ditch (diameter 4.5 m) with an interruption on the southeast side. The southwest side shows a recent disturbance. Central interment lost.

Grave 91   A probably closed circular ditch (diameter 4.5 m) with an recent disturbance at the northwest side. Central interment lost.

Grave 92   Circular ditch (diameter 5.2 m) with an interruption on the southeast side. Central interment lost.

Grave 93   Rectangular ditch (4.75 x 3.75 m) with an interruption at the east corner. Central interment lost.

Grave 94   Shallow pit (f. 1-90) with few cremation remains (8 gr), disturbed by the ditch of a grave monument from the Roman period (R-40). Without a peripheral structure.

Grave 95   Circular ditch (diameter 6.25 m) with an interruption on the southeast side. Central interment lost.

Grave 96   Circular ditch (diameter 4 m) with an interruption on the southeast side. Central interment lost.

Grave 97   Circular ditch (diameter 6 m) with an interruption on the east side. Central interment lost.

Grave 98   Part of a circular ditch (diameter 5.5 m) with an interruption on the southeast side. The ditch has been largely disturbed in recent times. Central interment lost.

Grave 99   The northwest part of a largely disturbed circular ditch (diameter 5.5). The presence of an interruption is uncertain. Central interment lost.

Grave 100   Circular ditch (diameter 6.4 m) with an interruption on the east side. Central interment lost.

Grave 101   Circular ditch (diameter 3.85 m) with an interruption on the east side. The south side shows a recent disturbance. Central interment lost.

Grave 102   Circular ditch (diameter 4.75 m) with an interruption on the east side. Central interment lost.

Grave 103   Circular ditch (diameter 4.5 m) with a recent disturbance at the east side. The presence of an interruption is uncertain. Central interment lost.

Grave 104   Circular ditch (diameter 4.9 m) with an interruption on the east side. Central interment lost.

Grave 105   Long-bed (length between 25 and 33 m, width 3.4 m) with open ends. The north end was disturbed in medieval times. Central interment lost.

Grave 106   Small parts of a recently disturbed circular ditch (diameter c. 4.25 m). The presence of an interruption is uncertain. Central interment lost.

Grave 107   Northwestern part of a recently disturbed circular ditch (diameter ?). The presence of an interruption is uncertain. Central interment lost.

Grave 108   Long-bed (length c. 22 m, width 5 m) with a rectangular north end (fig. 8). The south end shows a recent disturbance. Connected to the long-bed of grave 109. Central interment lost. Pottery from the ditch-fill: a) rim and wall fragments of an almost complete dish with 'haakrand' and decorated with grooved lines (fig. 10, no. 108a); b) 1 rim fragment and 30 roughened wall fragments probably of a Harpstedt-like pot (fig. 10, no. 108b). The sherds of both pots were found concentrated in the west ditch.

Grave 109   Long-bed (length c. 22 m, width 3 m) with probably a rectangular north end (fig. 8). Recent disturbances at the southern and northern end. Central interment lost.

Grave 110   The northeast part of a recently disturbed circular ditch (diameter c. 6.25 m). The presence of an interruption is uncertain. Central interment lost.

Grave 111   The northwest part of a recently disturbed circular ditch (diameter 4.5 m). The presence of an interruption is uncertain. Central interment lost.

Grave 112   Circular ditch (diameter 4.3 m) with an interruption on the southeast side. Central interment lost. Pottery from the ditch-fill: a) 7 secondarily burnt wall fragments. C14 date of charcoal from the ditch-fill: 2510 ± 35 BP (GrN-20594), 793-489/440-425 cal BC (2 sigma).

Grave 113   Circular ditch (diameter 3.5 m) with an interruption on the southeast side. Central interment lost.

Grave 114   Circular ditch (diameter 5 m) with an interruption on the south side. Connected to grave 108. Central interment lost. Pottery from the ditch-fill: a) 1 bottom and 10 roughened wall fragments, all secondarily burnt.

Grave 115   Circular ditch (diameter 4.25 m) with an interruption (orientation ?). Recent disturbance at the southeast side. Central interment lost.

Grave 116   Circular ditch (diameter c. 6.5 m) with a recent disturbance at the south and west sides. The presence of an interruption is uncertain. Central interment lost.

Grave 117   Small parts of a circular ditch (diameter c. 4 m). The presence of an interruption is uncertain. Central interment lost.

Grave 118   Circular ditch (diameter c. 6.5 m) with an interruption on the east side. The west side shows a recent disturbance. Central interment lost.

Grave 119   Circular ditch (diameter 3.6 m) with an interruption on the southeast side. Connected to the circular ditch of grave 120. Central interment lost. Pottery from the ditch-fill: a) 8 rim, 3 wall and 5 bottom fragments of a smooth-walled bowl with vertical comb decoration (fig. 10, no. 119a); b) 2 rim , 17 wall and 4 bottom fragments of a Harpstedt-like pot with a roughened belly, a smoothened neck and finger-tip impressions on the rim (fig. 10, no. 119b).

Grave 120   Round pit (f. 33-4) with cremation remains (1036 gr). Situated in the centre of a circular ditch (diameter 7 m) with an interruption on the east side. Pottery from the ditch-fill: a) 12 roughened wall fragments, all secondarily burnt.

Grave 121   Part of a circular ditch (diameter 6 m). The presence of an interruption is uncertain. Central interment lost.

Grave 122   Southern part of a recently disturbed circular (?) ditch (diameter c. 6 m). The presence of an interruption is uncertain. Central interment lost.

Grave 123   Disturbed shallow pit (f. 26-55) with cremation remains (24 gr). Situated within a circular ditch (diameter 10.1 m) with an interruption on the east side. The northeast part was disturbed in medieval times. The peripheral ditch is surrounded by a circle of originally 19 or 20 post-holes (10 or 11 are lost).

Grave 124   Small part of a circular (?) ditch, largely disturbed in medieval times. The presence of an interruption is uncertain. Central interment lost.

Grave 125   Disturbed shallow pit (f. 33-68) with few cremation remains (6 gr). Situated within a circular ditch (diameter 5.5 m) with an interruption on the southeast side and a medieval disturbance at the northwest side.

Grave 126   Disturbed shallow pit (f. 32-44) with cremation remains (18 gr). Without a peripheral structure.

Grave 127   Disturbed shallow pit (f. 33-59) with cremation remains (20 gr). Without a peripheral structure.

Grave 128   Probably closed circular ditch (diameter 3.25 m) with a recent disturbance on the northwest side. Central interment lost.

Grave 129   Parts of a recently disturbed circular ditch (diameter 3.75 m). The presence of an interruption is uncertain. Central interment lost.

Grave 130   Circular ditch (diameter 9.5 m) with a recent disturbance at the southeast side. The presence of an interruption is uncertain. Central interment lost. Pottery from the ditch-fill: a) 1 secondarily burnt rim fragment with smoothened neck and finger-tip impressions on the rim (fig. 10, no. 130a); b) 1 rim and 4 wall fragments of a smoothened biconical pot (fig. 10, no. 130b); c) 1 secondarily burnt, smoothened wall fragment; d) 2 secondarily burnt, roughened wall fragment; 6 secondarily burnt wall fragments (indet.).

Grave 131   Northern part of a largely disturbed circular ditch (diameter ?). The presence of an interruption is uncertain. Central interment lost.

Grave 132   Peripheral structure consisting of a circle (diameter 10.8 m) of originally c. 25 post-holes (11 recently disturbed) (fig. 8). No traces of a circular ditch. Central interment lost.

Grave 133   Probably closed circular ditch (diameter 5.25 m) with a recent disturbance at the northwest side. Central interment lost.

Grave 134   Circular ditch (diameter 6.5 m) with an interruption on the southeast side. Central interment lost.

Grave 135   Circular ditch (diameter 3.6 m) with an interruption on the east side. Central interment lost.

Grave 136   Circular ditch (diameter 4.8 m) with a recent disturbance on the southeast side. The presence of an interruption is uncertain. Central interment lost.

Grave 137   Parts of a recently disturbed circular ditch (diameter 16.8 m). The presence of an interruption is uncertain. Central interment lost.

Grave 138   Circular ditch (diameter 4.25 m) with an interruption on the east side. Recent disturbance at the northeast side. Pottery from the ditch-fill: a) 1 smoothened wall fragment. Central interment lost.

Grave 139   Disturbed shallow pit (f. 33-5) with cremation remains (52 gr). Situated excentrically within a circular ditch (diameter 4.8 m) with an interruption on the southeast side.

Grave 140   Oval pit (f. 33-1) with cremation remains (322 gr). Situated in the centre of a circular ditch (diameter 7 m) with an interruption on the southeast side. C14 date of charcoal from the grave pit: 2495 ± 35 BP (GrN-20595), 789-414 cal BC (2 sigma).

Grave 141   Circular ditch (diameter 5 m) with an interruption on the east side. Central interment lost (fig. 8).

Grave 142   The northwestern part of a recently disturbed circular ditch (diameter ?). The presence of an interruption is uncertain. Central interment lost.

Grave 143   The southern part of a recently disturbed circular ditch (diameter c. 6 m). The presence of an interruption is uncertain. Central interment lost.

Grave 144   Circular ditch (diameter 4.2 m) with a recent disturbance at the southeast side. The presence of an interruption is uncertain. Central interment lost.

Grave 145   Circular ditch (diameter 4 m) with a recent disturbance at the east side. The presence of an interruption is uncertain. Central interment lost.

Grave 146   The northeast part of a circular ditch (f. 35-79 en 28-21) with a diameter of c. 3.5 m. The presence of an interruption is uncertain. Central interment lost.

Grave 147   The northern part of a recently disturbed circular ditch (diameter ?). The presence of an interruption is uncertain. Central interment lost.

Grave 148   Circular ditch (diameter 2.8 m) with a recent disturbance at the southeast side. The presence of an interruption is uncertain. Central interment lost.

Grave 149   Disturbed shallow pit (f. 37-20) with cremation remains (29 gr). Situated in the centre of a circular ditch (diameter 5.5 m) with an interruption on the east side. The north side shows a recent disturbance.

Grave 150   Circular ditch (diameter 2.8 m) with an interruption on the southeast side. C14 date of charcoal from the ditch-fill: 2520 ± 40 BP (GrN-20596), 797-440 cal BC (2 sigma). Central interment lost.

Grave 151   The southern part of a circular ditch (diameter c. 4 m). The presence of an interruption is uncertain. Central interment lost.

Grave 152   Circular ditch (diameter 4.9 m) with a recent disturbance at the east side. The presence of an interruption is uncertain. Central interment lost.

Grave 153   The southern part of a recently disturbed circular ditch (diameter c. 4.75 m). The presence of an interruption is uncertain. Central interment lost.

Grave 154   The western part of a recently disturbed circular ditch (diameter c. 4.5 m). The presence of an interruption is uncertain. Central interment lost.

Grave 155   Circular ditch (diameter 4 m) with a recent disturbance at the northeast side. The presence of an interruption is uncertain. Central interment lost.

Grave 156   Circular ditch (diameter 4.5 m) with an interruption on the east side. Central interment lost.

Grave 157   Circular ditch (diameter 4.85 m) with a disturbance from the Roman period (ditch R-78) at the south side. The presence of an interruption is uncertain. Central interment lost.

Grave 158   Circular ditch (diameter 5 m) with a medieval disturbance at the southwest side. The presence of an interruption is uncertain. Central interment lost.

Grave 159   Circular ditch (diameter 5.6 m) with an interruption on the east side. Central interment lost.

Grave 160   Disturbed pit with cremation remains (4 gr). Mode of interment uncertain. Situated in the centre of a circular ditch (diameter 5.1 m) with an interruption on the east side.

Grave 161   Circular ditch (diameter 4.9 m) with an interruption on the southeast side. Central interment lost.

Grave 162   Circular ditch (diameter 5.2 m) with a medieval disturbance at the southeast side. The presence of an interruption is uncertain. Central interment lost.

Grave 163   Circular ditch (diameter 6.1 m) with an interruption on the east side. The northwestern part shows a recent disturbance. Central interment lost.

Grave 164   Closed circular ditch (diameter 1.75 m). Connected to the ditch of grave 163. Central interment lost.

Grave 165   Circular ditch (diameter 5.5 m) with an interruption on the southeast side and a disturbance from the Roman period at the west side. Surrounded by a circle of originally 14 post holes (5 are lost). Central interment lost.

REFERENCES

Annaert, R., 1984: Urnenveld te Ravels, *Archeologie* 1985-2, 127-129.

Appelboom, T.G., 1952: Onderzoek van een urnenveld. Nederweert (Limburg), *BROB* 3, 45-48.

Ascádi, G./J. Nemeskéri, 1970: *History of Human Life Span and Mortality*, Budapest.

Beex, G., 1952: Grafheuvels aan de weg langs het Huismeer te Knegsel, *Brabants Heem* 4, 14-18.

Beex, W., 1989: *Oud nieuws. Archeologische vondsten en vindplaatsen uit de Vroege en Midden Bronstijd in het Maas-Demer-Schelde-gebied* (unpublished MA thesis, University of Amsterdam).

Bodegraven, N. van, 1991: Nederzettingssporen uit de late bronstijd en de vroege ijzertijd op de Everse Akkers in St.- Oedenrode, in H. Fokkens/N. Roymans (eds), *Nederzettingen uit de bronstijd en de vroege ijzertijd in de Lage Landen*, Amersfoort (NAR 13), 129-139.

Broeke, P.W. van den, 1987: De dateringsmiddelen voor de ijzertijd van Zuid-Nederland, in W. A. B. van der Sanden/P. W. van den Broeke (eds), 101-119.

Engels, A./L. van Impe, 1984: Grafveld uit de ijzertijd te Kaulille, *AB* 258, 20-25.

Fontijn, D., 1996: Socializing landscape. Second thoughts about the cultural biography of urnfields, *Archaeological Dialogues* 3, 77-87.

Glasbergen, W., 1954: Barrow excavations in the Eight Beautitudes, *Paleohistorea* II, 1-134.

Hessing, W.A.M., 1989: Wijk bij Duurstede "De Horden": Besiedlung und Bestattungen aus der frühen Eisenzeit, *BROB* 39, 297-344.

Hulst, R.S., 1964: Een grafveld uit de voor-Romeinse ijzertijd te Nijnsel, gem. St.-Oedenrode, prov. Noord-Brabant, *BROB* 14, 74-83.

Impe, L. van/G. Beex/H. Roosens, 1973: Het urnenveld op "De Roosen" te Neerpelt: eindrapport, *AB* 145, 5-31.

Klei, P., 1993: *Voorlopig verslag opgraving Berkel-Enschot*, Tilburg (ITHO Archeologische Reeks 4).

Kooi, P.B., 1979: *Pre-Roman Urnfields in the North of the Netherlands*, Groningen.

Modderman, P.J.R., 1955: Een voorlopig onderzoek van een urnenveld op het Philips kampeerterrein, gem. Someren, N. Br., *BROB* 6, 66-70.

Modderman, P.J.R., 1963: Een grafheuvel met paarsgewijs gestelde palenkrans van het urnenveld op het Philips kampeerterrein, gem. Someren, N. Br., *BROB* 13, 571-575.

Modderman, P.J.R./L.P. Louwe Kooijmans, 1966: The Heidebloem, A Cemetry from the Late Bronze Age and Early Iron Age between Veldhoven and Steensel, Prov. Noord-Brabant, *APL* 2, 9-26.

Roymans, N., 1991: Late Urnfield societies in the Northwest European Plain and the expanding networks of Central European Hallstatt groups, in N. Roymans/F. Theuws (eds), *Images of the Past. Studies on Ancient Societies in Northwestern Europe, Amsterdam* (Studies in Prae- en Protohistorie 7), 9-89.

Roymans, N., 1995: The cultural biography of urnfields and the long-term history of a mythical landscape, *Archaeological Dialogues* 2, 2-24.

Roymans, N./H. Fokkens, 1991: Een overzicht van veertig jaar nederzettingsonderzoek in de Lage Landen, in H. Fokkens/N. Roymans (eds), *Nederzettingen uit de bronstijd en de vroege ijzertijd in de Lage Landen*, Amersfoort (NAR 13), 1-19.

Roymans, N./A. Tol, 1993: Noodonderzoek van een dodenakker te Mierlo-Hout, in N. Roymans/F. Theuws (eds), *Een en al zand. Twee jaar graven naar het Brabantse verleden*, 's-Hertogenbosch, 42-56.

Sanden, W. van der, 1981: The urnfield and the Late Bronze Age settlement traces on the Haagakkers at St.-Oedenrode (province of North Brabant), *BROB* 31, 307-328.

Sanden, W. van der, 1994: De funeraire en aanverwante structuren, in C. Schinkel, 199-218.

Sanden, W.A.B. van der/P.W. van den Broeke (eds), 1987: *Getekend zand. Tien jaar archeologisch onderzoek in Oss-Ussen* (Bijdragen tot de studie van het Brabantse heem 31), Waalre.

Schinkel, C., 1994: Zwervende erven. *Bewoningssporen in Oss-Ussen uit de Bronstijd, IJzertijd en Romeinse tijd. Opgravingen 1976-1986*, Leiden (unpublished phil. doc. thesis, University of Leiden).

Slofstra, J., 1991: Een nederzetting uit de Vroege IJzertijd op de Heesmortel bij Riethoven, in H. Fokkens/N. Roymans (eds), *Nederzettingen uit de bronstijd en de vroege ijzertijd in de Lage Landen*, Amersfoort (NAR 13), 141-151.

STIBOKA, 1981: *Toelichting bij Bodemkaart van Nederland. Schaal 1:50.000, Kaartblad 51, Oost-Eindhoven.*

STIBOKA, 1981: *Toelichting bij de Geomorfolochische Kaart van Nederland. Schaal 1:50.000, Kaartblad 51, Oost-Eindhoven.*

Tol, A., 1993: *Leven naast de dood* (unpublished MA thesis, University of Amsterdam).

Verlinde, A.D., 1987: Die Gräber und Grabfunde der späten Bronzezeit und frühen Eisenzeit in Overijssel IV, *BROB* 35, 170-341.

Verwers, G.J., 1964: A Veluvian bell beaker with remains of a cremation in a tumulus near Meerlo, *APL* 1, 17-24.

Verwers, G.J., 1966a: A Late Bronze Age/Early Iron Age urnfield at Goirle, Prov. Noord-Brabant, *APL* 2, 33-48.

Verwers, G.J., 1966b: A tumulus and an urnfield at Meerlo, Prov. Limburg, *APL* 2, 6-8.

Verwers, G.J., 1966c: Tumuli at the Zevenbergen near Oss, Gem. Berghem, Prov. Noord-Brabant, *APL* 2, 27-32.

Verwers, G.J., 1972: Das Kamps Veld in Haps in Neolithikum, Bronzezeit und Eisenzeit, *APL* 5.

Verwers, W.J.H., 1991: Archeologische kroniek van Noord-Brabant 1990, *Brabants Heem* 43, 116-118.

The Iron Age urnfield and settlement of Someren-'Waterdael'

Fokko Kortlang[1]

I   INTRODUCTION

One of the fields of research in the current Meuse-Demer-Scheldt (MDS) project is the study of the long-term transformations of the cultural landscape. The object of study is not merely the landscape

[1] I am indebted to Nico Roymans for his inspiring supervision of the investigation and his critical comments on the manuscript. I also wish to thank Paul van der Kroft and Edy Mulié (IO-Graph) for the digital processing and layout of the figures.

Fig. 1. Location of Someren in the Netherlands.

in a physical sense, but also as a mental construction of the former inhabitants.[2] In order to realize this research aim, a strategy was chosen in which several micro-regional projects in the MDS area form the starting-point. Here, the settlement history and the relation between man and landscape are studied on the basis of large-scale, long-term excavation projects together with field surveys, historical and historical-geographical research. In addition to Oss, Weert and Geldrop, the micro-region of Someren is now one of the main focuses of research within the South Netherlands project.

Since 1991, the IPP has been carrying out rescue excavations in Someren. Like so many municipalities in North Brabant, Someren is dependent on the arable land around the old village centre for its development plan. Extensive old arable complexes have fallen prey to new housing schemes in Someren in recent years. After the residential areas on the (south) west side of the village had been built towards the end of the 1980s, the arable land on the east side of the village centre was earmarked for development. In 1990, traces of an Iron Age urnfield were discovered during the construction of roads for the new development plan 'Waterdael'. In the course of 1991 and 1992, the IPP was able to excavate almost the entire urnfield. In addition to graves and traces of habitation from the Iron Age, settlement traces from the Roman period and High Middle Ages were also discovered.

Since 1991 an excavation campaign has taken place every year, varying in duration from several months to more than seven months (1994). The rescue excavations are carried out prior to the preparation of a new site for building. The excavation team generally consists of a small fixed group of IPP staff and several members of the local working group of amateur archaeologists. This team is supple-

---

[2] Roymans 1996, 240 ff. See for example Roymans (1995), in which a long-term perspective of the mythical landscape is given on the basis of archaeological, historical and folkloric information, with a number of urnfields from the MDS region as a starting-point. See also Roymans/Theuws and Roymans/Kortlang, this volume.

mented in the summer months by archaeology students from the various Dutch Universities.[3]

The excavation at Someren can be described as a typical '*es*' excavation. Underneath an anthropogenic '*plaggen*' soil of late-medieval origin, settlement traces can be observed on one level which – at the present stage of research – cover a time-scale from the Early Iron Age (ca 650 BC) up to and including the High Middle Ages (ca 1250 AD). Thanks to the protective effect of the *plaggen* cover, which in places is more than one metre thick, the traces have been relatively well preserved. The long time-span covered by the archaeological traces, together with the large scale of the excavations (at present an area of almost 20 hectares has been uncovered), enable us to sketch a diachronic picture of the habitation which may be regarded as representative for the central part of the MDS area.

This article deals with the urnfield of Someren-'Waterdael' and the associated Iron Age settlement traces encountered during the excavation campaigns of 1991 to 1997. The urnfield was the starting-point for the analysis for two reasons. A first pragmatic reason is that the analysis of the urnfield has been completed. This is in contrast to the settlement data, which are added to with every new excavation campaign. Although the processing of this material is gradually progressing, there is still a considerable backlog. With the temporary conclusion of the excavations in 1998, however, a preliminary balance can be drawn up. The second reason is that the Waterdael urnfield was almost entirely excavated, and is therefore a good starting-point for getting a grasp on all kinds of aspects of the living community, such as demography, social structure and ideas and values. The urnfield analysis serves as a basis for the interpretation of the settlement data.

In the following chapter the area around Someren will be discussed. The distribution pattern of archaeological sites will be dealt with against the background of the pre-modern cultural landscape. In addition, this chapter will give a brief impression of the excavation area east of the village centre. Chapter 3 provides an analysis of the urnfield. In addition to a description of traces and finds, an attempt is made to grasp the dynamics of the urnfield in time and space. Burial monuments and cremation graves form the basis for a demographic analysis and social interpretation. Chapter 4 outlines the Iron Age settlement traces. Topics such as houses, yards, structure and dynamics of the settlement will be briefly discussed. Finally, in chapter 5 some concluding remarks will be made. Urnfield and settlement are discussed in relation to each other in order to arrive at a comprehensive picture of the community which inhabited the coversand plateau east of the present village centre between about 650 BC and the beginning of this era.

[3]   The scientific direction was in the hands of Dr Nico Roymans. From the start, the author was in charge of the day-to-day management of the project. We are grateful to all students, volunteers and other persons who contributed in whatever way to the fieldwork. A special word of thanks is due to Martin, René, Jos, Will, Nell, André, Ad, Frans, and, last but not least, our crane operator Ton Luiten.
      The municipality of Someren and the Province of North Brabant funded an important part of the excavation. In addition, financial contributions were received from the Stichting Nederlands Museum voor Anthropologie en Praehistorie at Amsterdam, the University of Amsterdam, the Lionsclub Deurne-Asten-Someren and the Rabobank Someren. Without the enthusiastic efforts of the above-mentioned persons and the financial support of these institutions the investigation would never have been possible.

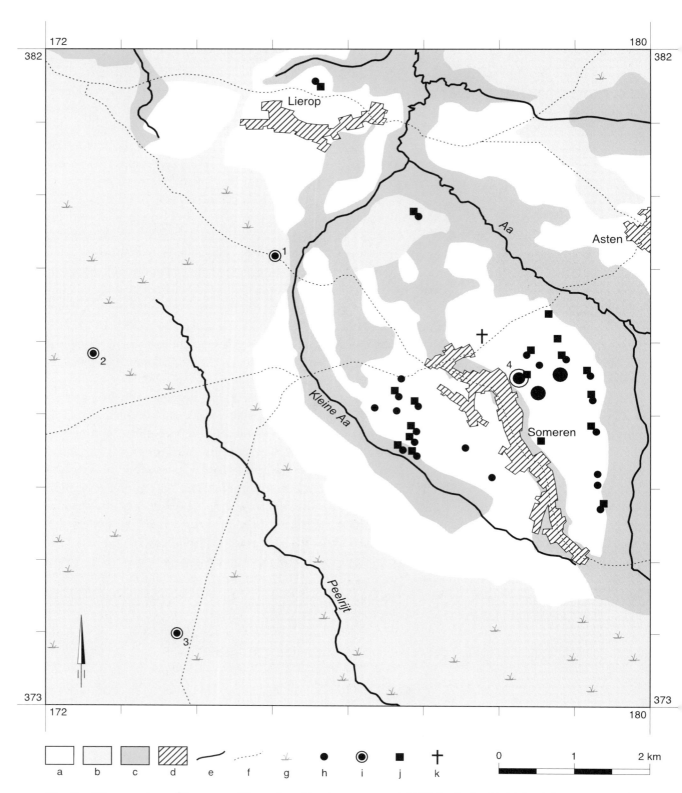

Fig. 2a. Micro-region of Someren. The cultural landscape around 1850 (scale 1 : 50.000) with overview of the findspots.

a. fields; b. heathland; c. grassland; d. major zone of habitation (village); e. river; f. major roads; g. wet zones; h. Iron Age site; i. Iron Age urnfield; j. Roman period site; k. medieval parish church.

1. 'Philips-kampeerterrein' urnfield; 2. 'Hoenderboom' urnfield; 3. 'Kraaijenstark' urnfield; 4. 'Someren-Waterdael' urnfield

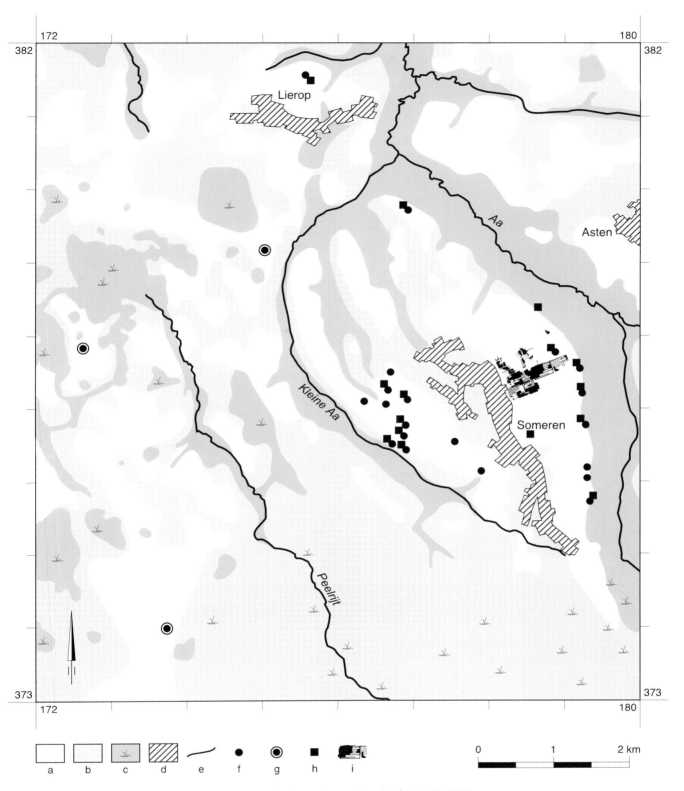

Fig. 2b. Micro-region of Someren. Geomorphological situation (scale 1 : 50.000).
a. higher coversand area; b. lower coversand area; c. stream valleys and marshy lowlands; d. major zone of habitation (village) around 1850; e. river; f. Iron Age site; g. Early Iron Age urnfield (ca 775-500 BC); h. Roman period site; i. excavated area 1990-1997

2 THE MICRO-REGION OF SOMEREN: LANDSCAPE AND ARCHAEOLOGY

2.1 THE AREA AROUND SOMEREN

Figure 2 (a and b) shows the pre-modern landscape of the micro-region of Someren based on 19th-century topographical maps. The figure is important for various reasons. First, the landscape underwent relatively few changes from the 13th/14th century until the end of the 19th century. Second, the pre-industrial use of land gives us an indication of the agrarian quality of the various landscape zones. For example, the wet-dry and fertile-infertile relations are easily visible. One object of research is the extent to which the patterns given by this map are also relevant to older periods. Finally, the map is indispensable to the evaluation of the distribution pattern of archaeological sites in the micro-region.

Morphologically, the area can be characterized as a gently undulating coversand landscape, the foundation for which was laid under the influence of the wind in the last cold phase of the Pleistocene (*Weichselian*). The stream valleys provide an intricate segmentation of the landscape. The pre-industrial cultural landscape of the micro-region of Someren can be roughly divided into two halves along a diagonal NW-SE line, coinciding with the river Kleine Aa. West of the line is an uncultivated zone of wasteland consisting of extensive heaths and peatbogs. The further south one goes, the wetter this area becomes. East of the line we find the cultivated zone with settlements, arable fields and (in the stream valleys) pasture- and haylands. From the Late Middle Ages until well into the 19th century heaths, fields and stream valleys formed the complements of the traditional agricultural system based on mixed farming with the production of manure as a major connecting element.

In the uncultivated zone there were, until the beginning of the 20th century, extensive areas of heath with marshy depressions, such as the Lierop, Someren and Strabrecht heaths. Large areas of this relatively infertile landscape were reclaimed in the first half of this century or planted with pine. In the marshy depressions peat had developed which was used as fuel from the High Middle Ages on. The great expansion of heaths took place in the Late Middle Ages and was linked with the growth of sheepbreeding and sod-cutting for the fertilization of the fields. Before then the vegetation appears to have consisted not only of heath but also of (poor quality?) deciduous forest. We have evidence that the zone of the later heathlands originally was an attractive habitat for prehistoric farming communities. The evidence includes several stray axe finds from the Neolithic and the locations of three urnfields, two of which certainly date from the Early Iron Age. It may be assumed that there were settlements in the vicinity of the urnfields. This zone was probably fairly intensively inhabited in the Late Bronze Age/Early Iron Age. Degradation of the sandy soils with a low loam content as a result of deforestation and the relatively extensive celtic field agriculture may have been the reason that habitation definitively stopped in this zone in the course of the Middle Iron Age.[4]

Within the cultivated zone, the coversand plateau on which the village of Someren is situated, is enclosed by the streams Kleine Aa and Aa. Together with a finer network of brooks running southeast-northwest they drained the area. The somewhat higher grounds around the village centre had

---

[4] The only Roman find from the heath area is a small hoard of 43 coins dated to around 100 AD. It was discovered in the immediate surroundings of the southernmost urnfield. Since the heath reclamations were usually carried out by hand, the chance is slight that conspicuous features such as a Roman Age cemetery were overlooked. See also chapter 5 and Roymans/Theuws, this volume.

been an attractive place for settlement since prehistoric times. In contrast to the areas of coarser sand in the west zone, this plateau consisted of sand with a higher loam content and therefore was less sensitive to soil degradation. Since the Middle Iron Age, the coversand plateaus in the cultivated area had been the most important areas for settlement. The stream valleys, on the other hand, were regularly submerged because of insufficient drainage in the winter months. Although they were important for all kinds of purposes, they were not suitable for permanent habitation. Originally the stream valleys were forested with alder carr. Not until the High and Late Middle Ages were they reclaimed and cultivated as hay- and pastureland. The reclamations led to better drainage, so that habitation became possible in lower-lying areas. Since the Late Middle Ages (13th/14th century) the entire sandy plateau between the Grote and Kleine Aa was almost permanently in use as arable land. Settlement had by then moved from the coversand plateau to the adjacent lower areas. The map (fig. 2) shows that in the 19th century the village of Someren was situated in an elongated and relatively wet zone of a former stream valley. Archaeological investigation has shown that this is a relatively modern situation; at any rate it does not predate the 13th century.

What immediately strikes one in figure 2 is the concentrations of findspots on the coversand ridges west and east of the village of Someren. Up to fifteen years ago, this distribution pattern was completely different. The coversand ridges on which a thick *plaggen* layer had developed since the Late Middle Ages due to intensive fertilization, formed 'blind spots' on the archaeological distribution map. Because of the thick arable layer, archaeological finds hardly ever surfaced during normal ploughing. This changed when the old arable land was built up. The frequent earth-moving regularly revealed traces and finds from the Iron Age, Roman period and the Middle Ages. Many of the findspots were registered by the local archaeologist, Jos Van der Weerden. The distribution pattern of archaeological sites is therefore strongly influenced by the 'blind spot effect' of the protective *es* cover on the one hand, and by the extent to which the old arable land has, in recent years, been destroyed by new building schemes and local sand extraction.[5] Whether it is representative or not, the map certainly shows that the coversand plateaus around the village centre of Someren had been attractive areas for settlement since late prehistory, as may be seen below.

2.2   THE EXCAVATION SITE

On the east side of Someren village there is an extensive complex of old arable land, situated on an elongated coversand plateau which is bordered on the east by the valley of the river Aa. The north part of the plateau has been badly affected by new village development in the past decades. Directly west of the Aa valley is the highest part of the arable complex (ca 29.00 + NAP), which bears the toponym 'Hoge Akkers' (High Fields). Towards the west the area gradually slopes down to ca 27.00 + NAP ('Lage Akkers': Low Fields). The post-medieval *plaggen* layer varies in thickness from 80 cm to over a metre.

During the Holocene, a dense mixed oak forest had developed on the relatively loamy coversand, which, under the influence of man, gradually became more open.[6] Although the area at the present

---

[5]   The radius of action and the period in which Jos Van der Weerden was active as an archaeologist in Someren also play a part here.

[6]   Cf. Janssen 1972. The many hundreds of traces of pits

left by fallen trees found on the excavation site are striking. They mainly date from before the Iron Age and indicate that the area must have been fairly wooded. The soil may be described as a moderpodzol, typi-

surface level appears to be relatively flat, on removal of the *plaggen* layer the subsoil is interspersed with former small peat bogs and depressions. These are Late-Pleistocene blown out basins varying in depth from several decimeters to over three metres in one case.[7] The shallow depressions periodically submerged in late prehistory, and must have been recognizable to man as zones with a different kind of vegetation, perhaps an alder carr type of cover. In the deeper (waterfilled) depressions peat had developed in the course of the Holocene. We have been able to demonstrate that in a number of these the peat was extracted in the High Middle Ages. Shortly afterwards – probably in the 12th or 13th century – most of the depressions were filled up by farmers and used as arable land. The rigorous reclamations carried out by medieval farmers had a levelling effect on the original micro-relief. As a result, the archaeological record was considerably depleted, particularly on the tops of the former sandy dunes. After the Late Middle Ages, however, the *es* cover preserved the archaeological remains from further destruction.

2.3   EXCAVATION METHOD

From the start the investigation at Someren has focused on the systematic excavation of sites threatened by new housing development. Excavation usually took place prior to the preparation of a section for building, by means of: a. the excavation of planned road trajectories; b. the digging of trial trenches 5-8 m wide and often hundreds of metres long and c. the excavation of larger areas. In addition to settlement sites and cemeteries, attention was focused on the off-site investigation of depressions, fields, ditch systems and old road patterns.

As already mentioned in the introduction, all traces of habitation dating from prehistory up into the Middle Ages are found on the same level immediately underneath the protective *es* cover. In order to reach as far as the 'legible' level, the post-medieval *es* cover was removed with the help of a crane. With regard to the interpretation of the traces, post-depositional anthropogenic processes (e.g. ploughing and reclamation) should be taken into account, which have led to the disappearance of the original surface layer. In the case of Someren, it may be stated that at least the first 20-30 cm of the original traces have been 'decapitated'. The first – and generally the only – excavation level is therefore some 20 to 30 cm below the original surface.

Between 1991 and 1997 almost 20 hectares of arable land were excavated in an area ca 1 by 0.75 km, following the above strategy. The excavated area forms an almost continuous west-east oriented transverse section through the coversand ridge from stream valley to stream valley. Apart from the Iron Age settlement traces which will be discussed below, the investigation revealed traces of some isolated farms and a somewhat larger settlement from the Roman period; two settlement nuclei from the Early Middle Ages as well as three hamlets and many scattered farmsteads from the High Middle Ages. Stray finds of flint artefacts indicate that hunter/gatherer groups inhabited the area in the Mesolithic. So far, no traces or finds are known from the period between the Mesolithic and the Early Iron Age. However, this seems to be due to a *Forschungslücke* rather than to a real hiatus in settlement. Despite the large-scale nature of the excavations, our knowledge of the local habitation is still incomplete.

cal of a forest floor. This soil was assimilated into the arable layer during later reclamations and is therefore no longer present.

[7]   Cf. Broertjes 1977, 21ff.

The first traces of the urnfield were discovered in the spring of 1990 during the construction of roads for the new housing scheme Waterdael. After reporting the discovery, the State Archaeological Service (ROB) carried out a two-week-long rescue excavation. A total of 21 graves and burial monuments (grave nos. 86-106) were investigated: 17 circular ditches; 1 long-bed and 3 graves without a peripheral structure. In the subsequent campaigns of 1991 and 1992, the IPP was able to excavate the remaining part of the cemetery almost entirely.

The necropolis extends over an area measuring over 350 m in length by a maximum width of ca 100 m. It is elongated in shape and is oriented more or less northwest-southeast. The graves could be recognized in the excavation area by the brownish-grey fill of circular, oblong or rectangular ditches enclosing the cremation graves (fig. 3). A total of 185 graves and/or burial monuments were excavated, including one inhumation grave. There must originally have been low mounds inside the ditch structures. However, these disappeared when the area was reclaimed in the High Middle Ages. As mentioned above, one should take into account the fact that the top layer (ca 30 cm) of the occupation level at the time has been assimilated into the medieval arable layer. One of the consequences of this is that shallow ditches may have been lost. This would appear to be the case in the empty zone directly east of long-bed no. 89 and at the northwest boundary of the cemetery.[8] What applies to the shallow ditches also applies to the less deeply dug cremation burials. Of the 185 graves and burial monuments, only 72 cremation graves (39%) have survived the post-depositional processes more or less intact. In a large number of cases only minimal cremation remains have been preserved, mostly in mole tunnels which penetrated to a deeper level at the place of the grave. Although not every peripheral structure still contained a grave, we may assume that each grave monument originally had a central burial.

For the rest, the cemetery has been preserved in a reasonably good condition. The settlement traces from the High Middle Ages in the north and south zones caused relatively little damage to the burials. Unfortunately, we did not have the opportunity to investigate a strip north side of the cemetery which had already been paved. Nor was it possible to excavate several 1- to 2-metre-wide strips on either side of the excavated road sections.

As far as lay-out, types of burial monument and cremation rite are concerned, the cemetery of Someren-Waterdael is typical of the urnfields belonging to the *Niederrheinische Grabhügelkultur* (NGK).[9] Generally, the body of the deceased was cremated on a funeral pyre. The deceased's relatives picked out (part of) the cremated bones from the remains of the pyre and collected them in an urn or a leather or textile cloth. The remains were then buried in a shallow pit, around which a ditch was usually dug. A low mound was raised over the cremation grave with the sand from the ditch and with sods brought from elsewhere.[10] It is surprising that at the Someren 'urnfield' the cremation remains

---

[8]   The latter zone has moreover been seriously disturbed by post-medieval sand-extraction strips.

[9]   For this term see Kersten 1948 and the discussion in

Roymans/Kortlang, this volume.

[10]   Little can be said about the height of the earth mounds. Most would seldom have been higher than

Fig. 3. Someren-Waterdael. Circular ditches stand out against the yellow coversand. The dark spot at the back of the excavation is a depression filled with peat (photograph Fokko Kortlang).

(with one possible exception) were never found in an urn. The remains were mostly discovered in the form of a compact lump (*beenderblok*) in a small pit (fig. 6c). Although there is no direct evidence for this, due to the poor conditions for conservation, we assume that they were originally buried in a cloth of perishable material.[11] The cremation remains are virtually free of charcoal, indicating that the bones were carefully collected.

Because the original surface is no longer present, the chance of finding pyre remains is minimal. The regular occurrence of charcoal in the ditch fills (sometimes in the form of small branches and twigs) indicates that cremation took place in, or in the immediate vicinity of the cemetery. In two cases we have evidence for the location of a pyre. In both cases this is a spot of red scorched sand, mixed with lumps of charcoal and small pieces of burnt bone. The first burnt spot was found at the bottom of the circular ditch (east side) around grave no. 68. From the fact that the ditch had already been dug when the fire was lit, it may be concluded that grave 68 already existed and that the crema-

one metre (cf. Holwerda 1913, 4 ff.). I assume that the three largest monuments on the south side of the cemetery would have had a more impressive appearance than the other graves. A height of 1.5 to 2 metres is quite possible. It is striking that the largest mound (grave 4) served in the High Middle Ages as a point of

orientation for the construction of a ditch which was probably used as a kind of basis for reclamation.

[11] We do, however, consider it possible, in view of the few intact graves, that the number of urn graves was originally higher, especially in the northeast part.

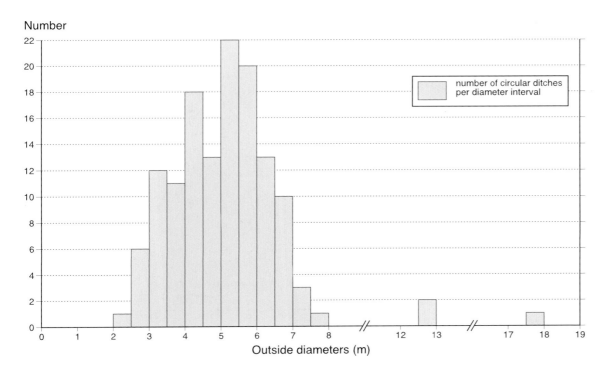

Fig. 4. Someren-Waterdael. Distribution of diameters of circular ditches.

tion remains of the pyre were intended for another grave monument. The second burnt spot was in the immediate surroundings of the cemetery, ca 30 m east of grave no. 15.

Grave gifts, following the general pattern in Dutch urnfields, are extremely scarce. Only a few cremation graves contain (sherds of) pottery burnt on the pyre. Some pottery (mostly fragmentary) was also discovered in the ditches around the graves. Both the burnt pottery and some burnt animal bone from five graves suggests that food was offered with the deceased, or that a ritual meal was held by the relatives at the cremation spot.

3.2   GRAVES AND BURIAL MONUMENTS

Various types of graves and burial monuments can be distinguished in the urnfield. With regard to the burial monuments, a distinction can be made on the basis of the peripheral structures around the mounds between graves surrounded by a circular ditch, graves with a rectangular ditch and graves with an elongated ditched enclosure on either side (so-called *langbedden* or long-beds). In addition, the cemetery has graves without a peripheral structure (so-called flat graves) of which it is not always certain whether they once had a low mound. One cremation grave was dug in the circular ditch of another grave (grave no. 108).[12] The graves themselves consist mainly of shallow pits with varying amounts of cremation remains. The diameter of the burial pits fluctuates around 30 cm with a depth

[12]   Another flat grave (185) was discovered in 1995 among Iron Age settlement traces several hundred me- tres southeast of the cemetery.

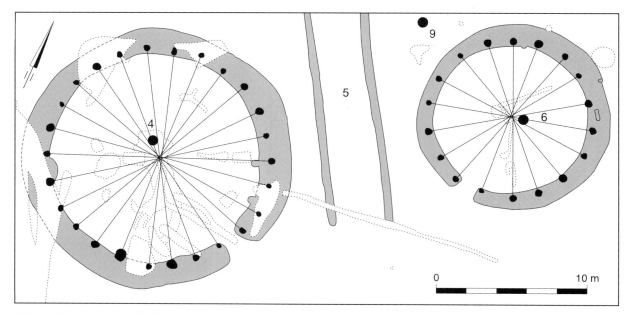

Fig. 5. Someren-Waterdael. Regularity of the post-circles of graves 4 and 6, shown by means of connecting lines.

of 40 cm at the most. Moreover, one inhumation grave was found in the urnfield dating from the final phase of the cemetery. The various categories will now be discussed in more detail.

Circular ditches
Burial monuments with a circular ditch represent the largest group in the cemetery. They generally lie close together and sometimes form compact clusters. Intersections are never found. All circular ditches have an opening in the southeast. The orientation of the openings varies from 95 degrees to 185 degrees from north on the map (fig. 7). Most circular ditches have an outer diameter of between 2 and 8 metres (fig. 4).[13] Considerably larger in size are the ditches belonging to three more or less aligned monuments on the south side of the cemetery (grave 4: ca 18 m; graves 6 and 7: ca 13 m). These burial monuments are also remarkable in another respect. At the bottom of the three ditches vague traces were found of a widely-spaced circle of 26, 18 and 21 posts respectively.[14] The post-circles show a high degree of regularity. By connecting the posts opposite each other with lines, a central intersection occurs approximately at the cremation grave (fig. 5). There are various methods of placing the posts in a way that a central intersection emerges, for instance by bringing the posts in one line via a central point.[15] Post-circles around a central grave are a regularly recurring feature in the urnfields of the MDS area. Most of them date from the Early Iron Age.[16] In most cases the diameter

[13] The depth of the ditches varies from several centimetres to 40 cm from the excavation surface. Most are 10 to 20 cm in depth. In order to calculate the original depths, at least 30 cm must be added to this.

[14] In the sections of the postholes which had been dug and then filled in again (diameter 30-50 cm), the post-cores could still be recognized. These were round in diameter and had a blunt base. The diameter of the posts varied from 10 to 20 cm (usually about 20 cm).

From the bottom of the ditch the posts could reach a depth of over 40 cm. This is 90 cm below the excavation surface, ca 120 cm under the occupation level of the time. The average distance between the posts was at grave 4: 185 cm, grave 6: 180 cm and grave 7: 175 cm. The diameter of the post-circles is 15 m, 11 m and 11.5 m respectively.

[15] For various methods, see Lohof 1991, 159-169.

[16] Cf. Van der Sanden 1994, 204-205; Tol, this volume.

of the circles is over 10 metres. Both circles of widely- spaced posts and picket-fences occur. Most of the post-circles are found on the outside of the circular ditch. In some cases a ditch is lacking. The post-circles of Someren-Waterdael are the only ones to be situated within the ditch. Although this could not be demonstrated conclusively, they appear to have been erected prior to the digging of the circular ditch and the raising of the burial mound. This might imply that they only functioned for a short time, for example, as a temporary demarcation of a sacred space. Although the length of time between the erection of the post-circle and the digging of the circular ditch cannot be indicated, this does support the idea that the burial ritual was a phased process.[17] If we assume that approximately 1/3 of the posts was in the ground and that they were placed before the ditches were dug, we can re-solve the above-ground section to a height of 2 to 2.5 metres. A construction with cross-beams con-necting the posts at the top is possible, but cannot, of course, be proved.

type of monument or interment	number		with cremation remains
circular ditches	135	(73 %)	43
long-beds	15	(8 %)	7
rectangular ditches	18	(10 %)	7
interment in peripheral ditch	1	(0.5 %)	1
flat(?) graves	15	(8 %)	15
inhumation grave	1	(0.5 %)	-
total	**185**	**(100 %)**	**72**

Table 1. Someren-Waterdael: different types of peripheral structures and interments.

Long-beds
Scattered over the urnfield, singly or in clusters, are fifteen elongated burial monuments which are re-ferred to as *langbedden*. Originally the long-beds consisted of a low, elongated mound bordered on ei-ther side by a ditch. In four cases, three parallel ditches form the peripheral structures of two flanking long-beds. The length of the monuments varies from 8 to 145 m. The width is between 3 and 5.5 m. In 7 cases a cremation grave was found on the longitudinal axis of the long-beds. The extremely long grave even contained two graves, one of which lay precisely in the middle. All the long-beds are ori-ented northwest-southeast. As a result, the southeast openings of the long-beds correspond to those of the circular ditches. They also more or less mark the longitudinal axis of the cemetery and the di-rection in which it expanded (fig. 7). However, the orientation of the long-beds is generally much more heterogeneous. In most urnfields, they follow the local relief and/or a prehistoric road.[18]

[17] Cf. Lohof (1991, 160-161) for some examples of Middle Bronze Age burial mounds with post-circles, and also the remark made by Annaert/Van Impe 1985, 4. As already mentioned, the traces were generally vague, and were only observed at the bottom of the ditches. At graves 4 and 6 several postholes were visi-ble at a higher level outside the ditch. Clear cutting of postholes by the ditch was not observed.

[18] Verlinde 1987, 186; Kooi 1979, 159 ff.; Roymans, this volume; Tol, this volume.

6a

6b

146

6c

Fig. 6. Someren-Waterdael. Photograph a: circular ditch of grave 7 intersected by the traces of a medieval farm-house. Photograph b: part of long-bed 5. Photograph c: compact lump of cremation remains in a small pit (photographs Fokko Kortlang).

Since the late Bronze Age (Ha A1), long-beds have been a widespread phenomenon within the urn-field cultures of the Northwest-European plain.[19] The range of forms is substantial. In the *Niederrheinische Grabhügelkultur* region, long-beds of the *Riethoven* and *Goirle* type (elongated ditched structures with more or less rounded short sides) are the most common.[20] Long-beds in which the short sides of the ditches are missing, were only known from Someren-Waterdael. Recently, howev-er, long-beds of the 'Someren type' were also discovered in the urnfields of Mierlo-Hout and in Weert, both within a radius of less than 15 km around Someren. The dating evidence suggests that this type of monument is characteristic for the Early Iron Age.[21]

[19] See for example Roymans/Kortlang, this volume, note 24, and further Verlinde 1987, 173 ff.; Kooi 1979, 130 ff.

[20] Verwers 1966, 46-57; see also however Verlinde 1987, 286 ff.

[21] Mierlo-Hout: Tol, this volume; Weert-Raak: Tol in preparation. Urnfields in the South Netherlands in which long-beds have been found with at least one short open side are: Kaulille (Engels/Van Impe 1985); Posterholt (Willems 1983, 221 ff.); Berkel-Enschot (Kleij 1993, 21). In all three cases the short sides of the long-beds could only be observed on one side. Only the long-bed of grave 89 at Someren-Waterdael possi-bly had a closing ditch on the north side, according to the amateur archaeologists who excavated it.

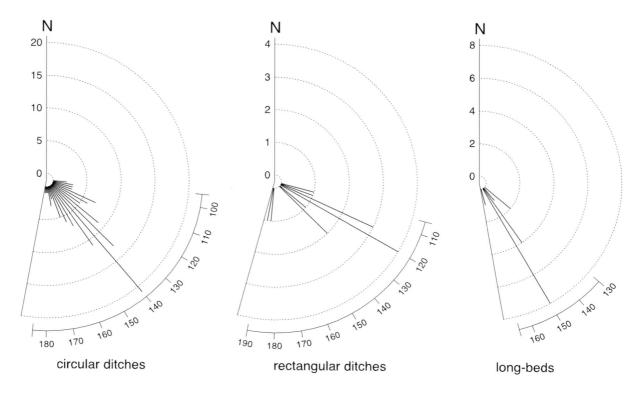

Fig. 7. Someren-Waterdael. Orientation of interruptions in circular ditches, rectangular graves and long-beds.

Rectangular ditches

Rectangular burial monuments are concentrated on the north side of the cemetery. In five cases we have composite monuments, consisting of two connected ditched structures. As far as could be determined, all ditches have an opening in the southeast. The sides of the separate rectangles measure between ca 4.5 and 8.5 m. Grave 179 is the exception, with 22 by 18 m. The monument is divided into two equal sections by means of a transverse ditch. It is somewhere in-between a more or less rectangular monument with an internal division and two flanking long-beds with a south-north orientation. In the southeast corner of the west 'long-bed' there is an opening. Unfortunately the monument could only partially be excavated. A cremation grave was not found, so that its function as a burial monument is not certain.[22] Judging from the context, an interpretation as burial monument is plausible. It might even have been a double burial. Parallels for grave 179 are rare. Only the enclosure

---

[22] See the discussion in Van der Sanden (1994, 205 ff.), in which several more monumental ditched structures (with post structures) in the cemetery of Oss dating from the Middle Iron Age are interpreted as cult places, also in view of the considerable amount of find material from the ditches and their exceptional size. However, I am of the opinion that these monuments were primarily intended as burial monuments, and that only at a later stage did the cult element (ancestor cult) prevail. A good example is monument R26 and annex R26a (with cremation grave). The post structures around both ditches were probably added at a later date. The absence of a cremation grave in R26 is probably due to postdepositional processes: a subrecent ditch runs through the centre of the monument.

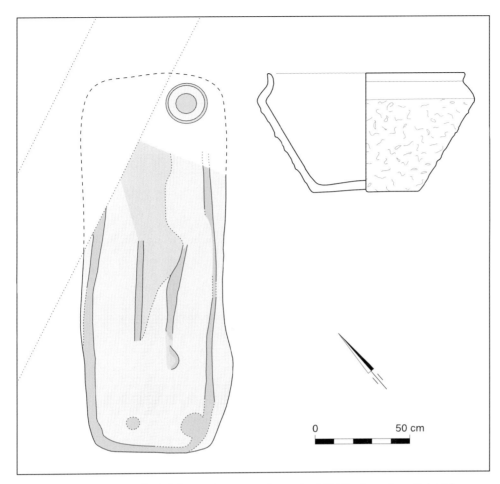

Fig. 8. Someren-Waterdael. Inhumation grave from the Middle Iron Age (5th/4th century BC). Grave, scale 1 : 20; roughened bowl, scale 1 : 4.

R2 in the cemetery of Oss-Ussen (province of North Brabant), which dates from the Middle Iron Age, is similar regarding size and form;[23] it lacks, however, a transverse ditch.

The (burial?) structure 163 in the northwest corner of the cemetery poses a problem. The structure is badly eroded, and only several metres of a ditch are left. It may have formed part of a long-bed or of a rectangular structure. Six shallow postholes probably also belong to the monument. Three of them lie parallel to the above ditch, at regular intervals, and then continue in a westerly direction at an angle of almost 90 degrees. The post structure supports the idea that this was once a rectangular ditched structure surrounded by a palisade. Further west, the site is too disturbed for any conclusion to be drawn about the size and function of the monument. A parallel for this structure is the enclosure R26 mentioned in note 22 from the Middle Iron Age at Oss-Ussen, which has been interpreted as a cult place.

[23] Van der Sanden 1994, 211-212. The enclosure is, however, seriously damaged, so that any possible cen- tral burial is missing.

Isolated cremation graves

16 cremation graves were found without any peripheral structure. They are referred to here by the term 'flatgraves', although some of them may originally have had a low mound. Grave 108 is the only one to have been dug in the circular ditch of an already existing burial mound (109). Most of the flat graves are situated in the periphery of the urnfield. Graves 148 and 166, situated in the northwest part, may have lost a possible peripheral structure due to the erosion of the site. In the case of graves nos. 87, 90 and 95, a monument is unlikely since the graves are far too close to another burial monument. Flat graves 16, 17 and 185 were discovered among Iron Age settlement traces. The location of graves 16 and 17 may be included in the border zone of the urnfield, but grave 185 lies beyond it.

An inhumation grave

A remarkable find is inhumation grave 184, discovered in the northwest border zone of the urnfield. Although the traces were vague, it was possible to distinguish traces of a coffin and possibly the silhouette of a body within a rectangular pit of ca 2.10 × 0.80 × 0.25 m (fig. 8). In the northeast corner of the pit (head end?) there was an earthenware pot which may originally have contained food or drink. The high carinated shoulder of the pot, which was roughened from the base to the polished shoulder, betrays the influence of Northern French *Marne* pottery.

Inhumation graves in these regions are an unusual phenomenon in the Iron Age. They are completely absent from the urnfields. The only examples from the Iron Age in the Netherlands are known from a small cemetery dating from the Middle Iron Age at Geldermalsen (province of Gelderland), excavated at the beginning of the 1990s.[24] In the *Hunsrück-Eifel-Kultur* (HEK) area and the Northern French region (*Marne culture*) inhumation remains the rule rather than the exception until well into La Tène B (400-250 BC).[25] The question arises whether the inhumation grave with 'Marne-type' pot from Someren-Waterdael should be interpreted as a Northern French influence. On the basis of the pottery, the grave can be dated in the 5th or early 4th century BC.[26]

3.3   POTTERY AND OTHER FINDS

As stated in section 3.1, the urnfields in the Lower Rhine area are characteristic for their lack of grave goods. This is the case in this cemetery too. Apart from pottery, which was mainly collected from the peripheral ditched structures, the finds are limited to a perforated amber bead (grave 30), some fragments of worked bone and antler (graves 50, 175) and six iron objects (graves 4, 6 and 175).

[24] Hulst in prep. The Iron Age cemetery (ca 60 x 40 m) consists of 16 cremation and 7 inhumation graves. No peripheral structures were observed. The richest grave (grave 1) was that of an adult woman (34-40 years). As grave gifts, she had around her neck a bronze *torque*, and around her right and left wrists respectively an open and a closed bronze bracelet. To the left of the head end there were three pieces of pottery an iron knife and a pig's rib. The date of the cemetery as a whole is between ca 450 and 400/375 BC. I take this

opportunity to thank Rudi Hulst for making his information available to me.

[25] For a survey of these regions see Roymans 1990, 217 ff.

[26] Oral communication Peter van den Broeke. According to Van den Broeke (1987, 33), the Marne influence on handformed pottery in the South Netherlands applies to his phases E (500-450 BC) and F (450-400/375 BC). No influences can be observed in phase H.

Pottery

Out of a total of 583 pottery fragments and 4 more or less complete pots it was possible to identify 107 different specimens. Only in 25 cases – those in which the profiles provided sufficient information – could the form of the pot be established (figs. 9 – 11). Two items of pottery were spindles. If we take a closer look at the variety of forms of the pottery, the first thing one notices is that the typical urn forms from the Early Iron Age, such as *Schräghals* pots and tall, roughened biconical pots of the Harpstedt type are lacking in the Someren-Waterdael urnfield.[27] The range of forms includes: open dishes (4 x); open to closed bowls (12 x); more or less closed pots (7 x) and several small cups.[28] Decoration of the pottery is regularly found: nail impressions on the rim (11 x), and also on the belly (11 x); combed decoration on belly and shoulder (5 x) and groove or scratch lines (2 x). All the pottery is tempered with pot grit, occasionally in combination with sand. Moreover, in 14 cases the surface of the pots is polished and in 20 cases roughcast. In four cases both techniques have been combined.

Only 9 times was pottery found in combination with cremation remains. With the exception of the pots from grave 88 and grave 90 (fig. 11, 88.1 and 90.1), this pottery had been secondarily burnt to varying degrees. It seems plausible to assume that in these cases the pottery was also burnt on the funeral pyre, either as a container with food and drink, or as the remains of a ritual meal consumed by the relatives during the cremation. Only the unburnt pot from grave 90 can be interpreted as an urn. This is less certain in the case of grave 88, because of the small size of the pot. In the remaining 62 graves the pottery was found in the peripheral ditches. It mostly consisted of stray sherds, although more complete pots were also found. The sherds in the ditches generally belong to one, occasionally to two or three specimens. A greater number was found in the circular ditch around grave 4, from which sherds from at least 9 pots were collected.[29] Remarkable are several potsherds, discovered in various peripheral structures, which show such a strong similarity that they could have come from the same pot. In these cases the peripheral structures in question are all situated in each other's proximity (e.g. 6.3 and 8.1) or even adjacent to each other (84 and 85; 135.1, 136 and 138; 144 and 145.1). Whether the distribution of these sherds is due to intentional action or to various kinds of postdepositional processes is uncertain.

29% of the pottery from the peripheral structures shows signs of secondary burning. A reasonable explanation for this is that the pottery had come into contact with the pyre before ending up in the ditch. In addition, some of the pottery may perhaps be interpreted as being settlement refuse – taking into account the fact that ditches make excellent artefact traps. For example, there are settlement traces

[27] Cf. the Early Iron Age urnfields of Beegden (Roymans, this volume) and Someren-'Philipskampeerterrein' (Modderman 1955; 1960/61), where most of the grave pottery (urns) consists of roughened pots of the *Harpstedter Stil* and *Schräghals* pots. Although the vast majority of central burials at Someren-Waterdael is no longer present, so that possible urns may be missed, we assume that the available pottery forms a representative sample.

[28] The difference in dishes, bowls and (tall) pots is based on Van den Broeke's classification (1980, 30): dish: maximum diameter > 2 x the height; bowl: max. diam. = 1.5 – 2 x the height; (tall) pot: max. diam. < 1.5 x height. Van den Broeke makes a further distinction between open pots (type I) and closed pots without neck (type II) and with neck (type III). A further definition is made on the basis of the pot profile in a single, bipartite and tripartite construction.

[29] It should be mentioned that this ditch also contained a fragment of a Late La Tène glass armring (fig. 12, 4.7) and that the pottery lay not only on the floor of the ditch but also at higher levels in the ditch fill. Some specimens may therefore be of later date.

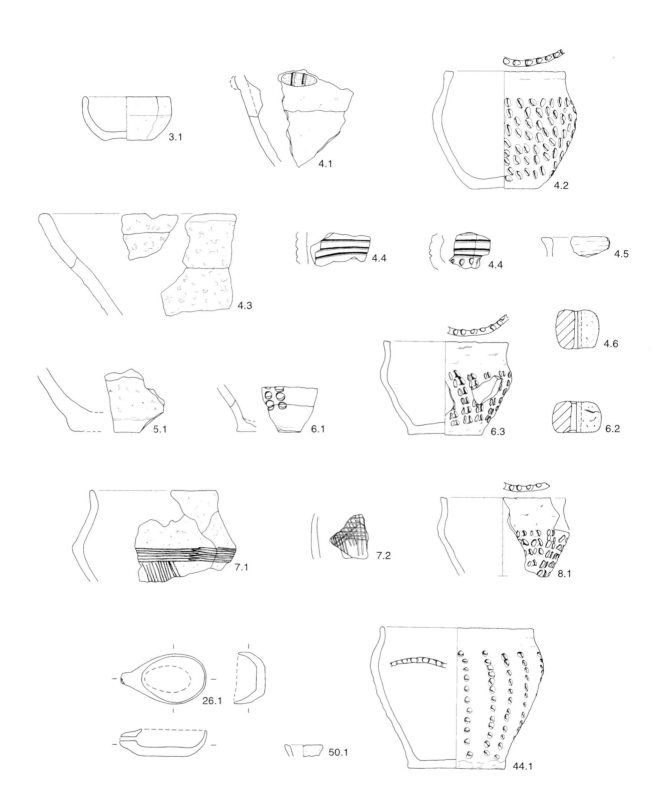

Fig. 9. Someren-Waterdael. Pottery from the cemetery. Scale 1 : 4, except spindle whorls 4.6 and 6.2: scale 1 : 2.

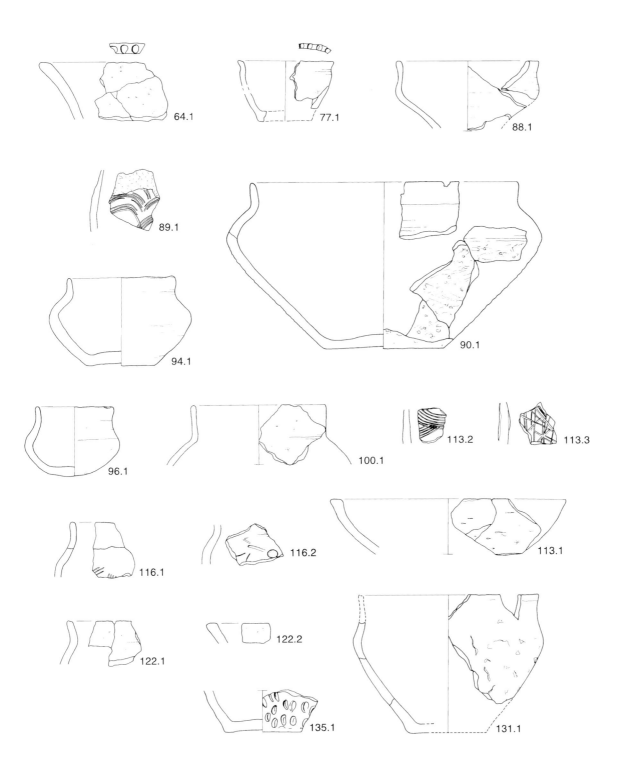

64.1

77.1

88.1

89.1

90.1

94.1

96.1

100.1

113.2

113.3

116.1

116.2

113.1

122.1

122.2

135.1

131.1

Fig. 10. Someren-Waterdael. Pottery from the cemetery. Scale 1 : 4.

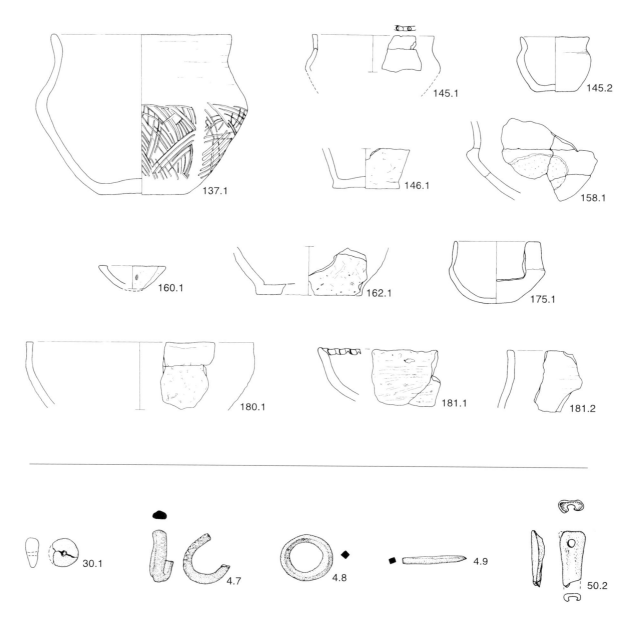

Fig. 11. Someren-Waterdael. Above: pottery from the cemetery (scale 1 : 4). Below: other objects (scale 1 : 2). 30.1 perforated amber bead; 4.7 fragment of a blue glass armring with applied thread of yellow glass paste (Late Iron Age); 4.8 iron ring; 4.9 iron pin; 50.2 perforated fragment of a metatarsus of a sheep(?)

in the southeast corner of the urnfield which date from an advanced stage of the Iron Age. Perhaps some of the sherds in the ditches can be explained in this way, but certainly not all of them. In particular, the more complete pottery, together with that found at a greater distance from the above-mentioned settlement traces, deserves an alternative explanation in the funerary sphere. One can imagine the material remains of ritual meals held by relatives as part of the burial ritual or of an ancestral cult.[30]

[30] Cf. Roymans/Kortlang, this volume, for several Late Bronze Age long-beds with an exceptional amount of pottery in the ditches. See also Van der Sanden 1994, 206 ff., for several rectangular structures (R26 and R49) from the Middle Iron Age at Oss. On the basis of the large quantities of finds (over 3300 sherds, sev-

Description of the pottery

Here follows a brief description of the most relevant pottery, shown in figures 9 to 11. The numbers correspond to the grave- and find-numbers.

3.1   Complete small open bowl. Secondarily burnt on the pyre(?). Origin: among cremation remains.

4.1   Wall fragment with doubly perforated knobbed ear, from the debris layer above the cremation grave. Secondarily burnt. Twelve other sherds probably come from the same pot. Dating: EIA (750-500 BC). Cf. Van den Broeke 1984, 87; Verlinde 1985, 281.

4.2   Bipartite pot, from belly to shoulder and on the rim decorated with fingertip impressions. From the debris layer above cremation grave. Secondarily burnt and distorted by fire. Dating: same context as 4.1.

4.3   Rimsherd from an open dish with a notch in the rim. Roughened to rim. From circular ditch; secondarily burnt. Dating: EIA(?). Cf. Van den Broeke 1984, 75 (fig. 12:3).

4.4   Two secondarily burnt potsherds with grooved decoration. One with fingertip impressions. Origin: circular ditch.

4.5   Rimsherd of a polished pot. Origin: circular ditch.

4.6   Fragment of a spindle. Origin: circular ditch.

5.1   Base fragment of roughened pot. Secondarily burnt. Origin: ditch of long-bed.

6.1   Base fragment of pot with fingertip impressions. Secondarily burnt. Origin: circular ditch.

6.2   Spindle, secondarily burnt. Origin: circular ditch.

6.3   Tripartite bowl. From base to shoulder decorated with vertical rows of double fingertip impressions and fingertip impressions on the rim. Secondarily burnt. Origin: circular ditch. Pottery identical to 8.1. Both parts probably belong to the same pot.

7.1   Tripartite pot(?) with combed decoration on shoulder and belly. Secondarily burnt. The potsherds were found with some cremation remains in two postholes of a 12th-century building. During construction of the building the cremation grave was destroyed. Both postholes were in the centre of the circular ditch.

7.2   Sherd with combed decoration. Origin: circular ditch.

8.1   Rimsherd of tripartite bowl, identical to 6.3. Possibly from the same pot. Origin: circular ditch.

26.1   Complete cup with spout, polished. Origin: from the fill of one of the smallest circular ditches. The cup may have served as a teat ('*biberon*') for a baby or young child. If so, the burial monument (without central interment) may perhaps be ascribed to a child.

44.1   Tripartite pot. From base to shoulder decorated with vertical rows of fingertip impressions and fingertip impressions on the rim. Origin: ditch of long-bed.

50.1   Rimsherd of small cup(?). Secondarily burnt. Origin: centre of a rectangular ditch, in an animal track with some cremation remains. Probably from a disturbed cremation grave.

64.1   Rimsherds of a dish or pot with everted rim; fingertip impressions on rim; roughened. Origin: circular ditch.

77.1   Small open bowl with fingertip impressions on rim. Origin: the sherds lay scattered over three locations in the circular ditch.

eral loomweights, a spindle and unburnt animal bone), he interprets these structures as cult places, by analogy with the *fossé à exposition* of the open-air sanctuary of Gournay-sur-Aronde. See also however note 22.

88.1   Bipartite bowl, polished. Origin: found among cremation remains in the centre of a circular ditch. Unburnt.

89.1   Polished sherd with combed decoration. Origin: ditch of long-bed.

90.1   Tripartite bowl, roughened to the shoulder and decorated with brush strokes. Polished from the shoulder. Origin: found in a flat grave together with cremation remains. Unburnt; probably an urn.

94.1   Almost complete tripartite bowl; polished; thick-walled. Origin: circular ditch.

96.1   Bowl with sagging base. Partly secondarily burnt(?). Origin: circular ditch.

100.1   Fragments of a tripartite pot with cylindrical neck. Some of the wallsherds are roughened. Shoulder and rim are polished. Three of the 25 sherds were secondarily burnt. Origin: circular ditch.

113.1   Conical dish. Exterior is smoothened. Origin: circular ditch.

113.2   Wallsherd with combed decoration. Origin: circular ditch.

113.3   Wallsherd with scratched decoration. Origin: circular ditch.

116.1   Rimsherd of a tripartite pot with combed decoration on transition belly/shoulder. Origin: circular ditch.

116.2   Wallsherd with dimple on the shoulder. Secondarily burnt. Origin: circular ditch.

122.1   Rimsherd of tripartite pot; polished. Origin: ditch of long-bed.

122.2   Rimsherd. Origin: ditch of long-bed.

131.1   Parts of a bipartite pot, roughened from base to shoulder, polished from shoulder. Part of the base and belly are secondarily burnt. Origin: circular ditch.

135.1   Base fragment with fingertip impressions. The pottery is identical to that from graves 136 and 138. Origin: circular ditch.

137.1   Parts of a tripartite pot with combed decoration on the belly. Polished from shoulder. On the belly, at regular intervals, there are vertical strips where the comb marks have been rubbed away. The combed decoration was applied before the pot was polished. Origin: bottom of the circular ditch.

145.1   Rimsherd of a tripartite pot with fingertip impressions on the rim. Secondarily burnt. Origin: these are two fragments which were found separately in the adjoining circular ditches of graves 144 and 145.

145.2   Complete small tripartite pot, found at the bottom of the circular ditch.

146.1   Base of a pot. Partly secondarily burnt. Origin: circular ditch.

158.1   Wall fragment of a tripartite bowl; polished. Has some 'Marne' characteristics. Origin: rectangular ditch. Date: 500-450 BC, Van den Broeke's Phase E (1987). See also ibidem: fig. 6, p. 34 for a virtually identical profile.

160.1   Small cup with impression of a grain of corn in the outer wall. Secondarily burnt. Found on the site of the cremation grave, in which only a few lumps of cremation remains were left.

162.1   Base sherd of a roughened pot. Origin: circular ditch.

175.1   Small bipartite bowl with sagging base. Secondarily burnt on the pyre(?). Origin: among cremation remains from a long-bed. Date: 500-450 BC, Van den Broeke's Phase E (1987). See also Van den Broeke 1984, fig. 9:6, p. 76.

180.1   Rimsherd of an open dish. Exterior roughened. Origin: square ditch.

181.1   Rimsherd of a roughened open dish with fingertip impressions on the inside of the rim. Brush strokes. Origin: square ditch.

181.2   Rimsherd of a polished pot. Origin: square ditch.

184.1   Tripartite bowl with carinated profile (fig. 8). Roughened from base to the polished shoulder. Typical Marne influence. Origin: inhumation grave. Date: Van den Broeke (1987) phase E/F; ca 500-400/375 BC.

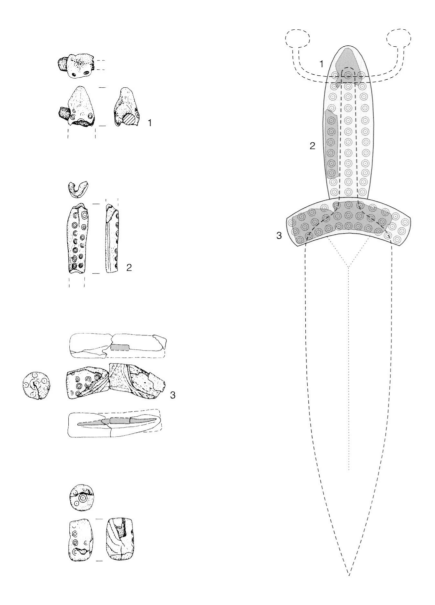

Fig. 12. Someren-Waterdael. Antler fragments with a point-circle decoration. Scale 1 : 2 (left). On the right: proposed reconstruction. The hatched parts indicate the recovered fragments (scale 1 : 2).

Amber

A perforated amber bead, 1.7 cm in diameter and 0.7/0.3 cm thick (fig. 11, 30.1) was found in the circular ditch of grave 30. A similar disc-shaped bead was found in inhumation grave 3 of the previously-mentioned cemetery of Geldermalsen. There the bead hangs from a bronze ring and is interpreted as an ear- or nose-ring.[31] Two amber beads are known from the settlement site at Haps (North Brabant) as stray finds.[32]

---

[31]   Hulst, in preparation.   [32]   Verwers 1972, 120, fig. 81.

Worked bone and antler

Among the scanty cremation remains of grave 50 was a perforated fragment of a *metatarsus*, probably of a sheep (fig. 11, 50.2). Its function is uncertain. It may have served as a pendant.

Cremation grave 175 contained a number of antler fragments from a red deer or a roe deer, which were decorated with a point-circle motif (fig. 12, 175.2). In one of the fragments there is an iron pin two centimetres long with a diameter of 0.5 cm. It was possible to fit several pieces of antler together. These have been reconstructed to form a ca 5 cm long, bent stick 1.5 cm in diameter. On the convex side there is a rectangular notch ca 1.0 cm in length and an estimated 0.3 to 0.4 cm in breadth. The concave side reveals a 4.2-cm-long groove which narrows at either end. In this way a continuous groove appears which is narrow on the convex side and wide on the concave side. On the basis of the fragments present, it is difficult to reconstruct the original object. We must take into account the fact that only a part of the burnt antler remains finally ended up in the grave. Moreover, the material has shrunk and become distorted by the heat. The iron pin in one of the fragments suggests that the decorated antler was originally part of a larger object. I would interpret the decorated antler remains as parts of an iron dagger, with the crooked stick described above separating the blade from the hilt (see reconstruction fig. 12). The other long antler fragment may have been a piece of the hilt which was originally pushed over the hilt tang and attached to it by means of iron nails. Possibly we have found one of them. The iron pin may even have formed part of an *antenna*, as known from the Haps specimen.[33]

Metal

Among the cremation remains of three graves were six iron objects.[34] All objects are cremation artefacts. A piece of iron from grave 175 has already been discussed above in connection with the decorated antler fragments. From grave 4 is an iron ring, 2.8 cm in diameter and a 3.4-cm-long iron pin, one side of which ends in a point (fig. 11, 4.8 and 4.9). The pin is not complete. The function of both objects is unclear.

Grave 6 contained several rusty lumps of iron which, after restoration, were transformed into three iron arrowheads (fig. 13, 14). The complete specimen is 8.4 cm in length. The shaft of the two other arrowheads has broken off. The blades are almond-shaped with a lightly-pronounced rib across the middle of the blade which continues as far as the shaft. The diameter of the round shaft-hole of the complete specimen is 0.6 cm. The blades measure 3.4 × 1.6 cm; 4.8 × 2.2 cm and 4.4 × 2.2 cm respectively.

In the Lower Rhine area, iron arrow- or spearheads from Iron Age burials are comparatively rare. The best parallels are the three arrowheads from grave 190 at Haps. These were found together with an *antennae* dagger and a *Kropfnadel* in a pit with cremation remains which was surrounded by a circular ditch of average diameter. Verwers dates the objects in the 6th or beginning of the 5th century BC (HaD2/LTA). Other examples from the Dutch Lower Rhine area are the arrow and/or spearheads from Nijmegen-Kops Plateau; Nijmegen-Trajanusplein (Gelderland); Overasselt (Gld) and Darp

[33] Verwers 1972, 55.62, especially fig. 3. Bone remains with circle and point decoration are only known at two Dutch findspots: Berkel-Enschot (NB), cremation grave 35/32, date: Early Iron Age (Kleij 1993, 31); Zevenbergen (NB), urn 3 tumulus I, date: Middle or Late Bronze Age (Verwers 1966, 29, fig. 5).

[34] Liesbeth Smits also observed a greenish (bronze?) discolouration on some bone fragments of a lower jaw and cheekbone from flat grave 2. Although no bronze remains were found in the grave, one may assume that a bronze object was also burnt on the pyre.

(Drenthe). The finds, all from cremation graves, are dated in the 6th and 5th century BC.[35]

What significance should be attached to the iron arrowheads of Someren-Waterdael? Let us first consider the function of the arrows. In the Dutch examples, a distinction can be made between lanceheads which served as thrust weapons on the one hand, and arrow- and spearheads which were launched as a projectile, by means of a bow or by hand, respectively, on the other hand. The difference between an arrow- and a spearhead is not always clear.[36] This is especially so in the case of heads with blades longer than about six centimetres. A distinction can be made on the basis of the internal diameter of the shaft.[37] With arrowheads this is usually less than one centimetre (0.6 to 0.8 cm), whereas the shaft diameter of spearheads is over one centimetre (1.2 – 1.3 cm). The Someren specimens certainly belonged to arrows, which may have been used for hunting as well as in the military sphere. Some authors give preference to their usage for hunting.[38] Since the arrows are generally found in a ritual context, it may be assumed that they had a symbolic significance. It is striking that the arrow- or spearheads are often found in threes. If we take a closer look at the contexts of the Dutch arrow- and spearheads, we can make several observations. The cremation graves of Nijmegen-Trajanusplein, Overasselt and Darp contain the remains of horse harnesses in addition to the arrows. The former burial even contained iron parts of a two-wheeled wagon, while the Overasselt grave contained a bronze *situla* and a bronze cup. Although there is no evidence for a monumental mound over these graves, their inventories can be associated with a Middle Iron Age elite. In contrast, the group of five cremation graves from the Middle Iron Age on the Kops Plateau at Nijmegen only produced arrow- and spearheads. Judging from the restricted size of the circular ditch around grave 72 (diameter 6.5 m), the burials did not have a monumental character. The same applies to grave 190 at Haps, where, apart from the grave goods, neither the burial monument nor the position of the grave in the cemetery indicates that the person buried here underwent any privileged treatment.

With this we return to the question of the symbolism of the Someren-Waterdael arrowheads. Apart from the arrowheads, grave 6 did not contain any other finds, although it should be noted that the grave had been truncated as a result of the medieval reclamation. In this respect the grave does not suggest an elite burial. Its context within a separate group of monumental circular ditches with post-circles does point to a special position held by the deceased person. Weapons in graves are often

---

[35] Iron arrow- and/or spearheads from the Netherlands: Haps: grave 190, see above (Verwers 1972, 55-62); Nijmegen-Kops Plateau (Fontijn 1995, 55-58): grave 72 with circular ditch (diam.: 6.5 m): 2 arrowheads, 4 spearheads and 1 lancehead; graves 78 and 79: both 3 spearheads, graves 81 and 83: both 1 spearhead. Date: 5th century BC; Nijmegen-Trajanusplein (Bloemers 1986, 77, 78): cremation grave 60/9: one lancehead and 1 to 2 arrow or spearheads among the iron remains of a two-wheeled wagon and horse harness. Date: 450-350 BC; Overasselt (Fontijn 1995, 58; De Laet 1979, 497): cremation grave with 3 spearheads, bronze *situla*, bronze cup and remains of horse harness. Date: 5th century BC; Darp-Bisschopsberg (= Havelte) (Kooi 1983, 197-208): 3 arrow- or spear-

heads found together with remains of horse harness in an urn. A second grave from the same site also contains three or four arrow- or spearheads, an iron dagger with bronze hilt and sheath, several iron and bronze rings, a bronze bracelet, and an urn. Date: 6th century BC.

[36] Fontijn 1995, 55.

[37] Krausse-Steinberger 1990, 89.

[38] Krausse-Steinberger 1990, 93 ff., bases the preference for hunting purposes on the occurrence in some grave inventories of blunt-headed arrows as well as the discovery of arrows with different kinds of wooden shafts in the *Fürstengrab* of Hochdorf, which might indicate a use for various kinds of game.

159

Fig. 13. Someren–Waterdael. Restorated iron arrowheads from cremation grave 6 (Photograph Mark Ydo).

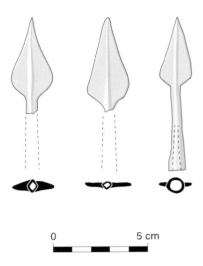

Fig. 14. Someren-Waterdael. Drawing of the iron arrowheads. Scale 1 : 2.

associated with a martial ideology, especially in the case of swords.[39] The same applies to lance-, spear- and arrowheads. This martial ideology appears to have been reserved for men. Although the cremation remains of grave 6 only provide information about the age of the deceased (30 – 60 years), it may be assumed that he was a man, particularly since the other graves belonging to this cluster (graves 3, 4 and 5) also contained the remains of adult males.

Summing up, we may state that the deceased man(?) was given three arrows (and perhaps a bow) by his relatives on his funeral pyre, which was quite unusual for this region. In view of the location and monumental nature of the grave, and the grave goods, the man held an important position within the local community during his lifetime. He had attained this position partly as a result of his qualities as a warrior and/or hunter. Moreover he possibly belonged to the group of people who founded the settlement, and may have been honoured as such after his death (see below). He would have died sometime in the late 7th or 6th century BC (HaD).

3.4   DATE OF THE URNFIELD

For dating the cemetery we have various categories of data at our disposal: a. the typochronology of the burial monuments; b. the mode of interment; c. the typochronology of the pottery and other finds; d. six C14 dates; e. two tree-ring datings from the settlement associated with the cemetery.

Starting with the first category, it may be stated that all circular ditches have an opening in the southeast segment of the ditch. This phenomenon is found in the Lower Rhine area from the Early Iron Age until into the Middle Iron Age. Before this time (Middle and Late Bronze Age) the circular ditches formed a closed circle.[40] In the Lower Rhine region, post circles around the central grave usual-

[39] See for example Roymans 1991, 58 ff.

[40] Beex 1960; Verwers 1972, 36; Verlinde 1987, 199 ff.

ly date from the Early Iron Age (second half 8th – 7th century BC).[41] Square graves first appear around 500 BC.[42] The more 'angular' form of the long-beds occurs since the beginning of the Early Iron Age.[43]

It has already been observed that urn burials in the cemetery of Someren-Waterdael are probably underrepresented, due to the fact that the central graves have only been preserved to a limited degree. On the other hand it is significant that the better-preserved cremations were always discovered without any remains of a ceramic container. Also because of the regular distribution of urnless graves over the cemetery, I assume that the rarity of urn graves is representative for the actual situation. Tol (this volume) – following Verwers – has already remarked that the number of urn burials increased sharply in the transition period between the Late Bronze Age and Early Iron Age. A shift toward urnless burials already appears to take place in the course of the Early Iron Age. Probably urn burials had already become the minority by the end of the 7th century.[44]

Only a small proportion of the pottery from the Someren cemetery provides chronological indications. We already observed that typical pot forms from the Late Bronze Age (pots with cylindrical necks or with *Kerbschnitt* decoration) but also Harpstedt and *Schräghals*-type pots, characteristic of the early phase of the Early Iron Age (ca 750 – 650 BC), are not found in the cemetery. Some dating value is provided by the sherd with a doubly perforated knobbed ear from grave 4 (fig. 9, 4.1) which can be dated in the Early Iron Age (ca 750 – 500 BC); the wall fragment of a bipartite bowl with Marne influence (fig. 11, 158.1) from a square ditch (Middle Iron Age, ca 500 – 450 BC) and the carinated pot from the inhumation grave (fig. 8, 184.1), which can be dated to between 500 and 400/375 BC.[45]

The iron arrowheads from grave 6 date from the 7th century BC at the earliest.[46] In view of the relatively young dates of the other Lower Rhine specimens (HaD/LTA), a 6th-century date seems more likely.

The relevance of the available C14 dates is limited. All six dates are in the notorious 'wiggle' period between ca 800 and 400 BC.[47] As a result, all values are around ca 2500 – 2400 BP. The dates fluctuate between 792 and 200 cal BC (2 sigma). In the table below, the C14 dates are calibrated according to Stuiver and Pearson's method.[48]

The above evidence leads to the conclusion that the Someren-Waterdael urnfield must be dated within the margins of the Early and Middle Iron Age. Relatively late (5th-century) elements make up the rectangular graves, some Marne-type pots and a C14 date (grave 148). Early elements (7th century) are less prominent: possibly only the urn from grave no. 90. The calibrated C14 values do not exclude a date before 700 BC, but on the basis of the other indices this is most unlikely. An important indication for the starting date of the cemetery is provided by the settlement evidence. Tree-ring dating of oakwood from two wells has yielded some precise dates. The felling date of the wood for the

[41]   See Tol, this volume.

[42]   Verwers 1972, 36-37; see further Hulst 1964, 81-82; Verlinde 1987, 204-206.

[43]   See for example the rectangular long-beds of Beegden (Roymans, this volume) and Someren-Philipskampeerterrein (Modderman 1953).

[44]   Tol, this volume; Verwers 1972, 44.

[45]   For references see section 3.3.

[46]   Pare 1991, 20. Almost all iron arrow finds from the Middle Rhine area however date from HaD or LTA (Krausse-Steinberger 1990).

[47]   Van den Broeke 1987, 24-26.

[48]   Stuiver/Pearson 1993. Use has been made of the radiocarbon calibration programme CAL-20 of the Dutch Centre for Isotope Research in Groningen.

grave no	context	14C date BP (GrN)	years cal BC 1 sigma (68.3 %)	years cal BC 2 sigma (95.4%)
4	charcoal from burial (circ. ditch)	2440 ± 30 BP (GrN-22200)	752-706 / 528-410	760-676 / 554-402
48	charcoal from burial (circ. ditch)	2510 ± 30 BP (GrN-22194)	774-760 / 680-548	792-752 / 730-528
68	charcoal from circular ditch	2380 ± 40 BP (GrN-22198)	512-440 / 420-392	754-692 / 534-382
108	charcoal from burial (flatgrave)	2520 ± 30 BP (GrN-22195)	774-760 / 638-548	792-752 / 706-528
148	charcoal from burial (flatgrave)	2320 ± 50 BP (GrN-22197)	408-356 / 288-210	434-340 / 326-200
175	charcoal from burial (long-bed)	2420 ± 40 BP (GrN-22196)	750-734 / 528-402	762-674 / 554-396

Table 2. Someren-Waterdael: 14C dates and calibrated dates (1 and 2 sigma confidence level) of some graves and a circular ditch from the urnfield.

first well, situated in the oldest zone of the settlement site, was 588 BC. The second well, several hundred metres east of the urnfield, contained secondarily used wood from a tree which was felled in 650/649 BC.[49] We shall stick to this date as a starting date for the urnfield. The final date is set at 400/375 BC, which does not contradict the youngest C14 dates. An additional argument is the fact that the rectangular grave structures are in the minority.

3.5 PHYSICAL-ANTHROPOLOGICAL ANALYSIS OF THE CREMATION REMAINS

Most of the grave pits were truncated or even completely destroyed by medieval reclamation activities, so that the quantity of cremation remains preserved is often only a small fraction of what was originally buried.[50] Moreover, it was rare for all the remains to be collected from the pyre. A *pars pro toto* principle seems to have been applied.[51]

The cremation remains from Someren were analysed by Liesbeth Smits (IPP). A survey of the relevant data can be found at the end of this article (appendix 2). The most important results have been summarized below.[52]

In almost 50% of the cremations less than 50 grams were preserved. The higher the weight, the greater the chance of establishing the age and sex of the deceased (fig. 15). In 52 cases it was possible to say something about the age, although with adults margins of 20 years must sometimes be allowed for! Sex determination was only possible for adult individuals (table 3). Of the 24 sex determinations, only 10 could establish the sex with certainty and 8 with some degree of certainty.

[49] The tree-ring dating was carried out by the Dutch Centre for Dendrochronology (Ring Foundation, ROB) in Amersfoort. Samples SOW 12345: 588 BC (summer); SWW 34567: 651 + 1 BC (autumn/winter); SWW 020: 635 + 20 ± 6 AD.

[50] Cremation weights from more or less complete graves: grave 3: 1271 g.; grave 10: 2333 g.; grave 4: 2570 g.; grave 48: 1983 g.; grave 108: 1295 g.; grave 175: 1182 g.

[51] The average weight of the bone remains of an adult after cremation in a modern crematorium is ca 2500 g. (Wahl 1982, 20). Only three complete graves from Someren-Waterdael approach this weight. Compare the weights of cremation remains from the graves at Beegden and Mierlo-Hout (both this volume).

[52] Age and sex determination was carried out according to the guidelines of the *Workshop of European Anthropologists* (1980). The method used is described in Menno Hoogland's contribution (Roymans, this volume).

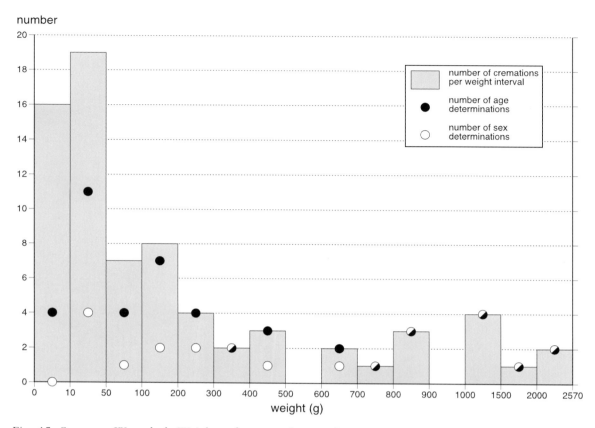

Fig. 15. Someren-Waterdael. Weights of preserved cremation remains. From 700 grams, information can be given as to the age and sex of each individual.

Extremely advanced ages are seldom found. Grave 88 contained the remains of a woman aged between 50 and 70 years. The most frequently found age group is 20-40 years. In accordance with the general trend, children, and certainly neonates, are greatly underrepresented.[53] Only 12% of the cremations could be attributed to children (0-14). Grave 142 contained the remains of an adult female and a neonate. It is not inconceivable that the woman was in an advanced stage of pregnancy when she died, or that mother and child died during labour. In three cases (graves 4, 6 and 48), pathological disorders to the bone were observed. In two cases this was *osteophytosis (arthritis)*. The third case concerned *osteophytes* on the cervical and thoracal vertebrae (neck and chest vertebrae) of the man buried in grave 4. *Osteophytes* are a common degenerative condition found in individuals over ca 35 years of age. Finally it may be stated that the *postcranial* skeletons of the men buried in grave 3 (long-bed), grave 4 (circular ditch with post-circle) and grave 5.1 (largest long-bed), appear to be relatively robust. It is striking that all three graves belong to the separate group of 5 monumental graves on the south side of the urnfield.

In six cremation graves small quantities of animal bone remains were found.[54] The worked animal bone material has already been described above. The other remains probably indicate that meat

[53] See Roymans, this volume, for references.

[54] Identification of the animal remains was carried out by Rick Maliepaard, IPP.

age group		number		remarks
neonate	(0-1)	1	(2 %)	together with remains adult female
children	(1-14)	5	(10 %)	3 x C; 2 x C/J
juveniles	(14-18)	2	(4 %)	2 x J?
adult males		12	(23 %)	6 x M; 6 x M?
adult females		6	(12 %)	4 x F; 2 x F?
adults indet		26	(50 %)	16 x A; 7x A?; 3 x A??
total number		**52**	**(100 %)**	

Tabel 3. Someren-Waterdael: age and sex distribution of the cemetery population (? = probable; ?? = possible).

grave	type of monument	sex	animal bones	remarks and meat-equivalent
4	circular ditch	M?	rib fragments of pig or sheep	breast
7	circular ditch	?	femur sheep	leg of mutton
50	square ditch	?	metatarsus sheep(?)	used as bone pendant (?)
148	flat grave	M?	humerus sheep	leg of mutton
175	long-bed	M	radius of a sheep; antler fragments of red deer or roe deer	decorated antler fragments
178	flat grave	F	pelvis, patella, tibia and 2 tarsalia of a pig	pig foot

Tabel 4. Someren-Waterdael. List of animal bones from cremation burials.

was burnt on the pyre. Now that cremation remains are being more systematically examined, it seems that animal remains in graves regularly occur. In the Dutch urnfields, these are mainly fragments of sheep/goat and pig. A flat grave from the (Middle?) Iron Age at Oss contained some poultry bones.[55]

[55] Cremation graves with animal bone fragments in urn-fields: St-Oedenrode grave 33 (child?): fragm. prox. radius sheep/goat (Van der Sanden 1981, 315); Oss: poultry bones among cremation remains (grave R 47?) (Van der Sanden/Van den Broeke 1987, 71). Burnt and unburnt bones from cattle, pig, sheep/goat, dog and poultry are found in Oss in various peripheral structures belonging to graves from the Middle or Late Iron Age (Van der Sanden 1994, 237 ff.); Mierlo-Hout: left forefoot of a pig and rib fragments of sheep or pig (Tol, this volume). Geldermalsen, inhumation grave 1 (female) contained a rib section (8 ribs) of a pig (Hulst, in prep.); Nijmegen-Trajanusplein, wagon grave 60/9: 7 g. animal remains of three young pigs (Bloemers, in prep.). Nijmegen Kops Plateau: LBA/EIA: 2 graves with remains of a medium-sized mammal and one grave with an animal tooth; MIA: graves 72, 74, 76, 79 and 87/36 respectively: animal?; pig; pig > 2 years; young pig; piglet and sheep/goat (verbal communication A. Cuijpers, ROB); Cuijpers (1994, 20) gives a survey of the animal remains from graves from eight cemeteries in Overijssel. In 5 graves there were the remains of red deer (without human remains?), roe deer, pig and possibly sheep, respectively. The remains in 9 other graves could not be identified more closely.

age group	CD	LB	RD	FL	total
neonate (0-1)	1	-	-	-	1
children (1-14)	1	-	1	3	5
juveniles (14-18)	2	-	-	-	2
adult males	6	5	-	3	14
adult females	6	-	1	2	9
adults indet	12	2	1	6	21
total number	**28 (21 %)**	**7 (46 %)**	**3 (16 %)**	**14 (88 %)**	**52 (28 %)**

Tabel 5. Someren-Waterdael. Age and sex distribution of the cemetery population in relation to the type of monument. Between brackets: percentages of interments in relation to the total number of graves within this monument type (CD = circular ditch; LB = long bed; RD = rectangular ditch; FL = flat grave).

In addition to the demographic aspects of the investigation of cremation remains, the results serve as a lead in the study of the symbolic significance of the various types of burial monuments and, with it, all kinds of social aspects of the society.[56] To conclude this section, I would like to compare the various sex and age categories with the type of burial monument in which they were found.

One first observation is that in tumuli with a circular ditch all age categories of both men and women are found. A comparison of the size of the circular ditches shows that there is generally no relation between their size and the age or sex of the deceased. In circular ditches with an average diameter (4 to 7 m.), there are men, women and children. A possible exception is the three largest ditches with post-circles on the south side of the urnfield (nos. 4, 6 and 7), which are possibly associated with adult males. The smallest circular ditches with a diameter of less than 3 metres were possibly intended for children. A second observation concerns the flat graves. Most of the flat graves in Someren contain the remains of adult individuals. Three of the five child graves are, however, flat graves. An overrepresentation of children in flat graves has also been observed in the case of the Beegden urnfield.[57] The results for the long-beds are equally surprising. In 5 of the 6 long-beds which could be identified as to age and sex, there were adult males (3 × M; 2 × M?). The largest long-bed (grave 5) contained both the grave of an adult male (grave 5.1, dug in the centre of the monument) and the grave of a second adult of indeterminate sex (grave 5.2). The sixth grave was *probably* that of an adult. The (cautious) conclusion is that long-beds were primarily reserved for adult males. I shall return to this later.

3.6   A DEMOGRAPHIC RECONSTRUCTION

With the data presented above and Acsádi and Némeskeri's formula[58] an attempt has been made to gain information about the size of the living community. The formula is: $P = k (D x e) / t$, where $P =$

---

[56] Cf. the discussion in Roymans/Kortlang, this volume.   [58] Acsádi/Némeskeri 1970.

[57] Roymans, this volume.

population; k = correction factor; D = number of interred persons; e = average life expectancy at birth; t = duration of the cemetery.

Several remarks must be made about the variables k, D, e and t. Table 3 shows an underrepresentation in the cemetery of persons younger than 18: only 16%, whereas the number of burials of non-adults as a result of a high infant mortality is between 45 and 60% in pre-modern societies.[59] We can explain this bias on the one hand by the fact that bodies of newborn infants possibly received a different kind of treatment, for example inhumation in the burial mound of a deceased relation, or burial on the house-yard. However, due to the poor conservation conditions for bone in the sandy areas, this is difficult to prove. On the other hand, the extreme underrepresentation of this age category can be explained by the limited number of well-preserved cremation graves, particularly in the smaller burial monuments. These were apparently more prone to erosion than the graves in the larger monuments. To compensate for the underrepresentation of newborn children the value 1.1 (10%) has been used as a correction factor (k).[60] We assume that deceased children over the age of ca one year did in fact undergo a cremation ritual and that they were buried in their own burial monument.

Graves and burial monuments are the starting-point for the calculation of the total number of deceased individuals (D). The Someren-Waterdael cemetery was more or less completely excavated. However, it should not be forgotten that a number (15 to 20) of graves had disappeared, especially on the northeast and northwest side of the cemetery. The total number of burials therefore amounts to ca 200 (without the correction factor (k) of 1.1). For premodern societies the average life expectancy at birth (e) is usually estimated to be 25 years.[61] The duration of the cemetery (t) is estimated at ca 250 years: from ca 650 to 400 BC. However, a continued use after 400 BC for one or two generations remains possible.

e = 25	D = 200	D = 225	D = 250
t = 225	24.5	27.5	30.5
t = 250	22	25	27.5
t = 275	20	22.5	25

Table 6. Someren-Waterdael. Calculation of the average size of the living population, with different values for the variables D (total number of interred persons) and t (duration of the cemetery). k = 1.1. The average life expectancy (e) is fixed on 25 years.

From the above table we may conclude that the living population of Someren consisted of a group of about 25 persons. Assuming a nuclear family with an average of 6 members, the Someren burial community must have included ca 4 households on average.

[59] Hessing 1989, 327; Caselitz 1986, 169. Even in comparison with the proportion of 38% non-adults in the Beegden urnfield (Roymans, this volume), the 16% for Someren-Waterdael is extremely low.

[60] This follows the example of Beegden (Roymans, this volume) and Wijk bij Duurstede (Hessing 1989).

[61] Caselitz (1986, 167-172) estimates an average life ex-

pectancy at birth of 32.4 years for the completely excavated North German urnfield of Hameln-Wangelister Feld (Late Bronze Age/Early Iron Age). In his view this is surprisingly favourable, certainly in comparison with a random sample survey of a number of cemeteries where an average value of 26.5 was obtained.

I want to conclude this chapter with a summarizing analysis resulting in a first social interpretation of the cemetery. If we examine the layout of the cemetery, the following observations can be made. The cemetery consists of an elongated, more or less continuous zone of burial monuments. In a spatial sense, a distinction can be made between the northern and the southern zone. In addition to circular ditches and long-beds, both zones also have square burial structures, although these are limited to two specimens in the southern zone. Regarding the spatial structure of both zones, several differences can be noted. In the northern part, the graves are compactly situated, enclosed by three shallow depressions. On the north side, the burial monuments mainly consist of square structures. The southern zone gives a more differentiated picture. The most striking feature is the colossal long-bed (grave 5) with a length of ca 145 m. and, entirely on the south side, the three large circular ditches with a post-circle (4, 6 and 7). Long-bed 5 forms a separate cluster together with these three graves, the small long-bed 3 and two other circular ditches (1, 8). If we take a closer look, we see a certain symmetry between the two monuments to the west (3 and 4) and to the east (6 and 7) of long-bed 5. This symmetry becomes even more obvious when one starts from the central burials themselves. The distance between graves 3, 4, 6 and 7 is in each case ca 25 m. Graves 4 and 6, on either side of long-bed 5, both measure 12.5 m. from the longitudinal axis of the long-bed. It is tempting to assume that this layout follows a specific spatial design. Long-bed 5 forms the backbone, along which the entire southern zone developed. One notices that the middle (and largest) cluster of graves is concentrated on the east side of long-bed 5, at the position of the central burial. A third cluster can be distinguished on the northeast side of long-bed 5, consisting of three long-beds (43 – 45) and three circular ditches (46 – 48). The zone west of the long-bed has no graves. Perhaps there was a road or path on this side.

On the basis of the above, an attempt can be made to outline the development of the cemetery (fig. 16). The oldest nucleus of the northern zone developed around 650 BC between three shallow depressions.[62] One of the first graves is the more monumental long-bed 89 (45 m.). In the course of the 7th/6th century, the area between the depressions was gradually filled in with circular ditches and long-beds. In the 6th/5th century this development continues in a northwesterly direction and subsequently in a northerly direction with mainly rectangular graves. Around 400/375 BC the last burial monuments were erected in the vicinity of the large rectangular grave 179.

The oldest burial monument in the southern zone is probably long-bed 5. With this long-bed as a basis, the development of the zone appears to continue from two or three nuclei:

– cluster A, on either side of the foot of long-bed 5. The development of this southerly nucleus (6 to 7 graves) probably took place within a timescale of one to two generations.[63]
– cluster B; the development of this central nucleus (33 graves) takes place to the east of long-bed 5 at the position of the central grave, ending with two rectangular monuments.

---

[62] This is based on the following considerations : the ditch around long-bed 89 is the only one with a closed short side, which possibly indicates an earlier dating than the 'Someren-type' long graves; the only known urn grave (90) comes from this zone; the C14 date of grave 108 is among the earliest of the urnfield (774-528 BC, 2 sigma).

[63] This is indicated by the strong similarity between the monumental graves 4, 6 and 7, and by planned layout of cluster A.

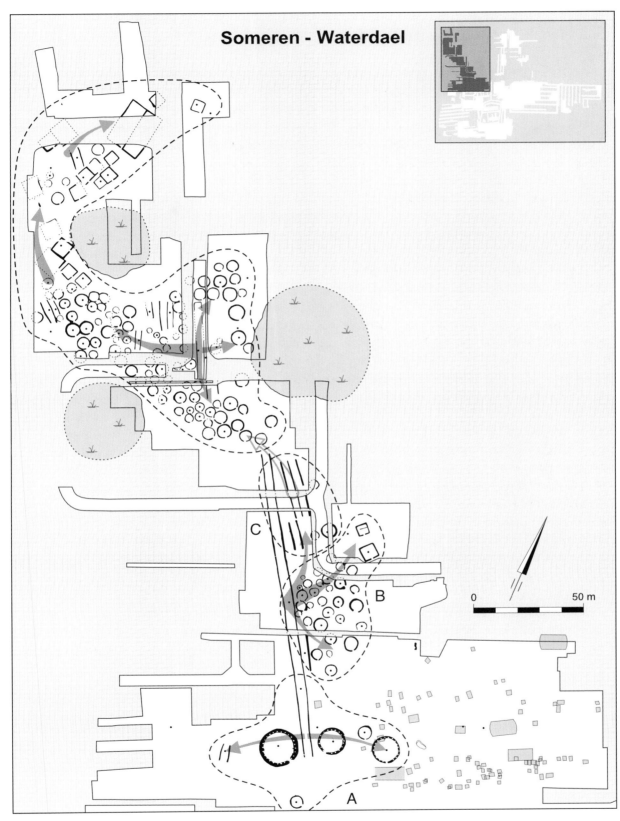

Fig. 16. Someren-Waterdael. Development of the cemetery between ca 650 and 400/375 BC.

– cluster C; the construction of long-beds 43-45 immediately next to long-bed 5 probably emphasized the kinship tie between the deceased and the man in long-bed 5.

For each zone we have a reasonable idea of the horizontal stratigraphy, based on some chronological
indications such as the rectangular burial monuments and the pottery. The oldest nuclei are characterized in both zones by large monumental structures. Although they develop more or less synchronical-
ly, the dating evidence does not allow us to establish the starting date of the southern zone with regard to that of the northern zone. We assume that both zones began to be used as a burial ground
more or less simultaneously in about 650 BC.

Central to the social interpretation is the assumption put forward in the introductory article that the
burial system is embedded in a wider system of ideas and values which reflect the society's views on
social reality and the wider cosmos.[64] It is against this background that the material evidence of the
burial ritual of Someren-Waterdael is understood. The cemetery formed within the dynamic settlement system (see below) a central and stable element in the territory of the local community. It reflected the collective identity of the local group, with the concept of ancestors forming a central notion. To the outside world, the cemetery with its ancestral graves served as a territorial marker, which
could be referred to if claims to the territory were disputed by other groups. The internal structure of
the Someren cemetery reveals, in addition to a distinction between a northern and a southern zone,
a variety of burial monuments that is comparable to those of other Lower Rhine urnfields. We assume that the basic variety of monuments reflects to some extent the social structure of local communities. The separate zones may be seen as the burial grounds of different family groups, the northern
zone being used by a larger number of nuclear families (3 on average) than the southern zone (1 family on average). With a more or less equal duration, this might explain the comparatively small number of graves in the southern zone. In addition to a large group of circular ditches and rectangular
graves of average size, the cemetery has a relatively small number of long-beds.[65] Elsewhere in this
volume it has been suggested that long-beds can be associated with the heads of nuclear families or
households. As a metaphor for the house and the nuclear family they had a more collective meaning
than the other burial monuments. During their lives, the heads of families (mainly men) played an
important part in the reproduction of relations between the ancestors, the land and the living community.[66] Moreover the cemetery contains a small group of burial monuments of more than average
size. These include the long-beds 5 and 89; the circular ditches with post-circle 4, 6 and 7, and possibly also the large rectangular monument 179.[67] The difference in size of these graves compared with
that of the other monuments is so great that there must be another underlying meaning. Apart from
grave 179 which belongs to the last phase of the urnfield, the other five specimens may be included
among the earliest monuments within the separate groups. The extremely large long-bed 5 of the
southern zone could be interpreted as the grave of the ancestral founding-father of the community as

[64] Roymans/Kortlang, this volume. Following Hodder
(1994, 74) we argue that: "Material culture does not
passively reflect society, but is actively manipulated to
construct society".

[65] A comparatively small number of long-beds has also
been established for a number of other cemeteries in
the MDS region (Roymans/Kortlang, this volume).

The ratio of long-beds to other graves in Someren is
about 1:12. For the cemetery as a whole this means an
average of 1.8 long-beds per generation (25 years).

[66] Roymans/Kortlang, this volume.

[67] This structure may also be interpreted as two adjoining
long-beds.

a whole. The urnfield of Beegden shows a similar picture. The largest long-bed 22/9 (55 m.), which can also be interpreted as a founder burial, is the oldest burial monument there.[68] Moreover the urnfield shows a spatial division between the graves of the various families, similar to the division into a northern and southern zone at Someren-Waterdael.

How can we explain the three large circular ditches (and possibly also the small long-bed 3) against this background? Did the persons buried here – probably all men – belong, just like the man in the large long-bed, to the very first newcomers? Were they close relatives of the person buried in long-bed 5 or did they derive their status from other achievements, being warriors and/or hunters (think of the arrowheads in grave 6)? It is clear that the meaning underlying the more monumental nature of the circular ditches and post-circles must have been different from that of the long-beds.

A final remark must be made about the flat graves. As has already been observed, the flat graves 16, 17 and 185 are situated among the nearby Iron Age settlement traces. There are various indications for dating the settlement traces, situated immediately east of the urnfield, in the Late Iron Age (ca 200 BC, see also below). This would mean that, after giving up the urnfield in the Middle Iron Age, the habitation either continued or returned to the area in the course of the Late Iron Age. It is possible that some of the flat graves were burials on house-yards. If the answer is affirmative, this means that there was a break with the tradition of burying the dead in the collective cemetery. Perhaps the (new?) inhabitants did not sense a direct ancestral link with the dead of the cemetery. Flat grave 148, located in the periphery of the northern zone should also be mentioned in this connection. This grave yielded a C14 date which is relatively late in the Middle Iron Age (see above). It is quite possible that flat graves were dug in the periphery of the cemetery until into the Late Iron Age, which are now missing, either due to postdepositional processes or to the fact that we did not have the opportunity of investigating a larger zone around the cemetery. This would have, of course, important consequences for the duration of the cemetery in relation to the settlement evidence.

4   SETTLEMENT TRACES FROM THE IRON AGE

4.0   INTRODUCTION

During the excavations over the past seven years, traces were found of ca 30 houses and several hundred outbuildings spread across an extensive area (ca 750 m × 500 m) south and east of the cemetery (fig. 17). They represent several dozen farmyards dating from the Early Iron Age up to and including the Late Iron Age. We assume that the houses from the Early and to a large extent also the Middle Iron Age are directly related to the cemetery. The buildings are distributed over two zones within the excavated area: a. an east zone containing mainly traces from the Early Iron Age, situated on the higher and sandier section of the plateau, and b. a west zone with traces dating mainly from the Middle and Late Iron Age, situated in the somewhat lower and more loamy section. From the highest point in the east (ca 27.50 + NAP) the archaeological level gradually declines in a westerly direction to about 26.00 + NAP. Several depressions of varying size and depth contribute to the varied micro-relief of the site. The relatively empty part between both habitation zones may partly be explained by the destructive influence of settlement traces of a medieval hamlet. The most northerly part of the area excavated (in the centre) was investigated at the beginning of the 1990s by the ROB. The results of this investigation are not yet available.

---

68   Roymans, this volume.

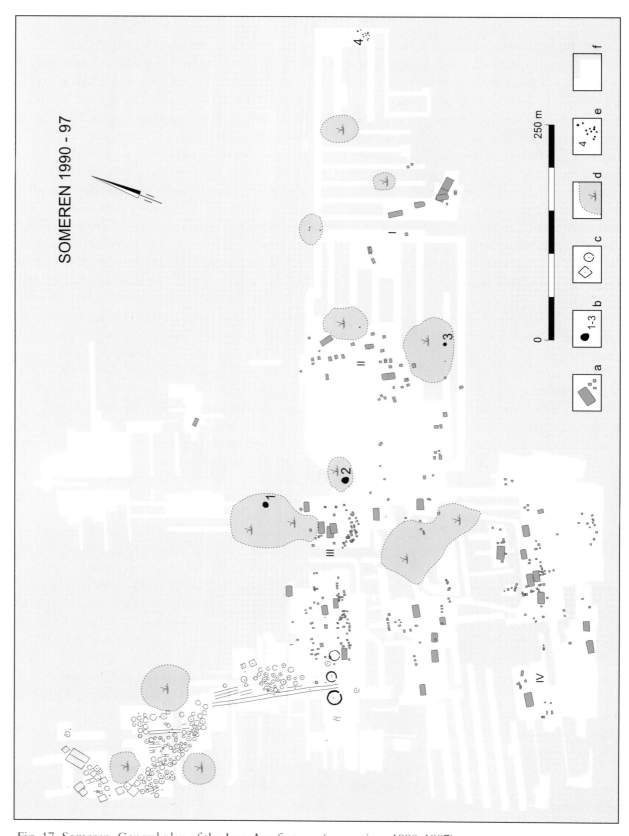

Fig. 17. Someren. General plan of the Iron Age features (excavations 1990-1997).
a. houses, sheds and granaries; b. wells (1-3); c. cemetery; d. depressions; e. storage pits; f. boundary excavated area. I-IV clusters of features mentioned in the text

The preservation conditions of the building traces vary. Especially the traces on the higher sections of the site were affected by medieval reclamation and levelling activities. The postholes of outbuildings such as barns and sheds have generally been better preserved than the postholes of main buildings. This can be explained by the fact that outbuildings had deeper foundations than main buildings because of their simpler above-ground construction. We assume that the number of main buildings is underrepresented due to the shallow depth of the postholes. Some clusters of traces with only outbuildings do indicate a farmyard but probably lack the main building for this reason.

The finds from the settlement site are mainly confined to pottery (including several spindles and loomweights), some natural stone (sandstone, quartzite) and quernstone fragments of tephrite. Surprisingly, the greater number of finds comes from the east zone. One explanation for this is that large pits which act as artefact traps are scarcely found in the west zone. The traces there mainly consist of postholes of limited size. It is significant that more than half of all the settlement pottery in Someren (ca 2500 sherds) comes from only a handful of pits within two house sites (building IA and ID/E).[69] For want of datable pottery, most of the buildings have been attributed to a certain period on the basis of typochronology of house-plans. In the following section a number of characteristic farmyards will be presented in chronological order as an example. Subsequently the structure and development of the settlement as a whole will be discussed.

4.1 HOUSE AND YARD

During the analysis of the settlement, the basic assumption was that, from an archaeological point of view, the yard consists of a main building, several outbuildings such as barns and sheds, and very occasionally a well. Boundaries in the form of ditch systems, palisades or fences are not present or were not preserved. A practical problem with interpreting clusters of settlement traces is that it is difficult to reconstruct contemporary structures of a yard – partly due to the absence of datable features. A cluster of traces may be the result of continuous habitation for several generations, or the regular – or incidental – return to the same location. The presence of a large concentration of outbuildings tells us more about a greater continuity in habitation and the relatively short life-span of such structures than about a large storage capacity and therefore surplus production.[70] An important lead in recognizing a longer period of habitation at the farmyard level is the extent to which the main building underwent archaeologically traceable repairs, or was simply replaced as a whole. In the following, we shall discuss examples of multi-phase as well as single-phase yards.

4.2 SETTLEMENT TRACES FROM THE EARLY IRON AGE: THE EASTERN ZONE

Cluster I

The oldest cluster of settlement traces was excavated in the most easterly part of the area (fig. 17, I). This is an elongated northwest-southeast zone (ca 140 × 40 m.) with postholes and larger pits. The most southerly section could not be excavated so far. The site is badly eroded, making it difficult in some cases for houseplans to be identified. This applies particularly to a group of post traces northeast

[69] As mentioned earlier, one must take into account the fact that ca 30 cm of the top layer is included in the medieval arable layer. Most of the settlement refuse in the arable layer has gradually disappeared due to erosion.

[70] Cf. Gent 1983, 243-267.

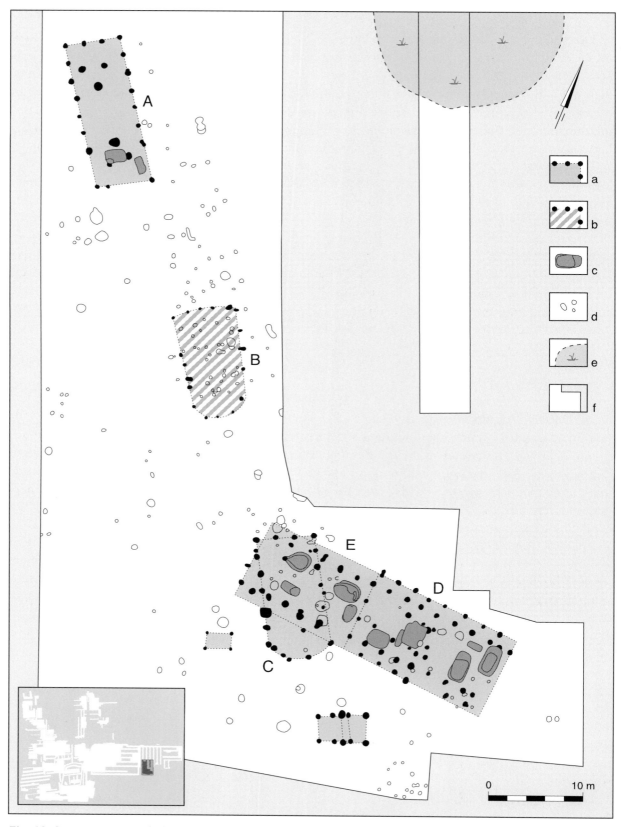

Fig. 18. Someren. General plan of the southern part of cluster I (Early Iron Age ca 650-600 BC). Scale 1 : 400. A – E: houses; a. postholes of building; b. probable house-plan; c. cellar pit; d. other traces; e. depression; f. boundary excavated area

174

of some larger outbuildings in the north part and building IB which will be discussed below. Figure 18 shows the south part of the zone. Four to five main buildings can be distinguished:

– *Building IA* (orientation NW-SE). A rectangular building ca 15.5 × 7 m. The outermost posts supporting the eaves are probably missing. The groundplan would originally have been wider (see also building ID/E). Four shallow postholes inside the building are probably part of the roof-supporting construction. The common house type in the Early Iron Age is the three- or four-aisled byre-house (*Wohnstallhaus*). Inside the house, on the south side, there are two rectangular pits with a flat bottom (2.25 × 1.25 × 0.50 m. and 1.90 × 0.80 × 0.50 m.). On the longitudinal axis there are two shallow basin-shaped pits. In the most southerly of these there were some burnt bones of a medium-sized dog in addition to some pottery.[71]
– *Building IB* (orientation NW-SE). The interpretation of this group of traces is uncertain. It was possibly a three- or four-aisled house (ca 11.5 × 6 m.) with a rounded short side on the south and a straight short side on the north. It is not clear which traces belong to the roof-supporting inner structure. Most of the traces are very shallow.
– *Building IC* (orientation NW-SE). The building (ca 13 × 6 m.) has a rounded short side on the south and a straight short side on the north. The inner structure is unclear. Within the plan there are several large pits. Their orientation, however, makes one suspect that they belong to building ID/E. For want of clear cuts it is not possible to establish whether building IC is younger or older than ID/E.
- *Building ID/E* (orientation W-E). The interpretation of this or these buildings is problematical. The east part (ID) measures 15 × 8.5 m. Due to the presence of six large rectangular pits it is not possible to establish what the roof-supporting construction was like. However, the north side provides information on the wall construction. This consists of a double row of posts, the inner row of which served as the house wall, while the outer row supported the overhanging eaves. There is no evidence of entrances. A row of four posts may have supported the closing west wall of the building. Since many post traces have disappeared, especially in the west part (IE), it is not certain whether this section belonged to the construction of building ID or whether it was a separate building. One could even doubt building IE, were it not that, as in building ID, there are several large pits which are parallel or at right angles to an (imaginary) long wall and thus have the same orientation as the pits in building ID. Moreover, the innermost wall posts appear to continue from ID to IE. If building IE was part of ID, there would be a ground-plan of ca 28 m. long and 8.5 m. wide.

This resembles the building structures from Wisch and Loon op Zand which were interpreted as a double house.[72]

The excavated zone as a whole represents the traces of two to three farmyards. The most northerly of these consisted of a main building (which could not be reconstructed) and two large SE-NW oriented barns (both 6 × 3 m.), one of which was later replaced by a larger barn 8.5 × 4 m. The section shown in figure 18 with the traces of 4 to 5 houses, one six-post and two four-post granaries, must be attributed to various yards, of which two at most were contemporaneous. Buildings IA and ID/E

---

[71] Identification Rick Maliepaard, IPP.

[72] Silvolde-mun. of Wisch (Groenewoudt/Verlinde 1989, 278); Loon op Zand, house 3 (Roymans/ Hiddink 1991, 115 ff.). The latter plan (ca 24 x 8 m.) is divided into two equal spaces by a (double?) row of posts. In both spaces, parallel to the long sides, there is a rectangular pit, which may be interpreted as a storage cellar.

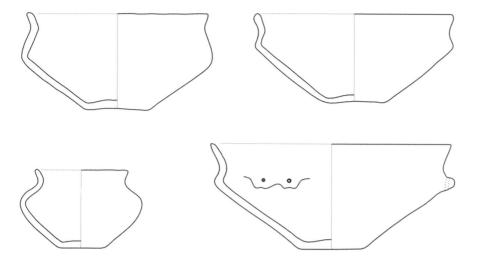

Fig. 19. Someren. Some almost complete pottery from a storage pit in house ID. Scale 1 : 4.

stand out because of the large pits inside the plans.[73] In the last decades, Early Iron Age houses with similar pits have been excavated in different places in the Lower Rhine area.[74] The number of pits in the house varies considerably. In some cases their number is so great that they cannot have been contemporaneous.[75] Possibly some of them were dug after the house had lost its dwelling function. The pits are generally interpreted as storage cellars. What might have been stored in the cellar pits of buildings IA and ID/E is unclear. On the one hand perhaps perishable foodstuffs like milk and meat products. This is perhaps indicated by three virtually complete bowls and a small cup which were found, together with a loaf-shaped tephrite quern, on the floor of the most easterly pit in building ID (fig. 19).[76] On the other hand, the pits may have served to store both sowing grain and grain for consumption. Some pits appear to have been quickly closed with clean sand after use. Others seem to have had a secondary usage as refuse pit. The fill of several pits in building ID/E consisted of red burnt sand and much charcoal, in addition to a large quantity of potsherds. Much of the pottery, including the sherds of a number of large storage pots, had been secondarily burnt to a high degree. Apparently the material had been exposed to fire. The house possibly met its end in a fire, or, after being abandoned, was intentionally set alight. On the basis of the pottery, the houses with storage cellars can be dated in the Early Iron Age, and more specifically, in Van den Broeke's phases B or C (650 BC − 575 BC).[77] They therefore belong to the earliest phase in relation to the urnfield.

[73]   The mainly rectangular pits at Someren vary in size from ca 1 x 0.60 m. to 3.75 x 1.75 m. The remaining depth varies from 0.20 to 0.75 m.

[74]   House-plans with storage cellars in the Lower Rhine area: St-Oedenrode (Kortlang 1987; Van Bodegraven 1991); Riethoven (Slofstra 1991, Vanderhoeven 1991); Loon op Zand (Roymans/Hiddink 1991); Silvolde, mun. of Wisch (Groenewoudt/Verlinde 1989, 278); Deventer (Verlinde 1991); Colmschate-Swormink (Groenewoudt/Verlinde 1989).

[75]   Cf. St-Oedenrode (Van Bodegraven 1991, 129 ff.). Riethoven-Heesmortel (Slofstra 1991, 141 ff.).

[76]   Illustrative in this respect are the sherds of three bowls with perforated walls, found in one of the cellar pits of house 3 at Loon op Zand. The perforated bowls may be associated with cheese-making (Roymans/Hiddink 1991, 124-125).

[77]   Van den Broeke 1987, 27 ff. The find material from the pits at Someren was studied by IPP student Conny van der Horst (Van der Horst 1997). As mentioned

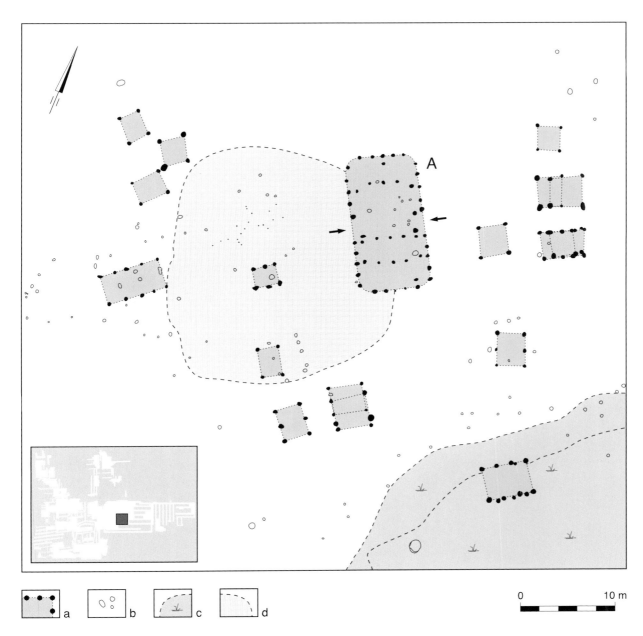

Fig. 20. Someren. General plan of an Early Iron Age farmyard of cluster II. Scale 1 : 400.
A. house; a. postholes of building; b. other traces; c. depression; d. 'dirt layer'

Cluster II.
The second cluster of settlement traces from the Early Iron Age is situated west of two natural depressions (fig. 17, II). Roughly speaking, three types of building can be distinguished. Two buildings can be interpreted as farmhouses. They are both NW-SE oriented and measure 15 × 7.5 m. and 9 × 5 m. respectively. The largest building (see below) is probably a farmhouse with a living section and a byre. This is less likely in the case of the other building in view of its smaller size. A third farmhouse may have been located further north, but few traces of it have been preserved. Large cellar pits inside the farmhouses, as in cluster I, are not found in this section. However, on the north side of the cluster,

three pits in a row were found, all of a similar size. There is no evidence for a building structure in the vicinity of the pits. The other types of building consist of four- and six-post granaries and some outbuildings of a larger size (7 × 3 m.; 5 × 3.5 m.). As to the function of the latter structures, not much can be said. They were possibly barns for storing crops and equipment, or stalls for small livestock. It is striking that, in contrast to the main buildings and most of the six-post granaries, they are SW-NE oriented. The traces in cluster II represent at least three farmyards. It is uncertain whether they existed contemporaneously. It is furthermore conceivable that a main building on the north side was erased from the archaeological record by later reclamations.

Judging from the distribution of the building traces, the southernmost yard (fig. 20) must have been about 60 × 60 m. in size. It consisted of a centrally situated main building (IIA) and seventeen outbuildings, which certainly did not all function at the same time. Several granaries were rebuilt on the same spot. The main building, however, shows no clear traces of repair or replacement of posts, so that we may assume that the farmyard was not used for longer than one generation (25 years). On the southeast side the yard is bordered by a shallow depression. This spot may have been quite wet, especially in the winter months. On the border between the depression and the higher area there is a zone of post traces which could not be attributed to building structures. They may have formed part of a kind of fence. Immediately west of the main building a humic layer was observed in the excavation pit, which was riddled with old mole and beetle tunnels. Apart from two granaries, the traces of several dozens of small, deeply driven in pointed stakes were found in this zone. Their fairly random distribution makes it likely that these were separate pickets to which small livestock (goats?) were tethered. The humic layer probably indicates a zone where livestock was kept for a long period. On such a well-manured spot the soil could become deeply burrowed through, especially by the ground fauna.

– *Building IIA* (15 × 7.5 m.; orientation: NW-SE) represents the common house type of the Late Bronze Age and Early Iron Age in the Lower Rhine basin.[78] The building has a four-aisled layout, formed by three rows of three inner posts set parallel to the short walls. The outer posts served as a support for the overhanging roof. Of the house wall on the inside only a few postholes remain. There is no wall trench. Two wide, opposing entrances in the middle of the long walls divide the house into two equal spaces. In view of the small number of inner posts, the north part was probably the living section and the south the byre. The posts set ca 3.5 m. from both short sides indicate a hipped roof construction.

The other buildings consist of 10 relatively large four-post granaries (2.5 × 2.5 m.; 3 × 3 m.); 5 six-post granaries (4.5-5 × 3.5 m.) and two larger structures (10- and 8-post) measuring 8 × 4 m. and 6 × 4.5 m. respectively. The four- and six-post structures are usually associated with the storage of crops,

above, more than 50% of the Iron Age find material at Someren comes from the pits of house IA and ID/E. House IA contained over 200 sherds of several dozen pots. The pits in plan ID/E contain nearly 2000 sherds of ca 170 pots. In five pits there were small fragments of pottery from the coastal area, used as packing material for sea salt (Van den Broeke 1986, 91-114). Spindles and (parts of) loomweights point to wool production. Worth mentioning are also fragments of several querns of sandstone and tephrite. Research into

the charred remains of cereals from the fill of some pits was not very successful: 20 grains of hulled barley; 1 seed of gold-of-pleasure; 2 seeds of millet; 1 hazelnut and 1 blackthorn nut were the result. A C14 date of charcoal from one of the pits produced the value 2520 ± 20 BP (GrN 22202). This is 675-591 / 583-553 cal BC (1 sigma) and 783-757 / 684-542 cal BC (2 sigma).

[78] Type 2B according to the typology of the Iron Age settlement at Oss (Schinkel 1994, part II, 1.1 ff.).

Fig. 21. Someren. General plan of farmyard III (Middle or Late Iron Age). Scale 1 : 400.
A – D: houses; a. postholes of building; b. well; c. other traces; d. hypothetical boundary of farmyard (by means of an earthen bank?); e. depression; f. boundary excavated area

hay and straw.[79] It is assumed that the granaries had a raised platform, partly to keep away vermin, and partly to protect the harvest produce from rising damp.

Pottery was hardly found at all on the plot. The Early Iron Age date was obtained on the basis of typological parallels for the main building. If the well found in the depression, over 50 metres south-east of the site, was built by the inhabitants of this farmyard, it provides us with a precise date of 588 BC (see also section 3.4).

4.3 SETTLEMENT TRACES FROM THE MIDDLE AND LATE IRON AGE: THE WESTERN ZONE

The zone containing the most traces, those of over 20 houses and several hundred outbuildings dating from the Middle and Late Iron Age, is located immediately east and south of the cemetery. This zone yielded hardly any pottery. The date of the buildings is based on several C14 datings and the typology of the houses.[80] The Late Iron Age traces appear to be concentrated mainly in the northwest section of this zone, directly east of the urnfield (see separate annex).[81] A brief description of two clusters of traces from this zone follows.

Cluster III (fig 17, III and fig. 21) consists of four houses, of which buildings III-A to C probably represent three successive phases of the same farm. House D may have been contemporaneous with one of the other houses. All houses are of the Haps type.[82] Especially the more deeply founded central posts and entrances have been preserved. The less deeply founded outer posts supporting the eaves were often only several centimetres deep – if present at all. A wall trench or inner posts marking the wall have not been preserved. The remaining buildings consisting of four- and six-post structures (57 altogether), are mainly concentrated in the southwest corner. They are often found in small groups. Some outbuildings had been replaced several times at the same spot. The sickle-shaped concentration of granaries in the southwest section appears to indicate an angular boundary of the farmyard. The orientation of a number of granaries also seems to be an indication. The southeast side of the yard is bordered by a small shallow depression. A well was dug here in the Iron Age which may have belonged to the farm, though an Early Iron Age date cannot be excluded.[83] The west boundary is probably situated

[79] Various postholes of granaries at Someren yielded charred seeds of hulled barley, emmer, millet, oats and flax (cf. Kortlang 1998).

[80] The houses are all of the 'Haps type' (Verwers 1972) with, as main features: a two-aisled internal division by means of 3 to 5 more deeply founded central posts; two opposed entrances in the middle of the long walls, dividing the house into a living section and a byre, and a hipped roof construction. This type corresponds to type 4 of Schinkel's typology for Oss (Schinkel 1994, part II, 13-15). An exception to this type is building B (separate annex) which has a four-aisled division and probably dates from the Late Iron Age.

[81] Apart from the scanty pottery, three C14 dates of carbonized corn and charcoal from the postholes of two

granaries point in this direction. Corn from granary post: 2070 ± 40 BP (GrN-22201), 182 – 14 cal BC (2 sigma); charcoal from the same posthole: 2190 ± 60 BP (GrN-23202), 382 – 66 cal BC. The date of the charcoal from another granary corresponds to this: 2160 ± 50 (GrN-23201), 364 – 50 cal BC.

[82] The houses have the following dimensions: house A: ca 12.5 x 7.5 m.; house B: 14 x 7.5 m.; house C: 16 x 7.5 m.; house D: ca 12 x 6 m.

[83] Tree-ring dating of the wood from the well did not produce a date. A well in a small depression north of yard III was dated in the Early Iron Age (ca 615 BC) on the basis of dendrochronological analysis of the wood. See also section 3.4.

Fig. 22. Someren. General plan of farmyard IV (Middle Iron Age). Scale 1 : 400.
A: house; a. postholes of building; b. other traces; c. boundary excavated area

east of an elongated (NW-SE) zone containing postholes. On the north side the yard is also bordered by a depression. If we adhere to the boundaries suggested above, this farmyard measures about 60 × 60 m. The position of the houses and the many 'granaries' would suggest a continuous occupation rather than a return to the farmyard after various intervals. Assuming a life-span of ca 25 years for the houses, the farmyard may have been in use for about 75 years. The average number of granaries per generation would then be around 15. The duration of a granary was, however, considerably less that of a house. The transecting plans of granaries show that they were sometimes replaced up to two times on the same spot. If we assume that this took place in one and the same generation, the number of granaries that were in use simultaneously can be reduced to about 5. A more precise date for the house sites than Middle or Late Iron Age cannot be given due to lack of dating material.

Fig. 23. Someren. A storage pit (left) and a well (right). Photograph Fokko Kortlang.

Finally, cluster IV is a fine example of a farmyard from the Middle Iron Age that probably functioned for only one generation (fig. 22). Because the house was built in a small depression, the traces
have been relatively well preserved. The house (IV-A) measures ca 16 × 8.5 m and is one of the few
examples where the wall posts have also been preserved. Five more deeply founded central posts supported the weight of the roof. Two opposing entrances divide the house into a living section and a
byre. It is not clear which section is the byre, probably the slightly longer east part. Around the
Wohnstallhaus traces were found of 11 four-post and 3 six-post structures. Two six-post structures
stand out for their exceptional length (5 and 6 metres respectively). The site did not produce any datable pottery. A C14 date of charcoal from the postholes is being analysed at the moment. Another
C14 sample from a pit ca 50 m. east of the site gave a date of 2310 ± 60 BP.[84]

4.4   OTHER TRACES

Two categories of traces have scarcely been mentioned so far: storage pits and wells. Storage pits are
cylindrical pits with a diameter of ca 1 m. and a flat bottom. The depth of the pits is dependent on the
degree to which the top layer of the feature has disappeared, but is usually over 0.5 m. Pits of this kind
are usually interpreted as storage pits for grain. In contrast to above-ground grain storage in granaries,
the pits were probably used for storing sowing seed.[85] If hermetically sealed, grain could be successfully

[84] GrN-23203: 406 – 354 / 296 – 208 cal BC (1 sigma);   [85] Bakels 1989, 10.
     520 – 192 cal BC (2 sigma).

182

stored for some time. Storage pits are regularly found in Bronze or Iron Age settlements on the higher sandy areas. In some cases layers of charred grain have been found at the bottom of the pits.[86] In Someren a total of 11 features can be interpreted as storage pits: a group of 9 pits on the highest, eastern part of the excavated area (fig. 17, 4 and fig. 23) and two pits in the central part at the transition zone of Early and Middle Iron Age features. The latter were found in the vicinity of a Middle Iron Age house, but need not date from the same period. In the immediate surroundings of the former group, no further building traces were encountered. It is not inconceivable that the pits were originally situated within a farmyard. Traces of buildings may have disappeared here due to the heavy erosion of the sandy ridge. Another possibility is that isolated pits were dug at the edge of a field. The nine pits are probably the result of the repeated annual storage of sowing seed, for which the pits were only used once. In section 4.3 the possibility was mentioned that some cellar pits in the buildings IA and ID/E had a similar function. However, the number of storage pits for the entire excavated area is extremely low. Apparently the above-ground storage of sowing seed in granaries was the rule rather than the exception. In the west zone no pits were found which were suitable for storing grain, which implies that underground storage in the Middle and Late Iron Age was no longer common.

An intriguing matter is that of the water supply for people and animals in the settlement. At places where the ground water is relatively close to the surface, as is the case at Oss, wells are regularly found in the farmyard. For the higher sandy areas the common picture is that wells were dug in depressions, often at some distance from the farmyard.[87] The latter case is partly confirmed in Someren:

[86] Roymans 1985; for some other examples, see Fokkens/Roymans (eds) 1991.

[87] Roymans/Fokkens 1991, 10, 11; Tol, this volume; Oss: Schinkel 1994, 245 ff. The wells at Oss mostly consist of a basin-shaped pit, sometimes lined with sods, in which a hollowed-out tree-trunk, wattle or a revetment of vertically-cleaved posts was placed. Unrevetted waterholes are also found here.

wells are not found in the farmyard. Three wells were discovered in depressions, two of them certainly date from the Early Iron Age. Moreover, at the bottom of the depressions in the east zone, ca 10 smaller waterholes were found with a diameter of 0.5 to 0.8 m. and a maximum depth of ca 0.5 m. They seem to have been used for the short-term water supply in times of extreme drought. The three wells consisted of basin-shaped (open) pits with a diameter of 4 to 6 m. and a depth of ca 2 m. below the excavation level. The revetments found at the bottom of the pits consist of a circle of pointed and/or cleaved oak and occasionally ash planks driven vertically into the soil. In the most northerly well (fig. 17, no. 1) secondarily used construction timber (oak) had also been used. Between the planks, which were set at some distance from each other, no traces of wattle were found. Well 2 had at least two phases. In the first phase it consisted of a construction of vertical wooden poles of alder with a horizontal wickerwork of twigs (fig. 23). At some stage this was replaced by a revetment as described above.

Although most of the depressions were incompletely excavated we must conclude that the number of wells discovered is minimal compared to the hundreds of years that the area was inhabited in the Iron Age. Even more striking than the few specimens from the Iron Age is the complete absence of wells from the Middle Iron Age. How was the water supply organized in this period? Were the wells of the west zone concentrated in a depression which we have not been able to find up to now? Or was the water fetched from the stream valley, further to the west? For the time being we have no answer to these questions.

4.5 STRUCTURE AND DYNAMICS OF THE SETTLEMENT

One first general remark must be made regarding the term settlement. The prevailing archaeological picture of settlements from the urnfield period in the Lower Rhine area is that of a diffuse spatial structure of isolated (single-phase) farmyards which, when the houses required replacing, or when the fields were exhausted, were moved to another location within the territory of the settlement. The urnfield was the fixed centrepoint (almost literally) of the local community in this dynamic system of 'wandering farmsteads'. The above suggests that private ownership of land was hardly developed, and that the emphasis lay on the collective ownership and use of land.[88] The model of wandering house-sites is mainly based on the results of the settlement and cemetery research at St-Oedenrode and Oss, together with the celtic field research in the north of the Netherlands.[89] Someren is the first settlement in the sandy areas where, in addition to an almost complete cemetery, a substantial part (ca 15 hectares) of the associated settlement territory has been investigated. We assume that the settlement traces are the archaeological results of one community which built its farmsteads in various parts of the settlement territory in the course of time. Although we are dealing here with a local variant of the generally accepted model, the research at Someren may provide an important contribution to a further elaboration of this model.

On comparison of the structure and composition of the farmyards in the west zone and those in the east, both similarities and differences can be observed. As a general similarity we may state that in both zones the average farmsteads consists of a main house (probably combining a living quarter and a

[88]   Roymans/Fokkens 1991, 11-13; Roymans/Kortlang 1993, 31.

[89]   Roymans/Fokkens 1991; St-Oedenrode: Van Bode- graven 1991, Van der Sanden 1981; Oss: Schinkel 1994; Harsema 1980, 1991.

byre) and a number of outbuildings. The size of the farmyards in the Early Iron Age will not have differed much from those of the Middle and Late Iron Age. Single- and multi-phased farmyards are found in both zones, although it is not always clear whether this implied a continuous habitation of the yard or the incidental return to the same spot. These were the similarities.

One first point of difference which has already been mentioned is the construction method of the houses: in the Early Iron Age they were of the three- or four-aisled type and in the Middle and Late Iron Age of the two-aisled 'Haps type'. A second difference is the orientation of the houses. Whereas the houses in the east zone are mainly NW-SE oriented, all the houses in the west zone are SW-NE, almost at right angles to the former. The third difference is the absence of large outbuildings (barns?) in the west zone.[90] The only outbuildings here are four- or six-post 'granaries' which, moreover, are usually smaller than those of the east zone (2.5 – 1.5 × 2 m. as opposed to 2.5 × 2.5 m. and 3 × 3 m.). The number of granaries appears relatively larger in the west zone, and they are also more concentrated. This can be explained by the fact that some farmyards in this zone were occupied for more than a generation, while the duration of a granary was substantially shorter than that of a house. A fourth difference concerns the structure of both settlement zones. Whereas the features in the east zone show little structure, the west part seems to be built up of several elongated SW-NE strips with farmyards, with relatively featureless zones in-between.[91] The orientation of the houses corresponds to that of the strips. Several rows of granaries on the north side of the west zone may indicate the hypothetical boundaries of these strips.[92]

With the latter observation in mind, I would again like to refer to the previously-outlined model of wandering house-sites against the background of the celtic field system practised at the time.[93] Although no traces of a celtic field complex (such as earthen banks etc.) were found at Someren due to later reclamations, the settlement structure in the west zone does seem to indicate it.[94] By analogy with the 'primary clearance units' described by Brongers for the celtic field complex of Vaassen (Veluwe), the supposed strips at Someren could imply a more systematic reclamation of this part of the coversand plateau.[95] The eastern settlement zone (Early Iron Age) provides no leads for reconstructing a celtic field system. Even though this does not mean that there was no pattern of small walled fields here, a more systematic reclamation of this zone remains completely out of the picture.

Summing up, it may be stated that, on the basis of the present information, the settlement pattern of the Early Iron Age at Someren fits in well with the general image of settlements from the urnfield period, namely that of scattered – usually single-phased farmsteads, which moved from time to time within the settlement territory. The early traces of habitation at Someren are to be found mainly on the higher parts of the coversand plateau. In the Middle Iron Age a certain contraction of habitation

---

[90] This was already observed by Schinkel in the case of Oss (Schinkel 1994, 250).

[91] Several empty zones were investigated by means of trial trenches. Unfortunately, due to encroaching house-building, several crucial blocks remained unexcavated, so that the 'strip hypothesis' is less certain.

[92] An alternative explanation for the structure-free zone in the north is the presence of a SW-NE oriented prehistoric road.

[93] It is assumed that the more systematic reclamation and exploitation of the sandy areas by means of a system of

small walled fields originated as early as the Late Bronze Age. Celtic fields are mainly known from the Veluwe and Drenthe. In recent years, several findspots of celtic fields have been discovered in the MDS area too, for example in Nederweert (Bruekers 1996, 199-213), Riethoven (Milikowski 1985, 79-85), Kaulille-Bosschellerheide, Maarlo, Gruitrode-Muisvennerheide (Van Impe 1977, 101-109) and Lommel-Riebosserheide (Vandekerchove 1994).

[94] Harsema 1980, 94 ff.

[95] Cf. Brongers 1976, 57 ff. and map 15.

occurs in the slightly lower part of the plateau. Although this cannot be demonstrated conclusively, a celtic field system seems to have formed a major structuring element in the layout of this settlement. The farmsteads, of which no more than three or four were contemporaneous, were in this case situated inside (a part of) the celtic field complex. A tendency toward clustering of the settlement traces in the Middle and Late Iron Age has already been observed in Oss and Haps.[96] With this, an impetus is given toward a settlement structure which was more tied to place as known from the Roman period. The farmyard III described above, which may date from the Middle or the Late Iron Age, is an example of a continuous habitation of a farmyard for several generations.

5 SOME CONCLUDING REMARKS

Round about 650 BC, several families settled with their goods and chattels on the coversand plateau immediately west of the river Aa. As far as we can establish, this part of the plateau was uninhabited on their arrival. The natural vegetation probably consisted of a mixed oak forest with some open spaces at the location of a number of shallow depressions. The first activities of the pioneers were to clear tracts of woodland so that they could lay out small fields and build some farmhouses.

Where did they come from? This group of people had probably split off from a community elsewhere in the area. They possibly originated from the region west of the river Kleine Aa (the later heath zone), from which several Early Iron Age urnfields are known (fig. 2a, 1-3).[97]

The pioneers of the virgin territory perhaps included the people who were later buried in the more monumental grave structures of the cemetery. The man in long-bed 5 may be regarded as the initiator and head of the group. After his death, he was buried in a colossal long-bed, 145 m. in length. As a metaphor for the house and the family, the long-beds had a more collective significance than the other graves. The extreme size of long-bed 5 in this sense emphasizes the status of the deceased as an ancestral founding father for the community as a whole. With the construction of the cemetery, the newly-founded community symbolicly claimed the surrounding area. The deceased were buried in the collective cemetery during a period of over 250 years. Whether the cemetery was still in use after 400/350 BC is less clear. From the settlement evidence there appears to have been continuity of habitation in the area until into the Late Iron Age. Several flat graves in the periphery of the cemetery possibly indicate a continuation of the tradition of burying the dead in or near the cemetery. However, three flat graves found at Late Iron Age house-sites may reflect a break with this tradition. The custom of building burial monuments in the form of small ditched mounds disappears.

---

[96] Oss: Schinkel 1994, 135, 189; Haps: Verwers 1972, 63 ff.

[97] One reason why this group split off may have been a combination of demographic and social stress, triggered by ecological and anthropogenic factors. The systematic removal of the natural vegetation together with a relatively extensive form of agriculture and possibly a deterioration of climate in about 800 BC led in the west part of the micro-region to a degradation of the soils (which were poor in loam) as a result of secondary podzolization. This resulted in the continuous shrinkage of the available area of arable land and an increase in the heath vegetation. Once the critical ecological and demographic threshold was reached, the splitting-off of groups to other (sparsely- or unpopulated) landscape zones was an adequate means of reducing social stress. Cf. Spek 1993; Theuws/Roymans, this volume. For climatic changes in the Late Bronze Age cf. Van Geel et al. in press.

In the course of the Middle Iron Age, the farmyards gradually shift from the south towards the northwest. Unfortunately, due to the new housing development, we were not in a position to investigate the zone on the east side of the cemetery. This would probably have yielded important information on the further course of habitation in the Late Iron Age. Evidence for habitation of the area in the Early Roman period is an inhumation grave, dug in about 20/30 AD in the middle of the east ditch of long-bed 45. The farmhouse which can probably be associated with the grave was discovered ca 75 m. further south. The traces of a second farmhouse were found several hundred metres to the east. The settlement evidence is not yet conclusive enough for us to be able to speak of continuous habitation from the Late Iron Age into the Early Roman period.

On the basis of the settlement and cemetery evidence a picture can be evoked for the Someren Iron Age community. The mixed farm was the subsistence basis of the community. The farmhouse, with a dwelling section and a byre, housed the family and a number of head of cattle. In addition to stock-breeding (cattle, pigs, sheep and/or goats and possibly horses), products of celtic field agriculture (including barley, emmer wheat, millet, pulses and oleiferous seeds) were the main source of food. Storage of these agricultural products took place in the farmyard, above all in four- and six-post structures. Calculations of the area of arable land required per household, consisting of six persons, fluctuates for the sandy areas between 6 and 9 hectares, assuming an annual 2/3 fallow section (4 to 6 hectares).[98] For a community of an average of four households this would amount to 24 to 36 hectares of arable land. The fallow fields could be grazed by the cattle, ensuring natural fertilization of the fields – be it to a limited degree. In addition, the cattle could be grazed outside the arable land, for example in and around the shallow depressions and in places where a heath vegetation had developed.

Fragments of tephrite querns from the Eifel region and several sherds of pottery from the coastal area, indicating the import of sea salt, bear witness to interregional exchange relations. This exchange which also included ornaments, tools and weapons will have been strongly embedded in social relations. As such, it illustrates the integration of the Someren community in wider social networks.

---

[98] Schinkel 1994, 256; Bakels 1989, 8; Harsema 1980, 98-99.

Appendix 1. Table of graves and burial monuments.
C= circular ditch; F= flatgrave; I= inhumation grave; L= long-bed; R= rectangular ditch.

grave number	monument type	inside diameter	outside diameter	length	width outside	width ditch	depth ditch	width opening	degrees from N.	weight cremation	sex	age	additional remarks
1	C	5.15	6.15	-	-	50	16	90	100	400	M?	>20	
2	F	-	-	-	-	-	-	-	-	433	M??	30-47	bronze-discolouration on cremation remains
3	L	-	-	8.20	4.50	70	20	320	165	1271	M	24-40	
4	C	14.25	17.95	-	-	200	40	115	115	2570	M	30-40	circle of 26 posts (within ditch)
5.1	L	-	-	144.50	4.60	40	15	325	150	1259	M?	20-40	see also grave number 5.2
5.2	L	-	-	-	-	-	-	-	-	847	F??	30-60	see also grave number 5.1
6	C	10.10	12.75	-	-	110	37	130	185	687	?	30-60	circle of 18 posts (within ditch)
7	C	11.00	12.85	-	-	10	22	60	155	193	?	30-50	circle of 21 posts (within ditch)
8	C	5.45	6.75	-	-	55	17	55	155	15	?	?	
9	F	-	-	-	-	-	-	-	-	118	?	A?	
10	L	-	-	17.40	4.40	90	30	275	150	2333	M?	24-28	alongside long-bed no. 5
11	C	4.65	5.70	-	-	55	20	70	170	7	?	?	
12	C	4.30	5.45	-	-	60	25	40	150	-			
13	C	2.55	2.90	-	-	35	5	45	135	-			
14	C	4.55	5.70	-	-	60	20	65	140	132	?	?	
15	C	5.70	6.90	-	-	65	20	60	140	-			
16	F	-	-	-	-	-	-	-	-	493	?	A?	
17	F	-	-	-	-	-	-	-	-	111	?	20-44	
18	C	4.35	5.05	-	-	40	5	?	?	22	?	?	
19	C	3.50	4.50	-	-	55	15	75	130	70	M??	A?	
20	C	5.55	6.75	-	-	70	25	?	?	16	F??	A?	
21	C	3.60	4.60	-	-	50	14	65	140	-			
22	C	2.60	3.30	-	-	35	12	80	110	-			
23	C	4.10	5.05	-	-	55	30	45	130	21	M?	20-40	cremation remains in medieval feature
24	C	2.60	3.30	-	-	40	10	45	140	-			
25	C	4.60	5.35	-	-	45	18	45	140	206	?	12-16	
26	C	2.00	2.60	-	-	30	10	?	?	?	?	?	few cremation remains
27	C	1.80	2.40	-	-	30	5	70	135	-			
28	C	3.45	4.35	-	-	50	30	80	150	-			
29	C	3.70	4.45	-	-	30	5	80	175	2	?	?	
30	C	3.60	4.50	-	-	45	15	45	180	-			amber bead in ditch
31	C	4.50	5.55	-	-	50	8	115	115	?	?	?	few cremation remains
32	C	4.05	5.30	-	-	65	25	60	135	26	?	?	
33	C	5.10	6.70	-	-	85	18	85	160	-			width opening >= 85 cm
34	C	3.20	4.30	-	-	50	10	135	135	-			
35	C	4.10	4.80	-	-	80	25	100	100	14	?	?	
36	C	2.60	3.30	-	-	35	8	75	145	-			
37	C	2.85	3.70	-	-	40	18	60	115	-			
38	C	4.10	5.60	-	-	65	16	?	100	2	?	?	ditch incomplete
39	C	3.50	4.00	-	-	25	5	?	?	-			ditch incomplete
40	C	4.20	5.20	-	-	50	15	?	140	-			ditch incomplete
41	C	3.70	4.60	-	-	45	10	45	115	-			
42	C	3.90	4.85	-	-	45	15	?	?	-			ditch incomplete
43	L	-	-	14.05	4.60	100	35	275	145	-			
44	L	-	-	28.10	3.85	80	20	250	145	-			
45	L	-	-	28.10	4.35	90	15	250	145	-			width N.: 325 cm; S.: 255cm; Roman-age grave intersects ditch
46	C	3.70	4.55	-	-	50	18	70	150	-			
47	C	3.25	4.20	-	-	50	22	60	120	-			

grave number	monument type	dimensions								weight cremation	sex	age	additional remarks
		inside diameter	outside diameter	length	width outside	width ditch	depth ditch	width opening	degrees from N.				
48	C	5.70	7.30	-	-	85	30	?	?	1983	F	30-40	
49	F	-	-	-	-	-	-	-	-	18	?	>±12	
50	R	-	-	5.55	5.40	22	60	60	135	61	?	?	perforated bone pendant
51	R	-	-	7.60	7.30	18	75	70	135	4	?	>±12	
52	C	4.80	6.05	-	-	10	55	85	140	-			
53	C	4.80	5.80	-	-	16	50	75	155	-			
54	C	4.85	5.85	-	-	14	50	90	160	-			
55	C	4.70	6.05	-	-	25	65	60	140	-			
56	C	5.80	6.95	-	-	18	60	85	140	12	?	J?	
57	C	5.25	6.15	-	-	10	45	85	105	-			
58	C	3.35	4.40	-	-	15	55	75	135	-			
59	C	3.75	4.50	-	-	5	40	?	?	?	?	?	few cremation remains
60	C	3.40	4.30	-	-	14	45	60	130	-			
61	C	3.40	4.40	-	-	20	55	50	125	-			
62	C	2.90	3.65	-	-	8	45	25	130	303	M?	A	
63	C	3.70	4.60	-	-	10	45	75	145	2	?	?	
64	C	4.10	4.95	-	-	12	45	60	125	290	F?	23-40	
65	C	5.40	6.35	-	-	24	55	85	140	27	?	A?	
66	C	3.15	4.05	-	-	10	45	70	120	-			
67	C	5.85	6.95	-	-	22	55	35	105	2	?	>10	
68	C	3.80	5.00	-	-	25	55	90	140	-			traces of a pyre(?) at the bottom of the ditch
69	C	5.30	6.55	-	-	17	55	115	140	-			
70	L	-	-	8.55	5.55	14	50	455	150	-			long-bed incomplete
71	C	4.15	5.10	-	-	20	50	60	155	2	?	?	cremation grave excentric (S.W.)
72	C	4.35	5.05	-	-	10	45	55	165	-			
73	C	2.80	3.45	-	-	15	40	55	95	-			
74	C	4.70	5.80	-	-	15	55	55	135	5	?	10-40	
75	C	3.15	3.95	-	-	18	45	50	160	?	?	?	few cremation remains
76	C	3.30	4.20	-	-	15	50	85	115	7	?	?	
77	C	4.10	5.20	-	-	15	55	85	125	-			
78	C	4.15	5.10	-	-	8	50	?	?	-			
79	C	3.40	4.20	-	-	8	40	?	?	-			
80	C	3.15	3.70	-	-	8	30	?	?	-			
81	C	4.00	5.00	-	-	18	50	75	135	-			diameter estimated
82	C	4.50	5.85	-	-	18	60	75	95	-			
83	C	2.90	3.55	-	-	7	35	?	?	-			
84	C	3.90	4.90	-	-	12	50	55	150	-			diameter estimated
85	C	4.85	6.05	-	-	25	65	60	135	5	?	?	
86	C	3.20	4.10	-	-	?	45	45	140	-			diameter estimated
87	F	-	-	-	-	-	-	-	-	29	?	?	
88	C	4.45	5.10	-	-	?	45	45	150	166	F?	50-70	
89	L	-	-	45.50	3.60	?	40	?	150	-			northern short side of ditch uncertain
90	F	-	-	-	-	-	-	-	-	241	?	12-15	
91	C	?	?	-	-	10	35	?	?	-			few cremation remains
92	C	2.25	2.65	-	-	4	20	?	?	-			
93	C	5.95	7.15	-	-	15	60	125	155	7	?	?	
94	C	4.05	5.05	-	-	18	50	90	145	-			
95	F	-	-	-	-	-	-	-	-	17	?	>2<7	

grave number	monument type	inside diameter	outside diameter	length	width outside	width ditch	depth ditch	width opening	degrees from N.	weight cremation	sex	age	additional remarks
96	C	6.50	7.80	-	-	20	65	115	130	-			
97	C	3.30	4.25	-	-	14	45	95	155	-			
98	C	5.70	6.80	-	-	15	65	85	170	-			
99	C	5.00	6.20	-	-	8	55	85	130	-			
100	C	4.75	5.85	-	-	?	55	80	130	-			
101	C	?	?	-	-	?	30	?	?	-			
102	C	4.80	5.85	-	-	6	55	?	135	-			opening assumed
103	C	5.00	6.40	-	-	15	65	105	150	?	?	?	few cremation remains
104	C	4.40	5.50	-	-	15	55	50	140	-			
105	C	4.60	5.75	-	-	14	55	55	140	-			
106	C	3.25	4.25	-	-	10	50	75	110	-			
107	C	4.65	5.60	-	-	20	50	?	?	92	?	?	no opening observed
108	F	-	-	-	-	-	-	-	-	1295	M	20-40	grave number 109 in ditch
109	C	4.70	5.75	-	-	25	55	40	160	-			see also grave number 108
110	C	2.40	3.20	-	-	5	40	?	?	-			diameter estimated
111	C	3.55	4.45	-	-	12	45	?	?	-			few cremation remains in centre
112	C	2.30	2.90	-	-	3	30	?	?	-			
113	C	2.90	3.80	-	-	20	45	?	?	-			
114	C	3.85	4.55	-	-	8	35	?	?	-			
115	C	2.85	3.65	-	-	15	40	80	105	-			
116	C	3.05	3.90	-	-	16	45	30	140	-			
117	C	2.35	3.05	-	-	16	35	55	160	20	?	?	
118	C	2.10	2.75	-	-	7	35	55	140	-			
119	L	-	-	7.80	2.95	12	50	195	145	490	?	A?	
120	L	-	-	14.15	3.75	10	55	235	150	-			see also grave number 121
121	L	-	-	12.85	3.05	6	35	215	150	701	M	20-40	see also grave number 120
122	L	-	-	9.30	2.95	10	40	190	150	?	?	?	few cremation remains
123	C	2.30	3.15	-	-	6	40	?	?	-			
124	C	3.25	4.10	-	-	8	40	50	120	20	?	J?	
125	C	3.15	3.95	-	-	6	40	?	?	?	?	?	few cremation remains
126	C	2.30	2.85	-	-	5	35	?	?	-			
127	C	4.75	5.60	-	-	8	40	?	?	-			
128	C	5.05	6.30	-	-	10	60	50	125	-			
129	C	4.30	5.40	-	-	20	55	60	130	-			
130	C	4.30	5.30	-	-	16	50	95	145	-			
131	C	5.00	6.20	-	-	20	65	55	150	-			
132	C	2.45	3.10	-	-	12	40	?	?	-			
133	C	2.75	3.35	-	-	5	35	?	?	-			
134	C	2.75	3.50	-	-	7	40	65	125	-			
135	C	3.35	4.25	-	-	14	45	95	140	-			
136	C	4.15	5.15	-	-	14	50	75	110	-			
137	C	5.25	6.50	-	-	20	60	95	140	39	F??	23-40	
138	C	4.35	5.35	-	-	20	50	65	120	-			
139	C	4.10	5.10	-	-	20	45	65	120	-			
140	C	5.00	6.05	-	-	12	55	?	?	20	?	?	
141	C	3.30	4.30	-	-	5	45	70	140	-			
142	C	5.05	6.15	-	-	20	55	90	115	608	F	23-40	with bone fragments of a neonate
143	C	4.20	5.55	-	-	20	60	50	135	52	?	A	
144	C	5.50	7.05	-	-	30	90	70	130	185	?	20-40	
145	C	5.20	6.90	-	-	32	80	60	115	53	?	?	
146	C	4.20	5.55	-	-	20	70	75	135	67	?	>18	
147	C	2.60	3.20	-	-	4	30	?	?	-			

grave number	monument type	inside diameter	outside diameter	length	width outside	width ditch	depth ditch	width opening	degrees from N.	weight cremation	sex	age	additional remarks
148	F	-	-	-	-	-	-	-	-	814	M?	30-60	
149	C	4.40	5.40	-	-	6	50	?	?	-			
150	L	-	-	11.15	4.25	10	65	185	130	?	?	?	see grave number 151 (few cremation remains)
151	L	-	-	11.80	3.10	12	50	205	130	?	?	?	see grave number 150 (few cremation remains)
152	C	4.00	5.20	-	-	15	60	55	135	126	M	A	
153	C	4.90	5.60	-	-	3	35	?	?	5	?	A?	
154	C	2.80	3.40	-	-	2	30	?	?	-			
155	C	4.10	5.20	-	-	10	55	55	170	-			
156	C	4.00	4.85	-	-	8	45	50	140	36	?	?	disturbed grave
157	R	-	-	6.15	6.15	18	50	70	120	3	?	?	cremation grave excentric
158	R	-	-	6.30	6.15	15	50	60	120	24	?	20-60	cremation in medieval feature
159	R	-	-	?	?	10	60	?	110	-			monument incomplete
160	R	-	-	8.40	7.75	22	65	60	105	?	?	?	few cremation remains
161	R?	-	-	?	?	8	35	?	?	-			grave monument uncertain
162	C	5.00	6.00	-	-	16	50	55	135	-			
163	?	-	-	?	?	3	45	?	?	-			grave with post structure (?)
164	C	4.80	5.50	-	-	3	35	?	?	-			
165	C	2.85	3.45	-	-	5	30	?	?	1	?	?	
166	F	-	-	-	-	-	-	-	-	108	?	20-40	
167	C	3.25	3.95	-	-	4	35	105	165	-			
168	R	-	-	7.20	6.80	20	50	50	130	-			some cremation remains in ditch
169	R	-	-	7.00	6.35	12	55	65	115	8	?	?	
170	R	-	-	6.15	6.05	10	55	?	115	-			connected to grave 169
171	R	-	-	4.70	4.60	8	35	?	?	18	F??	A?	opening disturbed
172	R	-	-	6.35	6.30	15	55	55	115	2	?	?	
173	R	-	-	5.90	5.30	12	60	80	120	-			opening in S.W.
174	C	5.00	5.80	-	-	8	40	70	120	-			
175	L	-	-	9.75	4.50	20	60	340	140	1182	M	23-40	decorated antler in grave
176	R	-	-	?	?	39	85	65	120	-			
177	R	-	-	?	?	15	55	?	?	-			
178	F	-	-	-	-	-	-	-	-	232	F	20-40	
179	R	-	-	22.00	17.75	25	70	75	190	-			double grave(?)
180	R	-	-	?	?	12	55	?	?	-			
181	R	-	-	5.90	5.75	15	50	75	185	-			
182	F	-	-	-	-	-	-	-	-	54	?	20-40	
183	F	-	-	-	-	-	-	-	-	32	?	12<40	
184	I	-	-	2.15	-	15	-	-	130	-	?	?	roughened tripartite bowl with carinated profile
185	F	-	-	-	-	-	-	-	-	817	F	20-40	excavation "Hoge Akkers" 1995

Appendix 2

Table of cremation remains

grave number	weight							fragmen-tation	calci-nation	sex	age	animal	additional remarks
	neuro-cranium	viscero-cranium	axial skeleton	diaphysis	epiphysis	residual	total						
1	26	12	20	167	10	165	400	4	4	M?	>20		PZ +2
2	49	9	8	83	34	250	433	4	5	M??	30-47		POE +1; PZ +1; CSM -1; sec. bronze discolouration
3	162	33	185	226	51	618	1275	6,4	4,5	M	24-40		POE +2; PZ +1; CSM +1; IIM +2; OI +2: robust
4	207	40	330	818	165	1010	2570	4	5	M	30-40	sheep or pig?	POE +2; PZ +2; SP +2; IM +2
5/1	70	4	40	300	55	790	1259	3,2	4,5	M?	20-40		RPN +1; CSM 0; PC skeleton rather robust
5/2	60	21	30	220	16	500	847	5,3	4	F??	30-60		PM +1; PP=female
6	65	6	63	230	8	315	687	5,4	4,5	-	30-60		osteophytosis on lumbal vertebra(?)
7	11	1	3	100	3	75	193	3,2	4	-	30-50	sheep	disturbed cremation in medieval post-holes
8	0	0	0	15	0	0	15		4,5	-	-		
9	0	0	5	50	8	55	118		4,5	-	A??		
10	120	30	300	520	63	1300	2333	6	4,5	M?	24-28		AS -1; IF -1; PZ +1; CSM 0; SP +2; AP+2
11	1	0	0	3	0	3	7	1	4	-	-		
14	17	0	0	38	2	75	132	3	4,5	-	-		
16	12	7	35	159	3	277	493	3,4	4,5	-	A??		
17	5	0	3	65	1	37	111	3	4,5	-	20-44		LA on the femur is robust
18	6	1	3	10	0	2	22	2	4,5	-	-		
19	2	1	35	2	0	30	70	2	4,5	M?	A??		AS +2
20	2	0	3	8	0	3	16	2	4	F?	A??		IIM −1
23	10	3	0	2	0	6	21	2	4	M??	20-40		CSM +1
25	8	1	2	10	0	185	206	2,1	4	-	12-16		teeth + closing of epiphyses
29	0	0	0	0	0	2	2	<2	4	-	-		
32	5	0	1	4	0	16	26	4	4	-	-		
35	0	0	0	0	0	14	14	<2	4	-	-		
38	0	0	0	0	0	2	2	<2	4	-	-		
48	115	35	135	500	48	1150	1983	4	4	F	30-40		AS -1; PZ -1; MO -1; minor osteophyto-sis
49	0	0	0	0	0	18	18	<2	4	-	>±12		older than 12 years ± 12 months
50	2	0	0	26	3	30	61		4	-	-	(sheep?)	perforated bone pendant (metatarsus sheep?)
51	0	0	0	0	0	4	4	<2	4	-	>±12		
56	0	0	0	0	0	12	12	<2	4	-	J?		Sutura metopica
62	9	3	6	55	0	230	303	3	4,5	M?	A		CSM +2
63	0	0	0	0	0	2	2	<2	4	-	-		
64	14	2	8	63	3	200	290	4	4	F?	23-40		RRPN +1; PZ -2; CSM 0; MO 0; MM -2
65	1	0	0	16	0	10	27	2	4	-	A?		
67	0	0	0	0	0	2	2	<2	4	-	>10		

grave number	weight							fragmentation	calcination	sex	age	animal	additional remarks
	neuro-cranium	viscero-cranium	axial skeleton	diaphysis	epiphysis	residual	total						
71	0	0	0	0	0	2	2	<2	4	-	-		
74	0	0	0	0	0	5	5	<2	4	-	10-40		Phalanx
6	0	0	0	0	0	7	7	<2	4	-	-		
85	0	0	0	0	0	5	5	<2	4	-	-		
87	0	0	0	0	0	29	29	<2	4	-	-		
88	8	1	13	67	2	75	166	5,2	4	F?	50-70		MO –2
90	25	4	20	115	10	67	241	3,4	4,5	-	12-15		teeth + closing of epiphyses
93	0	0	0	0	0	7	7	<2	4	-	-		
95	0	0	0	0	0	17	17	<2	4	-	2-7		
107	3	0	4	30	0	55	92	2	4	-	-		
108	95	40	250	260	120	530	1295	8	4,5	M	20-40		PM +2; CSM +2; MO +2; IIM +1; very robust
117	0	0	0	0	0	20	20	<2	4	-	-		
119	9	0	9	72	0	400	490	2	4	-	A?		
121	56	7	45	300	3	290	701	4	4	M	20-40		SP +1; IIM +1
124	0	0	0	0	0	20	20	<2	4	-	J?		thickness of skull + open sutures
137	16	3	3	11	0	6	39	5,3	4	F??	23-40		fragm. orbit slightly female
140	0	0	0	0	020	20	<2	4	-	-			
142	69	12	64	250	13	200	608	4	4,5	F	23-40		IIM -2; also some fragments of a neonate
143	9	0	5	18	0	20	52	3	4	-	A		
144	11	0	10	42	3	119	185	3,2	4	-	20-40		
145	3	0	3	47	0	0	53	2	4	-	-		
146	3	1	7	3	0	53	67	2,1	4	-	>18		age: full-grown M3-root
148	42	3	17	320	2	430	814	5,2	4	M?	30-60	Sheep	CSM + 1; MO + 2; IIM 0 (slightly male)
152	11	12	12	21	0	70	126	3,2	4	M	A		MO + 2; CM = robust
153	0	0	0	0	0	5	5	<2	4	-	A?		
156	3	1	5	11	16	0	36	3,2	4	-	-		
157	0	0	0	0	0	3	3	<2	4	-	-		
158	7	0	0	7	0	10	24	3	4	-	20-60		thickness of skull
165	0	0	0	0	0	1	1	<2	4	-	-		
166	11	1	3	17	76	0	108	3,1	4	-	20-40		
169	0	0	0	0	0	8	8	<2	4	-	-		
171	0	2	0	0	0	16	18	<2	4	F??	A?		PZ; impression: female
172	0	0	0	0	0	2	2	<2	4	-	-		
175	117	30	142	400	29	464	1182	6,5	4	M	23-40	sheep+roedeer	PM+1; PZ + 1; CSM 0; MO -2; SP + 2; IIM + 2
178	89	10	10	27	6	90	232	5	4	F	20-40	Pig	AS -2; MO -2. pig foot: fragmentation: 10
182	8	0	11	14	21	0	54	3	4	-	20-40		
183	0	0	0	0	0	32	32	3	4	-	12<40		thin LA; 12years or older
185	78	28	120	245	20	380	871	4,7	4,5	F	20-24		M(F)O -2; AM -1 (excavation "Hoge Akkers")

Abbreviations
AM = Angulus mandibula; AP = Angelo pubis; AS = Arcus superciliaris; CM = Condylus mandibula; CSM = Cristra supra mastoidea; IF = Inclinatio frontale; IIM = Incisura ischiadica major; LA = Linea aspera; MM = Margo mandibula; MO = Margo orbita; OI = Os ischii; POE = Protuberantia occipitalis externa; PP = Pars petrosa; PZ = Processus zygomaticus; RPN = Relief planum nuchale; SP = Sulcus preauricularis;

REFERENCES

Annaert, R./L. van Impe, 1985: Een grafheuvelgroep uit de ijzertijd te Klein-Ravels (gem. Ravels), *AB* I, 2: 37-41.

Ascádi, G./J. Némeskeri, 1970: *History of Human life span and mortality*, Budapest.

Bakels, C.C., 1989: *Een lading graan*, inaugurele rede, Leiden.

Bakels, C.C., 1994: Vruchten en zaden uit de ijzertijd-nederzettingen te Oss-Ussen, in K. Schinkel (eds), *Zwervende erven. Bewoningssporen in Oss-Ussen uit bronstijd, ijzertijd en Romeinse tijd. Opgravingen 1976-1986, I-II (catalogus)*, Leiden (diss.), 219-232.

Beex, G.A.C., 1960: *De urnenvelden cultuur in de Kempen*, Tongeren.

Bloemers, J.H.F., 1986: A cart burial from a small middle iron age cemetery in Nijmegen, in M.A. van Bakel/R.R. Hagestein/P. van de Velde (eds), Private Politics. A multi-disciplinary approach to 'Big Man' systems, *Studies in Human Society* 1, 76-95.

Bloemers, J.H.F./T. van Dorp (eds), 1991: *Pre- en Protohistorie van de Lage Landen*, Houten.

Bodegraven, N. van, 1991: Nederzettingssporen uit de late bronstijd en de Vroege ijzertijd op de Everse Akkers in St.-Oedenrode, in H. Fokkens/ N. Roymans (eds), *Nederzettingen uit de bronstijd en vroege ijzertijd in de Lage Landen*, NAR 13, 129-139.

Broeke, P.W. van den, 1980: Bewoningssporen uit de ijzertijd en andere perioden op de Hooidonkse Akkers, gem. Son en Breugel, prov. Noord-Brabant, *APL* 13, 7-80.

Broeke, P.W. van den, 1984: Nederzettingsvondsten uit de ijzertijd op De Pas, gem. Wijchen, *APL* 17, 65-105.

Broeke, P.W. van den, 1986: Zeezout: een schakel tussen West- en Zuid-Nederland in de IJzertijd en de Romeinse tijd, in: *Rotterdam Papers V*, p. 91-114.

Broeke, P.W. van den, 1987a: De dateringsmiddelen voor de ijzertijd in Zuid-Nederland, in W.A.B. van der Sanden/P.W. van den Broeke (eds), Getekend zand. *Tien jaar archeologisch onder zoek in Oss-Ussen*, 23-43.

Broeke, P.W. van den, 1987b: Oss-Ussen: het handgemaakte aardewerk, in W.A.B. van der Sanden/P.W. van den Broeke (eds), *Getekend zand. Tien jaar archeologisch onderzoek in Oss- Ussen*, 101-109.

Broertjes, J., 1977: Het ontstaan van de Brabantse vennen, in N. Roymans et al. (eds), *Brabantse Oudheden*, Eindhoven (Bijdragen tot de studie van het Brabantse heem, 16), 19-25.

Brongers, J.A., 1976: *Air photography and celtic field research in the Netherlands*, Amersfoort (Nederlandse Oudheden 6).

Bruekers, A., 1996: Een 'schaakbord van de goden'. Het prehistorische akkercomplex tussen 'de Zoom' en 'de Gebleekten', in A. Bruekers (ed.), *Nederweerts Verleden. Mensen, macht en middelen*, Nederweert, 199-213.

Caselitz, P., 1986: Die menschliche Leichenbrände des jünger-bronze- und ältereisenzeitlichen Gräberfeldes im 'Wangelister Feld", Stadt Hameln, Kr. Hameln-Pyrmont, *Neue Ausgrabungen und Forschungen in Niedersachssen* 17, 157-180.

Cuijpers, A.G.F.M., 1994: *Crematieresten uit de Late Bronstijd en Vroege IJzertijd in Overijssel*, Amersfoort (ROB Interne Rapporten 10).

Elerie, J.N.H./S.W. Jager/Th. Spek, 1993: *Landschapsgeschiedenis van De Strubben/Kniphorstbos. Archeologische en historisch-ecologische studies van een natuurgebied op de Hondsrug*, (Regio- en landschapsstudies nr. 1).

Engels, A./L. van Impe 1985: Het urnenveld op de Dorperheide te Kaulille (gem. Bocholt). *AB* I, 2, 33-35.

Fokkens, H./N. Roymans (eds), 1991: *Nederzettingen uit de bronstijd en vroege ijzertijd in de Lage Landen*, Amersfoort (NAR 13).

Fontijn, D.R., 1995: *Nijmegen-Kops Plateau. De lange-termijngeschiedenis van een prehistorisch dodenlandschap*, I-II (Catalogus), unpublished M.A. thesis, university of Leiden.

Geel, B. van/J. Buurman/H.T. Waterbolk (in press): Abrupte veranderingen in delta 14C rond 2700 BP in paleo-klimatologisch en archeologisch perspectief, in D. Hallewas et al.(eds.), *Dynamisch Landschap – Archeologie en geologie van het West-Nederlandse kustgebied*, Amersfoort

Gent, H., 1983: Centralized storage in later prehistoric Britain, *Proceedings of the Prehistoric Society* 49, 243-267.

Groenewoudt, B./A.D. Verlinde, 1989: Ein Haustypus der NGK und eine Vorratsgrube aus der frühen Eisenzeit in Colmschate, Gem. Deventer, *BROB* 29, 269-295.

Harsema, O., 1980: Het Drents Plateau. De latere prehistorische bewoning, in M. Chamalaun/H.T. Waterbolk (eds), *Voltooid verleden tijd? Een hedendaagse kijk op de prehistorie*, Amsterdam, 83- 102.

Harsema, O., 1991: De bronstijd-bewoning op het Hijkerveld bij Hijken, in H. Fokkens/ N. Roymans (eds), *Nederzettingen uit de bronstijd en vroege ijzertijd in de Lage Landen*, Amersfoort (NAR 13), 93-110.

Hessing, W.A.M., 1989: Wijk bij Duurstede 'De Horden': Besiedlung und Bestattungen aus der frühen Eisenzeit, *BROB* 39, 297-244.

Hodder, I., 1994: Architecture and Meaning: the exemple of neolithic houses and tombs, in M. Parker Pearson/C. Richards (eds), *Architecture and Order*, Cambridge, 73-86.

Holwerda, J.H., 1913: *Das Gräberfeld von 'de Hamert' bei Venlo*, Leiden.

Horst, C. van der, 1997: *Materiaalscriptie Nederzettingsaardewerk uit de IJzertijd uit Someren.* (Internal report IPP, Amsterdam).

Hulst, R.S., 1964: Een grafveld uit de voor-Romeinse ijzertijd te Nijnsel, gem. St.-Oedenrode, prov. Noord-Brabant, *BROB* 14, 74-83.

Impe, L. van/G. Beex/H. Roosens, 1973: Het urnenveld op 'De Roosen' te Neerpelt; eindrapport, *AB* 145, 5-31.

Impe, L., 1977: Sporen van oude akkersystemen in de Limburgse Kempen, in N. Roymans et al (eds), *Brabantse Oudheden*, Eindhoven (Bijdragen tot de studie van het Brabantse heem, 16), 101- 109.

Janssen, C.R., 1972: The palaeo-ecology of plant communities in the Dommel valley, North Brabant, Netherlands, *Journal of Ecology* 60, 411-437.

Kam, W.H., 1956: Vondstmelding van urnen, ontdekt nabij het ven "Kraayenstark", gem. Someren, *BROB* 7, 13-14.

Kersten, W., 1948: Die Niederrheinische Grabhügelkultur, *Bonner Jahrbücher* 148, 5-81.

Kleij, P., 1993: *Voorlopig verslag opgraving Berkel-Enschot*, Tilburg (ITHO Archeologische Reeks 4).

Kooi, P.B., 1979: *Pre-Roman urnfields in the North of the Netherlands*, Groningen.

Kooi, P.B., 1983: A remarkable Iron Age grave in Darp (municipality of Havelte, The Netherlands), *OMROL* 64, 197-208

Kortlang, F., 1987: *De Dommelvallei. Een Archeologische inventarisatie*, 's-Hertogenbosch.

Kortlang, F., 1998: *Het kaf van het koren. Een paleoethnobotanisch onderzoek naar verkoolde zaden en vruchten uit de IJzertijd te Someren.* (Internal report IPP, Amsterdam).

Krausse-Steinberger, D. von, 1990: Pfeilspitzen aus einem reichen Latène-A-Grab von Hochscheid, Kr. Bernkastel-Wittlich, *AK* 20, 87-100.

Laet, S.J., 1974/9: *Prehistorische kulturen in het zuiden der Lage Landen*, Wetteren.

Lauwerier, R.C.G.M./ G.F. IJzereef, 1994: Vee en vlees in de nederzettingen in Oss-Ussen (800 v. Chr – 250 na Chr.), in K. Schinkel (ed.), *Zwervende erven. Bewoningssporen in Oss-Ussen uit bronstijd, ijzertijd en Romeinse tijd. Opgravingen 1976-1986*, I-II Leiden, 233- 243.

Lohof, E., 1991: *Grafritueel en sociale verandering in de bronstijd van Noordoost-Nederland*, Amsterdam (phil. doc. thesis University of Amsterdam).

Milikowski, E., 1985: Archeologische luchtkartering van het gebied Eersel-Riethoven-Bergeijk, in J Slofstra et al. (eds), *Het Kempenproject 2; een regionaal-archeologisch onderzoek in uitvoering*, Waalre, 79- 85.

Modderman, P.J.R., 1955: Een voorlopig onderzoek van een urnenveld op het Philips Kampeerterrein, gem Someren, N.Br., *BROB* 6, 66-70.

Modderman, P.J.R., 1962/63: Een grafheuvel met paarsgewijs gestelde paalkrans van het urnenveld op het

Philips-kampeerterrein, gem. Someren, Noord-Brabant, *BROB* 12-13, 571-575.

Modderman, P.J.R./L.P. Louwe Kooimans, 1966: The Heibloem, a cemetery from the Late Bronze Age and Early Iron Age between Veldhoven en Steensel, prov. Noord-Brabant, *APL* 2, 9-26.

Pare, C.F.E., 1991: Swords, wagon graves and the beginning of the Early Iron Age in Central Europe, Marburg (*Kleine Schriften aus dem vorgeschichtlichen Seminar Marburg).*

Reynolds, P.J., 1974: Experimental Iron Age storage pits. An interim report, *PPS* 40, 119-131.

Roymans, N., 1985: Carbonized grain from two Iron Age storage pits at Neerharen-Rekem, *AB* I, 1, 97-105.

Roymans, N., 1988: Beegden, nederzetting en grafveld uit ijzertijd en Romeinse tijd, in H. Stoepker (ed.), Archeologische kroniek over 1987, *PSHAL* 124, 346-363.

Roymans, N., 1990: *Tribal Societies in Northern Gaul. An anthropological perspective,* Amsterdam (Cingula 12)

Roymans, N., 1991: Late urnfield societies in the Northwest European plain and the expanding networks of Central European Hallstatt groups, in N. Roymans/F. Theuws (eds), *Images of the past. Studies on ancient societies in Northwestern Europe,* Amsterdam (Studies in prae- en protohistorie 7), 9-89.

Roymans, N., 1995: The cultural biography of urnfields and the long-term history of a mythical landscape, *Archaeological Dialogues* 2, 2-24.

Roymans, N., 1996a: The sword or the plough. Regional dynamics in the romanisation of Belgic Gaul and the Rhineland area, in N. Roymans (ed.), *From the sword to the plough. Three studies on the earliest romanisation of Northern Gaul,* Amsterdam (Amsterdam Archaeological studies I), 9- 126.

Roymans, N., 1996b: The South Netherlands project. Changing perspectives on landscape and culture, *Archaeological Dialogues* 3, 231-245.

Roymans, N./ H. Fokkens, 1991: Een overzicht van veertig jaar nederzettingsonderzoek in de Lage Landen, in H. Fokkens/ N. Roymans (eds), *Nederzettingen uit de bronstijd en vroege ijzertijd in de Lage Landen,* Amersfoort (NAR 13), 1-19.

Roymans, N./H. Hiddink, 1991: Nederzettingssporen uit de bronstijd en vroege ijzertijd op de Kraanvensche heide te Loon op Zand, in H. Fokkens/ N. Roymans (eds), *Nederzettingen uit de bronstijd en vroege ijzertijd in de Lage Landen,* Amersfoort (NAR 13), 111-127.

Roymans, N./F. Kortlang, 1993: Bewoningsgeschiedenis van een dekzandlandschap langs de Aa te Someren, in N. Roymans/F. Theuws (eds), *Een en al zand. Twee jaar graven naar het Brabantse verleden,* 's-Hertogenbosch, 22-41.

Roymans, N./A. Tol, 1993: Noodonderzoek van een dodenakker te Mierlo-hout, in N. Roymans/F. Theuws (eds), *Een en al zand. Twee jaar graven naar het Brabantse verleden,* 's-Hertogenbosch, 42-56.

Sanden, W.A.B. van der, 1981: The urnfield and the Late Bronze Age settlement traces on the Haagakkers at St.-Oedenrode (prov. of North Brabant), *BROB* 31, 307-328.

Sanden, W.A.B. van der, 1994: De funeraire en aanverwante structuren, in K. Schinkel (ed.), *Zwervende erven. Bewoningssporen in Oss-Ussen uit bronstijd, ijzertijd en Romeinse tijd. Opgravingen 1976-1986. I-II (catalogus),* Leiden, 199-218.

Sanden, W.A.B., van der/P.W. van den Broeke (eds), 1987: Getekend zand. *Tien jaar archeologisch onderzoek in Oss-Ussen,* Waalre (Bijdragen tot de studie van het Brabantse Heem 31).

Schinkel K., 1994: *Zwervende erven. Bewoningssporen in Oss-Ussen uit bronstijd, ijzertijd en Romeinse tijd. Opgravingen 1976-1986. I-II (catalogus),* Leiden (phil. doc. thesis University of Leiden)

Slofstra, J., 1991: Een nederzetting uit de vroege ijzertijd op de Heesmortel bij Riethoven, in H. Fokkens/ N. Roymans (eds), *Nederzettingen uit de bronstijd en vroege ijzertijd in de Lage Landen,* Amersfoort (NAR 13), 141-151.

Spek, Th., 1993: Milieudynamiek en locatiekeuze op het Drents Plateau (3400 v. Chr.-1850 na Chr.), in J.N.H. Elerie et al., 169-236.

STIBOKA, 1981: *Bodemkaarten. Toelichting bij de Bodemkaart van Nederland. Schaal 1:50.000. Kaartblad 51 Oost-Eindhoven.*

STIBOKA, 1981: *Geomorfologische kaart en Toelichting bij de Geomorfologische kaart van Neder land. Schaal 1:50.000 Kaartblad 51 Oost-Eindhoven.*

Stuiver, M./G.W. Pearson, 1993: High-precision bidecadal calibration of the radiocarbon time scale, AD 1950-500 BC and 2500-6000 BC, *Radiocarbon* 35, 1-23.

Vandekerchove, V., 1994: 'Celtic Fields' in de Belgische Kempen, *Lunula* 2, 71-74.

Vanderhoeven, A., 1991: Botanisch onderzoek van de vroege-ijzertijd nederzetting op de Heesmortel bij Riethoven, in H. Fokkens/ N. Roymans (eds), 153-162.

Verlinde, A.D., 1987: Die Gräber und Grabfunde der Späten Bronzezeit und Frühen Eisenzeit in Overijssel IV, *BROB* 35, 231-412.

Verlinde, A.D., 1991: Huizen uit de Bronstijd en Vroege IJzertijd te Colmschate, in H. Fokkens/ N. Roymans (eds), 31-40.

Verwers, G.J., 1966a: Tumuli at the Zevenbergen near Oss gem. Berghem, Prov. Noord-Brabant, *APL* 2, 27-32.

Verwers, G.J., 1966b: Non-circular monuments in the southern Dutch urnfields, *APL* 2, 49-57.

Verwers, G.J., 1972: Das Kamps Veld in Haps in Neolithikum, Bronzezeit und Eisenzeit, *APL* 5.

Wahl, J., 1982: Leichenbranduntersuchungen: Ein Überblick über die Bearbeitungs- und Aussagemöglichkeiten von Brandgräbern, *Prähistorische Zeitschrift* 57, 1-125.

Wieberdink, G.L., 1989: *Historische Atlas van Noord-Brabant. Chromotopografische kaart des Rijks 1:25.000*, Den Ilp.

Willems, W.J.H., 1983: Posterholt, in: Archeologische kroniek van Limburg over de jaren 1980-1982, *PSHAL* 119, 221-225.

Workshop of European Anthropologists 1980: recommendations for age and sex diagnoses of skeletons, *Journal of Human Evolution* 9, 517-549.

Late Iron Age human skeletal remains from the river Meuse at Kessel: a river cult place?

Muuk E. ter Schegget[1]

I   INTRODUCTION: HUMAN BONES FROM RIVER CONTEXTS IN THE NETHERLANDS

In the Netherlands, a formal burial practice focused on cremation cemeteries is observed from the Late Bronze Age until well into the Roman period.[2] This applies particularly to the river area of the Central Netherlands and the sandy areas of the South and North Netherlands. From the northern

---

[1] I would like to thank L. and O. Stolzenbach for temporarily placing the skeletal material at my disposal and for their kind permission to have some of the bones dated; the Stichting Nederlands Museum voor Anthropologie en Praehistorie for financing most of the C14 datings; H. Schoorl for producing drawings 1-7 on computer; E. van der Kerff for improving figure 8; W. van der Sanden for pointing out to me the finds of human remains in the Drentse Aa; F. Laarman for showing me the human bones dredged from rivers now present at the ROB; and N. Roymans for critically reading earlier drafts of this article.

[2] Chronology in the Netherlands: Late Bronze Age 1100-800 BC; Early Iron Age 800-500 BC; Middle

Fig. 1. Location of Kessel in the Netherlands.

terp region too, there is increasing evidence for the existence of a cremation rite in which the burials took place outside the actual terp settlements. Inhumations in a cremation cemetery are rare. Examples from the Middle Iron Age are known from Geldermalsen and Someren.[3] In the West Netherlands, examples from the Roman period have only been recorded at Schagen, Spijkenisse and Valkenburg.[4] In the latter two cemeteries a number of inhumations, mainly of young children, are found among the cremation graves. However, the evidence for cremation cemeteries is so scarce for the coastal area of the West Netherlands that alternative mortuary practices, such as an excarnation rite by exposure, must be seriously considered.

Apart from a formal burial practice focused on cremation cemeteries, deviant forms of treatment of the dead can be found throughout the Netherlands. Isolated unburnt human bones and even complete skeletons are regularly found outside graves or cemeteries. They come from a diversity of contexts: from settlements, bogs and rivers.

Hessing gives a survey of uncremated human remains from settlement contexts in the Dutch coastal and river areas. More than 260 uncremated individuals are recorded from 61 locations, all dating from a period between 400 BC and 350 AD.[5] Van der Sanden inventories the North Netherlands bog bodies and skeletons.[6] So far, 56 bog bodies have been discovered in the North Netherlands, but there were undoubtedly far more. Ten bodies are dated in the Middle Ages or later. The remaining 46 bodies or parts of bodies, originating from 36 findspots, certainly or probably date to the Late Iron Age and Early Roman period. An initial impetus to describe human bone material from rivers is the series of articles on the so-called "River Valley People", in which some 150 river finds are anatomi-

Iron Age 500-250 BC; Late Iron Age 250-12 BC; Roman Period 12 BC-450 AD; Early Middle Ages 450-950 AD.

[3]   Kortlang, this volume.

[4]   Respectively Therkorn 1984; Smits 1992; Smits 1993.

[5]   Hessing 1993.

[6]   Van der Sanden 1990, 1992 and 1996.

Fig. 2. Findspots of human skeletal remains in river contexts in the Netherlands. After Erdbrink/ Meiklejohn/Tacoma 1993; Van der Sanden 1990, 1992, 1997; and unpublished data present at the ROB, Amersfoort.

1 Hagestein, 2 Maasvlakte/Europoort, 3 Hasselt, 4 Grafhorst, 5 Doesburg, 6 Zwolle, 7 Windesheim, 8 Welsum, 9 Deventer (Koerhuisbeek), 10 Borger, 11 Vianen, 12 Woerden, 13 Rijswijk, 14 Maurik, 15 Elst/Amerongen, 16 Lienden, 17 Rhenen, 18 Lathum, 19 Oosterbeek, 20 Nijmegen, 21 Hummelo, 22 Kerkdriel, 23 Rossum, 24 Heerewaarden, 25 Kessel, 26 Dreumel, 27 Maasbommel, 28 Tiel, 29 Kerk-Avezaath, 30 Zoelen, 31 Lobith, 32 Heteren, 33 Nederhemert, 34 Elst, 35 Valburg, 36 Arnhem, 37 Groessen, 38 Kekerdom, 39 Buggenum, 40 Asselt, 41 Beegden, 42 Roermond, 43 Bunde, 44 Assen (Deurzerdiep, Anreep), 45 Buinen

1	2	3	4		5
find place	river	bone	C14 years BP		period
Deurzerdiep 1	Drentse Aa	tibia	4000 ± 40	(GrA-2431)	Late Neolithic
Deurzerdiep 4	Drentse Aa	pelvis	2990 ± 40	(GrA-2430)	end of Middle Bronze Age
Elst 1/ Amerongen 3	Rhine	mandible	2900 ± 130	(Oxa-728)	end of Middle/Late Bronze Age
Hummelo 2	Oude IJssel	skull	2530 ± 90	(Oxa-616)	Early/Middle Iron Age
Beegden 1	Meuse	left femur	2450 ± 90	(Oxa-726)	Early/Middle Iron Age
Borger	Voorste Diep	skull	2060 ± 100	(Ua-1500)	Middle Iron Age/Early Roman period
Buinen	Achterste Diep	skull	1990 ± 70	(Oxa-3133)	Late Iron Age/Early Roman period
Rhenen 2	Rhine	skull	1640 ± 100	(Oxa-727)	Late Roman period/Early Middle Ages
Koerhuisbeek 2	IJssel	skull	1460 ± 80	(Oxa-669)	Early Middle Ages
Anreep 2	Drentse Aa	pelvis	1350 ± 40	(GrA-2439)	Early Middle Ages
Rhenen 1	Rhine	skull	1330 ± 110	(GrN-12079)	Early Middle Ages

Table 1. C14 dates from human skeletal remains from rivers in the Netherlands (except those from Kessel). After Gowlett et al. 1987; Hedges et al. 1992 and 1993; Van der Sanden 1992, 148 and 1997.

cally described.[7] Nevertheless, there is still no systematic inventory of human bones from Dutch rivers. The human skeletal remains are mostly found in the present bank zones of the great rivers such as the Meuse and IJssel (fig. 2). Many findspots are situated near the confluences of rivers. The majority of the skeletal remains consists of skulls and femora. Several findspots, such as Kessel and Roermond (fig. 2: 25, 42), show an accumulation of bone material and metal finds, especially weapons from the Iron Age.

Until recently, little attention was paid by archaeologists to the find material dredged up from rivers. It was often referred to as eroded finds without context, and therefore of little scientific value. The result of this attitude is that much undocumented material has been lost. Only since the end of the 1980s has a change set in. This began with a systematic interest in metal finds from river contexts dating from the Bronze Age, Iron Age and Roman period.[8] These contexts are often surprisingly rich in finds, which are virtually unknown in settlements and cemeteries. Metal objects from rivers are commonly regarded as depositions made out of religious motives.[9] However, the spectrum of finds from rivers is broader than only metal finds, and often includes pottery and animal and human bones. So far no systematic attention has been paid to the latter finds. A major problem with human – and animal – bone material from rivers is the dating. In contrast to metal objects and pottery, dredged bone material cannot be dated typochronologically. Up to now only a few C14 dates of human skeletal material are known in the Netherlands (table 1). They cover the period from the Neolithic to the Early Middle Ages.

The collection of human remains from the river Meuse at Kessel (fig. 2: 25) is now the only find complex in which a large quantity of skeletal remains can be analysed in probable association with other finds. The material from Kessel was systematically collected from 1991 to the end of 1993 on board of a dredger by the amateur archaeologists Leo and Olaf Stolzenbach. The finds include large quantities of pottery, some weapons, brooches, bronze cauldrons, harvest implements and both unburnt animal and human bones. This find complex is therefore suitable for starting the discussion on human remains from rivers. C14 dates of several human bones dredged up at Kessel show a range

[7] Erdbrink/Meiklejohn/Tacoma 1993 (with further references).

[8] Roymans 1990 (Late Iron Age metal finds) and 1992

(Late Bronze Age/Early Iron Age metal finds).

[9] E.g. Jankuhn 1967; Colpe 1970; Maringer 1974; Gladigow 1984; Pauli 1991.

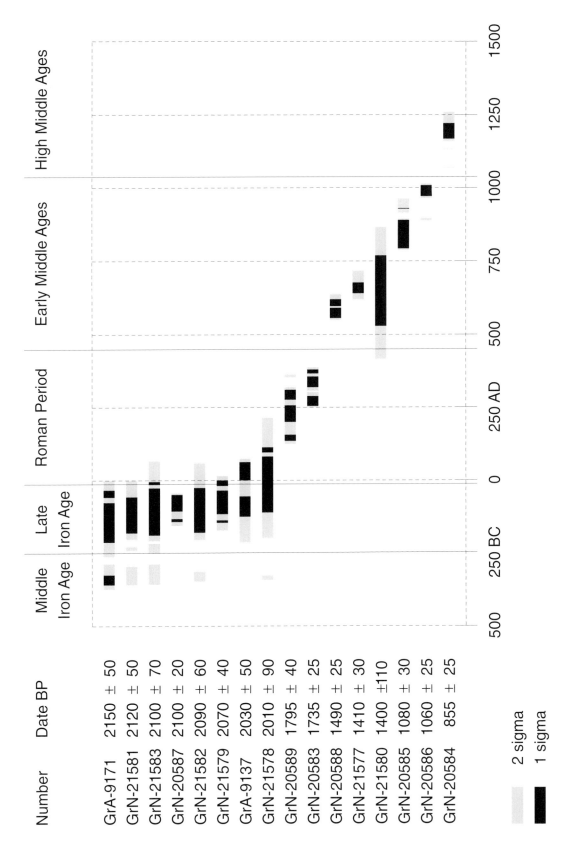

Fig. 3. Calibrated C14 datings from Kessel (listed in table 2). The black parts of the datelines indicate a probability of 68.3% (1 sigma), the grey parts 95.4% (2 sigma). Graph P. Haanen.

varying from about 360 cal BC to 1260 cal AD (fig. 3), though with a peak in the Late Iron Age and a less pronounced concentration in the Early Middle Ages. The majority of the finds (pottery and metal objects) dates from the Late Iron Age. The site of Kessel will be presented here as a case study.

2 THE DEPOSITION OF HUMAN REMAINS OUTSIDE FORMAL BURIAL PLACES IN NORTHWEST AND CENTRAL EUROPE

Apart from cemeteries, depositions of human skeletal material in Northwest Europe are known from a variety of contexts, such as bogs, rivers, settlements and sanctuaries. The deposition of (in)complete unburnt skeletons from the Late Bronze Age up to and including the Roman period does not, in many regions, correspond to the common burial ritual (cremation). Apparently there were deviant forms of mortuary treatment, which were reserved for only a small section of the population. These can be linked with the system of religious and cosmological ideas at the time and the ritual practices connected with them.

In settlements in West and Central Europe, human bone material has been found in pits and wells or in ditches.[10] It is striking that the ditches and pits with human remains are often found at entrances to, or at the outer limits of settlements, in liminal places. One can imagine that the dead, or parts of them, were deposited to mark – or confirm – a boundary. Especially in Britain and Northern France there is the practice of deposition of complete inhumations in disused storage pits. Such finds are interpreted as the remnants of a fertility rite.[11] On the continent, mainly isolated long bones and skulls are found in ditches and pits. Human skeletal remains are also occasionally found in deep pits inside Viereckschanzen, especially in Southwest Germany, Switzerland and France. These pits are interpreted as sacrificial pits. The ritual practices which confront us in the above situations include decapitation, exposure of the body in the open air (excarnation), secondary deposition of the entire defleshed body or parts of it, and probably also dismemberment.

Human remains are also found at public cult places which were thought to be the earthly domicile of divine powers and where ritual practices were performed. In Northern France, several pre-Roman cult places have been excavated. Remains of both articulated and unarticulated bones were encountered, showing that individual body parts, especially long bones and skulls, were deposited.[12] Sometimes the bones reveal traces of weapon cuts, decapitation or dismemberment. The complex ritual practices involved, such as secondary burial and manipulation of bodies, are difficult to interpret. In addition, most of the Late Iron Age sanctuaries yield weapons (sometimes rendered unusable), animal bones, fibulae and Celtic coins.

The category of human remains from watery contexts includes both peat-bog and river finds. Artefacts from (former) waters are usually encountered during hydraulic work, or turf, sand or gravel extraction. Most of the material from rivers has been collected during dredging activities. In peat-bogs, complete bodies are usually found, though sometimes also separate body parts, especially skulls. Most of the bog bodies come from the North European peat areas and date from the Late Iron Age and Early Roman period. They are usually connected with religious practices, and cannot be separat-

[10] Wait 1985; Wiedemer 1963.

[11] Cunliffe 1984, 1993; Brunaux 1988.

[12] Cadoux 1984; Brunaux 1988. Pre-Roman cult places in Northern France which have produced human skeletal remains are Gournay-sur-Aronde, Epiais-Rhus, Estrée-Saint-Denis, Ribemont-sur-Ancre, Digeon and Moeuvres. Cf. the list with references in Roymans 1990, 62-68.

ed from the deposition of a wide spectrum of other objects in bogs.[13] Many of the individuals whose bodies were found in the peat met an unnatural end. This is evident from the cut throats, nooses around the neck indicating strangling or hanging, smashed skulls and deep wounds caused by a sharp instrument in the chest. The sex ratio is predominantly male. There is a striking peak in the population of bog bodies in the Late Iron Age and Early Roman period, but an explanation for this phenomenon is hard to give. There may be a connection between votive offerings from Late Iron Age cult places in Northern France and those in the peat areas and river beds in Central and Northwest Europe. Finds from the northern peat bogs also include parts of carts, agricultural tools, weapons, coins, pottery and animal bones (mainly of cattle).[14] These peat finds are also interpreted as votive offerings, with the role of the southern cult places now being played by the peat moors.[15]

The find spectrum from Northwest-European rivers includes roughly the same categories as those from peat bogs and marshes: coins, weapons, bronze vessels, agricultural tools, animal and human remains. As for human remains in rivers, little is yet known. In the Netherlands and Germany almost all the attention goes to the metal finds; the possible presence of human skeletal remains is hardly mentioned, if at all.[16] Only in Britain efforts have been made to seriously include the human bone material in the analysis of river finds.[17] More than 350 human skulls are known from the Thames and its tributaries. C14 dating has shown that the deposition of skulls or heads took place from the Bronze Age up to and including the Anglo-Saxon period.[18] Most skulls are of adults, aged about 25 to 35; 60% of the population consists of young adult males. This evidently does not reflect a normal living population. Apart from skulls, many metal objects from the Iron Age were discovered, mainly weapons. The distribution pattern of both the weapons and the human bones suggests that certain sections of the rivers were selected for these depositions.[19]

In Switzerland, human remains were found at three locations in the river Zihl – at La Tène, Port and Cornaux. The scattered skeletal remains were found in combination with, among other finds, Late Iron Age weapons. The sites of La Tène and Port, possibly also that of Cornaux, are interpreted as probable cult places or Flussheiligtümer.[20] In the bed of the Zihl at La Tène, skulls and several complete human skeletons were found in association with the remains of wooden bridges and over 2,500 objects, more than one-third of which were weapons.[21] Among the other finds are parts of carts, tools, fibulae, coins, bronze vessels, pottery and animal bones. The human skeletal remains belong to nine individuals: seven men, one woman and one juvenile. One of the skeletons had a noose of hemp around the neck. Weapon cuts were observed on several skulls and on one of the femora, probably inflicted by a sword.[22] The Late Iron Age findspot at Port is similar to that at La Tène. Several complete skeletons, 150 swords and spearheads, harvesting tools and bronze vessels were recovered from the river bed. Several swords were bent. At Port, too, post remains of a wooden bridge or platform were found.[23] Near the remains of a wooden bridge[24] at Cornaux-Les Sauges, the skeletal remains of at least 18 individuals were excavated, including adult men and women and two children. Nine of the skele-

[13] Bradley 1990; Van der Sanden 1996.

[14] Prummel/Van der Sanden 1995, 84-123.

[15] Van der Sanden 1992, 47-49.

[16] Driehaus 1970; Zimmermann 1970; Torbrügge 1970-71; Wegner 1976; Roymans 1990, 84-90; idem 1992, 20-49; idem 1996, 15-20; Schalles/Schreiter 1993.

[17] Fitzpatrick 1984; Bradley 1990.

[18] Bradley/Gordon 1988, 503-509.

[19] Bradley/Gordon 1988, 506.

[20] Wyss 1974, 175 ff.; Brunaux 1988, 42-43; Bradley 1990, 156 ff.

[21] Vouga 1923; Raddatz 1952; Schwab 1974; Wyss 1974.

[22] Vouga 1923, 135-142.

[23] Wyss 1974, 181.

[24] The bridge is dendrochronologically dated to 143 BC.

tons were complete. Of the others, only the skulls or other parts were found. One skeleton of an adult man had a noose around the neck. Among the scattered skeletal remains were also Late La Tène swords, spearheads, axes, knives, pottery, fibulae, parts of horse gear and animal remains.[25]

In the South Netherlands, swords, mostly bent or broken, have been dredged up at various locations, though mainly from the Meuse at Kessel and Roermond. There are several striking similarities between the two sites. They both lie on the Meuse at or near the confluence with another river, the Waal and the Roer respectively. At both places a large quantity of human skeletal remains and bent or broken Late Iron Age weapons were dredged up.[26] From the Meuse at Roermond, about 75 human bones and bone fragments (mainly skulls and femora) are known, in addition to metal finds from the Bronze Age to the Early Middle Ages. The skeletal remains are mainly from (young) men, but women and some juveniles are also represented.[27] It is not clear to what extent there is a connection between the metal finds and these skeletal remains, since there are hardly any absolute dates for the bone material and there is no stratigraphical information.[28]

3 THE FIND COMPLEX FROM THE RIVER MEUSE AT KESSEL: GENERAL DESCRIPTION

Since the 1970s, the south bank of the Meuse at Kessel (province of North Brabant) has been intensively dredged for extracting sand and gravel. During the dredging operations, many archaeological objects have been found. At one place, at the entrance to the dredge pit at Kessel, human bone in combination with many metal objects and pottery sherds was brought to the surface. The greater part of the material belongs to the late phase of the Iron Age, but there is also material from the Roman period and the Early Middle Ages. The occurrence of human skeletal remains from these periods in a river context is remarkable. The present research addresses the question how these well-preserved and unburnt human remains are to be interpreted. In order to answer this question, an investigation was made into the dating and composition of the human skeletal remains with respect to the number of individuals, age, sex and traces of injury.

3.1 TOPOGRAPHY

The findspot at Kessel forms part of a larger zone, rich in finds, between Rossum and Lith in the Dutch river area (fig. 4). A large amount of archaeological material has been found in the bed of the Meuse and its present flood-plain, mainly dating from the Late Iron Age, the Roman period and the Early Middle Ages.[29] Significant is the position of the findspot at Kessel at one of the places where the Meuse and Waal flowed together in the Roman period.[30] It is assumed that, at Kessel, the Meuse still flows along roughly

[25] Schwab 1972; 1973, 59-70.

[26] At Kessel, 19 Late La Tène swords and/or scabbards were dredged up, and at Roermond, 10 Late Bronze Age swords and 5 Late La Tène swords (Verwers/ Ypey 1975; Roymans 1992, 27, table 1 and 40, fig. 13; and Roymans 1996, 15, fig. 1).

[27] Among others, Erdbrink/Meiklejohn/Tacoma 1975.

[28] A left femur (Beegden 1) from the Meuse southwest of Roermond has a C14 date of 2450 ±90 BP (OxA 726; *Archaeometry* 29, 1987, 125). This femur (794-392 cal BC at 2 sigma) is not from the same period as the swords.

[29] Information present at the ROB, Amersfoort; Roymans/Van der Sanden 1980, 192 ff.

[30] Henderikx 1986, 511-512.

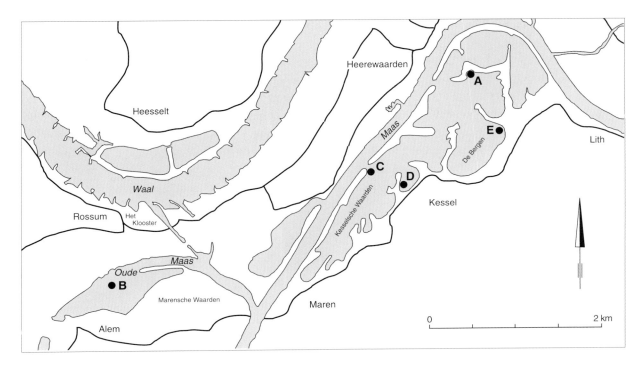

Fig. 4. River courses and the major find complexes between Rossum and Lith in the Iron Age and Roman period. After Roymans/Van der Sanden 1980, with additions.
A findspot with various find layers from the Late Iron Age at Lith (not eroded); B findspot of two Roman votive stones at Alem; C probable ritual find complex with human remains at Kessel (not eroded), discussed in this article; D remains of walls from a Late-Roman fort at Kessel (eroded); E Roman building debris (eroded), discovered in 1991.

the same bed as it did in the Late Iron Age.[31] On the sandy natural levees were scattered settlements.

In the 1970s, large-scale sand extraction began in the flood-plain along the south bank of the Meuse at Kessel and Lith. As a result, dredge ponds developed at Kessel (de Kesselsche Waarden) and at Lith (de Bergen). At present, the work has reached a final stage.

Along the Meuse at Kessel several separate find locations are known. At the entrance to this dredge pit (fig. 4,c) in a layer of clay mainly Late Iron Age finds were dredged up. According to the dredging crew, these included human bones, especially skulls. The dredged gravel could not be used at the time, and was placed in a depot 50 to 100 metres southwest of the original findspot. From this depot, which has always remained under the surface of the water, gravel has again been dredged since the beginning of the 1990s. Obviously, there can be no question of any stratigraphy.

3.2 THE FINDS

In general, the representativity of dredge finds poses a problem. It is not clear to what extent the documented finds reflect the original find complex.[32] However, in the case of Kessel, better information

---

[31] Henderikx 1986, 453.

[32] They are often chance finds made by the dredging crew; often only part of the dredged material is noticed by the crew, finds are selectively preserved and

is available because, for some years, amateur archaeologists collected material on a dredger from a shaking sieve with a mesh width of 16 mm.

The river finds from the Meuse date from the Palaeolithic[33] up to and including the Middle Ages. This shows that we are dealing with a complex situation and with many contexts. We shall restrict ourselves here to a description of by far the largest group of finds, namely the material from the Late Iron Age and the Early Roman period. The human bone material collected so far and the metal finds belong to a find complex of no more than 100 by 200 m in size, situated near the entrance of the dredge pit at Kessel. A small part is probably still in situ. The human skeletal material collected, over 650 bones and bone fragments, is undoubtedly only a fraction of the original number once deposited here as complete bodies or parts of bodies. In addition, over 100,000 animal bones were discovered. A rough estimate has been made of the composition of the animal population based on the number of mandibles.[34] The majority of bones are from cattle. Approximately one-fifth is from pig, about one-tenth from horse, and about 5% from sheep/goat and less than 1% from dog.

The – still virtually unpublished – metal finds include partly bent swords and scabbards, belt-hooks, an iron umbo, spearheads, axes, knives, parts of horse gear, fibulae, harvesting tools, an iron helmet and (fragments of) bronze vessels. In addition, an enormous quantity of fragmented handmade pottery was collected which can be dated in the (Late) Iron Age.

3.3 FIND CIRCUMSTANCES

The conservation of bone material in wet contexts is dependent on various factors. In anaerobic conditions, this material can be excellently preserved, especially when the bones are surrounded by water-saturated sediment or mud. In addition to environmental factors, conservation is also influenced by size and robustness of the individual skeletal parts. In general, teeth, the distal part of the humerus and complete bones remain well preserved. Less compact sections of bone, such as the proximal part of the humerus and vertebrae, remain less well preserved. The size of the bones also determines whether they are noticed. The question of whether bone material in watery surroundings is actually discovered during dredging activities therefore depends on both the characteristics of the bone and the nature and intensity of the dredging, not to mention the degree of interest of the dredging crew.

The river finds at the entrance to the dredge pit at Kessel were at the time dredged up from a depth of between 3.5 and 4.0 m +NAP. The majority of the finds came from a layer of clay 0.7 to 1.0 m below the present groundwater level.[35] The top of this layer never came above the surface; even in summer, it remained approximately 20 cm below the surface. The conservation of the bone tissue is generally good to very good. The majority of the human remains must therefore have been deposited in a wet context and immediately cut off from oxygen. The bones were probably covered later by new clay sediment.

The analysis of the exterior of the bones, enclosures and attachments provides some insight into the nature of the original layer of finds. It appears that most of the finds were originally in a layer of ex-

---

only few are reported (cf. Roymans/Van der Sanden 1980, 199 ff.).

[33] This is due to the great depth, up to 30 m, at which dredging took place.

[34] Pers. comm. O. Stolzenbach, June 1994.

[35] Pers. comm. O. Stolzenbach, who received this information from the dredging crew.

1	2	3	4	5	6
find number	GrN-number	bone fragment	sex	age	C14 years BP
Kessel 1997-2	GrA-9171	skull	?	30-50	2150 ± 50
MK 132/111	21581	skull with injury	male	30-40	2120 ± 50
MK 114	21583	skull	—	child	2100 ± 70
MK 359	20587	femur	male	adult	2100 ± 20
MK 93	21582	skull with injury	?	40-60	2090 ± 60
MK 166/479	21579	skull with injury	female?	40-60	2070 ± 40
Kessel 1997-1	GrA-9137	skull	male?	18-30	2030 ± 50
MK 196	21578	skull with injury	?	adult, <60	2010 ± 90
MK 361	20589	femur	male	adult	1795 ± 40
MK 355	20583	femur	male	adult	1735 ± 25
MK 360	20588	femur	male	adult	1490 ± 25
MK 478	21577	humerus with injury	?	adult	1410 ± 30
MK 135	21580	skull with injury	?	adult, <40	1400 ± 110
MK 357	20585	femur	female	adult	1180 ±30
MK 358	20586	femur	male	adult	1060 ±25
MK 356	20584	femur	female	adult, <30	855 ±25

Table 2. C14 dates from human bones found at Kessel. The find numbers refer to the catalogue (appendix).

tremely fine clay. The water must have had a limited flow velocity in order to enable the fine clay to subside. For this reason, the material cannot have been deposited in the middle of the river bed because the erosive force there is much greater. However, the water was not still either. The human remains seem to have been thrown into a virtually non-active bed of the Meuse, or into the soggy bank zone of the main bed at that time. The complete absence of traces of gnawing by dogs also indicates a deposition in open water. At any rate, the bones had not been dragged around by animals.

3.4 THE DATING OF THE HUMAN REMAINS

It is difficult to give a reliable date for the Kessel skeletal remains since it was not discovered in situ during a regular excavation, but was collected as stray finds. The dating evidence available for this bone material are the assumed association with datable finds and a series of C14 dates of individual bones.

The archaeological material dredged up together with the human skeletal remains mainly dates from the Late Iron Age. This would justify a dating of the majority of the find complex in that period.

A number of bones with a varying degree of conservation was selected for a C14 dating. Seven right femora were chosen in the first instance. In addition a series of six bones with traces of violence and one with evidence of malnutrition[36] were selected, namely six skull fragments and a humerus. It was investigated whether the external visual characteristics of a bone, such as colour, specific gravity and degree of erosion showed any relation to the C14 date.[37] The analysis revealed that neither the exterior nor the weight were a reliable relative means of dating.[38]

[36] A skull fragment of a child with pepperpot holes in the orbits (*cribra orbitalia*). This porotic hyperostosis was probably the result of an iron-deficiency anaemia (cf. Stuart-Macadam 1989).

[37] Ter Schegget 1994, 17-19.

[38] It is often assumed that heavy, mineralized bones are extremely old. That this is an incorrect assumption can be seen from the C14 dating of a heavy and mineral-

Fig. 5. Overview of the human skeletal remains dredged at Kessel. Photo M. Ydo.

The sixteen C14 dates show a distribution over about a millennium, with two separate peaks (fig. 3 and table 2): the first one in the Late Iron Age (eight bones) and a second one in the Merovingian[39] period (three bones). These C14 dates fit the pattern which we had of the periodization of this find complex on the basis of the datable archaeological material.

4 PHYSICAL ANTHROPOLOGICAL ANALYSIS OF THE SKELETAL REMAINS FROM KESSEL

In this research, approximately 650 bones and bone fragments were identified and analysed.[40] The skeletal material consists mainly of long bones and skull fragments. Only 3% of the long bones is complete, and not one of the skulls (fig. 5). This high percentage of fragmentation is mainly due to modern dredging activities, shown by the fact that most of the fractures are recent. The smallest bones from hands and feet are hardly represented (fig. 6). These are the parts which, if present at all, are easily overlooked during dredging. Only the slightly larger and harder heelbones were collected. Kneecaps are completely absent. Small and fragile parts of the skeleton such as vertebrae are hardly represented. Apart from the fact that these are easily overlooked during collection, the chance of vertebrae being preserved is not great. The same goes for shoulder blades.

ized femur (MK360) to around 600 AD (GrN-20588).

[39] Between 450-750 AD.

[40] In the catalogue, a list is given of the results of the analysis per bone. Each bone or bone fragment has a find number.

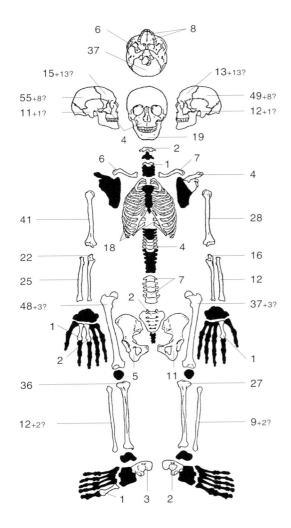

Fig. 6. The number of bones and bone fragments examined per skeletal element and per body half. Missing skeletal elements are indicated in black.

4.1 METHODS FOR THE ESTIMATION OF SEX AND AGE

Diagnosing sex is only possible with adult individuals. The skull and pelvis are generally used for this. Morphological characteristics which can be determined by means of visual inspection are, among other things, the robustness of the bones. The sexing of skeletons was carried out according to the recommendations of the Arbeitsgruppe Europäischer Anthropologen (AEA).[41] In addition, metrical characteristics may be used. For the metrical diagnosis of sex the following measurements were applied: the sagittal and transversal diameter of the head of the humerus and the head of the femur;[42] the femoral shaft circumference;[43] the bicondylar width and the popliteal length of the femur[44] and various measurements of the petrosal bone in the skull.[45] Methods based on metrical characteristics are simple and easily applied to fragmented skeletal material. Particularly the femoral shaft circumference is excellently suited for the sex estimation of adults. A determination of the length of the femur is often impossible because the ends of the bone are extremely vulnerable to damage and erosion. On

[41] Arbeitsgruppe Europäischer Anthropologen (AEA) 1979, 1-11.

[42] Bass 1984, 21-22; Ubelaker 1984, 44.

[43] Black 1978.

[44] Bass 1984, 173-174.

[45] Wahl 1982.

1 bone	2 male	3 probably male	4 indiff. or indet.	5 probably female	6 female	7 total adults	8 child / juvenile	9 total	10 MNI
mandible	5	2	6	3	1	17	2	19	19
maxilla	2	1	3	-	-	6	2	8	8
cheekbone	2	1	1	-	-	4	-	4	4
occipital bone	9	2	11	4	6	32	5	37	36
skull base	-	-	4	1	-	5	1	6	6
temp./petrosal bone	10	3	2	1	7	23	1	24	15
frontal bone	12	1	17	1	7	38	3	41	39
parietal bone	13	-	78	1	-	92	20	112	55
humerus	1	6	48	5	1	61	8	69	39
radius	1	7	21	3	-	32	5	37	25
ulna	3	9	22	3	-	37	1	38	22
femur	42	-	26	2	11	81	7	88	45
tibia	-	2	57	2	-	61	2	63	36
fibula	-	-	22	-	-	22	1	23	12
vertebrae	-	-	13	-	-	13	1	14	2
pelvis/sacrum	2	1	6	2	1	12	6	18	10
collar-bone	-	1	12	-	-	13	-	13	11
shoulder-blade	-	-	4	-	-	4	-	4	4
ribs	-	-	18	-	-	18	-	18	1
heelbone	1	1	-	2	1	5	-	5	4
metacarpals	-	-	4	-	-	4	-	4	2
metatarsals	-	-	1	-	-	1	-	1	1
unknown	-	-	7	-	-	7	-	7	1
total (n)	103	37	383	30	35	588	65	653	-
total (%)	15.8	5.7	58.7	4.6	5.4	90	10	100	-

Table 3. Classification according to sex and Minimal Number of Individuals (MNI) of the skeletal population of Kessel. Sex was only determined in the case of adult individuals.

the other hand, the shaft consists of thick and compact bone and is therefore solid and difficult to break. The circumference can almost always be measured.

In order to determine the age at death, use was made of a number of methods for age estimation as described by the AEA. These are based on: 1. epiphyseal closure of the long bones and the ossification of the various parts of the pelvis;[46] 2. tooth eruption;[47] 3. the wear of the dental elements;[48] 4. endocranial suture closure;[49] and 5. length of the long bones.[50] For young individuals, the methods for age estimation are mainly based on growth and development (1, 2, 4 en 5), for adult individuals on wear and degeneration (3).

[46] AEA 1979, 12-22.

[47] Ubelaker 1984, 46-47.

[48] Brothwell 1981, 64-72; Pot 1988.

[49] Vallois in Rösing 1977; AEA 1979, 19-20.

[50] AEA 1979, 16; Bass 1984; Ubelaker 1984, 46-53.

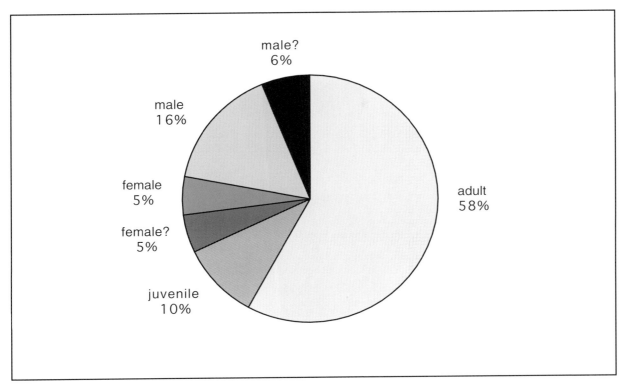

Fig. 7. Classification according to sex of the skeletal population of Kessel.

4.2 MINIMAL NUMBER OF INDIVIDUALS

The minimal number of individuals (MNI) that can be reconstructed on the basis of the bone remains studied is 55.[51] This number has been established on the basis of the right parietal bones of the skull (table 3). The number of left parietal bones is at least 49. The minimum number of individuals on the basis of the post-cranial skeleton (right femora) is 45. It was established that not one maxilla and mandible belonged together, so that the number of individuals on the basis of the teeth is 27. In reality, the number of individuals must have been much higher.

4.3 SEX

Approximately 90% of all bones belonged to adult individuals (n=588) and a third of these were sexed:[52] male, probably male, female and probably female (table 3 and fig. 7). The sex of 383 bones (65%) is undetermined or indifferent. A total of 138 bones and fragments could with certainty be attributed to a man or a woman. Of these bones, 103 came from male individuals and 35 from females. This ratio (75% male: 25% female) was also observed with the femora (see 4.5).

---

[51] Due to the find of new bones, the MNI has now risen to about 65 individuals.

[52] No attempt was made to estimate the sex of fibulae, vertebrae, shoulderblades, ribs, metacarpals and metatarsals, nor of the small, unidentifiable bone fragments (n=69).

age (in years)	percentage	number of bones
<23	14%	n=43
23-40	61%	n=184
30-60	4%	n=12
40-80	21%	n=64

Table 4. Age distribution based on the cranial suture closure.

4.4 AGE

Approximately 10% of all the bones came from young children and adolescents (n=65). The most reliable indication for the age at death of a pre-modern individual is provided by the teeth.[53] The age composition on the basis of the teeth (n=27) produces more or less the same picture as that of the total skeleton, namely 18% is younger than 20 years, and 82% is adult. The majority of the individuals, however, did not exceed the age of 30. Three children were aged between 4 and 12.5 years.

The age structure on the basis of the skull indicates that most individuals were not older than about 40 (table 4). Approximately 1/5 of the bones came from older individuals. Unusual are some skull fragments of young children, namely a newborn of 0 to 3 months and an infant of 1 to 2 years. In total bones of six infants, aged up to ten years have been found. One juvenile was about 15.

4.5 SELECTIVE DEPOSITION?

In an attempt to answer the question of whether whole bodies or certain parts of them were deposited, an investigation was made into the division between cranial and postcranial skeletal elements as well as the distribution of the relevant skeletal parts over the left and right halves of the body.

As far as the division between cranial and postcranial elements is concerned, there appears to be nothing unusual; there are no indications that individual skulls were deposited. The Minimal Number of Individuals, 55 on the basis of the skulls and 45 on the basis of the femora, points to a deposition of complete bodies.

However, of the postcranial skeleton more right bones and bone fragments were found than left. The question is whether this was just chance or whether there was some selective deposition of certain parts of the body. On separating left and right limbs according to sex we observed in the case of the femora a tendency towards an association of adult males with right bones. The numbers male/female and right/left femora were as follows:

---

[53] The skeletal remains examined included three complete and 16 less complete mandibles from 19 different individuals. Four of them contained no elements, mainly as a result of post-mortal loss. None of the eight maxilla (from different individuals) was complete.

	right femur		left femur	
male	26	(76.5%)	16	(69.6%)
female	8	(23.5%)	7	(30.4%)
total	34	(100%)	23	(100%)

By means of a statistical test[54] the probability of the numbers found was investigated, assuming that the chance of discovery of right bones is equal to that of left ones. On the basis of the data now available, we must ascribe the fact that there are more right bones than left ones to chance. The difference is just below the significance level.[55]

4.6 INJURIES AND MARKS ON BONES

For the interpretation of the archaeological context it is important to establish whether there are any injuries and marks on the bones (traumatic lesions). In other words, are there any indications that we are dealing with victims of violence? Every possible dent, notch and hole was carefully examined. It is difficult and sometimes even impossible to distinguish between ante-mortem injuries and post-mortem damage. Intensive and repeated microscopic observation of the bone material gives some insight into the nature of the traces. Particularly when the bone shows no signs of healing in the form of bone reaction, it is not always possible to establish the time the damage was inflicted, i.e ante- or post-mortem. For this reason the term peri-mortem trauma is used for possible ante-mortem traces of violence without any bone reaction.

The most important criterion used to distinguish between ante- and post-mortem injuries is the presence and colour of a patina; less conclusive is the degree of erosion of the bone surface. If the surface of a lesion has an identical patina to that of the rest of the bone, it is regarded as an old surface and a trauma inflicted prior to or immediately after death.[56] All traces with a deviant patina, colour, gloss etc. are classified as post-mortem damage or erosion. A great many damages to bones appear to have occurred recently during the process of dredging.[57]

The traces of weapon injuries to the skeleton were classified in four groups, depending on the sort of weapon that was probably used and the nature and form of the injury. Apart from the shape (transverse, oblique or spiral) of the lesion, the location of the injury on the bone is important. The weapon injuries were divided into the following categories.[58]

[54] Conover 1971; Ter Schegget 1994, 33-35.

[55] In the literature, a tendency towards relatively more right femora than left is often observed (for example Wilson 1992). For this reason we would recommend that human bone material found outside formal burial places be critically examined as to its composition.

[56] Rolle 1970, 52.

[57] These damages may date from the 1970s or 1990s.

The bone damage from the 1970s may give rise to confusion because the damaged surface has meanwhile become lightly patinated and the fractures themselves rounded off. Because of the latter, the occurrence of an eroded surface on damaged areas is in itself not a criterion for the advanced age of the damage.

[58] Brothwell 1981, 119.

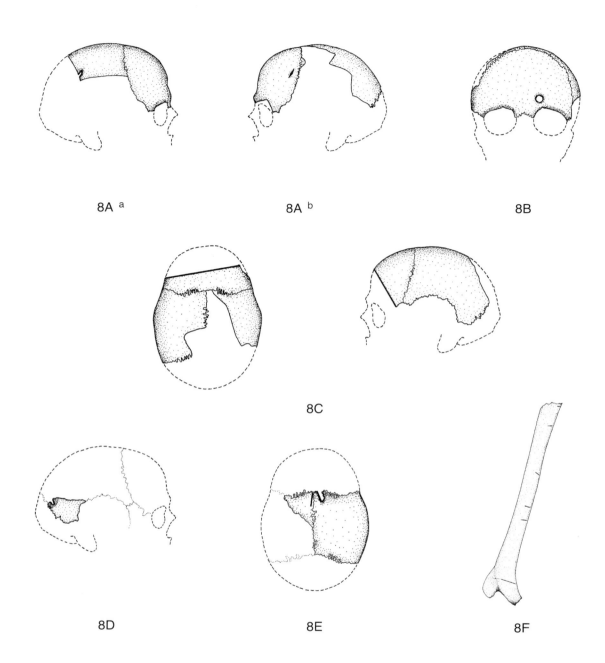

8A ᵃ   8A ᵇ   8B

8C

8D   8E   8F

Fig. 8. The position of injuries and marks on various bones:
A cut mark (a) and perforation (b) in the skull of an adult male (MK111/132), dated to the Late Iron Age (see also fig. 9); B hole above the left eye of an adult female (?) (MK166/479), dated to the Late Iron Age (see also fig. 10); C skull of an adult with part of the frontal bone cut off (MK93), dated to the Late Iron Age (see also fig. 11); D perforated parietal bone of an adult (MK196); dated to the Late Iron Age (see also fig. 12); E two cut marks in the skull of an adult (MK135), dated to the Early Middle Ages (see also fig. 13); F traces of blows on the front and outer side of the right humerus of an adult (MK478), dated to the Early Middle Ages (see also fig. 14)

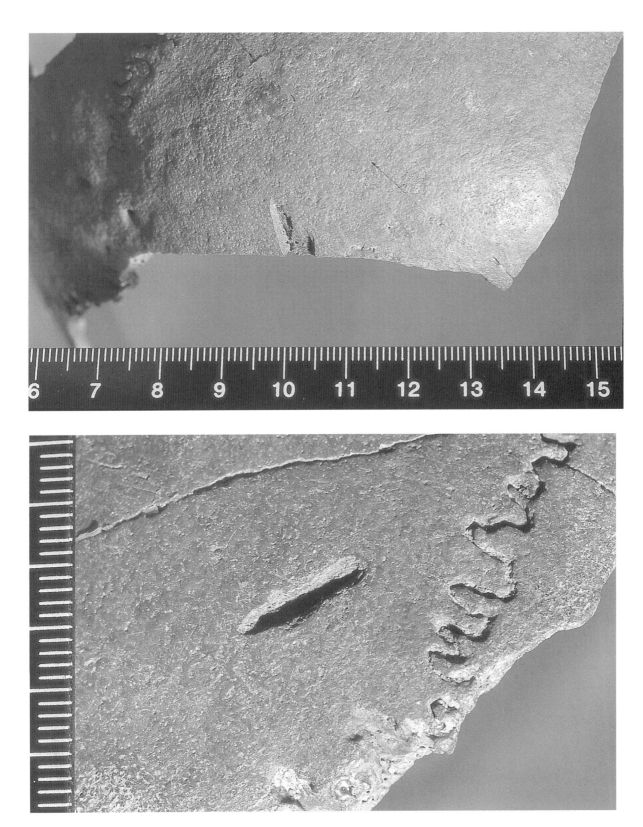

Fig. 9. Cut mark (a) and perforation (b) in the skull of an adult male (MK111/132), dated to the Late Iron Age. Photo M. Ydo.

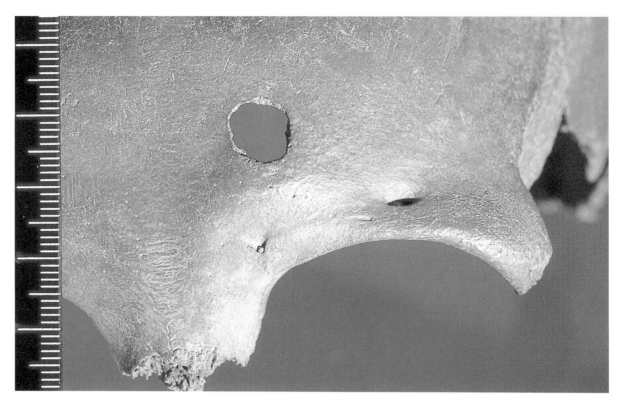

Fig. 10. Hole above the left eye of an adult female (?) (MK166/479), dated to the Late Iron Age. Photo M. Ydo.

1. Gross crushing by large stones or clubs. This may result in considerable deformation, and in the case of the skull, may show a primary depressed area from which subsidiary cracks radiate. An injury of this kind is usually fatal.
2. Less extensive fracturing by small clubs, maces and missile-stones. These smaller injuries are not usually fatal, so that signs of healing can be observed.
3. Piercing by spears, lances, daggers, javelins and arrows. Definite cases of ante-mortem perforation may usually be distinguished from post-mortem erosion by the well-defined shape of the hole. In the case of the skull vault, the perforation may be larger on the internal surface than externally.
4. Blow, gash or stab wound, caused by weapons with a sharp blade such as swords and axes. Sword injuries are generally narrower than those inflicted by an axe. A blow to the skull may be associated with secondary cracks. The injuries may appear as long, deep cuts, shorter and more superficial nicks or as small scratches caused by the sword glancing off the bone. Sharp-bladed weapons leave a definite trace in the form of one straight and one fragmented edge. A sword can also cut a round chunk off the skull resulting in a "pseudo-trepanation hole". Decapitation usually results in traces on the back of the head or one of the neck vertebrae.

The distribution of injuries over the skeleton can give insight into fighting technique. A man-to-man fight for example produces more injuries to the legs than to the arms, and more to the left than the right side.[59]

Injuries and marks on bones are clearly visible on 15 skeletal parts found at Kessel. Injuries caused

[59] Merbs 1989, 174.

218

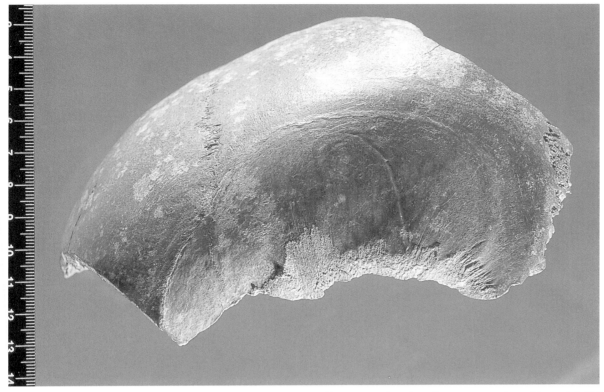

Fig. 11. Skull of an adult with part of the frontal bone cut off (MK93), dated to the Late Iron Age. Photo M. Ydo.

by blunt objects (cat. 1) were not observed. Dents (cat. 2) were only observed on parts of the skull. The majority of injuries was caused by pointed or sharp objects (cat. 3 and 4) such as a spear, lance, dagger, arrow, sword or axe. As far as the sex could be established, most injuries were found on adult males. Injuries caused by metal objects with a sharp blade, such as a sword or an axe (cat. 4), were only found on adult males or adult individuals of indeterminate sex.

Six bone fragments with traces of weapon injuries were dated by means of the C14 method (table 2). Four of them date from the Late Iron Age and two from the Early Medieval period.

Injuries to the skull were observed in nine individuals (fig. 8). Two adult males, younger than 40 years, have a peri-mortem dent in the middle of their foreheads. Both dents show no traces of recovery, such as small pits around the dent. The oldest of the two (MK98) has a round dent in the middle of the forehead with a diameter of about 1 cm. The younger (MK113) has an elongated to oval dent above the right eye, 1.5 cm in length and 0.5 cm in width.

In the case of a man of 30 to 40 years, two injuries to the skull were observed (MK111/132; fig. 8A and 9). This skull has a C14 date of 2120 ± 50 BP. On the upper left of the forehead there is an elongated perforation, with rounded edges and an identical patina to the rest of the skull. Particularly on the inside of the skull one can see that the hole was made in living bone. The perforation measures 1.1 cm on the outside and is 0.2 cm wide; the hole becomes smaller towards the inside of the skull. The triangular shape of the hole would appear to point to an injury caused by an arrow, dagger or spear. The second injury is sharp and probably inflicted by a sword. A section of the parietal bone with part of the trace of the gash has been broken off. The remaining part of the sword cut is 1.0 cm long and about 0.1 cm deep. No signs of healing were observed on either injury, which implies that they were inflicted simultaneously and were probably fatal.

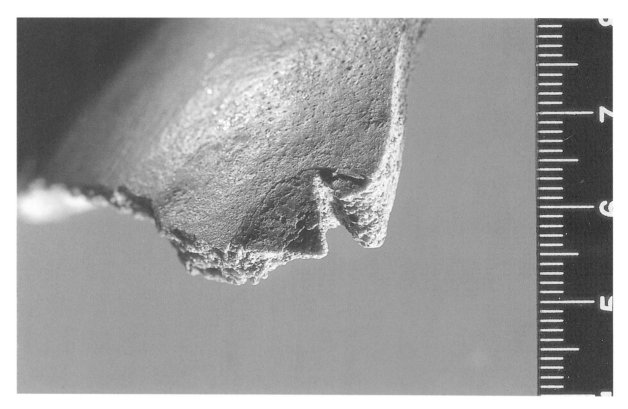

Fig. 12. Perforated parietal bone of an adult (MK196); dated to the Late Iron Age. Photo M. Ydo.

An older individual aged 40 to 60 years and probably female, has a round hole above the left eye (MK166/479; fig. 8,B and 10). A C14 dating of this skull gave 2070 ± 40 BP. The diameter of the hole is 0.8 to 0.9 cm and is larger on the inner side where recently some bone material has broken away. On the outer side, the edge looks 'old' and the surface has a similar patina to the rest of the skull. There are no signs of healing. The hole was probably caused by an arrow and would have been fatal.

Unusual is a skull with a hewn–off forehead (dated 2090 ± 60 BP). This faceless skull came from an individual of indeterminate sex, aged 40 to 60 years (MK93; fig. 8,c and 11). The surface of the cut has a shiny patina and is virtually straight and the edge is sharp. The injury appears to have been inflicted by a sword blow, in which the sword was worked back and forth. Possibly the line of fracture in the middle of the forehead was caused by the blow. In view of the surface of the cut which is not altogether regular, the possibility that the skull was manipulated peri- or post-mortem by removal of the face cannot be excluded.

A peri-mortal perforation with cracks is situated at the back right of the parietal bone of an adult individual under 60 (MK196; fig. 8, D and 12). The skull fragment which has a C14 dating of 2010 ± 90 BP, is so small that no further information on sex and age can be obtained. Although only a small section of the injury has been preserved, it can be clearly seen that the weapon entered the skull wall with great force or speed, causing it partly to shatter. The length of the hole is at least 0.7 cm (the rest has been broken away), the width is 0.2 to 0.3 cm. The surface of the perforation is 'old', i.e. ante- or peri-mortem. Judging from the shape of the injury and the force or speed with which it was inflicted, it would appear to have been caused by a spear or an arrow. No traces of healing were observed, so this injury will have been fatal.

On the top of the skull of an adult individual younger than 40 there are two long deep gashes (MK135; fig. 8,E and 13). This skull has a C14 date of 1400 ± 110 BP. Both cuts appear to have been

Fig. 13. Two cut marks in the skull of an adult (MK135), dated to the Early Middle Ages. Photo M. Ydo.

inflicted by the same weapon, an axe or a sword. The gash in the left parietal bone is 1.5 cm long and has a smooth surface. More or less perpendicular to the gash the skull has cracked over a length of 2.5 cm. The gash in the right parietal bone is 3 cm long with a continuing crack of 5 cm. This cut also has a smooth surface. The exact lengths of the injuries cannot be ascertained because the entire forehead is missing. Both gashes show no signs of healing and will have been fatal.

The six cases with probable ante- and peri-mortem injuries to arms and legs are less straightforward than those to the skull. A small perforation 0.3 to 0.4 cm in diameter was observed on a left humerus belonging to an adult (MK275). The small hole is located on the outside of the arm, near the shoulder. The colour indicates an 'old' surface and there are no signs of healing. In view of the specific shape of the perforation, it would appear to have been caused by an arrow- or spearhead.

On the front and outer side of a right humerus (dated 1410 ± 30 BP) of an adult, there are a number of incisions (MK478; fig. 8,F and 14). The lengths of the cuts vary from 1 to 2 cm. In the incisions, dents and scratches the surface is 'old' and eroded; there are no traces of healing to be seen. The cuts and scratches appear to have been caused by a sharp-bladed weapon, probably a sword. Judging from the position and depth of the cuts to the arm they were probably defensive traces.

On the front of the left femur of an adult of indeterminate sex there is a small perforation 0.4 to 0.5 cm in diameter (MK403). The hole closely resembles the perforation in the humerus described above (MK275). It has an 'old' surface and shows no traces of healing. The shape indicates an injury caused by an arrow or spear-head.

Three femur fragments from three different adults appear to have been hacked or sawn off (MK 397, 606 and 395). The two shortest fragments are 6 to 7 cm in length, and the longest is about 10 cm. The injuries are all on the outer side of the leg, so that a sword or axe cut is possible. One right

Fig. 14. Some traces of blows on the front and outer side of the right humerus of an adult (MK478), dated to the Early Middle Ages. Photo M. Ydo.

fragment was from a male; this bone has, in addition to a possible swordcut at right angles to the bone, a 1.5 cm-wide cut on the fore side, possibly caused by a sword glancing off it. The length of this cut is at least 3 cm. Its exact length cannot be determined because the bone has been cut off at the place of the blow.[60]

5   INTERPRETATION AND DISCUSSION

There are various possible explanations for the presence of skeletal remains in the river Meuse at Kessel. Leads for an explanation are the position of the findspot in the landscape, the composition of the find complex (animal and human bones, pottery, weaponry, bronze vessels, belt-hooks and other metal objects) and the characteristics and dating of the skeletal material itself. Possible interpretations are: 1. an eroded cemetery with inhumation burials; 2. an eroded settlement; 3. a battlefield; 4. a cult place.

1. An important argument against an interpretation of this find complex as an eroded inhumation cemetery is that the spot was used for centuries to deposit all kinds of objects. We would then be dealing with several eroded cemeteries which would be unlikely. In the second place it is significant that most of the bone material was not affected by river erosion. If we assume that most of the bones date from the Late Iron Age, there is a third argument against it. In contrast to the Early Middle Ages, cremation and not inhumation was the common burial ritual in the Lower Rhine area during the whole of the first millennium BC. Moreover, in the Late Iron Age the deposition of weapons, coins and bronze vessels in graves was most unusual. Finally, it can be concluded from the conservation of the bone material that it had been almost immediately cut off from oxygen, in other words, it was under water. The material seems to have been deliberately deposited in a less active bed of the Meuse. On the basis of these arguments the cemetery interpretation has to be rejected.

2. An important feature of settlement remains is the presence of traces of gnawing by dogs on the bones. The total absence of gnawing traces on the Kessel bones indicates direct deposition under water. For this reason, the skeletal material does not appear to originate from an eroded settlement. The composition of the find complex – particularly the presence of many valuable or prestigious metal objects – also argues against an interpretation as settlement material. The occurrence of such an abundance of metal ware is unusual in settlement contexts.

3. The age and sex division in combination with the traces of weapon injuries may point to a social group engaged in warfare. Part of the Iron-Age and Early-Medieval population even appears to have succumbed to force of arms. They were possible war victims. The greater part of the population consists of young adult males. However, there are also at least ten women, several children and a number of old individuals aged between 50 and 80. This would imply that the find complex was not a purely military one. The presence of many weapons – swords, spearheads, knives and axes – might indicate a

---

[60] Some other bones from Kessel have less obvious traces of injury. The only non-adult individual with a possible peri-mortem trauma is a 10 to 15-year-old child with a dent on the right parietal bone (MK176). This dent has a diameter of 1 cm at the most. At the back of the head of an individual 50 to 80 years old there is possibly part of a perforation (MK126). Only part is present because the rest has recently been broken off. The hole is to the right of the centre, has an old surface and shows traces of healing in the form of pitting. Since this skull fragment is rather weathered, it cannot be established with certainty whether this is an ante-mortem injury (a blow to the head) or post-mortem erosion.

battlefield interpretation. However, some of the swords were still in their scabbards or had been rendered useless by secondary bending. An important argument against a battlefield interpretation is the probable association of the human skeletal remains with large quantities of pottery and animal bones.

4. On the basis of the present information, we are inclined towards an interpretation of the material from Kessel as a ritual find complex belonging to a cult place of a certain regional importance. This interpretation provides the best explanation for the composition and relative wealth of the Late Iron-Age/Early-Roman finds collected near the entrance of the dredge pit at Kessel. Excavations of pre-Roman cult places elsewhere in Northern Gaul often yield a similar combination of considerable numbers of weapons, fibulae and coins, as well as large quantities of pottery, animal and often also human remains.[61] The find conditions at Kessel, as far as these could be reconstructed, confirm this ritual interpretation. The material appears to have been deliberately deposited in the river in accordance with a tradition of depositions in watery contexts which lasted for a long period in Northwest and Central Europe, and which attained a new peak in various regions in the Late Iron Age. As a result, Kessel belongs to the category of 'river cult places' which also includes the famous Swiss Iron-Age sites at La Tène and Port. The existence of this category of cult places is closely linked with the cosmological associations of rivers in Celto-Germanic and Gallo-Roman religion. Rivers could be worshipped as deities or were intimately linked with divine powers.

To what extent this cult place at Kessel was still significant in the Early and High Middle Ages, remains an open question. The presence at this site of human skeletal remains is difficult to interpret at the moment. Possibly an integral study of the early-medieval find material will provide new insights.

It falls outside the scope of this study to examine the ritual practices performed at Kessel and their social and religious backgrounds. In order to do this, we must wait for a full publication of the other finds. However, it may be stated that the presence of weaponry, the predominance of adult males in the skeletal population and the weapon injuries on some of the bones all point to a close connection between the rituals performed here and the domain of warfare. Many questions regarding the identity and cause of death of the persons deposited here must remain unanswered. Two main interpretations can be given. The first, referring to texts by classical authors, is that of the sacrifice hypothesis. Celts and Germans were familiar with the practice of human sacrifice, especially in situations of crisis when the victims were often prisoners of war.[62] The association of weapons with human remains in rivers may point in the direction of offerings made to the gods of war. Other finds in rivers, like harvest implements, seem to link the place with offerings to the fertility powers.[63] In the second interpretation, the human remains from rivers are linked with a deviant mortuary ritual, involving members of the local community instead of enemy outsiders. Elsewhere in this volume, Roymans and Kortlang hypothesize the existence – alongside the normal cremation rite practised in the urnfields – of an alternative way of disposing of corpses or certain parts of bodies in rivers.[64]

It may be clear from the above discussion that further investigation is essential if one wishes to arrive at better-founded conclusions on the phenomenon of human remains from rivers. On the basis of the scanty evidence at present at our disposal, these would appear to be ritual depositions in many cases, and this practice probably extended over a long period. The information for the Netherlands shown in table 1 covers the period from the Late Neolithic to well into the Early Middle Ages. However, because of the small number of C14-dated bones from river contexts nothing can yet be

[61] Cf. Roymans 1990, 82, table 4.4.

[62] Beck 1970; Davidson 1993, 96 ff.

[63] Merrifield 1987, 22-57; Davidson 1988, 26, 131-133;

Green 1993[2], 138-166.

[64] Roymans/Kortlang, this volume. See also the discussion in Bradley/Gordon 1988; Bradley 1990, 99-109.

said about the fluctuating 'popularity' of this depositional practice throughout time. We must also take into account the considerable variation in the number of individuals (or parts of them) deposited per location. In Kessel – and possibly also in Roermond – these are large quantities of human remains which form part of larger find complexes. In many other locations there appear to be isolated or small numbers of bones. One of the first tasks for future research is to describe the spatial and temporal patterning in the deposition of human remains in rivers.

Appendix

Descriptive catalogue of the human remains from the river Meuse at Kessel

Legend to the catalogue: the first column gives the find number; the second gives the part of the skeleton; the third column indicates the right and/or left side of the body; the fourth column gives the percentage of bone present (where 100% means a complete bone, P the proximal part – situated nearest to the centre of the body – of a long bone, D the distal part – situated away from the centre of the body – of a long bone and M the middle part); the fifth column indicates the sex (male, probably male, female, probably female or indifferent); the sixth column gives the skeletal age and the seventh column indicates the presence of traces of violence or injury, pathologies and some particularities.

1 no.	2 bone	3 R/L	4 % present	5 sex	6 age (in years)	7 trauma/pathology/other
01	mandible	R+L	99	female?	20-30	
02	mandible	R+L	100	male	18-25	
03	mandible	R+L	100	male	18-25	
04	mandible	R	25	indiff.	—	
05	mandible	R	60	indiff.	>18	
06	mandible	R	65	male?	25-30	
07	mandible	R	55	male	21-28	
08	mandible	R	50	(child)	7,5-12,5	
09	mandible	R	45	male	17-22	
10	mandible	R	30	indiff.	18-21	
11	mandible	R	30	female	18-25	
12	mandible	R	30	female?	18-25	
13	mandible	L	70	male?	22-25	
14	mandible	L	60	male	18-21	
15	mandible	L	40	indiff.	>18	
16	mandible	L	40	indiff.	>18	
17	mandible	R+L	40	(child)	4-8	
18	maxilla	L	50	(child)	7,5-12,5	
19	maxilla/cheekbone	R	50	male	18-25	
20	maxilla/cheekbone	R	50	male	21-28	
21	maxilla/cheekbone	R	50	-male?	25-28	
22	maxilla	L	50	—	25-35	
23	maxilla	L	40	—	18-25	
24	maxilla	L	40	—	25-28	
25	maxilla	L	50	(child)	15-18	
26	occipital bone	-	100	(child)	0-3 months	
27	occip./parietal bone	L	100	(child)	14-24 months	
28	occip./parietal bone	R+L	95	male	23-40	
29	occip./parietal bone	R+L	40	male	60-70	fits with no. 82
30	occip./parietal bone	R	50	—	50-60	
31	occip.bone/skull base	-	100	—	15-20	
32	occip.bone/skull base	-	100	female	23-40	
33	occip.bone/skull base	-	90	indiff.	>24	
34	occip./parietal bone	R	50	male	23-40	
35	occipital bone	-	100	male	<40	
36	occipital bone	-	100	male	<40	
37	occipital bone	-	100	male	<40	
38	occipital bone	-	100	male?	<40	

39	occipital bone	-	95	male?	<40	
40	occip./parietal bone	L	95	male	<40	
41	occipital bone	-	100	female	<24	
42	occipital bone	-	95	female	<40	
43	occipital bone	-	100	female?	<40	
44	occipital bone	-	95	female?	<40	
45	occipital bone	-	100	female	<40	
46	occipital bone	-	60	female	<40	
47	occipital bone	-	75	indiff.	<40	
48	occipital bone	-	75	indiff.	<40	
49	occipital bone	-	60	female	<40	
50	occipital bone	-	60	(child)	<20	
51	occipital bone	-	75	female?	adult	
52	occipital bone	-	50	indiff.	adult	
53	occipital bone	-	25	female?	<40	
54	occipital bone	-	25	—	—	
55	occipital bone	-	25	—	<40	
56	occipital bone	-	25	—	<40	
57	cheekbone	R	100	female?	adult	
58	skull base	-	100	—	adult	
59	skull base	-	100	—	>20	
60	skull base	-	100	—	>20	
61	temp./petrosal bone	L	100	female?	>20	
62	temp./petrosal bone	L	100	male	>20	
63	temp./petrosal bone	L	100	female	>20	
64	temp./petrosal bone	L	90	female	>20	
65	temp./petrosal bone	L	100	indiff.	>20	
66	temp./petrosal bone	L	100	male?	>20	
67	temp./petrosal bone	L	90	female	>20	
68	temp./petrosal bone	L	100	female	>20	
69	temp./petrosal bone	L	80	(child)	subadult	
70	temp./petrosal bone	L	90	female	>20	
71	temp./petrosal bone	L	50	female	>20	
72	temp./petrosal bone	R	100	male?	>20	
73	temp./petrosal bone	R	100	male	>20	
74	temp./petrosal bone	R	100	male	>20	
75	temp./petrosal bone	R	100	male	>20	
76	temp./petrosal bone	R	100	female	>20	
77	temp./petrosal bone	R	100	indiff.	>20	
78	temp./petrosal bone	R	100	male	>20	
79	temp./petrosal bone	R	100	male?	>20	
80	temp./petrosal bone	R	90	male	>20	
81	temp./petrosal bone	R	90	male	>20	
82	occip./temp./par.bone	R	70	male	60-70	fits with no. 29; post-mortem notch
83	temp./petrosal bone	R	100	male	>20	
84	temp./petrosal bone	L	50	male	>20	
85	mandible	R	55	indiff.	25-28	
86	mandible	R	30	female?	28-40	
87	occip./par. bone	R+L	50	—	50-70	
88	occipital bone	-	100	male	<40	
89	occipital bone	-	100	indiff.	<40	
90	occipital bone	-	60	indiff.	<40	
91	frontal/par.bone	R+L	90	male	40-70	
92	frontal/par.bone	R+L	75	male	23-40	

93	frontal/par.bone	R+L	60	indiff.	40-60	part of frontal bone cut off, by sword?; Late Iron Age (fig. 8,c and 11)
94	frontal bone	-	100	male?	<40	
95	frontal bone	-	100	female	23-40	
96	frontal bone	-	80	male	40-70	very robust
97	frontal bone	-	100	female	<40	
98	frontal bone	-	90	male	<40	dent in middle of forehead
99	frontal bone	L	50	indiff.	<40	
100	frontal bone	L	50	male	40-70	robust, looks petrified
101	frontal bone	-	10	indiff.	—	
102	frontal bone	-	15	female	—	
103	frontal bone	R	50	female	<40	
104	frontal bone	R	50	indiff.	<40	
105	frontal bone	R	50	female	<40	
106	frontal bone	L	50	male	40-55	
107	frontal bone	R	50	female	<40	
108	frontal bone	R	60	indiff.	<40	
109	frontal bone	R	15	male	—	light cribra orbitalia
110	frontal bone	R	40	(child)	<20	
111	frontal bone	R	80	male	30-40	fits with no. 132; perforation, due to arrow?; Late Iron Age (fig. 8,a and 9)
112	frontal/par.bone	R	30	male	60-80	
113	frontal bone	R	50	male	<40	dent above right eye
114	frontal bone	L	50	(child)	<20	cribra orbitalia; Late Iron Age
115	frontal bone	L	50	male	<40	
116	frontal bone	L	50	(child)	<18	
117	frontal/par.bone	R	30	male	40-60	
118	frontal bone	L	20	—	30-60	
119	frontal bone	L	15	indiff.	<40	possible cribra orbitalia
120	frontal bone	L	15	female	—	
121	frontal bone	R	40	—	<40	
122	frontal bone	R	60	—	23-40	
123	frontal/par.bone	R	10	—	40-70	
124	frontal bone	R	40	—	<40	
125	frontal bone	L	15	—	23-40	
126	frontal/par.bone	R+L	15	—	50-80	possible hole or erosion?
127	frontal/par.bone	R+L	15	—	40-60	
128	frontal bone	L	20	—	40-60	
129	frontal bone	-	10	—	—	
130	parietal bone	R+L	75	—	<20	
131	parietal bone	R+L	100	—	<40	
132	parietal bone	R+L	40	male	30-40	fits with n. 111; on right side cut mark due to sword; Late Iron Age (fig. 8,a and 9)
133	parietal bone	R+L	50	—	23-40	
134	parietal bone	R+L	40	—	55-80	petrified
135	parietal bone	R+L	75	—	<40	cut mark on right and left side, due to axe or sword; Early Middle Ages (fig. 8,e and 13)
136	parietal bone	R+L	20	—	<40	
137	parietal bone	R+L	45	—	40-60	
138	parietal bone	L	100	—	<40	

139	parietal bone	L	100	—	23-40	
140	parietal bone	L	100	—	<40	
141	parietal bone	L	100	—	<40	
142	parietal bone	L	90	—	<20	
143	parietal bone	L	80	—	<40	
144	parietal bone	L	80	—	<23	
145	frontal bone	L	40	—	<40	
146	parietal bone	L	10	—	<23	
147	parietal bone	L	10	—	<23	
148	parietal bone	L	20	—	<40	
149	parietal bone	L	25	—	<40	
150	parietal bone	L	15	—	23-40	
151	parietal bone	R	25	—	23-40	
152	parietal bone	L	50	—	30-50	
153	parietal bone	L	40	—	<40	
154	parietal bone	L	40	—	<40	fits with no. 183
155	parietal bone	L	20	—	<40	
156	parietal bone	L	40	female?	30-60	
157	parietal bone	L	40	male?	30-60	
158	parietal bone	L	20	—	<40	
159	parietal bone	R	20	—	<20	
160	parietal bone	L	20	—	—	eroded
161	parietal bone	L	20	—	adult	
162	parietal bone	L	20	—	<40	
163	parietal bone	L	20	male?	30-60	petrified
164	parietal bone	L	20	—	<23	
165	parietal bone	L	30	—	<40	
166	parietal bone	L	30	female?	40-60	fits with no. 479; round hole above left eye; Late Iron Age (fig. 8,b and 10)
167	parietal bone	L	40	—	<40	
168	parietal bone	L	30	—	23-40	
169	parietal bone	L	30	—	40-60	
170	parietal bone	R	75	—	<23	
171	parietal bone	R	80	—	<23	
172	parietal bone	R	99	—	<23	
173	parietal bone	R	99	—	23-40	
174	parietal bone	R	90	—	<20	
175	parietal bone	R	100	—	<40	
176	parietal bone	R	90	—	10-15	dent on right of forehead
177	parietal bone	R	75	—	<40	
178	parietal bone	R	20	—	23-60	
179	parietal bone	R	25	—	<40	
180	parietal bone	R	40	—	23-40	
181	parietal bone	R	40	—	<40	
182	not used number					
183	parietal bone	R	40	—	<40	fits with no. 154
184	parietal bone	R	40	—	<20	
185	parietal bone	R	50	—	<40	
186	parietal bone	R	50	—	<20	
187	parietal bone	R	25	—	<20	
188	parietal bone	R	30	—	adult	
189	parietal bone	R	20	—	<40	
190	parietal bone	R	40	—	adult	

191	parietal bone	R	40	—	<40	
192	parietal bone	R	10	—	adult	
193	parietal bone	R	15	—	<60	
194	parietal bone	R	40	—	20-30	
195	parietal bone	R	40	—	23-40	
196	parietal bone	R	25	—	<60	perforation due to arrow or spear; Late Iron Age (fig. 8,d and 12)
197	parietal bone	L	10	—	23-40	
198	parietal bone	R	20	—	<40	
199	parietal bone	R	25	—	subadult?	
200	parietal bone	R	25	—	<23	
201	parietal bone	R	10	—	adult	
202	occipital bone	-	20	—	<23	
203	parietal bone	-	15	—	adult	
204	parietal bone	-	10	—	<20	
205	parietal bone	-	10	—	adult	
206	parietal bone	-	10	—	adult	
207	parietal bone	-	10	—	<40	
208	parietal bone	-	5	—	<20	
209	parietal bone	-	20	—	>40	
210	parietal bone	L+R	20	—	>40	
211	parietal bone	-	10	—	<40	
212	humerus	R	100	male	>20-25	stature estim. 167.4-176.6 cm
213	humerus	R	95D	male?	>17-20	
214	humerus	R	95D	—	>16	
215	humerus	R	95D	—	>16	
216	humerus	R	95D	female?	>16-19	
217	humerus	R	95D	male?	>17-20	
218	humerus	R	95D	female?	>16-19	
219	humerus	R	95D	—	adult	
220	humerus	R	95D	male?	adult	
221	humerus	R	95D	—	adult	
222	humerus	R	95D	—	adult	
223	humerus	R	60D	—	adult	
224	humerus	R	50D	—	adult	
225	humerus	R	60D	—	adult	
226	humerus	R	70D	—	adult	
227	humerus	R	80D	—	adult	
228	humerus	R	80D	—	adult	
229	humerus	R	60D	—	subadult?	
230	humerus	R	80D	—	adult	
231	humerus	R	80D	—	subadult	
232	humerus	R	80D	—	subadult	
233	humerus	R	70D	—	adult	
234	humerus	R	90D	(child)	3.5-4.5	length of bone approx. 14 cm
235	humerus	R	40D	—	subadult	
236	humerus	R	40D	—	adult	
237	humerus	R	40D	—	adult	
238	humerus	R	40D	—	adult	
239	humerus	R	30D	male?	adult	
240	humerus	R	30D	—	adult	
241	humerus	R	30D	—	adult	
242	humerus	R	20M	—	adult	
243	humerus	R	30D	—	adult	

244	humerus	R	20D	—	adult	
245	humerus	R	20D	male?	>25	
246	humerus	R	50M	—	adult	
247	humerus	R	30M	—	adult	
248	humerus	R	50M	—	adult	
249	humerus	R	20M	—	adult	
250	humerus	R	100	female	>16-19	stature estim. 159.7-168.5 cm
251	humerus	L	95D	female?	>16-19	
252	humerus	L	90D	female?	>16-19	
253	humerus	L	90D	male?	adult	
254	humerus	L	90D	female?	adult	
255	humerus	L	90D	—	adult	
256	humerus	L	90D	—	adult	
257	humerus	L	90D	—	adult	
258	humerus	L	50D	—	adult	
259	humerus	L	90D	—	adult	
260	humerus	R	80D	—	subadult	
261	humerus	L	80D	—	adult	
262	humerus	L	80D	—	adult	
263	humerus	L	80D	—	adult	
264	humerus	L	80D	—	adult	
265	humerus	L	80D	—	adult	
266	humerus	L	80D	—	adult	
267	humerus	L	80D	—	adult	
268	humerus	L	70D	—	adult	
269	humerus	L	90D	(child)	7-10	length of bone 19.4 cm
270	humerus	L	90D	(child)	7-12	length of bone 19-20 cm
271	humerus	L	80D	—	adult	
272	humerus	L	60M	—	adult	
273	humerus	L	70M	—	adult	
274	humerus	L	50D	—	adult	
275	humerus	L	30M	—	adult	small hole, due to arrow or spear?
276	humerus	L	20D	—	>16	
277	humerus	L	20D	—	adult	
278	humerus	L	40M	—	adult	
279	humerus	L	40M	—	adult	
280	radius	R	100	male?	>22	stature estim. 166.4-175.8 cm
281	radius	R	100	female?	>22	stature estim. 160.7-169.1 cm
282	radius	R	90D	—	adult	
283	radius	R	90P	—	adult	
284	radius	R	90P	—	14-25	
285	radius	R	80M	—	adult	
286	radius	R	80M	male?	adult	
287	radius	R	80M	male?	adult	
288	radius	R	80D	female?	>22	
289	radius	R	70M	—	adult	
290	radius	R	60P	(child)	<14	
291	radius	R	60M	—	adult	
292	radius	R	60P	female?	14-25	
293	radius	R	50M	—	adult	
294	radius	R	60M	—	adult	
295	radius	R	50M	—	adult	
296	radius	R	60D	—	adult	
297	radius	R	60D	—	adult	

298	radius	R	60M	—	subadult?	
299	radius	R	60P	male?	adult	
300	radius	R	60M	—	subadult?	
301	radius	R	60P	male?	adult	
302	radius	R	50P	—	subadult?	
303	radius	R	60P	—	adult	
304	radius	L	100	male	adult	stature estim. 180.5-189.9 cm
305	radius	L	80M	male?	adult	
306	radius	L	80M	—	adult	
307	radius	L	80M	—	adult	
308	radius	L	80M	—	adult	
309	radius	R	70M	—	adult	
310	radius	L	70P	—	subadult	
311	radius	L	60D	—	adult	
312	radius	L	50P	male?	>18	
313	radius	L	60P	—	subadult	
314	radius	L	50D	—	adult	healed fracture?
315	radius	L	40P	—	adult	
316	radius	L	40M	—	adult	
317	ulna	R	100	male?	22-30	stature estim. 179.9-183.3 cm
318	ulna	R	100	male?	>22	stature estim. 180.6-190.0 cm
319	ulna	R	90M	—	adult	
320	ulna	R	80P	—	>18	
321	ulna	R	90P	female?	>18	
322	ulna	R	80P	female?	>18	
323	ulna	R	80P	male?	>18	
324	ulna	R	70P	—	>18	
325	ulna	R	70P	male?	>18	
326	ulna	R	70M	—	adult	
327	ulna	R	70M	—	subadult	
328	ulna	R	70M	—	subadult	
329	ulna	R	70M	—	subadult	
330	ulna	R	50P	—	adult	
331	ulna	R	40P	—	adult	
332	ulna	R	40P	male?	adult	
333	ulna	R	40P	—	adult	
334	ulna	R	30P	male?	>18	
335	ulna	R	25P	male	>18	
336	ulna	R	40P	—	subadult	
337	ulna	R	40M	male?	adult	
338	ulna	R	50M	male	adult	
339	ulna	L	100	female?	>22	stature estim. 158.9-166.5 cm
340	ulna	L	90P	—	>18	
341	ulna	L	90P	—	>18	
342	ulna	L	70P	—	adult	
343	ulna	L	70M	male?	adult	
344	ulna	L	70P	—	adult	
345	ulna	L	70P	—	adult	
346	ulna	L	70P	—	adult	
347	ulna	L	70P	—	adult	
348	ulna	L	70P	male?	adult	
349	ulna	L	70M	—	subadult	
350	ulna	L	50P	—	adult	
351	ulna	L	70M	—	adult	

352	ulna	L	60M	—	adult	
353	ulna	L	90M	(child)	6-10	length of bone approx. 15 cm
354	ulna	L	40M	male	adult	
355	femur	R	95M	male	>20	colour brown (320g, 37 cm); Late Roman period
356	femur	R	95M	female	subadult	light colour (183g, 34 cm); High or Late Middle Ages
357	femur	R	90M	female	adult	eroded, colour brown (165g, 31 cm); Early Middle Ages
358	femur	R	90M	male	adult	light brown (231g, 31 cm); Early or High Middle Ages
359	femur	R	80M	male	adult	grey-brown, heavy (230g, 30 cm); Late Iron Age
360	femur	R	80M	male	adult	eroded, colour brown, small pits, petrified (212g, 28 cm); Early Middle Ages
361	femur	R	60M	male	adult	grey-brown, round fracture areas (125g, 22 cm); Early or Middle Roman period
362	femur	R	50P	male	adult	
363	femur	R	75P	male	>20	
364	femur	R	95P	male	>20	
365	femur	R	90P	male	>20	
366	femur	R	90P	male?	>15	
367	femur	R	90D	female	>20	
368	femur	R	90M	male	>15	
369	femur	R	95D	male	>20	
370	femur	R	90P	male	adult	
371	femur	R	80P	male	>15	
372	femur	R	80P	male	adult	
373	femur	R	80P	female	adult	
374	femur	R	90P	indiff.	adult	
375	femur	R	75P	male	>20	three possible cuttings
376	femur	R	60P	male	>20	
377	femur	R	60P	female	adult	
378	femur	R	50P	indiff.	adult	
379	femur	R	50P	indiff.	>15	
380	femur	R	60M	male	adult	
381	femur	R	60M	male	adult	
382	femur	R	50M	indiff.	adult	
383	femur	R	60M	male	adult	
384	femur	R	50M	male	adult	
385	femur	R	50M	female	adult	
386	femur	R	60M	female	adult	
387	femur	R	40D	indiff.	adult	
388	femur	R	35M	indiff.	adult	
389	femur	R	35M	male	adult	
390	femur	R	25M	—	adult	
391	femur	R	25M	indiff.	adult	post-mortem dents
392	femur	R	25M	male	adult	
393	femur	R	25M	male	adult	
394	femur	R	25M	indiff.	adult	
395	femur	R	25M	female?	subadult	bone sawn through?
396	femur	R	25M	male	adult	post-mortem damage

397	femur	R	20M	male	adult	bone sawn through? cut mark??
398	femur	R	10P	—	>15	
399	femur	R	40D	male	>20	
400	femur	R	20D	—	>20	
401	femur	R	10D	—	15-30	
402	femur	L	90P	male	>15	
403	femur	L	90D	indiff.	>15	hole?
404	femur	L	90P	(child)	about 15	
405	femur	L	90P	indiff.	>15	
406	femur	L	90P	male	>15	
407	femur	L	80P	male	adult	rachitis
408	femur	L	80P	female	adult	
409	femur	L	60M	male	adult	
410	femur	L	70M	male	adult	
411	femur	L	80M	indiff.	adult	
412	femur	L	70M	male	adult	
413	femur	L	80M	male	adult	
414	femur	L	60M	indiff.	adult	
415	femur	L	50P	male	adult	
416	femur	L	80M	(child)	about 9	length of bone approx. 27 cm
417	femur	L	60M	female?	15-20	
418	femur	L	60M	—	subadult	
419	femur	L	60M	female?	subadult?	
420	femur	L	60M	indiff.	adult	
421	femur	L	40P	male	adult	
422	femur	L	40P	male	adult	
423	femur	L	40P	female	adult	
424	femur	L	60P	female	adult	
425	femur	L	50M	male	adult	
426	femur	L	50M	male	adult	
427	femur	L	40M	male	adult	
428	femur	L	40M	—	subadult?	
429	femur	L	40M	male	adult	
430	femur	L	40D	female?	subadult?	
431	femur	L	30D	—	adult	
432	femur	L	30P	—	adult	
433	femur	L	30M	female	adult	
434	femur	R	95M	(child)	3-4	
435	femur	L	50D	male	>20	
436	femur	L	30D	—	>20	
437	femur	L	5P	—	>20	
438	femur	L	10P	—	>20	
439	tibia	R	99P	female?	18-30	
440	tibia	R	95D	male?	>20	
441	tibia	R	95D	female?	>18	
442	tibia	R	90M	—	adult	
443	tibia	R	80M	male?	>20	post-mortem damage
444	tibia	R	80M	—	adult	
445	tibia	R	75M	—	adult	
446	tibia	R	75M	—	adult	
447	tibia	R	75M	—	adult	
448	tibia	R	75M	—	adult	
449	tibia	R	75M	—	adult	
450	tibia	R	50P	—	>18	

451	tibia	R	75M	—	adult	
452	tibia	R	75M	—	adult	
453	tibia	R	50P	—	adult	
454	tibia	R	40P	—	adult	
455	tibia	R	60M	—	adult	
456	tibia	R	75M	—	adult	rachitis
457	tibia	R	60M	—	adult	
458	tibia	R	40P	—	adult	
459	tibia	R	60M	—	adult	
460	tibia	R	50M	—	adult	
461	tibia	R	30M	—	adult	
462	tibia	R	60M	—	adult	
463	tibia	R	75M	—	adult	
464	tibia	R	60M	—	adult	
465	tibia	R	60M	—	adult	
466	tibia	R	75M	—	adult	
467	tibia	R	60M	—	adult	
468	tibia	R	60M	—	adult	
469	tibia	R	60M	—	adult	
470	tibia	R	30M	—	adult	
471	tibia	R	50M	—	adult	
472	tibia	R	30M	—	adult	
473	tibia	R	30M	—	adult	
474	tibia	R	30M	—	adult	
475	vertebra, atlas	-	-	—	adult	
476	vertebra, atlas	-	-	—	adult	
477	femur	L	80M	male	>20	
478	humerus	R	90D	—	adult	various cut marks, due to sword?; Early Middle Ages (fig. 8,f and 14)
479	frontal bone	-	100	female?	40-60	fits with no. 166; round hole above left eye, due to arrow?; Late Iron Age (fig. 8,b and 10)
480	tibia	L	100	—	>18	stature estim. 165.1 – 175.5 cm
481	tibia	L	90M	—	adult	
482	tibia	L	90M	—	adult	
483	tibia	L	90M	—	adult	
484	tibia	L	80M	—	adult	
485	tibia	L	70M	—	adult	
486	tibia	L	100	(child)	7-10	length of bone 20.7 cm
487	tibia	L	95M	(child)	8-10	min. length of bone 21-23 cm
488	tibia	L	80M	—	adult	
489	tibia	L	70P	—	adult	
490	tibia	L	70M	—	adult	
491	tibia	L	70M	—	adult	
492	tibia	L	60D	—	adult	
493	tibia	L	60M	—	adult	
494	tibia	L	60M	—	adult	
495	tibia	L	60M	—	adult	
496	tibia	L	60M	—	adult	
497	tibia	L	60M	—	adult	rachitis
498	tibia	L	70M	—	adult	
499	tibia	L	50M	—	adult	
500	tibia	L	30M	—	adult	
501	tibia	L	40M	—	adult	

502	tibia	L	30M	—	adult	
503	tibia	L	30M	—	adult	
504	tibia	L	30M	—	adult	
505	tibia	L	20M	—	adult	
506	tibia	L	20M	—	adult	
507	pelvis/sacrum	-	100	male	adult	
508	fibula	R	90M	(child)	2.5-4.5	min. length of bone 15.5 cm
509	fibula	R	95D	—	>17	
510	fibula	R	90M	—	adult	
511	fibula	R	80D	—	adult	
512	fibula	R	85M	—	adult	
513	fibula	R	80M	—	adult	
514	fibula	R	70M	—	adult	
515	fibula	R	50M	—	adult	
516	fibula	R	50M	—	adult	
517	fibula	R	40M	—	adult	
518	fibula	R	40D	—	adult	
519	fibula	R	20D	—	adult	
520	fibula	L	95D	—	>17	
521	fibula	L	80D	—	>17	
522	fibula	L	70D	—	>17	
523	fibula	L	80M	—	adult	
524	fibula	L	80M	—	adult	
525	fibula	L	50M	—	adult	
526	fibula	L	30M	—	adult	
527	fibula	L	50P	—	adult	
528	fibula	-	30M	—	adult	
529	fibula	-	30M	—	adult	
530	pelvis/sacrum	R	90	(child)	about 10	(os ilium)
531	pelvis/sacrum	R	40	male	>20	
532	pelvis/sacrum	R	30	female	25-34	
533	pelvis/sacrum	R	25	female?	25-39	
534	pelvis/sacrum	R	20	—	adult	
535	pelvis/sacrum	L	70	indiff.	17-24	
536	pelvis/sacrum	L	30	—	adult	
537	pelvis/sacrum	L	25	female?	25-39	
538	pelvis/sacrum	L	40	male?	adult	
539	pelvis/sacrum	L	15	indiff.	25-39	
540	pelvis/sacrum	L	20	indiff.	subadult?	
541	pelvis/sacrum	L	20	—	adult	
542	pelvis/sacrum	L	80	(child)	10-15	(os ilium)
543	pelvis/sacrum	L	50	(child)	about 10	(os ilium)
544	pelvis/sacrum	L	70	(child)	about 5	(os ilium)
545	pelvis/sacrum	L	90	(child)	5-10	(os ischii)
546	collar-bone	R	100	—	>21	
547	collar-bone	R	100	—	>21	
548	collar-bone	R	90	—	adult	
549	collar-bone	R	80	—	adult	
550	collar-bone	R	90	—	adult	
551	collar-bone	R	80	—	adult	
552	collar-bone	L	100	male?	>21	
553	collar-bone	L	90	—	adult	
554	collar-bone	L	80	—	adult	
555	collar-bone	L	80	—	adult	

556	collar-bone	L	80	—	adult	possible healed fracture
557	collar-bone	L	80	—	adult	possible healed fracture
558	collar-bone	L	70	—	adult	
559	shoulder-blade	L	30	—	adult	post-mortem damage on the back
560	shoulder-blade	L	30	—	adult	
561	shoulder-blade	L	30	—	adult	
562	shoulder-blade	L	30	—	adult	
563	vertebra, cervical	-	100	—	adult	
564	vertebra, thoracal	-	40	—	adult	
565	vertebra, thoracal	-	100	—	adult	
566	vertebra, thoracal	-	90	—	subadult	
567	vertebra, thoracal	-	95	—	adult	
568	vertebra, lumbar	-	100	—	adult	
569	vertebra, lumbar	-	95	—	adult	
570	vertebra, lumbar	-	95	—	adult	
571	vertebra, lumbar	-	100	—	adult	
572	vertebra, lumbar	-	80	—	adult	
573	vertebra, lumbar	-	90	—	adult	
574	vertebra, lumbar	-	50	—	adult	
575	pelvis/sacrum	-	20	—	adult	(first segment of sacrum)
576 - 594	ribs	-	-	—	—	18 ribs
595	heel bone	R	100	male?	>18	
596	heel bone	R	80	female?	>18	one individual with no. 599?
597	heel bone	R	100	female	>18	
598	heel bone	L	100	male	>18	
599	heel bone	L	80	female?	>18	one individual with no. 596?
600	metacarpal two	R	100	—	>18	
601	metacarpal three	R	100	—	>18	
602	metacarpal three	R	100	—	>18	
603	metacarpal two	L	90	—	>18	
604	metatarsal one	L	100	—	>18	
605	femur	-	75M	—	adult	
606	femur	-	10M	—	adult	bone sawn through?
607	femur	-	10M	—	adult	
608	bone unknown	-	-	—	adult	
609	bone unknown	-	-	—	adult	
610	bone unknown	-	-	—	adult	
611	bone unknown	-	-	—	adult	
612	fibula	L	30M	—	adult	
613	bone unknown	-	-	—	adult	
614	bone unknown	-	-	—	adult	
615	bone unknown	-	-	—	adult	

REFERENCES

Arbeitsgruppe Europäischer Anthropologen, 1979: Empfehlungen für die Alters- und Geschlechts-diagnose am Skelett, *Homo* 30, Anhang, 1-32.

Bass, W.H., 1984: *Human osteology: a laboratory and field manual of the human skeleton*, Columbia.

Beck, H., 1970: Germanische Menschenopfer in der literarischen Überlieferung, in H. Jankuhn (ed.), *Vorgeschichtliche Heiligtümer und Opferplätze in Mittel- und Nordeuropa*, Göttingen (Abhandlungen der Akademie der Wissenschaften Göttingen), 240-258.

Black, T.K., 1978: A new method for assessing the sex of fragmentary skeletal remains: femoral shaft circumference, *American Journal of Physical Anthropology* 48, 227-231.

Bradley, R., 1990: *The passage of arms. An archaeological analysis of prehistoric hoards and votive deposits*, Cambridge.

Bradley, R./K. Gordon 1988: Human skulls from the river Thames, their dating and significance, *Antiquity* 62, 503-509.

Brothwell, D.R., 1981: *Digging up bones. The excavation, treatment and study of human skeletal remains*, London.

Brunaux, J.-L., 1988: *The Celtic Gauls: gods, rites and sanctuaries*, London.

Cadoux, J.-L., 1984: L'Ossuaire Gaulois de Ribemont-sur-Ancre (Somme), premières observations, premières questions, *Gallia* 42, 53-78.

Colpe, C., 1970: Theoretische Möglichkeiten zur Identifizierung von Heiligtümern und Inter-pretation von Opfern in ur- und parahistorischen Epochen, in H. Jankuhn (ed.), *Vorgeschichtliche Heiligtümer und Opferplätze in Mittel- und Nordeuropa*, Göttingen (Abhandlungen der Akademie der Wissenschaften), 19-39.

Conover, W.J., 1971: *Practical nonparametric statistics*, New York.

Cunliffe, B., 1984: *Danebury: an Iron Age hillfort in Hampshire 1. The excavations 1969-1978: the finds*, London.

Cunliffe, B.W., 1993: *Fertility, propitiation and the gods in the British Iron Age*, Amsterdam (15e Kroonvoordracht).

Davidson, H.R.E., 1988: *Myths and symbols in pagan Europe. Early Scandinavian and Celtic religions*, New York.

Davidson, H.R.E., 1993: *The lost beliefs of Northern Europe*, London.

Driehaus, J., 1970: Urgeschichtliche Opferfunde aus dem Mittel- und Niederrhein, in H. Jankuhn (ed.), *Vorgeschichtliche Heiligtümer und Opferplätze in Mittel- und Nordeuropa*, Göttingen (Abhandlungen der Akademie der Wissenschaften Göttingen), 40-54.

Erdbrink, D.P/C. Meiklejohn/J. Tacoma, 1975: River valley people: fossil human remains from Limburg province in the Netherlands, *Proceedings van de Koninklijke Nederlandse Akademie van Wetenschappen* C 78/3, 226-264.

Erdbrink, D.P. Bosscha-/C. Meiklejohn/J. Tacoma, 1989: River valley people: fossil human cranial material from the Maurik area, *Proceedings van de Koninklijke Nederlandse Akademie van Wetenschappen* B 92/4, 267-312.

Erdbrink, D.P. Bosscha-/C. Meiklejohn/J. Tacoma, 1993: River valley people: fossil human remains from the Rhederlaag along the river IJssel, *Proceedings van de Koninklijke Nederlandse Akademie van Wetenschappen* B 96/1, 1-11.

Fitzpatrick, A.P., 1984: The deposition of La Tène Iron Age metalwork in watery contexts in Southern England, in B.W. Cunliffe/D. Miles (eds), *Aspects of the Iron Age in Central Southern England*, Oxford, 178-190.

Gladigow, B., 1984: Die Teilung des Opfers. Zur Interpretation von Opfern in vor- und frühgeschichtlichen Epochen, *Frühmittelalterliche Studien* 18, 19-43.

Gowlett, J.A.J. et al., 1987: Radiocarbon dates from the Oxford AMS system: datelist 5, *Archaeometry* 29, 131-132.

Green, M., 1993[2]: *The gods of the Celts*, Avon.

Hedges, R.E.M. et al., 1992: Radiocarbon dates from the Oxford AMS system: datelist 14, *Archaeometry* 34,148.

Hedges, R.E.M. et al., 1993: Radiocarbon dates from the Oxford AMS system: datelist 16, *Archaeometry* 35, 152.

Henderikx, P.A., 1986: The lower delta of the Rhine and the Maas: landscape and habitation from the Roman period to c.1000, *BROB* 36, 447-599.

Hessing, W.A.M., 1993: Ondeugende Bataven en verdwaalde Friezinnen? Enkele gedachten over de onverbrande menselijke resten uit de IJzertijd en Romeinse Tijd in West- en Noord-Nederland, in E. Drenth et al., *Het tweede leven van onze doden*, Amersfoort (NAR 15), 17-40.

Jankuhn, H., 1967: *Archaeologische Beobachtungen zu Tier- und Menschenopfern bei den Germanen in der Römischen Kaiserzeit*, Göttingen (Nachrichten der Akademie der Wissenschaften in Göttingen, I Phil.Hist. Klasse), 117-147.

Maringer, J., 1974: Flussopfer und Flussverehrung in vorgeschichtlicher Zeit, *Germania* 52, 309-318.

Merbs, C.F., 1989: Trauma, in M.Y. Iscan/K.A.R. Kennedy (eds), *Reconstruction of life from the skeleton*, New York, 161-190.

Merrifield, R., 1987: *The archaeology of ritual and magic*, London.

Pauli, L., 1991: Heilige Plätze und Opferbräuche bei den Helvetiern und ihren Nachbarn, *Archäologie der Schweiz* 14, 124-135.

Pot, Tj., 1988: Een gebitsonderzoek van het 18e-eeuwse grafveld St. Janskerkhof 1984, *Kroniek van bouwhistorisch en archeologisch onderzoek 's Hertogenbosch* I, 125-149.

Prummel,W./W.A.B. van der Sanden, 1995: Runderhoorns uit Drentse venen, *Nieuwe Drentse Volksalmanak* 112, 84-131.

Raddatz, K., 1952: Zur Deutung der Funde von La Tène, *Offa* 11, 24-28.

Rolle, R., 1970: Zum Problem der Menschenopfer und kultischen Anthropophagie in der vorrömischen Eisenzeit, *Neue Ausgrabungen und Forschungen in Niedersachsen* 6, 46-52.

Rösing, F.W., 1977: Methoden und Aussagemögligkeiten der anthropologischen Leichenbrandbearbeitung, *Archäologie und Naturwissenschaften* 1, 53-80.

Roymans, N., 1990: *Tribal societies in Northern Gaul. An anthropological perspective*, Amsterdam (Cingula 12).

Roymans, N., 1992: Late Urnfield Societies in the Northwest European Plain and the expanding networks of Central European Hallstatt Groups, in N. Roymans/F. Theuws (eds), *Images of the past. Studies on ancient societies in Northwestern Europe*, Amsterdam (SPP 7), 9-89.

Roymans, N., 1996: The sword or the plough. Regional dynamics in the romanisation of Belgic Gaul and the Rhineland area, in N. Roymans (ed.), *From the sword to the plough. Three studies on the earliest romanisation of Northern Gaul*, Amsterdam (Amsterdam Archaeological Studies 1), 9-126.

Roymans, N.G.A.M./W.A.B. van der Sanden, 1980: Celtic coins from the Netherlands and their archaeological context, *BROB* 30, 173-254.

Sanden, W.A.B. van der (ed.), 1990: *Mens en moeras. Veenlijken in Nederland van de Bronstijd tot en met de Romeinse tijd*, Assen.

Sanden, W.A.B. van der, 1992: Mens en moeras: het vervolg, *Nieuwe Drentse Volksalmanak* 109, 140-154.

Sanden, W.A.B. van der, 1996: *Through nature to eternity. The bog bodies of Northwest Europe*, Amsterdam.

Sanden, W.A.B. van der, 1997: Het kerkhof onder de autoweg. Menselijke resten uit de Drentsche Aa, *Nieuwe Drentse Volksalmanak* 114 , 171-179.

Schalles, H.-J./C. Schreiter (eds), 1993: *Geschichte aus dem Kies. Neue Funde aus dem Alten Rhein bei Xanten*, Köln (Xantener Berichte 3).

Schegget, M.E. ter, 1994: *Menselijke skeletresten in een ritueel vondstcomplex uit de IJzertijd in de Maas bij Kessel (gem. Lith)*, Amsterdam (unpublished M.A. thesis, University of Amsterdam).

Schwab, H., 1972: Entdeckung einer keltische Brücke an der Zihl und ihre Bedeutung für La Tène, *AK* 2, 289-294.

Schwab, H., 1974: Neue Ergebnisse zur Topographie von La Tène, *Germania* 52, 348-367.

Smits, E., 1992: Het grafveld van Spijkenisse-Hartel West. Het fysisch-antropologisch onderzoek, in A.B. Döbken (ed.), *Boorbalans* 2, 223-230.

Smits, E., 1993: Het fysisch-antropologisch onderzoek van het Romeinse grafveld te Valkenburg (ZH), in E. Drenth et al., *Het tweede leven van onze doden*, Amersfoort (NAR 15), 11-16.

Stuart-Macadam, P.L., 1989: Nutritional deficiency diseases: a survey of scurvy, rickets, and iron deficiency anemia, in M.Y. Iscan/K.A.R. Kennedy (eds), *Reconstruction of life from the skeleton*, 201-222, New York.

Therkorn, L.L., 1984: Schagen, Muggenburg, in P.J. Woltering (ed.), Archeologische Kroniek van Holland over 1983, I Noord-Holland, *Holland* 16, 215-216.

Torbrügge, W., 1970-71: Vor- und frühgeschichtliche Flussfunde; zur Ordnung und Bestimmung einer Denkmälergruppe, *Berichte der Römisch-Germanischen Kommission* 51-2, 1-146.

Ubelaker, D.H., 1984[2]: *Human skeletal remains. Excavation, analysis, interpretation*, Washington.

Verwers, G.J./J.Ypey, 1975: Six iron swords from the Netherlands, *APL* 8, 79-91.

Vouga, P., 1923: *La Tène*, Leipzig.

Wahl, J., 1982: Leichenbranduntersuchungen, *Praehistorische Zeitschrift* 57, 97-125.

Wait, G.A., 1985: *Ritual and religion in Iron Age Britain*, Oxford (BAR, Brit. Ser. 149).

Wegner, G., 1976: *Die vorgeschichtichen Flussfunde aus dem Main und aus dem Rhein bei Mainz*, Kallmünz (Materialhefte zur bayerischen Vorgeschichte, Reihe A, 30).

Wiedemer, H.R., 1963: Menschliche Skelettreste aus Spätlatène-Siedlungen im Alpenvorland, *Germania* 41, 269-280.

Wilson, B., 1992: Considerations for the identification of ritual deposits of animal bones in Iron Age pits, *International Journal of Osteoarchaeology* 2, 341-349.

Wyss, R., 1974: Grabriten, Opferplätze und weitere Belege zur geistigen Kultur der Latènezeit, in *Ur- und frühgeschichtliche Archäologie der Schweiz* 4, Die Eisenzeit, Basel, 167-196.

Zimmermann, W.H., 1970: Urgeschichtliche Opferfunde aus Flüssen, Mooren, Quellen und Brunnen Südwestdeutschlands, *Neue Ausgrabungen und Forschungen in Niedersachsen* 6, 53-92.

The archaeology and history of the *curia* of the abbey of Saint-Trond at Hulsel (province of North Brabant) (c. AD 700 - 1300)

Frans Theuws

Preface

This is the final report on the excavations of a part of a medieval settlement at Hulsel in the province of North Brabant (fig. 1) by the Instituut voor Pre- en Protohistorische Archeologie (IPP) of the University of Amsterdam. The excavations took place from September 16th to October 11th 1985 and from August 11 to 21th 1986. The settlement site is situated in a development area and all the archaeological remains would have been destroyed during building activities over the following years (fig. 2). Apart from these practical reasons, the site was chosen for reasons of research policy. This report was written in 1990-1991.

1   INTRODUCTION

The excavations of a medieval settlement at Hulsel are part of the Kempen project that started in 1980. The major research objectives of this project were the reconstruction of the settlement pattern and the settlement system in the Kempen region and the study of the processes of integration of the region into larger polities, mainly during Roman and medieval times.[1] The Kempen project has now been integrated in a larger IPP-project comprising all of the Southern Netherlands. In the Kempen-project the

---

[1] An introduction to the project and its goals are given in: Slofstra a.o., 1982; see also Slofstra 1983; Theuws 1986; Verhoeven/Vreenegoor 1991; Theuws 1991; Theuws/Bijsterveld 1991.

Instituut voor Pre- en Protohistorische archeologie of the University of Amsterdam concentrated on the medieval period, the Roman period is studied by the Archeologisch Instituut van de Vrije Universiteit in Amsterdam.

The archaeological study of medieval settlements and the cultural landscape in the Kempen region

Fig. 1. The location of Hulsel in the Netherlands.

began with little knowledge about the location of the settlements, their diversity, their size, the shape of the buildings and the pottery sequence. A few early-medieval cemeteries and some churches had been excavated, but as of 1980 they were not published or studied in a regional context. Local historical-geographers had reconstructed medieval settlements using 19th-century land registry maps, but on closer inspection these reconstructions proved to be unsatisfactory on many points, and they could not account for the socio-economic processes in the region that occurred during its integration in the Frankish empire in the Early Middle Ages and the duchy of Brabant in the High Middle Ages.[2] In both periods the region formed a peripheral area within the polities. The exact nature of the relations that emerged between central and peripheral regions within medieval polities of different organizational complexity was a major concern of the project and still is. Ultimately, the results are expected to contribute to a better understanding of medieval state formation processes.

The large-scale excavations of a complete medieval settlement near the church at Dommelen (1981-1983) provided information about the form of the buildings, the typo-chronology of the pottery, and the differentiation and location of settlements.[3] It soon proved that many (if not most) of the medieval settlements had undergone profound changes in their layout, or were relocated or abandoned.[4] The settlement pattern, even in a peripheral region, such as the Kempen, was much more complex and changed more often than was expected from the former historical-geographical models. An important result of the excavations at Dommelen was evidence that the churches standing in the middle of the

[2] On this literature see Steegh 1978; Maas 1991; Theuws 1989.

[3] Van Regteren Altena 1982; Theuws/Verhoeven/Van Regteren Altena 1988; Van Regteren Altena 1989; Theuws/Bijsterveld 1991; Theuws 1991.

[4] Theuws 1989, 180-187.

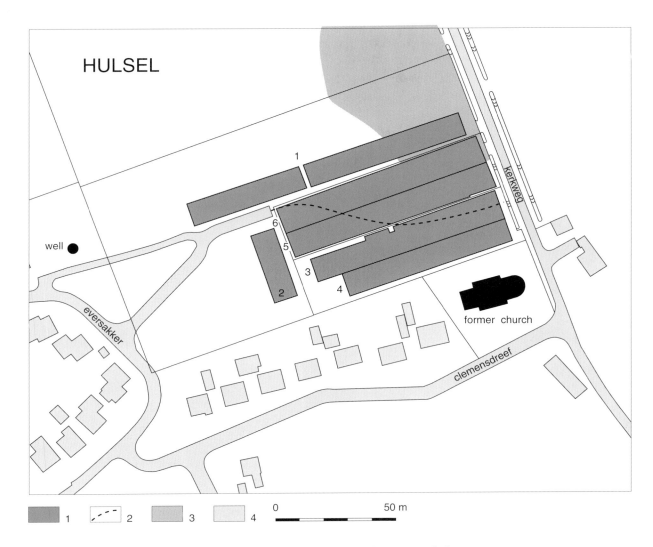

HULSEL

well ●

eversakker

clemensdreef

kerkweg

former church

1   2   3   4   0   50 m

Fig. 2. The location of the excavation trenches north of the church site at Hulsel.
1 excavation trenches with their number; 2 projected road; 3 boundary of the low-lying area north of the settlement; 4 modern buildings and roads

fields were perhaps not as isolated in medieval times as formerly assumed (fig. 3). It has been generally
thought that the isolated position of the church was the result of the cooperation of the inhabitants of a
few hamlets (each incapable of building and maintaining a church of their own) in building a church or
chapel, which was placed in the middle of the participating settlements. Around all the isolated churches
lay the arable fields of the settlements, which were thought to be as old as the medieval habitation itself
(second half of the 6th century). The church at Dommelen, however, proved to be at the location of a
settlement extant by the second half of the 7th century, which disappeared in the 13th century. It was
that settlement that could be excavated, because after it was abandoned or moved, the site was used for
arable land up to the 1980s when the whole area was slated for development.

The presence of the church and the discovery of 'rich' Merovingian burials belonging to an early
phase of the habitation prompted speculations about the type of the settlement it was.[5] It is supposed
now that the settlement may have been a part of an early-medieval villa in the hands of an ecclesiastical

5   Theuws 1986; Theuws 1991.

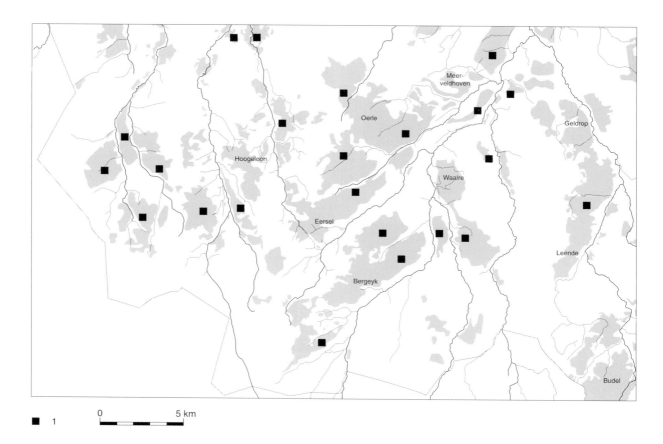

Fig. 3. The distribution of isolated churches on high-lying grounds in the Kempen region. The shaded areas represent the extent of the most fertile soils in the High and Late Middle Ages.
1 isolated church on high-lying ground. Waalre is situated on high-lying ground but is not isolated, other places with a church on low-lying ground are named on the map

institution or lay men, and that it continued to be a centre of a (relatively) large holding up to the High Middle Ages when the demesnes of the feudal era started to fall apart. Perhaps this model could explain the isolated position of other churches in other localities of the region as well. Thus, it should be tested whether traces of medieval settlements could be found in the vicinity of other isolated churches and, if so, whether these were founded by the late Merovingian/early Carolingian times, and if they disappeared in the 12th or 13th centuries. If settlements with a development comparable to that at Dommelen could be found, it would be important to ascertain their position in the local and regional settlement pattern and settlement hierarchy. Archaeological evidence alone would probably not suffice and would have to be supplemented with historical and new historical-geographical research. Dommelen proved not to be a good case for historical research, because no properties of early and high-medieval abbeys (essential to the availability of written sources) are mentioned in the written evidence. On the other hand, it appeared to be almost the only site in the region where a complete settlement could be excavated. An excellent comparable site is the isolated church of Oostelbeers; it should be preserved along with its surroundings. There are other partially destroyed sites, on the other hand, situated in parishes with demesnes of early- and high-medieval monasteries mentioned in the written sources. In an attempt to compare the historical evidence with archaeological evidence, excavations have taken place around the churches of Bergeyk, Oerle, Hulsel, and Bladel (fig. 4). The development of the settlement at Hulsel seems to be very similar to that of Dommelen. Other parish centres show a different development.[6]

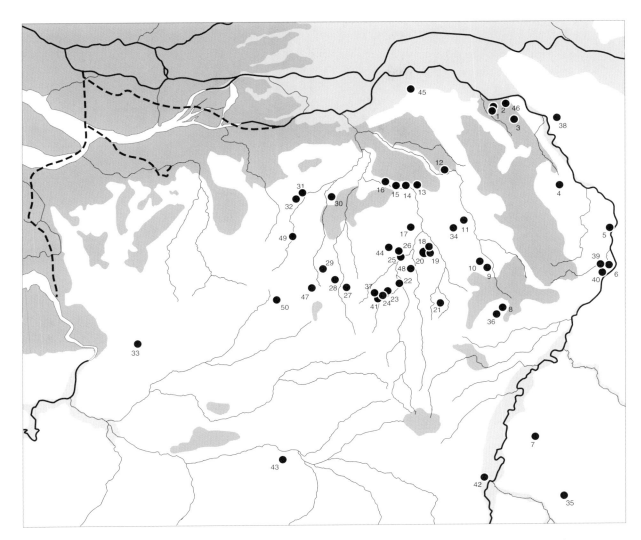

Fig. 4. The location of excavated medieval settlements in the Meuse-Demer-Scheldt region. See appendix 1.

The site at Hulsel was thus chosen for excavation not only for practical reasons, but also because in the written evidence there were indications that the monastery at Saint-Trond had an important estate (*curia*) in the village. Moreover it owned the church, which was thought to be an indication that the settlement that is supposed to have existed at that place was also in the hands of the monastery and that it was possible to excavate a part of a medieval *curia*. There is, however, also evidence, dating from early Carolingian times (AD 710), that the monastery of Echternach owned lands and woods in the village too (at *Hulislaum*, which is identified as Hulsel). The relation between the possessions of both monasteries was unclear. The analysis of the historical evidence, however, shed a new light on the relation between the possessions of both monasteries at Hulsel, which is of course of direct importance for the interpretation of the discovered archaeological remains.

The oldest name for Hulsel is thought to be *Hulislaum*. *Lauhum* (laum) is the dativus pluralis of the Germanic word *lauha*, which means wood on high-lying ground, *hulisa* is the name of a shrub: holly.[7] So the name means woods on high lying ground with lots of holly (Hollywood of the Kempen). In this

6   Theuws 1989   7   Gysseling 1960, 523.

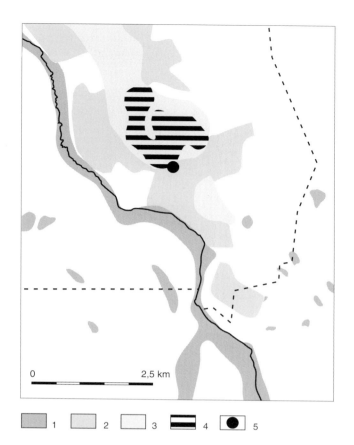

Fig. 5. Hulsel: the natural environment and location of the site (cf. fig. 38).
1 brook valley deposits; 2 high-lying relatively fertile soils (moist); 3 high-lying relatively fertile soils (dry); 4 extent of the löss deposit; 5 location of the excavated site

0   2,5 km

1   2   3   4   5

article the evidence from the excavations at Hulsel will be presented along with a reconstruction of the local settlement pattern and settlement system. The regional importance of the results of this analysis have already been discussed elsewhere.[8] First a short description of the natural environment in the parish will be given, followed by a detailed account of the available archaeological evidence. Thereafter the historical evidence will be analysed. In the final section a reconstruction is given of the developments in the local settlement pattern and settlement system.

2   THE NATURAL ENVIRONMENT

The natural environment and the landscape in the parish of Hulsel does not differ significantly from that of other parishes in the Kempen region.[9] Important for understanding the environmental frame- work of the settlement pattern are the hydrology (surface water as well as groundwater levels), the relief and the relative fertility of the various soil-types. The main characteristics of the hydrological system and relief, as well as the deposits at the surface in the region, are of Pleistocene date. In the relatively flat landscape of the Kempen region the relief is least important as such. No steep slopes occur and absolute differences between high-lying and low-lying lands are small. High-lying and low-lying refers first and

[8]   Theuws 1991.

[9]   A detailed description of the environmental situation in the parish of Dommelen and the vicinity of the exca-

vated medieval settlement is given in Theuws/ Verhoeven/Van Regteren Altena 1988, 238-270.

foremost to the relation between the surface and the ground water table. Almost the entire Kempen region is covered by late Pleistocene aeolian or fluvioperiglacial deposits (coversands).[10] In the stream valleys the coversands have been eroded, so that the Kempen region basically consists of local sand plateaus, intersected by stream valleys. The coversand layer is of variable thickness. In the northern part of the Kempen it seldom exceeds two metres. However, to the north of the village of Hulsel a deposit of more than two metres of loess and coversands consisting of fine sandy loam and loamy fine sand is present over a small area (fig. 5). The partly excavated medieval settlement lies on the southern edge of this deposit. These loamy sands are probably relatively fertile in comparison to the other coversands, and may have attracted habitation. Since the Late Middle Ages the deposit has almost entirely been covered with *Hoge Zwarte Enkeerdgronden* (old arable land, *plaggen* soil).[11] It is possible that the oldest arable fields were laid out in this area.

In the stream valleys peat was often formed in the Holocene period. As a consequence of the reclamation of large parts of the stream valleys after c. AD 1000, this peat has almost entirely disappeared.

An important element in the natural environment of Hulsel is a small stream, the Raamloop (fig. 5), running from the south-east in a north-westerly direction. The late-medieval habitation of Hulsel is oriented towards this stream and is situated along the northern stream valley slope (fig. 6). In the east another small stream, the Witvense loop, marks off the territory of Hulsel towards Netersel and Bladel (since late-medieval times the exact division between the parishes runs somewhat to the east of the stream, see fig. 6). To the north a small tributary of the Raamloop (in the *Baarschotten fields*) divides the arable land of Hulsel from that of two hamlets of Lage Mierde (Mispeleind and Braakhoek). The coversand plateau of Hulsel is thus surrounded by low-lying areas that are drained by three small streams.

The soils that developed in the coversands of the plateau consist mostly of wet podzolic soils (*Veldpodzolgronden* in the Dutch soil classification), which were probably already there in the Early Middle Ages. The higher parts of the plateau, as has been said, are covered by a man-made *plaggen* epipedon (*Hoge Zwarte Enkeerdgronden*) (fig. 5). Little is known about the soil conditions there before the early-medieval habitation started. It may be expected that originally *Holtpodzolgronden* (England: Typical brown podzolic soil) were present. The potential natural vegetation on these soils will have been Fago-Quercetum (a beech-oak forest) or Betulo-Quercetum (birch-oak forest). The natural vegetation on the lower-lying wet podzolic soils will have had a more open character with large patches of heather.

In a large part of the stream valley of the Raamloop a *plaggen* soil also developed, but under wet conditions (*Lage Zwarte Enkeerdgronden*). The meadows were probably fertilized with sod-mixed manure too since the Late Middle Ages or early modern times. In the southern part of the valley of the Raamloop and in the eastern valley, the original soils, *Gooreerdgronden*, are preserved. These soils develop under moist conditions and have an A1-horizon thinner than 50 cm, which is rich in humus, and with no red mottles within 35 cm below the surface. Originally the stream valleys will have had a marshy character where a wetland forest (alder carr) was present and where peat was formed. Only in the course of time

---

[10] Bisschops/Broertjes/Dobma 1985, 97-102.

[11] A description of the relevant Dutch soils, as well as a list of terms for comparable soils in surrounding countries is given in Theuws/Verhoeven/Van Regteren Altena 1988, 245-247 and Heidinga 1987, 82-84. *Plaggen* soil: (Dutch: *plaggendek* or *esdek*) = mineral earthy layer (A1 horizon), raised topsoil accumulated by the application of sod manuring (= old arable land). There is some debate on the dating of the start of sod-manuring which caused the raising of the surface. In the Meuse-Demer-Scheldt region sod-manuring was probably not generally applied befor the 13th century. See Heidinga 1987, 91-92; Theuws/Verhoeven/Van Regteren Altena 1988, 252-264; Theuws 1990, 52-54; Spek 1992.

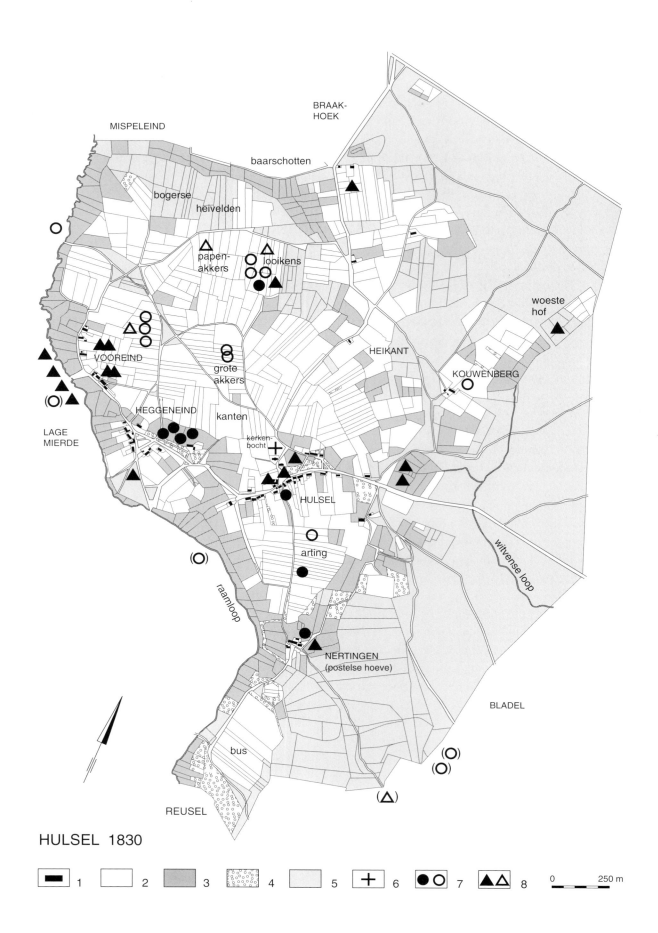

MISPELEIND

BRAAK-
HOEK

baarschotten

bogerse
heivelden

woeste
hof

papen-
akkers

looikens

HEIKANT

KOUWENBERG

VOOREIND

grote
akkers

HEGGENEIND   kanten

kerken-
bocht

LAGE
MIERDE

HULSEL

arting

witvense loop

raamloop

NERTINGEN
(postelse hoeve)

BLADEL

bus

REUSEL

HULSEL 1830

| ▬ 1 | ☐ 2 | ▨ 3 | ⬚ 4 | ☐ 5 | ✛ 6 | ●○ 7 | ▲△ 8 | 0 ▬▬ 250 m |

Fig. 7. Hulsel: the depression north of the settlement, which can still be seen in the field because of the different vegetation.

(most of it probably not before 1000 AD) the stream valleys were reclaimed and turned into hay fields (see fig. 6).

The excavation also provided some information about the environmental situation in the immediate vicinity of the settlement. Directly to the northeast a depression was present, which still can be seen in the field (figs. 2 and 7), even though attempts have been made during a land reallotment in the late 1960s and early 70s to fill it in, in order to improve local conditions which were too wet for modern agriculture. During the excavation this depression could be distinguished easily by the presence of the original wet podzolic soil that had developed in it. The A1-horizon had been preserved at places underneath the *plaggen* epipedon (fig. 27). The depression seems to demarcate the limits of the settlement towards the northeast. However, it cannot be ruled out that further to the north at the edge of this lower-lying area, and higher up the plateau, other medieval habitation took place. The presence of a wet or moist depression in the immediate vicinity of the settlement is similar to situations at Dommelen, Geldrop and Someren, where depressions were present near the settlements.[12] These depressions on higher ground were an important element for settlement location in the Early and High Middle Ages.

Fig. 6. Hulsel in 1830 according to the cadastral archives.
1 buildings; 2 arable land; 3 hay fields and meadows; 4 woods and trees; 5 heather fields; 6 excavation site;
7 rents of the abbey at Saint-Trond; open symbol: mentioned in 1813; 8 rents of the duke of Brabant, open symbol: mentioned in 1813

Fig. 8. Hulsel: trench 3 under excavation, looking west. In the foreground pit III-12, a few metres further to the left the well. To the right are the southern rows of postholes of buildings 1 and 2, and in the middle of the trench is the modern road.

After 1000 they were probably drained and then provided some grazing ground or grass land near the settlement. The ditches 5 and 6, situated in the depression, may have been dug in order to drain it.[13] The depression probably extended further to the east, for in 1830 the fields in that direction were used as grazing land or hay fields.

The original soil conditions at the site of the settlement itself are difficult to establish. The regular occurrence of red mottles or stains in the matrix indicate that moist conditions may once have been prevalent. Whether that was also the case during medieval habitation could not be established. Today, however, the groundwater level is relatively low. At the time of the excavation of the well (early October 1985) the groundwater level was about 1.90 m below the surface.

After the site was no longer inhabited, it was used as arable land. As a consequence of sod manuring a *plaggen* layer of variable thickness was formed. In the eastern part of the terrain, at the site of the depression, it reached a thickness of c. 80 cm; in the western part it is no more than 40 cm. The *plaggen* soil in

[12] Dommelen: Theuws/Verhoeven/Van Regteren Altena 1988, 254-258 (section wall 2 and the reconstruction in figs 15 and 16); Geldrop: Broertjes 1990, 21 and fig. 5, Bazelmans/Theuws 1990, figs 8, 13 and 16, Theuws 1993, fig.3. Someren: Kortlang, this volume.

[13] At Geldrop it has also been established that in the High Middle Ages the large depression next to the early- and high-medieval settlement sites was drained in the period after 1000 by digging ditches through the subsoil: Beex 1990, 41 and figs. 16 and 17.

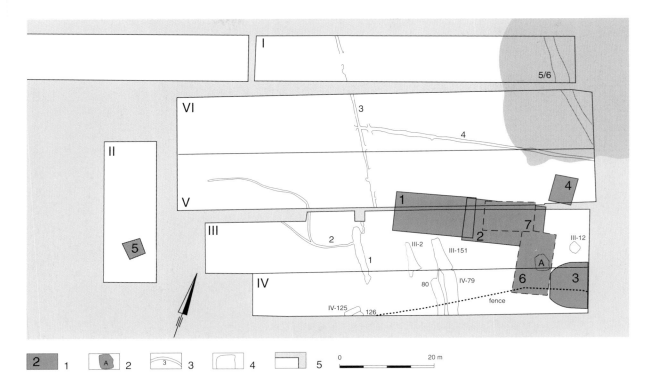

Fig. 9. The excavated structures at Hulsel and their numbers.
1 buildings; 2 the well; 3 ditches; 4 pits; 5 excavation trenches

the depression consists of three different layers. From top to bottom, they are a layer of black, humic sand (recent ploughsoil), a dark-brown, humic layer, and a light-brown, humic layer of sand (fig. 27). Beneath the *plaggen* epipedon, but on top of the fill of the ditches and on the original soil, is a layer of grey-black, humic sand, which seems to be the result of filling the depression in order to level the field for agricultural purposes. Similar developments in lower lying parts of the fields have been observed at Dommelen.[14]

The ploughlayer extends down to c. 30 cm below the original surface. Thus, the top 30 cm of the features are missing, which is quite disadvantageous to archaeological research because most of the finds may have been in the upper parts of the features. The cultural landscape in the parish of Hulsel will further be discussed in connection with the examination of the local settlement pattern in a section below.

3   THE FEATURES

The usual range of features for medieval settlements in the Kempen region were found at the site (fig. 12 and fig. 8). Most of the features were post-holes, only a few of which could be used in the reconstruction of building ground-plans and structures. Most of the post-holes cannot be interpreted, which is often the case in this kind of excavation. One well, several ditches and a number of pits, some of them long, rectangular, some oval or round in horizontal section, were also present. A track dated to the 17th-

---

[14] Theuws/Verhoeven/Van Regteren Altena 1988, 254-
258 (section wall 2).

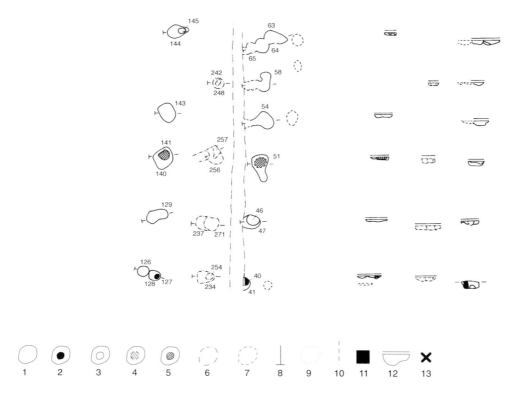

Fig. 10. Hulsel: building 1. Scale 1:200. The standard height is 26.50+ NAP.
1 post hole; 2 post-pipe observed both in horizontal and vertical section; 3 post-pipe only observed in horizontal section; 4 post-pipe only observed in vertical section; 5 secondary fill above post-pipe; 6 feature that possibly belongs to the structure; 7 feature that does not belong to the structure; 8 location of the vertical section; 9 recent disturbance; 10 limit of excavation trench; 11 feature of which no vertical section is drawn and only the depth is known; 12 elevation of a feature in relation to a standard height; 13 location of missing feature

19th centuries, which is shown in 19th-century maps, ran north-south through the centre of the excavation and was treated for reasons of time and money as a recent disturbance. It means that its filling was taken away mechanically in order to find older features underneath it, which were however hardly preserved. The criteria used for reconstructing the building ground-plans are discussed in detail in the publication of the medieval settlement at Dommelen.[15]

From the high density of post-holes in the southeastern part of the excavated area, four building ground-plans could be reconstructed, only one of which, building-groundplan 3, is considered to be a fully reliable reconstruction. Many simple structures may have been present in medieval farmyards, but to reconstruct them is nearly impossible. The groundplans of three uncertain structures have also been reconstructed, but it is not known whether they ever existed. Buildings 1 and 2 are of Carolingian date. Building 3 (a farmhouse) dates from the 12th century. Structure 4 cannot be dated exactly.

[15]   Theuws/Verhoeven/Van Regteren Altena 1988, 272-274.

Building 1 (figs. 9, 10)
Entire framework [16]
The evidence for the ground plan of this building is two rows of opposing post-holes. Cross-connections were presumably placed across each pair of posts. The post-hole opposite no. 58 seems to be missing, however post-holes 58 and 64 do not seem to belong to the original building-groundplan and were probably dug during a later repair of the building. If this is true, the distance between the westernmost pair of posts (nos 63 and 445) and the next pair to the east (nos 54 and 143) is larger than that between the other pairs. If the western pair is not taken into consideration, the average distance between the pairs of post-holes is c. 3 m. The opposing post-holes 140/141 – 51 and 129 – 46/47 are separated by 5 m, post-holes 126/127/128 – 40/41 are 4.60 m apart. The total length of the framework is 13.40 m.

Not much remained of the southern row of post-holes; post-pipes could not be recognized except in hole no. 128. Although the excavation level was the same, more remained of the northern row of post-holes and a post-pipe was discerned in hole 41. It is difficult to draw any conclusions on the shape of the post-holes and the position of the posts from this evidence. It is, however, clear that originally the holes were not deep, because the original surface was only 30 or 40 cm higher than the excavation level. The posts in these holes probably carried the weight of the roof. The groundplan may have extended further to the west, where post-holes may have been destroyed by the recent track (see below). In the present reconstructions buildings 1 and 2 are however of equal length, which may indicate that both building groundplans are complete.

In the centre of the building-groundplan a row of post-holes (nos 234/254, 237/271, 256/257, 242, 258), parallel (east-west) to the others, was situated, which might have belonged to the building. In each of these holes a post-pipe was present indicating that all the post-holes in the row originally belonged to a single structure. Post-pipes are, however lacking in most of the holes of the framework described above. There are no opposing post-holes to those of the central row to reconstruct a new building groundplan comparable to that described above. The function of the posts remains therefore obscure. It may have supported a beam or plate, that in its turn supported the cross-connections over the posts mentioned above.

The wall
Traces of a wall are absent. It could not be established with the available evidence whether the wall was constructed along the roof-posts mentioned above or at a short distance from the roof-posts. A few post-holes found on the northern side of the structure could belong to a wall. It is expected that the wall was at a short distance (c. 1.50 m) from the roofposts.

Entrances
Traces that might indicate the location of entrances were not seen. However, entrances could have been present between posts 143 and 140/141 and 54 and 51. The distance between the two pairs of post-holes is smaller than that between other pairs. Moreover holes 143 and 140/141 are relatively large.

---

[16]   The scheme and the terminology used for describing the building ground plans are given in appendix 2

Internal division
No direct indications were observed that provide information on the internal division of the building. If, however, the central row of post-holes belongs to the building, it might indicate a division in the building in two parts: one half with three central posts and one half with only one central post. The postulated entrance is right between these halves.

Unusual elements
None observed

Repairs
As has already been indicated above, post-hole 58 together with no. 64 might be the result of a repair of the building on the western side. Post-hole no. 126 might be a renewal of 127/128 or the reverse is the case.

The disappearance of the building
The absence of post-pipes in the holes except those of the eastern pair indicates that the posts may have been removed at a certain time. The building may have been torn down rather than left to disintegrate, or the posts may have been removed at a later date in order to clear the site.

Overcutting features
Not present

Measurements (see appendix 2)

1	–		18	26.39 m
2	–		19	–
3	13.40 m		20	east-west
4	4.92 m		21	3-aisled or 4-aisled
5	5.00 m		22	5 (later maybe 6)
6	4.60 m		23	0.24 m
7	4.55 m		24	round
8	2.30 m		25	straight line
9	1: 4.50 m; 2: 2,30 m;		26	none
	3: 3.30 m; 4: 3.30 m		27	–
10	–		28	–
11	–		29	–
12	–		30	–
13	–		31	–
14	–		32	no
15	–		33	67 m2
16	0.22 m		34	–
17	1.17 m		35	Carolingian

Building 2 (figs. 9, 11)
This building is situated immediately east of building 1. It probably replaced building 1 or no. 1 replaced no. 2. The positioning of the buildings along the same axis indicates that they were either erected near a boundary for whose existence there is no other evidence or that they were constructed in relation to each other.

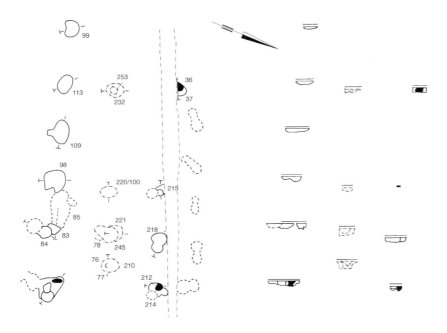

Fig. 11. Hulsel: building 2. Scale 1:200. The standard height is 26.55+ NAP. Legend: see figure 10.

Entire framework

The groundplan of this building is similar to that of no. 1. Two parallel rows of post-holes were all that remained of this building as well. It was east-west oriented. The post-holes were placed opposite each other, and cross-connections were probably placed on top of each pair of posts. These posts would have carried the weight of the roof. Post-holes opposite nos. 109 and 99 were not verified, because a bank had to be left between excavation trenches III and V. The total length of the framework is 13.90 m, the width varies between 5,50 and 5,75 m.

The post-holes are not very deep and their shape varies. Only in the easternmost pair (as in building 1) and in hole 36/37 could post-pipes be seen. The post-holes in the southern row are relatively large compared to their depth, a phenomenon which will come up for discussion later. The positioning of the posts could not be established definitely, although a vertical position seems likely.

A central row of post-holes (nos 210/76/77, 78/221/245, 100/220, 232/253) was also present in this structure, which, again, may have belonged to another structure whose plan and shape cannot be identified, or may well be a part of building 2.

The wall

Possible traces of a wall in the form of a row of small post-holes were found on the northern side of the framework. The distance between the row of small post-holes and those of the framework is c. 1.75 m to 2.00 m. If the small post-holes indicate the place of a wall, then the building had a two-aisled or perhaps a three-aisled groundplan. The small post-holes may, however belong to another structure (no. 7).

Entrances

Traces that might indicate the location of entrances were not found. There may, however, have been an entrance in the middle of the building between post-holes 98 and 109. Both holes are somewhat larger than the others.

Internal division
No direct indications were found that provide information on an internal division of the building. If, however, the central row of post-holes belongs to the building it is divided into two parts: one half with three central posts and one half with only one central post. The postulated entrance is in the middle.

Unusual elements
Not observed, unless pit 85 belongs to the building.

Repairs
The extra post-holes at the southeastern corner of the framework may indicate that the posts were renewed.

The disappearance of the building
The absence of post-pipes in the majority of the holes might indicate that the posts were removed.

Overcutting features
Not present

Measurements (see appendix 2)

1	–	18	26.45 m
2	–	19	–
3	13.90 m	20	east-west
4	5.61 m	21	3-aisled or 4-aisled
5	5.65 m	22	6
6	5.50 m	23	0.31 m
7	3.20 m	24	round
8	2.30 m	25	straight line
9	1: 3.00 m; 2: 2.75 m;	26	–
	3: 2.60 m; 4: 2.80 m; 5: 2.75 m	27	–
10	–	28	–
11	–	29	–
12	–	30	–
13	–	31	–
14	–	32	pit 85
15	–	33	78 m2
16	0.23 m	34	–
17	1.06 m	35	Carolingian

Concluding remarks on buildings 1 and 2
Although we will go into the dating of the buildings in more detail in a section below it seems clear that they are of early-medieval date and more particularly of Carolingian date (8th - 9th centuries). The groundplans can best be compared with those of Carolingian buildings in the settlement at Dommelen.[17] Carolingian building groundplans are relatively irregular compared to those of the previous (Merovingian) and later (high-medieval) periods. Their reconstruction therefore often contains a

number of uncertainties, that cannot be avoided or solved. Moreover, the reconstruction of the two groundplans at Hulsel is hampered by the fact that a bank of topsoil had to be left in place where the boundary between two fields (and a fence) was. Although some uncertainties remain, the reconstructions presented here seem to be relatively reliable. One argument is that both groundplans are almost identical. However, the danger of a circular argument is present here.

It has been difficult up to now to find any indications for an internal arrangement of medieval buildings in the Kempen region. For that reason it is a pity that it cannot be established definitely that the

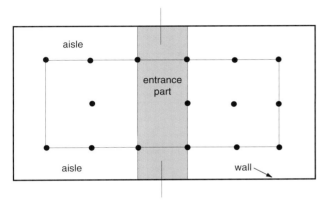

Fig. 12. Model of the ground plan of the Carolingian buildings at Hulsel in the case the central rows of posts belong to buildings 1 and 2.

central rows of post-holes belong to the buildings. They have a similar order in both buildings. If they belong to the buildings a clear division can be detected. The buildings are then divided into two parts: an eastern and a western part with an entrance in between. In the eastern part there are three central posts and in the western part there is one post in the middle. The eastern parts may have been stables, the western living quarters. The central space will have been the entrance area.

The buildings probably had aisles outside the framework. If the central row of posts belongs to the buildings they are four-aisled (fig. 12), if not they are three-aisled. It is difficult to reconstruct the buildings on the basis of the evidence now available. However, it can be expected that six pairs of boxframes caried the weight of the roof. It is also expected that the roof rested on plates placed lengthwise over the cross connections of the box frames. In view of the distances between the box frames, the roof construction probably was made independently from the positioning of the boxframes, which means that an unbound system of construction[18] was already applied in Carolingian times.

Building 3 (figs. 9, 13)
Entire framework
The excavations of the medieval settlements at Dommelen and Bladel-Kriekeschoor familiarized the groundplans of high-medieval (ca. 950-1300) farmhouses in the Kempen region to archaeologists.[19] Although building 3 has only been partially excavated, it is possible to reconstruct its groundplan. An important characteristic of the high-medieval farmhouses are the pairs of posts that are closely placed together in the short walls of the building. At times both posts are placed in a single large post-hole, as is

[17] The Carolingian building groundplans of this settlement have already been examined, but have not yet been published in detail, see Theuws 1991, 360.

[18] See for the discussion on this construction principle: Theuws/Verhoeven/Van Regteren Altena 1988, 274-289.

[19] Dommelen: Theuws/Verhoeven/Van Regteren Altena 1988, 274-289; Bladel Kriekeschoor: Van Dierendonk 1989. See also Geldrop: Beex 1990 with a provisional reconstruction. More general: Verhoeven/Vreenegoor 1991

the case in building 3 of Hulsel, although the vertical section of feature 43 was placed somewhat too far to the east to establish this definitely. It can be seen that the rectangular pit had two deeper parts, each of which must have contained a post. Postpipes were not seen, perhaps because of the eccentric position of the vertical section. The post-holes are deeper and larger than those of buildings 1 and 2.

The weight of the roof in this type of building is carried by the posts of the main framework, which, in this case, probably consisted of eight posts in two straight rows of four of which two pairs of posts were found (nos 22 and 19 and 1 and 4). The posts are placed opposite each other, so that a cross-beam can be placed on top of them. These constructions are termed box-frames.[20] Plates that carried the rafters of the roof must have been placed lengthwise on top of the cross-beams. The shape of the post-holes in vertical section is quite symmetrical, in horizontal section the shape differs per hole.

The wall

Traces of a wall, which could be expected at a short distance from the roof-posts, could not be identified with certainty. It is possible that to the north and the south of feature 43, two post-holes of cornerposts are present (nos 40/41 and 27 possibly also 28). The posts in these holes may also have been part of another (uncertain) structure (no 6).

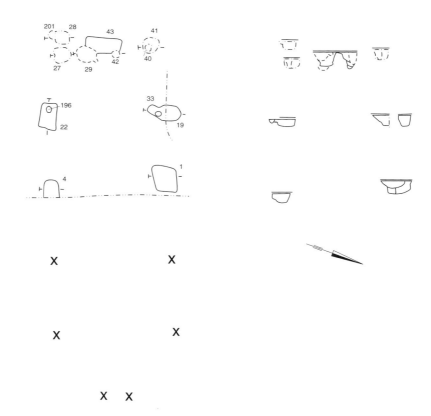

Fig. 13. Hulsel: building 3. Scale 1:200. The standard height is 26.60+ NAP. Legend: see figure 10.

[20] See Theuws/Verhoeven/Van Regteren Altena 1988, 277-280 for further details concerning the construction of these buildings.

258

Entrances
Traces that might indicate the location of entrances could not be identified with certainty.

Internal division
No observations.

Unusual elements
No observations.

Repairs
The western short wall of the building may have been repaired once (see under overcutting features).

The disappearance of the building
No post-pipes were seen. This indicates that the posts were removed at a certain time.

Overcutting features
Feature 43 is overcut by two pits (nos 29 and 42) which are relatively deep. They may have been dug during a repair of the western short wall of the building. The first lay-out could have consisted of posts in pits 40/41, 43 and 28; the second lay-out could have consisted of pits 40/41, 42, 29 and 27.

Measurements (see appendix 2)

1	c. 18.85 m	18	26.56 m
2	–	19	–
3	–	20	east-west
4	6.00 m	21	3-aisled
5	6.00 m	22	probably 4
6	6.00 m	23	–
7	3.85 m	24	–
8	3.65 m	25	probably straight line
9	1: 3.80 m; 2: 3.75 m	26	cornerposts westside?
10	1.10 m	27	–
11	–	28	–
12	–	29	–
13	–	3	one, in the lower part two
14	c. 4.50 m	31	–
15	–	32	–
16	0.62 m	33	c. 67,5 m2
17	1.52 m	34	–
		35	12th century (type A4)

Structure 4 (figs. 9, 14)
The reconstruction of the groundplan of this small structure, of which only six post-holes remain, is mainly based on the more or less isolated position of the group of post-holes immediately to the north of the main group of post-holes. Similar configurations of post-holes occur in almost all medieval settlements. They are often interpreted as six-post granaries, but they could equally well represent the framework of a small barn or aisled barn.[21] The six posts are placed in a north-south oriented rectangle 5.75 m long and 5.00 m wide. It is possible that post-hole 5/6 also belongs to the structure. The post-holes

were of varying depth and shape, and post-pipes were seen in two of the western post-holes.

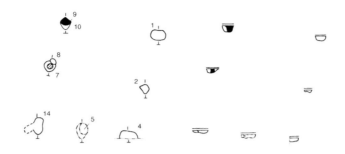

Fig. 14. Hulsel: structure 4. Scale 1:200. The standard height is 26.55+ NAP. Legend: see figure 10.

Uncertain structures

After having reconstructed the ground plans of building 1 to 4 a large number of post-holes remain that cannot be attributed to a particular structure. The problem of the 'remaining post-holes' is well known in settlement archaeology.[22] At Hulsel a relatively large number of deep dug post-holes remain. In an attempt to interpret these post-holes the following reconstructed plans of 'uncertain structures' are given. Their uncertainty is however so large that these structures cannot play any role in the reconstruction of the topography of the settlement.

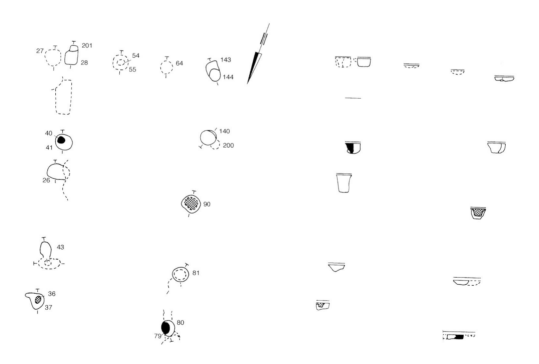

Fig. 15. Hulsel: uncertain structure 6. Scale 1:200. The standard height is 26.60+ NAP. Legend: see figure 10.

[21]   Theuws/Verhoeven/Van Regteren Altena 1988, 294-296.

Uncertain structure 5 (fig. 9 and fig. 42)
In the far western end of the excavation (trench II) a four-post structure was present. The posts were placed in a square with sides of c. 3.50 m to 4.00 m. This structure could date from medieval as well as post-medieval times, or is even of recent date.

Uncertain structure 6 (figs. 9, 15)
The groundplan of structure 6 consists of two, more or less parallel rows of post-holes that are north-

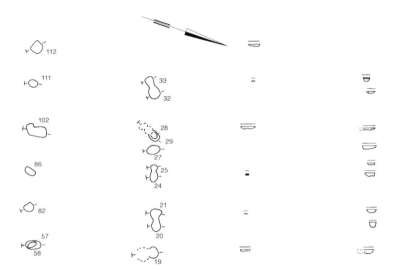

Fig. 16. Hulsel: uncertain structure 7. Scale 1:200. The standard height is 26.00+ NAP. Legend: see figure 10.

south oriented. The holes in both rows are situated opposite each other, although irregularities occur. The average distance between the posts in the western row is c. 3.60 m. The distance between the posts of each pair varies between 6.85 m and 7.65 m. The total length of the structure is 13.90 m. post-holes IV-28 and IV-40/41 could also have belonged to building 3. The depth of the post-holes and the 12th-century pottery sherds found in them, indicate that the postulated structure could date from the 12th-century. The structure was not necessarily a building. It can also be interpreted as a cattle-enclosure (corral), situated next to building 3. In other medieval settlements, similar enclosures have been observed at one end of a large building.[23] There is, however, no evidence that supports this interpretation definitely.

Uncertain structure 7 (figs. 9, 16)
The reconstruction of this ground plan is mainly based on the existence of the northern row of post-holes in which a number of twin post-holes occur. The row seems to belong to a particular structure. It might be attributed to building 2. In that case the row of post-holes must be interpreted as the remains of a wall that has been repaired once. If not, it might have belonged to another structure. A possible sug-

[22] See for instance Heidinga 1987, 15-17; Theuws/ Verhoeven/Van Regteren Altena 1988, 272-274.

[23] For instance: Dommelen stream-valley settlement: building 21 (Theuws/Verhoeven/Van Regteren Altena,

1988); Ermelo (Horst): buildings 10 and B13 (Heidinga 1987, fig. XIII); Vorbasse (Denmark) (Hvass 1986, 540).

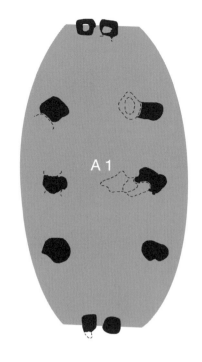

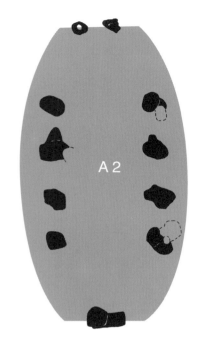

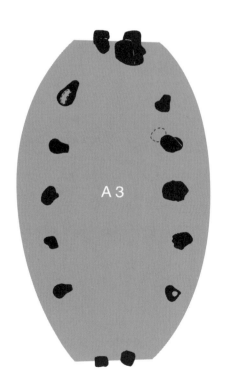

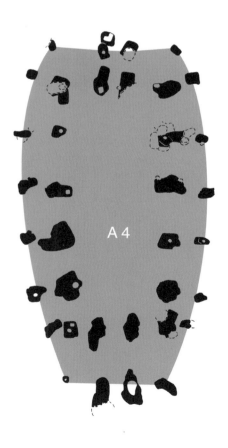

gestion is made here. To the south, another parallel row of post-holes can be reconstructed, although not much remained of the holes. Some of them might not be post-holes at all. The post-holes in each row are at an average distance of 2.14 m from each other. The distance between the post-holes in each pair varies from 6.20 m tot 6.55 m.

Concluding remarks on the buildings and structures

It is difficult to interpret early-medieval structures in functional terms. This is caused by the uncertainties in the reconstruction of the ground plans on the one hand and the absence of circumstantial evidence on the other. If the central rows of post-holes belong to buildings 1 and 2, they could almost certainly be interpreted as houses with a living and a stable part. Now, this must remain hypothetical, although the evidence from other settlements (Dommelen, Geldrop) suggests that other interpretations of their function (for instance as barns) are highly unlikely. Other evidence, for instance the presence of wells, that could have supported the interpretation as houses is absent.

Building 3 was most probably a farmhouse, with living-quarters and a stable, comparable to the farmhouses of type A2 (11th-12th centuries) at Dommelen (fig. 17). The well, which is contemporaneous with it, supports this interpretation. Neither the finds nor the configuration of the post-holes provide any further information on the internal arrangements and the use of the various parts of the buildings. Buildings 1 and 2 could be either farmhouses or barns. That they were barns is supported by the absence of associated wells, which are usually not far apart from the houses, and the absence of pottery sherds in the post-holes, which is often interpreted to mean that household activities were not performed in these buildings, an interpretation that need not be valid, as we will see later. On the other hand, if they are barns, they must have been more distant from their respective farmhouses than is usual.

3.2   WELL A   (feature III-4/6) (fig. 18)

A well, of the type typical in Kempen medieval settlements, was found not far from the northwest corner of building 3 in the centre of the plan of structure 6. It consisted of a hollowed out tree-trunk with a diameter of c. 70 cm. The lower part of the trunk (below 25.00 m+ NAP) was preserved to a depth of c. 24.50 m+ NAP. The total depth of the well must have been c. 2.50 m. The lower part of the well could not be studied properly due to rapidly inflowing ground water. The well was placed in a large pit of which the eastern wall probably had a stepped appearance; the western wall was vertical.

The fill of the well indicates that after it was abandoned the lower part was filled up with rubbish in a short time. Thereafter the well slowly decayed and collapsed, forming a funnel-shaped pit, which was then slowly filled up, but may have been levelled at a later time. The black humic layers in the lower part of the pit may indicate that it lay open for a certain time and that organic material accumulated (for instance leaves) or that some vegetation developed. The humic material could, of course, have been thrown in. The pit of the well was dug through the fill of one of the post-holes of structure 6. If structure 6 existed it is not likely that they were contemporaneous.

3.3   PITS
Pits of various shapes and sizes were present, but their different functions are difficult to establish.

Fig. 17. Building groundplans of farmhouses in the medieval settlement at Dommelen.
From top left to bottom right: type A1, type A2, type A3, and type A4

Pit III-12 (fig. 19)

A round pit with a diameter of c. 2.25 m was present directly north of building 3. When found, its depth was 80 cm, but its original depth must have been c. 1.20 m. It had a fairly flat bottom and slightly out-

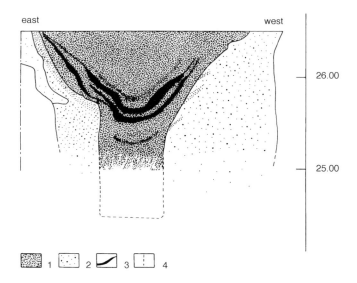

Fig. 18 Hulsel: the well, east-west section. The height is in metres above NAP. Scale 1:40.
1 the fill of the well; 2 the fill of the pit; 3 black humic sand; 4 total depth of the conserved wood.

ward sloping walls. The fill consisted of several layers of sand. The pit intersected an older (probably Carolingian) pit or post-hole. Large pits like this one are unusual in high-medieval settlements in the Kempen region. Its function is not clear.

Several long, rectangular pits were found in the central part of the excavation (fig. 20).

Pit III-151/IV-79

Pit III-151/IV-79 consisted of two parts. The northern part (III-151) was 7.25 m long, and the southern part (IV-79) was at least 10 m; both were 1.70-2.25 m wide. The pit had a flat bottom and slightly outward curving walls (fig. 21). The observed depth was c. 30 cm; the original depth must have been c. 60-70 cm. The lower part of the fill consisted of a black, very humic layer of sand (fig. 22). Beneath that, a

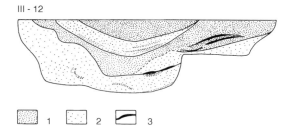

Fig. 19. Hulsel: pit III-12, vertical section. Scale 1:40.
1 grey-brown humic sand; 2 grey to yellow-brown, humic sand; 3 high concentrations of charcaol

layer of brown sand and a layer of grey or dark-grey sand were found. These layers are more probably the result of soil formation processes than the fill of the pit. On top of the black layer a layer of yellow-brown, mixed sand was present. Some time after the pit had been filled up a hole had been dug through pit 79, as could be seen in the southern wall of excavation trench IV (fig. 23). This must have occurred before the *plaggen* layer was formed, and may indicate that the pit(s) belonged to the medieval settlement. Pit 79 could not be excavated for lack of time.

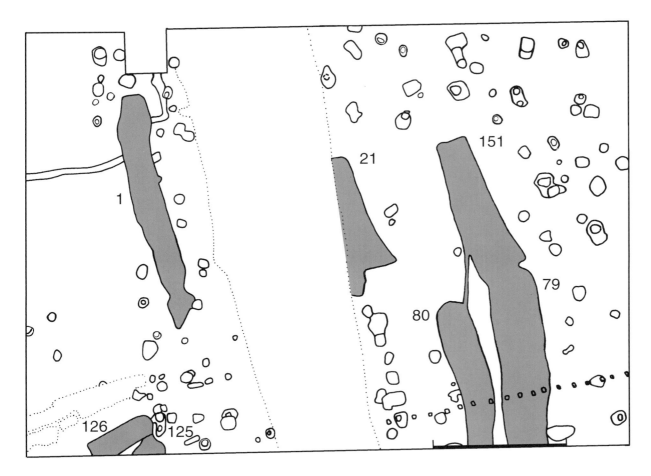

Fig. 20. The part of the excavated area with the elongated rectangular pits. Scale 1 : 200.

Pit III-2 (fig. 24)
Pit III-2 was c. 6.20 m long and 1.80 m wide and lay parallel to the northern part of pit III-151/IV-79. The depth was c. 70-80 cm, the original depth must have been c. 1.00-1.10 m. It had a fill similar to the

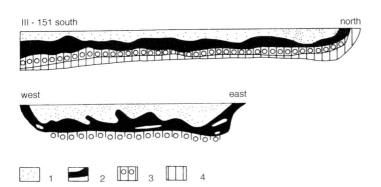

Fig. 21. Hulsel: pit III-151, north-south section (above) and west-east section (below). Scale 1:40.
1 yellow-brown sand; 2 black, very humic sand; 3 layer originated as a consequence of soil formation processes (A2 horizon); 4 soil formation (B horizon)

pits mentioned above and was probably in use at the same time or during a relatively short period.

Parallel to the southern part of pit III-151/IV-79 was a third pit (IV-80) with rounded corners. Its length was at least 8 m and it was c. 90 cm wide. Although it had a concave bottom, the fill was identical to the others. Its observed depth was c. 60 cm and its original depth would have been c. 1.00 m.

Fig. 22. Hulsel: pit III–151 in section, looking south.

Long, rectangular parallel pits were also discovered in the medieval settlement of Dommelen, but these were connected to each other by another ditch so that the whole system had the form of an H in plan view. It is thought that they were used for processing flax. Pits similar to those at Hulsel were found

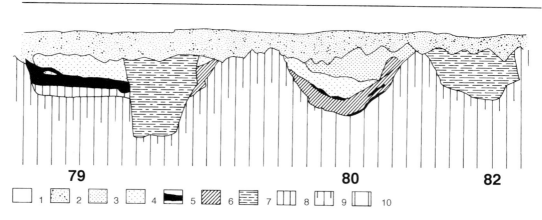

Fig. 23. Hulsel: part of the southern section wall of trench IV with vertical section of pit IV-79. Scale 1:40. 1 black humic sand (recent plough layer); 2 churned up light brown sand; 3 brown humic sand; 4 yellow sand; 5 black very humic sand; 6 black/brown humic sand; 7 fill of pitt; 8 grey sand (soil formation layer underneath the pit?); 9 B–horizon of wet podzolic soil in yellow sand; 10 undisturbed C–horizon, yellow sand

266

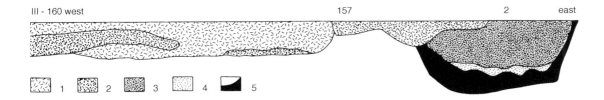

Fig. 24. Hulsel: pit III–160/157/2, west–east section. Scale 1:40.
1 churned up sand; 2 dark-brown, homogeneous, humic sand; 3 grey-brown, homogeneous, humic sand;
4 churned up sand containing iron pan concretions; 5 black, very humic sand

in the medieval settlement of Bladel-Kriekeschoor, but were associated with a building, which is not the case at Hulsel. The occurrence of the dark, black, very humic layer at the bottom of all pits at Hulsel may mean that their functions were similar. It does not seem that the layer developed after the pits were no longer in use as a result of an accumulation of humic material from the surrounding area. Nor does it seem that the pits were used specifically to dump refuse. Perhaps these pits were used to mix manure with other organic materials, such as sods, as was done in later times in stables with a sunken floor (Dutch: *potstallen*). Samples for ecological and phosphate analysis were taken, but have not been analysed yet. The results of this analysis may provide new information about the function of the pits. The total capacity of the pits was c. 40 m³.

Pits IV-125 and 126
In the southwestern part of trench IV two pits were found; pit 125 could only partially be excavated (fig. 25). Pit 126 was c. 3.70 m long, 1.20 m wide, and c. 35 cm deep. The fill consisted of homogeneous darkgrey-brown, humic sand. Pit 125 may have been of equal size and depth. The fill was more or less identical to that of no. 126, but the pit is somewhat younger.

Pit III-85 (fig. 26)
This pit is situated between two post-holes of building 2. It has a long oval form in horizontal section (c. 2 m long and 1 m wide). It has an irregular bottom. It seemed not to overcut any other post-holes, However, post-hole III-83 had a post-hole filled with clean sand which was at first not observed. Pit 85 clearly cut this fill and is thus younger than building 2 or contemporary with it.

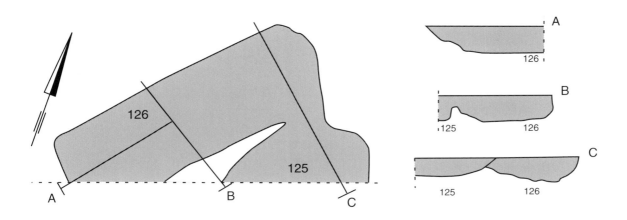

Fig. 25. Hulsel: plan and vertical sections of pits IV–125 and 126. Scale 1:50.

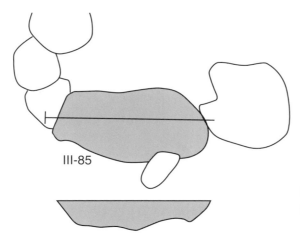

III-85

Fig. 26. Hulsel: plan and vertical section of pit III-85.
Scale 1:50.

3.4 DITCHES AND FENCES (fig. 9 and fig. 42)

Ditch 1 (feature III-171/IV-163)
It is not clear whether ditch 1 was intended as a short ditch or a large pit. It was c. 13 m long, 1.60 m wide and c. 55 cm deep. It had a fill of black, very humic sand.

Ditch 2
Ditch 2, found in the western half of the excavation was curvilinear, 30 cm wide, and c. 10 cm deep. It had been renewed at a certain time and laid out somewhat more to the north. In trench II, two parallel rows of very small holes were found, which were probably the remains of supporting stakes of a fence. A small track may have been present between them. The fences and ditch 2 are probably part of the same structure, but it is not clear whether they enclose a farmyard or a small field.

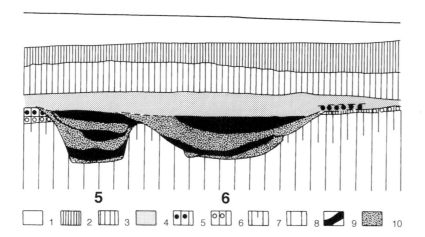

Fig. 27. Hulsel: ditch 5/6, vertical section. Scale 1:40.
1 black humic sand (recent ploughsoil); 2 dark-brown, humic sand (*plaggen* epipedon); 3 light-brown, humic sand (*plaggen* epipedon); 4 black, homogeneous, humic sand; 5 A1-horizon of a wet podzolic soil; 6 A2-horizon of a wet podzolic soil; 7 B-horizon of a wet podzolic soil; 8 C-horizon; 9 black, very humic sand (fill of the ditches); 10 grey, very humic sand (fill of the ditches)

Ditches 3 and 4

Ditches 3 and 4 are part of the same system of field boundaries. Ditch 3 ran in a north-south direction, while ditch 4 was oriented east-west, contiguous but not at right angles to ditch 3. They were probably in use at the same time, since one ditch did not cut into the fill of the other. The traces of a track ran parallel to ditch 3, but ditch 3 seems to be older. The northern, southern, and eastern ends of the ditches are not excavated. No ditches have been found that divide the field to the west of ditch 3. Ditches 3 and 4 seem to be younger representatives of field boundaries that may already have existed in the period in which buildings 1 and 2 were erected.

Ditches 5 and 6 (fig. 27)

In the lower-lying area to the north of the settlement parts of two ditches were found in approximately the same location. After ditch 5 was no longer in use and got filled up, a large part of its fill was dug up in constructing ditch 6. The older ditch was not recognized at excavation level, but was seen in the vertical sections. It stopped in the middle of trench I. Ditch 5 had a flat bottom, nearly vertical walls, and was c. 1 m wide; ditch 6 had a concave bottom, outward sloping walls; and was c. 2 m wide. They were both c. 60 cm deep and filled with layers of black and grey, very humic sand.

The fence around the church site (fig. 42)

In the southern part of the excavation a row of small holes indicate the stakes of a fence that enclosed the church site and the cemetery. Since the small post-holes cut into all other features except those of the track, the fence must have been built during or after the late-medieval period.

3.5   THE TRACK (fig. 42)

Traces of a track, running north-south, were found in the central part of the excavation. The traces include chart-tracks, ditches and churned up patches of sand. The track dates from early modern times, because it cuts into the features of the medieval settlement several times. Small rectangular pits from which sand was extracted were found in the southern part of the track in the lower part of the feature (not indicated on fig. 42). These pits may have been dug to improve the track. In the Kempen region sand tracks are still improved by digging holes along it in which the water could flow and from which sand could be thrown on the road to raise its surface. The holes could also have been dug at the border of a field before the track was laid out. The exact relation between the pits, ditch 3, and the traces of the track could not be established due to the deep disturbances caused by the use of the track. It was in use until recent times. During the land-reallotment, however, it was ploughed over and turned into arable land and pasture. Fragments of bricks and slate were recovered from the churned up fill.

A thin *plaggen* layer developed above the track showing that sod manuring of the fields also extended over the track, a phenomenon which has also been observed at Dommelen. Probably portions of the tracks in the fields were ploughed over and used for arable land, but then functioned as a track during harvest.

4   THE FINDS

Most of the finds consist, as usual, of pottery sherds. Unfortunately, they are too few to allow precise dating of the habitation. Other finds include some whetstones, fragments of millstones, a ploughshare, and a tile fragment. A. Verhoeven, who is analyzing the medieval pottery of the southern Netherlands,[24] provided valuable assistance in interpreting the ceramics found at Hulsel. In this section the finds will first be described. In the next section we will deal with the dating of the structures, which is not only dependent on the dating of the pottery finds.

4.1 THE POTTERY

The pottery recovered from the traces of the buildings and structures, the ditches, and the pits will be discussed first, followed by a discussion of the pottery from the remaining features. The analysis was focused on assigning the sherds to chronological types in an attempt to date the periods of site habitation. Other types of analysis were not deemed feasible, given the small amount of sherds available.

No pottery sherds were found in the post-holes of building 1. Only a small wall sherd of Andenne pottery was found in post-hole no. 98 of building 2. In post-hole 61 a sherd was found whose provenance and dating could not be determined, however, it is not certain that this post-hole belongs to building 2. A sherd of Carolingian date was found in post-hole no. 84, which seems to cut into 83 and finally, 2 wall sherds of Badorf-pottery were found in post-hole 99 that has been included in the groundplan of building 2.

Building 3
Ceramic sherds were found in all of the post-holes of building 3, although no rim or base fragments were present. It is sometimes difficult to attribute small wall sherds to a specific production centre or period. Six wall fragments were recovered from post-hole 1. These fragments belong to a group of pottery which is probably of local Kempen origin, and therefore called 'Kempen pottery'.[25] The post-hole also contained six wall fragments of Andenne pottery and an unclassifiable sherd. Post-hole 33 contained a few small sherds of South-Limburg pottery, post-hole 43 one sherd of South-Limburg pottery, post-hole 19 a sherd of Kempen pottery and an unclassifiable sherd, post-hole 22 an unclassifiable sherd, post-hole 196 a fragment of Paffrath pottery and an unclassifiable sherd, and post-hole 4 contained a sherd of South-Limburg pottery. In total c. 25 sherds were found. Considering that post-hole 43 was not excavated entirely and that only half the building was excavated, the amount of pottery sherds is comparable to that found in buildings of the same type at Dommelen. The pottery sherds of building 3 do not allow an accurate dating of the period it was in use. According to Verhoeven, the earliest 'Kempen pottery' dates from the second quarter of the 12th century. No ceramics of the 13th century were present. We will discuss the dating of the building in more detail later.

No pottery-sherds were found in the post-holes of structures 4 and 5.

[24] For information on the pottery production centres of the High Middle Ages and their imports to the Kempen region see the contribution of A. Verhoeven in Theuws/Verhoeven/Van Regteren Altena 1988. Further references to the pottery of Dommelen in this and following chapters concern information given in that publication. See also: Verhoeven 1985 and Verhoeven 1989.

[25] In the section below several terms for pottery found in medieval settlements will be used such as 'Kempen pottery' for which still no production centre is known (Verhoeven 1985, 47); 'Andenne pottery' produced in the Middle Meuse valley, with Andenne as the major production centre (Borremans/Warginaire 1966); 'South-Limburg pottery', produced in various production centres in South Limburg (Netherlands) (Bruyn 1962-63), and 'Paffrath pottery' produced at Paffrath (Lung 1955-56). For further information see Theuws/Verhoeven/Van Regteren Altena 1988.

Structure 6
In the post-holes of the uncertain structure 6 some pottery sherds were found, which all date from the 12th century. In the western row of post-holes no sherds were found. In post-hole IV-28 a wall fragment of South-Limburg pottery, in post-hole IV-41 2 wall fragments of Andenne- and 1 wall fragment of South-Limburg pottery, in hole III-26 1 wall fragment of South-Limburg pottery and in the core of post-hole III-34/35 a rim fragment of South-Limburg pottery (fig. 31, 4) were found. In post-hole III-90 an iron plough-share was found.

The finds from the well
The finds from the well are divided into three groups: a. those from the fill of the well; b. those from the lower part of the well itself; and c. those from the fill of the pit in which the well was placed. Group c may provide a terminus post quem for its construction, while group a may provide a terminus post quem for its abandonment.
A few wall sherds of South-Limburg pottery were found in the pit dug for the well. It could not be determined whether they were hand-made or wheel-thrown, which is important for their dating. A datable find is, however, a fragment of a high-collared rim (*manchetrand*, in Dutch) of a cooking pot of Andenne pottery. Eight high-collared rims were also found in the fill of the well (group a) (fig. 28, 1-4), a few of which may belong to the same pot, as well as a fragment of an outward curved rim, probably of

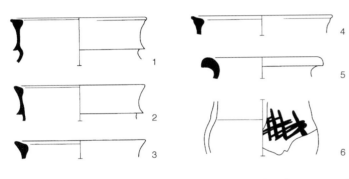

Fig. 28. Hulsel: the pottery finds from the well. Scale 1:4.
1-4 fragments of Andenne high-collared rims;
5 outward curved rim of Andenne pottery;
6 hand made beaker of South-Limburg pottery

a pitcher of Andenne pottery (fig. 28, 5) and a fragment of a hand-made beaker of South-Limburg pottery decorated with painted cross-hatched lines. The other finds consisted of three wall fragments of Paffrath pottery, 17 wall fragments of Andenne pottery, three fragments of South-Limburg pottery, one fragment of probably Carolingian pottery, a lump of iron, and a piece of basalt-lava, probably a fragment of a millstone. The dating of the well will be discussed below in combination with other features, although it can be said now that it was probably in use during the 12th century.

Pit III-12
A fragment of a high-collared Andenne rim, along with a lenticular base fragment and four wall sherds of the same fabric were found in pit III-12. One wall fragment of Paffrath pottery was also present. One rim fragment and three wall fragments of Carolingian Badorf-pottery and two other fragments of probable Carolingian date are considered to have been present at the site when the pit was dug or in use. Henceforth, such older finds will be referred to as 'residual finds'. They probably come from a small pit older than no. 12 that contained many Badorf sherds. No other finds were observed.

Pits III-151/152, III-2, IV-79 and IV-80
No finds were recovered from pits 151/152 and 79. It should be noted, however, that no. 79 was not completely excavated. That nothing was found during the cleaning of the horizontal sections and the

partial excavation of pit 151/152 may be related to the function of the pits. In pit III-2, on the other hand, three fragments of Andenne pottery, a rim fragment of probably 'local' Carolingian ceramics (fig. 29, 1) and three unclassifiable sherds, probably Carolingian in date, were found. The Carolingian pottery, again, will be residual finds. Pit IV-80 contained one fragment of Mayen pottery, one of Andenne, and an unclassifiable sherd.

Pits IV-125 and 126

Three wall fragments of Mayen pottery, a small wall fragment of Badorf pottery and one of Andenne pottery were found in pit 125. Pit 126 contained a rim fragment of a cooking pot of Dorestad type

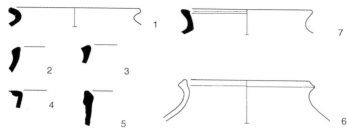

Fig. 29. Hulsel: pottery from various pits and ditches. Scale 1:4.
1 pit III-2; 2-3 pit IV-126; 4 ditch 1; 5 ditch 2; 6 ditch 5-6. Findnumbers respectively: III-2, IV-43, IV-43, IV-35, III-1, and VI-1.

WIII, but it is not of the well-known Mayen fabric (fig. 29, 2), and a sickle-form rim fragment (fig. 29, 3).[26] The rim fragment fig. 29, 3 belongs to the Meuse/regional group. It has some characteristics similar to those of the cooking-pots found at Huy in oven no. 1 at the Batta site, which date from the end of the 7th and the early 8th centuries.[27] A small pot with a rim comparable to the one in fig. 29, 3 was found in the cemetery at Fays (municipality of Achene, province of Namen, Belgium), but with a different fabric, dated to the second half of the 7th century.[28] Seven wall fragments of various fabrics and an unclassifiable sherd, probably of Carolingian date, were also present.

Ditch 1

Twenty-one wall fragments of Andenne pottery, a rim fragment, possibly of Carolingian date (Dorestad WIII?) (fig. 29, 4) and an unclassifiable wall fragment were found in ditch 1. A brick fragment was also recovered, but may come from the nearby early modern track in which many brick fragments were present. A whetstone completes the inventory of this ditch.

Ditch 2

An exceptional combination of finds comes from ditch 2: a rim fragment of a vessel of Badorf-pottery (type Dorestad WII) (fig. 29, 5); a brick fragment, a piece of *tefriet* (basalt-lava), a piece of bone; and two fragments of South-Limburg pottery in the northern branch of the ditch.

Ditch 5/6

As stated above, ditch 5 could only be seen after a large part of no. 6 had been excavated. It is expected that both were in use during a relatively short period. The finds of the two ditches were not collected separately. One fragment of a high-collared rim and c. 10 wall fragments of Andenne pottery were found. Approximately seven sherds from the South-Limburg production centres were present, one of them from period 3, as defined by Bruyn,[29] as well as two fragments of Paffrath pottery and a few

[26] Van Es/Verwers 1980. The further references to Dorestad concern this publication.

[27] Willems 1973, fig. 9, nos. 8-10.

[28] De Waele/Nyns 1984.

[29] Bruyn 1962-1963.

unclassifiable sherds. An important find from this ditch is a base fragment of a Merovingian biconical pot of soft-baked, sand-tempered clay, with a grey core and black surface (fig. 29, 6). Finally a piece of baked or sun-dried (local?) clay was found that resembles a piece of daub. But since it is tempered with fine sand it could be a base fragment of a local made early-medieval pot. A specimen of a comparable fabric has been found in a post-hole of a Merovingian building at Dommelen (A. Verhoeven, personal communication). These early finds must, however, be considered as residual finds.

The pottery in the remaining features
Most of the pottery comes from features that cannot be attributed to any structure. This pottery can be divided into two groups: pottery from the Early Middle Ages, mainly Carolingian in date (8th-9th centuries), and pottery from the High Middle Ages (mainly 12th century).

Much of the pottery from the Early Middle Ages is the well-known Badorf pottery. The rim- and wall fragments are all of the various specimens of the vessel Dorestad type WII (fig. 30, 1-6).[30] Pottery from the production centre at Mayen is present in the form of one rim fragment (fig. 30, 7). Some of the Carolingian pottery was probably produced in the Meuse valley, but this cannot be distinguished from the pottery that may have been locally made in the region. It consists mainly of wall fragments that are difficult to ascribe to a particular production centre. The pottery finds of Hulsel are not of a quality and quantity to deal in detail with the problems of the Carolingian pottery in the Kempen region.

One rim fragment of black polished, soft-baked pottery with a grey-reddish core from Hulsel is cer-

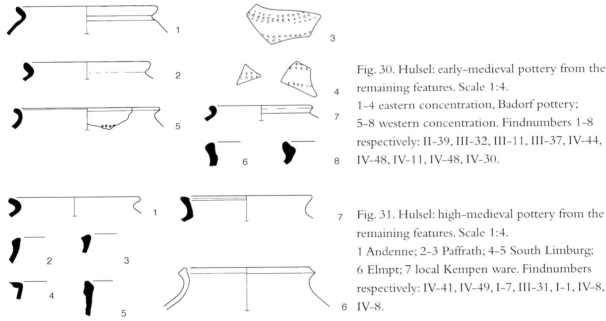

Fig. 30. Hulsel: early-medieval pottery from the remaining features. Scale 1:4.
1-4 eastern concentration, Badorf pottery;
5-8 western concentration. Findnumbers 1-8 respectively: II-39, III-32, III-11, III-37, IV-44, IV-48, IV-11, IV-48, IV-30.

Fig. 31. Hulsel: high-medieval pottery from the remaining features. Scale 1:4.
1 Andenne; 2-3 Paffrath; 4-5 South Limburg; 6 Elmpt; 7 local Kempen ware. Findnumbers respectively: IV-41, IV-49, I-7, III-31, I-1, IV-8, IV-8.

tainly of Merovingian date (fig. 30, 8) It may be the rim of a biconical jug like the one on the pot in grave 17 of the Merovingian cemetery at Beerlegem.[31] It also resembles the rim of a biconical jug from Krefeld-Gellep (type 144).[32]

The ceramics of the High Middle Ages consist mainly of sherds from the production centres in Andenne (fig. 31, 1), Paffrath (fig. 31, 2-3), and South-Limburg (fig. 31, 4-5). A rim fragment of a pitcher

---

[30] Van Es/Verwers 1980, 69-78.

[31] Roosens/Gyselinck 1975.

[32] Pirling 1966, 137.

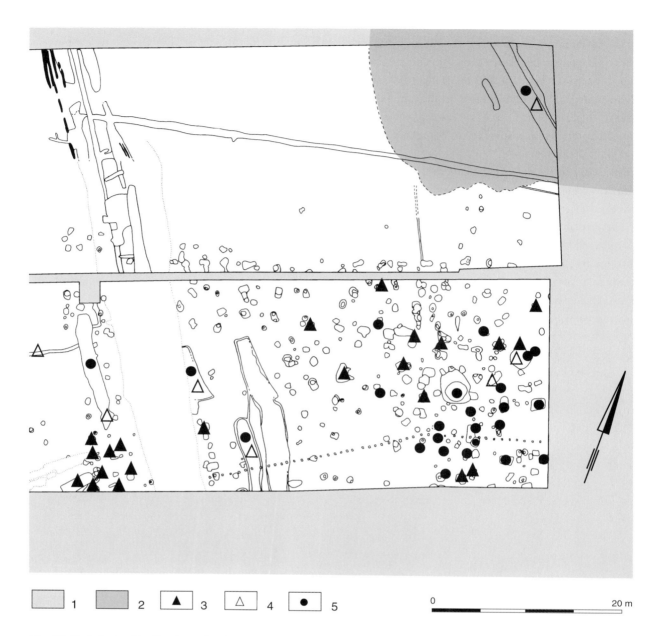

Fig. 32. Hulsel: the distribution of early- and high-medieval pottery and residual early-medieval pottery in high-medieval features over the site. Scale 1:400.

1 non excavated area; 2 low lying area; 3 early medieval pottery; 4 early medieval pottery, residual finds; 5 high-medieval pottery

with an engobe (iron-wash) on the outside from South-Limburg, dating from period 3 (early 13th century) as defined by Bruyn, belongs to this group (fig. 31, 5). A rim fragment and a number of wall fragments of a cooking pot of Elmpter or Elmpter-like ware along with a rim- and wall fragments of 'Kempen ware' (fig. 31, 6-7) were found in a post-hole that is probably younger than building 3. They are important for the dating of the structure. Elmpter ware is rare in Hulsel; one other fragment was found in the fill of the (early) modern track. It is a common type of pottery in the late 12th and 13th centuries.

The distribution of the two groups of pottery over the site is shown on fig. 32. The features from which high-medieval pottery was recovered are indicated with dots, and those with early-medieval pottery with triangles. Open triangles indicate residual early-medieval pottery in features dated to the High Middle Ages. The high-medieval pottery is mainly confined to the southeastern part of the excavation in the features of building 3 and its immediate vicinity.

The pottery of the early-medieval period (several dozens of sherds) appears in two concentrations, one in the eastern part of the excavation and one immediately southwest of the modern track. Close inspection of these two concentrations shows that their composition differs. The eastern group almost entirely consists of sherds of Badorf vessels WII. There are only two or three fragments of Mayen ceramics and other fabrics.

In the western group, some Badorf sherds are also present, but most of the items are Meuse or 'local' wares and Mayen pottery. Although the absolute number of sherds in each group is low, the difference can probably be explained in chronological terms, the western group being somewhat earlier than the eastern group, although not much is known about the respective ages of the Meuse valley and 'local' Carolingian wares. We will return to these concentrations while discussing the dating of the various structures and the settlement below.

Concluding remarks on pottery

On the basis of the description of the pottery finds it can be concluded that almost all the pottery used in the settlement came from production centres outside the region. Even the location of the production centre or centres of the so-called 'Kempen ware' may lie somewhere in the Meuse valley. Like the inhabitants of other Kempen settlements those of Hulsel had access to products from the Meuse valley and the Rhineland. How they obtained these goods is a matter of debate,[33] but the fact that they were included in a manorial system of agricultural production[34] (see the next chapter) gave them a place in a larger exchange network upheld by the land-owner. It gave even the inhabitants of such a small settlement as Hulsel in the Early and High Middle Ages a window on society outside their immediate environment.

4.2   OTHER FINDS

Three whetstones were found (in features II-19 and 171 and IV-29). Two of them are long and rectangular in section, and one is long and oval in section (fig. 33, 1-3). Specimen no. 3 is broken.
A fragment of a brick, curved rooftile (fig. 33, 4) similar to a Roman imbrex was present in post-hole 1 of building 3. All the sides of the fragment were burned, except the upper- and lower sides. It must have been reused, and may have been part of a pile of similar fragments that had been in contact with fire. Roman roof- and hypocaust tiles are found at various places in the Kempen region. They are regularly found on early-medieval sites. Brick tiles are not usual in a 12th century settlement since brick making, as far as we know now, was not done at that time in the region. Occasionally, however, they occur e.g. in 12th-century rural contexts like the settlement at Horst-Ermelo on the Veluwe.[35]

Another important find is an iron ploughshare (fig. 33, 5) found in a post-hole . The post-hole might be part of the uncertain structure 6. Its total length is 27 cm, the largest width is 12.8 cm. It probably dates from the 12th century. The presence of the ploughshare in a post-hole is remarkable. It can

---

[33]   Verhoeven 1990.

[34]   Theuws 1991.

[35]   Personal communication H.A. Heidinga IPP.

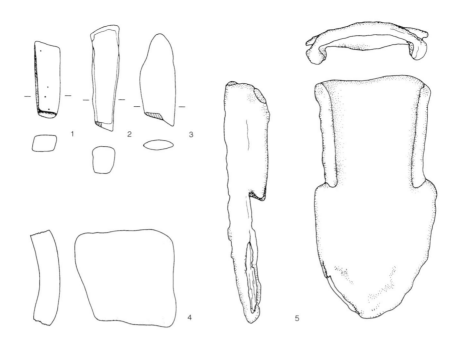

Fig. 33. Hulsel: non-ceramic finds. Scale 1 : 4. 1 - 3 grindstones; 4 Roman tile; 5 ploughshare

hardly be accepted that it got there by chance, as will have been the case with most of the other finds. If one accepts such an explanation then the ploughshare must have been lying around somewhere and have fallen into the hole that is not much bigger than the ploughshare itself. The chance that this could have happened is relatively small. The ploughshare must have been deposited in the post-hole on purpose, possibly as a votive or ritual deposit for whatever reason one might think of. Ploughshares and ploughs often play an important role in ritual activities in the medieval countryside.[36]

5   THE DATING OF THE STRUCTURES AND THE SETTLEMENT

In an attempt to date the habitation at this site it is easiest to start with the High Middle Ages and try to date building 3 on the basis of the pottery finds. The best material for dating the building comes from post-hole 1 in which six wall fragments of 'Kempen pottery' and six wall fragments of Andenne pottery were found. According to Verhoeven, the Kempen pottery is not older than the second quarter of the 12th century. The Andenne pottery may date from the 11th and 12th centuries. However, a closer look at post-hole 1 shows that no post-pipe was present; the fill indicates that the post was removed and the remaining pit filled up. The pottery sherds were probably thrown in at that time and provide a terminus post quem for the demolition of the building, which is the second quarter of the 12th century. An important observation is that post-holes 29 and 42 cut into post-hole 43 of the building. Both holes 29 and 42 could be the result of renewals of the posts in the western short wall of the building. It is, however, also possible that there is no relation between the post-holes and the building. In no. 29 sherds were found of Elmpt or Elmpter-like ware that must be dated to the late 12th or 13th centuries. This could mean that the building had been abandoned by that time or that the building was repaired during

[36]   Rooijackers 1987, 67-80.

that period. However, the absence of Elmpter ware, which was imported en masse to the Kempen region, in other post-holes of building 1 and elsewhere on the site indicates that this last possibility is unlikely and that the building was out of use at the end of the 12th century.

The absence at the site of Andenne cooking pots with sickle-shaped rims, common in the late 11th and early 12th centuries, indicate that the building was not erected before c. 1125. It must have been built shortly after that date, since Paffrath pottery is present. According to Verhoeven, Paffrath pottery was imported into the Kempen region in the late 11th and early 12th centuries. It is lacking in the rest of the 12th century. Building 3 would have been in use at least during the second and third quarters of the 12th century and possibly also in the last quarter.

Comparable farmhouses at Dommelen designated as type A2 date from the second half of the 11th and the first quarter of the 12th centuries and are succeeded by buildings of type A3 with five roof-posts in a curved line, which are typical for the period in which the Andenne pots with high-collared rims were common. Buildings of type A2 in Dommelen are associated with the Andenne sickle-form rims, which are absent in Hulsel. On the basis of the evidence from Hulsel it must be concluded that the buildings of type A2 were also in use after c. 1125.

The dating of building 3 corresponds more or less with that of the well. An Andenne high-collared rim, which dates from the second and third quarter of the 12th century, was found in the pit indicating that the well must have been dug after c. 1125. That the same type of rims were present in the fill of the well indicates that it was filled up not long after c. 1175 or before that date. The beaker of South Limburg pottery is handmade and should therefore be attributed to period I, as defined by Bruyn. The type of decoration seems to be common in the later phase of period I (XIId).[37] The best parallels for the outward curved Andenne rim are found in 12th-century contexts.[38] The well was probably in use during the second and third quarter of the 12th century.

The presence of a fragment of a high-collared rim and 10 wall sherds of Andenne pottery in ditches 5/6 indicates that the ditch was in use sometime during the 12th century. Theoretically it could have been in use in a later time as well, but 11 sherds of a type of pottery common in the 12th century is probably to many for them to be residual finds. Moreover there are no younger pottery sherds present. The same is true for pit III-12. The relatively large number of Andenne wall fragments in ditch 1 indicates that it was also in use in the 12th century.

A major problem is the dating of the large rectangular pits such as III-151. Three fragments of Andenne pottery, but also a number of sherds of Carolingian date, were found in pit III-2. In pit IV-80 a Carolingian sherd was found. The Andenne pottery could be present in a Carolingian pit as a consequence of animal activity in the soil; however, three Andenne sherds is too much of a coincidence to be ascribed to mole activity. The earlier pottery should be considered as residual material. If the pits were indeed of Carolingian date, they would probably have been overcut by later post-holes more than once. An indication that they are of high-medieval date is the fact that pit III-79 is overcut by a large pit or post-hole as can be seen in the southern section wall of the trench (fig. 23). This last pit is older than the *plaggen* layer that cannot have been present at the time of the digging of the pit. No traces of the *plaggen*

---

[37] Datings are often given in Roman figures for the centuries and letters for subdivisions of them. A an B mean first and second half of a century, lower cast letters stand for the respective quarters of a century.

[38] Borremans/Warginaire 1966: fig. 22, A11 a/d, no. 37; Lauwerijs 1981/82, fig. 2, no. 14;. Lauwereys/Petit 1967,

planche 1 four 3 nos. 18-19; planche III four 7, nos 1-2; planche IV interfours 1-7, nos. 5, 11, 14. Ovens nos. 1 and 7 belong to a late phase in the production at Wierde and may therefore be dated to the second half or late 12th and 13th centuries

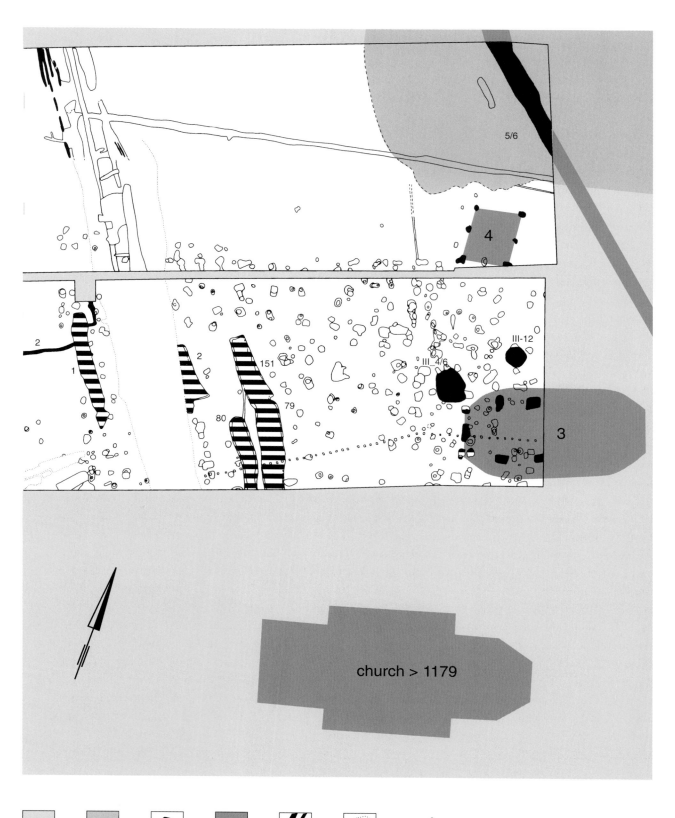

5/6

4

2

1

2

151

80

79

III-12

III 4/6

3

church > 1179

| | 1 | | 2 | | 3 | | 4 | | 5 | | 6 | 0 | 20 m |

layer were found in its fill. Finally, is is still possible that they are younger than the 12th century and that the Andenne pottery sherds too are residual finds. In that case they are dug after the settlement was abandoned and before the *plaggen* layer was created. However, the formation of this layer on these fields cannot be dated exactly. The pits are oriented along the same axis as the early modern road and ditch 3. This could be an argument to date them to the post-habitation period. Whatever is the case, the large pits seem to belong to a later phase of the habitation or to the late-medieval or early modern period.

The South Limburg sherds in ditch 2 may indicate that it was also in use along with the fence in the 12th century, although the evidence is not very convincing.

The following structures can be attributed to a 12th-century settlement phase: building 3, the well, pit III-2, ditch 1, ditch 5/6 and possibly ditch 2 (fig. 34). Of uncertain date are: pits III-151/152, 2, IV-79 and IV-80. The uncertain structure no. 6 is not taken into consideration here. If it existed it was probably of 12th-century date. The low quantity of pottery that can be dated to the 13th century indicates that this settlement phase did not last beyond the end of the 12th century.

Various explanations can be given for the almost total absence of finds in the post-holes of buildings 1 and 2. First of all, the post-holes were not very deep in comparison to those of building 3. Second, the absence of finds in the post-holes of these buildings could be related to their use. Third, the absence of finds may indicate that these buildings were the first that were built at this site so that no pottery from earlier occupation phases would have been incorporated into post-holes. Lack of habitation in the centuries following this settlement phase would prevent sherds from later occupation phases falling into in the post-holes. The few sherds found in one of the post-holes of building 2 may indicate that this was the younger one. Fourth, pottery from the occupation phase may have been present in the higher parts of the post-holes, which were destroyed by ploughing since the Late Middle Ages.

If the ground-plans of buildings 1 and 2 are compared to those of Dommelen, the best parallels are found among the buildings of the Carolingian period. In the Merovingian period the buildings there have small and shallow post-holes. In the Carolingian period relatively large and shallow post-holes and in the High Middle Ages (since c. 950), large and deep post-holes are common. The buildings at Dommelen date from the second half of the 8th and the 9th centuries. The early-medieval pottery from Hulsel supports this date. The Badorf vessel WII and the cooking pots WIII are generally dated to the second half of the 8th and the 9th centuries.[39] The Meuse valley and the 'local' Carolingian wares cannot be dated precisely. That Badorf ceramics are more numerous than Mayen sherds in the eastern part of the excavation may indicate that habitation there should be dated somewhat later in the Carolingian period (after c. 800?). Chronologically speaking, Badorf ceramics are in use longer than the Mayen ceramics, which gradually went out of use in the second half of the 8th century. Buildings 1 and 2 that are probably not contemporary, can be brought in connection with the eastern concentration of Badorf ceramics. It is, however, difficult to explain why Carolingian pottery is present in the remaining post-holes and not in those of the buildings. Perhaps a large part of the post-holes containing pottery sherds were dug on the farmyard during habitation. The habitation connected with the western group of Carolingian pottery may start somewhat earlier. No buildings of this part of the settlement could be reconstructed. Perhaps the (early) modern track destroyed the features of such a building. Pits IV-125 and 126 are likely to be of Carolingian date (fig. 35). The single Andenne sherd in pit 125 may have been transported downwards by a mole. The beginning and the end of the Carolingian habitation phase are difficult to establish. The ceramics of the 10th and 11th centuries as found in Dommelen are lacking

Fig. 34. Hulsel: high-medieval structures and ditches. Scale 1: 400.
1 non excavated area; 2 low lying area; 3 high-medieval features (hatched: possible high-medieval features; 4 high-medieval buildings (with number) and ditches; 5 track (possibly younger); 6 recent disturbance

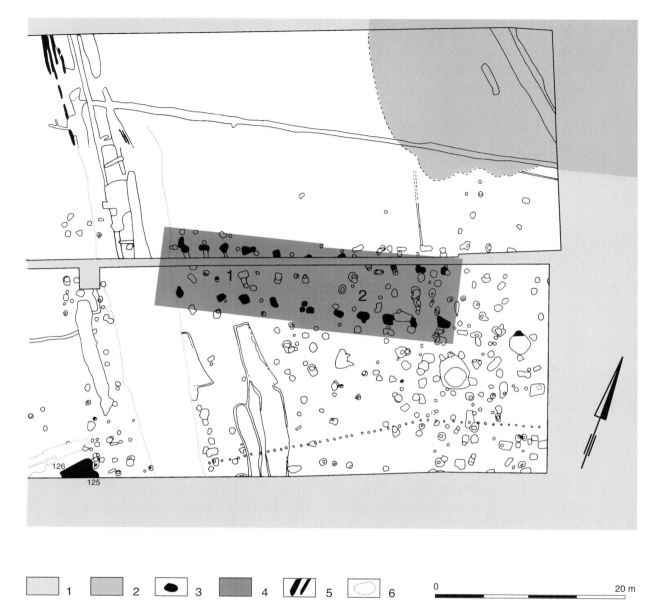

Fig. 35. Hulsel: early-medieval structures. Scale 1: 400.
1 non excavated area; 2 low-lying area; 3 early-medieval features ; 4 early-medieval buildings (with number); 5 track (younger); 6 recent disturbance

in Hulsel, which indicates that there is a gap in the habitation in this particular area of the settlement in that period.

Features that can be attributed to the Merovingian period are not found or identified at Hulsel (unless the uncertain structure 7 is dated in that period (fig. 16), but there are indications that habitation may have started in the first half of the 8th century or even somewhat earlier. Ceramics of Merovingian date were found in ditch 5/6 (fig. 29, 6) and in post-hole IV-204/207, a metre to the east of pit IV-125.

[39]   Van Es/Verwers 1980, 69-78 and 81-87.

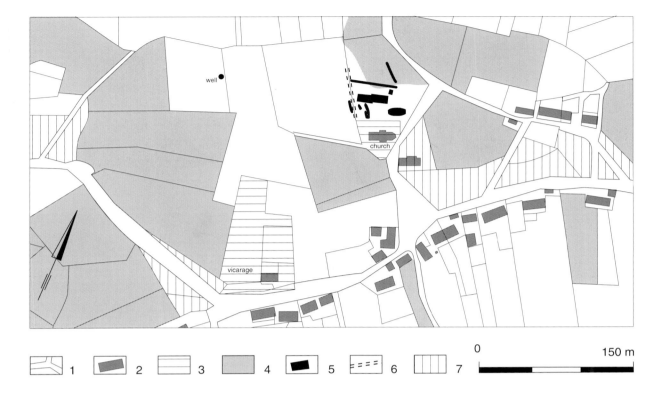

1	2	3	4	5	6	7

0   150 m

Fig. 36. Hulsel: a comparison of the topography of 1830 and the early- and high-medieval structures and ditches. 1 tracks in 1830; 2 buildings 1830; 3 property of the church of Hulsel; 4 low lying area; 5 buildings, ditches and pits from the Early and High Middle Ages; 6 track found in the excavation trenches; 7 communal property

(fig. 30, 8).[40] The rim fragment shown in fig. 29, 3 could date from the late 7th or first half of the 8th centuries. Finally the rim fragment fig. 29, 1 of 'local' Carolingian pottery resembles rims of Merovingian biconical pots and may, therefore, be dated to the first half of the 8th century.

It can be concluded that the habitation started at least in the first half of the 8th century or possibly somewhat earlier. The earliest habitation must, however, have taken place outside the excavated area.

6 THE LOCATION AND TOPOGRAPHY OF THE SETTLEMENT

Only part of the settlement at Hulsel has been excavated. In spite of this, some remarks about the location and the topography can be made. As has already been said in chapter 2, the settlement is situated near a lower-lying area which is situated to the north-east of it. This is a regularly recurring feature in the location of early- and high-medieval settlements in the Kempen region. However, the excavated part of the settlement is not situated on a particularly high part of the local sand plateau as is often the case. One might even say that it is on the edge of a lower-lying area to the south of it, that more or less forms an extension in eastern direction of the valley of the Raamloop. Other parts of the settlement may have been situated to the south of the church site as well as to the north along the depression. This depression

---

[40] The last mentioned rim fragment resembles, as has been said, that of pots of type 144 at Krefeld-Gellep, which are dated to the 7th century: Pirling 1966, 137.

Fig. 37. Hulsel: the church of Hulsel in 1825 (after Van Laarhoven 1975, 95).

was drained in the 12th century by digging ditches in it. The same activity could be observed at Geldrop where low-lying parts were also drained by digging trenches in them.[41] Early medieval activities in relation to these depressions have not been observed. It may therefore be expected that in general these low-lying areas on high ground were reclaimed for the first time in the High Middle Ages.

It is notable that the early-medieval features do not extend beyond an imaginary, east-west oriented line that seems to separate the settlement site from the wet area to the north. Both buildings 1 and 2 seem to respect this line. Although no ditch or fence has been found, it may be presumed that some kind of boundary, whatever its physical appearance, was present. The high-medieval features are not found either beyond this boundary. Ditch 4 may be related to this boundary although its date cannot be established. It is probably younger than the habitation phase. A boundary may have been present there

[41]   Beex 1990, 41 and 48-49.

since Carolingian times. During the 12th century, activities did not extend significantly beyond the line and when habitation disappeared the new field boundaries (ditches 3 and 4) have more or less the same orientation.

It could not be determined whether the early-medieval features were part of one or two farmsteads. One high-medieval farmstead has been found.

The *Kerkweg* now runs over the site of farmhouse 3. Its present course is, however, the result of modern alterations. In former times it was situated more to the east as can be seen on the land registry map of 1830 (fig. 36 and fig. 6). The main archaeological features are indicated on this map as well. The high-medieval features fit into the early 19th-century field pattern relatively well. The 12th-century farmstead is situated in the south-east corner of the field to the north of the church that may have been the yard of the 12th-century farm. If the ditches 5 and 6 are extended to the south in a straight line, they pass alongside the reconstructed farmhouse, which may indicate that the ditches served as the eastern boundary of the farmyard. Local informants told us that while building the Eversacker 8 house a well, probably made of a hollowed out tree trunk, was found (fig. 2). Such wells are typical for the Early and High Middle Ages; in late-medieval and modern times wells are often made with sods or with timber. Other evidence for habitation was not observed, but circumstances were, of course, not favourable. This well may indicate the location of another early- or high-medieval farmstead. On the other hand, it has been observed at Bladel-Kriekeschoor that these wells were also present in the fields.

The area to the north of the church was occupied only during the Carolingian period and the 12th century, two periods for which an expansion of the agrarian economy in western Europe has been postulated.[42] We may be dealing with extensions of a settlement during these periods. Whatever may have been the case, the presence of habitation in these periods may be an indication that agrarian expansion occurred at those times in the Kempen region too.[43] The hypothetic character of this conclusion must, however, be stressed, because internal characteristics of the settlement or even of a single farmstead, and specific local conditions may also have played a role in its topographical development.

An important element in the settlement, the church site, has not been investigated, because it is protected by the ancient monuments act and currently used as a small park. The late-medieval gothic, brick church or chapel (fig. 37) burned down in 1888, and a new church was built at another (the present) location. It would be worthwhile digging some trial trenches in order to try to establish the date of the oldest burials and, with some luck, the dates of the predecessors of the late-medieval church. The earliest burials and a possible wooden church are probably not much older than c. 1100. The excavations in the churches of Dommelen and Luyksgestel, which are of comparable status and are situated in parishes of comparable size, show that they are of that date or even somewhat younger.[44] The church, which is first mentioned in a document dated to 1179 (see section 7.1) and the cemetery are probably contemporaneous with farmhouse 3. The presence of a church in or near the settlement indicates that it must have had, at least in the High Middle Ages, a special status within the parish.

The archaeological research in Hulsel gave an answer to a number of questions raised in the introduction. First of all, it was shown that traces of a medieval settlement probably older than the church itself were present in the immediate vicinity of the isolated church. The settlement was probably found-

---

[42] See for instance the chapters by Fourquin in : G. Duby, ed., 1975: *Histoire de la France rurale. Tome 1. La formation des campagnes françaises des origines au XIVe siècle*, Paris, especially 340-363, 337-473.

[43] The results of the excavations in other parishes in the region (Bladel, Geldrop, Dommelen, Someren, Sint-Oedenrode) indicate this too. See also Theuws 1993; Roymans/Kortlang 1993; Arts 1993.

[44] Luyksgestel: Theuws 1981; Dommelen: unpublished.

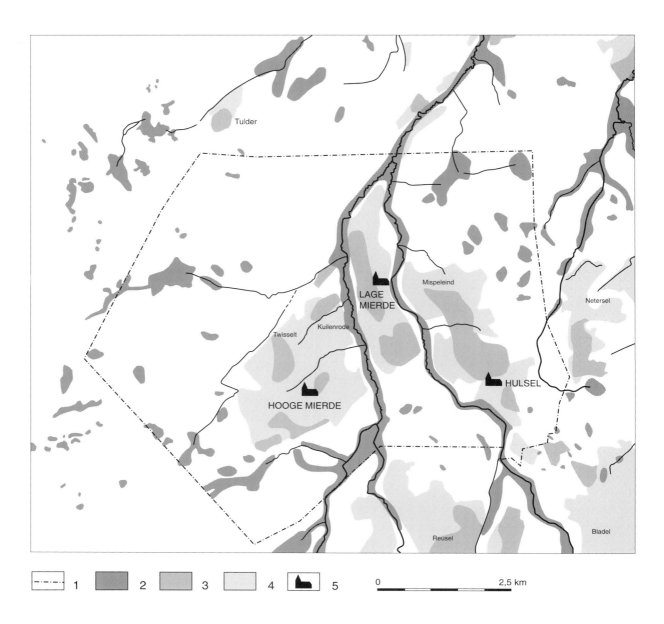

Fig. 38. The extent of the territory over which the elements of an early-medieval estate of the abbey of Saint-Trond at Hooge-, Lage Mierde and Hulsel could have been scattered. Indicated in dark grey are the brook valleys and fens and in light grey the relatively fertile, dry soils. Also indicated are the locations of medieval churches.
1 possible limits of the territory of the estate of the abbey at Saint-Trond; 2 brook valleys and fens; 3 high-lying relative fertile soils (dry); 4 high-lying relative fertile soils (moist); 5 location of medieval churches

ed in the (early?) 8th century and seems to have disappeared in the late 12th or early 13th century. It has not, however been established that there was continuity of habitation from the 8th/9th centuries to the 12th. In the next chapters we will try to gain a better view on its position in the local settlement system by studying the historical evidence and the settlement pattern.

7 HISTORICAL EVIDENCE FROM THE MIDDLE AGES ABOUT HULSEL

Although Hulsel was and still is a small village in the Kempen region, it boasts of being one of the first villages mentioned in the written sources of the region, together with the nearby village of Hapert and the hamlet of Hoksent in northern Belgium, province of Limburg. But there is also interesting historical evidence about the ecclesiastical holdings from the High and Late Middle Ages, some of which, with the help of census registers from the modern period, are possible to locate.

Hulsel is said to be mentioned for the first time in 710. In that year, Bertilindis, a member of an elite family in the pagus Texandrië donated part of her property in the Kempen region to Willibrord, the bishop of the Frisians and the abbot of the monastery at Echternach (Lux.).[45] Among the goods listed are: *vassalos sex cum tribus puellis et silvam in loco Hulislaum et quicquid ibidem legitime provenit*. It is generally accepted that *Hulislaum* can be identified with Hulsel near Bladel, although some doubts exist about the validity of this identification (see discussion below). Hulsel is indicated as a *locus*. The term may indicate a single settlement, but, in our opinion, a number of small settlements might be involved.[46] We know that Bertilindis possessed unfree people and a forest at a place called Hulsel, which may have belonged to a larger demesne of hers, a *villa*, several of which are mentioned in the region in contemporary charters. Unfortunately, nothing is known about the later history of the early-medieval demesne and the property of Willibrord in Hulsel. It is not mentioned in his so-called 'will' (from 726) in which he donates a large part of his possessions to the monastery of Echternach[47] nor in a list of rents of the abbey in Texandrië dating from the early 13th century.[48] So it is not known where the forest was situated and the *vassalli* lived. As said, it is possible that it was brought under the administration of one of the nearby *villae* of Echternach.

Nearly 500 years pass before Hulsel is mentioned again in the written sources. The high-medieval evidence concerns the church and the estate of the abbey at Saint-Trond in the village. The church history will be discussed first, because it can be directly related to the excavated settlement, and then we will try to locate the estate goods using the modern evidence.

7.1 THE CHURCH AT HULSEL

In 1179 Pope Alexander III brought the abbey at Saint-Trond under his protection.[49] All the properties and rights the abbey possessed were mentioned in the charter that was drawn up at that occasion. Among them was the (*altare*) *de Husela*, it means that the abbey possessed the church dedicated to Saint

---

[45] Camps 1979, no. 4. See also Ganshof 1954, Werner 1980, 139-58, Van Loon 1980 and Theuws 1988, 81-86. For the regional context of this donation see Theuws 1988, 81-86 and 299-318; Theuws 1991, 321-337.

[46] Theuws 1986.

[47] Wampach 1929-30, I2, no. 39. There is still some discussion about the authenticity of this document. See Koch 1970, 3-4, who does not doubt the fact that Willibrord donated a number of goods to the monastery of Echternach in 726/727. However, he recognizes that the present text of the charter is corrupt in some places. For

the latest discussion see: Rombaut 1989. Other places donated to Willibrord are not mentioned in the 'testament'. One reason may be that small properties were incorporated in larger villae. Some of these even originally belonged to these villae, but were partitioned off from it during the dividing of an inheritance, Theuws 1991, 339 note 177.

[48] Camps 1979, no. 134. See also Bijsterveld 1989a and 1989b.

[49] Camps 1979, no. 72.

Clemens. There has been some confusion about the identification of *Husela* with Hulsel, for on similar occasions, in 1107 and 1161, an *altare de Gunsela* was mentioned,[50] which refers to Woensel, now part of the town of Eindhoven, c. 20 km to the northeast of Hulsel. The *Husela* of the 1179 charter was thought to be a corrupt version of *Gunsela* and thus also identified with Woensel.[51] There was, however, one inconsistency. In the well-known records of the possessions and revenues of the abbey kept by abbot Willem of Rijkel in the middle of the 13th century, *Hulsele* or *Holsele* as well as *Gunsela* or *Gunsele* are mentioned.[52] *Gunsela* is always mentioned in combination with the large demesne of the abbey at Alem on the Meuse near 's-Hertogenbosch. Probably *Gunsela* was brought under the administration of the prior at Alem.[53] This situation already seems to have existed in the 12th century, for this combination seems to be present in the charters of 1107, 1161 and 1179. In 1107, the churches of Alem, *Gunsela*, Son, and Macharen are mentioned among others. In 1161, they are mentioned again, but not in 1179 when *Husela* appears. *Husela* (Hulsel) therefore seems to occupy a relatively independent position in relation to the *curia* at Alem. From this it may be deduced that *Gunsela* and *Husela* are different places and that Woensel and Hulsel were respectively referred to, and that the possessions and rights at Woensel were administered by the prior of Alem already by 1107. It is clear from the records of abbot Willem of Rijkel that the possession of the church meant that the abbey was entitled to tithes and had the right to nominate the village priest. In 1254 and 1259, some rents are also mentioned,[54] indicating that the abbey probably also had some land. In 1257 the tithes amounted to 12 *modii* of rye, or in some years only 10. In 1253 the collection of the tithes of the abbey was leased for a period of three years to the magister of the nearby priory at Postel for 13 *modii* of rye and 20 pounds of wax; in 1259, the collection of the tithes and the rents were again leased for three years to a priest called Lambertus.[55]

Now *Husela* and *Gunsela* are identified as separate locations an inconsistency arises in the records; however, it can probably be solved. Charters from 1255, 1270, and 1310, concerning the chapter of Hilvarenbeek (12 km. to the north of Hulsel) indicate that the dean was entitled to the tithes of Hulsel,[56] but also state that the chapter possessed these tithes long before. It is possible that the abbey at Saint-Trond did not own the entire tithe revenues from Hulsel and that they were shared between the abbey and the chapter of Hilvarenbeek. At the end of the 18th century, the tithes that were once in the hands of Saint-Trond were leased, and it appears that they included only half the tithes of Hulsel.[57] It is not clear who owned the other half, which is referred to as *Pastorietienden* (= vicarage-tithes); maybe it was the village priest. It is doubtful, however, that the 18th-century situation was identical to that in the 13th century. If the village priest was entitled to half the tithes, it is likely that they were originally owned by Saint-Trond, who nominated the priest. In 1253, there is mention in the records that part of the tithes had to be handed over to the investitus, the village priest, but it is a normal situation that at least one third of the tithes is for the benefit of the village priest.[58] Moreover, one gains the impression from the written evidence that both the abbey and the chapter each possess all the tithes in Hulsel, which is, of course, impossible, especially in 1255. It is also possible that two Hulsels are involved. Five kilometres to the southwest of Hilvarenbeek there is a small hamlet named Hulsel in the Belgium

[50] Camps 1979, no. 33 and 62. Camps 1979, no. 33 and 62.

[51] Camps in his edition of the charters in 1979 still does. See, however, Kesters 1979 on this problem.

[52] Pirenne 1896, passim.

[53] Bijsterveld 1989a, 15.

[54] Pirenne 1896, 165 and 353.

[55] Pirenne 1896, 323 and 353.

[56] Camps 1979, nos. 258, 324 and 810.

[57] State archives in North Brabant ('s-Hertogenbosch). Archives of the '*Commissie van Breda*', *rentambt* Saint-Trond, no. 760.

[58] Pirenne 1896, 323.

municipality of Poppel. It is most likely that the chapter possessed the tithes in this hamlet and that the abbey at Saint-Trond had the tithes of Hulsel near Bladel, as stated by written evidence of a later date. Camps identifies Hulsel mentioned in the charters of the chapter with the Hulsel of 710, which is generally accepted to be the Hulsel near Bladel. This identification of Hulsel can now be questioned. One can also question the identification of the *Hulislaum* of 710, where Bertilindis' properties were situated, with Hulsel near Bladel since it is based solely on identical names. Against the identification speaks the fact that in Hulsel near Bladel nothing is ever heard again of property or rights of any kind of the abbey at Echternach. On the other hand Echternach levied some rents in the village of Poppel in which the second hamlet of Hulsel is situated.[59] If the *Hulislaum* of 710 has to be identified with Hulsel near Bladel then Saint-Trond has probably obtained her possessions by taking over a part or the entire possessions of the abbey at Echternach. There are, however, no indications for such a transaction. Another possibility is that both Saint-Trond and Echternach obtained their properties from private persons in the Early Middle Ages. Although there are indications that in some places there is a relation between the properties of Echternach and Saint-Trond[60] it is more likely in the case of Hulsel that the goods donated to Echternach were situated in Hulsel near Poppel and those of Saint-Trond in Hulsel near Bladel.

The church of Hulsel appears in the ecclesiastical records of the 15th and 16th centuries as a *quarta capella*, which means that it had the lowest possible rank and was not a rich church.[61] Churches with this low rank seem to be of relatively late date (after AD 1000) and are often dependent on another higher-ranking church (*ecclesia integra* or *ecclesia dimidia*). The church of Hulsel could have been an appendix of Lage Mierde. The abbey of Saint-Trond was probably the (sole) owner of both the tithes of the village and the right to nominate the priest, a situation which usually indicates that the chapel was erected and the parish organized by the owner in question. The patron-saint of the chapel is Saint Clemens which also indicates that the chapel was erected by the abbey at Saint-Trond.[62] It seems to possess at least some rights on tithes already between 1108 and 1136 (see below) and it owns the church definitely in 1179.

There are indications that the villages of Hooge- and Lage Mierde and Hulsel were originally united in an estate of the abbey at Saint-Trond (fig. 38). Dirk II of Altena, who most likely was the *advocatus* of Saint-Trond in the Kempen region, had a number of possessions in Hooge- and Lage Mierde at the beginning of the 13th century, which could originally have belonged to an estate of Saint-Trond.[63] *Advocati* and administrators taking over possessions of the institutions they were supposed to protect are a common phenomenon in the Kempen region even in Hulsel as we will see below. Hooge- and Lage Mierde and Hulsel already formed a unity in the Middle Ages. They formed a single juridical district (*schepenbank*: aldermans court) and administered their common lands together.[64] This unity and the presence of the possessions of Dirk II of Altena can best be explained by assuming the existence of an estate of Saint-Trond, which may already have been in their possession since the Early Middle Ages. The cen-

---

[59] Camps 1979, no 134. See also Bijsterveld 1989a, 36 note 7.

[60] Bijsterveld 1989a, 16.

[61] Bannenberg, a.o., eds., 1968-1970, 367; Bijsterveld 1993, 7-11, 27-60.

[62] Bijsterveld 1989, 15.

[63] Camps 1979, nos 107-108. Before that, a certain Diederik van Hilvarenbeek also gave property to the monastery of Averbode that wasconnected to the church at Alem which was in the hands of Saint-Trond

(Camps 1979, no 91). See: Bijsterveld 1989a, 31; Bijsterveld 1989a, 21-22.

[64] See the introduction to the inventory of the archive of the Aldermens rolls of Hooge- and Lage Mierde and Hulsel (now in the State Archive at 's-Hertogenbosch). That the communal grounds of Hooge- and Lage Mierde and Hulsel formed a single whole appears from a charter (gemeyntbrief) of 19 august 1331 (Enklaar 1941, no 78).

tre of this estate was probably located either in Hooge- or (more likely) in Lage Mierde. The new chapel in Hulsel may have been created from this centre. If this reconstruction is valid Hooge- and Lage Mierde and Hulsel originally formed a parish.

The creation of a new chapel normally occurred on or near the centre of an estate, which in the case of Hulsel would mean that the excavated settlement was in the hands of the abbey at Saint-Trond at least in the High Middle Ages. There are some indications that Saint-Trond owned an estate at Hulsel.

7.2   THE ESTATE OF SAINT-TROND AT HULSEL

The first indications for the presence of an estate of Saint-Trond are the rents mentioned in the records of abbot Willem of Rijkel. More than 100 years before c. 1250, in the period between 1108 and 1136, a *villicus* illegally took possession of part of the rent, and a *dapifer* Hezelo usurped the tithes on flax, which he had to return.[65] Although it is not known what their exact positions were, it may be assumed that these persons were local stewards of the abbey at Hulsel. An important indication for the presence of a *curia* of Saint-Trond at Hulsel is found in a charter dating from 1280,[66] which was drawn up when Gozewijn Kenode sold some property of his at Bladel (a *domus* and *curtis*) and a rent at Arendonk to the Norbertinian abbey at Floreffe for the benefit of their dependent priory at Postel. The goods included lands that once belonged to *curiae* of the abbeys at Echternach and Saint-Trond and the seigneur of Herlaar. Although it is not known exactly where these *curiae* were located, it is known that the seigneurs of Herlaar had other possessions in the parish of Bladel (at *Elmeth*). In a list of rents collected by the abbey at Echternach, dating from the first quarter of the 13th century, Bladel and two other sites in the parish (*Herle* and *Elmeth*) are mentioned.[67] There are, however, no indications that Saint-Trond owned a *curia* at Bladel[68] and it is most likely that it was situated in the neighbouring parish of Hulsel. It is, of course, possible that some lands of a *curia* of Saint-Trond in Hulsel were situated in Bladel.[69]

A register from 1646 in the archives of the abbey at Saint-Trond lists the rents the abbey collected in the Kempen region.[70] These rents were due in several villages in the northern part of the Kempen and are listed under several headings, one of which is Hulsel.[71] The number of rents that had to be paid in Hulsel is by far the largest. Not only rents from Hulsel but also some from the neighbouring villages of Hoogeloon, Casteren, Vessem, and Bladel had to be paid here. This may indicate that the abbey formerly had a *curia* in the parish and that the rents were a last remnant of the abbey's possessions at Hulsel. Rents of this type are usually attached to particular fields irrespective of the owner, although sometimes there

[65]   De Borman 1877, 145.

[66]   Camps 1979, no 367.

[67]   Camps 1979, no 134.

[68]   Roymans 1979; Maas 1988.

[69]   In 1646 a rent of Saint-Trond was due for a farm near *Hofstad* in Bladel. This farm of the priory at Postel may have been the one that Gozewijn Kenode sold. Of all the farms that the monastery of Postel owned in the parish of Bladel, *Hofstad* is situated closest to Bladel, *Herle*, and *Elmet*, where rents of Echternach were due and the possessions of Herlaer were situated. This means that all the great landowners mentioned in the charter

of Gozewijn can be proven, with the help of other sources, to have had fields or collected rents in the vicinity of *Hofstad*.

[70]   State archive at Hasselt (Belgium, Province of Limburg). Archive of the abbey at Saint-Trond, no 6726, fol. 300-321; (abbreviated: AAST 6726).

[71]   The heading reads as follows: *Dit sijn die chijnsen die men den heere van St. Truiden jaerlyckx geldende is tot Hulsel op onser Lieve Vrouwen avont nativitatis.* The other headings concern: Eindhoven, Strijp, Stratum and Zeelst, Beers, Oerle, Schijndel, Vessem and Knegsel, and Oirschot. See also Kesters 1979, 26.

was an attempt to shift the rent from the fields to the houses, which were expected to be better security. Rents of this kind may have had a dual origin. They are sometimes due for occupying a part of the *curia*-lands. A number of rents may also have been paid for fields that once only nominally belonged to the curia but were reclaimed by private persons who paid a (low) rent as a recognition of the abbey's original right to the land. The rents of the first type can provide an idea of the area over which the *curia*-lands extended. The rents of the second type are of no help for the reconstruction of the extent of the cultivated area of the estate because they are of younger date. It is, however, difficult to distinguish between the different kind of rents. Taken together their distribution can provide a rough idea of the surface area over which the influence of the *curia* extended.

To locate fields for which rents are paid is difficult too, because the names of the fields are seldom given in the 1646 register and a special investigation is required to collect field names and then to locate them. Since it has not been possible to do this in sufficient detail to locate the fields exactly, they will be associated with a more general location. A few important observations can be made from the list of rents collected in Hulsel (see also fig. 6).

First of all, it appears that the abbot of the monastery at Postel had to pay a relatively large rent for his farm at Hulsel in comparison to other inhabitants (37.5 denier vs. 1 to 6 denier).[72]

Secondly, several persons had to pay a rent for *het goed* (= farm) *Ter Heggen*,[73] which altogether totalled 41.5 denier, and 5.5 oort. So, there were at least two (large) farms for which high rents had to be paid to the abbot of Saint-Trond.[74]

Third, a number of rents had to be paid by the villagers, at least one farmstead in the village was mentioned for which a rent had to be paid. Another rent was levied for a field in the *Arting*.[75]
Some rents cannot be located.[76] One of these was due for a field called *nieu huys en abt auder stede* (new house and abbots old house), the location of which might give a clue to the site of the former *curia*.

The high rents due for the farms of Postel and *Ter Heggen* probably indicate that either they originally belonged to Saint-Trond or that a lay man, or even the monastery of Postel itself, obtained the right to reclaim a large area and possess it as an allodial good, but, as has been said, had to pay a rent as a

---

[72] AAST 6726, fol 317r. The text reads as follows: *Heer Cornelis van Boesdonck abt tot Postel van sijn goed tot Hulsel 37,5 denier.* Van Boesdonk was the third abbot of Postel (from 1636 to 1650) after it became independent of the abbey at Floreffe (Belgium).

[73] Out of this farm the hamlet Heggeneind will have developed.

[74] AAST 6726, fol 318r: *Het goet ter Heggen 8,5 denier 1,5 oort, vanuut goet ter Heggen 11,5 denier 1 oort, fol 318v: vanut goet ter Heggen 8 denier 1 oort denier; fol 319v: dieselve uuten goet ter Heggen 5 denier 0,5 oort.*

[75] AAST 6726, fol 316v: *van sijn woninge daer hij in woont tot Hulsel ? denier; fol 317v: van den Aeltaersecker gelegen in de Ertinghe; fol 318r: uut de hoeve aen de straet; fol 318r: van de goede gheheten Loocken.* With Loocken probably a field in the *Looikens* is meant (see fig. 2).

[76] Apart from the fields mentioned in the previous notes a number of fields is recorded which cannot be located:

the *Vonderbroeckxen* which is mentioned three times (fol 318v). It concerns three parcels in a larger complex with the same name. The *Lovense bemt* is also mentioned three times (fol 316v, 319r). These fields are probably situated in the south of the parish or in the parish of Reusel on the other side of the Raamloop, for in that parish the farm *Loven* is situated. Finally, fol 317v: *eenen ecker gheheten nieu huys en abt auder stede.* A number of fields whose names are given are probably situated in Hulsel. However, since rents from several villages were collected at Hulsel it is not possible to determine the exact location of the following fields, fol 316r: *aen die plaetse den Zwanen*; fol 316v *uuten goeden ter Tommelen* (probably in Bladel); fol 317r *uuten Wyenhoff* (also fol 319r); fol 317r: *van den Berckecker*; fol 318r: *van den Langen gelegen in de gemeynte*; fol 317v: *uut Grastecker*; fol 320r *uut den Venecker.* Finally rents are mentioned from Hoogeloon, Hoogcasteren, Vessem, Casteren, and Bladel.

recognition of the rights the abbey of Saint-Trond had over the lands in the parish.[77] Either possibility would point to a process of diminishing influence of the abbey on the local level at Hulsel. The first farm came into the hands of another ecclesiastical institution (Postel) and therefore survived as a single farm until late in the 18th century, and the second farm (*Ter Heggen*) was subdivided. Before this point is further elaborated, an attempt is made to locate the fields and study the settlement pattern in Hulsel in more detail on the basis of the land registry of 1830 (fig. 6).

8   A SKETCH OF HULSEL IN THE EARLY 19TH CENTURY (fig. 6)

The location of the farm of the monastery at Postel called *Nertingen* is well known,[78] and the reconstruction of its demesne is not too difficult (see the next section). Most of the southern part of the parish was in the hands of the monastery at Postel, possibly since late-medieval times.

To the north of the farm lies a tract of arable land called the *Arting*. In 1830, arable fields were allocated to five categories according to their quality. Fields of the best quality (category 1) were not present at Hulsel. The fields in the *Arting* were all of category 2, which elsewhere in the parish is found only in a small area north and west of the church (the settlement area). The high quality of the arable fields and its old name may indicate that this area belonged to the oldest cleared parts of the parish. In the 17th-century administration of the monastery at Postel the farm at Hulsel is called *Nertingen*.[79] *Nertingen* and *Arting* are probably different forms of the same name. *Nertingen* could be a form in which the -*n* of the article *den* is attached to the name Arting (*den-Arting* = *Narting* is *Nertingen*). The name is probably older than the farm of Postel.

The fields in the *Arting* are situated at right angles along a track running north-south that begins in the centre of the village, where a small triangular square called the *Plaatse* and the major east-west road in the parish (*de Straat* = the street) intersect. In 1830, the church was at the northern end of the square. A larger 'public area' consists of the two rectangular plots surrounded by tracks to the east of the square, which more or less served as a village-green (fig. 36). A rent had to be paid to the duke of Brabant for the plot immediately to the east of the church.[80] The obligation to pay such rents often originated from the duke's consent to cultivate a part of the common heather fields, and usually indicate where, in late-medieval and modern times such fields are found, although there are older ducal rents in the Kempen region. These fields often encircle older (early- and high-medieval) cultivated fields and help to define the extent of older demesnes.[81] No ducal rents seem to have been paid for the *Arting* fields.

It is striking that almost all farmsteads of the village are situated to the south of the major road. Only one farm with a brewery lies on the northern side of the road for which a ducal rent had to be paid. Further to the west the village priest had his presbytery to the north of the road. It is as if 'something' prohibited the villagers from settling on the northern side of the road. This something may have been the public status of the fields on that side of the road east of the square and a special status of the area to the west of the square. Originally the lands may have been property of the abbey at Saint-Trond and belonged to the curia. The presence of the church lands north of the road may indicate this too. The

---

[77]   For parallel situations at Alphen see: Bijsterveld 1987 and Bijsterveld 1990/1991.

[78]   Roymans 1979.

[79]   See the next section.

[80]   State archives in North Brabant ('s-Hertogenbosch). Aldermens rolls Hooge- and Lage Mierde and Hulsel no 147, fol. 174-177 (1783).

[81]   Theuws 1989.

curved line of the village street indicates that it was going around fields that could not be crossed over.

Two small hamlets are situated to the west of the village centre along the road to Lage Mierde. In the first, Heggeneind, the farmhouses are grouped around a triangular green. The name of the hamlet may have been derived from the name of the farm *Ter Heggen* in the register of rents of Saint-Trond. This farm was probably located near this hamlet, or more likely, the hamlet grew out of the farm as it was subdivided, which would explain why several persons had to pay rents for the farm in 1646.

Further to the west is the hamlet of Vooreind (formerly Voort-einde, *voort* = ford) which is probably of fairly recent date (late medieval or modern) as is indicated by the large number of ducal rents to be paid for the fields and houses in this hamlet.

Most of the arable lands are situated to the north of the village centre and the two hamlets. The individual plots were grouped into four or five large fields in the land registry of 1830. Sometimes the individual plots have the same name as the larger fields, but other names may occur especially for the plots near the village and the hamlets. In the eastern part of the parish are the fields of Hulsel and Heikant, west of these are the *Grote Akkers* (= large arable fields) and *Kanten* that once seem to have been a single unit encircled by roads. To the north of the *Grote Akkers* are the *Papenakkers* and the *Looikens*. The fields of Hulsel, *Heikant*, the *Grote Akkers*, the *Papenakkers*, the *Looikens*, and the southeastern part of the *Kanten* are situated on the loess and coversand deposit of more than two metres thickness mentioned in chapter 2. It can be expected that of all the fields to the north of the village and the hamlets those of Hulsel, the northern part of *Heikant*, the *Grote akkers* and the southeastern part of the *Kanten* are the first to have been reclaimed because of the favourable soil conditions there. The arable fields of the hamlet Vooreind are located to the east and north of it. The fields directly to the north of the village and the hamlets are of good quality (category 3). Plots of heather are found around the arable fields (for instance the *Bogerse Heivelden* and the eastern part of the *Looikens*), which were probably in cultivation, though in an extensive form, in late-medieval or early modern times, but left fallow from the 16th to 18th centuries. Such tracts of fields can still be seen in nearly all Kempen villages. Also parts of the isolated farmsteads in the eastern heatherfields have been left fallow, which is indicated by the name of one of them: *Woeste Hof* (= lost farm).

The four scattered farmsteads in the north-east of the parish along the road to *Braakhoek* were built in the early 19th century.[82] The farmstead on the *Kouwenberg* and the one to the north of it are probably somewhat older.

The fields for which rents were paid to the abbey of Saint-Trond and the duke that can more or less be located are indicated on figure 6.[83] Three rents of the abbey are due from the *Vonderbroeksken*, a group of meadows that cannot be located exactly, but was probably situated near *Heggeneind* or east of the farm of Postel. Several ducal rents were paid for the *Vlasvenne*, which could refer to the *Venne* or *Ven* (= shallow lake or fen) east of the village, and for the *Lindt(Lijnd)einde,* which could refer to the western end of the village centre. These fields are not plotted on the map. Fields for which ducal rents were paid do not seem to have been present in the *Arting* or in the arable fields to the north of the village.

The fields for which rents were due to Saint-Trond occur all over the parish and their distribution is of no help in reconstructing the curia. The rents of the duke were mainly situated in Vooreind, in the centre of the village, and in the eastern part of the parish, i.e. at places where late-medieval and modern reclamations are found.

[82]   They are indicated as such on the cadastral map of
       the entire community of Hooge- and Lage Mierde and
       Hulsel. Private collection N. Roymans.

9 THE FARM OF THE PRIORY AT POSTEL (fig. 39)

9.1 HISTORICAL ASPECTS

In the southern part of the parish a farm of the priory at Postel is situated.[84] It is indicated in the written sources as *Nertingen*. The farm has left relatively little traces in the records even in those of the monastery itself.[85] In the middle of the 17th century, when Abraham Tempelaers functioned as steward, the farm yielded 109 guilders and 19 *stuivers*.[86] Somewhat earlier (the date of the document cannot exactly be established) it yielded: rye: 8 *mudden* (hectolitre); oats: 3 mudden, pork: 200 *stuivers*; butter: 40

[83] In the archives of notary Johan Franciscus Hoosemans a number of papers dating from 1813 is present that are part of an inventory of old rents which were due before the French revolution and the occupation of Holland by France which was going on at that time (Notary archives North-Brabant, Hooge- and Lage Mierde and Hulsel, no 4409). In Hooge- and Lage Mierde and Hulsel rents were due to the Duke of Brabant, the abbey at Averbode and the abbey at Saint-Trond which interest us here. They are attached to fields whose names are given. The names of the persons who had to pay for them are also given. This makes it possible in combination with the list of rents in the archive of the abbey to obtain a rough impression of the location of the fields concerned. An exact location can only be given after a detailed inventory of field-names has been made up. The following fields are listed (between brackets is the number of the document in dossier 4409, and an indication of the use of the field, a = arable, m = meadow, see also appendix 2): *de Langenakker* (a, 187), probably situated in the northern part of the *Arting*; *de Sluysbogt, de Daalakker* (a, 187), location unknown, the rents were paid by two persons living in the centre of the village (Hulsel itself) east of the Plaetse, their property lies immediately north and south of the village; *de Smeelakker* (a, 186), probably situated north-east of Vooreind; *het Gereslootje* (a, 186), location unknown; *het Aangelag* (a, 188), Cornelis Lemmens paid the rent, he lives at Vooreind; *de Smeel* (a, 189), probably north-east of Vooreind; *den Dessel* (m, 190), north of Vooreind near the stream; *de Hofstad* (a, 191), location unknown; *het Looyken* (a, 192), in the *Looikens*; *het Looyken* (a, 193), in the *Looikens*; *het Nieuwveld* (m, 194), it borders a field of Jan van de Heyden which were all situated in the south of the parish; *het Hoog Driesken* (m, 196), located as het

Nieuwveld; *het Looyken* (m, 197), in the *Looikens*; *de Smeelakker* (a, 197), probably north-east of Vooreind; *de Grootakker* (two fields with this name) (a, 198), located in the *Grote Akkers*; *het Veldeken* (m, 208), paid for by Jan de Leest who lives at the *Kouwenberg*; *het Hoogakkerken* (m, 208), location unknown; *het Trompbogt* (m, 208), location unknown.

[84] There exists no modern published study on the history of the abbey and the development of its patrimonium. Still, the works by Welvaarts (1878-79) and Prims have to be used in order to obtain an idea of Postel's history. An unpublished thesis however exists: J. Hermans, 1961: *De geschiedenis van de Premonstratenser gemeenschap te Postel*, Leuven. See also Hermans 1992-1993. Some remarks are also made by Welvaarts in his: *Geschiedkundige bijdragen over de voogdij van Molle*, Turnhout, 1891. Welvaarts also studied a number of villages where Postel had important possessions (see his bibliography in: Van Hoof 1978). De Groot studied watermills of Postel: I. de Groot, 1957: De watermolens van Venbergen en andere molens van de abdij Postel, *Analecta Praemonstratensia* 33, 302-317. Recently the study of the patrimonium of Postel has been taken up by analysing individual properties in several parishes, see for instance Maas 1991. Several other farms of Postel and their origins are now being studied, notably those at Bergeyk and Lierop. A detailed study of the farms at Reusel is disirable. Taken together the farms at Reusel, Hulsel and Bladel make up an important part of the patrimonium of Postel in the High and Late Middle Ages (see the map bijlage 3 to: Verhoeven/Theuws 1988). According to Welvaarts (1878-79, II-149) Postel also possessed a windmill at Hulsel. I have, however, not found any indications for this in the written evidence.

stuivers; eggs: 200, and 42 guilders.[87] The farm is also mentioned in the register of rents of Saint-Trond.[88] As has been said, a relatively large rent had to be paid to Saint-Trond.

The location of the farm in the south of the parish can be deduced from a description of the extent of a farm in the nearby parish of Reusel.[89] It concerns the farm *ten Eyndhoven* or the *Eindhoeve,* which is situated north of the road from Bladel to Reusel in the north-eastern part of the parish. That part borders Hulsel and Bladel.[90] The farm *Eyndhoven* is also situated next to other farms in Reusel and Bladel. So, it can be concluded that the farm *Nertingen* in Hulsel forms part of a larger complex of farms of Postel in the parishes Hulsel, Bladel and Reusel, and which are situated between the centres of these parishes. It concerns the farms *Nygem* or *Niddegem* (Bladel);[91] *Loven, Eyndhoven* and *Nieuwenhuisen* (Reusel) and finally *Nertingen* (Hulsel).

At what time *Nertingen* came into the hands of the canons at Postel is not known, but it can be expected that they obtained it somewhere in the 13th century. Maas suggests that Postel did not enlarge its patrimonium at Bladel to a considerable extent anymore after ca. 1300.[92] The same may apply for the Kempen region in general. Postel probably lost control over the farm quite soon after 1648 when the northern part of the duchy of Brabant came to be separated from the rest (in which Postel was situated) and was placed under the control of the *Staten-Generaal* of the new republic of the Seven Provinces (the separated part of Brabant was not one of them). In the northern part of Brabant almost all possessions of Roman Catholic institutions were confiscated (except those of foreign institutions like Echternach) and were administered by government stewards. One of the first will have been the above-mentioned Abraham Tempelaers. In the course of time many farms were sold and after being an ecclesiastical holding for several centuries they fell into private hands.[93] This must also have been the fate of the farm *Nertingen* for in 1830 three families lived on the estate. These families were partly related. It concerned those of Jan van der Heyden, Christiaan van der Heyden and the widow of Jan Koolen.[94] Jan and Christiaan van der Heyden were brothers and sons of Cornelis van de Heyden and Catharina Koolen who had at least three more dougthers.[95] So the properties of Jan and Christiaan were once united. This points to a situation in which Cornelis van der Heyden obtained the entire farm or a large part of it in

---

[85] For a short description of the archives see: Van Hoof 1978. A shadow archive on microfilm is provided for, which rests in the State Archive at 's-Hertogenbosch and the State Archive at Antwerp (Belgium) and partly in the Regional Archive (Streekarchief) at Eindhoven. The unpublished thesis of Hermans has not been used.

[86] Abbey archives Postel, dossier Bladel III (154).

[87] Abbey archives Postel, dossier Bladel III (154).

[88] See section 7.2.

[89] Abbey archives Postel, dossier Reusel, uninventarised. The date of the document is not known, probably 16th century.

[90] The description reads as follows: '*van daer coemende oestwaert aen eenen bempt den goidtshuyse toecommende die wordt gebruyckt met de hoeve genaempt Nertingen, gaende van daer oestwaert neffens diversche bempden (...), van daer noertwaert voerbij die voerschreven bempden totter heyden Postels erffenisse onder die hoeve Nygem* (onder Bladel), *van daer*

keerende oestwaert neffens diversche velden coemende voerbij het Weybroeck Postels erff onder die hoeve van den Nyeuwenhuyse, coemende zuytwaert aen den Reusels wech coemende van Bladel (...). Higher up in the document it appears that the farm *Eyndhoven* also borders the farm *Loven,* also a possession of Postel: *van daer keerende westwaert neffens den gemeynen wech tot noertwaert aen de hoeve ten Loeven, van daer gaende beneffens den Coolhoff een bochtken daerop staet den backboer van de voerschreven hoeve ten Loven.*

[91] For the farms in Bladel see: Roymans 1979; Maas 1988.

[92] Maas 1988, 59.

[93] The farms of Postel at Bladel were already sold to private persons before 1747, Welvaarts 1890, 102-104.

[94] Municipal archives Hooge- and Lage Mierde and Hulsel: Cadastral archive, Kadastrale legger.

[95] Municipal archives Hooge- and Lage Mierde and Hulsel, Cohier van Verpondingen 1777.

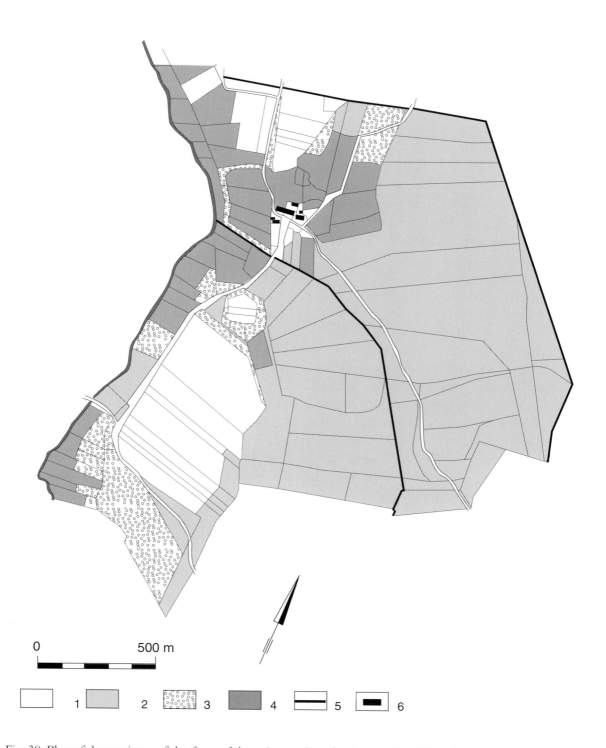

Fig. 39. Plan of the territory of the farm of the priory at Postel in the parish of Hulsel.
1 arable fields; 2 heather fields; 3 woods and trees; 4 brook valleys/hay fields; 5 field boundaries indicating the extent of the farm lands in two successive phases; 6 buildings in 1830

the middle or the second half of the 18th century, most probably directly from the state.[96] These three owners also have more or less one third of what might be the original site of the farmstead (see below). Thus the situation in 1830 described in the cadastral archives makes it possible to reconstruct the extent of the farm lands. One only needs to map the properties of the families mentioned above. It is now also possible to reconstruct the agricultural structure of the farm and to draw some conclusions regarding its topographical development.

9.2 THE TOPOGRAPHY OF THE FARM AND ITS AGRICULTURAL STRUCTURE

In fig. 40 the possessions of the three inhabitants living on the former farm of Postel are mapped. These properties are packed together in the southern part of the parish, and it is clear from the location of the individual fields that there has been a division of a larger whole. There are, however, a number of fields in the hands of other persons living in the village of Hulsel. Most of them belong to Adriaan Linkels. He could have been married to one of the doughters of Cornelis van de Heyden as well as the other men having fields in that part of the parish. That Adriaan Linkels (or rather his wife) also had a part in a division of fields can be deduced from the location of some of them. It appears now that the fields of these owners form an almost closed whole.

In the east this whole is bordered by a field boundary that runs in a more or less straight line from south to north over a distance of almost 600 metres. The northern end touches a similar east-west oriented boundary that runs in a straight line between various fields (compare fig. 40 with fig. 6). These boundaries are probably those of the farm of Postel since the Late Middle Ages or early modern times. To the west the farm lands reach as far as the Raamloop and to the south a boundary runs across the fields that is at the same time the parish boundary. Across the boundary lies the farm *Nygem* or *Niddegem*. A closer inspection of the field boundaries within the farm complex reveals that some of them run along a relatively large distance between the fields. They are more or less a reflection of the above described east and north boundaries (on fig. 40 they are indicated by a thick line). The territory of *Nertingen* has probably been enlarged once in a northern and eastern direction. The thick line thus probably indicates the maximum extent of the original farm. It is unfortunately not possible to determine the date of the enlargement. Together with the enlargement the farm itself will have been moved in a northern direction to the site of the three farms in 1830. They are then at a distance of c. 300 metres of the arable lands (de *Bus*) and there is no good explanation for the 'gap' between them. Immediately north of the large arable field is a small field entirely encircled by a broad bank planted with oak trees that is equally divided between three owners for which there is at first sight no specific reason. This field may, however, be the site of the medieval farm. The field, as well as a large part of the banks, is still present in the landscape and should be preserved as an important historical element in the landscape.

In 1830 the lands of the former farm were in use as arable, meadows, woodland, and heather (fig. 39). The main arable field is situated in the south (de *Bus*) and forms one large block. This is the original arable field of the farm. In the 'extension' some arable land is situated to the south of the *Arting*. The *Bus* is c. 8 ha. according to the land registry of 1830. The heather fields in the first phase are 13 ha, in the second phase c. 41.5 ha. The surface of the meadows is small in the first phase: c. 4 ha., in the second phase it is c. 9.3 ha. The farm *Nertingen* can be classified as a medium large farm. Large farms like the

---

96 Documents concerning this transaction could, however, not be found up to now.

0   500 m

| | 1 | | 2 | | 3 | | 4 | | 5 |

Fig. 40. Hulsel: the distribution of properties in 1830 of the land-owners occupying the former farm of the monastery at Postel.
1 field boundaries indicating the eastern and northern extent of the farmland in two successive phases; 2 the property of the widow of Jan Koolen; 3 the property of the widow of Christiaan van der Heyden; 4 the property of
Jan van der Heyden; 5 the property of Adriaan Linkels

one of Tongerlo at Hoogeloon have c. 16 ha. of arable land, small farms only 4 to 5 ha.[97] The 'extension' of the farm lands mainly concern heather fields and meadows. The heather fields were probably part of the common fields of Hulsel and may have been sold to Postel in order to raise money for the community.[98] The extension of the farm was clearly carried out in order to increase and/or secure the grazing and hayfields of the farm. The keeping of livestock (i.e. sheep) must have played an important role in the farm economy at that time. The extension may have taken place in the 14th century when sheep-keeping became more and more important in the Kempen region.

9.3   ARCHAEOLOGICAL FINDS NEAR NERTINGEN

At the site of the arable fields of the farm, finds from the Roman and Carolingian periods have been collected.[99] The finds from the Carolingian period consist only of a few sherds of cooking pots.[100] But since surface finds of Carolingian pottery are rare in the Kempen region, some importance may be attached to a few sherds. They can indicate habitation in Carolingian times in the immediate vicinity or on the site. Probably an isolated farmstead of the 'Geldrop-Hagelven'-type is located here.[101] There are, however no finds that indicate any continuity between this settlement and the farm *Nertingen*. It cannot be ruled out that there were isolated farms in that area both in the Carolingian period and the 12th century. Isolated farms like *Nertingen* seem to be new reclamations of the 12th and 13th centuries.[102] There are some indications on other sites in the Kempen region (notably at Bladel-*Heeleindse akker* and *Hooibergse akkers*) that some of these reclamations were situated at places where already in the 8th and 9th centuries farms were laid out, which were subsequently abandoned again sometime in the late 9th or 10th centuries. Such a development may have taken place at *Nertingen* too.

10   MEDIEVAL SETTLEMENT PATTERNS AND THE SETTLE-MENT SYSTEM

In order to reconstruct the early- and high-medieval settlement pattern a number of premisses must be accepted. First, the abbey of Saint-Trond founded the church. Second, the abbey did this in or near its *curia*. Third, the rents paid to the abbey provide an impression of the spatial extent of the influence of the demesne.

---

[97]   Van der Zee 1989; Kappelhof 1984, 92-93.

[98]   The selling of communal ground for this purpose is a normal practice in late-medieval and modern times, see: Leenders, 1987.

[99]   The finds are kept in various collections. Most of the Roman finds are at the Archaeological Institute of the Free University at Amsterdam. A number of finds is scattered over private collections. Some of the Carolingian finds are in the collection of K. Bazelmans (Bladel), which is now in the Eicha Museum at Bergeyk.

[100]   Roymans (1979, 22) mentions two wall-fragments of cooking pots of the type Dorestad W III (Van Es en Verwers 1980, 81-87). In the collection of K. Bazelmans

(Eicha-museum Bergeyk) are two rim-fragments of the same type of cooking pots.

[101]   Theuws 1991, 375.

[102]   Several of them have now been excavated in the province of North-Brabant at Bladel-'Kriekeschoor' (Van Dierendonck 1989); Sint-Oedenrode-'Houthem' (Heesters 1976); Sint-Oedenrode-'Cathelijne' (unpublished); Geldrop-'t Zand (Beex 1990). Similar reclamation farms at short distances from each other have been excavated at Sint-Oedenrode-'Everse Akkers' (Heesters 1973, Kortlang 1987) and Someren (Roymans/Kortlang 1993). For a recent overview on these settlements see Verhoeven/Vreenegoor 1991.

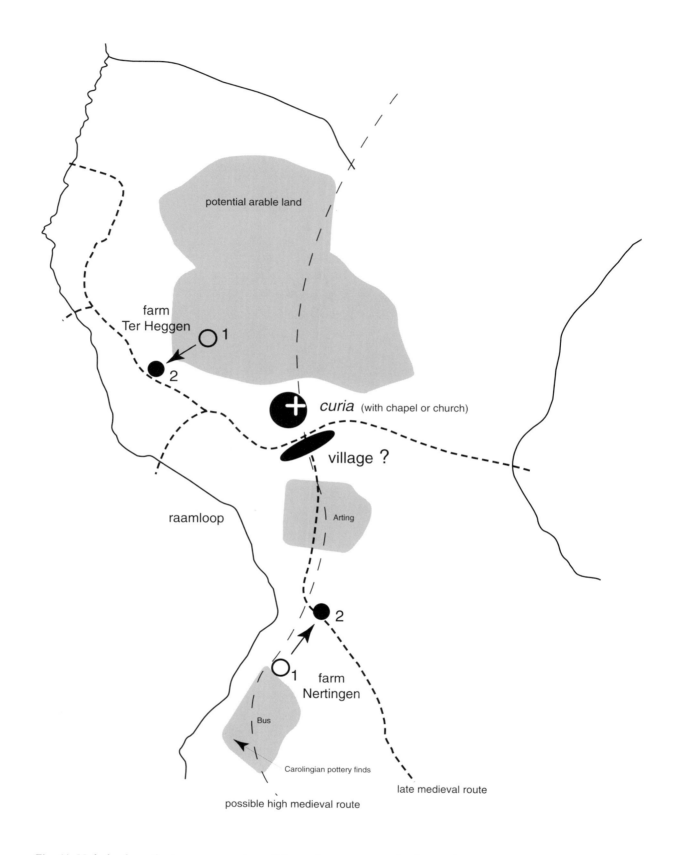

Fig. 41. Hulsel: a hypothetic reconstruction of the settlement pattern in the High Middle Ages.
1 possible high-medieval location; 2 late-medieval location

Based on these premisses, we can conclude that we have excavated a part of the centre of this *curia*, the fields of which (at least in high-medieval times) were situated to the north and south of it. As we have seen, this curia developed out of an early-medieval settlement, probably a part of a villa that, like others, came into being in late-Merovingian or early-Carolingian times (8th century).[103] By that time, habitation in the region had already been present for 100 years, as is indicated by the presence of the Merovingian cemeteries, which were already out of use when this settlement was probably founded.[104] The same holds true for the settlements at Dommelen, Bladel and Geldrop.[105] These settlements were qualified as 'local centres of the Dommelen type'. Most of them (like Geldrop and Dommelen) are secondary centres in a larger estate. Some may have been centres of the estate as a whole (Bladel). It is expected that these local centres were created on coversand plateaus where already Merovingian habitation was present and that they are the result of a reorganisation of landed property at the end of the 7th and 8th centuries. However, it cannot be excluded that a number of these settlements form the earliest medieval habitation at the plateaus. In that case they represent a new reclamation of the plateau.

In a section above we concluded that the *Hulislaum* of 710 is probably not to be identified with Hulsel near Bladel, but with Hulsel near Poppel in Belgium. So, the evidence in the charter cannot be used to demonstrate the presence of habitation at Hulsel near Bladel already at the end of the 7th and beginning of the 8th centuries.

On the basis of the evidence we have it is not possible to reconstruct in detail the development of the medieval settlement pattern and settlement system in the parish of Hulsel. Some ideas may, however, be put forward on this subject.

We do not know whether a settlement existed older than the one that was excavated, comtemporary with the Merovingian cemeteries. If so, it could be located in the *Arting* or perhaps in the relative fertile area in the northern part of the parish (*Kanten, Grote akkers*). The agricultural system of the Merovingian period on the sandy soils of the southern Netherlands and northern Belgium is hardly known. Probably agriculture in Merovingian times was not very intensive.

The exact location of a older Merovingian settlement can of course only be guessed at. What happened to such a settlement is unknown, but it will have gone out of use, as did the cemeteries, when the partly excavated settlement came into being.[106]

In view of the later evidence, indicating that Hulsel formed part of a larger estate of Saint-Trond, including Hooge- and Lage Mierde, it is most likely that the excavated settlement was created as a dependent settlement of a *villa*-centre at Hooge- or Lage Mierde. The peripheral position of Hulsel within the larger parish may point to such a development. That it became a *curia* later may have been the result of a loss of power by the abbey in the estate centre, so that it retreated to a peripheral settlement.

The formation of *villae* in the late 7th or early 8th century may have involved a process of increasing concentration of the local inhabitants (if Merovingian habitation was present). Later, new fields would have come under pasturage and cultivation as the number of *mansi* increased in the Carolingian period, a development that has been noted elsewhere in the Kempen region. We do not know at this stage of the research what a *mansus* exactly is and what it looked like in the field. The *mansi* (if they are to be considered as farmsteads) may have been scattered inthe fields. The few Carolingian pottery sherds found at the arable fields of the 'Bus' may indicate the presence of a Carolingian farmstead. There need

[103] Theuws 1991.

[104] Verwers 1987. See also Theuws 1988, 50-76 and Theuws 1991, 362-365.

[105] Theuws 1988, 225-250 (Dommelen) and 275-281

(Bladel); Theuws 1991 365-375, Theuws 1993 (Geldrop).

[106] Theuws 1991, 383-391.

not necessarily be continuity of habitation on that site from Carolingian times up to the Late Middle Ages, but the presence of a farmstead there may explain why a large rent had to be paid from the farm of Postel to Saint-Trond. It may have been old territory of the *villa* and *curia*, left fallow and reclaimed again in the 12th(?) century. Similar settlements elsewhere in the Kempen region seem to be abandoned in the late 9th and 10th centuries.[107] It is unlikely that the farm *Nertingen* developed directly out of such a Carolingian settlement, since this type of farm seems to date to the High Middle Ages. The name of the postulated Carolingian settlement, after it was abandoned, may have been used to refer to the area and was subsequently transferred to the new farm, creating the impression that the latter is very old. A similar development can explain why those high-medieval farms sometimes have early medieval -*heem* names like the nearby farm *Nygem* or *Niddegem.*

Nothing can be said about the division of the fields of the *villa* into different parts (*terra indominicata* vs. the fields of *mansi*). The problem of early medieval *villa*-formation and the transformations in the social organisation of the agricultural production in the Kempen region is, however, one of the research goals of the South Netherlands project.[108]

As the results of the excavation suggest, there was probably a temporary setback in agricultural activities in the 10th and 11th centuries, although local conditions may also have determined the changes in the topography of the settlement. It cannot be excluded that the settlement as a whole was lost in the 10th century, although we expect that there was continuity of habitation as in the other settlements of this type. A comparable development has been observed at Dommelen in the 10th century. Parts of the area under cultivation were probably left fallow and some *mansi* may have been lost.

The *curia* of Saint-Trond developed out of the Carolingian *villa* or part of a *villa* (fig. 41). This development was marked by an increase in agricultural activities, from the first quarter of the 12th century onwards. The old, lost fields were probably the first to be taken into cultivation again. The agricultural expansion may have been initiated and controlled by the abbey and other (elite) persons as well. At the same time a demographic expansion will have taken place. Then, as the archaeological evidence also suggests, the centre of the *curia* disappeared in the late 12th or early 13th century, probably following a loss of influence on the local level by the abbey at Saint-Trond. The chronicle of the abbey is full of accounts about the illegal activities of local stewards, who usurped the judicial and administrative rights as well as the lands and income of the abbey.[109] At Hulsel local stewards retained for themselves the rents and tithes paid. Some of these stewards were able to build up strong local positions in the Kempen region in the 11th and 12th centuries.[110] In the 12th- or 13th-centuries charters they often appear as the local seigneurs. At the same time that the abbey's rights were being diminished, the agrarian-economic system was developing towards a market-oriented economy. As a consequence, abbeys with large, scattered demesnes were forced, mainly in the 13th century, to lease their agricultural properties. The records of abbot Willem of Rijkel illustrate this change very well. These developments took place at the time when the duke of Brabant tried to bring the Kempen region within his sphere of influence, an attempt hampered by the strong positions that foreign abbeys and local elites had in the region. The loss of the influence that the great abbeys had on the local level in the 13th century may also have been the result of the duke's soliciting the loyalty of a part of the local elite (who were often the stewards on the abbey's demesnes), for instance, by raising their status through incorporation in the nobility in order to organize activities against the foreign abbeys. Later, the power of these local elites had to be broken too.

---

[107] There may be an exception at Eindhoven-'Blixembosch' (Arts 1993).

[108] See Theuws 1989, 288-285 and 299-316; Theuws 1991.

[109] Bijsterveld 1989, 16-24.

[110] Theuws 1989; Bijsterveld 1988; Bijsterveld 1989b.

These developments would certainly have had an impact on the settlement system at Hulsel. The old demesne of Saint-Trond may have started to fall apart in the 12th century. Two alternative lines of development could have taken place. First, the abbey could have saved a part of the old *curia* in the 13th century by reorganizing it as two farms to be leased, one of which came into the hands of Postel later. Second, and more likely, the abbey may have had to accept that an important lay man (maybe even its own steward) reclaimed a part of an area that nominally belonged to the *curia*, considered it as an allodial good, and paid a (token) rent as a recognition of the abbey's old rights.[111] Later, this lay man probably handed over the farm (*Nertingen*) to the monastery at Postel. The isolated position of the arable fields of the farm *Nertingen* point to a new reclamation in the High Middle Ages. The farmstead itself will have been located on the round plot near the arable fields (location 1 in fig. 41). This farm, then, existed side by side with the old *curia* near the church and another farm (*Ter Heggen*) that would also be of high-medieval date and located somewhere in the fields to the northeast of it. A large part of the lands of the *curia* came into the hands of the villagers who had to pay a rent for the possession of it. Moreover, in 1280, Gozewijn Kenode (and before him Godfried of Loven) possessed lands that once belonged to the *curia* of Saint-Trond, which also indicates that the *curia* had already, or was in the process of falling apart. The manor was probably not functioning as a centre of agrarian production anymore in 1280, which is in accordance with the archaeological evidence. Nothing remained of the *curia* other than a small administrative unit necessary to guarantee the collection of the rents through time. In modern times the collection of the rents and tithes was often leased and the rents probably had to be paid in a local inn. The judicial rights the abbey once had fell into the hands of the duke of Brabant, and sometime in the Late Middle Ages a local aldermans court (*schepenbank*) was formed, primarily for settling civil cases in Hooge- and Lage Mierde and Hulsel.

The settlement which we excavated to the north of the church may have been the centre of the *curia* of Saint-Trond, which was abandoned after the loss of the central agrarian, judicial, and administrative functions it had in the parish. The chapel attached to it remained and stayed in the hands of Saint-Trond, but came to stand in an isolated position. Such a development is identical to that in Dommelen. It is not known when the village to the south of the major road and the hamlets were formed, but it is expected that they all came into being in the later Middle Ages (from the 13th century onwards) after a moving of the 12th-century settlements from the high grounds to the edges of the stream valleys where they further developed into small hamlets in late-medieval and early modern times. Hamlets like Vooreind may even be of post-medieval date (fig. 6). Nor is much known about the relations between the (dependent) villagers and the abbey or its stewards in the *curia*. Further research in the Kempen region should concentrate on these problems by trying to excavate the settlements of the dependent farmers that were inhabited during the Early and High Middle Ages.

Finally, to come back to archaeology, some remarks should be made on the characteristics of the excavated settlement in relation to its postulated position in the settlement system. This position could only be determined on the basis of the presence of a chapel and its location within the parish. The excavated elements do not permit an identification of the settlement as a central place on the local level. For an archaeologist this is rather disappointing. One would expect larger farmsteads and larger barns in these kind of settlements compared to those of others. However, the farmhouse of the 12th century is not basically larger than that of other types of settlement, like the isolated farmsteads. Nor do the finds indicate a special status of the settlement, in fact they are rather poor. However, it is suggested that we did not excavate the central part of the settlement. The farmstead we excavated may have been a dependent farm that was, with others, situated around a main farm.

---

[111]   On such a development and allodial goods: Bijsterveld   1989, 29-30.

ACKNOWLEDGEMENTS

We are grateful to the following institutions and persons for their support of the excavations and the subsequent research: H. Jacobs in Hulsel and L. Verspaandonk in Reusel, who kindly permitted us to excavate in their fields; the municipal authorities of Hooge- en Lage Mierde and Hulsel (now municipality Reusel-De Mierden), who gave us permission to investigate their part of the site and gave other support in the field and gave access to their archives; the province of North Brabant and the University of Amsterdam who financed the investigation; W. Wimmers and R. Proos who were in charge of the excavation as part of their field training and made first evaluations of the uncovered remains; the many persons both students of archaeology and volunteers who assisted in the field; A. Verhoeven and H.A. Heidinga who read earlier versions of this paper and S. Loving who corrected the English of a first draft and Christine Jefferis who corrected the final version. Holger Schoorl assisted in preparing the layout of this article. This article was written with support of the Netherlands Organisation for Scientific research (NWO).

Appendix 1

(Places in fig. 4)

1	Escharen
2	Escharen
3	Haps
4	Venray-Sint Anthoniusveld
5	Grubbenvorst-Lottum
6	Blerick-Anthoniuslaan
7	Sittart-Haagsittart
8	Nederweert
9	Someren-Waterdael
10	Someren-Witvrouwenbergweg
11	Beek en Donk-Oude toren
12	Veghel-Scheffelaar
13	Sint-Oedenrode-Everse akkers
14	Sint-Oedenrode-Veghelseweg
15	Sint-Oedenrode-Cathelijnepad
16	Sint-Oedenrode-Houthem
17	Eindhoven-Blixembosch
18	Geldrop-'t Zand (site D)
19	Geldrop-Hagelven (sites A en B)
20	Geldrop-Kerkhof (site C)
21	Budel-dorp
22	Dommelen-Kerkakkers
23	Bergeyk-Bucht
24	Bergeyk-Eerselsedijk
25	Veldhoven
26	Veldhoven
27	Bladel-Kriekeschoor
28	Bladel-dorp
29	Hulsel
30	Moergestel
31	Goirle-Grote akkers
32	Goirle
33	Wijnegem (B.)
34	Lieshout-Nieuwenhof
35	Voerendaal
36	Weert-Laarderweg
37	Bergeyk-Ploeg
38	Gennep-Maaskemp
39	Blerick-Zaarderheiken
40	Blerick-Laurentiusstraat
41	Bergeyk-dorp
42	Neerharen-Rekem (B.)
43	Donk (B.)
44	Oerle-dorp
45	Oss-Ussen
46	Beers-Gassel
47	Reusel-dorp
48	Aalst-dorp
49	Hasselt (B.)
50	Oud-Turnhout

Appendix 2

1	Total length of the building
2	Largest width of the building
3	Length of the core of the building
4	Average width of the nucleus of the building
5	Largest width of a truss
6	Smallest width of a truss
7	Largest distance between two trusses
8	Smallest distance between two trusses
9	Average width of the bays
10	Distance between the two posts in the short west or north wall
11	Distance between the two posts in the short east or south wall
12	Largest width of the aisle on the north or west side
13	Largest width of the aisle on the south or east side
14	Width of the shorth wall on the west or north side
15	Width of the short wall on the east or south side
16	Average depth of the postholes of the core of the building below excavation level
17	Average diameter or length of a posthole of the core of the building

18	Average height of the excavation level in metres above Normaal Amsterdams Peil
19	Does the excavation level slope down?
20	Orientation of the building
21	Number of aisles including the central one
22	Number of trusses
23	Average thickness of the posts
24	Form of the posts (round or square)
25	Posts in a straight or bent/curved line?
26	Wallposts present?
27	Post M and N present?
28	Post P present?
29	Hearth present?
30	Posts in the short west or north side in one or two pits?
31	Posts in the short east or south side in one or two pits?
32	Other pits in the groundplan that are not part of the construction?
33	Floorspace in square metres of the core of the building
34	Floorspace in square metres of the entire building
35	Date

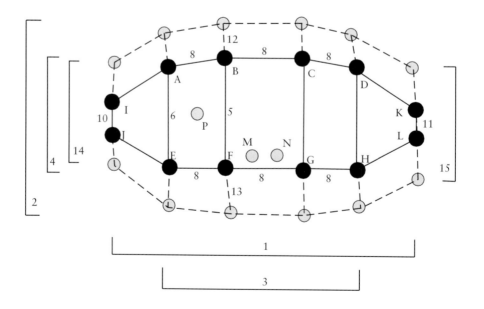

UNPUBLISHED HISTORICAL SOURCES

Municipal Archive Hooge- and Lage Mierde and Hulsel
Cadasteral archive: *Oorspronkelijk Aanwijzende Tafel* 1830
Kadastrale legger van grondeigenaren 1830
Cohier van Nieuwe erven 1801–1803
Cohier van verpondingen 1777

State Archive in North Brabant, 's-Hertogenbosch
Archive of the *Raad en Rentmeester Generaal* no. 208, Registre of rents in Hulsel 1646–1650
Archive of the *Commissie of Breda* no. 760
Documents concerning the leasing of the tithes of Saint-Trond in Hulsel Notary Archive (Hooge- and
Lage Mierde and Hulsel)
Notary J. F. Hoosemans no. 4409 *Minuutakten* nos. 4412–4425 *Minuutakten* 1817–20 december 1832
Aldermens rolls Hooge- and Lage Mierde and Hulsel. Several registers since 1770

State Archive in Limburg, Hasselt (Belgium)
Archive of the abbey of Saint Trond no. 6726 (1646), Fol. 309r–309v
Register of rents in Oerle Fol. 312r–314r
Register of rents in Vessem en Knegsel Fol. 316r–320r
Register of rents in Hulsel

Abbey Archive Postel (shadow-archive in the State Archive 's-Hertogenbosch)
Dossiers Reusel
Dossiers Bladel

PUBLISHED MEDIEVAL SOURCES

Bannenberg, G., e. a. (eds), 1968-1970: *De oude dekenaten Cuyk, Woensel en Hilvarenbeek in de 15de en 16de eeuwse registers van het aartsdekenaat Kempenland*, Nijmegen.

Borman, C. de (ed.), 1875: *Chronique de l'abbaye de Saint Trond*, Liège.

Camps, H.P.H. (ed.), 1979: *Oorkondenboek van Noord-Brabant tot 1312 I. De meierij van 's-Hertogenbosch (met de heerlijkheid Gemert)*, 's-Hertogenbosch.

Enklaar, D. Th. (ed.), 1941: *Gemeene gronden in Noord Brabant in de middeleeuwen*, Utrecht.

Koch, A.C.F., 1970 (ed.), 1970: *Oorkondenboek van Holland en Zeeland tot 1229. I Eind van de 7e eeuw tot 1222*, 's-Gravenhage.

Pirenne, H. (ed.), 1896: *Le livre de l'abbé Guillaume de Ryckel (1249-1272). Polyptique et comptes de l'abbaye de Saint Trond au milieu du XIIIe siècle*, Bruxelles.

Wampach, C., 1929/1930: *Geschichte der Grundherrschaft Echternach im Frühmittelalter. Untersuchungen über die Person des Grunders, über die Kloster- und Wirtschaftgeschichte auf Grund des Liber Aureus Epternacensis (698-1222)*, I1 and I2, Luxemburg.

REFERENCES

Arts, N., 1993: Middeleeuwse hoeven op Blixembosch bij Eindhoven, in N. Roymans/F. Theuws (eds), 1993: *Een en al Zand. Twee jaar graven naar het Brabantse verleden*, 's-Hertogenbosch, 106-115.

Acker, J. van, 1986: De Echternachteksten en Oud-Antwerpen, *Bijdragen tot de Geschiedenis* 69, 147-169.

Beex, W., 1990: Ontginningen in een feodale wereld, in J. Bazelmans/F. Theuws (eds) 1990: *Tussen zes gehuchten. De laat-Romeinse en middeleeuwse bewoning van Geldrop-'t Zand*, Amsterdam (Studies in Prae en Protohistorie 5).

Bijsterveld, A.J.A, 1989a: Een zorgelijk bezit. De benedictijnenabdijen van Echternach en Sint Truiden en het beheer van hun goederen en rechten in Oost-Brabant, 1100-1300, *Noordbrabants Historisch Jaarboek* 6, 7-44.

Bijsterveld, A.-J., 1989b: Het domein van de abdij van Echternach in Waalre en Valkenswaard; ontwikkeling en beheer ca. 1100-1400; in A. Verhoeven/F. Theuws (eds) 1989: *Het Kempenprojekt 3. De middeleeuwen centraal*, Waalre, (Bijdragen tot de studie van het Brabantse heem 33), 57-96.

Bijsterveld, A.J., 1990/1991: Alphen van Echternachs domein tot Bredase heerlijkheid, 1175-1312, I en II, *Jaarboek van de Geschied en Oudheidkundige kring van Stad en Land van Breda 'De Oranjeboom'* 43, 77-111; 44, 110-148.

Bijsterveld, A.J.A., 1993: *Laverend tussen Kerk en wereld. De pastoors in Noord-Brabant 1400-1570*, Amsterdam.

Bisschops, J.H./J.P. Broertjes/W. Dobma, 1985: *Toelichtingen bij de Geologische Kaart van Nederland, 1:50.000. Blad Eindhoven west (51W)*, Haarlem.

Borremans, R./R. Warginaire, 1966: *La ceramique d'Andenne. Recherches de 1956-1965*, Rotterdam.

Bruijn, A., 1962-1963: Die mittelalterliche keramische Industrie in Südlimburg, *BROB* 12-13, 357-459.

Bruijn, A., 1968: Zur Zeitbestimmung mittelalterlicher bemahlter Keramik, *Chateau Gaillard* 4, 45-47.

Dierendonck, R. van, 1989: Archeologie en historie van een ontginningshoeve: de Kriekeschoor bij Bladel, in A. Verhoeven/F. Theuws (eds), 1989: *Het Kempenprojekt 3. De middeleeuwen centraal*, Waalre (Bijdragen tot de studie van het Brabantse heem 33), 15-25.

Es, W.A. van/W.J.H. Verwers, 1980: *Excavations at Dorestad 1. The Harbour: Hoogstraat 1*, Amersfoort.

Ganshof, F.L., 1954: Grondbezit en gronduitbating tijdens de vroege middeleeuwen in het noorden van het Frankische rijk en meer bepaald in Toxandrië, *Brabants Heem* 6, 3-19.

Glasbergen, W., 1955: *Het rijengrafveld te Broekeneind bij Hoogeloon (N.Br.)*, Eindhoven (Bijdragen tot de studie van het Brabantse heem 6).

Gysseling, M., 1960: *Toponymisch woordenboek van België, Nederland, Luxemburg, Noord-Frankrijk en West-Duitsland (vóór 1226)*, Brussel.

Heesters, W., 1973: Uit de voorgeschiedenis van een Brabants dorp, *Brabants Heem* 19, 125-149.

Heesters, W., 1976: Archeologische sprokkelingen nr. 7; een zaalhuis in Olland, *Brabants Heem* 19, 66-68.

Heidinga, H.A., 1987: *Medieval Settlement and Economy North of the Lower Rhine. Archeology and history of Kootwijk and the Veluwe (the Netherlands)*, Assen/Maastricht.

Hendrikx, P.A., 1986: The lower delta of the Rhine and the Maas: Landscape and habitation from the Roman period to c. 1000, *BROB* 36, 445-599.

Hermans, J., 1992-1993: Abbaye de Postel à Mol, in U. Berlière e.a. (eds), *Monasticon belge, Tome VIII. Province d'Anvers*, Liège, 171-193.

Hoof, F. van, 1978: Het archief van de abdij van Postel, *Archief- en bibliotheekwezen in België* 49, 453-468.

Hvass, S., 1986: Vorbasse- Eine Dorfsiedlung während des 1. Jahrtausends n. Chr. in Mitteljutland, Dänemark, *Bericht der Römisch-Germanische Kommission* 67, 529-542.

Kesters, H., 1979: St. Truiden-Woensel, in W.H.A. Renders (ed), *Bijdragen tot de geschiedenis van Woensel*, Eindhoven, 19-33.

Kortlang, F., 1987: *Landschapsonderzoek. Archeologie. De Dommelvallei, een archeologische inventarisatie I en II*, 's-Hertogenbosch.

Laarhoven, J. van (ed.), 1975: *Het schetsenboek van Hendrik Verhees*, Den Bosch.

Lauwerijs, E., 1981/82: Un depotoir du XIIe siècle à Namur, *Bulletin du Cercle Archéologique Hesbaye-Condroz* 17, 195-202.

Lauwerijs E./G. Petit, 1967: Un atelier de potiers au Moyen Age, *Bulletin du Cercle Archéologique Hesbaye-Condroz* 7, 11-29.

Leenders, K.A.H.W., 1987: Van gemeynten en vroonten, *De Oranjeboom* 40, 44-78.

Loon, J. van, 1980: Actum publice in loco Bettinum Cale (703/4 en 710). Een nieuw onderzoek naar de oudste oorkonden betreffende zuidelijk Noord-Brabant, *Naamkunde* 12, 57-65.

Lung, W., 1955/56: Die Ausgrabungen nachkarolingischer Töpferöfen in Paffrath, Gem. Bergisch-Gladbach, *Bonner Jahrbücher* 155/56, 355-371.

Maas, A.J.P.M. 1991: Nederzettingsgeschiedenis van de Brabantse zandgronden, in A.-J. Bijsterveld/B. van der Dennen/A. van der Veen (eds): *Middeleeuwen in beweging. Bewoning en samenleving in het middeleeuwse Noord-Brabant*, 's-Hertogenbosch, 44-58.

Pirling, R., 1966: *Das Römisch-Fränkische Gräberfeld von Krefeld-Gellep*, Berlin. (Germanische Denkmäler der Völkerwanderungszeit, serie B 2).

Prims, F., 1935: *De onze-Lieve-Vrouweabdij der Norbertijnen te Postel*. Antwerpen.

Regteren Altena, H.H. van, 1982: De middeleeuwse nederzettingen op de Kerkakkers bij Dommelen, in J. Slofstra, e.a., *Het Kempenprojekt. Een regionaal-archeologisch onderzoeksprogramma*, Waalre (Bijdragen tot de studie van het Brabantse heem, 22), 114-124.

Regteren Altena, H.H. van, 1989: Opgravingen te Dommelen 1982-1984; in A. Verhoeven/F. Theuws (eds), 1989: *Het Kempenprojekt 3. De middeleeuwen centraal*, Waalre (Bijdragen tot de studie van het Brabantse heem, 33), 47-55.

Rombaut, H., 1989: De Echternachteksten betreffende Antwerpen: nieuwe argumenten, *Bijdragen tot de Geschiedenis* 72, 3-26.

Roymans, N., 1979: Op zoek naar Pladella villa, *Varia Historica Brabantica* 8, 1-47.

Roymans, N./F. Kortlang, 1993: Bewoningsgeschiedenis van een dekzandlandschap langs de Aa te Someren, in N. Roymans/F. Theuws (eds), 1993: *Een en al Zand. Twee jaar graven naar het Brabantse verleden*, 's-Hertogenbosch, 23-41.

Roosens, H./J. Gyselinck, 1975: *Een merovingisch grafveld te Beerlegem*, Brussel (Archeologia Belgica, 170).

Slofstra, J., e.a., 1982: *Het Kempenprojekt. Een regionaal-archeologisch onderzoeksprogramma*, Waalre (Bijdragen tot de studie van het Brabantse heem 22).

Slofstra, J., 1983: An antropological approach to the studie of romanization processes, in R. Brandt/J. Slofstra (eds), *Roman and Native in the Low Countries: Speres of Interaction*, Oxford (BAR International series, 184), 71-104.

Theuws, F., 1986: The Integration of the Kempen Region in the Frankish empire (550-750), *Helinium* 26, 121-36.

Theuws, F.C.W.J., 1988: *De archeologie van de periferie. Studies naar de ontwikkeling van bewoning en samenleving in het Maas-Demer-Schelde gebied in de vroege middeleeuwen*, Amsterdam.

Theuws, F., 1989: Middeleeuwse parochiecentra in de Kempen; in A. Verhoeven/F. Theuws (eds), 1989: *Het Kempenprojekt 3. De middeleeuwen centraal*, Waalre (Bijdragen tot de studie van het Brabantse heem 33), 97-216.

Theuws, F., 1993: Heren en boeren in vroeg-middeleeuws Geldrop, in N. Roymans/F. Theuws (eds), 1993: *Een en al Zand. Twee jaar graven naar het Brabantse verleden*, 's-Hertogenbosch, 88-104.

Theuws, F./A.Verhoeven/H.H. van Regteren Altena, 1988: Medieval Settlement at Dommelen, *BROB* 38, 229-430.

Verhoeven, A., 1985: Middeleeuws aardewerk uit Dommelen in een regionaal kader; in J. Slofstra, e.a.(eds) 1985: *Het Kempenprojekt 2. Een regionaal-archeologisch onderzoek in uitvoering*, Waalre (Bijdragen tot de studie van het Brabantse heem 27), 45-49.

Verhoeven, A., 1989: Middeleeuws aardewerk uit Bergeyk; in A.Verhoeven/F. Theuws (eds), 1989: *Het Kempenprojekt 3. De middeleeuwen centraal*, Waalre (Bijdragen tot de studie van het Brabantse heem 33), 217-243.

Verhoeven, A./E.Vreenegoor, 1991: Middeleeuwse nederzettingen op de zandgronden in Noord-Brabant, in A.-J. Bijsterveld/B. van der Dennen/A. van der Veen (eds): *Middeleeuwen in beweging. Bewoning en samenleving in het middeleeuwse Noord-Brabant*, 's-Hertogenbosch, 59-76.

Verwers, W.J.H., 1973: A Merovingian cemetery in Veldhoven, Province of North Brabant, *BROB* 23, 315-335.

Verwers, W.J.H., 1987: North Brabant in Roman and early medieval times 4. The Merovingian cemeteries, *BROB* 37, 173-223.

Waele, E. de/C.-H. Nyns, 1984: La nécropole mérovingienne de Fays à Achene, in *Activités 81 à 83 S.O.S. fouilles* 3, Bruxelles, 71-86.

Welvaerts, Th. Ign., 1878-79: *Geschiedenis van Postel naar haar eigene archieven*, I en II, Turnhout-'s-Hertogenbosch.

Welvaarts, Th. Ign., 1890: *Geschiedenis van Bladel en Netersel naar de archieven van Postels abdij*, Turnhout.

Werner, M., 1980: *Der Lütticher Raum in frühkarolingischer Zeit. Untersuchungen zur Geschichte einer karolingischer Stammlandschaft*, Göttingen.

Willems, J., 1973: *Le quartier artisanal Gallo-Romain et Merovingien de Batta à Huy*, Bruxelles (Archeologia Belgica, 148).

Zee, A. van der, 1989: Die hoeve tot Loen. Een 16de-eeuwse abdijhoeve in Hoogeloon; in A. Verhoeven/F. Theuws (eds), 1989: *Het Kempenprojekt 3. De middeleeuwen centraal*, Waalre (Bijdragen tot de studie van het Brabantse heem 33), 27-48.

Gift exchange, landed property, and eternity. The foundation and endowment of the Premonstratensian priory of Postel (1128/1138-1179)[1]

Arnoud-Jan A. Bijsterveld

> 'And anyone who has left houses, or brothers or sisters, or father or mother, or children, or land for the sake of my name will be repaid many times over, and gain eternal life' (Matthew 19:29)

1   INTRODUCTION

On Thursday August 1, 1140 a big crowd flocked to Postel (fig. 1) from all directions in order to be confirmed in their belief or to receive forgiveness of sins: noblemen, knights, and ordinary people, men and women, adults and children, by horse, on foot, in wagons with a pair or four-in-hand. The crowd was so large that knights and strong men could hardly prevent the over-enthusiastic public from trampling the bishop and the clergymen assisting him. Together with abbot Gerland of Floreffe they had come to the Kempen region to administer the dedication of the monastery church at Postel. The ordaining prelate was Siward, the Premonstratensian bishop of Uppsala in Sweden, who dedicated the church to the Holy Trinity, the Mother of God, and the holy confessor Nicholas. The bishop placed a part of St Agatha' s veil and relics of other holy martyrs, confessors, and virgins in the altar. The people had crowded to witness this and to contribute in the pious zeal. Numerous laymen came

[1] In writing this article I was advised by many, especially by Martien Dillo, Jos Bazelmans, Mayke de Jong, Ilana Friedrich Silber, and Henk Teunis, whom I wish to thank here. This contribution results from papers held at various occasions, such as the lecture series organized by Marco Mostert and Frans Theuws on 'Aristocratic power and ethics in the Middle Ages' at the University of Amsterdam (February 1, 1994), the

Fig. 1. The location of the abbey of Postel in northern Belgium.

forward, promised oblations, made gifts, and made vows on the altar which had only just been dedicated: *In desponsatione sua accesserunt multi dona donantes et vota voventes*.[2] Bishop Siward and the clergy accepted everything and he warranted its peaceful possession by means of his ban.[3]

At this pious dedication ceremony, one of the most powerful rituals known in the Middle Ages took place. The gift-giving ritual was a means of structuring religious, social, and political life. Not only through their presence, but primarily by giving landed property and valuable presents to endow the young monastery of Postel did numerous laymen demonstrate their active involvement in its foundation. They thus expressed their pious aspiration to be bounded to the religious community for ever. By donating money and landed property they entered into an association with the religious community and the holy power it represented. So far Dutch and Belgian historians have disregarded the possibilities of applying anthropological concepts and ideas to the study of gifts made by aristocrats to religious communities in the Low Countries during the Central Middle Ages. Yet, new con-

First International Medieval Congress in Leeds (July 6, 1994), and the Social Science Thursday Luncheon Seminar of the Institute for Advanced Study at Princeton (January 26, 1995). This text was partly written during my stay as a Visiting Scholar in the Department of History of Princeton University (1994-1995), which stay was made possible by a TALENT-stipend from the Netherlands Organization for Scientific Research (NWO) and a grant from the Van Coeverden Adrianistichting. My research project 'Gift exchange as an agent of social integration and political power in the Meuse-Demer-Scheldt area, *circa* 950 – *circa* 1250' is supported by the Foundation for History, Archaeology and Art History, which is subsidized by NWO. For an earlier version of this text see Bijsterveld 1997a.

[2] See for the word *votum*, which means a vow to God, and, more specifically, a votive offering or a sacred gift, Cappon 1995, 265-266 and n. 61.

[3] Camps 1979, 107-114, no. 69, ad datum <1173(?)>. See Hermans 1992-1993, 178; Steurs 1993, 129-131.

cepts on gift exchange and the settlement of disputes have shed new light on the relationship between the aristocracy and monasteries.[4] Inspired by seminal studies by American historians we propose to use anthropological concepts on gift exchange as a key to the analysis of a case from the Low Countries: the foundation and endowment of the Premonstratensian priory of Postel, today situated in Belgium, just south of the Dutch border, in the second and third quarter of the 12th century.

Gift exchange is defined as a series of ceremonial transactions of goods or services to create, to maintain or to restore relations between individuals or groups of people.[5] Reciprocity is an essential element of this exchange. A gift has the capacity to create the aforementioned relations because the initial gift obliges the recipient to return comparable gifts or services in the short or long term. These reciprocal obligations are summarized in the adage *do ut des*, 'I give so that you give'. Applied to a historical case, for example the medieval gift-giving by members of the aristocracy to monasteries, this anthropological concept draws the historian's attention to several aspects he or she might otherwise miss. In the first place it points to the importance of the returns or countergifts. These play a crucial role in the continuation of the relations brought about by gifts. Through the obligation to produce a countergift, the gift exchange is not restricted to one particular moment, but each act of gift giving is an episode in a continuous social relationship. In the historical context discussed here, gifts and countergifts consisted of landed property, money, objects, prayers, services, and human beings (like brides and oblates). A second aspect the anthropological conceptualization of gift exchange brings to light, is that gifts create lasting networks of relations: they act as a means of social integration or as a 'social glue'.[6] By giving landed property to religious communities the secular elite consolidated their reciprocal alliance. In this way gifts considerably contributed to medieval processes of social integration and the building up of power and lordship. The gift of landed property, in particular by aristocrats to religious institutions, thus constituted an important, if not the most important means to direct their often tumultuous and discordant relations into more orderly and more peaceful directions. The ceremonial and public character of gift-giving and its transcendent implications provided the donor with social prestige, which could be transformed into an increase in power. In the third place concepts on gift exchange draw attention to the immaterial aspects, that is the social, ideological, and religious meanings of the gift. In the medieval context the donors' desire for salvation is of course of crucial importance too.

A valuable concept in relation to gift exchange is that of the inalienable possession. Inalienable objects or objects bestowing identity acquire through their origin, value, or history of a person or a group a 'cultural biography' and a distinct 'historical identity'.[7] They symbolize or represent owners, or specific features of them, such as their power and virtues. In a certain sense these objects are even identical with them. Possessing such an object qualifies the holder: he or she derives his or her status and sometimes even his or her power from it. Even after giving such an object away, the donor and his or her associates kept some rights or kept the right to re-claim.[8] Some objects represent the constitutive parts making up a person according to the prevailing ideology, such as his body, his soul, his power or his honour.[9] Therefore, there is a meaningful connection between donor and donated object, involving different values. By donating an object these meanings can be expressed. Examples of

---

[4]   See Bijsterveld 1996. For a theoretical analysis of donations to monasteries in the medieval West see Silber 1995.

[5]   Kloos 1995, 34-36.

[6]   As shown by Rosenwein 1989, 202-207.

[7]   These ideas were formulated by Igor Kopytoff, as summarized by Appadurai 1990.

[8]   Weiner 1992.

[9]   Bazelmans 1996, 57-79, 210-217; Bazelmans 1997.

3 I I

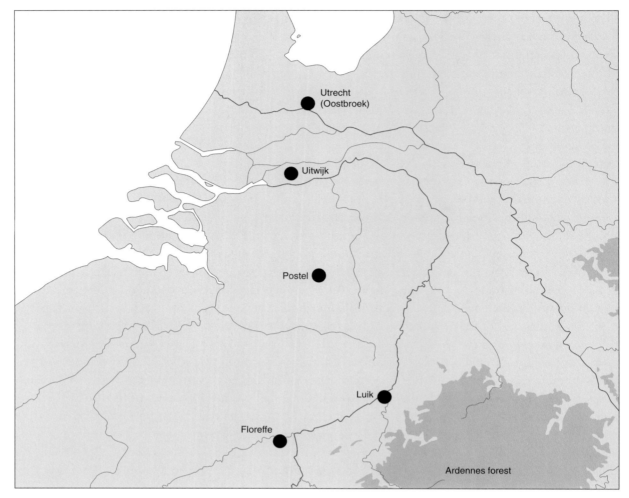

Fig. 2. Important places mentioned in the text.

inalienable possessions relevant to the European Middle Ages are arms, jewellery, monarchs' crowns and other regalia, relics, precious and holy books, objects connected with a princely descent, costly textiles, objects made of precious materials, names, stories and sagas, etcetera.[10] It is important to note that it not the object itself, but its context which makes it inalienable. Landed property can also be included, being the outstanding inalienable possession, as it can not be transferred physically to another person or place. Landed property was the focus of a group's identity, prestige, power, and history. It has the aura of eternity and is therefore, next to gold, the outstanding gift to create lasting relations between people. Landed property often represents the continuity of the group possessing it. In the Middle Ages this group is for instance an aristocratic kin group, which not only associated its identity with land, but also derived its name from this land or from the stronghold built on it. Even in the situation in which individual members held their own pieces of land, the land remained collective family property to some extent. Exclusive, individualized possession of land did not exist. Rather, one

[10] For relics see Geary 1994b; for silver objects Hardt
      1996; for books Palazzo 1997.

should conceptualize a property system which is characterized by joint ownership or ownership in common, based on overlapping claims.[11] When a member of such a group donated a piece of land to a monastery, the rest of the kin group (or at least a part of it) had to consent.[12] But even after the 'property' transfer had taken place, old family claims continued to rest on the land. That is why in the Middle Ages heirs of former owners, sometimes after several generations, often re-claimed land that at some point had belonged to the family patrimony. In judicial procedures the rights of the conflicting parties had to be established; rituals and ceremonies took place to reconcile them. The concepts of the inalienable possession and overlapping claims therefore are useful to understand the frequent disputes concerning gifts of landed property to monasteries.

This case study investigates the foundation and endowment of Postel priory, consisting of the donations made by a number of (mostly) aristocratic people. The difference between foundation and endowment has recently been explained by Christine Sauer: the founder or *fundator* is the donor of the *dos* or *fundus*, the piece of land on which a church or monastery was build.[13] He could claim the rights of the *patronus*, which often included the right of advocacy. The foundation is the initial donation, whereas the endowment consists of the contributions donors or *benefactors* made to create the material base for monastic life. After an analysis of the text informing us about the foundation and endowment of Postel priory, I will outline the foundation's religious and socio-political context. Next, I will try to answer several questions about the reciprocity of these gifts. With what intentions did the lay people in case donate? What did they expect from the conventuals who received their gifts, and what did they receive in return? I will also deal with the intentions and expectations the religious fostered when accepting these donations. What I want to explain is the way in which the socio-political interests and religious intentions of the lay donors on the one hand, and those of the conventuals on the other were brought into concordance through gifts and countergifts.

2   THE TEXT ON THE FOUNDATION AND ENDOWMENT OF POSTEL PRIORY

After Norbert of Gennep (also known as Norbert of Xanten; *circa* 1080-1134) had founded his first community at Prémontré in Northern France in the winter of 1119-1120, his order saw an unprecedented expansion, in, among other places, in what is now Belgium and the Netherlands.[14] Norbert was an active champion of the reformation of the canonical order, which had been going on since the 11th century. An earlier reform movement of regular canons that constituted a source of inspiration for Norbert, influenced the Low Countries too, namely the abbey of Kloosterrade near Aachen, also known as Rolduc, founded in 1104.[15] Norbert aspired to a monastic life and in 1121 he adopted for his order the complete Rule of St Augustine. In their houses the Premonstratensians combined a monastic way of life with that of the priestly and canonical order. They emphasized preaching and the care and cure of souls. Until his death in 1134 Norbert was the central figure in his order. He was intimately involved in the foundation of the first daughter houses of Prémontré and continued to direct them after his appointment as archbishop of Magdeburg in 1126. The first daughter house of

[11] Bouchard 1991, 7, 178-180. See also the debate triggered by Reynolds 1994, 53-74.

[12] On this *laudatio parentum* see White 1988.

[13] Sauer 1993, 21-32.

[14] Weinfurter 1984; Dekker 1984; Weinfurter 1989; Bond 1993; Bijsterveld 1997c.

[15] Gärtner 1991; Deutz 1992.

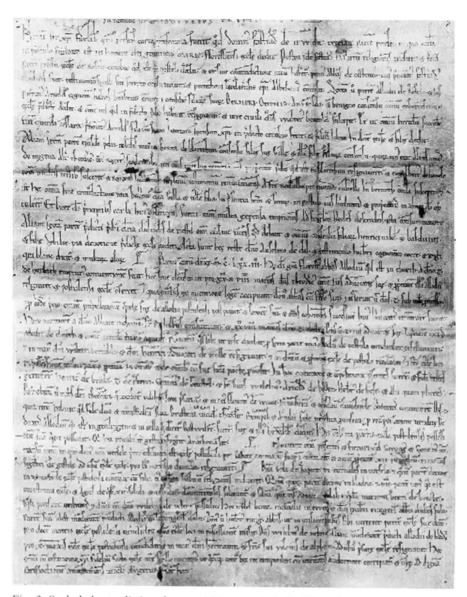

Fig. 3. Sealed charter listing the acquisitions on behalf of Postel priory [1173-1179] (Archive of the abbey of Postel, A *Abdij*, n. 1).

Prémontré was founded at Floreffe, on the river Sambre in the county of Namur in 1121-1122, on property donated by the count and the countess of Namur (fig. 2). The bishop of Liège adhered to the foundation in 1124. In 1128 the abbey received its first papal confirmation.[16] Ten years later, in 1138, the pope reconfirmed the property and privileges of the abbey of Floreffe. This time, among

16 The abbey's foundation took place on November 27, 1121; the first canons arrived on January 25, 1122. See Grauwen 1975, 5-14; Grauwen 1995; and also Kupper 1981, 367-368; Weinfurter 1984, 166-168. The foundation charter of November 27, 1121, ed. in Hugo 1734, I (Probationes), xlix-li; ed. Miraeus/Foppens 1723-1748, IV, 194-195; ed. Rousseau 1936, 8-11, no. 2. The episcopal charter of May 20, 1124, ed. Hugo 1734, I, li-lii; ed. Miraeus/Foppens 1723-1748, IV, 359-360. The papal confirmation of November 4,

the abbey's possessions 'the third part of Postel' is mentioned.[17] Here, at an unknown moment in or before 1140, a Premonstratensian community was founded from Floreffe. The priory of Postel would be elevated to the status of an abbey in 1616.[18] It was abolished by order of the French in 1797 and re-established in 1847.[19] Until about 1270, Postel monastery was a double monastery, housing male canons, lay brothers, and female lay sisters. The last nun at Postel is said to have died in 1317.[20]

The main source for reconstructing the monastery's early history is a charter-like text which was composed between 1173 and 1179 (fig. 3). This text, written at the initiative of Floreffe's canons, lists the possessions and rights which had been acquired for the benefit of the daughter house in Postel since the 1130s. We now have two clearly distinct versions of this text, which entailed diplomatic research with diverging outcomes by different scholars. The first version (henceforth indicated as I) is preserved in the form of a sealed charter as well as a transcript in the 13th-century cartulary of the abbey of Floreffe. The other version (henceforth: II) is only passed down as a transcript in the same cartulary.[21] According to V. Barbier, I is the abbreviated version of II.[22] For Camps the 'very arbitrary' formulary of both texts, the seal, and the script of no. I were suspect and therefore he branded both I and II as forgeries.[23] According to him, the sealed charter I could be 'a simple listing of the acquisitions of Postel until 1173, without any probative value or pretence thereof.' W. Steurs re-examined the texts and made a correct distinction between both texts.[24] He duly considers the sealed version I to be a so-called *notitia*. This is a written deed in which a transaction is recorded in an objective wording, that is, the person issuing the deed is not mentioned, and the acting person(s) or parties in the legal act are indicated in the third person.[25] According to him, there is no reason to suspect the seal nor the script. He dates the writing of version I between 1173 and 1179: the first year is mentioned in the text; in the last year the pope confirmed the possessions and rights listed in the text.[26] Version II, on the other hand, is regarded by him to be a forgery dating from the 1180s, meant to

1128, ed. Hugo 1734, I, lii; ed. Barbier 1892, II, 7, no. 9.

[17] (...) *tertiam partem Postulae.* The bull dates from December 21, 1138 (ed. Hugo 1734, I, lii-liv; ed. Miraeus/Foppens 1723-1749, IV, 120-121; see Barbier 1892, II, 9, no. 14; Ramackers 1972, I, 53). See also Hermans 1992-1993, 178; Steurs 1993, 118-119.

[18] Vienne 1996.

[19] The existing historiography on Postel is totally inadequate. See Welvaarts 1878-1879; Prims 1935. Unsatisfactory is Hermans 1992-1993.

[20] Hermans 1992-1993, 178-179; Steurs 1993, 120, n. 18.

[21] Camps 1979, 107-114, no. 69, ad datum <1173(?)>. H.P.H. Camps dubbed these versions 'I' and 'II'.

[22] Barbier 1892, II, 32, n. 1. Text I: 29-32, no. 47, ad datum 1173 (edition); text II: 32, no. 48, ad datum 1173 (précis).

[23] See note 21.

[24] Steurs 1993, 115-135.

[25] Declercq e.a. 1987, 264-265. There is, however, no consensus on the definition of *notitiae*, possibly because of their historical development. According to Guyotjeannin/Pycke/Tock 1993, 25, a *notitia* is 'un texte rédigé, en style objectif ou apparemment objectif, par le bénéficiaire d'une action juridique.' This last feature can often not be determined. See also Despy 1989, 589-590.

[26] Barbier 1892, II, 34-36, no. 54, dd. 1179 March 12; Ramackers 1972, II, 342-344, no. 203; Camps 1979, 116-117, no. 71 (fragment): (...) *parochiam, que uulgo Rosule dicitur, totam, preter sextam partem et in eadem parrochia curtem, que dicitur Rosule, et aliam curtem, que uulgo dicitur Postula, cum decima et appenditiis suis, quartam partem ecclesie et decime de Bladela et in eadem parrochia curtem de Uersele et allodium, quod uulgo dicitur de Helmedh, quartam partem ecclesie et decime, que uulgo dicuntur Kirkastele* (...): 'the parish, which in the vernacular is called Reusel, completely but for one sixth part, and in the same parish an estate called Reusel, and another estate, which in the vernacular is called Postel, with the tithe and its appurtenances, the fourth part of

take the edge off claims of previous owners and of farmers who lived on the properties in question.

M. Dillo proposes another solution.[27] According to him, text II is the transcript of a text which served as a draft for the sealed charter I. The abbey of Floreffe would have used this sealed instrument to send it to the pope to obtain a papal confirmation, which the abbey actually received in 1179. The sealed charter I was of course returned to the abbey. In contrast to Camps and Steurs, Dillo does not consider version I to be the *Vorlage* of II, but assumes that the now lost original version of II was the *Vorlage* of I.[28] Also, he sees no reason to consider one or both texts to be forgeries.

Although this is not the place to bring up all arguments to support Dillo's opinion, I want to point out the following. To contradict the supposition that one or both texts have been forged, one may observe that both texts have been transcribed on consecutive folios in the Floreffe cartulary, that is, first version I (considered by Dillo to be the text of the draft), and subsequently version II. Dillo's view also accounts for the fact that on several points II has a more correct wording than I.[29] The chronology of the gifts in II is internally consistent, which indicates that there was no falsification involved. The main differences between the sealed version and the draft are the following: in the first a charter concerning a settlement with Dietrich of Herlaar has been inserted; on the other hand, an exchange concerning goods in Reusel and the dedication charter are lacking. I will come back to all three points. The non-inclusion of the settlement with Dietrich of Herlaar in II can be explained by the fact that a separate charter on this was still available in the years 1173-1179. Accepting Dillo's views, I hereafter take the text of the draft (II) as the starting-point of my analysis.

The text of the draft can be divided in three parts.[30] The first part is labelled as a *carta* and was drawn up in the objective wording characteristic of a *notitia*. This text was recorded in the presence

---

the church and of the tithe of Bladel, and in the same parish the estate of Vorsel, and an allod, which in the vernacular is called 'of Elmt', the fourth part of the church and of the tithe, which in the vernacular are called Casteren'.

[27] Kindly communicated to me by M. Dillo. He carried out a diplomatic study of these texts while editing volume II of the forthcoming *Oorkondenboek van Noord-Brabant*.

[28] With this, Dillo returns to the opinion of Barbier 1892, II, 32, n. 1, who considered I to be 'l'abrégé du précédent' (= II).

[29] E.g.

Text I: (...) *terciam partem predii ecclesie de Rosole (...) dedit.*

Text II: (...) *terciam partem predii de Roselo et terciam partem ecclesie (...) tradidit.*

Text I: *Et Rogerus Scademule (...) pro emendo cultello (...) suscepit.*

Text II: *Et Rogerus Scademule (...) pro emendo cultello duos denarios (...) suscepit.*

[30] Part 1 (written down in 1173):
1. the first gift by Fastrad of Uitwijk (1128-1138)
2. the second gift by Fastrad of Uitwijk (1140)
3. a gift by Arnold called Brabent (1140) property and rights in Reusel
4. a gift by Berta of Blaarthem (1140-1173)
5. a gift by Didradis of Rixtel (1140-1173)

Part 2 (written down 1173-1179):
6. a gift by Gerung and Gocelin (1140-1173/1179) a sale by Gerung and Gocelin (1140-1173/1179)
7. a gift by Gela of Hapert (1140-1173/1179)
8. a sale by Abbot Hubert of Tongerlo (1156-1167) a sale by William of Vught (around the same time)
9. an exchange of landed property with Winand of Lohoven (*circa* 1173-1179).

Part 3: dedication charter dd. August 1, 1140.
Also records nine gifts on this occasion:
1. a gift by Fastrad of Uitwijk
2. a gift by Arnold [called Brabent]
3-9. seven gifts of sums of money by five men and two women.

of witnesses and mentions five related gifts. The first words are: *Notum sit Christi fidelibus quibus presens carta presentata fuerit quod* (...). The text is concluded with: *Acta sunt hec teste*, followed by the names of lord Anselm van Dil, Hubert called *Cocher*, and Witger called *Blanc*, and the message that other, anonymous witnesses had been present. Next the date is given: *Anno incarnationis Domini M° C° LXX° III°*, 'in the year of the Lord's incarnation 1173'. In the draft this date seems to belong to what precedes and therefore may provide a date to this deed. In the sealed version the date seems to belong to the inserted charter regarding the settlement with Dietrich of Herlaar. The second part of the draft, also a *notitia*, describes two gifts, three purchases, and one exchange. The introduction to this part reads: *Ne labatur a memoria inheritantium, per remedium scripti ad noticiam successorum transmittimus quod* (...), 'Lest it escapes from the memory of the heirs, by means of a written piece we transmit to the notice of the successors, that', and so on. There is no formal conclusion nor date, but the text must have been written down between 1173 and 1179. Parts one and two have also been included in the sealed version (I), with the exception of the recording of the exchange. The third and last part of the draft consists of the otherwise unknown charter concerning the dedication of the monastery church at Postel on August 1, 1140, the contents of which I briefly related in my introduction.[31] The form of this text is reminiscent of hagiography rather than of a charter, but there is no reason to doubt the correctness of what is recorded: it is all too easily forgotten that texts of this kind did not only have legal, but also sacred purposes. Steurs, in contrast, very confidently rejects this text's authenticity which 'mêle le vrai et le faux'.[32] Although he is willing to accept the facts on the dedication as being 'true', he rejects the rest as an account 'de facture littéraire, qui aurait plus sa place dans un roman hagiographique que dans une charte', and which should only have served 'pour sacraliser des donations que étaient contestées (...)'. I oppose his view that the description of events given in this text is 'en contradiction totale' with the contents of both lists of gifts. As in the case of Camps, Steurs' analysis too suffers from his exclusive fixation on the charter's formulary and legal purposes.

3 THE GIFTS TO POSTEL

The dedication of Postel's monastery church incited many to make gifts and vows (fig. 4). Nine of these gifts are listed in the dedication charter, and two of them, mainly involving landed property, are dealt with in more detail in the first part of the text. The remaining seven gifts were made by a nobleman, a priest, three men, and two anonymous women, and consisted of sums of money ranging from two to twelve *denarii*. All these gifts were made *super altare in Postulo*, on Postel's altar, and were meant to obtain salvation (*redemptio*).

With the exception of the seven gifts of money, all other transactions concerned landed property and/or appurtenant rights, such as the advowson of parish churches (the right to propose a new priest in case of a vacancy), tithes, and seigneurial rights. The oldest donation, recorded in the first part of the draft, took place at an unknown moment, when lord (*dominus*) and knight (*miles*) Fastrad of Uitwijk gave to the abbey of Floreffe the third part of an estate or manor (*predium*).[33] The church of

---

[31] The date is extensively recorded by giving the year of incarnation, the indiction, the epacts, and the years of government of the pope, the emperor, and the bishop of Liège. A similar precise date is also given by the chronicler of the *Annales Rodenses* in the case of the dedication year of the abbey church of Kloosterrade (1108), and of the year in which the priest Ailbert, founder of the abbey, died (1122) (Augustus/Jamar 1995, 88, 126).

[32] Steurs 1993, 129-131.

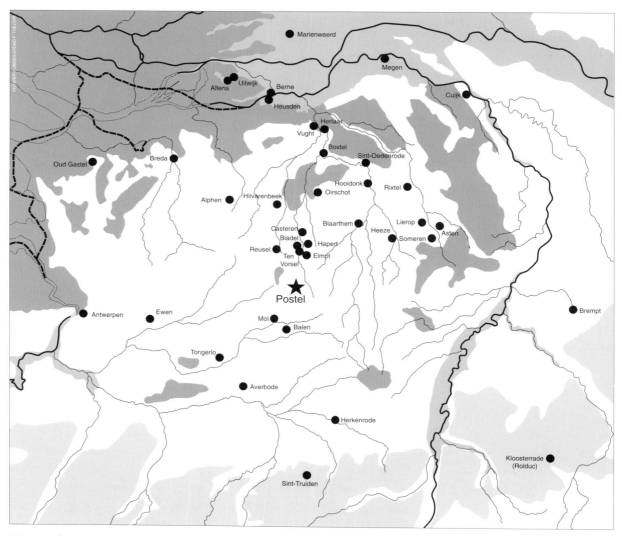

Fig. 4. The geographical 'scope' of the early endowment of the priory at Postel. Indicated are places where bene-factors lived or that are related to them and places where donations are located.

Postel was subsequently founded on this land, and a *cenobium* or monastery was built that became a daughter house of Floreffe. Fastrad can be regarded as the founder of Postel and his gift as the initial foundation. As the possession of the third part of Postel was not yet confirmed in the papal bull for the abbey of Floreffe of 1128, but is in the one from 1138, the initial gift by Fastrad can thus be dated between both years.

Floreffe's possession of 'a third part of Postel' was confirmed by the pope yet again in 1145, and by

33 On December 18, 1996, J.C. Kort pointed out to me that Fastrad's designation as both a *dominus* and a *miles*, as in the draft, is an anachronism for the time in which he lived, the second quarter of the 12th century. Therefore, according to Kort, the text is a forgery from the first decades of the 13th century. Indeed, ac-cording to Bonenfant/Despy 1958, 58-59, the title of *dominus* designates the nobles status of the bearer ('Ce qui paraît avoir (...) caracterisé le noble brabançon c'est sa qualité de *dominus*'; (...) 'la constante de la no-blesse aux XIIE et XIIIE siècles est la détention d'un village dont il porte le nom (...)'). This would be in

the emperor in 1151.[34] A second imperial charter, of 1152, briefly mentions 'the estate of Postel'.[35] Two papal bulls of 1155 and 1161 confirm the possession of 'the half of Postel'.[36] Finally, the bull of 1179 mentions 'the estate, which in the vernacular is called Postel, with the tithe and its appurtenances'.[37] From this it can be derived that between 1151 and 1155 the abbey of Floreffe acquired, next to the third part originating from Fastrad, a complementary sixth part of Postel. Furthermore, from the bull of 1179 we can deduce that the *curtis* Postel was situated in the parish of Reusel. As we have already mentioned, in the sealed version (I) of the text from the years 1173-1179 a charter (of 1173?) has been inserted. This ended the claims made by Dietrich of Herlaar, his sister, and all co-heirs to a sixth part of the allod of Postel.[38] Dietrich and his followers apparently challenged the deed through which he or his relatives had ceded this sixth part to the abbey, an act which must have taken place between 1151 and 1155.[39]

As we have already seen, Postel's monastery church was dedicated in 1140, and on this occasion the same knight Fastrad made a second donation. In the dedication charter this was recorded as the first gift to the monastery: *Primus miles Fastradus prima dona libere tradidit (...)*. According to the text of the draft, this pious gift consisted of the third part of an estate or manor (*predium*) at Reusel, north of Postel. The gift also included the third part of the church in this village and seigneurial rights on several plots of land. Next, the monastery acquired three one-sixth parts of the same estate in Reusel. According to the papal confirmation of 1179, the abbey of Floreffe indeed possessed five-sixths of the parish of Reusel, and a *curtis* of that name.[40]

---

contradiction with the quality of *miles*, because 'il n'y a point de *milites* avant 1200 dans la plupart des familles nobles du duché', save some exceptions after 1165 (*ibidem*, 33, 36). Therefore, the mention of a *dominus* as a *miles* in a text from the years 1173-1179 in itself does not have to be anomalous. But we can go even further: Tock 1997, 144, gives the example of charter of 1019 in which mention is made of a *nobilis miles*, which terms seem to be in contradiction. But, with reference to Barthélemy 1994, he insists on 'la complémentarité entre les deux termes, très tôt, dès le XIe siècle'. Indeed, Barthélemy 1994, 32 and 61, is convinced of the fact that 'La chevalerie et la noblesse s'articulent toujours ensemble' and that 'Parler de *miles nobilis* relève du pléonasme', and is not a contradiction at all!

[34] Bulls dd. 1138, December 21 (*tertiam partem Postulae*; ed. Hugo 1743, I, lii-liv; ed. Miraeus/Foppens 1723-1749, IV, 120-121) and dd. 1145, October 25 (*tertiam partem Postule*; ed. Barbier 1892, II, 10-11, no. 17; ed. Ramackers 1972, II, 169-170, no. 55). Imperial charter dd. 1151, [after September 17] (*terciam partem Postule*; ed. Hausmann 1969, 446-449, no. 258).

[35] Charter dd. 1152, December 28 (*curtem de Postule*; ed. Appelt 1975-1990, I, 67-68, no. 40).

[36] Bulls dd. 1155, April 22 and 1161, June 7 (*dimidiam partem Postule*; respectively ed. Ramackers 1972, II, 202-204, no. 76 and ed. Barbier 1892, II, 21-22, no. 37; ed. Ramackers 1972, II, 224-225, no. 93).

[37] Dd. 1179, March 12 (*aliam curtem, que uulgo dicitur Postula, cum decima et appenditiis suis*; ed. Barbier 1892, II, 34-36, no. 54; ed. Ramackers 1972, II, 342-344, no. 203).

[38] The charter concerns a *conventio et compositio*, a settlement. After Dietrich of Herlaar had promised to sell to Postel his rights to the allod Elmt (under Bladel) and to give up his claims on lands, watercourses, and meadows regarding a sixth part of the allod of Postel, a new conflict arose after the death of his mother Udehilt with his sister and her husband Florens of Voorne. They gathered to settle the case and to divide the inheritance. Dietrich kept his promise to Postel and to this end had also bound with an oath his *ministeriales* Brusten, Dietrich Stempel, and Amelius. In compensation of the sold inheritance, Dietrich gave to his sister and her husband an allod at Gerdingen (near Bree), and in the village of Baesweiler (15 kms. north of Aachen).

[39] See Steurs 1993, 122.

[40] See note 26.

The first of these three gifts, made by Arnold called Brabent, took place at the time of the church dedication in 1140; the two others some time later, but before 1173/1179. Arnold's donation is mentioned twice: in the first part of the text, and in the dedication charter, with reference to the first mention: (...) *secundus Arnoldus, ut superius dictum est* [*tradidit*]. Although Arnold gave 'his' sixth part of the *allodium* Reusel and of the advowson on the advice of his three sons Berner, Otto, and Arnold, and with the consent of all co-heirs, some heirs later contested this transaction. To end the quarrel, Arnold had his daughter Jutta enter the monastery and once again donated 'his' share in the estate as he had done before, now as 'the church's and his daughter's dowry'. After Arnold Brabent had ceremonially ceded his right to the aforementioned property, lord Walther Berthout accepted it 'in accordance with civil law'. Common law demanded for a layman as the monastery's representative to perform the seisinatery's advocate. Elsewhere it was usually the monastery's advocate who played this role. We encounter such a representative (or two representatives) in five transactions in both the draft and the sealed version of the text discussed here.[41]

The second donation, also a second sixth part of the *predium* Reusel, was made by a noble lady called Berta of Blaarthem; originally it was made for God's sake (*Deus principalis causa huius oblationis fuerit*). Berta's daughter Gisla, and Gisla's sons Alard of Megen, Dietrich, and Roger Scademule gave their consent and added to the donation another estate (*predium*) at Blaarthem.[42] However, problems arose in this case too, and a settlement with the heirs had to be arranged. The completion of this transaction presumably took many years: three generations were involved in it, and finally *frater* Rodulf, the *magister* in charge of Postel monastery at the time of Abbot Herman of Floreffe (1173-1194), had to interfere as well.[43] The settlement must have taken place between *circa* 1173 and 1179. The last donation of one-sixth of Reusel was made by Didradis of Rixtel, simply out of 'pious devotion' (*pia devotione*), with the consent of her children Henry, Baldwin, and Sibilia. With this the first part of the draft is concluded.

The second part of the text records first of all a donation which took place between 1140 and 1173/1179, as the brothers Gerung and Gocelin ceded to Postel a *mansus* of land, situated under Bladel, *pro salute anime sue* (*sic*), 'for the salvation of their souls'.[44] On this land the manor (*domus*) of Vorsel, one of Postel's most important estates, was later built.[45] Probably at the same time they sold a piece of land for the considerable sum of three marks and a half. Subsequently, the distinguished lady Gela of Hapert donated a piece of land at Vorsel and a tithe at Casteren on the occasion of her daugh-

---

[41] Besides in the donation of Arnold Brabent, in the donation by Berta of Blaarthem (Engelbert of Balen), at the conveyance by Gerung and Gocelin (Sigebert of Gestel), at the sale by William of Vught (lord Herman of Alphen and his brother Udo), and at the settlement with Dietrich of Herlaar (lord Walther Berthout and lord Henry, advocate of Mol) According to Heirbout 1997, 51, in Flemish feudal law, in case of a seisin by a corporate body, such as a church, the feudal lord seized a representative of that institution. This representative received the investiture not for himself but on behalf of the body he represented. The common expression for this is *ad opus*; here the expression *ad usus* is twice used.

[42] About the possible castle of this lineage at Blaarthem, see Arts e.a. 1996.

[43] Hermans 1992-1993, 181; Steurs 1993, 121, n. 24, 125. According to Prims 1935, 182, Rodulf was the successor to Godescalc, who became abbot of Berne in 1176 (see also Van der Velden 1986, 16). He probably acted as the *magister curie*, as the estate manager of a Premonstratensian *curie* was called.

[44] In text I rectified as: *pro salute animarum suarum*.

[45] Roymans 1979, 18-20.

ter Gerberga's entry into Postel monastery. This transaction also took place between 1140 and 1173/1179. Next follow the two remaining purchases. The first concerns one-fourth part of the tithes and of the advowson at Bladel, and rights in fields and a wood there, which property the noble lady Berta van Brecht equally shared with seigneur William of Vught. Berta had donated this property to the Premonstratensian abbey of Tongerlo on her entry as a nun into the monastery at Ewen, the abbey's nunnery, in the time of Abbot Hubert of Tongerlo (1156-1167).[46] He sold this property 'to put it to more profitable use for his monastery' for ten marks to the brothers of Postel. After that, sometime in the third quarter of the 12th century, William of Vught too sold his share to Postel for the same amount. William was a descendant of a noble lineage which named itself alternately 'of Vught' and 'of Oirschot', and which had possessions and rights in both places. These seigneurs are presumed to have founded the collegiate chapter of Oirschot in the 12th century.[47] The transaction last recorded concerns an exchange, that is an 'induced' donation followed by a countergift. This exchange has not been recorded in the sealed version. The transaction is interesting because it reveals something about the conventuals' attitude towards their neighbours benefactors. *Frater* Rodulf, *magister* of Postel between *circa* 1173 and 1194, ordered the priory's estate (*curia*) of *Lohoven* (under Reusel[48]) to be enclosed by a moat in such a way that outside the fence enough space remained for two plough-oxen to turn around.[49] In one place, however, near the house of a certain Winand, there was not enough space for this. In order to be able to dig the moat in a straight line, Rodulf asked to be given six or seven feet of Winand's land. Winand complied, but to stop the quarrel involving the succeeding heirs, the master compensated the given land with a stable near the cemetery of Reusel (on which Rodulf had built a *horreum* or barn), 'and so both [parties] remained in peace' (*et sic in pace uterque quievit*). So much for the text's contents, which informs us on fourteen donations, three purchases, and one exchange. From this enumeration we gain a clear impression of the temporal stratification of the entire text: it is the written recording of donations, transactions, and settlements which took place over a period of about forty years and which were written down at a single moment. Because of this, we might lose sight of this temporal stratification.

We can not escape going further into the chronology of the donations by the first benefactor and founder of Postel, Fastrad of Uitwijk. In my conviction the concept, which on this point is more detailed than the sealed version, renders the chain of events in an accurate way. The first donation by Fastrad (consisting of the third part of the land at Postel and directed to the abbey of Floreffe) took place between November 4, 1128 and December 21, 1138.[50] On this property the *ecclesia* – probably to be translated as monastery – of Postel was founded: (...) *in quo ecclesia de Postula fundata est* (...). After that (the draft reads: *Postea*) Fastrad made his second donation 'to the monastery which is in Postel' (*cenobio quod est in Postulo*), consisting of a third part of the estate at Reusel with appurtenances. Steurs holds the opinion that the draft's digression on the second donation of Fastrad (in which it is stated that Fastrad redeemed the property from his brother Hello at the division of the inheritance through exchange with other goods, and that none of the farmers or succeeding heirs will

[46]   Koyen/Van Dyck 1992-1993, 282-283.

[47]   Klaversma 1977-1979; Lijten 1991, 56-57, 60; Kappelhof 1995, 22-23.

[48]   See Theuws this volume.

[49]   For *Lohoven* see Camps 1979, 183-184, no. 115, dd. 1219, June (concerning the milling right of the water mill at Wolfswinkel under Bladel, which was claimed

by Winand of Lohoven, probably a descendant of the Winand mentioned here); 265-287, no. 186, dd. 1238, May 3. Roymans 1979, 23, mentions the toponym 'Looven', which, however, refers to a mere (*ven*) (see also Steurs 1993, 125, n. 38).

[50]   See note 17.

have any right to it any longer) is a forged addition to the 'authentic' account in the sealed version, and that this forgery served to take the edge off later claims.[51] However, in the same passage, in both the draft and the sealed version, mention is made of written proof, now lost, of this donation, which makes it plausible that these elements were taken from this document. As regards the content of the digression, one cannot raise objections. According to the dedication charter, Fastrad's second donation occurred at the monastery church's dedication on August 1, 1140. Consequently, the actual foundation of Postel priory can be dated to the years 1138-1140. During the next few decades Postel served, given the wording in the papal and imperial confirmation charters issued on behalf of Floreffe, as an outlying manor on which a church and a monastery were situated. This manor was Floreffe's property, and consequently the gifts made in the strict sense to the church or to the monastery of Postel, were regarded as the abbey's property.

After the dedication of the church of Postel, Fastrad, still according to the text of the draft, entered the Benedictine abbey of Oostbroek, near Utrecht (*His ita peractis idem miles Fastradus habitum religionis induit*), and had his pious gifts confirmed by a written testimony, sealed with the seal of Oostbroek's first abbot, to whom he owed obedience.[52] He placed his donations under the protection of Bishop Albero II of Liège (1135-1145).[53] This written testimony is now lost. The evidence indicates that Fastrad entered the abbey of Oostbroek after August 1, 1140, and before Albero's death (March 22, 1145). The sealed version (I), on the other hand, holds it that Fastrad entered the abbey after his first donation and made his second donation after that or on that occasion.[54] On his entry into Oostbroek, Fastrad, together with his wife Sophia, donated to this abbey property near Oud Gastel.[55] A.C.F. Koch dates this deed, in which Fastrad is referred to as 'surnamed *Scerebart*', between 1122 and the beginning of 1145, and maybe after September 7, 1130. Nothing in this charter opposes a more precise dating between August 1, 1140 and March 22, 1145. Accepting the accuracy of the contents of the Postel draft, we can considerably adjust the time limits of Fastrad's entry into Oostbroek and of his donation to this abbey.

From later information we can infer that Fastrad probably endowed both the abbey of Oostbroek and Postel priory with property in the vicinity of his ancestral holding at Uitwijk in the Land of Altena as well. A register, listing the damage caused by the so-called St Elizabeth's flood of 1421, also lists the loss by the abbey of Oostbroek of some 136 *morgen* (about 272 acres) of land with a chapel, a house, a barn, and a shed, called the manor and estate of Den Doorn, situated in the holm called the Grote Waard.[56] This property was located just north of Almkerk and 3 kms west of Uitwijk. In a charter of 1403, concerning lands in the village territory south of the former river called De Werken, also in the Land of Altena, the house of Postel is named as the adjacent landholder several times. Sixteenth- and seventeenth-century sources also mention possessions of Postel monastery here.[57] This

[51] Steurs 1993, 125-126, 129.

[52] (...) *primus abbas de Ostbruch, cuius prenominatus Fastradus obediens erat, testimonio sigilli sui scripto confirmavit* (...). Here Abbot Ludolf is meant. See Steurs 1993, 118-119.

[53] Kupper 1981, 499; Kupper 1982, 77-78. The bishops acted as the usual protectors of the young Premonstratensian foundations in the Low Countries (see Bijsterveld 1997c).

[54] *Postea idem Fastradus habitum religionis induit et terciam*

partem predii ecclesie de Rosole cenobio quod est in Postelo dedit. This version is corrupt: between *predii* and *ecclesie* at least the word *et* is missing. See also note 48.

[55] This donation was recorded in an inserted charter with a made up date: Koch 1970, 242-246, no. 122, ad datum [1122 (1130, September 7?) – beginning of 1145]. Leenders 1996, 236-238, for unclear reasons rejects the entire contents of this charter.

[56] Braams 1995, 55-56, n. 119, 137; Braams 1996, 94-96.

[57] Braams 1995, 44, n. 49, 46; Braams 1996, 96-97.

property may be identical to the *curtis de Werchina cum omnibus appendiciis suis*, in the possession of which the abbey of Floreffe was confirmed in 1179 and 1182 by popes Alexander III and Lucius III.[58] As this *curtis* was listed between the mill of Stipdonk and the *curtis* of Lierop, it has also been located in the vicinity of Lierop.[59] B.W. Braams, in contrast, assumes an identification with De Werken. This assumption is confirmed by the mention in the Floreffe obituary of *frater Johannes, conversus in Postula et provisor in Werkine*, deceased in 1341.[60] So, an outlying manor of Floreffe was indeed situated in De Werken. Given the proximity to Uitwijk, it is feasible that both Oostbroek's property, mentioned later, and Floreffe's 12th-century landed property here originate from Fastrad of Uitwijk's or his relatives' patrimony.

4   INTENTION AND SOURCES OF THE DRAFT OF 1173-1179

The drawing up of the text of the draft explicitly intended to prevent the transactions performed between *circa* 1138 and *circa* 1179 from slipping from the memories of the donors' heirs. This was no empty rhetoric, because Postel's conventuals were, as the text informs us, indeed vexed by conflicts with the donors' heirs. This list was almost certainly made at the instigation of the aforementioned *frater* Rodulf, *magister* of Postel in the last quarter of the 12th century. He ended both the conflict with Berta of Blaarthem's heirs and the controversy with Winand's heirs regarding Lohoven. Besides, he completed, according to the charter inserted in version I, probably in 1173, an agreement made earlier by the abbot of Floreffe with Dietrich of Herlaar by paying Dietrich the sum of 28 marks. In return, he gave up his position as *advocatus* or advocate, his allod of Elmt, and all claims he derived from his pretended possession of a sixth part of the allod of Postel.[61] Apparently the abbot of Floreffe had delegated Rodulf to put material things right at Postel. Therefore, in view of a papal confirmation, he had all transactions which had been carried out to the benefit of Postel, committed to writing in the draft.

In doing so, he used several texts which are now lost, in any case the sealed deed(s) of Fastrad's donations and the dedication charter of 1140. In the recording of the other donations too, he probably used notes from the abbey of Floreffe's archive.[62] One can think of *notitiae*, notes in a *liber traditionum* (a 'book of gifts'), and/or notes in an obituary. It is feasible that the individual gifts to Postel were recorded in *notitiae*, given the fact that the donations in the list of 1173-1179 have been registered in the objective wording characteristic of comparable 'informal' deeds. Separate *notitiae* have, however, not survived in either Floreffe's or Postel's archives. *Notitiae* or heavily abbreviated transcripts of charters were sometimes also written down in a *liber traditionum*.[63] It also happened that no separate written document was drawn up, but that the legal act was directly recorded in a *liber traditionum*. Finally, in obituaries or necrologies and in other liturgical codices brief notes, up to complete charters, concerning donations and other property transactions have been inscribed as well.[64] From the 12th century no *liber traditionum* of this kind nor an obituary of Floreffe or of Postel has been handed down. The oldest sur-

58   Camps 1979, 116-117, no. 71, dd. 1179, March 12; 122-124, no. 75, dd. 1182, January 15.

59   Künzel/Blok/Verhoeff 1988, 389. Identification with the later mentioned farm of Weerdingen, in Lierop: Bijsterveld 1989b, 21.

60   Barbier 1876, 216 (June 26).

61   See Van Dierendonck/Maas 1989.

62   See Steurs 1993, 128.

63   Johanek 1977; Molitor 1990; Guyotjeannin/Pycke/Tock 1993, 272-278.

64   Compare Lemaître 1993.

viving necrology of the abbey of Floreffe only dates back to the end of the fifteenth or the beginning of the sixteenth century.[65] Initially, the entries were restricted to the anniversaries of the abbey's abbots and of those of other Premonstratensian abbeys, as well as to anniversaries of the most important benefactors. Far from all donors nor all the abbey's own conventuals are listed. Of the oldest benefactors of Postel only Fastrad of Uitwijk, as Postel's founder, was granted an entry.[66] One way or the other, the 'list of gifts' of 1173-1179 is based on recordings in the form of *notitiae*. In some cases the information on several separate legal acts was summarized in a single record. This was the case with the donation by Berta of Blaarthem, for which we can observe four phases with time intervals between them: the initial gift by Berta, the additional gift of the property at Blaarthem, the renunciation by Berta's grandson Roger Scademule, and the one by Berta's daughter Gisla and her daughter.

The diplomatists' fixation on sealed charters and on establishing their so-called authenticity by method of their formulary, means of proof, and external features, has led to the negligence of numerous ways of 'non-authentic' recording of legal acts.[67] Well into the 12th century, various ways of putting property transactions down in writing and of guaranteeing the unchallenged possession of landed property in the future, were, next to the recording in 'authentic' (sealed) charters, far more frequent than can be gathered from the preserved charter collections and cartularies, let alone from modern editions of charters with their juridically biased stress on legally valid documents and 'correct' *formulae*. For contemporaries, however, the recordings of transactions in a so-called 'non-authentic' way, even those in monastic, canonical, and episcopal chronicles or liturgical books, had evidential value too.[68] After the 'victory' of the sealed charter in the course of the 13th century many of these 'non-authentic' recordings were destroyed or lost because they were no longer considered to be legally valid. In contrast to H.P.H. Camps, I am convinced that the text listing the transactions made to the benefit of Postel really had evidential value or at least pretended to have it.

5   THE CONTEXT: THE DONORS' MILIEU, THE SOCIAL-POLITICAL SITUATION, AND THE RELIGIOUS CLIMATE

The founder of Postel priory, Fastrad, originated, as has been said, from Uitwijk, situated in the Land of Altena in the Central Dutch river area, not far from the Premonstratensian abbeys of Berne and Mariënweerd. In 1108 a certain *Hubertus de Utwic* is mentioned among the nobles witnessing a charter issued by the bishop of Utrecht regarding a dispute over an estate situated between the rivers Lek and Linge.[69] The noble family Van Altena is probably a younger branch of the Van Uitwijk lineage. It is mentioned since 1143 and has played a prominent role in the Meuse-Demer-Scheldt area since then.[70] The motte-and-bailey castle of Altena was situated only 2.5 kms west of the Uitwijk castle, likewise on the small river Alm.[71] Apparently, Fastrad not only had property in the river area, but also more to the

[65]   Barbier 1876.

[66]   Barbier 1876, 280 (December 6): *Commemoratio Fastradi, monachi sancti Laurentii in Hostbruch, qui dedit nobis allodium de Postula et quartam partem ecclesie de Rosul.*

[67]   See now Guyotjeannin 1997.

[68]   See about this Kastner 1974, 83-96; Clanchy 1994, 154-156; Sot 1985, 21; Thissen 1989, 194-205; Molitor 1990, 72-88; Geary 1993; Geary 1994c, 81-114 ('Archival Memory and the Destruction of the Past'); Guyotjeannin 1996; Bijsterveld, in press.

[69]   Muller e.a., 1920-1959, I 257-258, no. 280, dd. 1108, August 9.

[70]   On the Van Uitwijk and the Van Altena lineage see, among others, Klaversma 1978, 12-13; Braams 1995, 52-56 and n. 119; Braams 1996, 94-97.

[71]   Hendriks 1990, 75-77, 82.

south, like many of his peers and fellow countrymen, who, through marriage and consanguinity, were related to the Kempen aristocracy. His contemporary Folcold, the founder of the Premonstratensian abbey of Berne (1134), was married to Bescela, who originated from Someren.[72] In the same period we observe the Van Cuijk family, who founded the Premonstratensian abbey of Mariënweerd in 1129, owning property in the Central Dutch river area as well as in the northeastern part of what is today the province of North Brabant, as well as in Asten and Lierop. The Van Cuijks were related to the Van Rode family, whose property was not only situated around Sint-Oedenrode and in Peelland, but also in the river area to the north and in the Kempen region.[73] The endowment of Postel priory was carried out by interrelated aristocratic families from the region in 1140 and between 1140 and 1173. A survey of Postel's benefactors, and of the intermediaries and witnesses mentioned, is a *tableau de la troupe* of the regional aristocracy of the northern part of the Meuse-Demer-Scheldt area of that time.[74] It regarded this area as their sphere of influence and power range, including the Central Dutch river area, where some of these families had their cradle and power base. Their familial and social networks linked all corners of this peripheral region and even crossed its boundaries. Some of these powerful people are titled *domini* and *domine*, 'seigneurs' and 'ladies', and *nobiles matrone*, 'noble matrons'.

The fact that the donors held the property donated by them to Postel in joint ownership, which means it originates from one inheritance, indicates that they were related. The estate of Postel (one part of which, next to Fastrad of Uitwijk's part, came from Dietrich of Herlaar and his family), the *allodium* or *predium* at Reusel, and the property at Vorsel are cases in point. The fragmentation must have resulted from inheritance patterns and marriage alliances. The donors represent at least the third generation of owners; they may have descended from an original proprietor who owned these properties undivided some fifty to sixty years earlier, that is around 1080. Although a lack of sources does not allow us to know the precise nature of the consanguinity and the alliances among these aristocrats, it is certain that they were not only in-laws and mutual friends, but were also related to families outside their own region. Incidentally we know more about the donors' familial background. Two of Berta of Blaarthem's grandsons, Alard, count of Megen, and Dietrich, are probably mentioned in other sources as well. A certain *Alardus de Megene* is a witness in a royal charter of 1145. Since 1196 at the latest he was succeeded as count of Megen by a certain William of Megen.[75] Alard's (half?)brother Dietrich has been identified with Dietrich [I] of Altena. He is mentioned as a witness in a charter is-

---

[72] Van Rij 1987, 94, 124, 128.

[73] Coldeweij 1981; Van Bavel 1993a, 163-180, 227-228, 262; Van Asseldonk 1996; Bijsterveld/Nissen, in press.

[74] Next to the donors and their relatives, the following persons are mentioned as intermediaries (who accepted the donation on behalf of the monastery, as apparently demanded by the prevailing law): lord Walther Berthout (twice), Engelbert of Balen, lord Henry, advocate of Mol, Sigebert of Gestel, lord Herman of Alphen and his brother Udo of Alphen. As witnesses are mentioned: lord Anselm of Dil, Hubert called *Cocher*, Witger called *Blanc*, and in the settlement with Dietrich of Herlaar, Henry of Breda, Dietrich of Altena, Gerald of Boxtel and his brother William, Arnold of Heusden, and Herbert of Heeze. The aforementioned Walther II Berthout of Grimbergen († 1180), together with his brothers Gerald II and provost Arnold, donated, also on behalf of a third party, property at Werchter to the Premonstratensian abbey of Middelburg between 1138 and 1155 (Koch 1970, 261-262, no. 136, dd. [1138 – circa 1155]; Baerten 1959, 25).

[75] Künzel/Blok/Verhoeff 1988, 247-248. Muller e.a. 1920-1959, I, 350-352, no. 388, dd. 1145, October 18; Camps 1979, 145-147, no. 85, dd. 1196; 151-152, no. 90, dd. 1200.

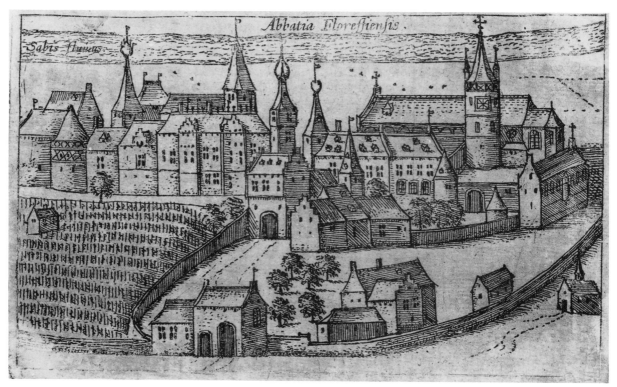

Fig. 5. View of the abbey of Floreffe. Engraving c. 1600 (from Gramaye 1608, 28).

sued by Bishop Hartbert of Utrecht in 1143 and in 1173 he witnessed the aforementioned settlement between Postel priory and Dietrich of Herlaar.[76] Like Alard of Megen he was a witness mentioned in the royal charter of 1145.[77] This Dietrich of Altena must have been related to Fastrad of Uitwijk. As we have seen, the castle of Altena is situated only 2.5 kms west of Uitwijk. As a supporting argument we mention the fact that, according to a charter from 1214, the aforementioned William, count of Megen, and his son Dietrich owned an allod at Rixtel, which links them to Didradis of Rixtel, one of Postel's other benefactors.[78]

The foundation of Postel was the last in a series of foundations of Premonstratensian monasteries in the northern part of present day Belgium and in the central and southern part of what is now the Netherlands. Between 1124 and *circa* 1140 seven Premonstratensian houses were built here, the abbey of St Michael's at Antwerp (1124), the abbey of Middelburg (1127; daughter of the abbey of Antwerp), the abbey Mariënweerd near Culemborg (1129; daughter of the abbey of Saint-Martin at Laon), the abbey of Tongerlo (*circa* 1133; daughter of Antwerp), the abbey of Berne (1134; daughter of Mariënweerd), the abbey of Averbode (1133-1135; daughter of Antwerp), and the priory of Postel (daughter of Floreffe) (fig. 5).[79] In most of these foundations an important role was played by the incumbent bishop of the diocese in which the monasteries were situated, that is the bishop of Cambrai for Antwerp and Tongerlo, the bishop of Utrecht for Middelburg, Mariënweerd and Berne, and the

[76] Koch 1970, 238-242, no. 121, dd. 1143, [October 7 or later].

[77] Melssen 1983, 17. See also Klaversma 1978, 10, 13; for the sources see Künzel/Blok/Verhoeff 1988: 64.

[78] Camps 1979, 180-181, no. 111; Coenen 1992, 23.

[79] See Bijsterveld 1997c.

bishop of Liège for Averbode and Postel. The bishops extended their protection to these young establishments. The *fundus* or *dos* was in most cases provided by one or several members of the regional aristocracy; only Averbode was founded by a lord with princely aspirations, that is by the count of Looz.

Over the last decades, several historians have investigated the backgrounds of the preference of the landed aristocracy in the German Empire for canons in general and for Premonstratensians in particular when founding a monastery.[80] This inclination can be explained by a coherent whole of familial, socio-political, and religious motives. To start with the first: the choice of founders in Northwestern Germany and the Low Countries for the order of Prémontré was inspired by the close relations which tied the bishops and the aristocratic families to Norbert of Gennep. The founding families were intimately linked among themselves, the bonds being based on kinship, friendship, and a shared geographic origin, which even bound together families in distant regions.[81] The active support by the bishops can be explained by the fact that Premonstratensian establishments, being monasteries of canons, were more integrated in the diocesan structure and could therefore count on more episcopal backing than the strictly monastic foundations could.[82] Some of the aforementioned bishops were close relatives of the founding families as well. Another advantage of regular canons over monks that may have been important in making a choice, was their active involvement in the care and cure of souls, that is, in *cura animarum* and in hospital work.[83]

The distinction between secular and regular canons, as well as the difference between secular and Premonstratensian canons, seems to have been of minor importance to the founders. The diocese of Liège is considered to have been a centre of the so-called *Kanonikerreform*, the revival and renewal of the canonical regimen, which culminated in the first decades of the 12th century. The first foundations of monasteries and chapters in the Meuse-Demer-Scheldt area since the Early Middle Ages were all communities of canons, starting with the abbey of Kloosterrade (Rolduc) in 1104, followed by the Premonstratensian foundations already mentioned, and the foundation of Hooidonk priory (between Son and Nuenen) from Kloosterrade in 1146. Both regimens of regular canons were based on the so-called Rule of St Augustine. How close to another they were in the eyes of the noble founders, can be illustrated by the case of the unsuccessful foundation of a daughter house of Kloosterrade at Berne in 1132. First, Folcold of Berne had invited two relatives of his, who as canons were members of the Kloosterrade community, to found a monastery in his castle. After this failed, without the slightest problem he invited the Premonstratensians of nearby Mariënweerd in 1134.[84] Familial connections were also decisive in the case of the foundation of Hooidonk priory. The priest Leo, a canon of Kloosterrade, built this monastery in 1146, with his abbot's permission, on a piece of land at Hooidonk, which he had received from his own brothers. A wooden chapel was dedicated there in 1148, but still Leo had to return to his mother house because his little monastery could not support itself. Hooidonk subsequently became a priory dependent on Kloosterrade.[85] Another of Kloosterrade's daughter houses, Ludingakerke in Frisia, was also a family foundation, by the Frisian lineage of Bishop Hartbert of Utrecht. He was closely connected to Kloosterrade, as his son Goswin had entered the abbey in 1136.[86]

The establishment of a number of secular chapters can probably be considered part of the same

[80] See Ehlers 1973; Kohl 1984; Zotz 1992; Parisse 1995.

[81] Kohl 1984; Van Bavel 1993a, 119, 123-124.

[82] Weinfurter 1977, 391-392; Ehlers 1973, 48.

[83] Weinfurter 1977, 393-394.

[84] Van Rij 1987, 97-100; Augustus/Jamar 1995, 154-156.

[85] Augustus/Jamar 1995, 192.

[86] Mol/Noomen 1996; Augustus/Jamar 1995, 162, 168, 188.

boom of foundations of regular canons. Again, it was almost invariably local and regional lords who took the initiative for these foundations, as at Hilvarenbeek (before 1157), at Sint-Oedenrode (before 1207, perhaps around 1150), and at Oirschot (before *circa* 1170).[87] In some cases they were even founded in the noble's castle, as at Berne, or in its proximity, as at Sint-Oedenrode. The differences between regular and secular chapters were not great. Some regular chapters originated from communities of secular canons. Other communities experimented with several rules. In any case, it is clear that the canonical regimen, be it of regular or secular canons, attracted the special attention and approval of the aristocrats. In the Meuse-Demer-Scheldt area and its immediate surroundings no monasteries were founded in which monks lived in accordance with a strict monastic rule. The Cistercian order, so successful elsewhere, did not have a single house in this region. The first abbey of Cistercian nuns was only founded at Herkenrode in 1182.

The choice for regular canons was perhaps motivated as well by the possibility that both men and women could enter into their monasteries: predominantly, the foundations resulted in double monasteries, housing male canons, lay brothers, and female lay sisters.[88] We observe several founders entering their own foundation, with or without their spouse. More frequent still are entries of the founders' son or daughter. These establishments thus permitted the founders to continue the family structure (the claims to the familial patrimony included) in a spiritual way. The lack of heirs played a role in some cases, like that of Folcold of Berne and his wife Bescela.[89] We should point here to the active role of aristocratic women in founding and endowing the monasteries of canons. Next to twelve men donating or selling property to Postel, three named and two anonymous *matrone* or aristocratic women acted as donors. This female involvement with Postel's endowment is remarkable but not exceptional. One third of those who donated to the abbey of Kloosterrade were women as well. Apparently, 12th-century women could convey immovable property or donate money on their own, that is without being dependent on their fathers, husbands, or sons. In accordance with the prevailing, so-called ligurian law of inheritance, daughters too were entitled to a portion in the paternal and maternal heritage. This explains the role women played in consenting to donations and in later contentions regarding property transactions, which does not differ from the role played by their male relatives. We can point to the part taken by Gisla and her daughter in the conflict concerning Berta of Blaarthem's gift, and to the arrangement Dietrich of Herlaar had to settle with his sister, after he had sold a part of their joint inheritance.

We also have to point to the possibility that donations to religious institutions were made to prevent the (further) fragmentation of the familial patrimony.[90] By donating this as a totality to a monastery or chapter, it was prevented from being divided among many members of a family. Parts of inheritances already split up were even joined again to endow a monastery. In this way the landed property, which, as has been said, represented the continuity of the founder's family, was kept together and was, above all, entrusted to the patron saint's supernatural protection. The foundation and endowment of the monastery can therefore be regarded as the perpetuation of the donor and his lineage by donating something of eternal value, that is landed property. The foundation and endowment of Postel may have been undertaken with this in the minds of the participants involved. The property

[87] Klaversma 1977-1979, 44, 90-91, 131-132.

[88] Van Schijndel 1971; Hagemeijer 1984; Janssens 1991, 19; Koch 1994, 10-12, 23-26; Venarde 1997: 67-70, 84, 133, 164-165, 177.

[89] The *Annales Rodenses* explain his wish to found a monastery by pointing to the fact he had no children (Augustus/Jamar 1995, 154).

[90] See Jahn 1988, 412; Hartung 1988; Reuter 1995, 171, 185.

donated indisputably originated from a single inheritance. Perhaps, by endowing Postel the founder and the benefactors aimed at keeping together their ancestral heritage. This doubtlessly implies too, that they continued to make certain claims on that property, in spite of (or more precisely because of) the donation to the monastery's patron saints. In this respect we should not forget that the remaining sixth part of the parish of Reusel, was not given to Postel priory and presumably remained in the ownership of (a member of) the donating lineage. Was this part the finger in the pie the family wanted to keep?

The aforementioned fact that the founder, in some cases accompanied by other members of his family, entered his own foundation, is a typical feature of the establishments mentioned. This was, for example, the case at Tongerlo, where the founder Gislebert entered, and at Berne, where Folcold and his wife Bescela became conventuals. Postel's founder, Fastrad of Uitwijk, did become a monk, but not at Floreffe, the mother abbey of Postel priory. He entered the Benedictine abbey of Oostbroek. Next to social and familial reasons, religious motives certainly played a role. People aspired to a personal reform or *conversio*, a radical break in their ways of life. By converting from a layman into a religious, an important step was taken by individuals into the interspace between sublunary life and the next world. Characteristic for an entry into a canonical foundation was the denial of social distinctions. We should think of the distinction between a married and unmarried status, and between male and female roles. Especially significant for the founders, was their asperation to bridge the gap between the social orders. Within the monastic community one strived to remove, or at least to level the distinction between noble and non-noble, and even the difference between free and unfree.[91] For this reason the distinguished but unfree order of *ministeriales* was particularly involved in these foundations, for instance at Kloosterrade. The statutes of Springiersbach and Kloosterrade therefore stressed that not worldly status, but personal merits should determine the rank of a person within the community of canons. In the religious climate of the time some *potentes* apparently critically questioned their own way of life and radically relinquished it. Out of religious motives they renounced wealth, the noble way of life, marriage, authority and the use of force, and embraced a *vita apostolica*, based on ideals of poverty, continence, and obedience. This 'poverty' was nevertheless a relative notion in practice: although one parted with one's property and donated it to the monastery, the involvement with the property continued, because sometimes one kept the usufruct of it, and often control over it.

The foundation and endowment of monasteries could also have political and economic benefits. Donations to a monastery not only entailed close and profitable bonds with the monastic community, but also social prestige and even political power in the lay world. Through gifts, which often took place in public ceremonies which were staged and ritualized acts of symbolic representation, aristocrats made themselves visible to their peers and lesser folk as magnanimous noblemen. Their alliance with the conventuals, and with the holy, transcendent power they represented, had a legitimizing function.[92] The goods given were henceforth inviolable and came under the patron saint's sacrosanct protection. This transformation of land from worldly into sacred property, ideologically strengthened the noble donors' position of power as well. Besides, by donating, they enlarged their network of alliances and thus their power range. Through their gifts, benefactors therefore acquired social capital made up of status and prestige.[93]

Furthermore, by virtue of early-medieval ideas on churches and monasteries as private property

[91]   Ehlers 1973, 38; Zotz 1992, 325-328.

[92]   Lauwers 1997, 191-194, 312-315, 325-329.

[93]   Social capital, according to Pierre Bourdieu (and cited

by Jacobs 1996, 151), is 'the complex of existing and potential resources resulting from having a more or less institutionalized, permanent network of relations

(the so-called *Eigenkirchen* and *Eigenklöster*), lay founders and their heirs often maintained particular rights of ownership and of disposition over the donated property. In general, it was not fully alienated.[94] I have already pointed to the possibility that donations to monasteries and churches were carried out to keep together the ancestral inheritance, in order to keep intact the power based on landed property. Donors therefore did not want to lose control over the goods given, but to keep at least part of this, even if it contradicted church legislation and often the recipients' wishes as well. Early- and high-medieval distinguished benefactors continued to regard donated land as part of their power base, and rather as a distinct, holy part, as it was owned and protected by a saint. Moreover, by virtue of 12th-century canon law the founders and their heirs were entitled to the right of the *patronus*. This covered influence on internal matters, such as the election of the abbot, interference with the monastery's property, claims to a part of the monastery's revenues included, and even to a certain extent participation in monastic life through the right to lodging in and maintenance by the abbey. This right was often exacted by powerful lords, and supplied willy-nilly by the conventuals, as we can read in the 12th-century Chronicle of the Benedictine abbey of Saint-Trond, which relates the unwelcome presence of both lay men and women in chapter-house and refectory.[95] When this abbey's prior had the cloister closed off so as to prevent laymen of either sex from walking in and out of the monastery, the abbey's female advocate, Countess Gertrud of Duras († 1114), protested, as she could no longer pass through the *claustrum* and the brothers' convent, as had been usual.[96] Her husband, the abbey's advocate, Count Gislebert of Duras, and his son Otto, were accommodated in the abbot's quarters between 1121 and 1123; the latter used these 'as if it was his own house' and, what is more, here, so close to the sacred church tower, he did not refrain from having intercourse with his young bride.[97]

Often the founder obtained the right of protector or advocate of the institution.[98] Advocacy implied the exercise of criminal justice on the monastery's domains and the military protection thereof in return for a profitable fief which served as a source of revenue. From the administration of justice revenues accrued to the advocate as well, usually one third of the fines and arrangements. Moreover, the advocate acted as an intermediary between donor and monastery in almost all property transactions. In this way he controlled the process of endowment by his peers. This role is very clear in the case of Count Adelbert of Saffenberg († 1110), who, as the donor of the foundation property of the abbey of Kloosterrade, reserved the abbey's advocacy for himself and his heirs. As the abbey's advocates, Adelbert, his son Adolf of Saffenberg, and the latter's son-in-law Henry of Limburg (since 1136), had a leading role in the process of the abbey's endowment in the first decades of its existence.[99] Advocacy was an important source of power for the aristocracy and a political instrument in consolidating its power. During the 13th century, therefore, advocacy rights often developed into seigneurial rights. The foundation and endowment of monasteries by the local and regional aristocra-

of mutual familiarity and appreciation – or from being a member of a group – which backs its participants with the collective ownership of the capital.' Relations and networks of relations are created and maintained by exchanging gifts.

[94] Jahn 1988, 412; Reuter 1995.

[95] De Borman 1877, I, 76, 131-133; Lavigne 1988, 59-60, 97-98.

[96] De Borman 1877, I, 135-136; Lavigne 1988, 100.

[97] De Borman 1877, I, 209; Lavigne 1988, 151. This happened during Abbot Rodulf's exile; after his return he had the abbot's residence, cause of much calamity to the abbey, demolished.

[98] See *L'avouerie en Lotharingie* 1984; Arnold 1991, 82-84, 167-168, 195-202; Sauer 1993, 27-30; Foote 1996. About the exercise of advocacy in the Meuse-Demer-Scheldt area see Bijsterveld 1989, 19-23.

[99] See Augustus/Jamar 1995, 88, 162-164.

cy in the Meuse-Demer-Scheldt area in the first half of the 12th century can be regarded as a remunerative way of 'keeping while giving'. In many instances the establishment grew into a noble *Hauskloster*, closely associated to the name-giving castle of the founding family and completely bound to it through hereditary advocacy.[100]

The socio-political situation of the 1130s, that is at the time of the foundation of Premonstratensian abbeys in the Meuse-Demer-Scheldt area, was particularly favourable for the political benefit of the regional aristocracy. The active involvement of an interrelated regional network of noblemen in the foundation and endowment of Postel priory emphatically puts the (nominal) territorial prince of those days in the shade. The count of Louvain as duke of Lower Lotharingia and margrave of Antwerp possessed the supreme authority of the region in question at least in name. In 1106 Emperor Henry V (1105-1125) had granted the duchy of Lower Lotharingia and the marquisate of Antwerp to Godfrey I, count of Louvain (1095-1139).[101] From then on, he represented the emperor's public authority in this part of the German Empire. However, from 1128 onwards, the counts of Louvain lived through a difficult period: in this year king Lothar III (1125-1137) took away from Godfrey I his ducal dignity and granted it to Walram II, count of Limburg (duke 1128-1139). The next year Godfrey lost the battle of Wilderen (near Duras) against the bishop of Liège and Walram of Limburg, which considerably decreased his power. His son Godfrey II (1139-1142) recaptured the ducal title, but only survived his father for three years. He left behind a one-year old son, Godfrey III (1142-1190), who could only establish his personal authority from 1155 onwards. During his minority his mother, Lutgard of Sulzbach, sister of the wife of Emperor Conrad III (1138-1152), acted as regent. This possibly accounts for the duke's aloofness during Postel's foundation phase and in the other Premonstratensian foundations.

After 1155 Godfrey pursued a very successful territorial policy, which made him into a supreme prince and ruler. In 1146, in a papal bull, he is mentioned as the holder of the *advocatia* of the abbey of Tongerlo. This resulted from the appointment by Emperor Conrad III of Godfrey II or III as the advocate of all abbeys in his realm, which must have taken place sometime between 1138/1139 and 1146.[102] Henceforth, a close connection between the duke and the Premonstratensian abbeys in his duchy would exist, which revealed itself among other things in the duke's generosity. By virtue of his

[100] Zotz 1992, 318.

[101] Bonenfant/Bonenfant-Feytmans 1968; Genicot 1975, 92-93; Kupper 1981, 163, 468-469; Steurs 1993, 119; Bijsterveld 1997c.

[102] According to an undated charter, King Conrad granted Duke Godfrey and his successors the advocacy of all 'churches and ecclesiastical persons' and their properties within the duchy of Lotharingia (*sub principatu Lotharingie*), which is unveracious. According to the last editor, F. Hausmann, this charter is a forgery from the later 13th century (Hausmann, 514-515, no. 296; see Werner 1991: 410-411 and n. 252). However, the oldest, fifteenth-century copy reads *sub ipsius dicionibus*, 'within his realm' instead, which, according to P. Bonenfant, makes the appointment 'tout à fait vraisemblable' (Bonenfant 1935, 356-358 and n. 6;

Bonenfant and Bonenfant-Feytmans 1968, 1146-1147, 1151 and n. 1, 1154; Genicot 1975, 84, 89-91. See also Van Uytven 1958-1959; Avonds 1982, 457; Bijsterveld 1989a, 18). The *datum post quem* of the duke's appointment is Conrad's election as king of the Romans on March 7, 1138, or, in all likelihood, the reappointment of Godfrey II as duke in the second half of 1138 or early 1139; the *terminus ante quem* is given by the papal bull for the abbey of Tongerlo of March 15, 1146. This bull states with regard to the abbey's *advocatia: Prohibemus autem ut ipsius loci advocatiam nullus usurpet, sed dominus Lovanie, qui pro tempore fuerit, sicut a carissimo filio nostro Cunrado Romanorum rege rationabiliter statutum est, absque aliqua exactione vobis et rebus vestris patrocinium prebeat* (Erens/Koyen 1948-1958, I, 5-8, no. 3, dd. 1146, March 15). In 1154

advocacy the duke from then on supervised the process of the abbeys' endowment, which increasingly provided him with control over the regional aristocracy. For instance, in the charters of the abbey of Tongerlo from about 1160 onwards, we observe him acting as the one who executed and confirmed almost all donations. The advocacy of the Premonstratensian abbeys in his realm constituted a pivotal determinant in expanding his authority over the aristocracy in the northern part of his duchy. During the first eighty years of Postel's existence, however, the duke of Brabant did not directly interfere in the priory's affairs. Only from 1215 onwards did Duke Henry I (1190-1235), who, from the end of the 12th century, started to call himself, next to duke of Lower Lotharingia, also duke of Brabant, begin to lavishly donate to Postel monastery and to further its interests.[103] Indeed, only since *circa* 1190 had this duke actually started to extend his authority to the northeastern part of his sphere of influence, that is, roughly speaking, to the later Bailiwick ('Meierij') of 's-Hertogenbosch.[104]

In the same second quarter of the 12th century, the bishop of Liège too undeniably lost power.[105] Until about 1120, the diocese of Liège was held to be a bastion of imperial policy. Since the tenth century, the bishop of Liège had been one of the pillars of the so-called *Reichskirche*.[106] From 985 onwards, the emperor had invested the bishop of Liège with the authority of a count in some regions, but the latter also pretended to have worldly power outside his counties; in any case he acted here as the representative of public authority, that is, of the emperor.[107] The course of the Investiture Controversy, the defeat of Emperor Henry IV (1056-1105; who died at Liège in 1106), the assumption of power of his son Henry V, who hardly interfered in this part of his empire at all, and Henry's designation of the count of Louvain as duke of Lower Lotharingia and margrave of Antwerp in 1106, brought about considerable shifts in the constellation of power in this part of the German Empire, to the detriment of the bishop's power. The compromise of the Concordat of Worms (1122) opened up a new period of Liège's adjustment and accommodation to the altered political and religious circumstances. Public authority slipped out of the bishop's hands into the hands of worldly princes and local *potentes*. As a result of the weakening of public authority on a supralocal level, in combination with social and economic developments, local and regional aristocrats claimed more independence; *milites*, knights, and *ministeriales* broke out of the old structure of the dependent *familia* and established themselves in the lower ranks of the aristocracy. D. Foote calls this process of a replacement of the imperial church by 'a comital church', 'in which regional princes thoroughly dominated the bishopric'.[108] The social and political circumstances of the second quarter of the 12th century created a political vacuum of which the local and regional aristocracy could take advantage. The 'crisis of identity' of the bishop of Liège and the political problems of the duke in this period offered the local and regional aristocracy an exquisite opportunity to act more independently. They particularly did so by founding new monasteries, which, in the region under scrutiny were almost without exception houses of the order of Prémontré. The oldest charters of these monasteries clearly show us that is was not the bishop or the duke, but the lower ranking seigneurs and the count of Looz who furnished the larger

Emperor Frederick I Barbarossa granted the duke the advocacy of the abbey of Park as well (ed. Appelt 1975-1990, I, 134-137, no. 81, d.d. 1154, June 17).

[103] Miraeus/Foppens 1723-1748, IV, 534, dd. [*circa* 1215] (= Barbier 1892, II, 70, no. 147, dd. [*circa* 1218]); Camps 1979, 181-182, no. 112, dd. 1215; 183-184, no. 115, dd. 1219, June; 212-213, no. 139, dd. 1227.

[104] See the paragraph on the integration of the Kempen region into the duchy of Brabant in Theuws 1989, 193-200; and Steurs 1993, 385-387.

[105] For this episode, see Foote 1996.

[106] Kupper 1981, 141-145.

[107] Constable 1980, 189, 193, 208; see also Genicot 1975, 84; Theuws/Bijsterveld 1992, 124-136; Foote 1996; Kupper 1997.

[108] Foote 1996: 9-11, 12-13, 22.

part of their endowments. This may be regarded as the religious, social and political manifestation of a rising order.

6   THE DONORS' MOTIVES

Can we, after having analysed the general socio-political and religious circumstances, say something about the particular intentions of the donors to Postel? For analytical purposes I will distinguish spiritual, material, legal, and political aspects of the donors' intentions and motives. In reality, these constitute an inextricable whole: in medieval pious gift-giving worldly and otherworldly motives inseparably converged. The religious beliefs and doctrines as well as the social implications and functions of the gift are all necessary, constitutive ingredients of the desired bonds between conventuals and the rest of society. This emphasis on the multifacetedness and multivocality of the gift recalls Mauss's famous characterization of gifts as 'total social phenomenons'.[109]

The religious motives of the donations to Postel are explicitly expressed, such as the desire for redemption (in the dedication charter), further piety and devotion (mentioned three times), and the concern for one's own salvation (mentioned once).[110] On two occasions a gift accompanied a daughter's entry into the monastery. Their families expected them to pray, together with their fellow conventuals, for the souls of their relatives and in this way make a spiritual return for the 'dowry' they brought with them on entering the monastery. It is clear that these religious motives were most prominent. We may assume that the donor held well-determined ideas about the meaning of what the scribe who wrote this text expressed as 'out of pious devotion' or 'for the salvation of his/her soul'. Although some historians have disposed of phrases like these as mere formulas and have taken their religious meaning for granted, recent studies have stressed their crucial significance.[111] Since Late Antiquity, ecclesiastical authors have stressed the redeeming capacity of giving alms and of the *donatio pro anima* and these ideas will not have escaped 12th-century laymen.[112] What the donor expected from monks and canons were, first of all, prayers for the salvation of his soul (*pro anima*) and the eternal celebration of his memory (*commemoratio*) in the liturgical services within their community, which would accelerate his redemption in the hereafter. Through his gifts he assured himself of good spiritual relations with the conventuals, and, through them, with the transcendent world, personified by the monastery's patron saint. As religious specialists the canons, monks, or nuns by their prayers would take care of the salvation of his soul and of the souls of his relatives, not only of the living ones, but also of his ancestors and of his future offspring. In the Middle Ages donations were the crucial means to maintain relations with de-

---

[109]   Mauss 1973, 147: 'Dans ces phénomènes sociaux "totaux" (...) s'expriment à la fois et d'un coup toutes sortes d'institutions: religieuses, juridiques et morales – et celles-ci politiques et familiales en même temps; économiques (...); sans compter les phénomènes esthétiques (..) et les phénomènes morphologiques (..)'. See Schmid 1985, 60, 66-67; and, above all, Silber 1995, 225-229.

[110]   At the church dedication the donors promised *se singulis annis redempturos*; Fastrad had confirmed in writ-

ing *illud quod pie egerat*; of Berta van Blaarthem's donation God was the *principalis causa*; Didradis of Rixtel made her gift *pia devotione*; Gerung and Gocelin donated *pro salute anime sue*.

[111]   Bouchard 1991, 75-76; Holdsworth 1991, 6-7; Parisse 1996.

[112]   See, about the development of the Christian ideology regarding the redeeming capacity of giving alms and the practice of the pious gift, Jobert 1977, 141-225; Bijsterveld 1996; Lauwers 1997, 69-89, 173-182.

ceased relatives.[113] Therefore, gifts to conventuals were meant to ensure the donor's good relations with God and all saints in heaven as well as with his relatives who had already entered the afterlife. In many *arengae*, that is the introductions to charters in which the religious motivation of the recorded transaction is stated, thoughts are expressed about the eternal reward the donor could expect in the hereafter for the gift of his temporal goods during his earthly life.[114]

But apart from these religious intentions, material, legal, and socio-political concerns were also involved in these donations. Berta of Blaarthem's heirs had to be compensated 'at high cost', and the two brothers who donated their farmstead 'for their soul's sake' also received a considerable amount of money in return for a piece of land. That religious and material motives could go hand in hand is clear from a charter of the year 1155, recording a transfer of property to the abbey of Floreffe. It is stated that the donor made his donation 'partly for the salvation of his soul, and partly by intervention of fair trade'.[115] What this donor gained materially by this gift, is not specified.

But more important than a material compensation for the ceded property to the benefactor, seems to have been the compensation for the hereditary rights relatives claimed. Three times the conventuals of Postel had to compensate heirs for their consent to the donation, or to end the quarrel raised by them some time after the transaction had taken place. In the case of Arnold Brabent's donation, he had to renew it because of the 'quarrel among all succeeding heirs'. To stop this, he now represented the donation as the gift of a dowry on his daughter's entry into the monastery. Although Berta of Blaarthem's daughter and three grandsons had consented in her donating landed property in Reusel and in Blaarthem, and although the transaction had taken place lawfully 'before many witnesses', it appeared necessary to give to one of the grandsons, Roger Scademule, a symbolic compensation for his renouncement. In the church of Brempt, some 80 kms from Postel (and 16 kms east of Roermond), *frater* Rodulf, the monastery's *magister* handed 'two pennies to buy a knife' over to him. This ceremony must therefore have taken place sometime between 1173 and 1179. The two pennies were probably the compensation for the knife he had put on the church's altar as a symbol of his renouncement.[116] Next, his mother Gisla and his sister also offered their hereditary and property rights 'to God on an altar', but this time the cession took place in the Postel monastery church, in the presence of the monastery's brothers and sisters. This woman and her daughter presumably had to be compensated with some money too. The last case concerning the compensation of heirs deals with the compensation the conventuals made for the small piece of land (*pro recompensatione illius terre*) ceded by Winand, who made it possible for a straight moat to be dug around one of Postel's estates. In this case the *magister* of Postel provided a return 'to stop the quarrel with the succeeding heirs'.

It is not easy to indicate the principle on which the claims of these heirs were based. Written or otherwise fixed laws of property and of inheritance did not exist. Although donations of landed property certainly were governed by unwritten, common law on property transactions, we cannot speak of a system of real property law governing the alienation of land before the 13th century.[117] This common law was dynamic as it was passed on orally. These 12th-century aristocratic families obviously held notions according to which patrimonial landed property was regarded as a joint and in-

[113] Geary 1994a; McLaughlin 1994, 251-252, 254-256; Lauwers 1997.

[114] Fichtenau 1957, 137-147; Jobert 1977, 215-216; White 1988, 154-155; Parisse 1996.

[115] Camps 1979, 93-95, no. 58, dd. 1155; 94 r. 27-28: (...) *partim pro salute anime sue, partim rationabilis inter-*

ventu commertii (...). See Bijsterveld 1989b, 19-20. For other examples see Bouchard 1991, 218.

[116] On the knife as a symbol used in property transactions, see Bijsterveld 1997b.

[117] White 1988, 130-176; Bouchard 1991, 178-180; Reynolds 1994, 53-74.

alienable possession. When a member of the family, man or woman, donated part of this to a monastery, the other beneficiaries most closely involved (or at least a number of them) had to give their consent. But even if this had taken place and the donor had lawfully parted with a piece of the family's patrimony, heirs could continue to claim a certain right to it. In any case, the receiving conventuals had to do justice to the rights and claims of the donors' heirs, that is in a concrete as well as symbolic way. Next to the religious motives described above, an appropriate compensation of the heirs seems to have been an important part of the donors' expectations when donating landed property to monasteries and saints.

As far as the politically inspired motives of Postel's benefactors are concerned, we can only express them in general terms. Unfortunately too little is known about the actual exercise of power and of lordship by aristocratic lineages in the Meuse-Demer-Scheldt area during the 12th century. In this regard, it is necessary to investigate the exercise of protective or advocacy rights of the young Premonstratensian foundations before the duke of Brabant exercised these. In the case of St Michael's abbey at Antwerp, the duke only acted as *dominus et advocatus*, 'lord and advocate' of the abbey and its possessions in 1154, thirty years after its foundation.[118] We already saw that the duke of Brabant possessed the *advocatia* of the abbey of Tongerlo in 1146. Given the duke's age at the time, about ten years, this advocacy cannot have been a personal exercise of authority. From the start the abbey of Averbode came under the jurisdiction of the bishop of Liège; the count of Looz, the abbey's founder, only acted as its advocate from the mid-1150s onwards, which advocacy was recognised by the duke of Brabant.[119] Only in the case of the abbey of Averbode do we observe the usual pattern of the founder assuming the advocacy, albeit only after some time. With the other Premonstratensian foundations it was the duke who, in the second instance, a few decades after their establishment, took over the advocacy. He did this by virtue of imperial designation and not because of his involvement with the foundation. Before that, in the period between the actual foundation and the duke's appearance, the judicial and military powers deriving from advocacy were in all probability exercised by the founders and their heirs. The protection in spiritual affairs was exercised by the bishop. In the case of Postel, the heirs and relatives of Fastrad of Uitwijk will therefore as advocates have assisted the monastery in the exercise of criminal justice and the military protection of the monastery's property. In this regard, attention should be drawn to the advocacy rights of the allod of Elmt, under Bladel, which Dietrich of Herlaar renounced on behalf of Postel priory in 1173. Apparently, the donor who ceded property to a monastery, usually kept in his possession its advocacy rights.

[118] Goetschalckx 1909, 26-27, no. 13, dd. 1154; see *ibidem*, 22-24, no. 11, dd. 1154.

[119] See Benedixen 1996, 193-199. For the charter evidence see Evers s.a., 19-20, no. 11, dd. 1154: charter issued by Count Louis I of Looz (1138/1140-1171), in which he calls himself *legitimus Averbodiensis ecclesie advocatus* (according to Janssens 1990, 29-32, 44-45, this charter is a forgery). According to a charter of 1155, regarding a donation of property at Maaseik (Evers s.a., 21-22, no. 12, dd. 1155), *elegit me* (= the count of Looz) *ecclesia Averbodiensis ibi in advocatum*. In 1160 (Evers s.a., 24-25, no. 14, dd. 1160) he calls himself *advocatus prefati claustri* and *comes et advocatus*. The charter of 1162, regarding the property at Maaseik (Evers s.a., 28-29, no. 17, dd. 1162), contains the remarkable phrase which records that the abbot of Averbode has elected and accepted Count Louis of Looz as this property's advocate *quia sue ecclesie amicus et defensor extitit*. In contrast, the papal bull for the abbey of 1139 stated that the abbey 'would have nobody else than the bishop as its advocate' ([...] *nec aliquem preter episcopum habeat advocatum*; Evers s.a., 8-10, no. 4, dd. 1139, April 16; compare Janssens 1990, 26-28).

We can be brief about the Postel canons' intentions when receiving gifts of land and appurtenant rights from lay benefactors. In the text in question no mention is made of the canons' and nuns' desire to acquire a stable economic foundation for their community. It is clear, however, that the Premonstratensian convents that were founded in the Low Countries during the 12th century were very well capable of adapting to the rapidly changing economic and social situation of that century.[120] They succeeded in acquiring the landed property necessary to take an active part in the economic boom witnessed by this region after about 1125 (fig. 6). What the scribe does express in this text is the monastery's concern to maintain good relations with the donors and their relatives. They bought off Berta of Blaarthem's heirs at high cost to obtain their consent with her donation and their renouncement of the property involved. They compensated for the piece of land ceded by Winand to stop the quarrel with his heirs, with the intended result that 'both parties remained in peace'. The canons and nuns of Postel monastery were obviously very eager to acquire and preserve the goodwill of the aristocrats surrounding their community, even if this meant that they had to spend a lot of money or had to return a piece of property as a countergift.[121] Peace and stability were a *conditio sine qua non* for a young religious community like Postel's and good relations with their neighbours were the essential means to obtain these.

8   THE RETURNS OF THE CONVENTUALS

What did the donors expect as returns for their gifts?[122] Here too, for analytical reasons, I will distinguish the spiritual from the material. As we have seen, most benefactors presumably expected to enter into a spiritual relationship with the religious community, either by becoming members of the *confraternitas* or fraternity of the monastery, or by being actually admitted into the community. Sometimes donors made stipulations in their charters that in the future they wanted to retire into the monastery to spend their last years or days as a monk or a canon. As a return for their gift, they were promised the monks' or canon's habit on their deathbed.[123] In the text concerned no mention is made of gifts on the occasion of a donor becoming a canon or a nun in Postel monastery. Postel's founder, Fastrad of Uitwijk, as we have seen, did not become a canon at Postel, but a monk in the Benedictine abbey of Oostbroek instead. We also mentioned the distinguished lady Berta of Brecht, who took the veil in the Premonstratensian nunnery of Ewen and whose entry gift to the abbey of Tongerlo was later sold to Postel by the abbot of Tongerlo.[124] The text does record two gifts made on the occasion of daughters becoming nuns in Postel. Through the dowry or accompanying gift provided by their relatives, they 'bought' themselves into the community, which would provide them with lifelong maintenance and lodging.

---

[120] Despy 1974-1975; Lohrmann 1985; Verhulst 1985; Van Bavel 1993b.

[121] Bouchard 1987, 218-219; Teunis 1997.

[122] Holdsworth 1991, 12-13; Bouchard 1991, 71-72; Teunis 1997.

[123] In the *necrologium* of the abbey of Floreffe numerous anniversaries of these brothers, sisters, and lay brothers

ad succurrendum have been recorded. See Barbier 1876, 13, 19, 24, 25, 29, 30, 39, 45, 47, 50-51, 52, 55, 60, 62, 66, 69, 195, 197, 199, 201, 203, 206, 212, 218, 219, 222, 225, 228, 246, 250, 256, 257, 258, 262, 264, 265, 278, 279, 285.

[124] Steurs 1993, 118, 123.

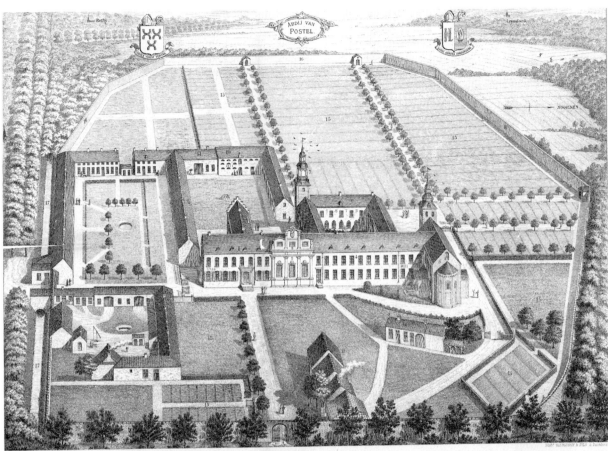

Fig. 6. The abbey of Postel c. 1875. To the right is the late 12th/13th century romanesque church (from Welvaarts 1878-1879).

The other pious donors will have been admitted into some kind of spiritual relationship with Postel's canons and nuns. This could sometimes take a tangible form, when a benefactor was promised a burial in the monastery church or graveyard, or meals in the refectory. But most of all it was the community's prayers that lay donors hoped to receive. These are, according to O.G. Oexle, 'als Gegengaben zu verstehen für die vielfaltigen geistigen und materiellen Gaben, die monastischen Gruppen ihren Gründern und Stiftern verdankten und durch die sie Tag für Tag materiell und spirituell in ihrer Existenz gehalten wurden'.[125] Donors thus expected that the conventuals would pray for the salvation of their souls and of those of their relatives, deceased, living, or yet to be born. The religious' prayers for benefactors could take place in the ceremonies known as the Chapter Office (the *officium capituli*) and the Office for the Dead, held daily, in the daily Mass, or in the private masses offered by priestly monks and canons, during which they were prayed for individually.[126] The promise of eternal commemoration as a member of the spiritual community of monks or canons and benefactors was a powerful means to ensure salvation.[127]

[125] Oexle 1983, 29.
[126] Holdsworth 1991, 17-18; Lauwers 1997, 117-119.
[127] See Geary 1994c.

Symbolic material returns given by the monastic community to the donors, according to the text studied, could consist of small sums of cash money (the two pennies to buy a knife), or of a piece of land. These returns were explicitly meant to appease discontented heirs. In her study of the 12th-century Cistercian monasteries in Burgundy, Constance Bouchard reserves for this kind of symbolic material returns from the monks the expression 'countergifts'. They appear in 10 percent of all gift transactions she studied and could be 'anything from a cow or horse to a sheep, a cloak, or a small sum of money'.[128] In 90 percent of the time however, the countergift consisted of a small amount of money paid in cash, 'appreciably less than the market value of the property involved'. Bouchard stresses the symbolic value of the countergift and therefore regards it as 'an expression of the monks' goodwill and, even more important, as a concrete representation of the transfer and of the prayers the monks would be offering'. 'A countergift from the monks to a man who had just made a pious gift was a sign that they found his gift acceptable and symbolized their concern and affection for him.' Bouchard found only a few cases in which those who consented received a countergift of their own. So in Burgundy most countergifts seem to have been given to the donors themselves. But Bouchard nevertheless concludes that 'a countergift could also serve as a concrete sign that a relative had indeed agreed to the original gift.'[129]

From an anthropological point of view, the countergifts as described by Bouchard and others are part of a more encompassing set of returns which are essential to the reciprocal gift. The countergift was not just an obligation automatically resulting from the initial gift. The need for the gift's recipient to affirm his prestige and his rank in society through a countergift, explains this return better than mere obligation.[130] The returns from the conventuals were mainly of a spiritual nature, that is prayers, but could also be of a material nature, that is money, goods, and land. To say it in the words of Constance Bouchard, by their gift-giving 'laymen gave property to the monks in return for something of value. But here the return from the monks was not the money of pawn, lease, or sale transactions, but rather the goodwill and inclusion in prayers which friendship with the monks entailed'.[131] Meals in the refectory, the permission to enter the *claustrum*, or even the (temporary) admission into the community, were granted as returns as well. In contrast, Barbara Rosenwein does not think it 'necessary to seek for concrete counter-gifts, such as donations in return for prayers or burial privileges'.[132] In her opinion, to explain donations 'the social meaning of gift giving alone is enough', and 'the gift in itself was its own reward.' She probably underestimates both the expectations of the donors which at times were quite concrete, as well as the symbolic meaning of the countergifts. Material countergifts appear more often than not to have been an essential part of gift exchange between laymen and conventuals. However, it remains an open question to what extent spiritual returns had to be accompanied by symbolic countergifts, or, in other words, to what extent an obligation existed to reward donations with material countergifts.[133] Bouchard indicates that in any case countergifts were more common than their explicit mentions in charters suggest. As the countergift was not an integral part of the transfer of property, it was not always recorded in the charters designed to record the transaction, but the same is true of the prayers.[134] Laymen and religious presumably ex-

[128] Bouchard 1991, 87-94.

[129] Bouchard 1991, 89. See also Bouchard 1987, 219. According to Tabuteau 1988, 115-119, in Normandy 'the countergift (...) was both an inducement and a compensation to a donor or a confirmer', and as such part of a legal settlement. See also Teunis 1997.

[130] Lauwers 1996, 75.

[131] Bouchard 1991, 93.

[132] Rosenwein 1989, 138-139, 204.

[133] See also Reuter 1995, 181-182.

[134] Bouchard 1991, 90-92.

changed, much more often than the preserved written documents suggest, objects and money as an element of, or, more accurately, as symbols of their ongoing spiritual and social bond. According to Henk Teunis, '(b)y making a countergift *in caritate* the monastery (of Noyers in the Touraine – AJAB) was trying to induce the donor (...) to perpetuate his benevolent attitude in the future. It was a means not only to define an equal and balanced agreement, but to guide the monastery's partner in the direction the monastery wanted. (...) Seen in this way, gift and countergift were the means *par excellence* to influence and control, as far as possible, each other's behaviour'.[135]

9   CONCLUSION

Summing up, we can say that, through their gifts to monasteries, benefactors wanted to establish lasting reciprocal bonds ('confraternity') with the conventuals. This friendship between laymen and monks, canons and/or nuns, phrased in religious terms, had both a socio-political and a spiritual side to it. A sound association with the religious in this world was considered to be a foreshadowing of a sound association with God and His saints in the hereafter, and moreover, with all relatives who had already passed the gates of eternity. Vice versa, it was of primary importance to the monks, canons, and nuns to maintain sound relations with their lay benefactors, who as more or less powerful people could both protect and ruin their community. This relationship was expressed in the religious' daily prayers for all who had been admitted into confraternity with the community. And in the way the donor's worldly property symbolized the bond with the religious, the religious' returns, consisting of prayers, could be symbolized in a material way. These countergifts could be intended for the benefactors themselves, or, as in the text discussed here, for the heirs. After all, they inherited the bonds their ancestors had established. Hence, it was of crucial importance to Postel's canons to continue these by showing their benevolence. This probably explains their efforts to appease the donors' heirs by supplying returns in exchange for their consent and renouncements.

The combination of spiritual and socio-political intentions of the donor, and of spiritual and symbolic material returns by the religious are two sides of one and the same coin. As has been said before, several, inseparable meanings underlie gift exchange. However, the donor's most explicit objective remained the creating of a spiritual bond with the hereafter through the religious' prayers. In exchange for temporal property he hoped to acquire eternal life and to be commemorated in the monastery's prayer services until the end of time.[136] By donating something of eternal value, that is ancestral landed property, he made a gift which in a certain sense represented the eternal life he could expect in return. In the same way, the religious' material compensations represented the prayers on the donor's behalf. The transcendent relations between donor and religious in this way found their equivalent on this side of death. Gifts and countergifts served to create, maintain and reproduce lasting, peaceful and stable bonds between laymen and their heirs on the one hand, and religious on the other, and, moreover, between donors and the afterlife, that is with God, His saints and the dead. The stability and peace brought about by these gifts, both in this world and in the hereafter, were in the mutual interest of both aristocratic laymen and religious.

A complex whole of religious and socio-political motives underlay the donations made by a number of regional aristocrats from the area between the rivers Meuse, Demer, and Scheldt to found and

[135] Teunis 1997, 88.

[136] For a summary of these services, see Holdsworth 1991, 16-18.

endow Postel priory in the second and third quarter of the 12th century. This resulted in a strengthening of a network of social and religious bonds, that is between donors and religious, between donors and the ecclesiastical authorities of the region, and among aristocrats themselves. Part of these relations had a heavenly, everlasting parallel. After the roaring days of the Investiture Contest, in a period of religious and political transformation, the 12th-century regional elite and Postel's canons tried to establish new connections. By reciprocal gift-giving and through entering into close relations, they once more aimed at creating some order in a turbulent society and at assuring peace both here and in the hereafter. It was the duke of Brabant who, after some decades, would gratefully employ this new order to establish his authority.

REFERENCES

Published medieval sources

Appelt, H. (ed.), 1975-1990: *Monumenta Germaniae Historica. Diplomata X. Friderici I. Diplomata*, Hannover.

Augustus, L./J.T.J. Jamar (eds), 1995: *Annales Rodenses. Kroniek van Kloosterrade. Tekst en vertaling*, Maastricht (Publikaties Rijksarchief Limburg 3).

Barbier, J. (ed.), 1876: Nécrologe de l'abbaye de Floreffe de l'ordre de Prémontré, au diocèse de Namur, *Analectes pour servir à l'Histoire Ecclésiastique de la Belgique* 13, 5-70, 190-286.

Barbier, V. (ed.), 1892: *Histoire de l'abbaye de Floreffe de l'ordre de Prémontré*, Namur.

Borman, C. de (ed.), 1877: *Chronique de l'abbaye de Saint-Trond*, Liége.

Camps, H.P.H. (ed.), 1979: *Oorkondenboek van Noord-Brabant tot 1312. I De meierij van 's-Hertogenbosch (met de heerlijkheid Gemert)*, 's-Gravenhage.

Erens, M.A./H.M. Koyen (eds), 1948-1958: *De oorkonden der abdij Tongerloo. Tekstpublicatie*, Tongerlo.

Evers, H. (ed.), s.a.: *De oorkonden der abdij van Averbode*, s.l.

Goetschalckx, P.J. (ed.), 1909: *Oorkondenboek der Witheerenabdij van s.-Michiels te Antwerpen I*, Eekeren/Donk.

Hausmann, F. (ed.), 1969: *Monumenta Germaniae Historica. Diplomata IX. Conradi III. Diplomata*, Wien/Köln/Graz.

Hugo, C.L. (ed.), 1734: *Sacri et canonici Ordinis Praemonstratensis Annales* (etc.), Nanceii [Nancy].

Koch, A.C.F. (ed.), 1970: *Oorkondenboek van Holland en Zeeland tot 1299. I Eind van de 7e eeuw tot 1222*, 's-Gravenhage.

Lavigne, E. (ed.), 1988[2]: *Kroniek van de abdij van Sint-Truiden. 1ste deel: 628-1138. Vertaling van de Gesta Abbatum Trudonensium*, Leeuwarden/Maastricht, 1986[1] (Maaslandse monografieën 43).

Miraeus, A./J.F. Foppens (eds), 1723-1748[2]: *Opera diplomatica et historica*, Louvain/Brussels.

Muller, S./A.C. Bouman/K. Heeringa/F. Ketner (eds), 1920-1959: *Oorkondenboek van het Sticht Utrecht tot 1301*, Utrecht/Den Haag.

Ramackers, J. (ed.), 1972[2]: *Papsturkunden in den Niederlanden (Belgien, Luxemburg, Holland und Französisch-Flandern)*, Berlin 1933-1934[1], Nendeln/Liechtenstein (Abhandlungen der Gesellschaft der Wissenschaften zu Göttingen. Philologisch-Historische Klasse. Dritte Folge 8-9).

Rij, H. van (ed.), 1987: Het stichtingskroniekje van de Abdij van Berne, in *Egmond en Berne. Twee verhalende historische bronnen uit de middeleeuwen*, 's-Gravenhage (Nederlandse Historische Bronnen 7), 87-143.

Rousseau, F. (ed.), 1936: *Actes des comtes de Namur de la première race 946-1196*, Bruxelles.

Velden, G. van der (ed.), 1986: *Het Necrologium Bernense van Arnold van Vessem uit 1574, aangevuld met de namen van de abijdleden tot 1986*, Heeswijk.

Literature

Appadurai, A., 1990[3]: Introduction: commodities and the politics of value, in A. Appadurai (ed.), *The social life of things. Commodities in cultural perspective*, Cambridge etc., 1986[1], 3-63.

Arnold, B., 1991: *Princes and territories in medieval Germany*, Cambridge etc.

Arts, N., e.a., 1996: *De kastelen Blaarthem en Gagelbosch bij Eindhoven*, Eindhoven (Archeologisch en historisch onderzoek in Eindhoven 1).

Asseldonk, M. van, 1996: Het graafschap Rode. Bouwsteen van het middeleeuwse kwartier Peelland, *Brabants Heem* 48, 59-66.

Avonds, P., 1982: Brabant en Limburg 1100-1403, in D.P. Blok e. a. (eds), *Algemene Geschiedenis der Nederlanden. 2. Middeleeuwen*, Haarlem, 452-482.

L'avouerie en Lotharingie, 1984: *L'avouerie en Lotharingie. Actes des 2es Journées Lotharingiennes. 22-23 octobre 1982. Centre Universitaire Luxembourg*, Luxembourg (Publications de la Section historique de l'Institut G.-D. de Luxembourg 98).

Baerten, J., 1959: De Berthouts in de XIIe eeuw, *Handelingen van de Koninklijke Kring voor Oudheidkunde, Letteren en Kunst van Mechelen* 63, 17-29.

Barthélemy, D., 1994: Qu'est-ce que la chevalerie, en France aux Xe et XIe siècles?, *Revue historique* 118, 15-74.

Bavel, B.J.P. van, 1993a: *Goederenverwerving en goederenbeheer van de abdij Mariënweerd (1129-1592)*, Hilversum.

Bavel, B.J.P. van, 1993b: Stichtingsplaats, ontginning en goederenverwerving. De economische ontwikkeling van Norbertijner abdijen in de Nederlanden (12de – 13de eeuw), in *Ideaal en werkelijkheid. Stichtingsplaatsen en ontginningsactiviteiten van Premonstratenzers in de Nederlanden. Verslagen van de derde contactdag. Abdij van Tongerlo zaterdag 15 mei 1993*, Tongerlo, 44-53.

Bazelmans, J.G.A., 1996: *Eén voor allen, allen voor één. Tacitus' Germania, de Oudengelse Beowulf en het ritueel-kosmologische karakter van de relatie tussen heer en krijger-volgeling in Germaanse samenlevingen*, Amsterdam.

Bazelmans, J., 1997: De waarde van geschenken in het Oudengelse gedicht 'Beowulf', in A. Komter (ed.), *Het geschenk. Over de verschillende betekenissen van geven*, Amsterdam, 91-107.

Benedixen, B., 1996: Einige Notizen zu den Anfängen des Doppelklosters Averbode im 12. Jahrhundert, *Analecta Praemonstratensia* 72, 171-199.

Bijsterveld, A.J.A., 1989a: Een zorgelijk bezit. De benedictijnenabdijen van Echternach en St. Truiden en het beheer van hun goederen en rechten in Oost-Brabant, 1100-1300, *Noordbrabants Historisch Jaarboek* 6, 7-44.

Bijsterveld, A.-J., 1989b: De hof van Lierop. De oudste bezittingen van de abdij van Floreffe en de priorij van Postel in Lierop en Asten, 1155-1306, in T. Maas (ed.), *Lierop 'n beeld van een dorp*, Lierop, 17-26.

Bijsterveld, A.J.A., 1996: Middeleeuwse vrome schenkingen als instrument van sociale integratie en politieke machtsvorming. Een historiografisch overzicht, *Tijdschrift voor Geschiedenis* 109, 443-464.

Bijsterveld, A.J.A., 1997a: *Dona dantes et vota voventes*. De stichting en dotatie van het norbertijnenklooster te Postel (1128/1138-1179), *Analecta Praemonstratensia* 73, 5-47.

Bijsterveld, A.J.A., 1997b: Een handschoen op het altaar. De betekenis van het middeleeuwse ritueel van grondschenking, in A. Komter (ed.), *Het geschenk. Over de verschillende betekenissen van geven*, Amsterdam, 58-73.

Bijsterveld, A.J.A., 1997c: Een nieuwe orde? De politieke en religieuze ontwikkelingen in het Maas-Demer-Scheldegebied in de elfde en twaalfde eeuw en de stichting van norbertijnenabdijen in het tweede kwart van de twaalfde eeuw, in S. van de Perre (ed.), *Norbertijnen in de politiek. Verslagen van de zevende contactdag. Abdij van 't Park zaterdag 26 april 1997*, Brussel, 9-38.

Bijsterveld, A.J.A., in press, The Commemorating Functions of Chronicles. Patrons and Gifts in Chronicles from the Diocese of Liège, Eleventh-Twelfth Centuries, *Revue Bénédictine*, in press.

Bijsterveld, A.J.A./P.J.A. Nissen (eds), *Rondom Rode. Macht, religie en cultuur in Peelland, circa 1000-1300*, in press.

Bijsterveld, A.-J.A., in press, The commemoration of Patrons and Gifts in Chronicles from the Diocese of Liège, Eleventh-Twelfth Centuries, *Revue Benedictine* 109 (1999).

Bond, J., 1993: The Premonstratensian order: a preliminary survey of its growth and distribution in medieval Europe, in M. Carver (ed.), *In search of cult. Archaeological investigations in honour of Philip Rahtz*, Woodbridge, 153-185.

Bonenfant, P., 1935: Note critique sur le faux diplôme d'Othon Ier de 947 conférant l'avouerie de Gembloux à Lambert, comte de Louvain, *Bulletin de la Commission royale d'Histoire* 99, 337-364.

Bonenfant, P./A.M. Bonenfant-Feytmans, 1968: Du duché de Basse-Lotharingie au duché de Brabant, *Belgisch Tijdschrift voor Filologie en Geschiedenis* 46, 1129-1165.

Bonenfant, P./G. Despy, 1958: La noblesse en Brabant aux XIIe et XIIIe siècles, *Le Moyen Age* 64, 27-66.

Bouchard, C.B., 1987: *Sword, Miter, and Cloister. Nobility and the Church in Burgundy, 980-1198*, Ithaca/London.

Bouchard, C.B., 1991: *Holy Entrepreneurs. Cistercians, Knights, and Economic Exchange in Twelfth-Century Burgundy*, Ithaca/London.

Braams, B.W., 1995: *Weyden en zeyden in het broek. Middeleeuwse ontginning en exploitatie van de kommen in het Land van Heusden en Altena*, Veessen/Wageningen.

Braams, B.W., 1996: Uithoven en ander geestelijk bezit in Noord-Brabant ten noorden van de Oude Maas, 1100-1300, *Historisch-Geografisch Tijdschrift* 14, 90-99.

Cappon, C.M., 1995: Eine donatio post obitum mit Treuhändern: die Schenkung von Dietrich von Ulft zugunsten des Klosters Camp (um 1138). Einige Aspekte der Vorgeschichte des Testaments in den Niederlanden, *Zeitschrift der Savigny-Stiftung für Rechtsgeschichte. Germanistische Abteilung* 112, 245-270.

Clanchy, M.T., 1994[2]: *From Memory to Written Record. England 1066-1307*, Oxford/Cambridge, 1979[1].

Coenen, J., 1992: *Van Ricstelle tot Aarle-Rixtel. De Geschiedenis van Aarle-Rixtel*, Aarle-Rixtel.

Coldeweij, J.A., 1981: *De Heren van Kuyc 1096-1400*. Tilburg (Bijdragen tot de Geschiedenis van het Zuiden van Nederland 50).

Constable, G., 1980: Monasticism, Lordship, and Society in the Twelfth-Century Hesbaye: Five Documents on the Foundation of the Cluniac Priory of Bertrée, in G. Constable, *Cluniac Studies*. London (Variorum CS 109) (earlier in *Traditio* 33, 1977, 159-224).

Declercq, G., e.a., 1987: L'informatisation de la "Table chronologique" d' A. Wauters. Méthodologie du nouveau répertoire des documents diplomatiques belges antérieurs à 1200, *Bulletin de la Commission royale d'Histoire* 153, 223-302.

Dekker, C., 1984: De komst van de Norbertijnen in het bisdom Utrecht, in C.M. Cappon e. a. (eds), *Ad fontes: opstellen aangeboden aan prof. dr. C. van de Kieft ter gelegenheid van zijn afscheid als hoogleraar in de middeleeuwse geschiedenis aan de Universiteit van Amsterdam*, Amsterdam, 167-186.

Despy, G., 1974-1975: Les richesses de la terre: Cîteaux et Prémontré devant l'économie de profit aux XIIe et XIIIe siècles, *Problèmes d'Histoire du Christianisme* 5, 58-80.

Despy, G., 1989: Les chartes privées comme source de l'histoire rurale pendant les temps mérovingiens et carolingiens, in H. Atsma (ed.), *La Neustrie. Les pays au nord de la Loire de 650 à 850. Colloque historique international*, Sigmaringen (Beihefte der Francia 16) I 583-593.

Deutz, H., 1992: Norbert von Xanten bei Propst Richer im Regularkanonikerstift Klosterrath, *Analecta Praemonstratensia* 68, 5-16.

Dierendonck, R.M. van/A.J.P.M. Maas, 1989: Archeologie en historie van een ontginningshoeve: De Kriekeschoor bij Bladel, in A. Verhoeven/F. Theuws (eds), *Het Kempenprojekt 3. De middeleeuwen centraal*, Waalre (Bijdragen tot de studie van het Brabantse Heem 33), 15-25.

Ehlers, J., 1973: Adlige Stiftung und persönliche Konversion. Zur Sozialgeschichte früher

Prämonstratenserkonvente, in *Geschichte und Verfassungsgeschichte. Frankfurter Festgabe für Walter Schlesinger*, Wiesbaden (Frankfurter Historische Abhandlungen 5), 32-55.

Fichtenau, H., 1957: *Arenga. Spätantike und Mittelalter im Spiegel von Urkundenformeln*, Graz/Köln (Mitteilungen des Instituts für Österreichische Geschichtsforschung. Ergänzungsband 18).

Foote, D., 1996: Taming monastic advocates and redeeming bishops: the *Triumphale* and episcopal *Vitae* of Reiner of St. Lawrence, *Revue d'Histoire Ecclésiastique* 91, 5-40.

Gärtner, W., 1991: Das Chorherrenstift Klosterrath in der Kanonikerreform des 12. Jahrhunderts, *Zeitschrift des Aachener Geschichtsvereins* 97, 33-220.

Geary, P., 1993: Entre gestion et *gesta*, in O. Guyotjeannin/L. Morelle/M. Parisse (eds), *Les cartulaires. Actes de la Table ronde organisée par l'Ecole nationale des chartes et le G.D.R. 121 du C.N.R.S. (Paris, 5-7 décembre 1991)*, Paris (Mémoires et documents de l'École des chartes 39), 13-26.

Geary, P., 1994a: Exchange and Interaction between the Living and the Dead in Early Medieval Society, in P.J. Geary, *Living with the Dead in the Middle Ages*, Ithaca/London, 77-92 (earlier as: Échanges et relations entre les vivants et les morts dans la société du Haut Moyen Age, *Droit et Cultures* 12, 1986, 3-17).

Geary, P.J., 1994b: Sacred Commodities: The Circulation of Medieval Relics, in P.J. Geary, *Living with the Dead in the Middle Ages*, Ithaca/London, 194-218 (earlier in A. Appadurai (ed.), *The social life of things. Commodities in cultural perspective*, Cambridge etc., 1986[1], 1990[3], 169-191).

Geary, P.J., 1994c: *Phantoms of Remembrance. Memory and Oblivion at the End of the First Millennium*, Princeton.

Genicot, L., 1975: Monastères et principautés en Lotharingie du Xe au XIIIe siècle, in L. Genicot, *Études sur les principautés lotharingiennes*, Louvain (Université de Louvain. Recueil de travaux d'histoire et de philologie, 6e série, fascicule 7) 59-139 (earlier as: Empire et principautés en Lotharingie du Xe au XIIIe siècle, *Annali della Fondazione Italiana per la storia amministrativa* 2, 95-172).

Gramaye, J., 1608: *Antiquitates Comitatus Namurcensis* etc, Louvain.

Grauwen, W.M., 1975: Norbert et les débuts de l'abbaye de Floreffe, *Analecta Praemonstratensia* 51, 5-23.

Grauwen, W.M., 1995: Norbert en de stichting van Floreffe, 1121, *Analecta Praemonstratensia* 71, 25-36.

Guyotjeannin, O., 1996: De la surinterprétation des sources diplomatiques médiévales. Quelques exemples français des alentours de l'an mil, *Enquête. Anthropologie, histoire sociologie* no. 3, 153-162.

Guyotjeannin, O., 1997: "*Penuria scriptorum*". Le mythe de l'anarchie documentaire dans la France du nord (X[e]-première moitié du XIe siècle), *Bibliothèque de l'École des chartes* 155, 11-44.

Guyotjeannin, O./J. Pycke/B.-M. Tock, 1993: *Diplomatique médiévale*, Turnhout, (L'atelier du médiéviste 2).

Hagemeijer, P., 1984: Samen, maar wel apart. Vrouwen en dubbelkloosters in de Noordelijke Nederlanden, 1100-1400, *Jaarboek voor Vrouwengeschiedenis* 5, 111-130.

Hardt, M., 1996: Silbergeschirr als Gabe im Frühmittelalter, *Ethnographische-Archäologische Zeitschrift* 37, 431-444.

Hartung, W., 1988: Adel, Erbrecht, Schenkung. Die strukturellen Ursachen der frühmittelalterlichen Besitzübertragungen an die Kirche, in F. Seibt (ed.), *Gesellschaftsgeschichte. Festschrift für Karl Bosl zum 80. Geburtstag*, München, I, 417-438.

Heirbaut, D., 1997: De procedure tot overdracht van onroerende goederen in het oud-Vlaamse recht: enkele feodale voorbeelden uit de dertiende eeuw, *Handelingen der Maatschappij voor Geschiedenis en Oudheidkunde te Gent, nieuwe reeks* 51, 37-59.

Hendriks, J.P.C.A., 1990: *Archeologie en bewoningsgeschiedenis van het Land van Heusden en Altena*, Almkerk.

Hermans, J., 1992-1993: Abbaye de Postel à Mol, in U. Berlière e.a. (eds), *Monasticon belge. Tome VIII. Province d'Anvers*, Liège, 171-193.

Holdsworth, Ch., 1991: *The Piper and the Tune: medieval patrons and monks*, Reading (The Stenton Lecture 1990).

Jacobs, M., 1996: Sociaal kapitaal van buren. Rechten, plichten en conflicten in Gentse gebuurten (zeventiende – achttiende eeuw), *Volkskundig Bulletin* 22, 149-176.

Jahn, J., 1988: Tradere ad sanctum. Politische und gesellschaftliche Aspekte der Traditionspraxis im agilolfingischen Bayern, in F. Seibt (ed.), *Gesellschaftsgeschichte. Festschrift für Karl Bosl zum 80. Geburtstag*, München, I, 400-416.

Janssens, H., 1990: De stichtingsoorkonden van de abdij van Averbode (1133-1139), gevolgd door enkele verdachte oorkonden uit de twaalfde eeuw, *Analecta Praemonstratensia* 66, 5-47

Janssens, H., 1991: De premonstratenzers en hun abdij te Middelburg (12de-16de eeuw), in A. Wiggers e.a. (eds), *Rond de kerk in Zeeland. Derde verzameling bijdragen van de Vereniging voor Nederlandse Kerkgeschiedenis*, Gouda/Delft, 17-36.

Jobert, Ph., 1977: *La notion de donation. Convergences: 630-750*, Paris.

Johanek, P., 1977: Zur rechtlichen Funktion von Traditionsnotiz, Traditionsbuch und früher Siegelurkunde. in P. Classen (ed.), *Recht und Schrift im Mittelalter*, Sigmaringen (Vorträge und Forschungen 23), 131-162.

Kappelhof, T., 1995: Vught in de middeleeuwen (900-1300). Het raadsel van de twee kerken, in J. van den Eijnde (ed.), *Vught vanouds*, Vught (Vughtse Historische Reeks 3), 7-32.

Kastner, J., 1974: *Historiae fundationum monasteriorum. Frühformen monastischer Institutionsgeschichtsschreibung im Mittelalter*, München (Münchener Beiträge zur Mediävistik und Renaissance-Forschung 18).

Klaversma, T., 1977-1979: De heren van Vught en Oirschot in de 12de en 13de eeuw, *Campinia* 7 (1977-1978) 43-45, 90-92, 131-133, 178-180; 8 (1978-1979) 47-49, 104-106, 148-151, 210-211.

Klaversma, T., 1978: De geslachten van Altena en Horne tot ca. 1300, *Publications de la Société Historique et Archéologique dans le Limbourg* 114, 7-61.

Kloos, P., 1995⁶: *Culturele Antropologie. Een inleiding*, Assen.

Koch, E.M.F., 1994: *De kloosterpoort als sluitpost? Adellijke vrouwen langs Maas en Rijn tussen huwelijk en convent, 1200-1600*, Leeuwarden/Mechelen (Maaslandse Monografieën 57).

Kohl, W., 1984: Die frühen Prämonstratenserklöster Nordwestdeutschlands im Spannungsfeld der großen Familien, in L. Fenske/W. Rösener/Th. Zotz (eds), *Institutionen, Kultur und Gesellschaft. Festschrift für Josef Fleckenstein zu seinem 65. Geburtstag*, Sigmaringen, 393-414.

Koyen, M./L.C. Van Dyck, 1992-1993: Abbaye de Tongerlo, in U. Berlière e.a. (eds), *Monasticon belge. Tome VIII. Province d'Anvers*, Liège, 263-375.

Künzel, R.E./D.P. Blok/J.M. Verhoeff, 1988: *Lexicon van Nederlandse toponiemen tot 1200*, Amsterdam.

Kupper, J.-L., 1981: *Liège et l'église impériale XIᵉ-XIIᵉ siècles*, Paris (Bibliothèque de la Faculté de Philosophie et Lettres de l'Université de Liège 228).

Kupper, J.-L., 1982: Leodium (Liège/Luik), in S. Weinfurter/O. Engels (eds), *Series episcoporum ecclesiae occidentalis ab initio usque ad annum MCXCVIII. Series V. Germania. Tomus I. Archiepiscopatus Coloniensis*, Stuttgart, 43-83.

Kupper, J.-L., 1997: Episcopus-advocatus. Sur l'exercice du pouvoir épiscopal dans l'ancien évêché de Liège, in *Centre de Recherches en Histoire du Droit et des Institutions. Cahier 7. La souveraineté*, Bruxelles, 13-25.

Lauwers, M., 1996: Le "sépulcre des pères" et les "ancêtres". Notes sur le culte des défunts à l'âge seigneurial, *Médiévales. Langue, texte, histoire* 31, 67-78.

Lauwers, M., 1997: *La mémoire des ancêtres, le souci des morts. Morts, rites et société au moyen âge (diocèse de Liège, XIe-XIIIe siècles)*, Paris (Théologie historique 103).

Leenders, K.A.H.W., 1996: *Van Turnhoutervoorde tot Strienemonde. Ontginnings- en nederzettings-geschiedenis van het noordwesten van het Maas-Schelde-Demergebied. 400-1350. Een poging tot synthese*, Zutphen.

Lemaître, J.-L., 1993: Les actes transcrits dans les livres liturgiques, in O. Guyotjeannin/L. Morelle/M. Parisse (eds), 1993: *Les cartulaires. Actes de la Table ronde organisée par l'Ecole nationale des chartes et le G.D.R. 121 du C.N.R.S. (Paris, 5-7 décembre 1991)*, Paris (Mémoires et documents de l'École des chartes 39), 59-77.

Lijten, J., 1991: De heren van Oirschot, in H.J.M. Mijland/L.M. van Hout/J.P.J. Lijten (eds), *Oog op Oirschot*, Oirschot, 52-87.

Lohrmann, D., 1985: Die Wirtschaftshöfe der Prämonstratenser im hohen und späten Mittelalter, in H. Patze (ed.), *Die Grundherrschaft im späten Mittelalter*, Sigmaringen (Vorträge und Forschungen 27), 205-240.

Mauss, M., 1975[5]: Essai sur le don. Formes et raison de l'échange dans les sociétés archaïques, in M. Mauss, *Sociologie et anthropologie*, C. Lévi-Strauss (ed.), Paris, 1950[1], 143-279 (earlier in *L'Année Sociologique*, seconde série, 1 (1923-1924), 30-186).

McLaughlin, M., 1994: *Consorting with Saints. Prayer for the Dead in Early Medieval France*, Ithaca/London.

Melssen, J.Th.M., 1983: Een verdwenen parochie...of hoe Eindhoven een Keulse bisschop van haar grondgebied bande, *Brabants Heem* 35, 11-21.

Mol, J.A./P.N. Noomen, 1996: De stichting van de augustijner koorherenabdij Ludingakerke en haar relatie met Rolduc, in S. Zijlstra e.a. (eds), *Vroomheid tussen Vlie en Lauwers. Aspecten van de Friese kerkgeschiedenis. Achtste verzameling bijdragen van de Vereniging voor Nederlandse Kerkgeschiedenis*, Delft, 11-46.

Molitor, S., 1990: Das Traditionsbuch. Zur Forschungsgeschichte einer Quellengattung und zu einem Beispiel aus Südwestdeutschland, *Archiv für Diplomatik* 36, 61-92.

Oexle, O.G., 1983: Die Gegenwart der Toten, in H. Braet/W. Verbeke (eds), *Death in the Middle Ages*, Leuven (Mediaevalia Lovaniensia. Series I, Studia 9), 19-77.

Palazzo, É., 1997: Le livre dans les trésors du moyen âge. Contribution à l'histoire de la *Memoria* médiévale, *Annales. Histoire, Sciences Sociales* 52, 93-118.

Parisse, M., 1995: La petite noblesse et les nouveaux ordres. Les bienfaiteurs de Riéval en Lorraine (XIIe-XIIIe siècles), in E. Mornet (ed.), *Campagnes médiévales: L'homme et son espace. Etudes offertes à Robert Fossier*, Paris (Histoire ancienne et médiévale 31), 455-471.

Parisse, M., 1996: Une enquête à mener: la spiritualité des nobles au miroir des préambules de leurs actes, in C. Duhamel-Amado/G. Lobrichon (eds), *Georges Duby. L'écriture de l'Histoire*, Bruxelles, 307-316.

Prims, F., 1935: *De Onze-Lieve-Vrouwe-Abdij der Norbertijnen te Postel*, Antwerpen (Campinia Sacra 4).

Reuter, T., 1995: Property transactions and social relations between rulers, bishops and nobles in early eleventh-century Saxony: the evidence of the *Vita Meinwerci*, in W. Davies/P. Fouracre (eds), *Property and Power in the Early Middle Ages*, Cambridge, 165-199.

Reynolds, S., 1994: *Fiefs and Vassals. The Medieval Evidence Reinterpreted*, Oxford.

Rosenwein, B.H., 1989: *To Be the Neighbor of Saint-Peter. The Social Meaning of Cluny's Property, 909-1049*, (Ithaca/London).

Roymans, N., 1979: Op zoek naar Pladella villa, *Varia Historica Brabantica* 8, 1-47.

Sauer, C., 1993: *Fundatio und Memoria. Stifter und Klostergründer im Bild. 1100 bis 1350*, Göttingen (Veröffentlichungen des Max-Planck-Instituts für Geschichte 109).

Schijndel, Th.M. van, 1971: De premonstratenzer koorzusters: van dubbelkloosters naar autonome konventen, in *Gedenkboek Orde van Prémontré 1121-1971*, Averbode, 161-177.

Schmid, K., 1985: Stiftungen für das Seelenheil, in K. Schmid (ed.), *Gedächtnis, das Gemeinschaft stiftet*, Zürich, 51-73.

Silber, I.F., 1995: Gift-giving in the great traditions: the case of donations to monasteries in the medieval West, *Archives européennes de sociologie* 36, 209-243.

Sot, M., 1985²: *Gesta episcoporum. Gesta abbatum*, Turnhout, 1981¹ (Typologie des sources du moyen âge occidental 37).

Steurs, W., 1993: *Naissance d'une région. Aux origines de la Mairie de Bois-le-Duc. Recherches sur le Brabant septentrional aux 12ᵉ et 13ᵉ siècles*, Bruxelles (Académie royale de Belgique. Mémoire de la Classe des lettres. Collection in-8°, 3ᵉ série tome 3).

Tabuteau, E.Z., 1988: *Transfers of Property in Eleventh-Century Norman Law*, Chapel Hill/London.

Teunis, H.B., 1997: The Countergift *in Caritate* According to the Cartulary of Noyers, *The Haskins Society Journal. Studies in Medieval History* 7 (1995), Woodbridge, 83-88.

Theuws, F.C., 1989: Middeleeuwse parochiecentra in de Kempen 1000-1350, in A. Verhoeven/F. Theuws (eds), *Het Kempenprojekt 3. De middeleeuwen centraal*, Waalre (Bijdragen tot de studie van het Brabantse Heem 33), 97-216.

Theuws, F./A.-J. Bijsterveld, 1992²: Der Maas-Demer-Schelde-Raum in ottonischer und salischer Kaiserzeit, in H.W. Böhme (ed.), *Siedlungen und Landesausbau zur Salierzeit*, Sigmaringen, 1991¹ (Römisch-Germanisches Zentralmuseum, Forschungs-Institut für Vor- und Frühgeschichte, Monographien Band 27) I 109-146.

Thissen, B., 1989: Het oudste toltarief van Koblenz. Een bijdrage tot de bronnenkritiek, in P. Bange/P.M.J.C. de Kort (eds), *Die fonteyn der ewiger wijsheit. Opstellen aangeboden aan prof. dr A.G. Weiler ter gelegenheid van zijn 25-jarig jubileum als hoogleraar in de Algemene en Vaderlandse Geschiedenis van de Middeleeuwen aan de Katholieke Universiteit Nijmegen*, Nijmegen (Middeleeuwse studies 5), 180-222.

Tock, B.-M., 1997: Les mutations du vocabulaire latin des chartes au XIᵉ siècle, *Bibliothèque de l'École de chartes* 155, 119-148.

Uytven, R. van, 1958-1959: Kloosterstichtingen en stedelijke politiek van Godfried I van Leuven (1095-1139), *Bijdragen tot de geschiedenis der Nederlanden* 13, 177-188.

Venarde, B.L., 1997: *Women's monasticism and medieval society. Nunneries in France and England, 890-1215*, Ithaca/London.

Verhulst, A., 1985: L'intensification et la commercialisation de l'agriculture dans les Pays-Bas méridionaux au XIIIe siècle, in *La Belgique rurale du moyen-âge à nos jours. Mélanges offerts à J.-J. Hoebanx*, Bruxelles, 89-100.

Vienne, L., 1996: Rumoldus Colibrant, eerste abt van Postel (1545-1626), *Trajecta* 5, 26-43.

Weiner, A.B., 1992: *Inalienable Possessions. The Paradox of Keeping-While-Giving*, Berkeley/Los Angeles/Oxford.

Weinfurter, S., 1977: Neuere Forschung zu den Regularkanonikern im Deutschen Reich des 11. und 12. Jahrhunderts, *Historische Zeitschrift* 224, 379-397.

Weinfurter, S., 1984: Norbert von Xanten als Reformkanoniker und Stifter des Prämonstratenserordens, in K. Elm (ed.), *Norbert von Xanten. Adliger, Ordensstifter, Kirchenfürst*, Köln, 159-183.

Weinfurter, S., 1989: Norbert von Xanten und die Entstehung des Prämonstratenserordens, in *Barbarossa und die Prämonstratenser*, Göppingen (Schriften zur Staufischen Geschichte und Kunst 10), 67-100.

Welvaarts, T.I., 1878-1879: *Geschiedenis der abdij van Postel naar hare eigene archieven*, Turnhout.

Werner, M., 1991: Der Herzog von Lothringen in salischer Zeit, in S. Weinfurter (ed.), *Die Salier und das Reich. 1. Salier, Adel und Reichsverfassung*, Sigmaringen, 367-473.

White, S.D., 1988: *Custom, Kinship, and Gifts to Saints. The* Laudatio Parentum *in Western France, 1050-1150*, Chapel Hill/London.

Zotz, Th., 1992: Milites Christi: Ministerialität als Träger der Kanonikerreform, in S. Weinfurter e.a. (eds), *Reformidee und Reformpolitik im spätsalisch- und frühstaufischen Reich. Vorträge der Tagung der Gesellschaft für Mittelrheinische Kirchengeschichte vom 11. bis 13. September 1991 in Trier*, Mainz (Quellen und Abhandlungen zur Mittelrheinischen Kirchengeschichte 68), 301-328.

Local communities in their landscape in the rent district of Eersel/Bergeyk (14th-16th centuries)

Daniel Vangheluwe

I   INTRODUCTION

There are few periods in the history of the Meuse-Demer-Scheldt area in which the society and the cultural landscape have undergone such radical changes as in the 13th and 14th centuries. Putting it simply, it is a transition from a 'feudal' society to an early-modern one, in which social, economic and mental structures were so subject to change that people in the 15th century may have regarded the 12th-century society in the same region as primitive. The rise and rapid growth of the towns and the improvement of agricultural technology are but two of the visible elements of this process. The construction of many new churches and towers is another. Archaeological research of this period is, however, only possible to a certain extent, for the settlements from this period are the same as the present ones. The traces of habitation from the 13th and 14th centuries have, in part, been destroyed by later building, or are inaccessible. Many churches were moved in the 19th century, so that archaeological investigation of the remains of medieval churches and cemeteries is possible, although the latter have been neglected up to now. The development of the arable fields has become better known because they have been regarded recently as an object of research during the large-scale settlement investigations in the area. The development of the haylands and the cultural landscape in the stream valleys on the other hand have hardly been studied at all, although drastic changes must also have taken place in these parts of the landscape.

    The absence of archaeological research into the 13th and 14th centuries is still insufficiently compensated by historical research into the structures of a peasant society of this period.[1] The result is that

---

[1]   In the past, attention has been devoted to institutional and legal-historical aspects of rural society, see for example Bezemer 1889; Enklaar 1941; Kerremans 1949; Martens 1952; Jansen 1955; Byl 1965; Spierings 1984

Fig. 1. The location of Eersel and Bergeyk.

we have insufficient information about such an interesting period of transformation as the 13th and 14th centuries. An important reason for this lack of in-depth historical research is of course the scarcity of written sources on the one hand and the fact that those sources which are available only provide the desired information after extremely intensive study. A flying start in the research into this period in the Meuse-Demer-Scheldt region was made by Peter Hoppenbrouwers, whose monumental study of the late-medieval land of Heusden may be considered a milestone in the analysis of the structures characterizing a peasant society. Similar research is lacking for other parts of the Meuse-Demer-Scheldt region, in particular the sandy areas. In the following, an attempt will be made to initiate such an investigation by means of an analysis of the rent registers of the Duke of Brabant and the registers of the Cth penny[2] from the 16th century of the rent district of Eersel, which was later divided into the districts of Eersel and Bergeyk (fig. 1).

The focus of the research is still on the 14th and 15th centuries, so that the 13th century which is so crucial remains an enigmatic period. We are aware of the fact that this study is only a first step in a more comprehensive investigation of social and landscape structures in the Late Middle Ages. We also realize that the research presented here must necessarily precede a more profound analysis of man-environment and subject-object relations in the Late Middle Ages and the way in which these relations were represented.

as well as the recent general work of Steurs 1993. Recent research on the Middle Ages in the region has focused on older periods or on the latest Middle Ages.

See for instance Bijsterveld this volume and the new literature referred to there.

2   Cth penny is the translation of *Honderdste penning*.

2 RESEARCH GOALS AND SOURCES

2.1 INTRODUCTION

The historical geography of the villages of the Kempen has for many years been an object of research. The research, which was mainly directed towards the collecting of field names, has gradually broadened to include questions on the economic, social, administrative and mental structures in rural areas. There are three main issues in this contribution. The first concerns the development of the cultivated land in the area. How large was the cultivated area which was divided into parcels, what was its development in the whole area and in individual hamlets? After a period of radical expansion of the cultivated area, the development in the period under study falls under the direction of the Duke of Brabant.[3] The second concerns power structures. Who were the owners of the land and how did they deal with each other? Are there any changes in the power structure and, if so, what caused them? The third question concerns the administration and in particular the aldermen's court. The relative wealth of the aldermen will be discussed, and in particular whether the elite could be distinguished from the rest of the population on the basis of the amount of land they owned. Was the social stratification of the rural communities (as established on the basis of landownership) reflected in this governing body?

In this study we shall demonstrate how the information collected provides insight into the history of the landscape, and the economic and social development. All these factors have made the landscape what it now is.

The main sources on which this study is based are the rent registers of the Duke of Brabant from the 15th and 16th centuries, supplemented by some other sources such as the register of the Cth Penny of Alva from 1569 and a rent register from Thorn. We shall discuss the use of land as it can be deduced from the rent registers on the basis of information on the location and size of the cultivated land parcelled out[4] and of information about the owners. We shall see that in 1450 the area of arable land of many hamlets was already equal in size to that of the 19th century, and some hamlets were even larger in 1450 than at the beginning of the 20th century. The rent register of 1450 is the tangible result of the greatest expansion of cultivated land ever to take place in this region, and that in barely one century.

The study of the rent registers calls for a specific approach. One of the rent registers contains 4000 different names of those liable for rent and about 2000 rents. Without a systematic approach with an index of names of persons research is impossible. We shall first discuss the sources and then we shall explain the processing of data necessary before turning to the presentation of the results of the analysis.

2.2 THE RENT REGISTERS OF THE DUKE OF BRABANT OF THE DISTRICT OF EERSEL AND THEIR ANALYSIS.

As stated above, the rent registers of the Duke of Brabant are the most important sources in this study. The rent registers have a closing date, which we use to refer to them, but they cover a period of 75 to 100 years prior to this date.

---

[3] By direction I do not mean that the duke was the initiator, but that his permission was required for reclamation, and that he regulated things from a distance.

[4] The cultivated land exists of arable fields, hayfields and meadows. It stands in opposition to the undivided common, uncultivated land in use as pasture.

Property charged with rents has its origin in the domanial period, when the rent was paid by the *laat* (unfree peasant) for the use of his lord's land.[5] The rents in the Duke of Brabant's rent registers are of later date. They are annual payments which (largely) arose as a result of reclamations. These reclamations took place on the common heath where the Duke of Brabant exercised his public rights on unreclaimed lands the so-called *wildernisregaal*, originally a royal right to all undivided and unreclaimed land. When a farmer reclaimed part of the common heath he paid a small amount to the duke: the rent. So the rents are not payments for the leasing out of land. The rents were at first paid in natura, for example in loaves, chickens, and later money which was subject to inflation because it was a fixed amount. The monetary unit in which the amount of rent was expressed was the *denier* (pennies). Once it had been established, the amount always remained the same, but its value devalued greatly and eventually became far less than the lease or rent price. To the duke, the rent was mainly symbolic. It was an expression of his bond with the land, to which he could assert certain rights. We shall come back to the actual value of the rents later.

The oldest rent register[6] which we used for the study was closed in 1450 and must have been copied from an older register shortly before this date. It covers a period of about 75 years prior to the final date. The register is written in Latin, and begins thus*: Census domini ducis in Eersel...* It is a so-called *netboek*, fair copy which was not used to register the annual payments but which served as evidence for rights of ownership. It is written by a single hand, with the exception of some additions regarding new reclamations in the period 1430-1440. It contains about 150 folios written on both sides, alphabetically ordered according to the first name of the payers of rents. The text is subdivided into entries recording al property charged with a rent per rentpayer in 1450. The rent remained attached to the parcel even after a transfer of property as a result of inheritance or sale. With the aim of proving ownership rights, the previous owners were also mentioned. On average, at least three generations of owners are named, and occasionally even older owners, omitting those in between. The following is an example of an entry in the rent register of 1450[7]*: Wilhelmus filius johannis killarts pro symone filio johannis filii johannis killarts ex parte gerardi filii johannis nagels et elisabet liberi filii godefridi filii meeus de hereditate johannis filii johannis heystecke ex parte vicinorum de eyke westerhoven et achel 4d nov.*

In the above quotation, Willem the son of Johan Killarts is the last owner and rentpayer. The previous owner was Simon son of Johan Killarts who had acquired his property from the inheritance of Gerard Nagels and Elisabeth, both children of Godefridus son of Meeus. The latter acquired his property from the inheritance of Johan Heisteks and the property was taken from the commons of Bergeyk, Westerhoven and Achel. In view of the mention of the village of Achel in this entry, this parcel must have been reclaimed from the common at Borkel near Achel.

The rent register refers to the large rent district of Eersel and contains circa 700 entries concerning 2269 parcels and in which 3238 different persons are mentioned. On average a person is mentioned twice, although the spelling is not always clear and occasionally alternative names are used. Usually the names of individuals are treated formally in the text, and a first name is always found together with the patronym and a stable family name.[8]

The second rent register has 3 July 1543 as its closing date.[9] The register records five generations of owners, thus bridging the period to the previous rent register of 1450. As a result, corresponding en-

5   Godding 1987, 162-195.

6   *Algemeen Rijksarchief Brussel, Archief van de Rekenkamer* (General State Archive, Brussels, Archive of the auditors office) no. 45044 (*Censier Eersel*) (dating from 1450). Henceforth: ARBR 45044 (1450).

7   ARBR 45044 (1450), f56r3.

8   Vangheluwe 1994a.

9   ARBR 45052 (1521). At the end, Jan Bax the steward of the 'state lands' of Brabant, testifies that on 3 July

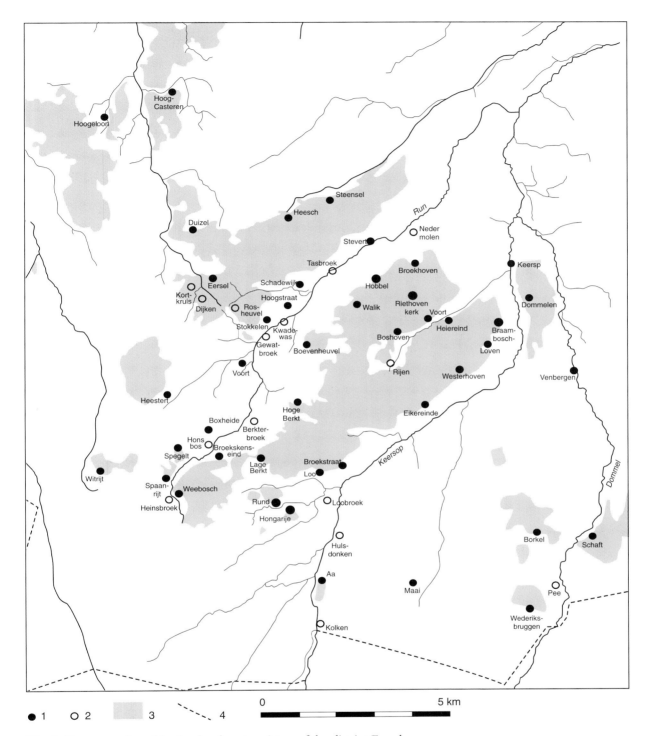

Fig. 2. Places mentioned in the ducal rent registers of the district Eersel.
1 hamlets where rents of the duke of Brabant are present; 2 hayland areas where rents of the duke of Brabant are present; 3 the extent of the late medieval and early modern arable fields mentioned in the ducal rent registers of the district of Eersel; 4 national border

tries in the registers can be traced. The register contains additions made in another hand. It was probably copied from a register ca 18 years older.[10] The second rent register has 1605 rent entries and 3747 different owners, and only comprises the rent district of Bergeyk between the brooks Run and Dommel (fig. 2) which is separated from the rent district of Eersel. The new rent district includes the villages of Bergeyk, Westerhoven, Riethoven, Dommelen, Borkel and Schaft and their hamlets. Although the territory of this rent register is smaller, more persons are mentioned, thus covering more generations than in the older rent register.

The third rent register of the Duke of Brabant dates from 1627 and concerns the rent district of Bergeyk. It was probably made in connection with the leasing out of Bergeyk by king Philip IV to Gerard of Brouchoven.[11] The entries refer to a page and rent number of an older rent register, which unfortunately no longer exists. However, this lost register appears to be a copy of the register we have just discussed, and the rent entries are in the same order in both. On the basis of the rent amounts which remained the same, the corresponding rents can be traced in both books. The younger register gives more field names and better place indications, such as the hamlet where the field is situated. In addition, its use as a meadow or hayland, farmyard or arable field is mentioned. As a result we are able to situate the property in the old rent registers better. However, one must use these results with caution because the pledge of a rent or the field to which it was attached does not always remain the same.[12]

The two remaining sources used in the study are a rent register of 1566 from the abbey of Thorn and the tax register or book of the Cth penny of 1569. The main part of the property described in the rent register of Thorn is situated in the western part of Bergeyk. The abbey which apparently also possessed rights to unclaimed lands, gave permission for land to be reclaimed at the same time as or earlier than the duke.

The book of the Cth penny of 1569 registers all property per owner including its use and location.[13] Moreover, a distinction is made between owners and leaseholders. The registration of the property is an important addition to the information from the rent registers which only concerns newly-reclaimed property subject to a ducal rent or a rent from Thorn.

1543 the book with 157 pages is *gecollacioneert tegens den gelijcken chijnsboek dien ick tersaken mijnre officien dagelijks ben gebruyckende ende zij bevonden accorderende*.

[10] For this, two arguments may be brought forward. In the first place, we observe that without the additions the fourth generation in the rent register is the same as in the register of 1450 (we assume 25 years per generation). In the second place we see that, according to the register, Daniel, son of Johan of Vlierden, is the most recent owner of the *Spegelt*, if we disregard an addition. The transfer of the farm *ter Spegelt* to Johan of Vlierden took place, according to the protocols of the aldermen's court of 's-Hertogenbosch in 1497. In the period 1497 to 1543, the year that Jan Bax signs, there

may already have been two new transfers. It is also possible that Daniel van Vlierden was the owner until ca 1425.

[11] De Schrijver 1965, 12. It is found in ARBR under no. 50850 as *Censier Lommel*.

[12] If the relation with the original pledge is lost, *het aangelag* (farmyard) is often used as a new pledge.

[13] *Algemeen Rijksarchief Den Haag, Archief van de Raad van State* (General State Archive The Hague, Archive of the Council of State), no. 2166LL (1569). Henceforth ARRS 216 (1569). Transcriptions were made by the author of the books of the Cth penny of the municipalities of Eersel, Steensel, Casteren, Bergeyk, Riethoven, Westerhoven, Borkel and Schaft.

All the information from the rent registers is stored in a relational database.[14] The database consists of two main files containing the personal information of the rentpayers and the data on all the fields for example the use, toponyms, location etc. The link between the two main files makes it possible to retrieve the property of each rentpayer. Conversely, the list of successive owners of a field (a pledge) can be traced. In this way, much can be reconstructed such as the possession of property charged with rent per rentpayer in a certain hamlet, and the property structure (in 1569) per hamlet. We shall give an example to illustrate the possibilities of this method. Searching for property under the name of *Skustings* (*des Kustings*) and the patronym *Willem* in the relational database shows that Willem son of Willem Skustinks with the surname Scordels (alderman from 1395-1424[15]) passed on his property charged with rent to his 4 children: 3 unmarried daughters: Aleide, Elizabet, Maria, and to a son, Willem. The inheritance of the fields situated at Schadewijk and de *Dijken* in Eersel was divided in 4 equal parts, each with a rent of thirteen pennies and one halfpenny.

2.4   THE PROCESSING OF THE DATA FROM THE RENT REGISTERS

Before considering the results of the research we shall first discuss the method of locating the fields in the rent registers, since it plays an important part. Direct indications are not always available, so that we had to make use of our knowledge of local toponymy. For example, the toponym *super platem* from the rent register refers to the hamlet Hoogstraat situated near the hamlet of Schadewijk in Eersel. Next we shall indicate how a periodization was applied on the basis of the successive owners per rent entry.

2.4.1 THE LOCATION OF THE FIELDS CHARGED WITH RENTS

The duke's rent registers are not consistent in their reference to the location of the parcels.[16] Sometimes field names are mentioned which, thanks to the results of toponymical studies,[17] can be ascribed to certain hamlets. In order to ascribe fields to specific hamlets, different procedures must be followed. We shall briefly discuss the methods used.

The location of the parcels is determined by means of a fixed procedure, in which every subsequent step is less certain. The first step and the most important indication is to see whether a field name has been recorded with the parcel. If we can then trace the hamlet in this way, this determination of the location is the most precise. The second step only concerns the parcels from the rent district of Bergeyk (approximately half of the parcels). It is possible to find a link between these parcels and those from the rent register of 1627.[18] Since this rent register indicates the hamlet in which the owner lives and where his fields are situated, the location of the corresponding parcel in the older

---

[14]   Vangheluwe 1990a.

[15]   In aldermen's deeds present in the archive of the Abbey of Postel (henceforth: AP) there is the variant: *willem skustinks willems scordels zoon*. *Skustinks* is the family name on the mother's side and *Scordels* the fam-

ily name on the father's side.

[16]   I rely here also on the information from the collection of field names collected by G. van der Aalst of Eersel.

[17]   Vangheluwe 1989a.

[18]   Vangheluwe 1992.

rent registers can be ascertained. Toponyms in the rent register of 1627 in some cases even allow the parcel to be traced on the cadastral map of 1830. By means of this method 70% of the parcels in the rent district of Bergeyk can be found. The third step is to reconstruct per hamlet networks of relations between persons who can be related to each other either on the basis of identical patronyms, or on the basis of a transmission of land or by inheritance.[19] In each network one or more persons are found with a parcel whose location we have already discovered via the field name in the previous step. We use this evidence to link the network with a hamlet. In this step all the parcels in a network are assumed to belong to the hamlet of that network, in the absence of further information. It should be stated here that this third and last step yields the least precise location. Consider, for instance, the possibility that one owner has inherited land in two or more hamlets. He then belongs to two or more networks which are combined via his person to form a larger network. As a result, the difference between these hamlets is in danger of becoming blurred. This problem occurs frequently in the later rent district of Eersel. We have partly solved the problem by making the location as unambiguous as possible and by keeping the networks small.[20] Naturally this procedure is very time-consuming. After the transcription of the text and the input of data into the computer, this is what took most time. Checks on the basis of other sources show that this method works well. For example, it is possible to distinguish the locations of parcels from Casteren, Eersel, Duizel and Steensel. For these villages we cannot rely on the second step. Parcels from the hamlets of *Dijken* and *Plaatse* in the centre of Eersel cannot, however, be distinguished from each other by means of networks because these hamlets are too close together and make use of the same complex of fields.[21]

With the help of the procedure described above, we were able to establish a location for each parcel. Subsequently we gave each owner a domicile on the basis of the hamlet where he inherited most. If an owner's property is scattered over several hamlets we assume that he lived in the hamlet linked to his network. The underlying assumption is that people dwelled where they had their strongest family ties. In case of doubt, one can take the most centrally situated hamlet within a person's scattered property. Parcels far from an owner's domicile are probably rented out.

2.4.2 DIVISION INTO PERIODS

The rent registers mention successive owners, which makes periodization possible. Generally a field changed hands as a result of inheritance. Consequently there is a time lapse of one generation span between the old and new owner. We assume an average period of 25 years per generation, and this corresponds to a period in the rent register. An average of three successive owners were noted in the rent register of 1450, so the register describes a period of c. 75 years. This can be proved on the basis of a number of cases in which the date of sale has been recorded.[22] In order not to lose track of the chronology, we have allocated a number to each person: 1 to 4 in the order young to old. As a result, each individual from the rent register is placed in a time context. We made use of this notation to trace developments and tendencies. We stress that this time number per individual can only be indicative for the period in which he/she managed his/her property: a person who lived at the transi-

[19] For example when a transfer of ownership is indicated by *pro* or inheritance by *ex parte* and *de hereditate*.

[20] If we rigorously apply a (Dbase) programme which searches for networks, it turns out that 90% of the names are in a network.

[21] This is the *Midakkers* complex.

[22] Vangheluwe 1992, 6.

tion between for example periods 1 and 2 may appear alternately in the former and in the latter period. We allocated every individual to a period. This means that persons at a transition between 2 periods are allocated the period in which they were first encountered in the rent register.

The indication by period also proved useful when distinguishing between persons of the same name. In the file of owners, each individual has a name, time number and place. The combination of all 3 is unique. Individuals with the same name and same place of residence may therefore differ by period. In distinguishing between persons, we used the criteria of the same name, time, place and family relation. The nomenclature in the rent registers is consistent and formal which makes it possible to identify persons.[23] The stability of the family names is good, making the source interesting from a genealogical point of view. The conclusion is that it is possible to build up a database of distinguishable persons.

2.4.3 THE WAY IN WHICH THE EXTENT OF THE PROPERTY CHARGED WITH RENTS IS DETERMINED

Finally we discuss a method which we have developed to determine the surface area of the parcelled out cultivated land in the rent registers. A simple assumption is that the amount of rent for a parcel is in proportionate to its size. In the study of the properties charged with rent by the abbey of Thorn in Bergeyk we assumed that the amount of rent was commensurate with the surface area.[24] The duke's rent register of 1525 offers a unique opportunity to prove this assumption. In the rent register the new parcels, the so-called *uitvangen*, are noted with their area and amount of rent. The area is mentioned sometimes in *roeden*, sometimes in *bunder*[25] and *roeden*. The *uitvangen* have various rents and surface areas, making it possible to see whether the amount of rent is related to the surface area of the parcel. The graph in fig. 3 shows that this assumption is correct, and also that a parcel for which a rent of 1 penny had to be paid had a surface area of 0.5 *lopense* or 33 *roeden*. For one *bunder* therefore 12 pennies or one *solidus* (*schelling*) were due. From fig. 3 it follows that one *bunder* must be equated with 400 *roeden*, which is also known from other sources. Similar details of new parcels in the rent register of 1450 reveal the same measurements so that these may be considered valid for the period preceding 1400, because the rent register covers a period of c. 75 years.

Two currencies are used in the rent registers: the old and the new (or ordinary) *denieren*. With one of the new parcels or *uitvangen* it says: *de quarta bonario in eyndrijt..2 denari veti*,[26] an a little further on: *de vuytfang de novo recepto de quarta bonario..3 denieren novo*. From this it follows that the old penny was worth 3/2 of the new penny. This must have been the result of a devaluation as a result of which the annual rents were raised for new grants of land. A study by Verhulst has demonstrated that in certain demesnes of the Saint Bavo's abbey in Ghent which were situated close to the abbey, the rents of new grants of land already amounted to one *solidus* (Flemish) per *bunder* in the second half of the 12th century.[27] With this standard for the new pennies we can estimate the size of a property charged with rent just as precisely as the land surveyors of the time.

---

[23]   Hoppenbrouwers 1992, 139-145.

[24]   Vangheluwe 1989b.

[25]   One *bunder* is locally c. 1.2 hectares which is 6 *lopense* or *lopenzaad* and 198 *roeden*. One *lopense* is 0.2 hectare,

one *roede* is 60m².

[26]   ARBR 45044 (1450), folio 110v, par 5.

[27]   Verhulst 1958, 216-218, 255-256, 305-307.

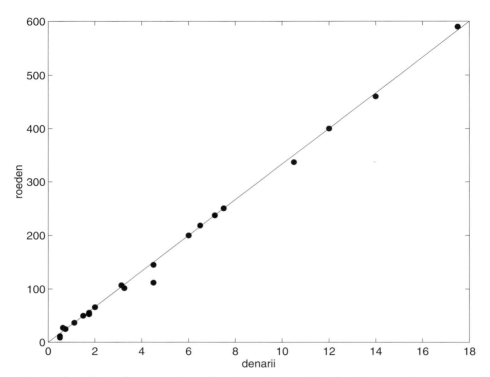

Fig. 3. The relation between the surface (*in roeden*) and height of the rent (in pennies) of new reclaimed areas (*uit-vangen*) in the rent register of 1525.

In 1300 the Duke of Brabant gave 20 *bunder* of pastureland in Oirschot to the abbey of Park near Leuven from which he had borrowed money.[28] This is of importance to this study because it was mentioned at the transmission of land that an annual rent had to be paid of 12 *denari Leuvens* per *bunder*, which is exactly the amount we deduced above for the denieren novo in the rent registers. On these grounds it may be assumed that in 1300 the new penny was already a means of payment, and that the old penny dated from before 1300. According to Godding, the rents of the new grants of land increased in the course of the 13th century to two *solidi* (Flemish?) per *bunder* and the amount of one *solidus* per *bunder* was introduced in the second half of the 12th century.[29] This means that the new penny was already in use as currency in the 13th century, possibly even as early as about 1200, and that the old penny was very probably used as such before 1200.

From a study of the value of issue of the Brabant penny it appears that its weight in silver drops from two Flemish *deniers* in 1210 to one Flemish *denier* between 1235 and 1280.[30] This may correspond with the various values of rents which we discovered for properties charged with rents in Bergeyk. The rents of Thorn are six *deniers* per *bunder*[31] and those of the duke 12 *deniers* per *bunder*. This appears to be linked with the above-mentioned devaluation of the Brabant penny between 1210 and 1280. On the basis of this, the grants of land controlled by the abbey of Thorn can be dated to before 1235, and those of the duke in new *deniers* after this date. The first grants of land by the duke in old *deniers* may already have taken place before 1235.

[28]   Camps 1979, nos. 588 and 646 (1300) and 773 (1303).

[29]   Godding 1987, 163.

[30]   Ghijssens 1976, 37. The system based on the pound is

abandoned in the case of the coins from Brabant after 1210.

[31]   Vangheluwe 1989b.

It is now clear that local toponymical studies and the method described above of determining the surface area of property charged with rent provide insight into the reclamation history and the use of land in the Kempen in the Late Middle Ages.

2.5 THE BOOK OF THE HUNDREDTH PENNY

The book of the Hundredth Penny is a register which was specially made for the collection of war taxes, the so-called *Honderdste Penning*. The book was realized under the authority of the Spanish governor Alva, and for Bergeyk begins as follows: *Dit sijn de quoyten van de C penninck van alle on-roerende goeden gemaeckt den 9 decembris anno 1569 ende nu wederom gedundeert bij parceelen elck landt ende groese besunder den 17 Octobris anno 1571.*[32]

We know from the sources that things were very efficiently organized during Alva's administration. The owners probably had to fill in information on their parcels on preprinted forms with the assistance of the assessors. Casteren was assessed anew.[33] The assessors came from South Brabant and were much stricter or more precise than the local assessors, either because the latter did not know the exact size of the parcel in metric terms or because it was not the custom to measure land or because buying and selling did not occur frequently (in contrast to inheriting land) so that in the case of a sale, people were not accustomed to doing this on the basis of exact measurements or size. Moreover, we must also take into account the fact that in some registers such as those of the hamlets mentioned above, the size of the fields is deliberately filled in too small. We shall return to this later with the register of the hamlet of Weebosch.

The book of the Cth Penny of the various villages in the Kempen always begins with a list, per hamlet, of the leaseholders with a complete specification of the fields, meadows and heaths belonging to their farms. After that the owners follow with their farms. The surface area of each parcel is described in *lopenzaad*[34] and the location can sometimes be even more precisely traced because the field name is given. The persons to whom a field has been rented out are also named, but not always per hamlet. Since we wish to follow the development of the area of cultivated land per hamlet, this occasionally poses problems. In the case of Eersel, this was solved as follows. The problem arises mainly with the old arable lands which are centrally located with regard to the hamlets. The division of the properties per hamlet over the various arable lands in Eersel can be seen in table 1. For the rented out fields no division per hamlet is known (table 1, column 6). We want to divide the rented out parcels over the hamlets so that we can establish the total area of arable land per hamlet. We can determine the size of the rented out area per hamlet by assuming that the proportion of rented out parcels of a hamlet in an arable complex is the same as the proportion of parcels owned.

[32]   In translation: These are the amounts of the C[TH] penny on all immovable goods settled on the 9th of December anno 1569, and now it is done again for each parcel of arable and meadow in particular, on the 17th of October anno 1571.

[33]   ARRS: *Boek van de Honderdste Penning, De Hoeven die in Pact vuytgegeven zijn in den Dorpe van Casteren* (1569).

[34]   One *lopenzaad* is the area that could be sowed with the contents of a barrel. Locally it is 0.2 hectares in size.

arable complex	1	2	3	4	5	6
Veldhoven	20	142	0	103	0	13
Midekker	29	76	3	0	86	134
Stokkelsekker	0	0	74	8	0	16
Eindekker	15	0	0	0	113	13
Steenselekker	18	0	0	0	0	0

Table 1. The division in *lopenzaad* of the properties owned per hamlet (columns 1-5) over the arable areas and the division of the rented out parcels over the arable areas (column 6) from the book of the Cth Penny of 1569. Column 1 Hees; column 2 Schadewijk; column 3 Stokkelen; column 4 Dijken; column 5 Plaatse; column 6 rented out parcels

Table 1 gives a survey of the main arable areas of Eersel. The location of the *Stokkelsekker* is clear: it belongs to the hamlet of Stokkelen, the *Midakker* is less obvious, this area is tilled from Schadewijk and Hees as well as from the centre of Eersel. It is therefore situated in between these hamlets to the north of Schadewijk and to the south of Hees. The name of the area, *Midekker* points to a central location. The *Veldhoven* area lies somewhere between the hamlets of Hees, Schadewijk and *Dijken*. We assume that it is situated more in the direction of Steensel and east of the Midakkers. The rented out parcels are allocated to the hamlets in the same ratio as the properties owned. The hamlet of Hees, for example, receives a portion 29/(29+76+3+86) of the total area of the rented parcels. The same has been done for the other areas in table 1.

2.6 SOME OBSERVATIONS PRIOR TO THE INVESTIGATION OF THE DEMOGRAPHIC DEVELOPMENT

From the rent registers information may be derived as to the demographic development. Our starting point is that the number of rentpayers is linked with the number of inhabitants and with the number of households. Periodization of this information produces population figures over the period 1400-1525 which were subsequently compared with the hearth counts from the census registers.[35] How do we estimate the number of households on the basis of the number of owners? We used the book of the Cth Penny of 1569 from which both numbers can be derived. For the village of Bergeyk, 392 different owners and 268 houses were mentioned in 1569. From the networks reconstructed on the basis of the rent registers it appears that approximately 15% of the rentpayers live outside the rent district. We assume this to be the case with the information in the book of the Cth Penny and calculate for Bergeyk 333 owners resident in the municipality, which is more than the 268 hearths, in other words the number of hearths in Bergeyk is 268/333=80% of the number of owners living in the municipality. Because houses are sporadically mentioned in the duke's rent registers, we must derive the number of houses indirectly from this source: first we take 85% of the number of rentpayers, thus eliminating the number of rentpayers resident outside the rent district, then we take 80% of these to find the number of households.[36] This does not produce equally reliable figures for all hamlets. In some hamlets, the divided culti-

---

[35] Cuvelier 1912-1913.

[36] In doing so, we assume that the percentage of 80% remains constant in this period as a ratio between the number of hearths and the number of owners resident there.

vated land consists almost entirely of property charged with rent. In these cases the figures are extremely reliable and a demographic trend can be seen. In other hamlets with relatively few ducal rents, possibly a large proportion of the owners also pays a (small) ducal rent, so that the number of rentpayers and the number of owners may correspond here too, but not necessarily.

After this introduction, we turn to the results of the investigation into the development of the parcelled out cultivated land in the region and the role played in this by the large landowners.

3   THE OLDER 'DUCAL' RECLAMATIONS[37]

From the above it appears that the size of the fields charged with rent and the amount of the rent are related. Two currency units were used, the old and the new penny. The new penny came into use roughly after the middle of the 13th century, and the old penny dates from before this time. By looking at the

Hamlet	total in *deniers*	part in old *deniers*	percentage old *deniers*	Hamlet	total in *deniers*	part in old *deniers*	percentage old *deniers*
Aa	328	128	39	*Kortkruis*	178	37	21
Berkt	667	13	2	*Kwadewas*	72	0	0
Berkt Lage	193	0	0	Loo	535	0	0
Berkterbroek	392	0	0	*Loobroek*	83	0	0
Bladel	24	0	0	Hoogeloon	295	15	5
Boxheide	213	0	0	Loven	406	49	12
Borkel	1285	218	17	*Maai*	64	16	25
Boshoven	226	11	5	Nedermolen	199	13	6.5
Boevenheuvel	573	6	1	*Pee*	11	0	0
Braambos	18	0	0	Riethoven kerk	6	0	0
Broekhoven	444	29	6.5	*Rijen*	90	7	7.5
Broekskenseinde	369	0	0	Rosheuvel	134	21	16
Broekstraat	182	0	0	Run	19	0	0
Dijken/Plaatse	575	115	20	Schadewijk	747	82	11
Dommelen	329	23	4	Schaft	765	306	40
Duizel	413	21	5	Spaanrijt	37	0	0
Eersel	157	0	0	Spegelt	339	0	0
Eikereinde	428	90	21	Spijker	13	0	0
Gewatbroek	25	0	0	Steensel	1179	35	3
Hapert	62	0	0	Stevert	173	0	0
Heesch	425	42	10	Stokkelen	1006	101	10
Heestert	236	5	2	Straat Hoog	48	18	37
Heiereinde	167	7	4	*Tasbroek*	116	0	0
Heinsbroek	24	0	0	Venbergen	100	0	0
Hobbelen	13	0	0	Vessem	36	0	0
Hongarije	13	0	0	Voort	576	86	15
Honsbos	76	0	0	Walik	127	18	14.5
Hulsdonk	560	252	45	Wederiksbruggen	290	0	0
Hoog Casteren	662	40	6	Weebosch	1152	0	0
Keersop	304	100	33	Westerhoven	215	0	0
Kolken	448	383	65	Witrijt	248	0	0

Table 2. The amounts of the rents due in the hamlets and some hayland complexes (in new pennies) and the ratio of old rents and new rents from the duke's rent register ARBB 45044 (1370-1450).

property for which rent was paid in old pennies, we get an impression of the size of the fields charged with ducal rents which was reclaimed before circa 1200/1250. It is possible that old arable land which was taken by the duke from old abbeys such as the one at Echternach is included in this group. The old cultivated land must have been more extensive than can be determined with the help of the ducal rent registers because there were other large landowners already present in this area. The size of the cultivated land for which rent was paid in new pennies indicates how much new land was reclaimed from the wilderness since c. 1250. It should be mentioned that, apart from the duke, other large landowners occasionally asserted their rights to the wilderness. The abbey of Thorn possessed parts of it in Bergeyk and granted this as property charged with rent to be reclaimed before or at the same time as the duke. We shall return to this later. The amounts due to the duke are shown per hamlet in table 2. In the second column of this table the total amount of the rent is shown, expressed in new pennies. In the third column the amounts of the rents are given in old pennies.[38] The relative proportion of the old pennies in the fourth column is calculated as a proportion of the size in columns 3 and 2.

The table also includes hayland areas in order to differentiate as much as possible according to place (fig. 2): the *Berkterbroek* is a hayland area between *Heinshovel* and Berkt, *Gewatbroek* is a hayland area south of Stokkelen, *Heinsbroek* is the farmstead of Postel op de Voort in Eersel, *Honsbos* is a hayland area between Boxheide and Lage Berkt, *Hulsdonk* is a hayland area between het Loo and the Aa in Bergeyk, *Kolken* is a hayland area between the Aa and Lommel, *Kwadewas* is the hayland area near Stokkelen, *Loobroek* is a hayland area in Dommelen, *Maai* is a hayland area south of Bergeyk, *Nedermolen* is a hayland area along the Run at Steenvoort, *Pee* is a hayland area along the Dommel at Borkel, *Rijen* is a hayland area between the fields at Boshoven, Run is a hamlet near het Achtste Loo in Bergeyk, the *Tasbroek* is a hayland area along the Run at Schadewijk. *Wederiksbruggen* is an old name which we assume refers to the hamlet of Achterste and Voorste Brug south of Borkel.

From table 2 it can be seen that in around 1300 there were already relatively many fields charged with ducal rents in the hamlets of Aa, Keersop, Schaft and Hoogstraat and in the hayland areas of *Hulsdonk*, *Kolken* etc. (fig. 4). In Borkel and the hamlets of Hees, Kortkruis, Schadewijk, Stokkelen and Voort, the hamlet of Walik and the hamlet of Loven, the old rents account for 10 to 20% of the later total number. Finally, from table 2 it appears that in many of the hamlets the duke had not granted any land in the (first half of the) 13th century.

It would appear that reclamation under the direction of the duke was begun from the village of Lommel in the south.[39] This is evidenced by the high percentages of old pennies for the haylands toward Lommel in the southern part of the valley of the Keersop. It is known that the duke, as part of his policy of integrating the region into his principality, had already granted limited town rights (vrijheid) to Lommel before 1250.[40] From here, possibly at the same time, new ducal reclamation bases were developed in the south of Eersel (in the hamlets of *Dijken*, *Kortkruis*, Schadewijk, Hees, Stokkelen and Voort), in Borkel and in Keersop. The conclusions are supported for Eersel by the mention of aldermen in Eersel in 1254.[41] With regard to the other villages such as Schaft and the

---

[37] By ducal reclamations we do not indicate reclamations conducted by the duke, but reclamations by others under the formal direction of the duke as sovereign overlord

[38] The old pennies are converted to new pennies by multiplying by the factor 1.5.

[39] Steurs 1993, 328.

[40] Steurs 1993, 328.

[41] Camps 1979, no. 254 (1254): *coram sculteto nostro Wellino de Busco ducis et scabinis de Eersele ac aliis hominibus nostris.* See also Melsen 1989, 59.

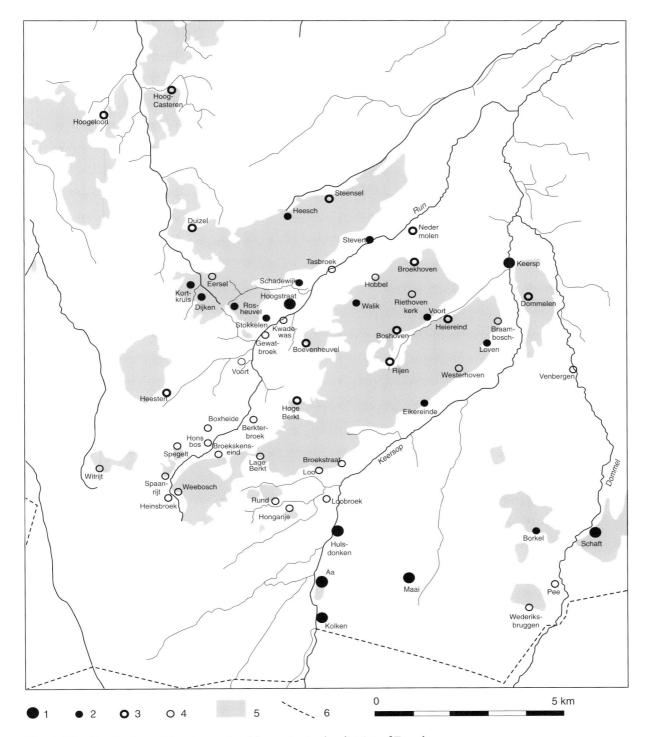

Fig. 4. The distribution of ducal rents in old pennies in the district of Eersel.
1 hamlet or area where more than 25% of the ducal rents are in old pennies; 2 idem, more than 10%; 3 idem, less than 10 %; 4 hamlets and areas with no ducal rents in old pennies; 5 the extent of the late medieval and early modern arable fields; 6 national border

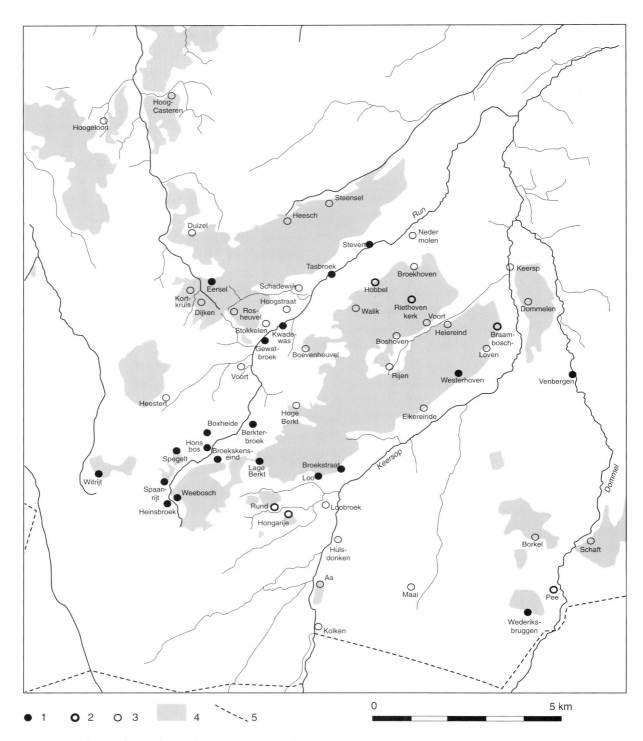

Fig. 5. Hamlets with ducal rents in new pennies only.
1 hamlets with only rents in new pennies, more than 20 pennies; 2 idem, less than 20 pennies; 3 other hamlets and areas; 4 the extent of the late medieval and early modern arable fields; 5 national border

hamlets of Keersop and Hoogstraat we are poorly informed by other sources about any possible early ducal influence.

The early influence of the duke is present in marginal areas in the parish of Bergeyk as well as the parish of Eersel. The great arable complexes on which important large landowners from bygone days (in many cases since the Early Middle Ages) probably still had a firm grasp remained closed to ducal interference. The distribution of the old rents reflects superbly the tension and interaction between old and new rulers in the region in the 13th century. There are also many hamlets where exclusively rents paid in new pennies are found (fig. 5). Ducal influence here is therefore relatively recent. It concerns in particular the most westerly part of the parish of Bergeyk (with the hamlets Weebosch, Witrijt, Lage Berkt) the hayland areas in the valley of the Run and of course the old centres including Westerhoven, Broekstraat and Eersel.

Finally the rents paid in *hoenders* imposed by the duke on houses in several hamlets in Eersel are worth mentioning. Table 3 gives a survey of them. From the occurrence of rents such as 1/12 *hoender* the consequences of successive inheritances become clear. These *hoender* rents are only found in hamlets in the rent district of Eersel, not in those of the rent district of Bergeyk.

Hamlet	number of hoenders
Dijken en Plaatse	11.2
Hees	0.2
Heestert	1.0
Kortkruis	5.3
Rosheuvel	3.0
Schadewijk	3.6
Stokkelen	14.3
Straat, Hoog-	1.5
Voort	5.5

Table 3. Hoender rents in Eersel from rent register no. 45044 of the duke (1450).

4 THE YOUNGER 'DUCAL' RECLAMATIONS (AFTER CA 1200/1250)

The question to which we attempt to find an answer in this chapter is: what developments with regard to reclamations are there after circa 1200/1250 and where does the cultivated land increase? What part does the duke play in this? In view of the large number of individuals that we are able to identify in the rent registers in which, as we shall see later, almost every individual with any property of significance is mentioned, we may expect conclusions to be drawn on the property structure. On the basis of the periodization we can ask questions relating to tendencies and developments in the property structure within the hamlets and outside them.

The rent register of 1450 contains information about the hamlets in the rent district of Eersel, including Bergeyk. The rent register of 1525 only contains information about the rent district of Bergeyk which came into existence in about 1460 due to the separation of the rent district of Eersel. We compare the size of the cultivated area from these rent books with that of the book of the Cth Penny of Alva. The latter source gives all the fields even those on which there are no ducal rents. By comparing surface area of the fields in this register with that of the fields in the ducal rent registers we can discover the proportion of reclamations under ducal control and compare it with the size of the old cultivated land which already existed before the reclamations. Regarding the latter, for the villages discussed here, in particular the property of old abbeys such as those at Echternach and Saint Trond, and the younger abbeys at Thorn and Saint Jacques at Liège is of importance.[42] Finally, the property of two Liège chapters, Saint Bartholomy and Saint Jean, is important.[43] To what extent were these monasteries able to maintain their property or perhaps even to expand it? The information on the old monasteries, especially from the period 1000-1300 is scanty, but perhaps we can trace the cores of their old property.

In table 4 a comparison is made between the size of the cultivated land granted under the duke's authority and that of the total area of arable land as registered in the book of the Cth Penny (fig. 6). With these data we can compare the sources. It is striking that eight hamlets have significantly less land in the duke's rent register than in the book of the Cth Penny (fig. 6). These hamlets are at the top of table 4. They are the centres of Bergeyk and Eersel with the hamlets of Eikereinde, *Dijken* and *Plaatse*, as well as Westerhoven, the hamlets of Hobbel, Heiereinde and Walik in Riethoven, the hamlets of Lage Berkt and Broekstraat in Bergeyk and the hamlet of Hoog Casteren.

The remaining hamlets in table 4, numbered 6, 9, 11-30, remained more or less (nr. 6 less than the others) the same size in 1569 or decreased. The latter is found in the case of the hamlets numbered 20-30 in table 4. For the hamlets numbered 31-32 no information could be found in the book of the Cth Penny. With Borkel and Weebosch the difference is so great that we are doubtful whether the surface area noted in the book of the Cth Penny is correct. As has already been discussed in the introduction, a check was made at Casteren when the book of the Cth Penny was being drawn up which revealed that the size of the parcels had been underestimated. This is to be expected particularly in villages like Casteren, Weebosch and Borkel because, as we shall see later, use was made of relatively unfertile land in these hamlets. This kind of parcel may well have been left out in the rent register.

In the hamlets 1-5, 7, 8 and 10 in table 4, the area charged with ducal rent is relatively small compared with the whole area. From this it follows that in these hamlets other large landowners also levied rents. In the hamlets 6, 9 and 11-29 in table 4, the surface area of the fields charged with ducal rents is virtually equal to or even larger than the total area of arable land in 1569. We therefore conclude that in these hamlets the duke was the sole owner of rents (fig. 7). These are often secondary hamlets, situated in a peripheral position with regard to the old centres. In the period 1200-1400, the duke granted lands to many villages for common use.[44] In this period, the individual parcels mentioned in the rent registers must also have been granted. From table 4 it may be concluded that it was these reclamations which led to the development and expansion of the hamlets 12-29. For the hamlets 1-11 in table 4 there must have been an old core of cultivated land present to some degree. In these hamlets the 'ducal' reclamations only contributed to the expansion in a relatively small way. As a result, we must attribute the area of cultivated land in these centres to reclamations which were carried out under the authority of large landowners other than the duke.

For the hamlets which developed entirely under the direction of the duke, it is useful to make use of the periodization data from the rent registers. By periodizing this information, the size of the area of cultivated land in the rent register of 1450 can be reconstructed for the periods around 1400, 1425

---

[42] Theuws 1989; Theuws/Bijsterveld 1991 and Bijsterveld 1996.

[43] Theuws/Bijsterveld 1991; see also Bijsterveld 1996.

[44] Enklaar 1941; Theuws 1989, 204.

no.	Hamlet	surface area 1450	surface area 1525	1525 minus 1450	surface area 1569	1669 minus 1450	1569 minus 1525
1		**2**	**3**	**4**	**5**	**6**	**7**
1	Eikereinde (Bergeyk)	42	43	1	211	169	168
2	*Dijken* and *Plaatse* (Eersel)	44	–	–	202	158	–
3	Hoog Casteren	55	–	–	200	145	–
4	Broekstraat	18	32	14	142	124	110
5	Westerhoven	16	14	-2	101	85	87
6	Broekhoven	41	56	15	87	46	31
7	Lage Berkt	15	–	–	58	43	–
8	Heiereinde	16	21	5	53	37	32
9	Loo	57	83	26	92	35	11
10	Walik+ Hobbelen	14	22	8	46	32	24
11	Boxheide	23	–	–	45	22	–
12	Schadewijk	68	–	–	90	22	–
13	Witrijt	25	41	16	40	15	-1
14	Hoge Berkt	101	–	–	110	9	–
15	Hees	38	–	–	46	8	–
16	*Kortkruis*	14	–	–	21	7	–
17	Schaft	43	47	4	47	4	0
18	Boshoven	25	25	0	27	2	2
19	*Maai*	4	–	–	4	0	–
20	Heestert	21	–	–	19	-2	–
21	Voort	38	–	–	36	-2	–
22	Loven	40	27	-13	35	-5	8
23	Aa + *Kolken*	34	35	1	20	-14	-15
24	Steensel	170	–	–	155	-15	–
25	Hongarije	48	–	–	17	-31	–
26	Borkel	116	154	38	81	-35	-73
27	Stokkelen	104	–	–	69	-35	–
28	Boevenheuvel	50	–	–	14	-36	–
29	*Hulsdonk*	62	–	–	20	-42	–
30	Weebosch + *Broekskenseinde*	178	191	13	58	-120	-133
31	Duizel	29	–	–	–	–	–
32	Dommelen	67	70	3	–	–	–

Table 4. Comparison of the surface area of cultivated land granted by the duke with the total area of cultivated land from the book of the Hundredth Penny.
Column 2 the surface area of the rent register of 1450; column 3 the surface area of the rent register in 1525; column 4 the difference between columns 2 and 3; column 5 the surface area of the book of the Hundredth Penny; column 6 the difference between columns 5 and 2; column 7 the difference between columns 5 and 3. All surface areas are expressed in hectares

and 1450, and in the rent register of 1525 for the periods around 1475, 1500 and 1525. The end of the development can be shown with the information from the Cth Penny register of 1569. The development of the surface area is shown in figures 8 and 9 for the hamlets 11-29 in table 2 which, as we have concluded, developed under the duke's authority. In figure 8 the hamlets and villages are listed which came under the new rent district of Bergeyk. The remaining hamlets which came under the rent district of Eersel (since ca 1467) are shown in figure 9. Figure 8 shows little growth in the

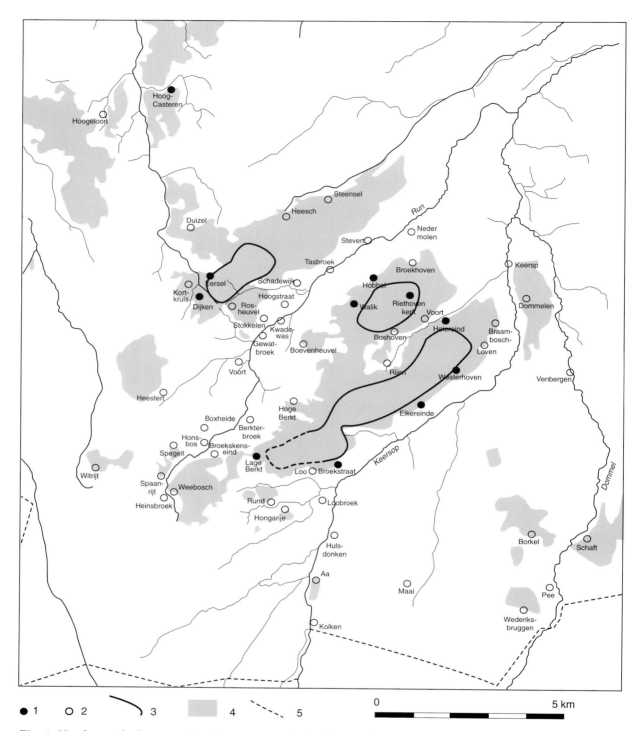

Fig. 6. Hamlets with almost no ducal rents present in the district of Eersel.
1 hamlets with almost no ducal rents; 2 other hamlets; 3 extent of the arable fields belonging to hamlets with almost no ducal rents (ancient core of arable fields); 4 extent of the arable fields in late medieval and early modern times; 5 national boundary

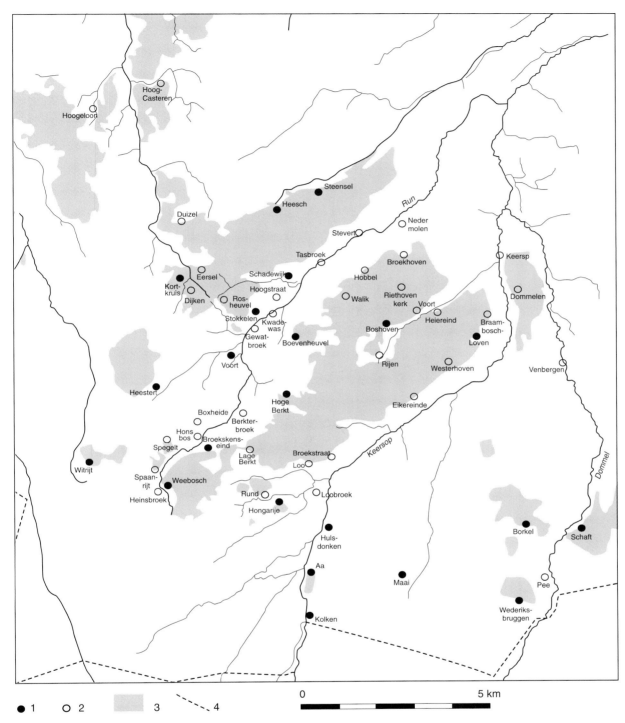

Fig. 7. Hamlets and areas with relatively many or exclusively fields with ducal rents.
1 hamlets and areas with many or exclusively fields with ducal rents; 2 other hamlets; 3 the extent of the late medieval and early modern arable fields; 4 national border

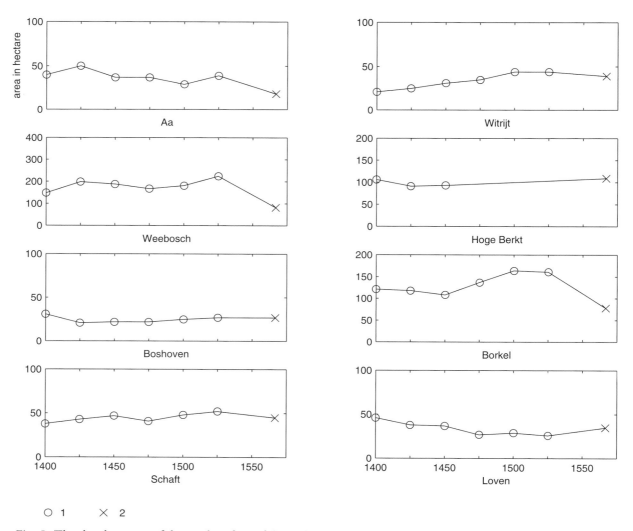

○ 1   ✕ 2

Fig. 8. The development of the total surface of the arable and hayland fields in hectares in late medieval and early modern times in different hamlets.

1 figures from the rent registers; 2 figures from the register of the Cth penny

surface area of cultivated land. The size of the cultivated land even diminishes in the period 1525–1569, especially in the hamlets of Aa, Weebosch, Witrijt and the villages of Borkel and Schaft. The increase at the hamlet of Witrijt and at Borkel between 1450 and 1500 indicates new reclamations or the re-use of poor ground. Some hamlets had much marginal land which possibly reverted to heaths in bad times, and depending on the economic situation were again taken into use. In figure 9 we see various developments: for the hamlets of Stokkelen and Heestert a decrease in the cultivated land for the hamlets of Hees, Schadewijk, *Kortkruis* and Boxheide, an increase. It appears that different developments took place in different hamlets. Generally speaking, the area of cultivated land in the rent district of Eersel remains stable as far as the ducal rent registers show.

The development of the area of cultivated land per hamlet clearly shows what has already been stated: from 1400 to 1569 there is little growth. The hamlet of Witrijt is one of the few hamlets in the study area to show a steady growth of circa 18 hectares in 1400 to circa 40 hectares in 1500. Elsewhere there is only the reclamation of small fields (the so-called *uitvangen*).

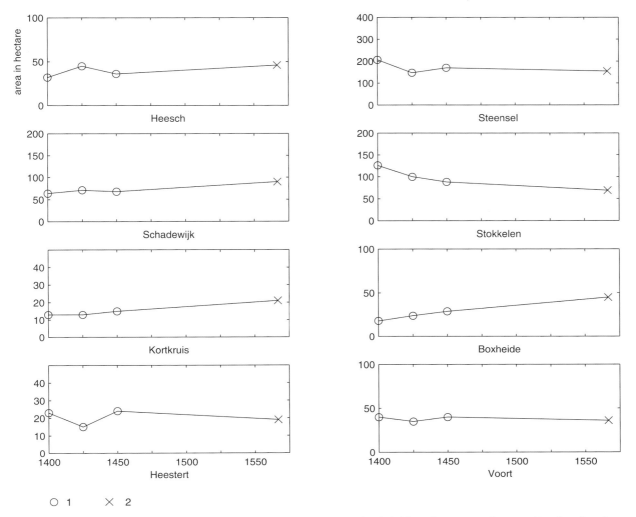

Fig. 9. The development of the total surface of the arable and hayland fields in hectares in late medieval and early modern times in different hamlets in the parish of Eersel.
1 figures from the rent registers; 2 figures from the register of the Cth penny

This conclusion is supported by the size of new reclamations, recorded as so-called *uitvangen*, for which the year of reclamation, the place and the surface area have been recorded. We have already made use of these data in the conversion of amounts of rent into surface area. The area of the *uitvangen* has been cumulatively plotted in time in figure 10. The increase of the arable area over the period 1400-1525 as a result of these reclamations is only 4% for Bergeyk over a period of almost 100 years, so we can draw the important conclusion that expansion of the cultivated land via reclamations under ducal control was therefore concluded before 1400.

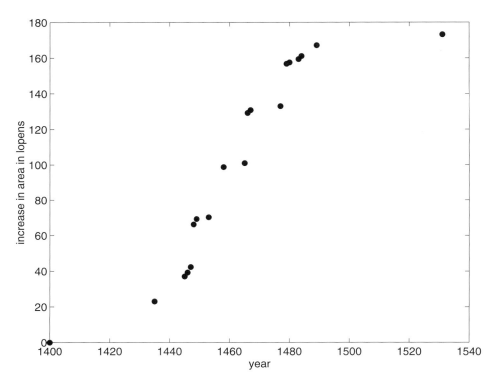

Fig. 10. The cumulative increase of new cultivated land (*uitvangen*) in the parish of Bergeyk.

5   DEMOGRAPHIC DEVELOPMENTS

The census registers are an important source for the demographic development in the region.[45] We can add the ducal rent registers to these as a source. We assume that the number of rentpayers is connected with the number of inhabitants and with the number of households in the hamlets and villages which arose and developed entirely under the duke's authority. As indicated in section 2.6, the number of households for these can be estimated from the number of rentpayers. We can periodize this count, which gives us a continuous series of figures for the period 1400-1525, indicating the general demographic development. However, in a number of hamlets rents were not only paid to the duke. In Bergeyk there are also other owners of rents such as Thorn, the abbey of Saint Jacques and the chapters of Saint Lambert and Saint Jean at Liège. Nevertheless, the number of households can be estimated for Bergeyk as a whole (the present village), so that a comparison with the census registers is possible. The section west of the centre developed from land handed out by the duke and by the abbey of Thorn.[46] The number of rentpayers and the number of households for this section can be derived from the rent registers of the duke and of Thorn.[47] For the section east of the centre (and in-

[45]   Cuvelier 1912-1913.

[46]   Vangheluwe 1989b, see also Theuws 1989.

[47]   The rentpayers of the duke and of Thorn (see e.g. Vangheluwe 1988) lived scattered over the hamlets and sometimes owners paid rents to both 'lords' so that a double count can occur when we add up the number of

households from both sources. This double count can be avoided as follows. The probability that a rentpayer of Thorn does not occur in the ducal rent register is determined by the ratio of the size of both areas. The owners of only one parcel (31% of the total number of owners) provide the greatest contribution. We calculate

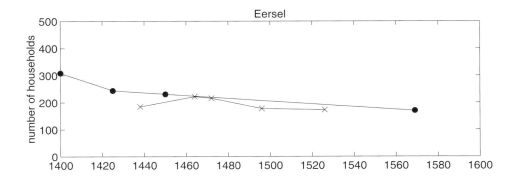

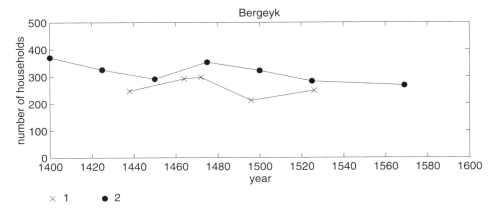

× 1   ● 2

Fig. 11. The development of the total number of households in Eersel and Bergeyk as determined on the basis of the rent registers and the register of the Cth penny and the register of hearths.
1 register of hearths; 2 rent registers and register of the Cth penny

cluding the centre) we do not have sufficient information from 1450. For the number of households in this section we fall back on the book of the Cth Penny which is of later date (1569). From this book it appears that the number of owners at Eikereind (east of the centre) in Bergeyk is 61% of the number in west Bergeyk (without Weebosch). We also apply this percentage in 1450, thus implicitly assuming that both parts of Bergeyk developed equally demographically between 1450 and 1569. The population figures estimated in this way are shown in table 5, for the east and west parts of Bergeyk and for Weebosch and Witrijt. The two latter hamlets are completely charged with ducal rents, so that the population figures follow directly from the ducal rent registers. The sum of these figures produces the number of households or hearths for the entire village of Bergeyk in 1450 and 1525.

We proceed in the same way for the village of Eersel. We have seen that in Eersel the reclamations under the duke's authority took place everywhere except in the centre. The development of the centre was determined by the handing out of land by large landowners already present in the area, for

this probability from the ratio of the surface areas of both areas to be 0.31 *702/(702+1385)=0.1043. The number of rentpayers for the area including Thorn is therefore 1.1043 times larger than the number of rentpayers to the duke alone. The number of rentpayers to the duke in west Bergeyk in 1525 is 184 and including

Thorn 203. The number of households is 80% of the number of rentpayers after a correction of 15% for the owners living outside the rent district. The number of households including the rent district of Thorn is then 203*0.8*0.85=138. It is used in table 3 to calculate the ratio.

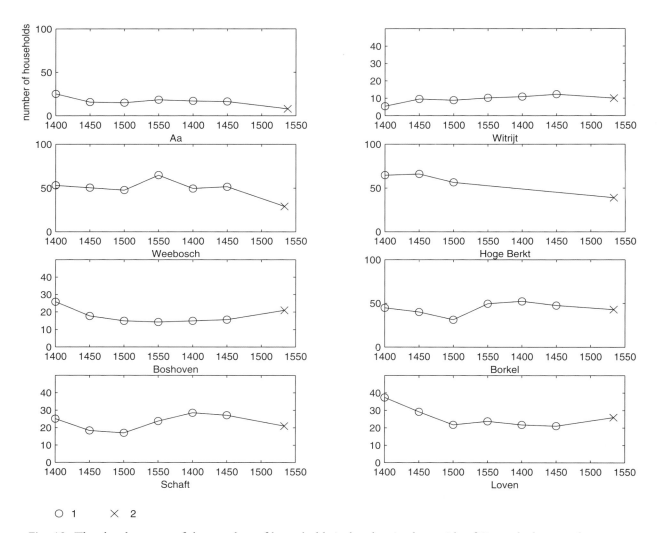

Fig. 12. The development of the number of households in hamlets in the parish of Bergeyk that are almost entirely covered with ducal rents.
1 figures from the rent registers; 2 figures from the register of the Cth penny

which we have no information. For data from the centre of Eersel we fall back on the book of the Cth Penny.[48] The result is shown in table 5.

How do the numbers of households compare with the numbers of hearths (which we equate with households) in the census registers? The comparison is shown in table 6. Unfortunately the dates of the periodization in the rent registers differ from the dates of the count in the census registers. We have plotted the results on a graph in figure 11 and summarized them in table 6. From figure 11 and table 6 it appears that in general the figures from the rent registers are slightly higher than those of the census reg-

---

[48] The number of houses in the centre of Eersel *(Dijken* and *Plaatse)* is 70% of that elsewhere in the municipality, as shown by the book of the C[TH] Penny. The part outside the centre developed under the duke's authority, and we conclude on the basis of the ducal rent registers that in 1450 there were 200 rentpayers for this part. As a result, we estimate the number of rentpayers in the centre of Eersel in 1450 to be 70% of this number. The number of households follows from the number of rentpayers by multiplying this by a factor 0.8.

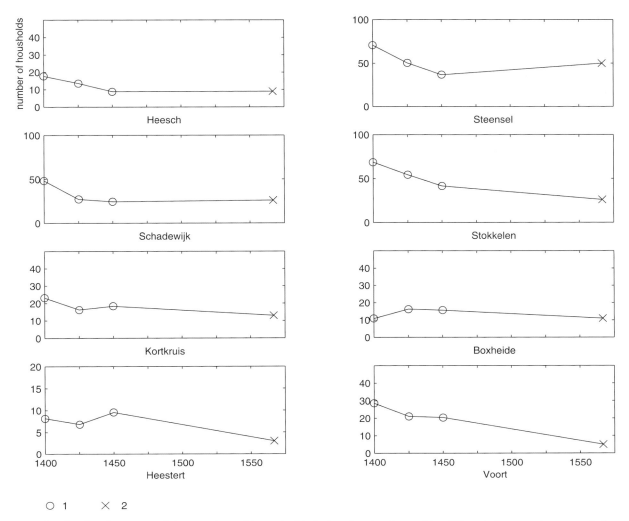

○ 1   ✕ 2

Fig. 13. The development of the number of households in hamlets in the parish of Eersel that are almost entirely covered with ducal rents.

1 figures from the rent registers; 2 figure from the register of the Cth penny

isters.[49] Both sources show that the population decreases between 1440 and 1569. This is slightly clearer in the case of Eersel than it is for Bergeyk. The decrease in the number of hearths is sharpest between 1400 and 1450. This is perhaps connected with the plague of 1437-1439. Both sources indicate a temporary increase of the population between 1440 and 1470 in Eersel and Bergeyk. The number of hearths in Bergeyk in 1464 is 292 (see table 6) and it rises to 298 in 1472, after which we see a decrease to 149 hearths in 1526. The years 1440-1470 are considered to have been extremely prosperous, they were the heyday of Burgundian culture.[50] From the rent registers it appears that the Kempen region also shared in this increase of prosperity. The prosperous period of 1440-1470 is ascribed to a higher purchasing power, peace, a stable currency and a controlled burden of taxation. We can differentiate the

49   With the census registers it is not clear whether the total number of hearths in 1438 includes the houses of the poor. We support the interpretation of the re-

searchers that the census register gives the total number of hearths.

50   Blockmans/Prevenier 1997.

area	1450		1525	
	1	2	1	2
Weebosch and Witrijt	79	54	89	60
Western Bergeyk (incl. Thorn)	217	147	203	138
Eastern Bergeyk (61%)	–	90	–	84
Entire Bergeyk	–	291	–	283
Eersel without *Dijken/Plaatse*	200	136	–	–
Dijken and *Plaatse* (70%)	–	95	–	–
Entire Eersel	–	231	–	–

Table 5. The number of rentpayers and the number of households in separate parts of the villages of Bergeyk and Eersel in 1450 and 1525.
1 number of rentpayers; 2 number of households

year	Eersel census register	Eersel rent register/ Cth penny book*	Bergeyk census register	Bergeyk rent register/ Cth penny book*
1400	–	308	–	370
1425	–	244	–	325
1438	185	–	247	–
1450	–	231	–	291
1464	222	–	292	–
1472	216	–	298	–
1475	–	–	–	353
1496	178	–	212	–
1500	–	–	–	322
1525	–	–	–	283
1526	173	–	249	–
1569 *	–	170	–	268

Table 6. The number of households as derived from various sources for the villages of Eersel and Bergeyk. The year 1569 is from the book of the Cth Penny.

population data from the rent registers according to the hamlets. The data are of special importance for the hamlets which developed under ducal authority. Figures 12 and 13 show the development of the population per hamlet for Bergeyk and Eersel, as it can be derived from the ducal rent registers. For the hamlets in Bergeyk, Westerhoven and Riethoven, Borkel and Schaft which developed under ducal authority and which are reflected in figure 12, there is no clear picture. The hamlets of Aa and Hoge Berkt and, to a lesser extent Weebosch, show a decreasing number of households. For Weebosch, Borkel and Schaft the revival of 1480 which continues through 1500 can be seen. Boshoven and Loven have a reasonably stable number of households, and at Aa the population increases only to decrease again after 1525. In general, we get the impression that the population in these hamlets decreases from 1525 to 1569. The results for the hamlets which developed under the duke's authority in Eersel and Steensel are shown in figure 13. For these hamlets we lack the data from 1525, so that it is more diffi-cult to trace the development of the population. Here, as in Bergeyk, there is a predominant picture of a decreasing population from 1450 to 1569, with five hamlets showing a decrease and two remaining stable. Only in the village of Steensel does the population increase. In figures 12 and 13 it can be seen that the number of households sharply decreases especially in the period 1400-1450.[51]

Now that we have described the development of the cultivated land and the population it is useful to investigate what the proportion of property charged with ducal rents is to the property charged with rents of other, often religious institutions in the study area.

6   OLD CULTIVATED LAND AND NEW OLD AND NEW RULERS

At the top of table 4 one can find the hamlets with a relatively small number of ducal rents. These are the hamlets where we hope to find rents of other, usually religious institutions. We assume that these hamlets were partly in the hands of old abbeys. Since the ducal rents are of more recent date, these hamlets with a large section of their cultivated lands appear to be the old medieval centres. What can the information on ducal rents tell us about the older property and does this correspond to what is already known about the property of old abbeys? We shall examine this for a number of hamlets in the study area.

We begin in Bergeyk: the centres in Bergeyk and Westerhoven were in the hands of the bishop of Liège. This property was handed over to the abbey of Saint Jacques[52] ,(at Bergeyk and Westerhoven), the chapters of Saint Jean[53] and Saint Lambert[54] (at Bergeyk at the *Kept* and on the *Berg*) and the abbey of Thorn[55] (op de Berkt). The maps in figures 2, 5 and 6 show where the Duke of Brabant imposed rents. From rent registers and other sources we conclude that the duke together with Thorn handed out land in the western part of Bergeyk.[56] In the centre of Bergeyk, the abbey of Saint Jacques predominates,[57] but the duke gains ground together with the abbey of Postel in *Runspade*, the surroundings of the castle and the watermill and in de *Rijen* north of the *Enderakkers*[58], therefore everywhere on the periphery of what appears to be the property of Saint Jacques in Bergeyk. From the field name *De Hoeven* at the *Enderakkers* (Eikereinde) we may conclude that the duke also handed out land here too.[59] Since the territory of the abbey of Saint Jacques in Bergeyk is surrounded by ducal reclamations, we assume that the abbey in Bergeyk played little part in expanding the cultivated area, perhaps because it could no longer assert any rights to the communal and unreclaimed lands. In a previous publication we have demonstrated how the old abbeys of Thorn and Saint Jacques gradually lost and

---

[51] The question is whether the assumed ratio of 0.8 between the number of hearths and the number of rent-payers always remained the same.

[52] Theuws 1989, 140 and epilogue (205); that the chapter of Saint Lambert also appeared to have rents in Bergeyk supports this conclusion.

[53] Lahaye 1942, 279; see also Theuws/Bijsterveld 1991, 130-136 and the map Abb. 6; Bijsterveld 1997.

[54] ARRS: *Quoyer van Westerhove van de honderste penninck*: here it mentions that *Jannes Meester Willemps heeft eenen*

chijns gepacht onder Bergheyck toebehoorende den Capittel Sint Lambrechts tot Ludick voor 9 gulden tsiaers.

[55] Franquinet 1881. See also Theuws 1989, 132-137.

[56] Vangheluwe 1992, 12.

[57] Theuws 1989, 121-122.

[58] This can be seen from e.g. toponyms in ARBR 50850, see also Vangheluwe 1992, 12.

[59] The distribution of the field name Hoeven in Bergeyk would appear to indicate this.

Fig. 14. The western arable fields of Bergeyk between Hoge Berkt, Lage Berkt, Loo and Broekstraat and the hay fields of Berkterbroek, and the distribution of fields with rents to be paid to the abbey of Thorn on the basis of the cadastral map of c. 1830.
1 building; 2 field boundaries; 3 streams; 4 heath (common pasture); 5 fields with rents to be paid to the abbey at Thorn

gave up the jurisdiction over their old possessions in Bergeyk.[60] If we look at the profit, a rent yields circa 100 times less than the tithe because of devaluation, whereas this was not so at first (when the rent was still a reasonable recompense for the use of the land). As a result of devaluation, the handing out of land charged with a rent lost importance and the levy of tithes became increasingly attractive due to the increasing area of land. The abbeys were allowed to levy tithes on the new lands (the so-called new tithes). The imposers of tithes including abbeys such as Echternach and Saint Jacques also profited from the recent ducal reclamations. There may even have been a deal in which the abbeys exchanged the jurisdiction which they had, of old, for the tithes on the newly-reclaimed lands, the duke increased his power. The policy of the duke is linked to this via the foundation of rent districts and administrative districts and the granting of limited town rights (vrijheden).

The same picture can be seen in the village of Westerhoven. The village with its cultivated land owes an important part of its rents to the abbey of Saint Jacques.[61] The hamlet of Loven to the east consists entirely of fields with ducal rents (fig. 7). Here too little was done by the abbey with regard to the reclamation of communal lands and a completely new hamlet developed as a result of the handing out of land by the duke. The abbey of Tongerlo which was strongly associated with the duke owns a leased out farmstead in Westerhoven, probably at Loven.[62]

Situated in a line towards the southwest from the hamlet of Loven, several new hamlets developed from ca 1200-1250 on: Klein Borkel, Borkel-Kapel, Voorste- and Achterste Brug (see figure 2). The arable lands of Borkel-Kapel, with the chapel in the centre, are still clearly recognizable on the topographical map of 1898. From the comparison of the surface area of cultivated land from the rent registers and the surface area on the topographical map of 1898 it appears that these hamlets already had their 19th-century size at the beginning of the 15th century.

East of Borkel, on the other side of the Dommel, is the village of Schaft. The most important owner of rents here is the duke. 40% of the ducal rents in this village appear to consist of valuta current before 1250 (the old pennies). This can be explained by the location of the village on the boundary with the property of the count of Gelre, an important rival of the duke. The duke will have attempted to reinforce his position on this boundary early on. Another large landowner in this area is the abbey of Echternach. The abbot refers to the duke as reengenoot (somebody with whom you have a common border), which may be seen as confirmation that the duke of Brabant controlled the hamlet of Schaft at an early date, which is also evidenced by the presence of many rents in old pennies (fig. 4).[63]

If we return to the west part of Bergeyk, we come to Hoge Berkt where the field complex known as De Hoeve is a reclamation under direction of the duke. To the hamlet of Hoge Berkt belong fields for which rents are paid to the abbey of Thorn (fig. 14). The same can be seen at the hamlet of Lage Berkt and at meadows in Broekstraat (for example Dode Vloet) and the haylands of Berkterbroek. The parcels

[60] Vangheluwe 1993, see also Theuws 1989, 132-143.

[61] Theuws 1989, 122 and appendix 2.

[62] Steurs 1977, 21 (Etats des biens (de Tongerlo) 1401 à 1500) and 457, (Etats des biens (de Tongerlo) 1475 à 1515, see also ARRS: Quoyer van Westerhove van de honderste penninck.

[63] Bijsterveld 1989, 67-69.

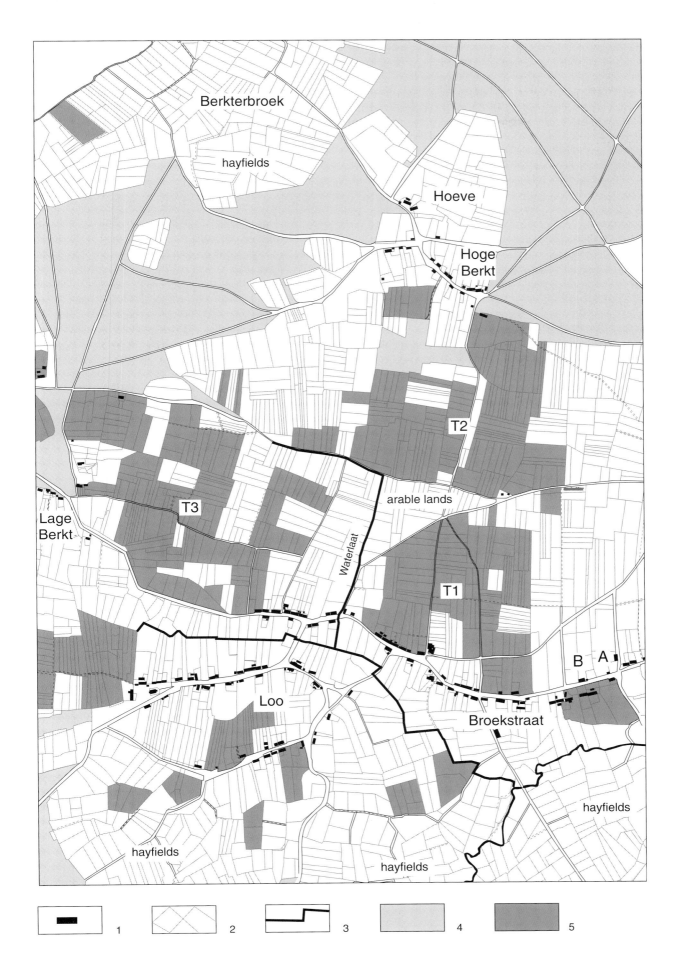

Berkterbroek

hayfields

Hoeve

Hoge
Berkt

T2

arable lands

T3

Waterlaat

Lage
Berkt

T1

B A

Loo

Broekstraat

hayfields

hayfields

hayfields

| | 1 | | 2 | | 3 | | 4 | | 5 |

with rents of each of them are situated close together here and are intermingled. Thorn probably had claims to the communal lands which predated the duke's rule and which made it possible for new rents to be created.[64] Haylands and marshes such as *Berkterbroek* and *Duivelsbos* on either side of the river Run which belonged to the communal lands, appear to belong to two owners of rents: the duke and the abbey of Thorn. However, it is striking that in Berkterbroek hardly any rents from Thorn are to be found, while there are many in the arable complex of Berkt. On the other hand one finds many ducal rents in *Berkterbroek*. This distinction between arable fields and haylands points to a difference in the time of reclamation of both types of cultivated land, in the sense that the haylands are younger and were reclaimed under the duke's authority. More generally, this means that the proportion of rents show what has long been surmised, namely that the wetlands were reclaimed far later than the high dry land. This can also be seen in the distribution of rents from Thorn in the arable area between Hoge Berkt, Lage Berkt, Loo and Broekstraat. These rents were not scattered at random over the area, but are located in three large complexes (fig. 14: T1-T3) with, in-between, areas without Thorn rents. The areas without Thorn rents hardly differ, from a environmental point of view, from those with Thorn rents. This similarity is the result of the centuries-long manuring of fields with deep litter manure since the Late Middle Ages which results in a physical levelling of the arable area. From the investigation of field names, however, another structure emerges. Many parcels between blocks T1 and T3 are called Waterlaat, named after a drain dug in a probably low-lying area.[65] The course of this drain can be reconstructed and is represented in fig. 14. The picture now presented is that the western arable area between Lage Berkt, Hoge Berkt, Loo and Broekstraat originally had more relief than is now the case, and that there were three small plateaus in the landscape with fields charged with Thorn rents, and in-between them low areas which were reclaimed later. It may be assumed that the ducal rents of Loo and the two Berkts must be sought in these low-lying areas. The question though is whether the Thorn rents can be considered reclamation rents. After all, archaeological investigation elsewhere in the region has revealed that these hills in the old arable complexes were inhabited and reclaimed as early as the Early Middle Ages. The western arable area, however, does not seem to belong to the central arable lands of Bergeyk which are to be found north of the village centre and Broekstraat. In the peripheral arable areas there may have been a hiatus in the habitation and cultivation in the late Carolingian period and in the 10th century. In the latter case, the Thorn rents are in fact reclamation rents because in that case a re-reclamation of the area in the late 10th, 11th and 12th centuries took place. If there was no interruption in the habitation in the late Carolingian period, it would have to be assumed that the Thorn rents and the ducal rents are partly of a different nature because part of the Thorn property charged with rents then was old arable land which was converted into property charged with rents. After all, Thorn was only founded as an abbey in the late 10th century and possibly acquired existing farmsteads in the western arable area. The situation in the western arable area of Bergeyk suggests that the ducal rents in other old centres mainly applied to the low-lying areas and the haylands. In contrast to the abbey of Saint Jacques, the abbey of Thorn apparently took the trouble to maintain old claims to uncultivated lands and possibly reached a compromise with the duke on this matter.

On the far side of the river Run and the above-mentioned haylands is the hamlet of Voort, in the territory of Eersel, with the leased out farmstead of Postel, named *Heinshovel*.[66] The cultivated area

---

[64]   Vangheluwe 1992, 12.

[65]   Borings to establish whether there are wet or dry soils under the arable cover can provide a simple solution.

[66]   ARRS: *Quoyer van Eersel van de honderste penninck*, folio 4r: the site of the farmstead is not specified, but the site of the other farmstead of Tongerlo in Eersel at Schadewijk is indicated from which this identification follows. The farmstead is now called *Hertheuvelse Hoef*, see also Steurs 1977, 20.

belonging to the hamlet is entirely charged with ducal rents from before 1250, showing that the hamlet already existed in the 13th century.

We return to Bergeyk to the hamlet of Broekstraat. In this hamlet there are two large leased out farmsteads: A. one belonging to the abbey of Postel and B. one belonging to the abbey of Tongerlo (fig. 14).[67] In 1362 the latter abbey also owns several fields charged with rent on the Langvoort, a hayland area situated between Broekstraat and het Loo.[68] The abbey came into possession of these lands by an endowment by Jan of Gemert who (as an intermediary) had acquired them from a local seigneur, Hendrik Boyfas.[69] This Boyfas also owned the local tithes and half of the patronage rights in the church of Bergeyk. The property charged with rents of the abbey also included a large farmstead situated to the west of the church of Bergeyk.[70] This farmstead probably goes back to the same Hendrik Boyfas. The rent paid by this farmstead is in old pennies, so that it must date at any rate from before 1200/1250. Boyfas possibly came into possession of this property as a steward or as a avower of one of the religious institutions of Liège. The abbey of Tongerlo had to pay rent for the land belonging to its leased out farmstead in Broekstraat to the three most important authorities in Bergeyk: the abbey of Saint Jacques, the abbey of Thorn and the Duke of Brabant. The two other large landowners apart from the duke who imposed rents in Broekstraat are the abbey of Saint Jacques and the abbey of Thorn. The abbey of Tongerlo is therefore the least important owner of rents in Broekstraat.

From Broekstraat we come to het Loo which consists of various hamlets which all owed rent to the Duke of Brabant and the abbey of Thorn. Hongarije, one of the hamlets at het Loo, is referred to as *Eikenhovel* in the rent register. The hamlet has a block of parcels called the *Hoeve*.[71] This is a toponym which we link with reclamations under ducal authority. The toponym is found everywhere, for example in Duizel[72] and at Witrijt[73], where the duke was the owner of rents. Further in a southerly direction there are haylands along the river Keersop called the *Hulsdonken* and the hamlet de Aa which are also completely charged with ducal rents, as is the area south of it, referred to in the rent register as the *Kolken*.[74] We are well informed about the latter area because of border disputes between Bergeyk and Lommel.[75] We have already focused attention on old ducal rents in this area dating from before 1250. Possibly the duke extended his sphere of influence from Lommel northward into our study area. In this area we also find a Jonkvrouwe Aleide from Lommel who owes rent, and who is related to the above-mentioned local seigneur Boyfas.

To the west of het Loo lies the hamlet of Run[76] where we find rents due to the Duke of Brabant and the abbey of Thorn. West of de Run we find the hamlets of *Broekskenseinde* and Weebosch. The former is characterized by large landownership. Allochthonous seigneurs such as the Lippens, Van Baasts and Van Vlierdens[77] exploit here between 1375 and 1525 an estate, *Ter Spegelt*,[78] of 15 *bunder*,

---

[67] Theuws 1989, 123-124 and appendix 1; Vangheluwe 1991.

[68] Vangheluwe 1990b.

[69] Theuws 1989, 116-124.

[70] Vangheluwe 1990b, 20.

[71] Vangheluwe 1989a, area 30, Hongarije south of Achterste Loo.

[72] See *Chromotopografische kaart des Rijks* (published as: *Historische Atlas van Noord-Brabant*, Den Ilp, 1989), map 706 of 1898: *Donkse Hoeven*, see also toponym *ter Donk* (156v4) and *aan die Donk* (91r4 and 146v5) in

ARBR 45044 (1450).

[73] Vangheluwe 1989a, area 33: Kleine Witrijt.

[74] This area now lies in the Belgian municipality of Lommel.

[75] Van de Boer 1990.

[76] Nowadays this hamlet is called: *de Rund*.

[77] ARBR 45044 (1450), f116v2, ARBR 45052 (1521) f21r.

[78] The estate is still recognizable as a unit on the 1830 map and is now called: *De Zandhoef*.

and the of Bladels and of Bruhezes an estate of 15 *bunder*.[79] These seigneurs, together with the inhabitants of the hamlet of Weebosch owe rent to the Duke of Brabant (see table 4). A little further away is the hamlet of Witrijt which developed out of two large farmsteads called Kleine and Grote Witrijt, as an island in the expanse of heath. In 1400 this hamlet is still growing, which is unusual (see figure 8 and table 4). Because the rents on Weebosch and Witrijt are exclusively specified in new pennies we assume that the reclamations under the duke's authority mainly date from after circa 1250.

North of Weebosch we come to the territory of Eersel in the hamlet of Boxheide, where the abbey of Averbode, one of the new Premonstratensian abbeys,[80] owns a leased out farmstead 16 *bunder* in size.[81] The hamlet is almost entirely charged with ducal rents. Nearby is the hamlet of *Heestert* which differs from the rest because its area of arable land was smaller in 1900 than it was in the 15th and 16th centuries. In 1450 and 1569 the hamlet had several owners and thus several houses and a surface area of 19 ha.[82] In 1900 6.5 ha was left,[83] and an old farmstead with that name, situated in the woods on the road from Eersel to Postel still exists. With 30 owners in around 1400, we estimate the number of houses in the hamlet of *Kortkruis* to be circa 24. In 1569 there are 20 houses.[84] From table 4 it appears that the largest owner of rents was the duke, and since the hamlet has no rents in old currency from before 1250, we conclude that the area of cultivated land belonging to the hamlet must have been largely reclaimed after 1250.

The centre of Eersel[85] is called the *Plaatse* in the book of the Cth Penny, and is now called *Hint*. Both hamlets appear to till on a centrally-situated arable complex called *Midakkers*, which is located north of the church and Schadewijk.[86] Eersel became a centre for the duke with a court, the privileged status of *vrijheid* (*libertas*) and the right to hold an annual fair.[87] The duke owned a large feudal estate of 97 *lopenzaad* (19 hectares) called `s Hertogen Hofstad ('the duke's homestead'),[88] which we locate in the centre (the *plaatse*) with land at *Midakkers* and Boxheide. From charters we know that the abbey of Echternach must have owned property in Eersel, donated by Saint Willibrordus.[89] Echternach also owned half the great tithes of Eersel.[90] Eersel still appears on a list of farmsteads and property charged with rents of the abbey from the first quarter of the 13th century,[91] but later we find no reference to the Echternach property there. Echternach probably still owns the property in 1450, for in table 4 it appears that the fields charged with ducal rents in *Dijken* and the *Plaatse* is half the surface area in Alva's rent register, which we assume to be valid for 1450. The percentage of old rents of 20% in the rent register indicates that the duke gradually extended his influence both before and after 1250.

To what extent Eersel had an administrative as well as an economic function for the region we do not know. The function of Eersel as a court and market-place at any rate offered prospects for this. The habitation around the typical market square may have consisted of merchants and craftsmen. It is possible that the *hoender* rents mentioned above were connected with this status of the village.

[79] ARBR 45044 (1450), f103r3 and ARBR 45052 (1521), f83r and f145r.

[80] See Bijsterveld in this volume.

[81] ARRS *Quoyer van Eersel van de honderste penninck*, 4.

[82] ARRS *Quoyer van Eersel van de honderste penninck*, 11.

[83] Measured on the *Chromotopografische kaart des Rijks* (published as: *Historische Atlas van Noord-Brabant*, Den Ilp, 1989), map 722 of 1898.

[84] ARRS *Quoyer van Eersel van de honderste penninck*, 12-14.

[85] We have included the hamlet of *Dijken* with the centre of Eersel because it proved difficult to separate the owners of these two hamlets on the basis of the networks.

[86] At the present traffic intersection het *Stuivertje*.

[87] Vangheluwe 1993, 5-17.

[88] Melsen 1989, 86.

[89] Camps 1979, no. 9 (726-727).

[90] See ARRS *Quoyer van Eersel van de honderste penninck*, 1.

[91] Camps 1979, no. 134 (1175-1225).

[92] The arable complex of Stokkelen is called *Stokkelseakkers* in 1569, see ARRS *Quoyer van Eersel van de honderste penninck*.

East of the centre of Eersel lies the hamlet of Stokkelen. This hamlet has its own field complex[92] south of the church of Eersel. The area of arable land belonging to the hamlet is entirely charged with ducal rents, and early on aldermen of Eersel are mentioned as coming from this hamlet.[93] The same applies to the hamlet of Schadewijk[94] with the hamlet of Hoogstraat in between.[95] A corn windmill stands in the hamlet. As we know, the hamlet of Hoogstraat developed in the 13th century. North of it is the hamlet of Hees where there was property belonging to Echternach. Worthy of mention is the large leasehold farmstead of Tongerlo at Schadewijk.[96] South of Schadewijk on the boundary with Bergeyk is the hamlet of Boevenheuvel like an island in the middle of the heath between Bergeyk and Eersel. The hamlet is almost entirely charged with ducal rents (see table 4). One of the old owners at Boevenheuvel is *Gerard de Eyke*, who has a conflict in 1295 with the abbey of Saint Jacques.[97] 150 years later (!) he is mentioned in the rent register *as Gerardi de Eyke et alys suis hereditaribus ex parte sua* with a rent of 24 pennies altogether on land situated on the Eersel side of Boevenheuvel.[98] Apparently the fact that such a person once owned the land affects its valuation. He transfers this land to common neighbours showing that the distance between the local nobility and the commoners cannot have been great and that it was no longer possible to preserve the heritage. The son of this Gerard, Hendrik Boyfas, sells his property in the centre of Bergeyk to Jan of Gemert, who in turn donates it to Tongerlo. After 1300 the Van Eiks are no longer important as local seigneurs in Bergeyk.[99]

North of the centre of Eersel lies the village of Duizel with the block of fields known as the *Hoeve*. This field name is a common one in the region for a reclamation under ducal authority. In this village, the duke is less important than a large landowner from the past, the chapter of Saint Bartholomy at Liège which owns the patronage and other 'feudal' rights.[100] The abbey of Tongerlo collects not only rents but also a fourth of the tithes here. How the abbey came to do so is unclear. North of Duizel is Hoogcasteren which is completely charged with ducal rents (see table 4). The abbey of Postel has several leased out farmsteads there.[101]

To the east lies the village of Steensel which, according to the information in table 4, is entirely charged with ducal rents. Steensel also illustrates that ducal rents are perhaps not always to be equated with reclamation. After all, we must assume that parts of Steensel had been reclaimed since as early as the Early Middle Ages, and that traces of habitation are to be found since the 7th century in the areas around the previously isolated church tower, as is also the case in such situations in other parts of the Meuse-Demer-Scheldt region. How the duke was able to hand out so many fields charged with rents in Steensel is difficult to ascertain; possibly the rents included those which may have originated from a previous large landowner. Only if there was a hiatus in habitation at Steensel in the late-Carolingian

[93] Camps 1979, no. 834 (1311): *Universis presentis litteras inspecturis Mercelis scultetus in Oerle, Godefridus dictus Scadeken, Henricus filius quondam Bulen, Petrus Faber, Iohannes Sutor, Tilmannus Carpentator, Iohannes de Stoclo, Theodericus filius Henrici de Stocloe, scabini in Eersele, veritas noticiam cum salute..*

[94] Camps 1979, no. 832 (1310): *Godefridum dictum Scadeken en Henricum de Schadewijc.*

[95] This hamlet is small and difficult to distinguish in the networks from the hamlet Schadewijk, and for this reason the two have been combined.

[96] ARRS *Quoyer van Eersel van de honderste penninck*, 18r;

see also Steurs 1977, 20 (*Etats annuels des biens* (de Tongerlo) *de 1401-1500*).

[97] Camps 1979, nos. 524 and 544.

[98] ARBR 45044 (1450), folio 94r3 with a rent of 15 new pennies and folio 96v3 with 9 new pennies.

[99] Theuws 1989, 110-118.

[100] Daris 1875, 178-179; see now also Bijsterveld 1997.

[101] ARRS *Quoyer van Casteren van de honderste penninck: De Hoeven die in Pact vuytgegeven zijn in den Dorpe van Casteren*, it is however not clear which of these farmsteads are located in Hoogcasteren and which in Kerkcasteren.

period and the 10th century would re-reclamation have taken place in the 11th and 12th centuries, but even in this case it cannot have been carried out under ducal authority. The aristocratic families who are mentioned in this village would have become dependent on the duke. The hamlet of Stevert, previously known as Steenvoort, is almost entirely subject to ducal rents. The same applies to the neighbouring hamlet of *Nedermolen*. Mention is made of fishing rights in the millpond.[102]

If we compare the surface area of the hamlet of Broekhoven onder Riethoven in the rent register with that in the book of the Cth Penny (see table 4), it appears that the duke imposed rents on about half the cultivated land in around 1450. The abbey of Echternach, which was of old the owner of rents in this hamlet,[103] qualifies as the owner of the other half. We see here the same development as in Bergeyk: old abbeys do not take part in new reclamations, thus losing importance as local authorities. The property charged with ducal rents in Broekhoven increased between 1450 and 1525 by about 37%, probably due to reclamation of the hayland areas in the direction of *Nedermolen*.

The hamlets Walik and Hobbelen, which we have combined because of their small size were charged with ducal rents for 30% in 1450 and for 48% in 1525 (see table 4). The centre of Riethoven is not clearly present in the duke's rent registers, though the hamlet of Heiereinde, also called *Riethovereinde*, is. We assume that the rents at Heiereinde must still have been in the hands of the abbey of Saint Jacques in Liège for three reasons: first, from a later rent register[104] of 1563 it appears that this abbey owned a large block of property charged with rents in Riethoven, second, only a small part of the hamlet is charged with ducal rents (see table 4) and third, the property links up geographically with the other possessions of Saint Jacques in Westerhoven and Bergeyk[105] (together they form a large complex on higher-lying arable land). From the above we have already seen that the abbey of Saint Jacques was capable of keeping its right of property intact. The abbey's rent register contains few toponyms and is not very informative as to the locations of parcels. At the beginning of the same stream valley from which Riethovereinde derives its name is the hamlet of Boshoven, the whole of which was given out for reclamation by the duke. On the other side of Riethovereinde on the brook Keersop lies the hamlet of Keersop. A number of parcels belonging to this hamlet are situated at Heiereinde as a result of which the cultivated lands of both hamlets interlap. Interesting in the Keersop hamlet apart from the watermill, is the property of aristocratic families, including a certain Udeman Udemans married to Mechtelt, daughter of Henrik of Boxtel[106] and the Herlaars who owned the watermill. The hamlet has old rents (see table 2) so that we assume that the duke exercised his influence here at an early stage.

Finally we arrive at the village of Dommelen. We do not have any information about it from the book of the Cth Penny, so that it is uncertain what the duke's influence as owner of rents would have been. The cultivated area from the rent registers (67 hectares) is small compared with that in 1900 (225 hectares).[107] We assume that the cultivated lands remained about the same from 1500 to 1900, so that the duke would not have been the biggest owner of rents in Dommelen. Excavations around the old chapel in Dommelen revealed settlements from the period 650-1250, which point to the presence of older property pre-dating the ducal reclamations.[108]

---

[102] ARBR 45044 (1450), f60r1: *ex parte arnoldi de nedermolen de piscatua in gurgite ant molendino*.

[103] Camps 1979, no. 134 (1175-1225), see also Bijsterveld 1989, 62.

[104] Rechterlijk Archief Bergeyk (RAB) no. 219 (1563); see also Theuws 1989, 208: 300 rent entries in Bergeyk, 170 in Riethoven and 156 under Westerhoven and Borkel.

[105] Theuws 1989, 208.

[106] Theuws 1989, appendix 3, the mill on the Keersop is a fief from the seigneurs of Herlaar.

[107] Taken from the *Chromotopografische kaart des Rijks* (published as: *Historische Atlas van Noord-Brabant*, Den Ilp, 1989).

[108] Theuws/Verhoeven/Van Regteren Altena 1988.

384

The hamlet of Venbergen with a watermill on the river Dommel, situated near Dommelen, is frequently mentioned in the ducal rent registers. The watermill belongs to the abbey of Postel,[109] an abbey protected by the duke. The rent registers show that the hamlet which had approximately 10 owners in 1400, becomes smaller: both the surface area and the number of owners appear to have decreased sharply by 1900. In 1900 the hamlet has 4 houses and the watermill.[110]

In conclusion, it may be stated that the information from the rent registers supplements the picture we already had of the development of the area. We get an impression of small-scale communities consisting of many large and small hamlets. A considerable part of the cultivated lands developed from reclamations carried out by private individuals under the authority of the dukes of Brabant in the 13th and, in the case of some, in the 14th century. As a result of this development a process is initiated which was to radically transform the relations between the inhabitants and their surroundings.

7   THE AVERAGE SIZE OF THE PROPERTY

The question occupying us now is what is the surface area of cultivated land per owner? In the first place, there is the matter of consistency between sources. In the second place there is the question whether there is any difference between the hamlets and whether any conclusions can be drawn as to the intensity of land use. On the basis of property hardly any conclusions can be made as to management. Nevertheless, differences in the landownership structure between the hamlets may provide an indication of the differences in management and of acquiring an income.

With this objective in mind, table 7 was compiled. The table shows the average property in hectares per owner as derived from the rent registers and the book of the Cth Penny[111]. For the hamlets not entirely charged with ducal rents, the property from the rent registers has been omitted. In these hamlets the owners have more property than mentioned in the rent registers. As a result we can only compare the sources for the hamlets which are entirely charged with ducal rents. The two rent registers from 1450 and 1525 give a consistent picture: there are no great differences between the average properties from either source. At Witrijt 2.8 hectares was owned in both years, whereas the property at Loven was 1.3 hectares in 1450 and 1.0 hectares in 1525. There are occasionally striking differences between the property from the book of the Cth Penny and the rent registers. In Borkel the property from the rent registers is 2.8 or 2.7 hectares, and from the book of the Cth Penny 1.7 hectares. In some hamlets the property from the rent registers is substantially larger than in the book of the Cth Penny, in others the reverse is the case. As we have already stated, the lower figures from the book of the Cth Penny of Steensel, Borkel and Weebosch can be explained by an incorrect entry in the book of the Cth Penny. In these hamlets, which are situated on relatively less fertile soils, the average property in the rent registers is larger than in the case of other hamlets, indicating less intensive cultivation of the land and the use of fallow periods. With this form of land use, it is conceivable that the surface area was underestimated or entered as being smaller for tax purposes. At Boxheide,

---

[109] Welvaarts 1878, 197-198, see also Bots/Melotte 1977, 74.

[110] See cadastral map of 1830 in Melotte/Molemans 1979.

[111] Owners not resident in the study area are not included. In the rent registers this is done by correcting the number of owners by 0.85. In the books of the Cth

Penny we take the number of houses (owned and rented) and divide it by 0.8. This is the ratio between the number of owners resident in the study area and the number of hearths as seen from a study of the book of the Cth Penny from Bergeyk.

Hoge Berkt, Heesch, Aa and Stokkelen, the property from the rent registers is significantly smaller than from the book of the Cth Penny. We do not exclude the possibility that in these hamlets an average increase in property took place between 1450 and 1569. We shall see this tendency also when we examine the property and balance of property of the rent registers per period in the next chapter.

If we look at the differences between the hamlets themselves, we notice that some have a small average property, such as Boshoven, Loven, Walik and Heiereinde. This property is consistently small in all the sources, as for instance in Boshoven.

Hamlet	1450	1525	1569	Hamlet	1450	1525	1569
Eikereinde	-	-	2.3	Heesch	1.5	-	4.1
Dijken and *Plaatse*	-	-	2.2	Schaft	2.2	1.5	1.8
Hoog Casteren	-	-	1.8	Boshoven	1.2	1.4	1.0
Broekstraat	-	-	2.7	Voort	1.6	-	5.1
Westerhoven	-	-	1.4	Loven	1.3	1.0	
Broekhoven	-	-	2.1	Aa	1.6	1.9	2.7
Heiereinde	-	-	1.2	Steensel	3.7	-	2.5
Loo	-	-	2.7	Borkel	2.8	2.7	1.7
Walik en Hobbelen	-	-	1.4	Stokkelen	1.7	-	2.6
Boxheide	1.5	-	3.2	Boevenheuvel	3.2		3.9
Schadewijk	2.2	-	2.6	Weebosch en *Broekskenseinde*	3.4	3.4	2.3
Witrijt	2.8	2.8	2.3	Duizel	2.0	-	-
Hoge Berkt	1.3	1.4	2.5	Dommelen	1.5	1.6	-

Table 7. The amount of cultivated land per owner in hectares, calculated from the information in the duke's rent registers of 1450 and 1525 and the book of the Hundredth Penny of 1569.

We do not expect that the farms in these hamlets were enlarged by the additional leasing of land, but rather that the income was increased by small-scale domestic industry, such as weaving, or by hiring oneself out as a labourer on a large farmstead. A small property may also point to extra earnings in the field of crafts, barrel- or basketmaking, for example. Craftsmen often had their own land just for the sake of owning it or as an emergency measure, as appears from the rent registers, where even a miller owns land.

Dijken and Eikereind, in other words parts of the centres of the villages of Eersel and Bergeyk, where the marketplace is expected (de *plaatse* in local dialect), have property of 2.2 hectares which does not differ from other hamlets which must have had an agrarian character. On the basis of this, one may assume that, apart from the marketplace, these centres were no different from the other hamlets and that farming would have predominated. As a result, the crafts must have been scattered over the hamlets and a concentration of crafts in local village centres would not have been likely.[112]

We end with the conclusion that the average agrarian property was very small: the average for the entire area was 2.44 hectares in 1569 and 2.09 hectares in 1450. The small amount of property indicates that small (mixed) farms predominated in the region. An in-depth study of Woensel in the 18th

---

[112] The names in the rent register point to this, names referring to a profession are frequently found throughout.

century shows the same picture. In 1810, the property per farmer is 2.41 hectares.[113] From this, it may be concluded that the late-medieval period of welfare and prosperity was based not so much on the divided cultivated land but on sheepbreeding on the large commons. The arable and hayland area, it appears, were exclusively reserved for individual subsistence and for keeping one or two cows. The integration of the region in an urban mercantile economy, as a result of which the Kempen farmers were able to acquire an additional income, makes it possible for such a radical reduction and fragmentation of the cultivated and hayland area to take place. Moreover, archaeological evidence indicates that from the 13th century on, the arable land was more intensively fertilized so that the yield per hectare rose and that it underwent more thorough tilling, digging perhaps instead of ploughing, in order to achieve an even higher yield.[114] This constellation and the form of land use is highly dependent on the presence of a textile market with a need for local wool. When the demand for local wool began to diminish and the contact between the Kempen and the market centres was disrupted due to external causes, the Kempen farmers possibly got into difficulties because their small areas of divided cultivated land were not big enough to rely on when attempting to keep up a farm. This resulted in a process of impoverishment and demographic decline. In the next chapter we shall discover that the average size of the farms did gradually increase again. Moreover, there is a complex relation between agrarian and craft activities. There is perhaps a light 'industrialization' of the countryside linked with the development of textile centres in the Brabant Kempen.[115]

8   THE PROPERTY STRUCTURE

8.1   PROPERTY STRUCTURE IN GENERAL

The information from the rent registers of the duke of Brabant in the study area enables us to map the property structure of a number of hamlets which were almost completely charged with ducal rents. We present the property structure as a frequency division into 9 classes of size. We have applied almost the same division in size of property as Hoppenbrouwers in his study of the Land of Heusden.[116] However, instead of using the morgen as a unit of measurement we use the hectare. In 1569 the property in the book of the Cth Penny consists mainly of cultivated land, with only a few entries of property in money. Here, the surface area of the landed property is taken as a measure of the owner's prosperity and social status.

The frequency distribution of different sizes of property complexes was compared with those made by Hoppenbrouwers for the Land of Heusden.[117] In table 8 we present the property structure from this study of the municipalities of Herpt, Oud-Heusden and Heesbeen where small to very small landownership prevailed.[118] These resemble most the property structure from the rent registers, an example of which is given in table 9 for the hamlets in Bergeyk which developed under ducal authority.[119] The picture sketched by Hoppenbrouwers of the Land of Heusden is more diverse than in our

---

[113] Van de Brink 1996.

[114] Theuws/Verhoeven/Van Regteren Altena 1988, 256-257. Spade traces like these have been found in many places and in different levels of the plaggen layer. See also Bieleman 1992, 96.

[115] See Jansen 1982.

[116] Hoppenbrouwers 1992, 325.

[117] Hoppenbrouwers 1992, 325.

[118] One *morgen* is 0.85 hectares.

[119] These hamlets are : Aa, Hoge Berkt, Boevenheuvel, Weebosch and *Broekskenseinde*, Hongarije, *Hulsdonk, Kolken*, Witrijt.

category in *morgen*	Herpt 1543-44		Oud-Heusden1556	
	number	percentage	number	percentage
< 1	7	23	17	18
1 tot 2	9	29	23	25
2 tot 3	7	23	14	15
3 tot 4	1	3	9	10
4 tot 5	4	13	6	6
5 tot 7.5	3	10	16	17
7.5 tot 10	0	0	2	2
>=10	0	0	6	6

Table 8. Frequency distribution of landed property in about 1550 in the Land of Heusden (after Hoppenbrouwers 1992, 325).

category in hectares	1450 number (212)	1450 relative percentage	1525 number (199)	1525 relative percentage
< 1	113	53.3	87	43.7
1- 2	40	18.9	35	17.6
2 -3	18	8.5	27	13.5
3 -4	8	3.7	14	7.0
4 -5	6	2.8	7	3.5
5 -6	6	2.8	13	6.5
6 -7	6	2.8	5	2.5
7-8	5	2.3	2	1.0
> 8	10	4.7	9	4.5

Table 9. Frequency distribution of landed property for that part of Bergeyk that is largely charged with ducal rents. Information derived from the ducal rent registers no. 45044 (1450) and no. 45052 (1521).

category in hectares	1400 number (400)	1400 relative percentage	1425 number (301)	1425 relative percentage	1450 number (271)	1450 relative percentage
0-1	223	55.7	144	47.8	113	41.7
1-2	90	22.5	78	25.9	69	25.5
2-3	32	8.0	35	11.6	40	14.8
3-4	15	3.8	15	5.0	13	4.8
4-5	12	3.0	9	3.0	13	4.8
5-6	5	1.3	6	2.0	4	1.5
6-7	6	1.5	1	0.3	2	0.7
7-8	8	2.0	2	0.6	5	1.8
> 8	9	2.3	11	3.7	12	4.4

Table 10. Frequency distribution of property in that part of the municipality of Eersel that developed under ducal authority. Information derived from rent register no. 45044 (1450).

study area. In the Land of Heusden there are municipalities where small landownership predominates, such as the municipalities mentioned above, but there are also municipalities such as Eethen with far larger landowners (over 5 *morgen* of land). Our study area rather shows a uniform picture of very small landownership. From table 9 it can be seen that 53.3% of the owners in 1450 had property of less than one hectare.[120] In Herpt in the year 1543-1544 (see table 8) 23% falls in the lowest category of less than one *morgen* (0.85 hectares) and 22% of the neighbours owns half the land. Tables 8 and 9 show both the numbers per category and the percentage per category.

Comparison of the data from 1450 and 1525 in table 9 shows that the property structure changed between 1450 and 1525. A tendency can be observed toward a larger average size of property at the beginning of the 16th century. Whereas in 1450 53.3% still owns less than one hectare, in 1425 this has decreased to 43.7%. The change is mainly found in the lowest categories up to 6 hectares, above this the size of the property hardly changes. In 1450 only 4.7% of the owners has more than 8 hectares of arable land. In 1525 this is still approximately the same, with 4.5%.

This raises the question whether this change in size of property had already begun before 1450. We can answer this question by making use of the periodization of the rent register prior to 1450. In this rent register we can clearly distinguish two older generations which we date to about 1425 and 1400 (25 years per generation). The property structure for these generations are shown in table 10 for the hamlets in the municipality of Eersel which are largely charged with ducal rents.[121] From table 10 it becomes clear that the tendency toward larger property had already started before 1450. Whereas in 1400 55.7% of the owners had less than one hectare, in 1450 it is only 41.7%. At the upper level of the categories of prosperity a development can also be observed. In 1400 we see that 2.3% owns more than 8 hectares. This group increases in number from 3.7% in 1425 to 4.4% in 1450. In all the categories of prosperity, from small to large, we observe an increase in the average size of farms from 1400 to 1450.

The above development is also reflected in the average size of property in the hamlets which developed under the duke's authority, both in the municipalities of Eersel and in Bergeyk. The total development is illustrated in figure 15, which also includes the surface area of property per owner from the book of the Cth Penny.[122] Figure 15 shows that the average area of property quickly increases from 1400 on, less quickly after 1450 and that it finally remains stable at 2.8 hectares at the beginning of the 16th century.

In the previous section we saw that inhabitants of some hamlets had less property than that mentioned above. The centres of Eersel and Bergeyk, as can be seen from the book of the Cth Penny, appear to have a somewhat smaller surface area of property, that is between 2.2 to 2.3 hectares, in 1569. The smaller average area of property in these hamlets points to other forms of income, such as domestic crafts or contract work (labourer on a larger farm). The ownership of one hectare which exists in some hamlets is under the subsistence level of a household (6 persons). Increase of the average area of cultivated land from 1400 to 1500 indicates that the agrarian character of the region intensified. More farms appear (from necessity?) which acquire their income exclusively from agriculture. With regard to craft, a specialization develops in which income is obtained more from craft activities and

---

[120] This picture corresponds to the Flemish sandy area in the 16th century: Bieleman 1992, 95-96.

[121] These hamlets are: Stokkelen, Schadewijk, Voort, Hees, Duizel, Boevenheuvel, Boksheide, Steensel, *Rosheuvel*, Heestert and Hoogeloon. They also include

the haylands of *Tasbroek, Gewatbroek, Honsbos, Nedermolen, Kwadewas*.

[122] This property is also calculated for the hamlets which developed under the duke's authority.

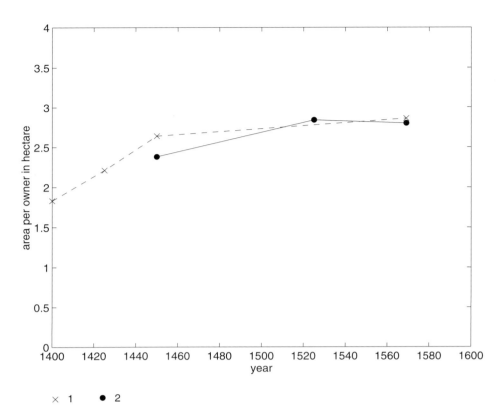

Fig. 15. The development of the average area of arable and hay fields per owner in Bergeyk (dots) and Eersel (crosses).

less from agricultural activities. For instance, a farmer who used to sit behind his loom in the winter season now does this all the year round. In the study area too, the weaving of linen sheets on farms becomes popular, witness the supply of *vlessen lakens* as part of the rent to the abbey of Tongerlo from 1544 on.[123]

8.2   THE ALDERMEN

Finally we come to the last subject of this analysis: how do the notables differ from the rest of the population? Persons belonging to this category are identified on the basis of one or more of the following factors: 1. bearing a title such as *magister,* 2. owning much land, 3. holding a public office, like the aldermen of the local court, 4. protocolling in the capital of the district Den Bosch, 5. holding in tenure a large leased out farmstead belonging to a religious institution. The rent registers provide information on the first two factors. Aldermen's charters in the archive of the abbey of Postel over the period 1350-1450 provide an outcome for factor 3: the charters always begin with : *Wij schepenen...* followed by the names of all the aldermen, *...oorkonden dat voor ons komen is...*etc. [124]

[123] Archive of the abbey at Tongerlo, lease contract of the farmstead in Bergeyk to Jan Haecxkens (1544).

[124] We aldermen ... record that before us appeared ... etc.

During an earlier investigation[125] we established that in the second half of the 14th century almost all the aldermen came from hamlets in the municipality of Eersel, particularly from Stokkelen, *Dijken* and Schadewijk. After 1400, aldermen are also mentioned from other hamlets, especially from the Bergeyk section of the court. In other words, the aldermen first come from those corners of the district which were under strong ducal influence, particularly to the south of the centre of Eersel. We have summarized this result in table 11.

period	contribution of Eersel	contribution of Bergeyk	unknown	total number
1347-1370	80%	2%	18%	84
1371-1390	74%	2%	21%	42
1391-1410	79%	13%	9%	56
1411-1430	47%	33%	20%	49
1431-1450	39%	30%	31%	71

Table 11. The distribution of aldermen according to origin from Eersel or Bergeyk in the aldermen's court of Eersel in the period 1350-1450.

In the 14th century we often see the same aldermen who had a one-year term of office returning to the aldermen's court. After about 1400 this becomes rare, and if an alderman returns it is only once. Because an increasing number of hamlets supply an alderman after 1400, it becomes more difficult to return to the aldermen's court because of the large number of hamlets desiring representation.

At this stage, Bergeyk is not yet a *vrijheid* like Eersel. It only receives this status from Charles the Bold around 1467, at the same time as the separation from the court of Eersel took place. The late date is probably connected with the dominant position of the old abbeys in Bergeyk. The abbey of Saint Jacques and the chapters of Saint Lambert and Saint Jean at Liège and the convent at Thorn, which exercise power at Bergeyk since c. 1000 AD, succeed in maintaining their influence and protecting it from the Duke of Brabant.

8.3   THE PROPERTY OF THE ALDERMEN

What position did the aldermen occupy in social life? What part did they play in it? Did they hold a prominent position and did they come from a certain social group? By looking at the landed property of the aldermen as a group on the basis of the data from the ducal rent registers, we can attempt to form an impression. It should, however, be mentioned that the ownership of cultivated land is not always indicative for the wealth of a person. After all, income from sheepbreeding and the sale of wool which appear to be significant for 15th-century prosperity cannot be revealed in this way. The names of the aldermen are taken from aldermen's charters in the archive of the abbey of Postel over the period 1350-1450.[126]

The majority (80%) of the names of aldermen mentioned in the charters can be traced in the ducal rent registers.[127] The rent register only mentions the property charged with ducal rents which is in the

[125] Vangheluwe 1993, 5-17.

[126] Archive of the abbey at Postel, charters Bergeyk.

[127] This is possible by paying attention to the patronyms and surnames which are used consistently, especially in

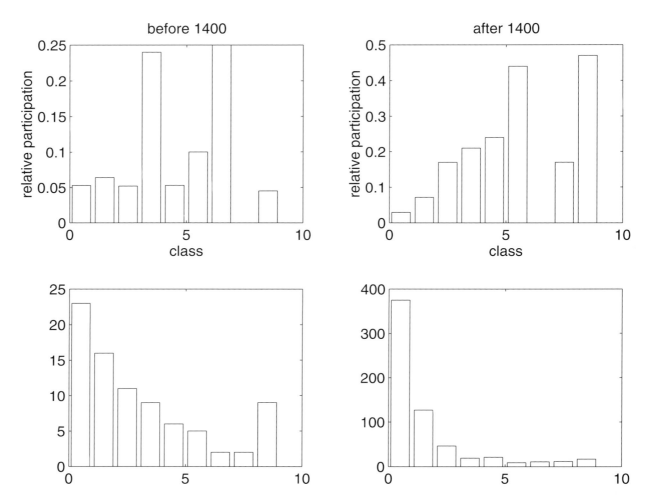

Fig. 16. The relative distribution of owners over different property classes for the population as a whole as well as the members of the aldermens court. Upper left: the relative distribution of aldermen over property classes in the second half of the 14th century; upper right: the relative distribution of aldermen over property classes in the first half of the 15th century. Lower left: number of aldermen per property class in the period 1350-1450; lower right: the distribution of owners over different property classes c. 1450.

hands of the aldermen. We conclude that many aldermen come from hamlets where ducal rents are predominant. For this reason, the ducal rent register may help in gaining some insight into the landed property and the related wealth of the aldermen. Table 12 gives a frequency distribution of the aldermen per property class. The same division is shown in figure 16. The figure consists of 4 histograms, of which the top two are discussed later. The distribution of property among the aldermen is shown in figure 16 in the bottom left histogram and, in comparison, the distribution of property of the court is shown at the bottom right, for the part almost entirely charged with ducal rents.

the rent register. The year of the charter and the period in the rent register must also correspond. For instance, a charter of 1442 names the alderman: *Loye arnts Loys zoon was*, who appears in the rent register as:

lodovis filius arnoldi loys... The year 1442 of the charter falls within the period 1425-1450 in the rent register, making identification almost certain.

no.	class in hectares	number of aldermen	relative proportion of aldermen	relative participation in aldermen's court in percentages
1	0-1	22	26.8	1.3
2	1-2	16	19.5	2.4
3	2-3	11	13.4	4.6
4	3-4	9	11.0	8.4
5	4-5	6	7.3	7.6
6	5-6	6	7.3	11.3
7	6-7	1	1.2	3.6
8	7-8	2	2.4	5.7
9	>8	9	11.0	12.0

Table 12. Frequency distribution of the aldermen per property class, from rent register 45044 (1450). The last column gives the relative attendance per class at the aldermen's court of Eersel from 1350-1450.

The two relative distributions clearly differ, and one notices that though a large area of property is not predominant among the aldermen, it is clearly present. The aldermen own an average of 3.5 hectares as opposed to 2.4 hectares for the population as a whole. These averages are considerably below those of jurors (Dutch: *gezworenen*) in Oud-Heusden at the end of the 15th century, where the size of property is 6.6 Rhenish *morgen* (1 Rhenish *morgen* is 0.85 hectares or circa 4 *lopenzaad*), slightly above the average of 5.8 *morgen* for all villagers.[128]

The frequency division per class among the aldermen in our study area clearly differs from that of the total population (see figure 16 bottom right). The progression in numbers of the classes of prosperity is far less for the aldermen than for the population. The higher classes are less populated and this produces, by definition, a lower number of aldermen for the wealthier classes. From this it follows that from the higher classes there are more participants in the aldermen's court in terms of percentage than from the lower classes. We obtain the relative participation in the aldermen's court per property class by dividing the number of aldermen by the number of owners. This relative number per property class is found in the far right column of table 12. It is also illustrated in figure 16, with a distinction between the period before 1400 in which the aldermen mainly come from Eersel, and the period after 1400 in which they also come from Bergeyk. It is clear that, from the lower to the higher property classes, participation in terms of percentage rises until a maximum of 25% is reached. For the period after 1400 the participation of the higher property classes appears to increase.

We conclude that the lowest classes have fewer representatives in the aldermen's court in proportion to their numbers. Nevertheless, they are in number the largest group in the court because their cohort is the largest.

Even though the aldermen's court is mainly occupied by small landowners, this does not exclude the fact that the wealthier members may have had the actual power. The members of the court had to change every year. In this case one would expect to measure the influence of the wealthy persons by

[128] Hoppenbrouwers 1992, 525.

the number of years that they were in office. A correlation between the number of years that a person was an alderman and the size of his property is not present (the correlation coefficient is < 0.1). The aldermen's court must therefore have been a reasonably democratic and mixed assembly of very wealthy and less wealthy villagers. By way of illustration: the aldermen's court in 1436 consisted of the following members: Willem Willems Scoerdels zoon from the centre of Eersel in class 2, possibly the chairman,[129] Peter Becker from Duizel with 22 *deniers* in class 3, Ansom Utenbosch[130] from Steensel with a very large property of 160 *lopense* in the highest class 9, Jan van der Roten at Berkt in Bergeyk in class 7, Peter van der Voort from Stokkelen or Broekhoven in class 5, Mijs Mijs Schenens zoon who we cannot trace in the register and Henrik Martens at Eikereinde in Bergeyk in class 2. We therefore find in a court persons with a very wide range of property.

A small property is no obstacle to holding the office of alderman together with persons who are extremely wealthy for this district, although one should not forget that persons with little cultivated land may nevertheless have been relatively wealthy. This says something about the mutual relations in the hamlets. Without doubt there was a layered society: this is apparent from the title of *magister* in the rent register and the odd aristocrat. These layers can also be seen in a platform where we might expect it: the governing body of the region. The wealthier and therefore the notables are more likely to be found in the aldermen's court. Their absolute number is smaller than expected, however, and the majority of the members is from the lower classes. This is possibly linked with the greater participation of all hamlets after circa 1400: this points to the existence of a system of circulation: every hamlet then has the right to send a representative to the aldermen's court. In the smaller hamlets, people were highly dependent on each other and there were often family ties. In these small communities of neighbours people treated each other equally, which implies that the most suitable neighbour or family member was sent to the aldermen's court as a representative and not necessarily the wealthiest. This explains the more or less equal participation of all property classes in the aldermen's court and the democratic relations. The same phenomenon of democratization of authority also appears to exist within the local communities in the Land of Heusden in the 15th century.[131]

The situation in the 14th century in which the hamlets of Stokkelen, Schadewijk and the centre of Eersel (*Dijken* and *Plaatse*) control the aldermen's court is clearly different from that after 1400. By tradition these hamlets were accustomed to supplying aldermen ever since the establishment of the aldermen's court, and they continue to do so throughout the 14th century. These are the hamlets from which the ducal expansion began. Nevertheless, they were no larger or more important than the other hamlets which would participate later in the 15th century. The influence of the aldermen's court clearly increased in the 15th century and now extended over the entire study area, which is indicative for the period in which the dukes controlled the villages. It can be seen in the participation of all hamlets in the aldermen's court. That Bergeyk splits off as a separate district from Eersel in around 1467 would seem to be a logical conclusion to this development.

[129] This alderman possibly owned other property since he comes from an area where there are other rents as well as those of the duke.

[130] ARBR 45044 (1450): in the rent register he is mentioned 19 times as: *ancelm filius ancelm utenbos*.

[131] Hoppenbrouwers 1992, 526: in 1375 many extremely wealthy neighbours hold the office of juror in Oud-Heusden and Heesbeen, however, in the 15th century this office appears to have been highly democratized.

In the above analysis a picture is sketched of local societies and their landscapes on the basis of a number of ducal rent registers as well as the registers of the Cth penny from the 16th century.

In the first place, the rent registers offer insight into the late-medieval reclamation activities which take place mainly on two fronts. The first is that of the peripheral hamlets which, in the period in which reclamations took place under ducal authority (i.e. since the 13th century), came almost completely into being. Weebosch and Borkel are examples. The second front is that of the low-lying wetland areas which were reclaimed to become haylands. This can be demonstrated clearly in the case of the hamlets surrounding the western arable area at Bergeyk. It also becomes clear that this wave of reclamation came to a halt before 1400. After this date, only small, insignificant parcels were reclaimed, which are referred to in the rent registers as *uitvangen*.

In the second place, the registers throw light on the ducal policy of which reclamation obviously formed a part. In parishes with many important landowners from the distant past, including important ecclesiastical institutions, we see that the duke extends his influence in these parishes via reclamations in peripheral areas, and that, as the director of these reclamations he takes over the position of these institutions. At Bergeyk we can trace his activities from Lommel in the southern valley of the Keersop, at Eersel south of the village centre in the vicinity of Stokkelen where the first aldermen came from, and in the valley of the Run.

In the third place, the registers give an image of the rural community in the Late Middle Ages. It is the image which develops after a radical transformation of the cultivated landscape since the early 13th century, one which is familiar to us from archaeological investigation. A significant element of this transformation is the physical movement of the settlements from the high areas to the edges of the stream valleys and the development there of the hamlets which we have described here. This also entailed the reorganization of the old settlement/arable areas and the application of new fertilization techniques which will have resulted in a considerable increase in the yield per hectare. It is striking that the cult places and cemeteries, in which the ancestors were buried, were not moved but left behind as solitary beacons in the landscape, symbols of the old situation. All this was probably accompanied by a substantial increase in the population which reached its peak in the 14th century and probably decreased again after 1400, judging from the decrease in number of households. We assume that the family structure remained more or less constant in the 13th to 15th centuries. The effects of the transformation process were extremely far-reaching, both in social-political-economic practice as in the ideas on relations between man and environment, although the rent registers do not provide much information on the latter aspect.

It is important to observe that not only society but also the cultivated landscape were subject to drastic fragmentation. In the 14th century a great many small settlements grew up, with households disposing of an average of only 2.4 hectares of arable land, and more than half of them with less than one hectare at their disposal. The supposed reduction of the average area of arable land per household and the small size of it in the 14th to 16th centuries may be linked with various factors. For example: 1. demographic growth and a system of inheritance in which all children inherit an equal part, as a result of which disintegration of property occurs. Whether this legal equality of all children always led in practice to a division of property among all the children cannot be stated at present. 2. Improved fertilization techniques (sod manuring) which brought about an increase in yield per hectare and which permit a reduction in the area of arable land per household. 3. The integration of the area in an urban-mercantilist economy resulting in other sources of income being tapped (wool trade) enabling people to earn a living. 4. The increase on craft activities and the light 'industrialization' of the country mainly via textile workers in their homes which allows a reduction of the arable land to be carried out.

The development of small local communities with their fragmented property which was reduced per household did not prevent them from undergoing a period of economic prosperity in the 14th and 15th centuries which was probably connected with the growth of the textile industry in the south of the duchy of Brabant. It was also expressed in the religious building activities in this period. The economic growth did not entail any extreme differences in the ownership of cultivated land. Large farms are the exception. Nor is it possible to determine on the basis of landed property alone whether there were significant differences in wealth. Important positions within the village community were not exclusively held by the wealthy, as can be seen from an investigation into the property of aldermen. Although the likelihood of a wealthy alderman being a member of the court was greater, the proportion of less wealthy landowners in the council of aldermen was always higher. Village communities were fairly democratic in the sense that almost everyone was poor. Here too, one must query the extent to which the formal complement of the council reflects the actual power relations inside a village, because 'informal' power networks remain hidden from us. A distinction between formal and informal power is perhaps unfortunate for such communities in which much would have been settled via personal networks, but may be helpful in forming an idea. This idea of the structures of a peasant society from the 13th to the 15th century in the sandy areas of the Meuse Demer Scheldt region is still in its early stages. It will be important to recognize what are the local variations and what are the structural elements. Not all villages have the same power relations or were reclaimed to the same extent under ducal authority. Nevertheless, research like that presented here offers the possibility of philosophizing in more abstract terms about the use of the landscape in the Late Middle Ages from a long-term perspective of this issue, the initial impetus to which has been given in the introduction to this volume.[132]

[132] I wish to express my gratitude to P. Hoppenbrouwers, A.-J. Bijsterveld and F. Theuws for their critical remarks on earlier versions of this article, and to Christine Jefferis for translating the text into English. The maps were drawn by F. Theuws.

ABBREVIATIONS

ARBR = *Algemeen Rijksarchief Brussel, Archief van de Rekenkamer* (General State Archive Brussel, Archive of the auditor's office [of the duchy of Brabant in Brussels])
ARRS = *Algemeen Rijksarchief Den Haag, Archief van de Raad van State* (General State Archive The Hague, Archive of the Council of State)
RAH = *Rechterlijk Archief 's-Hertogenbosch* (archive of the aldermen's court 's-Hertogenbosch)
RAB = *Rechtelijk Archief Bergeyk* (archive of the aldermen's court, Bergeyk)
AP = Archive of the abbey at Postel
AT = Archive of the abbey at Tongerlo

UNPUBLISHED HISTORICAL SOURCES

General State Archive Brussel, Archive of the auditor's office (of the duchy Brabant in Brussels) (ARBR)
45044, *censier Eersel* (1450)
45052, *censier Bergeyk* (since 1521)
50850, *censier Lommel* (1627)

General State Archive The Hague
Archive of the Council of State nr. 2166LL,
Quoyer van Westerhove van de honderste penninck
Quoyer van Eersel van de honderste penninck
Quoyer van Bergeyk van de honderste penninck(1569)

Archive of the abbey at Postel
Charters Bergeyk.

Archive of the abbey at Tongerlo
Deeds and administration regarding property in Bergeyk

Regional Archive Southeast North–Brabant
Archive of the aldermen's court in Bergeyk

Private collection Gerit van der Aalst
Unpublished collection of placenames in Eersel extracted from different sources

REFERENCES

Published historical sources
Camps, H.P.H. (ed.), 1979: *Oorkondenboek van Noord-Brabant tot 1312. De meierij van 's-Hertogenbosch (met de heerlijkheid Gemert)*, 's-Gravenhage.
Cuvelier, J., 1912-1913: *Les dénombremonts de foyers en Brabant (XIVe-XVIe siècles)*, Bruxelles.

Franquinet, G.D. (ed.), 1881: *Beredeneerde inventaris der oorkonden en bescheiden van de adellijke abdij Thorn berustende op het provinciaal archief van Limburg*, Maastricht.

Enklaar, D. Th., 1941: *Gemeene gronden in Noord-Brabant in de middeleeuwen*, Utrecht.

Lanaye, L., 1942: Fragments d'un polyptique de la collegiale Saint-Jean Évangeliste à Liége de l'an 1250, *Bulletin de la Commission Royale d'Histoire* 107, 199-292.

Vangheluwe, D., 1989a: *Toponiemische Verzameling Bergeyk*, (unpublished typescript edition Archive Museum Eicha, Bergeyk).

Vangheluwe, D., 1990a: *Index op het cijnsboek van de hertog van Brabant* (nr 45044), (unpublished typescript edition Archive Museum Eicha, Bergeyk).

Literature

Bezemer, W., 1889: *Bijdrage tot de kennis van het oude cijns- en grondrentenrecht in Brabant*, 's-Hertogenbosch.

Bieleman, J., 1992: *Geschiedenis van de landbouw in Nederland 1500-1950. Verandering en verscheidenheid*, Meppel/Amsterdam.

Blockmans, W./W. Prevenier, 1997: *De Bourgondiers, de Nederlanden op weg naar eenheid, 1384-1530*, Amsterdam/Leuven.

Boer, A. van de, 1990: Vechtend om Kokaertskolk, *Te lommel op die Campine* 3, 55-81.

Bots, J.J.W.M./H.E.M. Melotte, 1977: *Van Wedert tot Valkenswaard. Een historiebeschrijving van Valkenswaard in twee delen*, Valkenswaard.

Brink, G. van de, 1996: *De grote Overgang. Woensel 1670-1920*, Nijmegen.

Bijsterveld, A.-J., 1989: Het domein van de abdij Echternach in Waalre en Valkenswaard. Ontwikkeling en beheer, ca. 1100-1400, in A. Verhoeven/F. Theuws (eds), *Het Kempenprojekt 3. De Middeleeuwen centraal*, Waalre (Bijdragen tot de Studie van het Brabantse Heem 33), 57-96.

Bijsterveld, A.-J., 1996: 'Dusela villa Taxandrie'. Een drietal onopgemerkte oorkonden betreffende Duizel uit de elfde en de dertiende eeuw, *Noordbrabants Historisch Jaarboek* 13, 156-207.

Byl, R., 1965: *Les jurisdictions scabinales dans le duché de Brabant des origines à la fin du Xve siècle*, Bruxelles.

Daris, E.J., 1875: *Notices historiques sur les églises du diocèse de Liège*, vol 6, Liège, 178-79.

Ghijssens, J., 1976: Le denier de Brabant des XIIe et XIIIe siecles, Premiere partie: les données; Deuxième partie: la verification, *Bulletin Cercle d'etudes Numismatiques*, 13-1/2, 3-13, 32-37.

Godding, P., 1987: *Le droit privé dans les Pays-Bas meridionaux du 12e au 18e siecle*, Brussel.

Hoppenbrouwers, P.C.M., 1992: *Een Middeleeuwse Samenleving. Het Land van Heusden(ca. 1360-ca.1515)*, (Historia Agriculturae XXV), Groningen.

Jansen, H.P.H., 1955: *Landbouwpacht in Noord-Brabant in de 14de en 15de eeuw*, Assen.

Jansen, H.P.H., 1982: Handel en Nijverheid 1000-1300, in *Algemene Geschiedenis der Nederlanden* 4, 87-111.

Kerremans, Ch., 1949: *Étude sur les circonscriptions judiciaires et administratives du Brabant et les officiers placés à leur tête par les ducs, antérieurement à l'avènement de la maison de Bourgogne (1406)*, Brussel.

Martens, M., 1954: *L'administration du domaine ducal au moyen age (1250-1406)*, Brussel.

Melotte, H.E.M./J. Molemans, 1979: *Noord-Brabantse Plaatsnamen, Monografie 1 Valkenswaard*, Waalre.

Melsen, J.T.M., 1989: Het wapen van Eersel, een historische verkenning, in A. Dams/F.J.P. Huybregts/J. Spoorenberg (eds), *Eersel, Duizel, Steensel. Drie Zaligheden*, Hapert, 49-74.

Schrijver, de R., 1965: *Jan van Brouchoven Graaf van Bergeyk*, (Verhandelingen van de Vlaamse Akademie voor Wetenschappen 57), Brussel.

Spierings, M.H.M., 1984: *Het Schepenprotocol van 's-Hertogenbosch 1367-1400*, Tilburg.

Steurs, W., 1977: *Les Sources de l'economie Rurale dans le Quartier d'Anvers et dans la Seigneurie de Malines jusqu'en 1500*, (Publications du Centre Belge d'Histoire Rurale 42), Louvain.

Steurs, W., 1993: *Naissance d'une region. Aux origines de la mairie de Bois-le-Duc. Recherches sur le Brabant septentrional aux 12ᵉ et 13ᵉ- siecles*, Bruxelles.

Theuws, F.C./A. Verhoeven/H.H. van Regteren Altena, 1988: Medieval Settlement at Dommelen, Parts I and II, *BROB* 38, 229-430..

Theuws, F.C., 1989: Middeleeuwse parochiecentra in de Kempen 1000-1350, in A. Verhoeven/F. Theuws (eds), *Het Kempenprojekt 3. De Middeleeuwen centraal*, Waalre (Bijdragen tot de Studie van het Brabantse heem 33), 97-216.

Thoen, E., 1988: *Landbouweconomie en Bevolking in Vlaanderen gedurende de late Middeleeuwen en het begin van de moderne Tijden. Testregio: de kasselrijen van Oudenaerde en Aalst*, Gent

Vangheluwe, D., 1988: *Een rekonstructie van het cijnsgoed te Bergeyk: resultaat vergelijking cijnsboek van Thorn met het boek van de Hondedrste Penning*, (unpublished typescript edition Archive Museum Eicha, Bergeyk).

Vangheluwe, D., 1989b: *Een reconstructie van het cijnsgoed van Thorn te Bergeyk*, Brabants Heem 41, 26-32.

Vangheluwe, D., 1990b: Historisch-geografische verkenning in Bergeyk, *Rosdoek* 55, 20-28.

Vangheluwe, D., 1991: De Pachthoeve van Tongerlo te Bergeyk, *Rosdoek* 61, 3-23.

Vangheluwe, D., 1992: Vergelijking van twee Hertogelijke cijnsboeken te Bergeyk, *Te Lommel op die Campine* 18-1, 6-21.

Vangheluwe, D., 1993: Historisch onderzoek van de Dingbank Eersel 1350-1450, *Rosdoek* 68, 5-17.

Vangheluwe, D., 1994: Historisch onderzoek van de Dingbank Eersel 1350-1450. Deel III, Namen, *Rosdoek* 70, 4-13.

Vangheluwe, D., 1994: Historisch onderzoek van de Dingbank Eersel 1350-1450. Deel IV: Doorgifte van het erfgoed nader bekeken, *Rosdoek* 72, 13-25.

Vangheluwe, D., 1996: *Beroepen uit cijnsboek 45044, Merckenswaert jaarboek 1996*, Valkenswaard, 200-241.

Verhulst, A., 1958: *De Sint-Baafsabdij en haar grondbezit (VIIe-XIVe eeuw), Brussel*.

Welvaarts, T.I., 1878: *Geschiedenis der abdij van Postel naar hare eigene archieven*, Turnhout/'s-Hertogenbosch.